Teacher Edition

VISIONS

Language ✦ Literature ✦ Content

Mary Lou McCloskey

Lydia Stack

THOMSON

HEINLE

Australia ✦ Canada ✦ Mexico ✦ Singapore ✦ United Kingdom ✦ United States

VISIONS TEACHER EDITION BOOK A
Mary Lou McCloskey and Lydia Stack

Publisher: *Phyllis Dobbins*
Director of Development: *Anita Raducanu*
Director, ELL Training and Development: *Evelyn Nelson*
Developmental Editor: *Tania Maundrell-Brown*
Associate Developmental Editor: *Yeny Kim*
Associate Developmental Editor: *Kasia Zagorski*
Editorial Assistant: *Audra Longert*
Production Supervisor: *Mike Burggren*
Marketing Manager: *Jim McDonough*
Manufacturing Manager: *Marcia Locke*
Photography Manager: *Sheri Blaney*
Development: *Weston Editorial*
Design and Production: *Proof Positive/Farrowlyne Associates, Inc.*
Cover Designer: *Studio Montage*
Printer: *R.R. Donnelley and Sons Company, Willard*

Cover Image: *© Danny Lehman/CORBIS*

Printed in the United States of America.
   3 4 5 6 7 8 9 10   08   07   06   05   04

For more information, contact Heinle, 25 Thomson Place, Boston, Massachusetts 02210 USA, or you can visit our Internet site at http://www.heinle.com

For permission to use material from this text or product contact us:
Tel   1-800-730-2214
Fax   1-800-730-2215
Web www.thomsonrights.com

ISBN: 0-8384-5285-X

Contents

VISIONS

Language Acquisition through Literature and Content

Visions is a four-level language development program
that supports students from the pre-literacy level
through transition into mainstream classrooms.

By incorporating literature with content, students are
taught, and have ample practice with, the skills they need
to meet grade-level standards while being introduced to
the academic language needed for school success.

Visions has been student-tested and teacher-approved to ensure that learners have the best materials to guide them in their language acquisition.

Features:

- **4 levels:** Newcomer (Basic)
  Beginning (A)
  Intermediate (B)
  Advanced/Transition (C)

- **Basic Language and Literacy book for non-schooled and low-beginning students** provides systematic language development as well as literacy instruction.

- **Staff development handbook and video** is designed for easy program access.

- High-interest, low-level **literature and content-based readings** motivate students.

- **Scaffolding throughout all four books** uses a three-pronged approach to meeting the standards: Introduce, Practice, Assess.

- **Writing activities** reinforce and recycle strategic skills.

- **Quality assessment materials** and ExamView® test generating software are aligned with state standards.

- **Technology** reinforces listening/speaking, reading skills, and phonemic development.

- **Heinle Reading Library** gives students practice in independent reading with stories tied to Student Book themes.

Here's what teachers around the country have to say:

"All chapters were very relative to the themes. The vocabulary building activities are excellent!"

Minerva Anzaldua
Martin Middle School, Corpus Christi, TX

"Great ESL strategies for any level!"

"Clear directions for students!"

Gail Lulek
Safety Harbor Middle School, Safety Harbor, FL

"This is the type of literature and language series I've been looking for! I really like how each activity flows together and keeps the theme together."

Elia Corona
Liberty Middle School, Pharr, TX

"The readings were well-written. Students can relate and understand."

"The chapter goals and selections are clear and relevant to students' needs."

"The activities help students understand literary conventions."

James Harris
DeLeon Middle School, McAllen, TX

"The themes are well-developed. They provide conceptual frameworks within which students can understand the literature and learn language."

"The skills and information presented are important for students' academic success."

"The chapters are excellent because every activity has accessible vocabulary for ELL."

Donald Hoyt
Cooper Middle School, Fresno, CA

Components-At-A-Glance

Visions: Teacher Edition "Your guide to Standards-based instruction"

For Students		Basic Book	Book A	Book B	Book C
Student Book	offers accessible, authentic literature with a balance of fiction and nonfiction, including excerpts from novels, short stories, plays, poetry, narratives, biographies, and informational and content-based readings.	●	●	●	●
Activity Book	provides reinforcement of state standards and includes practice and expansion of skills and content presented in the Student Book.	●	●	●	●
Student Handbook	serves as a reference guide for students. It features listening, speaking, reading, writing, and viewing checklists, as well as grammar, vocabulary, and research reference information.	●	●	●	●
The Heinle Reading Library	offers 18 classic stories that are tied to every theme of *Visions* and designed for student independent reading. Examples include: *The Red Badge of Courage, Moby Dick, David Copperfield, Pride and Prejudice, 20,000 Leagues Under the Sea, Little Women.*		●	●	●
Student CD-ROM	provides an opportunity for practicing, reteaching, and reinforcing listening/speaking skills, reading skills, and phonemic awareness.	●	●	●	●
Audio CD*	features all reading selections recorded for building listening/speaking skills, fluency, and auditory learning.	●	●	●	●
Newbury House Dictionary with CD-ROM	helps students develop essential dictionary and vocabulary building skills. Features a pronunciation CD-ROM and a companion Web site.		●	●	●
More Grammar Practice	helps students learn and review essential grammar skills.		●	●	●
Web site (http://visions.heinle.com)	features additional skill-building activities and reference tools for students, including vocabulary activities, syllabication worksheets, and word lists.	●	●	●	●

*Also featured on Audio Tape.

For Teachers		Basic Book	Book A	Book B	Book C
Teacher Edition	contains point-of-use lesson suggestions, ongoing assessment, and multi-level activities developed specifically to state standard requirements.		●	●	●
Teacher Resource Book	provides easy-to-use and implement lesson plans aligned with state standards. Additional support includes graphic organizers to support lesson activities, CNN® video transcripts and Video Worksheets for students, and summaries of each reading in English and translated into Cambodian, Haitian Creole, Hmong, Chinese, Spanish, and Vietnamese. School-Home Newsletters, in English and the six languages, encourage family involvement. This component is also available on CD-ROM for teacher customization.	●	●	●	●
Assessment Program	features diagnostic tests and standards-based assessment items to ensure accountability, and tracking systems to monitor student progress. The Assessment Program is available on CD-ROM with the ExamView® test-generating software, designed to create customizable tests in minutes.	●	●	●	●
Transparencies	offers graphic organizers, reading summaries, and grammar charts for interactive teaching. The Basic Book Transparencies also include sentence builders, phonemic awareness, and syllabication.	●	●	●	●
Staff Development Handbook and Video	provide step-by-step training for all teachers. The video includes actual footage of classroom teaching.	●	●	●	●
CNN® Video	features thematic news segments from today's headlines to help build listening and content comprehension through meaningful viewing activities.	●	●	●	●
Web site (http://visions.heinle.com)	features additional teaching resources and an opportunity for teachers to share ideas and techniques with an online community.	●	●	●	●

Scope and Sequence

Unit 1: Traditions and Cultures

Chapter	Build Vocabulary	Text Structure	Reading Strategy	Spelling/Punctuation/Capitalization	Build Reading Fluency	Elements of Literature	Word Study	Grammar Focus	From Reading to Writing	Across Content Areas
1. "Family Photo" by Ralph Fletcher, and "Birthday Barbecue" by Carmen Lomas Garza p. 2	Learn Words for Family Members	Poem and Personal Narrative	Compare and Contrast	Capitalization: Names and titles; Spelling: Plurals	Rapid Word Recognition	Recognize First-Person Point of View	Identify Compound Words	Use Present Continuous Tense Verbs	Write a Personal Narrative	Math: Analyze a Bar Graph
2. "Coyote" by Andrew Matthews p. 14	Learn Words for Animal Sounds	Folktale	Read Aloud to Show Understanding	Punctuation: Periods at the end of sentences; Spelling: Irregular plural nouns	Reading Key Phrases	Understand Author's Purpose	Use a Thesaurus or Synonym Finder to Find Synonyms	Identify Subjects and Verbs in Sentences	Write a Narrative	Science: Learn About Food Chains
3. "Thanksgiving" by Miriam Nerlove p. 26	Learn Words for Foods	Poem	Describe Mental Images	Capitalization: Holidays; Spelling: To/Two/Too; Spelling: Plurals for words ending in -fe; Capitalization: I	Echo Read Aloud	Identify Rhyme	Analyze the Suffix -ful	Use Subject Pronouns	Write a Narrative About a Holiday	Social Studies: Read a Map
4. "Turkish Delight" by Hamdiye Çelik p. 42	Identify Words That Show Time	Personal Narrative	Compare Text Events with Your Own Experiences	Capitalization: Towns, cities, and countries; Spelling: Abbreviations of measurements	Reading Chunks of Words	Instructions	Recognize Root Words and the Suffix -ish	Use the Verb To Be with Complements	Write a Personal Narrative	The Arts: Design a Turkish Rug
5. "Sadako and the Thousand Paper Cranes" by Eleanor Coerr p. 54	Identify Words About Setting	Novel Based on a True Story	Identify Cause and Effect	Spelling: Adverbs ending in -ly; Punctuation: Apostrophes with contractions; Capitalization: Titles	Adjust Your Reading Rate for Quotations	Understand Characterization	Recognize Adjectives Ending in -ed	Recognize Possessive Nouns	Write a Fictional Narrative	Math: Learn Geometric Shapes and Vocabulary

Apply and Expand

Listening and Speaking Workshop p. 68	Viewing Workshop p. 69	Writer's Workshop p. 70	Projects p. 72
Present a Narrative About Your Favorite Holiday	View and Think: Compare and Contrast Cultures	Write a Personal Narrative About a Trip	1. Create a Poster About a New Tradition 2. Give a Cross-Cultural Presentation

Unit 2: Environment

Chapter	Build Vocabulary	Text Structure	Reading Strategy	Spelling/ Punctuation/ Capitalization	Build Reading Fluency	Elements of Literature	Word Study	Grammar Focus	From Reading to Writing	Across Content Areas
1. "Here Is the Southwestern Desert" by Madeleine Dunphy p. 76	Use Context to Understand Vocabulary	A Poem	Describe Images	Spelling: desert/dessert Spelling: Long vowel sounds and the -ed suffix Spelling: Ou sound Capitalization: First word in a sentence	Echo Read Aloud	Recognize Free Verse	Recognize Word Origins	Identify the Simple Present Tense	Write a Poem About the Environment	Science: Learn About Types of Climate
2. "Subway Architect" by Patrick Daley p. 92	Take Notes as You Read	Interview	Distinguish Facts From Opinions	Spelling: It's vs. Its Punctuation: Italics for emphasis Spelling: Schwa sound and r-controlled vowels	Repeated Reading	Understand Character Motivation	Learn About the Prefix Sub-	Identify and Punctuate Questions	Write a Personal Narrative	The Arts: Design a Mural
3. "Why the Rooster Crows at Sunrise" by Lynette Dyer Vuong p. 106	Understand Words in Context	Fable	Identify Main Idea and Details	Punctuation: Quotation marks for dialogue Punctuation: Semicolons	Read Silently	Review Personification	Learn About Words with Multiple Meanings	Identify Object Pronouns	Write a Fable	Science: Learn About Conservation
4. "Gonzalo" by Paul Fleischman p. 118	Use Word Squares to Remember Meanings	Narrative Fiction	Draw Conclusions	Capitalization: Titles of people and books, names of countries, peoples, languages Punctuation: Italics Spelling: I before e	Audio CD Reading Practice	Discuss the Theme	Use the Dictionary	Recognize and Use Comparative Adjectives	Write Narrative Fiction	Science: Learn About Plants
5. "Rain Forest Creatures" by Will Osborne and Mary Pope Osborne p. 132	Use Text Features	Informational Text	Outline Information to Understand Reading	Punctuation: Exclamation points Spelling: Consonant before -le	Adjust Your Reading Rate to Scan	Examine Visual Features	Learn Word Origins	Identify the Subject and Verb of a Sentence	Write an Informational Report	Social Studies: Read Pie Charts

Apply and Expand

Listening and Speaking Workshop p. 144	Viewing Workshop p. 145	Writer's Workshop p. 146	Projects p. 148
Perform an Interview	View, Compare, and Contrast: Respond to Media	Write Rules	1. Make a Poster of a Special Environment
			2. Prepare and Present a News Report

Unit 3: Conflict and Cooperation

Chapter	Build Vocabulary	Text Structure	Reading Strategy	Spelling/ Punctuation/ Capitalization	Build Reading Fluency	Elements of Literature	Word Study	Grammar Focus	From Reading to Writing	Across Content Areas
1. "We Shall Overcome" p. 152	Learn Words About Freedom	Song Lyrics	Make Inferences	Punctuation: Comma between city and state	Adjust Your Reading Rate to Memorize	Recognize Repetition	Recognize Homographs	Talk About the Future Using *Will* and *Shall*	Write Lyrics for a Song About the Future	The Arts: Learn About Types of Songs
2. "Zlata's Diary" by Zlata Filipović p. 162	Find Antonyms in a Thesaurus	Diary	Recognize Sequence of Events	Punctuation: Commas in dates Spelling: *There, they're, their* Capitalization: Letter greetings and closings	Reading Silently	Identify Tone	Form Contractions	Use Verbs with Infinitives	Write Your Opinion	Social Studies: Learn the Points of the Compass
3. "The Peach Boy" by Suzanne Barchers p. 176	Define Words Related to Nature	Play	Analyze Cause and Effect	Punctuation: Colon Spelling: Silent *w* before *r* Punctuation: Comma for direct address	Read Aloud to Engage Listeners	Recognize Problems and Resolutions	Identify Homophones	Use Compound Sentences With *and*	Write a Summary	Science: Classify Fruits and Vegetables
4. "Talking in the New Land" by Edite Cunhã p. 190	Use Synonyms to Find Meaning	Personal Narrative	Summarize to Recall Ideas	Spelling: Abbreviations of addresses Punctuation: Italics for words from other languages Spelling: Silent *gh* before *t* Capitalization: Family members' names	Rapid Word Recognition	Analyze Characters	Learn the Prefix *Dis-*	Use *Could* and *Couldn't*	Write to Solve a Problem	Language Arts: Learn About Graphic Features
5. "Plain Talk About Handling Stress" by Louis E. Kopolow, M.D. p. 206	Learn Words Related to Stress in Context	Informational Text	Identify Main Idea and Details	Punctuation: Colon to introduce a list Spelling: *Ph→/f/* and silent *p* Punctuation: Quotation marks Capitalization: Headings	Adjust Your Reading Rate to Scan	Use Headings to Find Information	Locate Meanings, Pronunciations, and Origins of Words	Recognize Complex Sentences with *If*	Write an Informational Text	Language Arts: Learn Different Meanings of *Conflict*

Apply and Expand

Listening and Speaking Workshop p. 222	Viewing Workshop p. 223	Writer's Workshop p. 224	Projects p. 226
Literary Response: Report Your Favorite Selection	View, Compare, and Contrast: Learn About the Civil Rights Movement	Response to Literature: Write a Review of Literature	1. Create a Storyboard
			2. Present a Radio Program

Unit 4: Heroes

Chapter	Build Vocabulary	Text Structure	Reading Strategy	Spelling/ Punctuation/ Capitalization	Build Reading Fluency	Elements of Literature	Word Study	Grammar Focus	From Reading to Writing	Across Content Areas
1. "The Ballad of Mulan" p. 230	Evaluate Your Understanding of Words	Legend	Make Predictions	Punctuation: Italics, hyphen, and exclamation point Spelling: Silent *k* in *kn*	Repeated Reading	Determine Main and Minor Characters	Use the Suffix *-ly* to Form Adverbs	Use Prepositional Phrases	Write a Legend	Social Studies: Use Map Features to Read a Map
2. "Roberto Clemente" p. 242	Recognize Baseball Terms	Biography	Use Chronological Order to Recall and Locate Information	Spelling: Abbreviations	Reading Chunks of Words	Recognize Third-Person Point of View	Understand the Prefix *un-*	Identify Prepositional Phrases of Time	Write a Biography	Science: Learn About Earthquakes
3. "Nelson Mandela" by Jack L. Roberts, and "The Inaugural Address, May 10, 1994" by Nelson Mandela p. 252	Infer Meanings of Homonyms	Biography and Speech	Draw Inferences	Spelling: *Ew* for long /u/ Punctuation: Hyphens in numbers Punctuation: Ellipses	Echo Read Aloud	Analyze Style in a Speech	Identify the Suffix *-ion*	Recognize Commands with *Let*	Write a Persuasive Speech	Social Studies: Read a Timeline
4. "My Father Is a Simple Man" by Luis Omar Salinas, and "Growing Up" by Liz Ann Báez Aguilar p. 266	Use Word Squares to Remember Meaning	Poem	Compare and Contrast	Spelling: *Ui* for the long /u/ sound, *ch* for the /k/ sound Punctuation: Commas to separate dependent adjective clauses Spelling: Silent *t* before *ch*	Audio CD Reading Practice	Recognize Imagery	Identify the Suffix *-er*	Recognize Reported Speech	Write a Poem	Social Studies: Read Advertisements for Jobs

Apply and Expand

Listening and Speaking Workshop p. 280	Viewing Workshop p. 281	Writer's Workshop p. 282	Projects p. 284
Give a Descriptive Presentation	View and Think: Compare and Contrast Biographies	Write a Biography	1. Interviews About Heroes
			2. Be a Hero

Unit 5: Explorations

Chapter	Build Vocabulary	Text Structure	Reading Strategy	Spelling/ Punctuation/ Capitalization	Build Reading Fluency	Elements of Literature	Word Study	Grammar Focus	From Reading to Writing	Across Content Areas
1. "Eye to Eye" by Sylvia Earle p. 288	Use Context to Identify Correct Homophones	Personal Narrative	Draw Conclusions	Spelling: *Oa* for the long /o/ sound	Read Silently	Analyze Figurative Language	Recognize Compound Adjectives	Recognize and Use the Simple Past Tense	Write a Personal Narrative	Science: Identify Types of Scientists
2. "The Fun They Had" by Isaac Asimov p. 298	Explore Multiple Meaning Words	Science Fiction	Make Inferences from Text Evidence	Capitalization: Months Spelling: *Gh* for the /f/ sound Spelling: Silent *t* and silent *l*	Rapid Word Recognition	Analyze Setting	Use the Latin Root Words to Find Meaning	Use Dependent Clauses with *Because*	Write an Ending to a Science Fiction Short Story	Science: Define Internet Terms
3. "Using the Scientific Method" by Stephen Kramer p. 312	Use a Dictionary to Locate Meanings and Pronounce Words	Informational Text	Recognize Cause and Effect Relationships	Punctuation: Periods for vertical lists Punctuation: Colon for times Spelling: *Qu* for the /kw/ sound	Read Aloud to Engage Listeners	Recognize the Style of Direct Address	Use Greek Word Origins	Use *Might* to Show Possibility	Write an Informational Text	Science: Learn About Sleep
4. "The Solar System" p. 326	Use Different Resources to Find Meaning	Informational Text	Summarize Information	Capitalization: Planets Spelling: Abbreviations for temperature Spelling: Irregular plurals Punctuation: Apostrophe for possession Spelling: *Ea* for the long /e/ sound	Adjust Your Reading Rate to Scan	Explore Graphic Aids	Recognize Words and Sounds with the Spelling *oo*	Identify Superlative Adjectives	Outline an Informational Text	Science: Compare Planet Orbits

Apply and Expand

Listening and Speaking Workshop p. 344	Viewing Workshop p. 345	Writer's Workshop p. 346	Projects p. 348
Give an Oral Report About Your Community	View and Think: Discuss What People Are Exploring	Write a Research Report	1. Explore Sources to Answer Science Questions
			2. Give a Presentation About an Explorer

Unit 6: Connections

Chapter	Build Vocabulary	Text Structure	Reading Strategy	Spelling/ Punctuation/ Capitalization	Build Reading Fluency	Elements of Literature	Word Study	Grammar Focus	From Reading to Writing	Across Content Areas
1. "Esperanza Rising" by Pam Muñoz Ryan p. 352	Understand Words in Context	Fiction	Make Inferences	Spelling: Silent *u*	Read Silently and Aloud	Analyze Characters	Distinguish Denotative and Connotative Meanings	Identify Possessive Adjectives	Write a Fiction Story	Social Studies: Learn About Land Forms
2. "Honus and Me" by Dan Gutman p. 362	Learn Words About Emotion	Fiction	Identify the Main Idea and Details	Spelling: Voiced vs. unvoiced *th*; Spelling: Abbreviation; Capitalization: Names of public places; Spelling: Silent *h* after *w*	Rapid Word Recognition	Recognize Style, Tone, and Mood	Use a Thesaurus or Synonym Finder	Understand the Past Perfect Tense	Write a Paragraph	Math: Use Multiplication
3. "The Boy King" by Andrea Ross p. 378	Look Up Syllables and Meanings of Words	Biography	Identify Cause and Effect	Punctuation: Hyphens in compound adjectives; Spelling: Open and closed syllables	Repeated Reading	Discuss Themes Across Cultures	Recognize the Suffix *-ian*	Understand Modal Auxiliaries	Write a Biography	Social Studies: Identify Symbols
4. "It Could Still Be a Robot" by Allan Fowler, and "High-Tech Helping Hands" by Jane McGoldrick p. 390	Distinguish Denotative and Connotative Meanings	Informational Text	Paraphrase to Recall Ideas	Spelling: *Oi* vowel sound; Spelling: Syllable boundary patterns; Punctuation: Dash	Reading Chunks of Words	Analyze Text Evidence	Learn Adverbs of Frequency	Use Adverbs of Frequency	Write a Persuasive Essay	Science: Read an FAQ Web Page

Apply and Expand

Listening and Speaking Workshop p. 404	Viewing Workshop p. 405	Writer's Workshop p. 406	Projects p. 408
Give a Persuasive Speech	View and Think: Compare Presentations of Technology	Write a Persuasive Letter to the Editor	1. Tell a Story About Your Culture
			2. Make an Advertisement of a Robot

Scientifically Based Research in the *Visions* Program

The *Visions* program was developed utilizing current, scientifically based research findings of the most effective methods to teach language mastery. The references for each section below identify specific areas within the *Visions* student materials where the research has been applied.

Vocabulary Development

Research shows students need to consistently work on vocabulary in three critical areas (Anderson, 1999) and to meet standards (California Dept. of Education, 1998).

Word Meaning: Students study vocabulary meanings and concepts, relate them to prior experience, and record them in their personal dictionary. See *Build Vocabulary* sections.

Word Identification Strategies: Students learn important skills such as context clues, roots, and affixes. See *Word Study* sections.

Vocabulary Across Content Areas: Students learn key words in science, math, and social studies in the *Content Connection* and *Across Content Areas* sections.

Reading Comprehension

Strategies: Reading strategies such as fact/opinion, cause/effect, prediction, summarization, and paraphrasing need to be directly taught before the reading, practiced during the reading, and then evaluated (Anderson, 1999). See *Reading Strategy* sections.

Types of Questions: Readings that are followed by literal, inferential, and evaluative comprehension questions develop higher order thinking skills (Fowler, 2003). See *Reading Comprehension* sections.

Reading Fluency

The ability to read rapidly, smoothly, and automatically while adjusting rate and reading with expression (Mather and Goldstein, 2001) defines reading fluency. English language learners and at-risk students need systematic scaffolding activities with repeated oral reading to become fluent readers (De la Colina, Parker, Hasbrouck, Lara-Alecia, 2001). See *Build Reading Fluency* sections.

Rapid Word Recognition: Practice of this skill can increase students' fluency (Cunningham and Stanovich, 1998; Torgesen et al., 2001).

Reading Chunks and Key Phrases: This helps ELL and at-risk students become more fluent and to understand what they read.

Adjusting Reading Rate: Students learn to vary reading rate according to the purpose and type of text.

Repeated Reading: Students reread words, phrases, and passages a specific number of times (Meyer and Felton, 1999) for consistent, positive support of effectiveness in increasing reading fluency (National Reading Panel, 2000). Six minutes a day of repeated oral reading practice (Mercer, et al., in press) was found to be highly effective in increasing fluency.

Reading Silently and Aloud: Practice and support using the teacher, a peer (Li and Nes, 2001), and the Audio CD (Blum, Koskinen, Tennant, and Parker, 1995) has been proven to increase reading fluency.

Sheltered Content Instruction

Using the strategies from Cognitive Academic Language Learning Approach (CALLA) and the Sheltered Instruction Observation Protocol (SIOP), students apply learning strategies to help them succeed academically in their content area classes. See *Use Prior Knowledge* and *Content Connection* sections.

Spelling Instruction

Students are taught orthographic patterns and frequently used words in conjunction with the readings. Students who receive direct instruction in word analysis and how to analyze speech sounds and spell words are more successful in reading and writing (Whittlesea, 1987). See *Visions Activity Book* and *Teacher Edition.*

Traits of Writing and Oral Presentations

Students can learn to write and give oral presentations with greater success when they are based on the model presented in their reading and when they are made cognitively aware of the traits that good writers and presenters use. In *Visions*, students write and present narrative, descriptive, technical, and persuasive writing, as well as research reports. Students analyze types of text structure used in various writing models. The writing process is used throughout. See *Text Structure, Writing Workshops,* and *Listening and Speaking Workshops.*

References

Anderson, Neil. *Exploring Second Language Reading*. Boston, MA: Heinle, 1999.

Becker, H. and Hamayan, E. *Teaching ESL K-12: Views from the Classroom*. Boston, MA: Heinle, 2001.

Blum, I.H.; Koskinen, P.S.; Tennant, N.; and Parker, E.M. "Using Audio Taped Books to Extend Classroom Literacy Instruction into the Homes of Second-language Learners." *Journal of Reading Behavior* 27 (1995): 535–563.

California Department of Education. *English-Language Arts Content Standards for California Public Schools Kindergarten Through Grade Twelve*. Sacramento, CA: 2001.

California Department of Education. *Strategic Thinking and Learning*. Sacramento, CA: 2001.

Chamot, A. and O'Malley, J. *The CALLA Handbook Addison-Wesley*. Reading, MA: 1995.

Cognitive Academic Language Learning Approach (CALLA) <http://www.writing.berkely.edu/TESL-EJ/ej07/r5.html>.

Cunningham, A.E. and Stanovich, K.E. "What Reading Does for the Mind." *American Educator* 22 (1998): 1–2, 8–15.

De la Colina, M.G.; Parker, R.I.; Hasbrouck, J.E.; Lara-Alecia, R. "Intensive Intervention in Reading Fluency For At-Risk Beginning Spanish Readers." *Bilingual Research Journal* 25 (2001): 503–38.

Fowler, B. *Critical Thinking Across the Curriculum Home Page* "Blooms Taxonomy and Critical Thinking (Questions)." Longview Community College, 1996. 22 January 2003 <http://www.kcmetro.cc.mo.us/longview/ctac/blooms.htm>.

Li, D., and Nes, S. "Using Paired Reading to Help ESL Students Become Fluent and Accurate Readers." *Reading Improvement* 38 (2001): 50–61.

Mercer, C.; Campbell, K.; Miller, M.; Mercer, K.; and Lane, H. in press. "Effects of a Reading Fluency Intervention for Middle Schoolers with Specific Learning Disabilities." *Learning Disabilities Research and Practice.*

Meyer, M.S., and Felton, R.H. "Repeated Reading to Enhance Fluency: Old Approaches and New Directions." *Annals of Dyslexia* 49 (1999): 283–306.

National Reading Panel. *Teaching Children to Read: An Evidence-based Assessment of the Scientific Research Literature on Reading and Its Implications for Reading Instruction* (National Institute of Health Publ. No 00-4769) Washington, DC: 2002 National Institute of Child Health and Human Development.

Nixon, Susan. *Six Traits Writing Assessment Home Page*. 22 January 2003 <http://6traits.cyberspaces.net>.

Short, Deborah J., and Echevarria, Jana. *ERIC Clearinghouse on Languages and Linguistics*. "Sheltered Instruction Observation Protocol: A Tool for Teacher-Researcher Collaboration and Professional Development." 1999. 22 January 2003 <http:// www.cal.org/ericcll/digest/sheltered.html>.

Torgesen, J.K.; Alexander, A.W.; Wagner, R.K.; Rashotte, C.A.; Voeller, K; Conway, T.; and Rose, E. "Intensive Remedial Instruction for Children with Severe Reading Disabilities: Immediate and Long-term Outcomes from Two Instructional Approaches." *Journal of Learning Disabilities* 34 (2001): 33–58.

The *Visions* Assessment Program was designed to ensure standards-based accountability for teachers and students alike. It begins with a Diagnostic Test to assess what students already know and to target students' needs in specific skill areas. The Assessment Program ensures ongoing as well as summative evaluation with the Chapter Quizzes, Unit Tests, and Mid-Book and End-of-Book Exams. Portfolio Assessment is also taken into account to measure the students' overall progress.

VISIONS Assessment Program		
	Name	**Purpose of Assessment**
Entry Level	**Diagnostic Test**	To enable teachers to ascertain their students' proficiency skills in vocabulary, reading, grammar, spelling, and writing, and to do a Needs Analysis in order to target specific instructional needs.
Monitor Progress	**Chapter Quizzes**	To monitor students' ongoing progress in vocabulary, grammar, reading, and writing. There are 27 Chapter Quizzes.
	Unit Tests	To monitor students' ongoing progress toward meeting strategies and standards in vocabulary, grammar, reading, and writing at the end of each unit. There are 6 Unit Tests.
	Mid-Book Exam	To monitor students' ongoing progress toward meeting strategies and standards in vocabulary, grammar, reading, and writing as taught throughout the first three units of the book.
	Student Resources Checklists	To promote student responsibility in meeting the standards. Students self-assess their strengths and weaknesses for purposes of reteaching if necessary.
Summative	**End-of-Book Exam**	To measure students' achievement and mastery in meeting the standards in vocabulary, reading, and writing as taught throughout the book.
Additional Tools to Monitor Progress	**Peer Editing Checklists**	To collaboratively involve classmates in giving and gaining feedback on their progress toward meeting the standards in writing.
	Active Listening Checklist	To collaboratively involve classmates in giving and gaining feedback on their progress in the area of listening and speaking during oral presentations.
	Teacher Resources Listening, Speaking, Reading, Writing, Viewing, and Content Area Checklists	To track ongoing progress of students in all domains of the standards, and to serve as a vehicle in planning instruction.
	Reading Fluency	To check students' progress in learning to read silently and aloud with expression, and to adjust their reading rates according to the purpose of their reading.
	Rubrics	To evaluate students' overall performance using a fixed measurement scale and a list of criteria taken from formal and informal outcomes. These rubrics should be part of each student's permanent record.
	Portfolio Assessment	To involve students in self-reflection on their progress in meeting their learning goals. This ongoing assessment is a collection of student work that exhibits the student's best efforts and progress.
	ExamView ® CD-ROM	To empower teachers to choose and customize test items to meet students' targeted needs; items chosen may be used to retest after intervention activities.

VISIONS

Language ◇ Literature ◇ Content

Mary Lou McCloskey

Lydia Stack

THOMSON
™
HEINLE

Australia ◇ Canada ◇ Mexico ◇ Singapore ◇ United Kingdom ◇ United States

VISIONS STUDENT BOOK A
Mary Lou McCloskey and Lydia Stack

Publisher: *Phyllis Dobbins*
Director of Development: *Anita Raducanu*
Director, ELL Training and Development: *Evelyn Nelson*
Developmental Editor: *Tania Maundrell-Brown*
Associate Developmental Editor: *Yeny Kim*
Associate Developmental Editor: *Kasia Zagorski*
Editorial Assistant: *Audra Longert*
Production Supervisor: *Mike Burggren*
Marketing Manager: *Jim McDonough*
Manufacturing Manager: *Marcia Locke*
Photography Manager: *Sheri Blaney*
Development: *Proof Positive/Farrowlyne Associates, Inc.; Quest Language Systems*
Design and Production: *Proof Positive/Farrowlyne Associates, Inc.*
Cover Designer: *Studio Montage*
Printer: *R.R. Donnelley and Sons Company, Willard*

Cover Image: *© Danny Lehman/CORBIS*

Printed in the United States of America.
   3 4 5 6 7 8 9 10   08   07   06   05   04

For more information, contact Heinle, 25 Thomson Place, Boston, Massachusetts 02210 USA, or you can visit our Internet site at http://www.heinle.com

For permission to use material from this text or product contact us:
Tel   1-800-730-2214
Fax   1-800-730-2215
Web   www.thomsonrights.com

ISBN: 0-8384-5247-7

Reviewers and Consultants

We gratefully acknowledge the contribution of the following educators, consultants, and librarians who reviewed materials at various stages of development. Their input and insight provided us with valuable perspective and ensured the integrity of the entire program.

Program Advisor

Evelyn Nelson

Consultants

Deborah Barker
Nimitz High School
Houston, Texas

Sharon Bippus
Labay Middle School
Houston, Texas

Sheralee Connors
Portland, Oregon

Kathleen Fischer
Norwalk LaMirada Unified
School District
Norwalk, California

Willa Jean Harner
Tiffin-Seneca Public Library
Tiffin, Ohio

Nancy King
Bleyl Middle School
Houston, Texas

Dell Perry
Woodland Middle School
East Point, Georgia

Julie Rines
The Thomas Crane Library
Quincy, Massachusetts

Lynn Silbernagel
The Catlin Gabel School
Portland, Oregon

Cherylyn Smith
Fresno Unified School District
Fresno, California

Jennifer Trujillo
Fort Lewis College
Teacher Education Department
Durango, Colorado

Teresa Walter
Chollas Elementary School
San Diego, California

Reviewers

Jennifer Alexander
Houston Independent School District
Houston, Texas

Susan Alexandre
Trimble Technical High School
Fort Worth, Texas

Deborah Almonte
Franklin Middle School
Tampa, Florida

Donna Altes
Silverado Middle School
Napa, California

Ruben Alvarado
Webb Middle School
Austin, Texas

Sheila Alvarez
Robinson Middle School
Plano, Texas

Cally Androtis-Williams
Newcomers High School
Long Island City, New York

Minerva Anzaldua
Martin Middle School
Corpus Christi, Texas

Alicia Arroyos
Eastwood Middle School
El Paso, Texas

Douglas Black
Montwood High School
El Paso, Texas

Jessica Briggeman
International Newcomer Academy
Fort Worth, Texas

Diane Buffett
East Side High School
Newark, New Jersey

Eva Chapman
San Jose Unified School
District Office
San Jose, California

Elia Corona
Memorial Middle School
Pharr, Texas

Alicia Cron
Alamo Middle School
Alamo, Texas

Florence Decker
El Paso Independent School District
(retired)
El Paso, Texas

Janeece Docal
Bell Multicultural Senior High School
Washington, DC

Addea Dontino
Miami-Dade County School District
Miami, Florida

Kathy Dwyer
Tomlin Middle School
Plant City, Florida

Olga Figol
Barringer High School
Newark, New Jersey

Claire Forrester
Molina High School
Dallas, Texas

Connie Guerra
Regional Service Center 1
Edinburg, Texas

James Harris
DeLeon Middle School
McAllen, Texas

Audrey Heining-Boynton
University of North Carolina-
Chapel Hill
School of Education
Chapel Hill, North Carolina

Carolyn Ho
North Harris Community College
Houston, Texas

Donald Hoyt
Cooper Middle School
Fresno, California

Nancy A. Humbach
Miami University
Department of Teacher Education
Oxford, Ohio

Marie Irwin
University of Texas at Arlington Libraries
Arlington, Texas

Mark Irwin
Cary Middle School
Dallas, Texas

Erik Johansen
Oxnard High School
Oxnard, California

Marguerite Joralemon
East Side High School
Newark, New Jersey

Karen Poling Kapeluck
Lacey Instructional Center
Annandale, Virginia

Lorraine Kleinschuster
Intermediate School 10 Q
Long Island City, New York

Fran Lacas
NYC Board of Education (retired)
New York, New York

Robert Lamont
Newcomer Center
Arlington, Texas

Mao-ju Catherine Lee
Alief Middle School
Houston, Texas

Leonila Luera
Pharr-San Juan-Alamo ISD
Pharr/San Juan, Texas

Gail Lulek
Safety Harbor Middle School
Safety Harbor, Florida

Natalie Mangini
Serrano International School
Lake Forest, California

Linda Martínez
Dallas Independent School District
Dallas, Texas

Berta Medrano
Pharr-San Juan-Alamo ISD
Pharr/San Juan, Texas

Graciela Morales
Austin Independent School District
Austin, Texas

Karen Morante
School District of Philadelphia
Philadelphia, Pennsylvania

Jacee Morgan
Houston ISD
Houston, Texas

Lorraine Morgan
Hanshaw Middle School
Modesto, California

Dianne Mortensen
Pershing Intermediate School 220
Brooklyn, New York

Denis O'Leary
Rio del Valle Junior High School
Oxnard, California

Jeanette Page
School District of Philadelphia (retired)
Philadelphia, Pennsylvania

Claudia Peréz
Hosler Middle School
Lynwood, California

Yvonne Perez
Alief Middle School
Houston, Texas

Penny Phariss
Plano Independent School District
Plano, Texas

Bari Ramírez
L.V. Stockard Middle School
Dallas, Texas

Jacqueline Ray
Samuel High School
Dallas, Texas

Howard Riddles
Oak Grove Middle School
Clearwater, Florida

R.C. Rodriguez
Northside Independent School District
San Antonio, Texas

Randy Soderman
Community School District Six
New York, New York

Rita LaNell Stahl
Sinagua High School
Flagstaff, Arizona

Dean Stecker
School District of Palm Beach County
West Palm Beach, Florida

Mary Sterling-Cruz
Jackson Middle School
Friendswood, Texas

Rosemary Tejada
Carlsbad High School
Carlsbad, California

Camille Sloan Telthorster
Bleye Middle School
Houston, Texas

Vickie Thomas
Robinson Middle School
Plano, Texas

Claudio Toledo
Lynwood Middle School
Lynwood, California

Christopher Tracy
Garnet-Patterson Middle School
Washington, DC

Lydia Villescas
Pharr-San Juan-Alamo ISD
Pharr/San Juan, Texas

Stephanie Vreeland
T.A. Howard Middle School
Arlington, Texas

Jennifer Zelenitz
Long Island City High School
Long Island City, New York

We wish to thank the students at the following schools who helped us select high-interest readings at an appropriate language level. Their feedback was invaluable.

Student reviewers

Cooper Middle School
Fresno, California

De Leon Middle School
McAllen, Texas

Garnet-Patterson Middle School
Washington, D.C.

Hanshaw Middle School
Modesto, California

Intermediate School 10 Q
Long Island City, New York

Jackson Middle School
Friendswood, Texas

L.V. Stockard Middle School
Dallas, Texas

Liberty Middle School
Pharr, Texas

Martin Middle School
Corpus Christi, Texas

Memorial Middle School
Pharr, Texas

Newcomer Center
Arlington, Texas

Nimitz High School
Houston, Texas

Oak Grove Middle School
Clearwater, Florida

Oxnard High School
Oxnard, California

Pershing Intermediate School 220
Brooklyn, New York

Samuel High School
Dallas, Texas

Serrano International School
Lake Forest, California

Silverado Middle School
Napa, California

T.A. Howard Middle School
Arlington, Texas

Trimble Technical High School
Fort Worth, Texas

Contents

To the Student

We hope you like *Visions*
We wrote it for you
To learn speaking, reading, writing,
And listening, too.

You'll read all kinds of things —
Stories, poems, and plays,
And texts that will help you understand
What your content teacher says.

Use this book to "grow" your English,
To talk about what you write and read.
Use it to learn lots of new words
And new reading strategies you'll need.

Good authors, good activities,
And especially your good teachers,
Can also help you learn grammar and writing,
And lots of other language features.

So please open this book
And learn everything you can.
Then write and show us how far you've come
Since you first began.

M.L.M. and L.S.

http://visions.heinle.com

Mary Lou McCloskey

Lydia Stack

Unit Materials

Activity Book: *pp. 1–40*
Audio: *Unit 1; CD 1, Tracks 1–6*
Student Handbook
Student CD-ROM: *Unit 1*
CNN Video: *Unit 1*
Teacher Resource Book: *Lesson Plans, Teacher Resources, Reading Summaries, School-Home Connection, Video Script, Video Worksheet, Activity Book Answer Key*
Teacher Resource CD-ROM
Assessment Program: *Quizzes and Test, pp. 7–22; Teacher and Student Resources, pp. 115–144*
Assessment CD-ROM
Transparencies
The Heinle Newbury House Dictionary/CD-ROM
More Grammar Practice workbook
Heinle Reading Library: *The Legend of Sleepy Hollow*
Web site: http://visions.heinle.com

Visions Staff Development Handbook

Refer to the Visions Staff Development Handbook for more teacher support.

Unit Theme: Traditions and Cultures

1. **Clarify the theme words** *Say: A tradition is a certain way people behave in a special situation. Can you name some traditions for Halloween?*
2. **Use personal experience** *Ask: What family traditions do you have for birthdays? Do you think birthdays are celebrated differently in different cultures or countries?*

Unit Preview: Table of Contents

1. **Use the table of contents to locate information** Ask questions about the chapters in this unit. *Ask: How many chapters are in this unit? What page is Chapter 1 on? Who is the author of the selection in Chapter 2?*
2. **Connect** *Ask: Which titles interest you?*

UNIT 1

Traditions and Cultures

UNIT OBJECTIVES

Reading
Compare and contrast a poem and a personal narrative • Read aloud to show understanding as you read a folktale • Describe mental images as you read a poem • Compare text events with your own experiences as you read a personal narrative • Identify cause and effect as you read historical fiction

Listening and Speaking
Tell about and act out a party activity • Present a dramatic reading • Tell what you are thankful for • Distinguish fact from opinion • Perform a dialogue

View the Picture

1. **Art background** Diego Rivera (1886–1957) painted pictures and murals with traditional Mexican themes. Using realistic but simple subjects and strong colors, Rivera recorded the celebrations and traditions of farmers, workers, and their families. This oil painting shows a traditional religious parade of children going through a town asking for "posada," or shelter, to represent Joseph and Mary's search in Bethlehem.

2. **Art interpretation** Point out that the color and light in the painting look very bright even though the scene takes place at night. *Ask: What message did Rivera paint by making a night scene look like day?* (children carrying candles give off special light; days will start growing longer and giving more light)

   a. **Explore and describe themes** Ask students to discuss why Rivera chose to reflect the wise men in the pool. (the Christmas theme)

   b. **Art interpretation** Have students explain how this painting tells a story about Mexican customs or traditions. *Ask: What is happening in the picture? Why are the children carrying candles?*

   c. **Use personal experience** *Ask: Have you been in a procession or march?*

   d. **Connect to theme** *Say: The theme of this unit is* traditions and cultures. *What examples of tradition and culture do you see in this painting?*

Children Asking for "Posada" (La Procesión), Diego Rivera, oil painting. 1953.

View the Picture

1. What are the people in this picture doing?
2. Do you know about this tradition?
3. What other traditions do you know about?

In this unit, you will read poems, personal narratives, a folktale, and historical fiction about different traditions and cultures. You will learn about the features of poems, narratives, and fiction. You will also practice writing these forms.

1

ASSESS

Have students draw a picture of a traditional parade. *Say: Try to use a part of the art on this page in your drawing, such as the season or the colors.*

Grammar

Use present continuous tense verbs
- Identify subjects and verbs in sentences
- Use subject pronouns • Use the verb *to be* with complements • Recognize possessive nouns

Writing

Write a personal narrative • Write a narrative • Write a narrative about a holiday • Write a fictional narrative

Content

Math: Analyze a bar graph • Science: Learn about food chains • Social Studies: Read a map • The Arts: Design a Turkish rug • Math: Learn geometric shapes and vocabulary

CHAPTER 1

Into the Reading

Chapter Materials

Activity Book: *pp. 1–8*
Audio: *Unit 1, Chapter 1; CD 1, Tracks 1–2*
Student Handbook
Student CD-ROM: *Unit 1, Chapter 1*
Teacher Resource Book: *Lesson Plan, Teacher Resources, Reading Summary, Activity Book Answer Key*
Teacher Resource CD-ROM
Assessment Program: *Quiz, pp. 7–8; Teacher and Student Resources, pp. 115–144*
Assessment CD-ROM
Transparencies
The Heinle Newbury House Dictionary/CD-ROM
Web site: http://visions.heinle.com

Objectives

Preview Read the objectives aloud. *Ask: Is there an objective you already know?*

Use Prior Knowledge

Discuss Family Celebrations

Brainstorm List and discuss family celebrations.

Answers

1. *Sample answers:* birthdays, anniversaries
2. *Sample answers:* **a.** My brother's high school graduation. **b.** With a party.

Family Photo

a poem by Ralph Fletcher

Birthday Barbecue

a personal narrative and a painting by Carmen Lomas Garza

Objectives

Reading Compare and contrast a poem and a personal narrative.

Listening and Speaking Tell about and act out a party activity.

Grammar Use present continuous tense verbs.

Writing Write a personal narrative.

Content Math: Analyze a bar graph.

Use Prior Knowledge

Discuss Family Celebrations

Prior knowledge is something that you already know. Use your prior knowledge to help you understand new information.

Families often come together to celebrate a holiday or an important event.

1. With a partner, list events that families celebrate in different regions and cultures.
2. Talk about a family celebration that your culture has.
   a. What event do you celebrate?
   b. How do you celebrate?
3. Use a storyboard to show pictures of a family celebration. Label each picture.
4. With your classmates, compare and contrast your storyboards.

Family Celebration

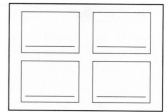

MULTI-LEVEL OPTIONS *Build Vocabulary*

Newcomer Have students draw or bring in pictures of their families. Tell them to use the pictures to complete their webs. Say and write the word for each family member. Help students pronounce words correctly. Have students work in pairs to practice family words using their webs for clarification.

Beginning Ask students to draw or bring in pictures of family members. Have them use the pictures to complete their webs. Then point to family members on the webs. Ask students to say the word for the family member as you point to each drawing or picture.

Intermediate Tell students to draw or bring in pictures of family members. Have students work in pairs. Ask each student to identify the family members and say one sentence about them. For example: *This is my mother. She is a doctor. That is Uncle Juan. He lives in Dallas.*

Advanced Have students work in pairs. Ask them to take turns describing a family celebration and the roles that each member plays. On the board, write model sentences: *My little cousin was a flower girl at my sister's wedding. My aunt always bakes special pies.*

Build Background

Piñatas

Background is information that can help you understand what you hear, see, or read.

A *piñata* is a clay or paper container that people fill with candy or gifts. It is often shaped like an animal or a star. At birthday parties in Mexico and some other countries, people hang a piñata from the ceiling or a tree. Children try to break open the piñata by hitting it with a stick while their eyes are covered.

SOCIAL STUDIES

Content Connection
Mexico is a country to the south of the United States.

Build Vocabulary

Learn Words for Family Members

When you learn new words, you **build your vocabulary.**

1. In your Personal Dictionary, draw the web shown.
2. With a partner, fill in words for family members.
3. If you don't know a word, ask other students or your teacher for help.
4. For help with pronunciation, ask your teacher or a classmate for help.

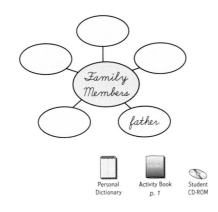

Personal Dictionary   Activity Book p. 1   Student CD-ROM

Chapter 1   Family Photo *and* Birthday Barbecue   **3**

Home Connection

Build Vocabulary Have students ask family members to identify their favorite holidays. Invite students to make two-column charts. In the left column, they can write words such as *mother, brother,* or *aunt,* for the family members. As an alternative, they can draw the family members. On the right, they can write the word for the person's favorite holiday or draw a symbol of it. Ask volunteers to share their charts.

Teacher Resource Book: *Two-Column Chart, p. 44*

Learning Styles
Musical

Build Background Invite students to share songs that are part of their family's celebrations.

Build Background

Piñatas

1. **Use personal knowledge** Ask: *Does anyone know how to make a paper piñata? How could you make one from a paper bag?*
2. **Use a map** Refer students to the map in their books and identify the three countries. *Ask: What are these bodies of water called? What are some other countries in Central America?*
3. **Content Connection** Mexico City is the capital of Mexico. It is located near the center of Mexico. *Ask: Has anyone ever visited Mexico?*

Build Vocabulary

Learn Words for Family Members

Teacher Resource Book: *Web, p. 37; Personal Dictionary, p. 63*

1. **Use a word web** Have students fill in their webs. Then ask a volunteer to draw his/her web on the board. Write other family words on the board that students may need.
2. **Reading selection vocabulary** You may want to introduce the glossed words in the reading selections before students begin reading. Key words: *generations, barbecue, teenagers, comforting, encouraging.* Instruct students to write the words with correct spelling and their definitions in their Personal Dictionaries. Have them pronounce each word and divide it into syllables.
3. **Multi-level options** See MULTI-LEVEL OPTIONS on p. 2.

 **ASSESS**

Have students write two sentences describing their family.

Text Structure

Poem and Personal Narrative

1. **Share personal experiences** Tell a brief story of a celebration you attended. Ask students to identify the features of the narrative in your story.

Reading Strategy

Compare and Contrast

Teacher Resource Book: *Venn Diagram, p. 35; Two-Column Chart, p. 44*

1. **Model compare and contrast strategy** Have students look at the art on p. 1. Ask them to compare and contrast it to the celebration on p. 5. Record their ideas on a two-column chart.
2. **Use a graphic organizer** Fill in the Venn diagram on the board.
3. **Multi-level options** See MULTI-LEVEL OPTIONS below.

ASSESS

Ask: How do poems and narratives look different? (Poems have stanzas; narratives have paragraphs.)

Text Structure

Poem and Personal Narrative

The **text structure** of a reading is its main parts and how they fit together.

1. "Family Photo" is a **poem.** As you read, look for these features of a poem:

Poem	
Experiences	the author's life, thoughts, and feelings
Images	words that make pictures in your mind
Structure	sections called "stanzas"; stanzas are not always complete sentences

2. "Birthday Barbecue" is a **personal narrative.** A narrative tells about things that happen. As you read, look for these features of a personal narrative:

Personal Narrative	
Experiences	the author's life, thoughts, and feelings
Details	words that describe true information, things, and actions
Pronouns	use of *I, we, us,* or *me*
Structure	paragraphs

Student
CD-ROM

Reading Strategy

Compare and Contrast

A **reading strategy** is a way to understand what you read. You can become a better reader if you learn good reading strategies.

When you **compare** two or more things, you see how they are similar. When you **contrast,** you see how they are different.

1. As you read or listen to the audio recording of "Family Photo" and "Birthday Barbecue," compare and contrast the characters (the people) and the events (the things that happen) in the two stories.

2. Copy the Venn Diagram on a piece of paper. Use it to compare and contrast as you read.

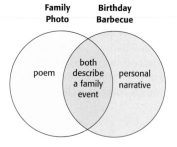

Family Photo — Birthday Barbecue
poem | both describe a family event | personal narrative

4 Unit 1 Traditions and Cultures

Student
CD-ROM

MULTI-LEVEL OPTIONS *Reading Strategy*

Newcomer Have two volunteers stand in front of the class. Point to something that is the same about each student, such as eye color or height. *Say: same, different.* Have students point to other similarities and differences as you say *same* or *different.* Then ask students to say *same* or *different* as you point to similarities and differences.

Beginning Have two volunteers stand before the class. Ask students to identify similarities and differences using phrases such as *same eyes, different hair.* Explain that the students are comparing and contrasting.

Intermediate Have pairs of students examine the picture of a family celebration on p. 5. Ask each pair to compare and contrast two people shown in the picture. Have students identify three similarities and three differences between the two people.

Advanced Have pairs of students look at the art on p. 5. Ask them to select two of the people and identify as many similarities and differences between the two as possible. Provide time for pairs to share their findings with the class.

Family Photo

a poem by Ralph Fletcher

Birthday Barbecue

a personal narrative and painting
by Carmen Lomas Garza

5

Reading Selection Materials

Audio: *Unit 1, Chapter 1; CD 1, Tracks 1–2*
Teacher Resource Book: *Reading Summary,*
 pp. 65–66
Transparencies: #1, *Reading Summary*

Suggestions for Using Reading Summary

- Introduce new vocabulary or cognates.
- Cut the summary into strips, or jumble the sentences on an overhead transparency. Students put the sentences in order.
- Practice the reading strategy.
- Students read aloud or with a partner.
- Students paraphrase the summary.
- Students do a cloze activity.
- Students create a visual or graphic organizer, such as a timeline or storyboard, to illustrate the summary.
- Students paraphrase the summary.

Preview the Selections

1. **Interpret the image** Tell students that the photo relates to both the poem and the personal narrative that they will read. *Ask: What is happening in this photo? What prediction can you make about the readings from this photo?*
2. **Connect** Remind students that the unit theme is *traditions and cultures.* Ask them how the picture relates to the theme.

Content Connection
The Arts

Ask students to bring in photos of family celebrations. Invite them to identify the celebrations and what the people are doing (eating special foods, playing musical instruments, playing games, opening gifts). As an alternative, students may talk about photos they have seen of other families.

Learning Styles
Interpersonal

Ask: How do the people in the picture feel? How do you know? Have students use what they know about celebrations along with visual clues, such as the expressions and actions of the people in the picture, to identify likely feelings (happy, excited, pleased). Have them discuss in small groups.

Read the Selection

1. **Use text features** Explain the purpose and use of the stanza numbers. Then direct students to glossed words. Clarify meanings as needed.
2. **Choral reading** Have small groups do choral readings of different stanzas. As groups of students read aloud together, remind them to read at the same pace so they sound like one voice.
3. **Make inferences** *Say: The author says this is one last picture before they "head off in different directions." Where do you think they will go? Do you think any of them live far away?*
4. **Identify text images** *Say: The author uses words to create pictures. What images are there in this poem?* (The family members as ripples in a pond, spreading out from the stone the grandparents threw.)

Sample Answer to Guide Question
The characters mentioned in the poem (not the picture) include: Grandma and Grandpa, a baby cousin, and kids.

See Teacher Edition pp. 434–436 for a list of English-Spanish cognates in the reading selection.

Audio
CD 1, Tr. 1

Family Photo
a poem by Ralph Fletcher

1 One last picture
before we head off
in different directions.

2 One last group shot of
all of us, **smirking,**
with **rabbit ears.**

3 Three **generations,**
kids on shoulders,
a baby cousin on my lap.

4 And in the middle
Grandma and Grandpa
who started all this.

5 We're all **ripples** in a pond
spreading out
from a stone they threw.

> **Compare and Contrast**
>
> Who are the characters in this poem? After you read "Birthday Barbecue" on page 8, compare and contrast the characters.

smirking smiling in a way that shows you feel smarter or better than someone else
rabbit ears when people hold their fingers in the shape of a "V" behind someone's head, like the ears of a rabbit

generations any of the different age levels in a family, such as grandparents, parents, and grandchildren
ripples little waves

6 Unit 1 Traditions and Cultures

MULTI-LEVEL OPTIONS *Read the Selection*

Newcomer Play the audio. Read the poem again, emphasizing words for family members: *cousin, Grandma, Grandpa.* Write these words on the board. Play the audio again. Tell students to raise their hands when they hear these words. *Ask: Is the poem about a family?* (yes) *Is the cousin grown up?* (no) *Are Grandma and Grandpa in the picture?* (yes)

Beginning Read the poem aloud to students. Then have them reread the poem chorally. *Ask: What is the poem about?* (a family) *Who is sitting on the writer's lap?* (his cousin) *Who started the family?* (Grandma and Grandpa)

Intermediate Have students do a paired reading. Seat students side by side in pairs. Direct them to take turns reading aloud. *Ask: Why did the family take a picture?* (The family members were going away.) *How are family members different?* (Some are younger; some are older.) *Why are the grandparents in the middle?* (They started the family.)

Advanced Have students read the poem silently and then read aloud in pairs. *Ask: Why does the writer say "We're all ripples"?* (He means that the younger people all came from the grandparents.) *Compare and contrast this family with yours.* (Sample answer: I have a baby cousin, but my family is smaller.)

Read the Selection

1. **Identify the structure of a poem** *Say: Does a poem have paragraphs?* (no, stanzas) *Remember that stanzas do not have to be complete sentences. What makes a complete sentence?* (subject and verb) Look at each stanza and discuss why it is not a complete sentence. You may want to talk about how each stanza could become a sentence.

2. **Teacher think aloud** *Say: Let me look at the first stanza. Does it have a subject? Yes, one last picture. Is there a verb? No. How could I make this into a sentence? Here is one last picture before we head off in different directions.* Have students discuss each stanza in the same way.

3. **Present a dramatic interpretation** *Say: Each poem has its own rhythm. You can change it slightly, just like a musician or rapper does a song. Can you read the poem aloud with a rap beat?* Give students the opportunity to do a dramatic reading of the poem.

4. **Multi-level options** See MULTI-LEVEL OPTIONS on p. 6.

About the Author

Evaluate information about the author Read the biography to students. Define *novels* and *nonfiction*. **Ask:** *When did he start writing stories?* (in junior high) *What does* "building my city of words" *mean?* (writing; *a city of words* is a story)

About the Author | **Ralph Fletcher (born 1953)**

Ralph Fletcher grew up in a big family. His family members told many stories. Fletcher started writing in junior high school. After college, he traveled around the world. Then he went back to school and studied writing. Now Fletcher writes poems, novels, and nonfiction. He says, "I love to write. I love getting up every morning and . . . playing with stories, trying to build my city of words."

➤ Based on "Family Photo," how do you think Ralph Fletcher feels about his family?

Chapter 1 Family Photo *and* Birthday Barbecue **7**

A Capitalization

Names and titles

Tell students that the first letter in a name is always capitalized. *Ask: What letters in the author's name are capitalized?* (R and F) *Why does the word* Grandma *begin with a capital letter?* (It is the name that the children call their grandmother.) *Can you find another name in the poem that is capitalized?* (Grandpa) Explain that the important words in titles of poems, stories, and books and the first word of a sentence also start with

capital letters. *Ask: What letters in the title are capitalized?* (F and P)

Apply Write on the board: *family photo is a poem by ralph fletcher. it tells about grandma and grandpa's family.* Ask students to decide which letters should be capitalized.

Read the Selection

1. **Teacher read aloud** Read paragraph 1 aloud as students read along silently. *Ask: Why is the family together?* (for a birthday) *What did they do before the party?* (filled a piñata, baked a cake, built a barbecue)

2. **Explore the influence of color** *Ask: What are the main colors used by the artist? What mood do the colors create? Why are these good colors for this celebration? What message is the artist trying to tell by using these colors?*

Sample Answer to Guide Question
In the poem, someone is taking a picture to celebrate a family gathering. In the narrative, everyone is celebrating a birthday, but family members are doing different things.

See Teacher Edition pp. 434–436 for a list of English-Spanish cognates in the reading selection.

Audio
CD 1, Tr. 2

Compare and Contrast

Compare and contrast what happened in "Birthday Barbecue" with what happened in "Family Photo."

Birthday Barbecue
a personal narrative by Carmen Lomas Garza

1   This is my sister Mary Jane's birthday party. She's hitting a piñata that my mother made. My mother also baked and decorated the cake. There she is, bringing the meat that's ready to cook. My father is cooking at the **barbecue,** which he designed and built himself. My grandfather is **shoveling** in the coals of **mesquite wood.**

barbecue a place for cooking food outdoors
shoveling using a shovel to move or pick up something

mesquite wood a type of wood used in cooking food outdoors

8   **Unit 1** Traditions and Cultures

MULTI-LEVEL OPTIONS *Read the Selection*

Newcomer Read the selection aloud. Emphasize the words: *sister, mother, father, grandfather, uncle, cousin, grandmother.* Reread the selection. Ask students to point to the family member in the picture as each is mentioned. *Ask: Is this about a boy's party?* (no) *Is the grandmother at the party?* (yes)

Beginning Have students look closely at the picture. Then do a paired reading of the selection. *Ask: Who is having a birthday?* (the sister) *Who is cooking the meat?* (the father and grandfather) *Who is the grandmother holding?* (a baby)

Intermediate Ask pairs to read together. Have each student read one paragraph. *Ask: How is Mary Jane celebrating her birthday?* (with a family party) *Why are there two people at the barbecue?* (One is cooking; one is putting coals on the fire.) *Why was the uncle trying to get the child to hit the piñata?* (to make him feel better)

Advanced Have students read the selection silently. Then *ask: Why is the family together?* (to celebrate the girl's birthday) *Why do you think grandmother takes care of the babies?* (She loves babies and is good at caring for them.) *What will the family probably do next?* (eat the food the adults are making)

2   Underneath the tree are some young **teenagers,** very much in love. My great uncle is **comforting** my young cousin, who was crying, and **encouraging** him to hit the piñata. My grandmother is holding a baby. She was always holding the babies, and feeding them, and putting them to sleep.

---

teenagers people between the ages of 13 and 19
comforting making someone feel better

encouraging giving strength or hope to, urging

About the Author

Carmen Lomas Garza (born 1948)

Carmen Lomas Garza was born and grew up in Texas. She is a painter. She has also written books with her stories and her paintings. Garza first discovered art from her mother, who was a painter. She says, "My mother Maria was the first artist I saw paint. I thought she was making magic." Garza's artwork and stories help her celebrate her Mexican-American culture.

➤ Why do you think Carmen Lomas Garza wrote about and painted a picture of her sister's birthday party? Describe the colors, shapes, and lines in the painting. How do they influence Garza's message?

Chapter 1 Family Photo *and* Birthday Barbecue **9**

 Spelling

Plurals

Explain that plurals are words that mean more than one. **Say:** *Many plurals are made by adding an -s to a noun.* Write on the board: *1 teenager, 2 teenagers.* **Say:** *To make a plural of a noun that ends in a consonant and -y, drop the -y and add -ies.* Write: *1 baby, 3 babies.*

    Apply Write on the board: *party, cake, family, granny, tree.* Have students work in pairs to write the plural of each word.

Evaluate Your Reading Strategy

Compare and Contrast *Say: You have practiced an important reading strategy. Now you can decide how well you have done. Does this statement describe how you read?*

> When I read a poem and a narrative, I compare and contrast them. Comparing and contrasting helps me understand how things are the same or different.

Read the Selection

1. **Paired reading** Have students read the selection in pairs. Tell them to read alternating sentences aloud as they sit side by side with their partners.
2. **Connect to theme** *Say: The theme of this unit is* traditions and cultures. *What traditions do you see in this painting?*
3. **Multi-level options** See MULTI-LEVEL OPTIONS on p. 8.

About the Author

Analyze facts Read the paragraph aloud. *Ask: Where did Carmen Lomas Garza grow up?* (Texas) *Who influenced her to begin painting?* (her mother) *What does she compare painting to?* (making magic) *What culture did she grow up in?* (Mexican-American)

Across Selections

▌ Teacher Resource Book: *Venn Diagram, p. 35*

Draw a Venn diagram on the board. Ask students to compare and contrast the two selections. (Compare: family gatherings, three generations, babies, happy people. Contrast: different text structures; the poem is about the end of the gathering and everyone is together; in the narrative, everyone is doing something different.) Have a volunteer record the information in the Venn diagram.

Spelling, Punctuation, Capitalization

After the Reading Comprehension section, students will practice spelling, punctuation, and capitalization in the Activity Book.

Reading Comprehension

Question-Answer Relationships

Sample Answers

1. There are the grandparents, parents, grandchildren, cousins, aunts, and uncles.
2. They are sitting in the middle.
3. Mary Jane is the author's sister. She's celebrating her birthday.
4. She baked and decorated the cake, and she brought out the meat.
5. She's bringing it to the barbecue.
6. The author means that the grandparents started the family, which has grown and spread out.
7. They both show a barbecue, but the painting has more details than the text.
8. She loves them. She always holds them and takes care of them.
9. They are happy readings because people seem happy together. They are smiling and celebrating.

Build Reading Fluency

Rapid Word Recognition

Rapid word recognition is an excellent activity for students who struggle with irregular spelling patterns. Time students for 1 minute as they read the words in the squares aloud.

Reading Comprehension

Question-Answer Relationships (QAR)

You can understand readings better if you answer different kinds of questions about them.

"Right There" Questions

1. **Recall Facts** In "Family Photo," who is in the family photo?
2. **Recall Facts** In "Family Photo," where are Grandma and Grandpa sitting?
3. **Recall Facts** In "Birthday Barbecue," who is Mary Jane? What is she celebrating?

"Think and Search" Questions

4. **Identify** In "Birthday Barbecue," name three things that the mother did.
5. **Draw Conclusions** In "Birthday Barbecue," where do you think the mother is bringing the meat?

"Author and You" Questions

6. **Interpret** Look at stanza 5 of "Family Photo." What do you think the author means?
7. **Compare and Contrast** How are the painting and the text in "Birthday Barbecue" similar and different?
8. **Draw Conclusions** In "Birthday Barbecue," how do you think the grandmother feels about babies? Explain.

"On Your Own" Question

9. **Identify Mood** Do you think "Family Photo" and "Birthday Barbecue" are happy readings? Why or why not?

Activity Book p. 2   Student CD-ROM

Build Reading Fluency

Rapid Word Recognition

Rapidly recognizing words helps increase your reading rate. It is an important characteristic of effective readers.

1. With a partner, review the words in the box.
2. Read the words aloud for one minute. Your teacher will time you.
3. Count how many words you read in one minute.

one	built	threw	who	threw	one
cousin	who	built	threw	who	threw
who	made	cousin	one	made	cousin
threw	threw	who	cousin	one	made
made	cousin	one	made	built	who

10 Unit 1 Traditions and Cultures

MULTI-LEVEL OPTIONS *Elements of Literature*

Newcomer Point to yourself and *say: I.* Stand beside a student, point to both of you and *say: we.* Pick up a book and *say: my book.* Ask students to point to themselves whenever they hear *I*, *my*, or *we* as you say sentences such as: *My birthday is in May. I want to have a party. We will have fun.*

Beginning Play a follow-the-leader game with students. For example, *say: I am happy*, and make an appropriate facial expression. Have the class respond by repeating your sentence with the correct pronoun, such as: *We are happy.*

Intermediate Ask students to pretend to be Mary Jane in "Birthday Barbecue" and talk about her birthday party. Direct students to use sentences such as: *I had a birthday party. My family was there. We hit the piñata.*

Advanced Have pairs of students role-play an interview using information from About the Author on p. 9. Remind students that the person acting as the author must answer in the first person. For example, one student might ask: *Where did you live?* The other student might respond: *My family lived in Texas when I was born.*

Listen, Speak, Interact

Tell About and Act Out a Party Activity

When people listen and talk to each other, they **interact.**

In "Birthday Barbecue," the author describes what people are doing at a birthday party.

1. Work with a partner. Choose a birthday party activity.
2. What happens during the activity? Write or draw the details in order.
3. Practice telling and acting out the activity with your partner.
4. Tell the class about your activity. Then act it out if possible.

5. What birthday activities did you learn about? How are they similar to and different from the activities in the selection?

> *Break a Piñata*
> 1. Hang a piñata.
> 2. Cover someone's eyes.
> 3.
> 4.

Elements of Literature

Recognize First-Person Point of View

Literature is something that an author writes for someone to read. Authors use many different ways to express themselves. These ways are the **elements of literature.**

A kind of literature is a **genre.** Poems and personal narratives are examples of genres.

In the narrative genre, the **narrator** tells the story. Sometimes the narrator is a person in the story.

<u>I</u> hang a piñata. <u>I</u> cover <u>my</u> sister's eyes. <u>My</u> sister tries to hit the piñata. The piñata breaks. <u>We</u> pick up the candy.

A story written like this has **first-person point of view.** Look at the underlined words in the example. When the narrator uses words like *I, my,* and *we,* the story is in **first-person point of view.**

In your Reading Log, write one sentence from "Birthday Barbecue" that shows first-person point of view.

First-Person Point of View	
Who	**Pronouns that Are Used**
The narrator describes events.	I, me, my, we, us, our

Reading Log   Activity Book p. 3   Student CD-ROM

Chapter 1 Family Photo *and* Birthday Barbecue   **11**

Listen, Speak, Interact

Tell About and Act Out Party Activities

1. **Brainstorm** Have students brainstorm other activities they can do at a birthday party.
2. **Newcomers** Choose one party activity to do with this group, such as bringing out the birthday cake. Write key words on the board, such as *cake, candles, blow, wish.* Have students practice describing and acting out the activity.

Elements of Literature

Recognize First-Person Point of View

1. **Review personal pronouns** Write on the board: *I, you, he, she, it, we, they.* Point out first-, second-, and third-person subject pronouns. Repeat for object pronouns: *me, you, him, her, it, us, them.* Model sentences using pronouns.
2. **Clarify terms** Give students time to read the explanation. Point out the terms in boldface and ask students what they mean. Clarify meanings as needed.
3. **Multi-level options** See MULTI-LEVEL OPTIONS on p. 10.

 ASSESS

Write two sentences from "Family Photo" (p. 6) that show first-person point of view. Use a different pronoun for each sentence.

Cultural Connection

Have students work in pairs. Ask them to use pictures and text in library books to identify birthday traditions across the world. Ask students to tell about or act out two traditions that they discover. Have them locate on a map where the traditions are practiced.

Learning Styles
Kinesthetic

Engage students in playing a few games commonly played at birthday parties in this country, such as "Pin the Tail on the Donkey" or "Musical Chairs." Invite students to share descriptions or drawings of activities from birthday celebrations in other countries. Engage the class in doing some of these activities, if possible.

Word Study

Identify Compound Words

Make a word chart Read the definitions and examples of compound words. Then have students work in pairs to find the compound words in the reading selection.

Answers

3. grand, mother, grandmother, grand, father, grandfather

Grammar Focus

Use Present Continuous Tense Verbs

Describe actions Direct students to the painting on p. 9. Have them describe what is happening in pairs. Remind them to use the present continuous tense.

Answers

Possible answers: She's hitting a piñata . . . My father is cooking at the barbecue . . . My grandfather is shoveling in the coals . . . My great-uncle is comforting my young cousin . . . My grandmother is holding a baby.

ASSESS

Write on the board: *bring, paint, hold.* Have students write the sentences with these verbs using the present continuous tense.

Word Study

Identify Compound Words

Words can have several parts. In this section, you will learn what the different parts mean.

A **compound word** is a word made of two words. Look at the chart.

1. Copy the chart in your Personal Dictionary.
2. Find compound words in "Birthday Barbecue" that fit the meanings.
3. Write the separate words and the compound words in the chart.

First Word	Second Word	Compound Word	Meaning
birth +	day ⇒	birthday	the day of your birth
+	⇒		the mother of one of your parents
+	⇒		the father of one of your parents

Personal Dictionary   Activity Book p. 4   Student CD-ROM

Grammar Focus

Use Present Continuous Tense Verbs

Grammar is the way that a language is put together.

A **present continuous tense verb** tells about an action that is happening now. It uses the verbs *am, is,* or *are* plus a verb ending in *-ing.* For example:

My father <u>is cooking</u>.

Present Continuous Tense		
I	**am**	cook**ing**.
He/She/It	**is**	cook**ing**.
We/You/They	**are**	cook**ing**.

1. Find two more sentences in paragraphs 1 and 2 of "Birthday Barbecue" that use present continuous tense verbs. Write them on a piece of paper. Circle the present continuous verbs.
2. Write your own sentence about something happening in the classroom right now. Use a present continuous tense verb. Circle it.

Activity Book pp. 5–6   Student Handbook   Student CD-ROM

MULTI-LEVEL OPTIONS *From Reading to Writing*

Newcomer Have students draw family celebrations. Help them label themselves in the illustrations by using the words *I* and *me.* Assist them in using present continuous tense verbs, such as *am eating, is singing, are playing,* to label some of the activities shown.

Beginning Have students write captions for their illustrations of family celebrations. Suggest sentence formats such as: *I am (verb). We are (verb). My mother is (verb).*

Intermediate Have students identify all the continuous verbs in "Birthday Barbecue." Then have them list continuous tense verbs to describe activities shown in their own pictures. Instruct students to use their lists as resources for ideas to include in their narratives.

Advanced Remind students of the compare and contrast activities in this chapter. Point out that writing can be made more interesting by including comparisons. Write on the board: *I am eating a big bowl of ice cream. I am eating a bowl of ice cream as big as a mountain.* Ask students to include a few comparisons.

From Reading to Writing

Write a Personal Narrative

After you read literature in school, you often write about it. This section shows you how to do this.

Draw a picture of a family celebration or a party. Put yourself in the picture, too. Write a personal narrative about the picture.

1. Write in the first-person point of view. Use *I, me, my, we, us,* or *our* to show that you are the narrator.
2. Use present continuous tense verbs.
3. Write one paragraph.

Activity Book
p. 7

Student
Handbook

Across Content Areas

Analyze a Bar Graph

Content areas are the subjects you study in school. Math, science, social studies, language arts, and other arts such as music and drawing are content areas.

A **bar graph** is a graph that shows amounts. This bar graph shows the number of different family members in Pablo Garcia's family. To read the bar graph, look at a family member at the bottom of a bar. Then find the number that corresponds to the top of the bar.

1. How many aunts does Pablo have?
2. How many sisters does he have?
3. Which bar has the most members?
4. Which bar has the fewest members?
5. Make a bar graph like this to show your own family members.

Activity Book
p. 8

Student
CD-ROM

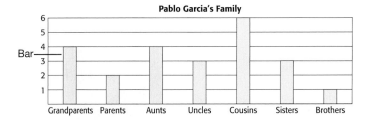

Pablo Garcia's Family

Bar

Grandparents Parents Aunts Uncles Cousins Sisters Brothers

From Reading to Writing

Write a Personal Narrative

1. **Model** Demonstrate how to do the activity. Bring in a photo or draw a simple picture of yourself at a celebration. Tell a first-person narrative about the picture.
2. **Multi-level options** See MULTI-LEVEL OPTIONS on p. 12.

Across Content Areas: Math

Analyze a Bar Graph

Define and clarify Direct students to the graph. Point out the heading across the top, the labels under each bar, and the numbers on the side.

Answers
1. 4 aunts 2. 3 sisters 3. cousins 4. brothers

ASSESS

Have students write two sentences describing their family.

Reteach and Reassess

Text Structure Draw a chart. Label the columns: *"Features," "Family Photo," "Birthday Barbecue."* Under *"Features,"* write: *details, experiences, images, paragraphs, pronouns, stanzas.* Help students check off the features found in each selection.

Reading Strategy Have students recall the party in "Birthday Barbecue." Ask them to place drawings or phrases on a Venn diagram comparing this event with a party they know about.

Elements of Literature Tell students to pretend to be Ralph Fletcher and tell about the picture in "Family Photo." Remind them to use first person.

Reassess Have students create side-by-side sketches of a classroom party and a family party. Then have them point to elements that are similar or different or make a list of continuous tense verbs comparing and contrasting activities in the two parties.

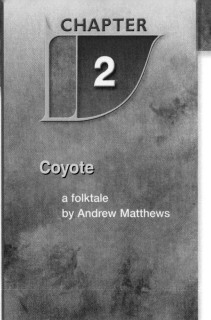

Chapter Materials

Activity Book: *pp. 9–16*
Audio: *Unit 1, Chapter 2; CD 1, Track 3*
Student Handbook
Student CD-ROM: *Unit 1, Chapter 2*
Teacher Resource Book: *Lesson Plan, Teacher
    Resources, Reading Summary, Activity Book
    Answer Key*
Teacher Resource CD-ROM
Assessment Program: *Quiz, pp. 9–10; Teacher
    and Student Resources, pp. 115–144*
Assessment CD-ROM
Transparencies
The Heinle Newbury House Dictionary/CD-ROM
Web site: http://visions.heinle.com

Objectives

Preview Read the objectives aloud. Ask
students to name folktales they know.

Use Prior Knowledge

Share Knowledge About Coyotes

1. **Preview** Ask students if they have ever
   seen or heard a coyote. Have them share
   what they know about coyotes.
2. **Provide facts** Explain that the coyote is
   also called a prairie wolf or a brush wolf.
   They are native to the western part of North
   America.

Answers
a. T b. F c. T d. T

Coyote

a folktale
by Andrew Matthews

Objectives

Reading Read aloud to show
understanding as you read a folktale.

Listening and Speaking Present a
dramatic reading.

Grammar Identify subjects and verbs
in sentences.

Writing Write a narrative.

Content Science: Learn about food chains.

Use Prior Knowledge

Share Knowledge About Coyotes

What do you know about coyotes?

1. Copy each statement below on a
   piece of paper.
   a. Coyotes live in many parts of the
      United States.
   b. Coyotes have no fur.
   c. Coyotes hunt for food during
      the night.
   d. Coyotes can live in very
      cold places.
2. Decide if each statement is true
   or false. Write *T* if you think a
   statement is true. Write *F* if you
   think a statement is false.

3. Share your answers with a partner.
   Do your answers match? Ask your
   teacher if you need help.

Coyote

MULTI-LEVEL OPTIONS *Build Vocabulary*

Newcomer Direct attention to
the photo of a coyote on p. 14.
Point to the picture and make a
howling sound. Invite students to
imitate the sound one time. *Say:
howl.* Introduce the words *growl,
yelp,* and *bark* in the same way.
Ask students to name animals
that make each sound.

Beginning Write the
vocabulary words on the board.
Demonstrate the meaning of each
by making the sound. Have
students work in pairs. Tell them
to take turns saying sentences
such as: *Coyotes howl,* after
which the other partner will act
out the sentence.

Intermediate Engage students
in a discussion of sounds coyotes,
dogs, and wolves make and why
animals make these sounds. Have
them work in pairs to make up a
sentence telling when an animal
might make each sound. For
example, *say: My dog barks when
he is happy to see me.*

Advanced Ask pairs to write
short descriptions of howls,
growls, yelps, and barks heard on
an imaginary camping trip. Have
pairs share their stories. One
student can be the narrator and
the other can provide sound
effects.

Build Background

Stories with Animals

People of all cultures tell stories. Some of these stories have animals in them. Sometimes the animals talk and do other things that animals cannot do.

Some stories tell about nature. For example, they might tell about the beginning of the ocean or Earth. Most people do not believe that these stories are true.

In the story you are going to read and listen to, the first coyote creates Earth. After you read or listen to "Coyote," talk about stories you have heard from different regions of the United States and other cultures. How are they similar or different?

Content Connection
Culture includes the ideas, activities (such as art, foods, clothing), and ways of behaving that are special to a country, people, or region.

Build Vocabulary

Learn Words for Animal Sounds

Animals make sounds, and languages have words for those sounds. Here are some words for sounds that dogs, coyotes, and wolves make.

1. Listen as your teacher says the words.
   a. howl
   b. growl
   c. yelp
   d. bark
2. Now listen as your teacher makes the animal sounds. Can you match the words above with the sounds?

3. Work with a partner. Make one of the animal sounds and have your partner say the word for it.
4. Write the words in your Personal Dictionary.
5. Do you know the word for *bark* in another language? What is it?

Personal Dictionary   Activity Book p. 9   Student CD-ROM

Community Connection

Learning Styles
Visual

Build Vocabulary Have students identify animal sounds they hear in their community. Place these on a two-column chart. Show the word for the sound along with the animal that makes it. Depending on the community, students may identify sounds such as the cooing of pigeons, the mooing of cows, the meowing of cats, or the chirping of robins.

Build Background Divide the class into groups. Give each group illustrated fables and folktales from various cultures. Invite students to notice how animals and other elements of nature are shown in the illustrations in these books.

Build Background

Stories with Animals

1. **Use personal knowledge** *Ask: What animal stories do you know?*
2. **Clarify terms** *Say: The ocean is part of nature. What other things are part of nature?*
3. **Content Connection** Have students give examples of special art, food, or clothing that are popular in their cultures.

Build Vocabulary

Learn Words for Animal Sounds

Teacher Resource Book: *Personal Dictionary, p. 63*

1. **Use sounds** Read the words to students. Have them repeat after you. Check for correct pronunciation. Repeat for animal sounds.
2. **Reading selection vocabulary** You may want to introduce the glossed words in the reading selection before students begin reading. Key words: *rainbow* (see front cover of book for picture), *divided, soared, galloped, howled.* Instruct students to write the words with correct spelling and their definitions in their Personal Dictionaries. Have them pronounce each word and divide it into syllables.
3. **Multi-level options** See MULTI-LEVEL OPTIONS on p. 14.

ASSESS

Divide the class into small groups. Have each group write one question about this page. After a few minutes, have groups exchange questions and answer them.

Text Structure

Folktale

1. **Use graphic organizers** Review features of a narrative. Read the paragraph and direct students to the chart.
2. **Multi-level options** See MULTI-LEVEL OPTIONS below.

Reading Strategy

Read Aloud to Show Understanding

1. **Pair reading** Have students read the material aloud in pairs.
2. **Discuss reread strategy** *Ask: Do you use this strategy in other subject classes? Does it help you to read aloud?*

ASSESS

On the board, write: *characters, setting, plot,* and *ending.* Have students write definitions for each.

Text Structure

Folktale

"Coyote" is a **folktale.** A folktale is a **narrative** (a story) that people tell to their children and grandchildren.

Look at the chart. It shows some distinguishing features of a narrative.

Look for and analyze these features as you read or listen to "Coyote."

Narrative

> **Beginning**
>
> *Who* is in the story? These are the **characters.**
>
> *Where* and *when* does the story take place? This is the **setting.**

↓

> **Middle**
>
> *What* happens? This is the **plot.**

↓

> **End**
>
> *How* does the story end? Are the characters happy? Sad?

Student CD-ROM

Reading Strategy

Read Aloud to Show Understanding

When you do not understand something you read, try reading it aloud to yourself. Follow these tips:

1. Reread the part of the selection aloud.
2. Ask yourself these questions:
   a. What happened in this part of the reading?
   b. What will happen next?

3. Go on to the next part of the reading.
4. Use this strategy as you read "Coyote."

Student CD-ROM

16   Unit 1 Traditions and Cultures

MULTI-LEVEL OPTIONS *Text Structure*

Newcomer Direct students to the picture on p. 17. *Ask: What do you see in the picture?* (a coyote, the moon, bushes, a rock, etc.) List words on the board. *What animal is in the picture?* (a coyote) Have students point to the coyote in the picture. *Where is the coyote?* (on a rock)

Beginning Direct attention to the picture on p. 17. *Ask: Do you see a character?* (coyote) *What is the coyote doing?* (howling) *Why is it howling?* (lonely, calling friends, hungry) *What is the setting?* (on a rock, at night)

Intermediate Direct attention to the illustration on p. 17. *Ask: Who is the character in this folktale?* (coyote) *What is the setting?* (on a rock, at night) Ask students to share any folktales or stories they know about coyotes. Point out the beginning, middle, and end of any story they tell.

Advanced Have students look at the picture on p. 17. Ask them to make predictions about the characters, setting, and plot of the story. Then ask if they can predict how the folktale ends. Tell students that they will read the story to check their predictions.

Coyote

a folktale by Andrew Matthews

17

Reading Selection Materials

Audio: *Unit 1, Chapter 2; CD 1, Track 3*
Teacher Resource Book: *Reading Summary,*
   pp. 67–68
Transparencies: #1, *Reading Summary*

Suggestions for Using
Reading Summary

- Introduce new vocabulary or cognates.
- Cut the summary into strips, or jumble the sentences on an overhead transparency. Students put the sentences in order.
- Practice the reading strategy.
- Students read aloud or with a partner.
- Students paraphrase the summary.
- Students do a cloze activity.
- Students create a visual or graphic organizer, such as a timeline or storyboard, to illustrate the summary.
- Students paraphrase the summary.

Preview the Selection

1. **Use photographs** *Say: Look at the photograph. What kind of animal is this? What is its setting? Why do you think it is howling? Why do you think this photograph was chosen to match a folktale?*
2. **Interpret the image** Talk about the composition of the photo. Introduce the terms *foreground, background, contrast.*
3. **Connect** Tell students that this folktale will be about a coyote. *Ask: Have you ever seen a coyote? What animals are similar to coyotes?* (fox, wolf, dog) *How are coyotes and dogs similar and different?*

Content Connection
Technology

Bookmark pages about coyotes on Internet encyclopedias and other online resources. If possible, provide time for students to look at the pictures and read about coyotes.

Learning Styles
Intrapersonal

Ask students to draw or write concerning their feelings about coyotes. Ask them why people are often curious or afraid or have other strong emotions about these animals.

Read the Selection

1. **Read aloud to understand** Read the guide question and the introduction. Read the selection. Then have students reread it with you chorally.
2. **Paired reading** Have pairs practice reading aloud. Then ask several to read aloud to the class. Ask them to read using expression.

Sample Answer to Guide Question
He wants to run. He made the sky.

> See Teacher Edition pp. 434–436 for a list of English-Spanish cognates in the reading selection.

Audio
CD 1, Tr. 3

Prologue

This story is from the folktales of the American Indians of the western and southwestern United States.

1   At the start of things, it was dark. Dark lay on dark and all was black and **still.** Then, into the stillness came a small sound, a quiet sound. It got bigger, louder, and stronger until it filled the darkness. The sound was Coyote's howl.

2   Coyote grew around the howl. First came his mouth with its sharp, white teeth, then his head with its bright eyes, then his body, bones, and fur. Last of all came a tail. Coyote blinked his eyes at the darkness.

3   "My legs want to run, but I can't run through the dark!" he said.

4   He breathed a wind in the shape of a shell. He turned the shell upside down and with a shake of his head he **flung** it into the air and made the sky.

> **Read Aloud to Understand**
>
> Read paragraphs 3 and 4 aloud. What does Coyote want to do? What did he make?

---

still   not moving   **flung**   threw with force, threw hard

18   Unit 1 Traditions and Cultures

MULTI-LEVEL OPTIONS *Read the Selection*

Newcomer Read the Reading Summary aloud. Then play the audio. Point to these elements in the story as they are mentioned: *Coyote, dark, sky, sun,* and *earth.* **Ask:** *Is the story about Coyote?* (yes) *Does Coyote want to run?* (yes) *Does Coyote make a lamp so he can see?* (no) *Does Coyote make the sun?* (yes)

Beginning Read the selection aloud. Use the pictures, facial expressions, and gestures to support meaning. Then *ask: Who is the main character?* (Coyote) *What is Coyote's problem?* (too dark to run, there is no ground) *What does he make?* (sky, sun, moon, earth)

Intermediate Have students do a paired reading. **Ask:** *Describe the setting at the beginning of the story.* (It is dark and silent.) *Why did Coyote howl?* (He is upset that he can't run.) *What did he make to solve his problem?* (sky, sun, moon, earth)

Advanced Have students read in pairs. **Ask:** *Why couldn't Coyote run in the dark?* (He was afraid he would bump into things or fall and hurt himself.) *How did he solve his problem?* (He made the sky and put the sun and moon in it.) *Predict Coyote's next problem.* (He needs a reason to run.)

5   Coyote took colors to the five corners of the Earth and then he waited. The colors grew into the sky and bent together in the first **rainbow.** The rainbow **divided** the day from the night.

6   Coyote howled a **disk** of burning gold and put it into the sky to be the Sun. He howled a disk of **gleaming** silver and put it into the sky to be the Moon.

7   "My legs want to run, but there's nothing to run on!" he said.

8   Coyote **bared** his teeth and growled. The hard sound of the growl turned into rocks and hills and mountains. Coyote growled more softly. His growl made forests and grassy **prairies.**

> **Read Aloud to Understand**
>
> Read paragraphs 7 and 8 aloud. Coyote can't run. Why? What does Coyote make?

---

rainbow   a curve of bright colors that sometimes forms
   in the sky after a rainstorm
divided   separated, split
disk   a thin, flat circle

gleaming   shining brightly
bared   showed
prairies   large areas of flat or slightly hilly grassland
   with tall grasses and few trees

Chapter 2 Coyote   **19**

Read the Selection

1. **Teacher read aloud** Read the selection aloud. Use variations in voice and gestures to dramatize the text. For example, read "Coyote growled more softly" in a quiet voice.

2. **Repetition as a literary device** Ask a student to read paragraph 7. *Ask: Where did Coyote say something like this before?* (paragraph 3) *How are they the same?* ("My legs want to run, but . . .") *Why do you think repetition is useful in a folktale?* (Folktales were often told, not read. Repetition makes it easier to remember and retell the story.)

3. **Multi-level options** See MULTI-LEVEL OPTIONS on p. 18.

Sample Answer to Guide Question
He can't run because there is no ground to run on. He creates the ground.

✐ Punctuation

Periods at the end of sentences

Explain that sentences always end with ending punctuation. *Say: Sentences that tell something end in periods. Find a telling sentence in paragraph 1 that ends with a period.* (At the start of things, it was dark.) *Say: Sentences that give commands also end in periods. What is a command that Coyote might have given to the sun?* (Get into the sky.) *What mark would be at the end?* (a period)

Read the Selection

1. **Use art to predict** Have students look at the illustration and name animals they know. (hares, deer, bison, and coyote) *Ask: What will these animals do in the folktale?*

2. **Reciprocal reading** Read the tale aloud. Then read each paragraph and have students ask you questions, becoming "teachers."

3. **Expand vocabulary application** Write the glossed verbs on the board. *Say: The hares darted. What other animals can dart?* (cats, dogs, birds) *When does a person dart?* (playing football, soccer, etc.) Ask questions for all of the verbs.

Sample Answer to Guide Question
He made animals.

---

9   Coyote blinked his eyes at the world.

10   "My legs want to run, but I have no one to run with!" he said.

11   So he yelped. **Hares darted** across the prairies, deer and **bison galloped.** Mice **scuttled** across the forest floor and great bears **lumbered** through the **undergrowth.** Coyote yelped again and salmon leapt from the rivers, beavers **bustled** through the water. Mountain lions padded over the hills while eagles **soared** above them on dark wings.

12   "My legs want to run, but I have no one to run from!" said Coyote.

> **Read Aloud to Understand**
>
> Read paragraph 11 aloud. Did Coyote make animals or water and hills?

hares animals that are like rabbits, but larger	**scuttled** moved very quickly
darted moved very quickly	**lumbered** ran or walked in a heavy way
bison large animals with four legs, hairy coats, and short, curved horns	**undergrowth** short plants growing under trees
galloped ran very quickly	**bustled** hurried
	soared flew through the air easily

20   Unit 1 Traditions and Cultures

MULTI-LEVEL OPTIONS *Read the Selection*

Newcomer *Ask: Did Coyote have anyone to run with?* (no) *Did Coyote make elephants?* (no) *Did Coyote use clay to make people?* (yes) *Did the folktale have a happy ending?* (yes)

Beginning *Who did Coyote make to run* with *him?* (hares, deer, bison, mice, bears, salmon, beavers, lions, eagles) *Who did Coyote make to run from?* (people) *What did Coyote use to make people?* (clay) *What did Coyote tell the people to do?* (wake up, gather food, build homes, have children)

Intermediate *Why did Coyote make animals?* (so they could run with him) *How did Coyote make animals?* (by yelping) *Why did Coyote make people?* (to chase him, to make his life challenging or interesting) *How did Coyote make people?* (He made them from clay.)

Advanced *How do you think Coyote was feeling in paragraph 1? Why?* (lonely because there was no one else on Earth) *How did Coyote solve his problem?* (He made other animals and people.) *How did Coyote feel at the end of the story? Why?* (He was happy because he wasn't lonely anymore.)

13　　He found a river with a high **bank** made from soft, red clay. With his sharp claws, Coyote dug in the bank and made heaps of clay. Then he breathed on them. The heaps of clay began to **stir.** They grew and changed shape until, finally, they became the first people.

14　　"Wake up!" Coyote said. "You must gather corn and fruits for food; you must hunt animals for meat. You must build homes and fill the world with your children. And wherever you go, I shall run from you. You will never catch me, but you will hear me at night when I howl at the Moon."

15　　And Coyote ran through the world he had made, barking and howling for joy.

Read Aloud to Understand

Read paragraphs 14 and 15 aloud. Who is Coyote speaking to? How does Coyote feel at the end?

---

bank　the land at the edge of a river　　　　**stir**　move slightly

About the Author

Andrew Matthews (born 1948)

Andrew Matthews is from Great Britain. At first, he was an English teacher. He left teaching to become a writer. He is interested in reading, listening to music, and wolves. He is a member of Great Britain's Wolf Conservation Society (a group that works to protect wolves). Matthews also helps create the society's magazine, "Wolf Print."

➤ How did Andrew Matthews's interest in reading, music, and wolves affect his story "Coyote"?

Chapter 2　Coyote　**21**

th Spelling

Irregular plural nouns

Remind students that they learned about forming plurals by adding -s and -ies in Chapter 1. *Say: Some plurals are not spelled with -s or -ies at the end. Some plurals have special spellings. Find the plural for* mouse *on p. 20.* (mice)

　Apply Write on the board: *child, person.* Have students find the plural form of these nouns on p. 21. (children, people)

Evaluate Your Reading Strategy

Read Aloud to Understand *Say: You have practiced an important reading strategy. Now you can decide how well you have done. Does this statement describe how you read?*

> If I do not understand something when I read it, I reread it aloud and ask myself questions.

Read the Selection

1. **Shared text reading** Have students listen to the story once. Then have them read aloud together from a shared text, such as a Big Book, an overhead transparency, or a chart.
2. **Discuss plot** Have students ask you questions about the last paragraphs to understand actions.
3. **Summarize** Tell students to follow along in their books as you read the story. Then have small groups summarize the folktale and present their summary to the class.
4. **Multi-level options** See MULTI-LEVEL OPTIONS on p. 20.

Sample Answer to Guide Question
Coyote's talking to the people he created. He's feeling joyful.

About the Author

Analyze facts Read the paragraph aloud. *Ask: What is the author interested in besides writing?* (reading, listening to music, and wolves) *What is* Wolf Print*?* (The Wolf Conservation Society's magazine)

Across Selections

Literary genres *Say: This folktale is a narrative. What other narrative did we read?* ("Birthday Barbecue") *Which one is fiction and which is non-fiction?* ("Birthday Barbecue" is non-fiction; "Coyote" is fiction.)

Spelling, Punctuation, Capitalization

After the Reading Comprehension section, students will practice spelling, punctuation, and capitalization in the Activity Book.

Beyond the Reading

Reading Comprehension

Question-Answer Relationships

Sample Answers

1. It was dark and still.
2. Coyote does.
3. He creates himself.
4. After himself, 4 times.
5. Animals appear.
6. He doesn't create houses or machines.
7. He repeats the same pattern of creation 4 times after the Coyote creates himself. Each time, he presents Coyote's problem by writing, "My legs want to run, but . . ." Then he has Coyote create something that solves the problem.
8. Yes. According to this folktale, they were considered very powerful.
9. There are many possible answers. For example, in Aesop's fable, "The Mouse Who Saved a Lion," a small animal saves the King of the Jungle from a hunter. It is similar to "Coyote" because it portrays an animal showing great power.
10. It is the story of how Coyote howled himself into being, and then howled and yelped other animals, natural things, and people into being. He created them so he wouldn't be lonely and so he could have fun.

Build Reading Fluency

Reading Key Phrases

Explain that reading key phrases helps improve reading fluency. Ask students to listen as you model reading key phrases before they practice aloud with a partner.

Reading Comprehension

Question-Answer Relationships (QAR)

"Right There" Questions

1. **Recall Facts** What is the world like at the beginning of "Coyote"?
2. **Recall Facts** Who makes the world in "Coyote"?

"Think and Search" Questions

3. **Determine Sequence of Events** What is the first thing that Coyote creates?
4. **Identify** How many times does Coyote make things?
5. **Determine Causes and Effects** What happens after Coyote yelps?

"Author and You" Questions

6. **Identify** Name some things that Coyote does *not* create in this story.
7. **Analyze** How does the author organize and present his ideas?

"On Your Own" Questions

8. **Make Inferences** Do you think coyotes were important to American Indians of the southwestern United States? Explain.
9. **Compare Oral Traditions** Many folktales are told out loud. What stories have you heard that tell about something in nature? What culture or region is the story from? How is it similar to "Coyote"?
10. **Paraphrase Text** How would you tell someone what "Coyote" is about in your own words?

Activity Book
p. 10

Student
CD-ROM

Build Reading Fluency

Reading Key Phrases

Reading key phrases will help you learn to read faster. Fluent readers group or phrase words as they read.

1. Read these phrases aloud.
2. Raise your hand each time you read the phrase "Coyote howled."

Coyote howled	Coyote blinked	Coyote barked
Coyote yelped	Coyote barked	Coyote howled
Coyote barked	Coyote howled	Coyote growled
Coyote growled	Coyote yelped	Coyote yelped

MULTI-LEVEL OPTIONS *Elements of Literature*

Newcomer Bring in television program guides. Draw a two-column chart labeled *entertain* and *inform*. Explain the terms. Have students work in small groups. Ask them to find three programs that entertain and three that inform. Have volunteers write the show titles on the chart. Discuss students' preferences.

Beginning Ask students to copy the words *entertain, inform, opinion,* or *persuade* into their Reading Logs. Have them create a simple icon to cue the meaning of each word. Encourage students to refer back to these icons as they list selections and authors' purposes in their Reading Logs.

Intermediate Have students write a sentence in their Reading Log to identify the author's purpose and explain why they think so. (The author's purpose for "Coyote" was to entertain. He told an unusual idea about how the world started.)

Advanced Remind students about comparing and contrasting. Ask students to enter selection titles and authors' purposes into their Reading Logs. Ask them to compare and contrast selections from this unit with other selections they have read. Instruct them to compare purpose and theme.

Listen, Speak, Interact

Present a Dramatic Reading

Long ago, people told folktales like "Coyote" to each other. They probably used their voices and bodies to show meaning and make the story exciting for listeners.

1. The class will form four groups. Each group will present a reading of one page of "Coyote."
2. In your group, decide which part each person will read.
3. Practice your reading with your group. Use your voice and body to show meaning and make the presentation enjoyable.
4. Group members may act out certain events while you read.
5. Present your reading for the rest of the class. If possible, videotape your performance. Be sure to listen as the other groups present.
6. How did the readings affect you as you listened? What parts of the readings caused this effect? Did you interpret meaning from voices and body movements?

Elements of Literature

Understand Author's Purpose

An **author** is a person who writes something. When you write, you are an author. When authors write something, they have a **purpose.** The purpose tells *why* they wrote it.

Here are some purposes for writing.
   a. *To entertain.* For example, the author has a funny or an unusual story to tell.
   b. *To inform.* For example, the author tells us about how coyotes live.
   c. *To express an opinion.* For example, the author tells us why he or she thinks coyotes are beautiful animals.

   d. *To persuade.* The author writes because he or she wants us to do something. For example, the author wants us to give money to protect coyotes.

1. Work with a partner. What is the author's purpose in writing "Coyote"? Sometimes there is more than one purpose.
2. Think about "Birthday Barbecue" in Chapter 1. What is the author's purpose in writing it?

Activity Book p. 11   Student CD-ROM

Chapter 2   Coyote   **23**

Listen, Speak, Interact

Present a Dramatic Reading

1. **Understand directions** Make sure students understand what to do in their groups. Monitor groups as they plan and practice.
2. **Interpret literature** Point out that the way they present their part is an interpretation of what the author meant.
3. **Newcomers** Include one newcomer in each of the groups. Help them find appropriate ways to participate in the drama, such as acting out an action that is repeated.
4. **Express opinions** Before presentations, write on the board: *I felt curious/surprised/ impressed/entertained/interested.* Students can use the words to answer Question 6.

Elements of Literature

Understand Author's Purpose

1. **Teacher think aloud** Model thinking through the first question. *Say: Did the author of "Coyote" want to entertain us? Yes. Was the folktale informative? Not really. Did Andrew Matthews express an opinion? No, it was just a story. Did he want to persuade us? No. So, what is the author's purpose?* (to entertain) Have students work in pairs to answer the next question.
2. **Multi-level options** See MULTI-LEVEL OPTIONS on p. 22.

Answer
2. *Example:* The author's purpose in "Birthday Barbecue" was to inform.

 **ASSESS**

Have students retell the story in their own words.

Cultural Connection

Invite a few volunteers to tell, in another language, about a story they know or something that happened to them. Tell them to use their voices and bodies to express and act out the meaning of their stories. Afterward, have the class discuss the meaning they got from the accounts. Ask them to identify specific uses of voice and gesture that helped them understand even if they did not know the language. Explain that this is called *non-verbal* or *body language.*

Learning Styles
Musical

In preparation for planning their own dramatic readings, have students listen to the audio of "Coyote." Ask them to notice the changes in voice the reader uses to communicate different feelings. Have students practice actions that could be used to communicate those feelings.

Word Study

Use a Thesaurus or Synonym Finder to Find Synonyms

1. **Identify synonyms** Read the explanation. Have students work in pairs to use a thesaurus to look up *dart* and *scuttle*.
2. **Clarify meaning and usage** Ask students to read the synonyms to clarify the meanings. Have students check to see if the listing also includes any usage notes that explain the proper use of the words.
3. **Locate pronunciation** Have students locate the pronunciation of *thesaurus* in the glossary in the Student Handbook and practice pronouncing it.

Answers
2. a. threw b. quiet c. piles

Grammar Focus

Identify Subjects and Verbs in Sentences

Identify parts of speech Have pairs of students write simple sentences, exchange them with another pair, and identify the subjects and verbs.

Answers
1. Coyote-howled 2. He-found 3. mice-scuttled

ASSESS

Write 3 sentences on the board. Have students copy them and circle the subject and verb.

Word Study

Use a Thesaurus or Synonym Finder to Find Synonyms

Synonyms are words with similar meanings. You can use synonyms to make your writing more interesting. Look at these synonyms from the selection:

Hares <u>darted</u> across the prairies.

Mice <u>scuttled</u> across the forest floor.

Both of these underlined words refer to a way of moving quickly.

You can find synonyms for words in a **thesaurus** or **synonym finder.** Both of these reference sources list words in alphabetical order, beginning with *A* and ending with *Z*. A list of synonyms is given next to each word.

You can find on-line versions of these references on the Internet.

1. Read the sentences and the list of words below.
   a. He <u>flung</u> the shell into the sky.
   b. Then a small sound filled the <u>stillness</u>.
   c. Coyote made <u>heaps</u> of clay.

   > ate   threw   smelled   quiet   car
   > story   birds   stones   piles

2. Choose the word that is the synonym of each underlined word.
3. Use a thesaurus to check your answers. (For *flung*, look up *fling*.)

Activity Book   Student
p. 12   CD-ROM

Grammar Focus

Identify Subjects and Verbs in Sentences

A complete **sentence** has a subject and a verb. The **subject** of a sentence is who or what the sentence is about. The **verb** describes the action, or what happens in the sentence. Look at this example:

Coyote blinked his eyes.

Coyote is the subject. The sentence is about Coyote. *Blinked* is the verb. It tells what Coyote did.

Find the subject and verb in each sentence.

1. Coyote howled a disk of gold.
2. He found a river with a high bank.
3. The mice scuttled quickly.

Activity Book   Student   Student
pp. 13–14   Handbook   CD-ROM

MULTI-LEVEL OPTIONS *From Reading to Writing*

Newcomer Give pairs of students three pieces of paper on which to draw the beginning, middle, and ending of their narratives. Help them label the pictures with words and phrases. As students share their stories, introduce synonyms. For example, Student: *The rabbit hopped.* Teacher: *I can see him leaping.*

Beginning Have students work in small groups. Help groups use a flowchart similar to the one on p. 16 to plan the character, setting, events, and ending of their narrative. Have students prepare a short skit based on their story flowchart.

Intermediate After students have completed their narratives, set up peer-editing conferences. Ask students to check each other's sentences to be sure each has a subject and verb.

Advanced When students have completed first drafts of their narratives, remind them of what they learned about using synonyms to make their writing more interesting. Ask each student to underline three words he or she wants to look up in a thesaurus to see if there is a more interesting choice.

From Reading to Writing

Write a Narrative

Use your imagination to write a narrative about an animal that creates something in nature. Your animal can talk and have other special abilities.

Tell your story in one or two paragraphs. Give it a title (a name).

1. Make sure your story has a beginning, a middle, and an end.

2. Choose your words carefully to be sure that your story makes sense.

3. Be sure to capitalize and punctuate your story correctly to strengthen its meaning.

Activity Book
p. 15

Student
Handbook

Across Content Areas

Learn About Food Chains

Some animals eat other animals. Coyotes, for example, hunt (chase and kill) and eat other animals such as hares. Animals that hunt are called **predators.**

What do hares eat? They eat plants. Plants, hares, and coyotes make up a **food chain.** A predator like a coyote is often at the top of a food chain. Coyotes eat hares. Hares eat plants.

Make another food chain with these three words:

Fish   People   Insects

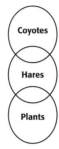

Coyotes

Hares

Plants

Activity Book
p. 16

From Reading to Writing

Write a Narrative

1. **Brainstorm** Read the instructions for the activity. Then brainstorm a list of animals they could write about. Talk about what animals could do.
2. **Pre-writing** Students may find it helpful to make some sketches of their animal character before writing their story.
3. **Pair work** Have students practice telling their stories in pairs before writing them. Instruct them to ask questions to clarify the story. Demonstrate this with one student first.
4. **Multi-level options** See MULTI-LEVEL OPTIONS on p. 24.

Across Content Areas: Science

Learn About Food Chains

Define and clarify Help students define *predators* and *food chain.* Then have students draw a new food chain for fish, people, or insects.

Answer
People eat fish. Fish eat insects.

 ASSESS

Have students name two predators and write a sentence about what each one eats.

Reteach and Reassess

Text Structure Draw a flowchart like the one on p. 16. Have students use it to record what happened at the beginning, middle, and end of "Coyote." Ask them how the author made the beginning and ending interesting. Have students identify the specific events in the middle of the story.

Reading Strategy Present students with a short, but challenging, piece of text. Work with them to use the steps on p. 16 to clarify its meaning.

Elements of Literature Present a variety of books from your school or classroom library. Ask students to predict the author's purpose based on the title, art, and text features.

Reassess Read aloud a brief folktale. Ask students to identify the author's purpose and retell the important ideas in the beginning, middle, and end.

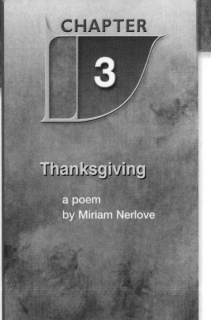

CHAPTER

3

Thanksgiving

a poem
by Miriam Nerlove

Into the Reading

Chapter Materials

Activity Book: *pp. 17–24*
Audio: *Unit 1, Chapter 3; CD 1, Track 4*
Student Handbook
Student CD-ROM: *Unit 1, Chapter 3*
Teacher Resource Book: *Lesson Plan, Teacher Resources, Reading Summary, Activity Book Answer Key*
Teacher Resource CD-ROM
Assessment Program: *Quiz, pp. 11–12; Teacher and Student Resources, pp. 115–144*
Assessment CD-ROM
Transparencies
The Heinle Newbury House Dictionary/CD-ROM
Web site: http://visions.heinle.com

Objectives

Preview Read the objectives aloud. *Say: We will learn these objectives in Chapter 3. Is there any objective you know already?*

Use Prior Knowledge

Talk About Holidays

1. **Brainstorm** Read the paragraph aloud. Have students say "Happy New Year" in other languages. Then brainstorm and record other holidays and celebrations.
2. **Pair work** Have students complete the chart in pairs.

Objectives

Reading Describe mental images as you read a poem.

Listening and Speaking Tell what you are thankful for.

Grammar Use subject pronouns.

Writing Write a narrative about a holiday.

Content Social Studies: Read a map.

Use Prior Knowledge

Talk About Holidays

A holiday is a special day. It is a day to celebrate events or important people. For example, New Year's Day is a holiday in many cultures. People celebrate the beginning of the new year on New Year's Day.

In the United States, people say "Happy New Year" on that day. What do you say in your region or culture?

1. Copy the chart on a piece of paper.
2. Think about holidays that your family or friends celebrate. List two holidays.

3. Write what people celebrate on each holiday.
4. Share your chart with a partner.

Holiday	What People Celebrate
New Year's Day	the new year

MULTI-LEVEL OPTIONS *Build Vocabulary*

Newcomer One by one, point to the photographs on p. 27. Say the name of each and ask students to repeat it after you. Then say the foods again and ask students to point to the correct picture. Introduce students to The Heinle Basic Newbury House Dictionary. Model how to locate meanings and pronunciations of unfamiliar words or to clarify meaning or usage. Have students look up the new vocabulary words.

Beginning Model pointing to one of the photographs of food on p. 27. Smile and *say: I like turkey.* Point to another. Frown and *say: I don't like pumpkin.* Have students follow your lead by pointing to the foods and indicating personal preferences through sentences and facial expressions.

Intermediate *Say: Sometimes, I eat a turkey sandwich for lunch.* Ask students to work in pairs. Ask them to use the food words on p. 27 to talk about their personal preferences in food.

Advanced Have students write a paragraph about foods that people eat for Thanksgiving dinners in this country. Ask them to use the words on p. 27 and add other foods they know and like.

Build Background

Thanksgiving

Thanksgiving is an important holiday in the United States. On Thanksgiving, people give thanks for the good things in their lives. Many people eat a big meal with family members and friends.

Content Connection

In the United States, people celebrate Thanksgiving on the fourth Thursday of November.

On Thanksgiving, people remember the story of the Pilgrims. The Pilgrims came from England to live in the Americas in the 1600s. At first, the Pilgrims did not have enough food. The Native Americans showed the Pilgrims how to grow and find food. Later, they shared a feast (a very big meal) together. The Pilgrims gave thanks for the food and their new home.

Build Vocabulary

Learn Words for Foods

On Thanksgiving, people eat many different foods.

Look at the food words and the pictures. Match each word with its definition. Use a dictionary to check your work.

1. pumpkin	2. cornbread	3. turkey
4. cranberries	5. nuts	6. pie

Definitions

a. bread made from corn

b. a type of meat from a bird

c. a dessert with a crust and a sweet filling

d. a big, orange fruit

e. seeds with a hard shell around them

f. small red fruit

The Heinle Newbury House Dictionary

Activity Book p. 17

Student CD-ROM

Home Connection

Build Vocabulary Invite students to bring in favorite family recipes using any of the foods listed on p. 27 if possible. Provide time for students to share the recipes and tell when their families eat these foods.

Learning Styles
Visual

Build Background Point out that some things from nature are used to make foods for Thanksgiving and to decorate for this and other fall holidays. Have students look through books and bookmarked Web sites to see examples such as pumpkins, cornstalks, fall leaves, and dried corn.

Build Background

Thanksgiving

1. **Visualize** *Say: Close your eyes and think of Thanksgiving. What images and words come to mind?*

2. **Content Connection** The first Thanksgiving was held by the Plymouth colonists in 1621. In 1863, President Lincoln declared Thanksgiving a national holiday.

Build Vocabulary

Learn Words for Foods

Teacher Resource Book: *Personal Dictionary, p. 63*

1. **Preview vocabulary** Have students repeat the food words after you. Check for correct pronunciation.

2. **Use a dictionary** Introduce students to The Heinle Newbury House Dictionary. Walk them through the Introduction on pp. xiii–xxii. These notes instruct students on how to use a dictionary to clarify meaning, pronunciation, and usage.

3. **Use other sources** Tell students that dictionaries are also available online and as CD-ROMs. The CD-ROM version of The Heinle Newbury House Dictionary is found on the inside back cover. Students will find meanings, pronunciations, derivations, and usage notes in these other sources.

4. **Reading selection vocabulary** You may want to introduce the glossed words in the reading selection before students begin reading. Key words: *plenty, gathered, wonderful, mood, stuffed, wishbone.* Instruct students to write the words with correct spelling and their definitions in their Personal Dictionaries. Have them pronounce each word and divide it into syllables.

5. **Multi-level options** See MULTI-LEVEL OPTIONS on p. 26.

Answers
1. d 2. a 3. b 4. f 5. e 6. c

ASSESS

Have students write four words related to Thanksgiving.

Text Structure

Poem

1. **Review** *Ask: What other poem have we read?* ("Family Photo") *What features of a poem do you remember?* (experiences, images, stanzas, rhymes)
2. **Multi-level options** See MULTI-LEVEL OPTIONS below.

Reading Strategy

Describe Mental Images

Describe images Ask students to close their eyes and *ask: Can you imagine what a feast looks like? Think of your own Thanksgiving. Picture the table in your mind, the food, and who is there.* Have students draw their mental images or describe them to you.

ASSESS

Have students give two pairs of rhyming words.

Text Structure

Poem

"Thanksgiving" is a **poem**. A **poet** is a person who writes a poem. Look at some features a poem can have.

Poem	
Rhyme	words with the same ending sound; for example: The winter was **cold** and the house was **old.**
Rhythm	a beat, like a drum sound in music
Stanzas	groups of lines
Vivid Language	words that help you see, hear, smell, touch, and taste what the poet is describing

Look for these features as you read the selection. Think about how the vivid language helps you to make pictures in your mind and understand the poem. Also notice how the words rhyme and have rhythm.

Student
CD-ROM

Reading Strategy

Describe Mental Images

"Thanksgiving" has many words that help you form **mental images.** Mental images are pictures that you form in your mind. Read these lines from the poem:

> so they held a great feast with plenty to eat.

> There was <u>cornbread</u> and <u>nuts</u>, <u>berries</u> and <u>meat</u>.

The underlined words help you picture the feast in your mind. They tell you what foods were at the feast. Draw a picture of your mental image of this stanza.

Describing mental images can help you understand and enjoy a poem better. Follow these tips to describe mental images:

1. Stop after you read each stanza. Think about mental images that you formed.
2. Describe your mental images or present a dramatic interpretation of your images to the class.

Student
CD-ROM

28 Unit 1 Traditions and Cultures

MULTI-LEVEL OPTIONS *Text Structure*

Newcomer Read a simple rhyming poem to students. Have them first tap out the rhythm. Then ask students to raise their hands when they hear pairs of rhyming words.

Beginning Write a few lines of a simple rhyming poem, such as "Roses Are Red." Work with students to label a pair of rhyming words, a stanza, and examples of vivid language.

Intermediate Have students read the information on the chart. Then ask them to predict some pairs of rhyming words they might find in a poem about Thanksgiving. Work with them to make a cluster map on the board of sensory images they predict might be found in a poem about this holiday.

Advanced Discuss the features of a poem as described on p. 28. *Ask: Why do you think a writer would choose this format to write about a topic?* (to focus on senses and feelings; to use words to create a mood or an image)

Thanksgiving

a poem
by Miriam Nerlove

29

Reading Selection Materials

Audio: *Unit 1, Chapter 3; CD 1, Track 4*
Teacher Resource Book: *Reading Summary, pp. 69–70*
Transparencies: #2, *Reading Summary*

Suggestions for Using Reading Summary

- Introduce new vocabulary or cognates.
- Cut the summary into strips, or jumble the sentences on an overhead transparency. Students put the sentences in order.
- Practice the reading strategy.
- Students read aloud or with a partner.
- Students paraphrase the summary.
- Students do a cloze activity.
- Students create a visual or graphic organizer, such as a timeline or storyboard, to illustrate the summary.
- Students paraphrase the summary.

Preview the Selection

1. **Describe art medium** *Ask: What is this picture made of? How can you tell?*
2. **Describe style** *Say: This painting is in a realistic style. Things and people are painted as they appear in real life. Describe some of the details.*
3. **Evaluate the effect** *Ask: What feeling do you get from this painting? What is the mood?*
4. **Connect** *Say: Every family has a different kind of Thanksgiving.* Have students describe their own Thanksgiving celebrations. Remind them that the theme of this unit is *traditions and cultures.*

 Cultural Connection

Display a small world map on a large piece of chart paper or poster paper to form a wide border. Write *Thanksgiving* on the border. Draw a line or run a piece of string from the word to the United States. Ask students to identify harvest festivals in countries they have visited or lived in, such as Pongal (India) and Crop-Over (Barbados). Write these in the border and use a line or string to connect the holidays with the countries.

Learning Styles
Intrapersonal

Ask students to draw or write a journal entry describing how they feel about Thanksgiving or another holiday their family observes. Ask them to show or tell what makes this holiday important to them.

Read the Selection

1. **Use the illustration** *Ask: Who are these people? What can you learn about them from this picture?* (They are poor; they arrived during a cold season; their boat is small; they look worried/happy.)

2. **Use prior knowledge** *Ask: What do you already know about the Pilgrims? What ocean did they cross? Where were they from?*

3. **Paired reading** Have pairs practice reading aloud. Then ask several to read aloud to the class. Ask them to read using expression.

Sample Answer to Guide Question
I see a big table with lots of food. I see my family sitting around the table.

> See Teacher Edition pp. 434–436 for a list of English-Spanish cognates in the reading selection.

Audio
CD 1, Tr. 4

Describe Mental Images

What mental images do you form when you hear the word *Thanksgiving?*

1 Thanksgiving! It's time for Thanksgiving!

2 Each year in November we like to remember . . .

3 the Pilgrims, who came such a long time ago,
to build and to live here, to work and to grow.

30 Unit 1 Traditions and Cultures

MULTI-LEVEL OPTIONS *Read the Selection*

Newcomer Play the audio. Point out the rhyming words. Then *ask: Is this poem about Thanksgiving?* (yes) *Is Thanksgiving in October?* (no) *Does the holiday remember Pilgrims who came here long ago?* (yes) *Did Native Americans help the Pilgrims?* (yes)

Beginning Do a paired reading of the part of the poem on these pages. Then *ask: What month is Thanksgiving in?* (November) *Who came to this country long ago?* (Pilgrims) *Who helped them?* (Native Americans) *What did Native Americans teach the Pilgrims to do?* (get food)

Intermediate Have students do a paired reading. Then *ask: What made life hard for the Pilgrims when they first came to this country?* (They didn't know how to find food. They got sick.) *How did they learn to grow and hunt for food?* (from the Native Americans)

Advanced Have students read the poem in pairs. Then *ask: How does the poet feel about Thanksgiving? How can you tell?* (The exclamations at the beginning show the poet is excited.) *Why did Native Americans teach the Pilgrims to get food?* (They probably saw the Pilgrims suffering and wanted to help.)

Read the Selection

1. **Use the illustration** *Ask: What is happening in the picture? What is this Native American teaching the Pilgrim?*

2. **Choral reading** Play the audio for stanzas 1–6. Then divide the class in three groups and have each group read a stanza aloud with you.

3. **Identify features of a poem** *Say: One feature of a poem is that often there are rhyming words. Can you find all of the rhyming words?* Have students write the word pairs on the board.

4. **Multi-level options** See MULTI-LEVEL OPTIONS on p. 30.

Sample Answer to Guide Question
I see a snowy winter picture with sick children and old people.

Describe Mental Images

What mental images do you form after reading stanza 4? What words help you form these mental images?

4   They hadn't much food and the winter was cold.
    The Pilgrims got sick—both the young and the old.

5   But Native Americans knew what to do.
    The Pilgrims were taught many things that were new.

6   They grew corn and pumpkins to last the whole year.
    They also caught fish, **hunted** turkey and **deer.**

---

hunted   killed for food   **deer**   an animal with hooves that lives in forests

---

A Capitalization

Holidays

Write *Thanksgiving* on the board. Underline the first letter and *say: The names of holidays begin with capital letters.*

   Apply Ask students to name holidays they celebrate. List these on chart paper. Use one color marker for the capital letter at the beginning of each word and a different color marker for the remainder of the word.

Read the Selection

1. **Use art to preview** Direct students to the art. Have them ask you questions about the picture.
2. **Choral reading** Play the audio. Then have students read the stanzas aloud with you.
3. **Relate to personal experience** *Say: When the Pilgrims came, they didn't know how to grow the local crops or how to get enough food. Who helped teach them? When you moved to a new place or school, who helped you? If a new person came today to our class, how could we help him/her?*

Sample Answer to Guide Question
Students may respond with numbers from 10 to 100.

7   The people were thankful for food they had grown . . .

8   so they held a great feast with **plenty** to eat.
There was cornbread and nuts, berries and meat.

9   Then **neighbors** and Pilgrims **gathered** to share
the Thanksgiving meal they all had **prepared.**

> **Describe Mental Images**
>
> How many people do you picture in your mind at the feast?

---

plenty more than enough	**gathered** came together
neighbors people who live close to one another	**prepared** made

32   **Unit 1**   Traditions and Cultures

MULTI-LEVEL OPTIONS *Read the Selection*

Newcomer *Ask: Did the Pilgrims thank the Native Americans?* (yes) *Did they have a special meal?* (yes) *Did they eat oranges?* (no) *Do we celebrate Thanksgiving today exactly the way that the Pilgrims did?* (no)

Beginning *Ask: Who prepared the first Thanksgiving meal?* (Pilgrims) *What is one food they ate?* (cornbread) *How does the boy in the poem celebrate Thanksgiving?* (with a big dinner) *Where does he have his special dinner?* (at Grandma's house)

Intermediate *Ask: How is our Thanksgiving similar to the Pilgrims'?* (We have big meals with some of the same foods.) *Why do you think the boy is in a hurry?* (He is excited about having a special dinner at his grandmother's house.)

Advanced *Ask: What do you think the guests talked about at the first Thanksgiving?* (how grateful they were to learn how to raise and find food) *What can you tell about the boy? Explain.* (He's helpful. He helped make the pies.) *What do you predict will happen next?* (The family will eat Grandmother's meal and have pie for dessert.)

Read the Selection

Teacher Resource Book: *Two-Column Chart, p. 44*

1. **Use art to compare and contrast** On the board, draw a two-column chart labeled *1621* and *Now.* **Say:** *This is a very different kind of Thanksgiving. What are the differences?* Have students compare the two illustrations and write the differences on the board.

2. **Use resources** While reading this poem, have students research information about the Pilgrims and Plymouth Plantation. Have them use an encyclopedia. They can write down information they learn and report back to the class.

3. **Shared reading** Play the audio or read aloud. Have students listen as they follow along in their texts. Instruct them to join in for the rhyming words by reading the last word of every line aloud.

3. **Multi-level options** See MULTI-LEVEL OPTIONS on p. 32.

Sample Answer to Guide Question
They drive there. They walk. They take the subway.

10 Now we remember that **feast** our own way,
with the special big dinner we're having today.

11 We work in the kitchen, Mother and I,
and **bake** not just one, but *two* pumpkin pies!

12 We're off to Grandma's. "Mother, let's go!
Please hurry up—we're going too slow."

> **Describe Mental Images**
>
> How do you think Mother and the boy get to Grandma's? Do they drive? Walk? What image do you form in your mind?

---

feast a large meal   **bake** cook in an oven

Chapter 3 Thanksgiving **33**

 Spelling

To/Two/Too

Say: Some words are pronounced the same, but they are spelled differently and have different meanings. Have students reread stanzas 11 and 12. Ask them to locate *two. Say: This word means a number.* Then have students find the word *to. Say: This word gives information about* where. Finally, help students locate the word *too. Say: This word means* also. *Sometimes it tells about* amount.

Apply Write the following sentences on the board:

Native Americans went (to/too/two) the first Thanksgiving feast.

(To/Too/Two) of the foods they ate were meat and cornbread.

They ate (to/too/two) much food.

Have students copy the sentences with the correct word. (to, Two, too)

Read the Selection

1. **Describe how art supports the text** Direct students to the art. Ask students to describe what they see. *Ask: Whose house is this? Who are these people? Can you tell what will happen next in the poem?*
2. **Paired reading** Have students practice reading the stanzas aloud to each other.

Sample Answer to Guide Question
The pie tastes sweet; it smells delicious; it looks brown and orange and round; "warm" and "smell so good and so sweet."

> **Describe Mental Images**
>
> How do you think the pumpkin pie tastes? Smells? Looks? What words help you form these mental images?

13 The warm pumpkin pies smell so good and so sweet,
I **sneak** a small piece of the **piecrust** to eat.

14 We finally arrive at a little past four—
the whole family's waving at Grandma's front door.

15 There's Grandma and Minnie, her little gray cat,
Uncle Bob, Aunt Marie, cousins Laura and Matt.

---

sneak   do something so that other people cannot see you

piecrust   the outside pastry that holds the filling of a pie

34   Unit 1   Traditions and Cultures

MULTI-LEVEL OPTIONS *Read the Selection*

Newcomer *Ask: Did the family eat dinner at noon?* (no) *Is Minnie the boy's cousin?* (no) *Was the family happy during their dinner?* (yes) *Did everyone eat a lot?* (yes)

Beginning *Ask: What did the boy taste before the meal?* (pie) *When did the family have dinner?* (four o'clock) *Who were the other children at the celebration?* (Laura and Matt) *Who cut up the turkey?* (Uncle Bob)

Intermediate *Ask: What foods did the family have that were also at the first Thanksgiving feast?* (meat and berries) *When the family says, "Enough," what do they mean?* (They don't want more food.)

Advanced *Ask: Do you think mother knew that the boy had a bit of the pie before they got to Grandma's? Explain.* (no, because the poet used the word *sneak*) *What do you think will happen next? Why?* (Some of the family will eat the pie even though they are full. Pumpkin pie is a special and delicious part of a Thanksgiving meal.)

16 We sit down to eat in a **wonderful mood.**
We say that we're thankful for **plenty** of food.

17 Uncle Bob **carves** the turkey and uses a knife
that is one of the biggest I've seen in my life!

18 We **gobble** the food down, we eat till we're **stuffed.**
When Grandma says, "More?" we tell her, "Enough!"

Describe Mental Images

What do you think the table looks like after the family finishes eating? Which words help you form this mental image?

wonderful very good; very pleasing	**carves** cuts into pieces or slices
mood how someone feels	**gobble** eat in a quick and hungry way
plenty a lot of	**stuffed** a feeling of being very full from eating

Chapter 3 Thanksgiving **35**

Read the Selection

1. **Describe mental images** Discuss the guide with students. Have them give as much detail as possible.
2. **Choral reading** Play the audio. Then have students read the stanzas aloud with you.
3. **Multi-level options** See MULTI-LEVEL OPTIONS on p. 34.

Sample Answer to Guide Question
The table is full of empty plates and dishes; napkins are rolled in balls; glasses are almost empty; "gobble the food," "we're stuffed," and "enough."

 Spelling

Plurals for words ending in -fe

Say: There is a special way of making nouns that end in -fe mean more than one. Direct students to stanza 17. Write on the board: *Uncle Bob uses a knife. Say: If Aunt Marie were using a knife, too, we would say, "They are both using knives."* Write *knives* on the board. Point out that the *-f* is changed to *-v* before adding the *-s.*

Apply Point out the word *life* in the second line of stanza 17. Write *life* on the board. Ask students how to make this word plural. (lives)

Read the Selection

1. **Listening for rhythm** *Say: Poetry has its own rhythm. Listen to the entire poem and listen for the rhythm.* Play the audio or read aloud. Students can listen with eyes closed or while reading along in the book.

2. **Paired reading** Have students practice reading the entire poem in pairs. Ask them to use rhythm and feeling as they read.

Sample Answer to Guide Question
A table full of empty cups and plates. They might be worried that Baby Laura would drop the cup or possibly get hurt.

19 But now comes the pie—and I know that it's good.
I waited to eat it as long as I could.

> **Describe Mental Images**
>
> What mental image do you form after you read this stanza? Are the people worried that Baby Laura will drop the cup?

20 When we're finished with dinner, it's time to clean up—
Watch out! Baby Laura has Uncle Bob's cup!

21 I pick up the **wishbone** that's dried on a dish.
Matt and I pull—will Matt get the wish?

---

watch out be careful

wishbone a bone in some birds that is shaped like a Y; people play a game with a wishbone: the person who breaks off the largest piece of the wishbone gets to make a wish

36 Unit 1 Traditions and Cultures

MULTI-LEVEL OPTIONS *Read the Selection*

Newcomer *Ask: Does the family eat pie for dessert?* (yes) *Does the baby have Uncle Bob's pie?* (no) *Did Matt win the wishbone game?* (no) *Did the boy have fun on Thanksgiving?* (yes)

Beginning *Ask: What did the family have for dessert?* (pumpkin pie) *What did the family do after the meal?* (clean up) *Who plays the wishbone game with the boy?* (Matt) *Who won the game?* (the boy)

Intermediate *Ask: How did the boy know the pie was good?* (He had sneaked a piece on the way to Grandma's.) *Why did someone say, "Watch out!"* (It's dangerous for a baby to grab a cup.) *What does the boy's wish mean?* (He enjoyed the family's celebration.)

Advanced *Ask: What probably happened after someone said, "Watch out!"?* (They probably took the cup away from the baby.) *Why did the family dry out the wishbone?* (to make it easier to break) *What do you think the boy will say to his friends about his family's holiday?* (that it was fun and the food was tasty)

Describe Mental Images

What mental image do you form when you read the words "I win!"? Is the boy smiling? Jumping up and down? Doing something else?

22 I win!
I make my own wish and I know what to say:
May next year's Thanksgiving be just like today!

About the Author

Miriam Nerlove (born 1959)

Miriam Nerlove was born in Minneapolis, Minnesota. She started her career as an illustrator (a person who draws pictures to go with text). She now writes poetry for young people. Many of Nerlove's poems are about holidays. She also writes about history.

➤ Why do you think Miriam Nerlove wrote a poem about Thanksgiving? To entertain? To describe? To teach? What questions would you want to ask Nerlove?

Chapter 3 Thanksgiving **37**

Read the Selection

1. **Use personal experience** Ask students what they do when they have eaten a big meal and still want a delicious dessert.
2. **Choral reading** Have students read the poem aloud. Have small groups or pairs read different stanzas.
3. **Multi-level options** See MULTI-LEVEL OPTIONS on p. 36.

Sample Answer to Guide Question
The boy is smiling and laughing. He's pleased with himself.

About the Author

1. **Analyze facts** After students have read the paragraph, *ask: What is an illustrator?* (Someone who draws pictures to go with text.) *What does the poet like to write about?* (holidays and history)
2. **Draw conclusions** Discuss the guide question. Remind students that an author can write for several purposes.

Across Selections

Teacher Resource Book: *Venn Diagram, p. 35*

Literary genres Ask students to compare and contrast "Thanksgiving" with "Family Photo" on p. 6. Have them work in pairs to chart ideas on a Venn diagram. (Similarities: both poems rhyme and are about family celebrations. Differences: "Thanksgiving" is longer and more detailed; it's about a specific holiday.)

Spelling, Punctuation, Capitalization

After the Reading Comprehension section, students will practice spelling, punctuation, and capitalization in the Activity Book.

A Capitalization

Direct students to stanza 19. *Ask: What word does the boy use to talk about himself?* (I) *Is the pronoun I capitalized?* (yes) Point out that the pronoun *I* is always capitalized, even if it is in the middle of the sentence.

Apply Have students write three sentences comparing themselves to the boy in the poem. Ask students to use the pronoun *I*. (The boy likes pumpkin pie. So do I.)

Evaluate Your Reading Strategy

Describe Mental Images *Say: You have practiced an important reading strategy. Now you can decide how well you have done. Does this statement describe how you read?*

As I read, I use words in the text to form mental images or pictures in my mind. Describing mental images helps me understand what I read.

Beyond the Reading

Reading Comprehension

Question-Answer Relationships

Answers

1. They didn't have much food and it was very cold.
2. Native Americans
3. at his Grandma's
4. two pumpkin pies
5. Grandma, Minnie (Grandma's cat), Uncle Bob, Aunt Marie, cousins Laura and Matt
6. Native Americans
7. They gathered for a feast, they shared food, and they ate some of the same foods.
8. Yes, because he wants to get there quickly, and he looks forward to next year.
9. Yes, because she creates a very positive, warm scene.
10. Students may talk about different feasts and family gatherings that they celebrate in countries they have visited or lived in.
11. How many Pilgrims came to Massachusetts? What kind of houses did they live in? How did they make friends with the Native Americans?

Build Reading Fluency

Echo Read Aloud

Model reading aloud with expression. Read one line at a time. Ask the class to read (echo) the same line you just read before going on to the next line or sentence.

Reading Comprehension

Question-Answer Relationships (QAR)

"Right There" Questions

1. **Explain** Why did the Pilgrims get sick?
2. **Recall Facts** Who taught the Pilgrims how to grow food?
3. **Recall Facts** Where do the boy and his mother celebrate Thanksgiving?
4. **Recall Facts** What do they take to the dinner?
5. **Recall Facts** Who else is at the dinner?

"Think and Search" Questions

6. **Make Inferences** Who was living in America when the Pilgrims arrived?
7. **Compare** How is the family's Thanksgiving similar to the Pilgrims' Thanksgiving?

"Author and You" Questions

8. **Make Inferences** Do you think the main character likes Thanksgiving? Explain.
9. **Understand Author's Perspective** Do you think the author likes Thanksgiving? Explain.

"On Your Own" Questions

10. **Connect Your Experiences** Do you know of a celebration like Thanksgiving in another culture? How are they the same? How are they different?
11. **Form Questions** What information would you like to find out (research) about the Pilgrims?

Activity Book
p. 18

Student
CD-ROM

Build Reading Fluency

Echo Read Aloud

Effective readers learn to read with feeling. Echo reading helps you read with feeling and expression. Your teacher reads a line. Then the class reads (echoes) the same line aloud. Turn to page 30.

1. Listen to your teacher read.
2. Read the same line aloud with expression.
3. Continue listening and reading.

38 Unit 1 Traditions and Cultures

MULTI-LEVEL OPTIONS *Elements of Literature*

Newcomer Reread stanzas 10 to 15 aloud emphasizing the rhyming words. Then reread the lines slowly and have students echo the rhyming words after you say them.

Beginning Read stanzas 10 through 12 aloud. Write the rhyming words as you say them. Then reread the stanzas stopping before you get to the final word of each line. Ask students to say the rhyming word as you point to it.

Intermediate Have students work in pairs to locate and write down six pairs of rhyming words from the poem. Tell them to sort the words into pairs that have similar spellings (life/knife) and pairs that do not (enough, stuffed).

Advanced Ask students to examine the rhyming word pairs in the poem. Tell them to notice the pattern the poet used for rhyming lines. Have students write four to six lines of rhyming poetry about a holiday of their choice.

Listen, Speak, Interact

Tell What You Are Thankful For

When you are thankful, you are happy about the good things in your life.

1. List three things that you are thankful for on a piece of paper.
2. Choose one thing on your list. Tell the class why you are thankful for it. Give evidence and examples to support your ideas and to make them clear.

What I Am Thankful For
1. *my home*
2. *my big sister*
3. *my healthy family*

3. Take notes as you listen to your classmates. Write down their main ideas (the most important things that they say) and their supporting evidence (information that shows that the main ideas are correct).

Elements of Literature

Identify Rhyme

Poems often have words that **rhyme.** Words that rhyme have the same ending sounds. The words *bad* and *mad* rhyme.

1. With a partner, choose a page of the selection that you like.
2. Find the rhyming words on your page. Be sure you know how to pronounce them. Ask your teacher if you are not sure.
3. With a partner, practice reading these stanzas aloud. Ask your partner to tell you if you pronounce the rhyming words correctly or not.

4. As you read, show meaning with your voice and gestures.
5. Read your stanzas to the class.
   a. Read loudly enough for everyone to hear.
   b. Read slowly enough for everyone to understand.
   c. Use a medium pitch—your voice should not be too high or too low.
   d. Use a tone of voice that expresses your feeling about the poem.

Activity Book
p. 19

Student
CD-ROM

Chapter 3 Thanksgiving **39**

Listen, Speak, Interact

Tell What You Are Thankful For

1. **Brainstorm** Have a student read the directions. Then brainstorm and list student ideas on the board. Circle one item to tell the class about, giving evidence or examples from your own experience.
2. **Newcomers** Reread the directions with this group. Have them draw pictures that show what they are thankful for. Help them write key words to label their descriptions.

Elements of Literature

Identify Rhyme

1. **Present a dramatic interpretation** Have students work in groups to prepare different stanzas from the poem. Ask them to practice using rhythm, intonation, and dramatic energy.
2. **Multi-level options** See MULTI-LEVEL OPTIONS on p. 38.

✓ ASSESS

Have students select one stanza from the poem to read aloud. Ask them to pick a stanza in which they can show feeling and drama.

Content Connection
The Arts

Have groups create a mural of things for which they are grateful. In addition to showing people and items, have them choose colors, shapes, lettering styles, and symbols that communicate the idea of thankfulness. Provide time for groups to share and explain their creations.

Learning Styles
Musical

Provide time for students to listen to a few songs used in the observance of various holidays. Have students note the rhyming pattern the songwriter used.

Word Study

Analyze the Suffix *-ful*

1. **Analyze the suffix *-ful*** Explain that the suffix *-ful* is very similar to the meaning of *full*.

2. **Apply** Write on the board: *hope, color, thought*. Have students add the suffix *-ful* to each and tell a partner what the new word means.

Answers

2. careful = b. full of care; wonderful = a. full of wonder; joyful = c. full of joy.

Grammar Focus

Use Subject Pronouns

1. **Use subject pronouns** Write on the board: *The Pilgrims were from England. They came in 1620. Say:* Pilgrims *is a noun;* they *is a pronoun.*

2. **Identify parts of speech** Remind students that pronouns *take the place* of nouns in sentences. That is why nouns and their pronouns usually do not appear in the same sentence.

Answers

1. **a.** It was very big. **b.** They were delicious. **c.** We like turkey.

ASSESS

Write on the board: *My sister cooks the turkey. My aunt and uncle eat together.* Have students change the subject noun to a subject pronoun. (She cooks the turkey. They eat together.)

Word Study

Analyze the Suffix *-ful*

A **suffix** is a group of letters added to the end of a word. A suffix changes the meaning of the word. The suffix *-ful* means "full of."

thank**ful** means "full of thanks"

1. Copy the chart in your Personal Dictionary.

2. Match each word in the chart with the correct definition below. Write the definitions in the chart.
   a. full of wonder
   b. full of care
   c. full of joy

3. With a partner, write a sentence for each word.

4. Use resources, such as a dictionary, or ask your teacher to help you correctly spell other words that have the suffix *-ful*.

First Word	Suffix	New Word	Definition
thank +	-ful ⇒	thankful	full of thanks
care +	-ful ⇒	careful	
wonder +	-ful ⇒	wonderful	
joy +	-ful ⇒	joyful	

Personal Dictionary | The Heinle Newbury House Dictionary | Activity Book p. 20 | Student CD-ROM

Grammar Focus

Use Subject Pronouns

A **noun** is a part of speech that stands for a person, a place, or a thing. *Girl, school,* and *backpack* are nouns.

A **pronoun** is a part of speech that takes the place of nouns. In Chapter 2, you learned about the subjects of sentences. **Subject pronouns** can be used in place of nouns that are subjects. The subject pronouns are *I, you, he, she, it, we,* and *they*.

Native Americans knew what to do. They knew what to do.

They takes the place of Native Americans.

1. Rewrite these sentences so that they have a subject pronoun.
   a. The turkey was very big.
   b. The pies were delicious.
   c. My brother and I like turkey.

2. Write three sentences using subject pronouns.

Activity Book pp. 21–22 | Student Handbook | Student CD-ROM

MULTI-LEVEL OPTIONS *From Reading to Writing*

Newcomer Write each of the following on a separate piece of unlined paper: *What? When? Why? How?* Give each student a set of these papers. Ask students to choose a holiday his or her family celebrates and create drawings to show the holiday and when, why, and how it is observed.

Beginning Have students copy one of each of the questions from 1a, p. 41, onto a sheet of unlined paper. Tell them to underline the question words (what, when, why, how). Ask them to draw pictures to answer each question. Then have students write phrases to tell what they have drawn.

Intermediate Have students use the model on p. 41 to plan key information to include in their paragraphs. Then tell them to close their eyes and see their mental images of the holidays they have selected. Ask students to open their eyes and add details of their mental images to their writing.

Advanced Have students draft paragraphs. Then ask them to read aloud their writing to a partner. Have the listener close his or her eyes and form mental images about the paragraph. Ask the listeners to describe these mental images to the writer. Ask writers to consider whether any details from these images should be added to the paragraph.

From Reading to Writing

Write a Narrative About a Holiday

Choose a holiday that your family celebrates. Write one paragraph about the holiday.

1. Ask yourself these questions:
   a. What is the important holiday? When do we celebrate it? Why do we celebrate it?
   b. How do we prepare for the holiday?
   c. How do we celebrate the holiday?
2. Write your narrative. Use the model to help you.
3. Write a title for your narrative.
4. Use singular and plural nouns and pronouns correctly to show people, places, or things.

Title _____

_____ is an important holiday. My family celebrates it on _____. We celebrate it because _____. To prepare, we _____. On the holiday, we celebrate by _____.

5. Use a resource, such as a dictionary, to help you correctly spell words in your paragraph.

The Heinle Newbury House Dictionary

Activity Book p. 23

Student Handbook

Across Content Areas

Read a Map

The Pilgrims came to the New World by ship. Because of bad storms, the Pilgrims did not land where they wanted to go. Look at the map and answer the questions.

1. Where did the Pilgrims want to go?
2. Where did they land?
3. Look in an **atlas** (a book of maps) or on the Internet to find out how far it is from Plymouth Colony to Virginia. Take notes.

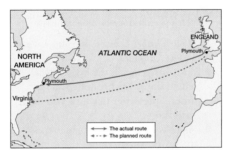

Activity Book p. 24

From Reading to Writing

Write a Narrative About a Holiday

1. **Brainstorm** Read the instructions for the activity. Then brainstorm different holidays they could write about.
2. **Pair work** After students have written their narratives, have them exchange papers and give each other feedback. Tell them to check that there is a title, the first sentence is indented, and correct punctuation and spelling is used.
3. **Multi-level options** See MULTI-LEVEL OPTIONS on p. 40.

Across Content Areas: Social Studies

Read a Map

Use a map Read the paragraph aloud. Explain the phrases "on course " and "blown off course." Have small groups summarize information from the paragraph and map using these phrases.

Answers
1. Virginia 2. Plymouth 3. approximately 450 miles

ASSESS

Have students write two sentences about the Pilgrims and their journey.

Reteach and Reassess

Text Structure Prepare a nursery rhyme or short rhyming poem. Have students identify rhyming words, stanzas, and descriptive words.

Reading Strategy Ask students to close their eyes and recall a recent school celebration or event. Have them open their eyes and draw or describe their mental images of the occasion.

Elements of Literature Copy a short poem on the board. Read the poem aloud to students. Discuss the meaning and rhyming words. Have students perform an expressive choral reading of the poem.

Reassess Write a language experience story about a classroom party. Have students copy the story and underline food words, descriptive words, and subject pronouns. Tell them to use a different color marker for each type of word.

CHAPTER 4

Turkish Delight

a personal narrative
and recipe
by Hamdiye Çelik

Into the Reading

Chapter Materials

Activity Book: *pp. 25–32*
Audio: *Unit 1, Chapter 4; CD 1, Track 5*
Student Handbook
Student CD-ROM: *Unit 1, Chapter 4*
Teacher Resource Book: *Lesson Plan, Teacher
    Resources, Reading Summary, Activity Book
    Answer Key*
Teacher Resource CD-ROM
Assessment Program: *Quiz, pp. 13–14; Teacher
    and Student Resources, pp. 115–144*
Assessment CD-ROM
Transparencies
The Heinle Newbury House Dictionary/CD-ROM
Web site: http://visions.heinle.com

Objectives

Preview Read the objectives. *Ask: What is
something new you will learn?*

Use Prior Knowledge

Discuss Everyday Activities

Define terms Give an example of chronological
order by describing what you did this morning.
Monitor students as they complete the chart.

Use Prior Knowledge

Discuss Everyday Activities

In "Turkish Delight," the narrator
describes everyday activities. They are
presented in the order in which they
occur. This is called **chronological order.**

1. Make a chart like the one shown on
   a piece of paper.
2. List your activities during a typical
   school day. Use chronological
   order—the order in which you do
   each thing.
3. Share your chart with a partner. Is
   the order you do things the same or
   different from your partner?

Time	Activities
6:00 A.M.	
10:00 A.M.	
12:00 P.M.	
3:00 P.M.	
6:00 P.M.	
8:00 P.M.	
10:00 P.M.	

42 Unit 1 Traditions and Cultures

MULTI-LEVEL OPTIONS *Build Vocabulary*

Newcomer Ask students to
make three simple drawings of
something they do at 7 A.M.,
4 P.M., and 8 P.M. Help them label
the drawings *In the morning,
After school, At night.* Shuffle the
drawings and exchange them
with another student. Have each
student put the pictures in the
correct order.

Beginning Ask students to fold
a large piece of paper into fourths.
Have them draw one event (listed
on p. 43, question 1 a–d) in each
quarter. Tell them to label their
drawings with the highlighted
words: *after, during, then, after.*
Ask students to cut apart the
fourths and arrange them in
chronological order.

Intermediate Have students
work in pairs. Instruct one partner
to copy sentences *a* and *b* on
two slips of paper and the other
partner to copy sentences *c*
and *d* on two other slips of paper.
Have students work together to
determine the correct chronological
order. The sentences may then be
copied into their Personal
Dictionaries.

Advanced Have students write
five sentences about what they do
after school. Remind them to use
the transition words presented on
p. 43 along with other transition
words, such as *before, next,* and
finally.

Build Background

Turkey

Turkey is a country that is partly in Europe and partly in Asia. Turkey has big cities and small towns. It also has rich farmland. Turkey is famous for its colorful ceramic dishes and tiles. Turkish handmade rugs are known around the world.

Content Connection

Turkish Delight is a sweet, chewy dessert made of nuts, fruit, and sugar. In Turkey, it is called *lokum*.

Build Vocabulary

Identify Words That Show Time

Sometimes an author organizes the story in chronological order. In "Turkish Delight," the author uses transition words that show this time order. Knowing the meanings of these words will help you analyze when events (things that happen) take place.

1. In your Personal Dictionary, write the following sentences.
   a. <u>After</u> school, I come home.
   b. <u>During</u> the week, I go to school in the mornings.
   c. <u>Then</u> I help my family with the housework.
   d. <u>After</u> the housework is finished, I do my homework.
2. Use clues in the sentences to rewrite the sentences into chronological order.

Personal Dictionary   Activity Book p. 25   Student CD-ROM

Chapter 4 Turkish Delight   **43**

Home Connection

Build Vocabulary Have students meet in pairs to tell each other about what they did the previous weekend. Ask students to use transition words, such as *first, then, later, after, during, next,* and *at last* in their accounts.

Learning Styles
Visual

Build Background Help students locate Turkey on a world map. Have them point to or tell what countries and bodies of water surround Turkey. Ask them to compare its size and shape with that of the United States and countries they have visited or lived in.

Build Background

Turkey

1. **Use a map** Direct students to the map of Turkey. Ask them to locate the capital (Ankara) and name the bodies of water surrounding the country (Black Sea, Mediterranean Sea).
2. **Connect to theme** *Say: The theme for this unit is traditions and cultures. Do you know any traditional foods or products from Turkey?*
3. **Content Connection** *Say: Food is an important part of a culture and tradition. Can you name a traditional food from a culture or region that uses fruit or nuts?*

Build Vocabulary

Identify Words That Show Time

Teacher Resource Book: *Personal Dictionary, p. 63*

1. **Use time words** Have students discuss their daily routines. As they speak, write any time words they use on the board. Point out that these words tell the order the events happened. Remind students to use the simple present tense for habits and routines.
2. **Reading selection vocabulary** You may want to introduce the glossed words in the reading selection before students begin reading. Key words: *clever, complaints, role model, regions, misunderstandings, income, apricots.* Instruct students to write the words with correct spelling and their definitions in their Personal Dictionaries. Have them pronounce each word and divide it into syllables.
3. **Multi-level options** See MULTI-LEVEL OPTIONS on p. 42

Answers
2. b, a, c, d

ASSESS

Ask students to write two sentences about Turkey.

Text Structure

Personal Narrative

Review Review features of a personal narrative. Remind students that "Birthday Barbecue" was also a personal narrative.

Reading Strategy

Compare Text Events with Your Own Experiences

1. **Use graphic organizer to compare** Direct students to the illustration on p. 45. Have them work in pairs to observe similarities between themselves and the girl in the picture. Have students prepare their Venn diagrams and begin to fill it in based on their discussions and information from paragraph 1.
2. **Multi-level options** See MULTI-LEVEL OPTIONS below.

ASSESS

Have students write a question about the form of a personal narrative. Collect and redistribute the questions. Have small groups answer several questions each.

Text Structure

Personal Narrative

"Turkish Delight" is a **personal narrative.** The chart shows the distinguishing features of a personal narrative.

Look for these features as you read "Turkish Delight."

Personal Narrative	
First-Person Point of View	pronouns *I, me, we, us*
Personal Details	true information about the author

Student CD-ROM

Reading Strategy

Compare Text Events with Your Own Experiences

You can understand text events better when you compare them with your own experiences.

1. Read or listen to the audio recording of paragraph 1 of "Turkish Delight." How are you similar to Hamdiye? How are you different from Hamdiye?
2. As you read or listen to each paragraph in the selection, compare your experiences with Hamdiye's. Organize your answers in a Venn Diagram.

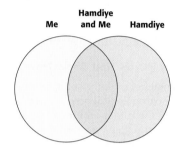

Student CD-ROM

MULTI-LEVEL OPTIONS *Reading Strategy*

Newcomer Read the paragraph aloud using story art and gestures to reinforce meaning. Make comparisons between the character and yourself. For example, point to Hamdiye, then point to Turkey on a map. Point to yourself and then to the United States. Have students compare themselves to the character using your model.

Beginning Have students point to Hamdiye in the illustration on p. 45 and say a word to indicate one of her traits, such as *thirteen*. Ask them to point to themselves and say their own age. Continue with other traits. Demonstrate how to put these one-word descriptions on the Venn diagram.

Intermediate Have students begin to record similarities between Hamdiye and themselves on the Venn diagram. As you read the selection, ask students to identify evidence from the selection that proves the character possesses the traits they identify. (likes reading— reads after doing housework)

Advanced Have students use the information on their Venn diagrams to write paragraphs comparing and contrasting themselves with Hamdiye.

Turkish Delight

a personal narrative and recipe
by Hamdiye Çelik

45

Reading Selection Materials

Audio: *Unit 1, Chapter 4; CD 1, Track 5*
Teacher Resource Book: *Reading Summary,
pp. 71–72*
Transparencies: #2, *Reading Summary*

Suggestions for Using Reading Summary

- Introduce new vocabulary or cognates.
- Cut the summary into strips, or jumble the sentences on an overhead transparency. Students put the sentences in order.
- Practice the reading strategy.
- Students read aloud or with a partner.
- Students paraphrase the summary.
- Students do a cloze activity.
- Students create a visual or graphic organizer, such as a timeline or storyboard, to illustrate the summary.
- Students paraphrase the summary.

Preview the Selection

1. **Art background** *Ask: How does the choice of this photograph represent the meaning of the text? What is the author doing? How would you describe her?* Then prompt students to ask you some questions.
2. **Compare media** *Ask: What if it were a painting instead? Would it seem as real? Would it be as interesting?*
3. **Connect** Tell students that this personal narrative is written by a real person. *Ask: When have you written a personal narrative? What was it about?*

 Content Connection
Social Studies

Provide time for students to look at books and online resources that show and tell about life in Turkey. Have students make predictions about how a 13-year-old girl may spend a weekday in Turkey.

Learning Styles
Kinesthetic

Tell students that they will read about things Turkish children know how to make, including rugs and fruit treats. Invite students to show something they know how to make. They can provide a simple demonstration, if possible. As an alternative, they can simply act out the steps involved.

Read the Selection

Teacher Resource Book: *Venn Diagram, p. 35*

1. **Paired reading** Read the first two paragraphs. *Ask: How old is Hamdiye? What is she like?* Have students reread in pairs.
2. **Use a graphic organizer** Have students continue to fill in information on their Venn diagrams.
3. **Identify words that show time** Ask students to identify the words in paragraph 2 that show time.

Sample Answer to Guide Question
I stay in school for lunch. I go to school in the mornings and in the afternoons.

See Teacher Edition pp. 434–436 for a list of English-Spanish cognates in the reading selection.

Audio
CD 1. Tr. 5

Compare Text Events with Your Own Experiences

How is your school day similar to or different from Hamdiye's?

1   My name is Hamdiye Çelik. I am 13 years old. I live in the town of Dargeçit in the southeastern part of Turkey. I have black hair and dark skin. I am a rather **reflective** and **clever** person. I respect my **elders** and love **youngsters.** I like reading poetry and playing volleyball.

2   During the week, I go to school in the mornings. When I return home at noon, I help my family with housework first and then eat lunch. I live with my four sisters and my mother. We all help each other. After the housework is finished, I do my homework, read, and play. Since my father died years ago, we live on a very **limited budget** and barely survive. But I have no **complaints.**

3   My mother is a hardworking, honest woman, who helps everyone, and for this reason, she is my **role model.** I am very happy to have such a family.

reflective   very thoughtful
clever   intelligent
elders   people older than you
youngsters   boys and girls older than babies and younger than teenagers

limited   restricted, a small amount
budget   money set aside for a purpose
complaints   expressions of unhappiness about something
role model   a person who is an example of success for young people

46   Unit 1   Traditions and Cultures

MULTI-LEVEL OPTIONS *Read the Selection*

Newcomer Draw clocks on the board showing 9 A.M., noon, and 3 P.M. Play the audio. Point to the relevant clock and act out Hamdiye's activities as they are described. *Ask: Does the girl go to school all day?* (no) *Does she come home at noon?* (yes) *Does she help her family?* (yes) *Does her family make coats?* (no)

Beginning Read the Reading Summary. Then have students do a paired reading. *Ask: Where does Hamdiye live?* (Turkey) *What does she do in the morning?* (go to school) *What does she do in the afternoon?* (help her family) *What do Hamdiye's sisters do to help the family?* (make rugs)

Intermediate Have students do paired readings. Then *ask: How does Hamdiye help at home?* (She does chores before she plays.) *How is spring different from winter for the family?* (In spring they work in someone's fields; in winter they stay home.) *If a kilim has red dots on one side, what would be on the other?* (red dots)

Advanced Have students read silently. *Ask: How is Hamdiye like her mother?* (Both help others.) *Does Hamdiye go to school in spring? Explain.* (No, because that is when the family leaves town.) *If the Hamdiye goes to weaving classes, will she likely do well? Why?* (Yes. She is clever and works hard.)

4   When spring comes, we go to fields in other **regions** to plow or collect cotton or **hazelnuts.** When winter approaches, we return to our town, and for the rest of the year, we live on the money we saved.

5   Our handmade Turkish kilims and carpets are famous worldwide. In **rural** villages, there are community centers especially for helping girls and women learn how to earn money. Two of my sisters took kilim and carpet weaving classes at one center. This is how they **contribute** to our family **income.**

> **Compare Text Events with Your Own Experiences**
>
> Reread paragraphs 4 and 5. What do farmers grow where you live?

> What's a *kilim?* A kilim is a hand-woven rug that is exactly the same on the front as on the back. **Doubly** useful!

regions areas of a country	**contribute** give to
hazelnuts nuts from a hazel tree that you can eat	**income** money earned from working
rural related to the countryside, not the city	**doubly** twice the amount of

Chapter 4 Turkish Delight   **47**

Read the Selection

Teacher Resource Book: *Two-Column Chart, p. 44*

1. **Shared reading** Play the audio. Have students join in when they can.
2. **Read for information** Draw a two-column chart. Label the left column "Topic" and the right one "Facts." Under "Topics" write the following words, each one corresponding to a paragraph: *1. Hamdiye 2. Weekday routine 3. Her mother 4. Spring work 5. Kilims and carpets.* Have students work in groups. *Say: Reread the narrative. Find 2 or 3 facts about each topic. Copy the chart and fill in the information.* When students have finished, have one group put their chart on the board.
3. **Compare text with your own experiences** Read the guide question and give students time to think about their answers. Then elicit answers and write them on the board. *Ask: What do we plant in our region? What do farms grow? When do they harvest or collect the crop?*
4. **Multi-level options** See MULTI-LEVEL OPTIONS on p. 46.

Sample Answer to Guide Question
vegetables, cotton, wheat, rice, fruit

A Capitalization

Towns, cities, and countries

Point out that the first letter of the names of towns, cities, and countries is capitalized. Have students locate *Dargeçit* in paragraph 1. Tell students it's the name of Hamdiye's town. *Ask: What other word in the paragraph begins with a capital letter and is the name of a place?* (Turkey) Write on the board: *The capital city of turkey is ankara. Ask: What words should start with capitals?* (Turkey, Ankara)

Apply Ask several students to identify countries they were born in. Write sentences such as: *Luis was born in ponce, puerto rico.* Have students tell you where to place capital letters.

Read the Selection

1. **Reciprocal reading** Play the audio. Divide students into small groups. Have students take turns being the "teacher." Instruct the "teacher" to read the selection aloud and ask other students questions about each paragraph.
2. **Compare traditions** Read the guide question. *Ask: Which traditions did the author write about? Do you have any of the same traditions? Do you think your rituals are similar or different? Why?*

Sample Answer to Guide Question
We also have the tradition of visiting sick people in my community. We celebrate weddings and have funeral services, too.

Compare Text Events with Your Own Experiences

Compare Turkish traditions with the traditions of your community.

6   In Turkey, our traditions and **rituals** have an important place in our lives. Some of our traditions are wedding celebrations for young couples, visiting sick people, and **funeral services.** They are signs of help and **solidarity** in our society. During religious holidays, people who are angry with each other forget and forgive old **misunderstandings** and, instead, live in **tolerance** and love.

Sweet Golden Treats

7   Turkey grows lots of **apricots.** People pick the apricots, then lay them out to dry—everywhere you look there's a beautiful orange glow! Here's a **yummy** way to eat Turkish apricots. Remember to ask an adult for help in the kitchen.

---

rituals   ceremonies to mark a serious or special event or day
funeral services   ceremonies for remembering people who have just died
solidarity   a feeling of togetherness or having the same opinions as others in a group

misunderstandings   disagreements, arguments
tolerance   acceptance, especially of beliefs and behavior that is different
apricots   small, peachlike fruits
yummy   good tasting

48   Unit 1   Traditions and Cultures

MULTI-LEVEL OPTIONS *Read the Selection*

Newcomer *Ask: Is there a special time to forgive people in Turkey?* (yes) *Are apricots a special treat in Turkey?* (yes) *Is this a recipe that tells how to make an apple treat?* (no) *Is the treat sweet?* (yes)

Beginning *Ask: What is a Turkish tradition or ritual that is similar to traditions and rituals in many countries?* (weddings, visiting the sick, funeral services) *What kind of fruit grows in Turkey?* (apricots) *When do you put whipped cream on the treat?* (after the apricots cool)

Intermediate *Ask: What happens during Turkish holidays?* (People come together.) *How do people celebrate religious holidays?* (by forgiving people they are angry with) *What is the reason for soaking the apricots in the recipe?* (to make the dry fruit soft) *How are the treats decorated?* (with whipped cream and nuts)

Advanced *Ask: What is the orange glow the author mentions?* (apricots drying in the field) *Why does the author suggest getting an adult to help with the recipe?* (to be safe while using a stove) *When do you think people use this recipe? Explain.* (For holidays, because it is on a page about holidays.)

Kaymakli Kayisi (Cream-filled Apricots)

8 dried apricots
½ cup (1¼ **dl**) water
1 cup (2½ dl) sugar
2 **T** lemon juice
1 cup (2½ dl) whipped cream
1 T chopped **almonds**

Compare Text Events with Your Own Experiences

Have you ever made or eaten a recipe like this one? Explain.

8   Soak apricot halves in water for two hours to soften them. Mix water, sugar, and lemon juice in a pan and **bring to a fast boil** over medium heat. Carefully add the apricots using a spoon and cook for 5 minutes. Turn off heat. Scoop the apricots from the pan and arrange on a plate. Let cool. **Dab** some whipped cream on each apricot. Sprinkle with chopped almonds. **Dig in!**

dl deciliter, a unit of measurement in the metric system	**bring to a fast boil** heat the liquid until it bubbles a lot
T tablespoon, a large spoon used to measure recipe ingredients	**dab** put a small amount
almonds nuts often used in dessert recipes	**dig in** eat and enjoy

Chapter 4 Turkish Delight **49**

 Spelling

Abbreviations of measurements

Call attention to the abbreviation *dl* in the recipe. Read aloud the glossary entry for *dl*. Explain that this is a short way of writing *deciliter*. Point out the use of *T* in the recipe. Help students determine its meaning using the glossary.

Apply Have students find abbreviations in other recipes. Using the glossed words on p. 49 as a model, help students create a classroom chart of abbreviations.

Evaluate Your Reading Strategy

Compare Text with Your Own Experiences
Say: You have practiced an important reading strategy. Now you can decide how well you have done. Does this statement describe how you read?

> I ask myself how my experiences are similar to events in the reading. When I compare text events with my experiences, I use what I know to better understand what I read.

Read the Selection

1. **Use art to predict** *Say: We are going to read a recipe. First look at the picture. What ingredients are in this recipe?* (apricots, sugar, water, lemon juice, almonds, whipped cream)
2. **Shared reading** Play the audio for the recipe. Have students join in by taking turns reading the ingredients and steps.
3. **Compare measures** Show students examples of measuring spoons and cups that are used in the recipe.
4. **Relate to own experience** Have students share recipes they know or have made. Point out that it is important to know specific amounts and directions.
5. **Multi-level options** See MULTI-LEVEL OPTIONS on p. 48.

Sample Answer to Guide Question
I've eaten my mother's desserts. I've helped my parents make special treats on holidays.

Across Selections

Compare points of view *Ask: What other narratives have we read with first-person point of view?* ("Birthday Barbecue") *What was the point of view in "Coyote"?* (third-person)

Spelling, Punctuation, Capitalization

After the Reading Comprehension section, students will practice spelling, punctuation, and capitalization in the Activity Book.

Beyond the Reading

Reading Comprehension

Question-Answer Relationships

Sample Answers

1. Hamdiye Çelik
2. Dargeçit
3. They weave kilims and carpets.
4. She eats lunch.
5. She has black hair and dark skin. She likes reading poetry and playing volleyball.
6. I learned that families are important and they help each other out. I learned that Turkish rugs and kilims are famous worldwide.
7. weddings, visiting the sick, and funeral services
8. She thinks they are important.
9. She loves children. Her mother is her role model. Her family lives on very little money. They have to leave their town to find work in other regions.
10. Family is also important in my culture. We also celebrate weddings, have funeral services, and visit sick people. We don't eat apricots very much. We go to school all day long.

Build Reading Fluency

Reading Chunks of Words

Explain that reading chunks of underlined words helps improve reading fluency. Ask students to listen as you model reading chunks before they practice aloud with a partner.

Reading Comprehension

Question-Answer Relationships (QAR)

"Right There" Questions

1. **Recall Facts** Who tells this narrative?
2. **Recall Facts** In which city does Hamdiye live?
3. **Recall Facts** How do Hamdiye's sisters earn money?

"Think and Search" Questions

4. **Describe the Sequence of Events** What does Hamdiye do after she finishes the housework?
5. **Describe** Describe Hamdiye. What does she look like? What does she like?
6. **Determine Characteristics of Culture** What did you learn about Hamdiye's culture?

"Author and You" Questions

7. **Identify Themes** What are some important traditions in Hamdiye's community?
8. **Draw Conclusions** How do you think Hamdiye feels about the traditions she describes?

"On Your Own" Questions

9. **Connect** What do you think are the best parts of Hamdiye's life? What do you think are the hardest parts?
10. **Compare and Contrast** In what ways is your culture similar to Hamdiye's? In what ways is it different?

Activity Book
p. 26

Student
CD-ROM

Build Reading Fluency

Reading Chunks of Words

Reading chunks or phrases of words is an important characteristic of fluent readers. It helps you stop reading word by word.

1. With a partner, take turns reading aloud the underlined chunks of words.
2. Read aloud two times each.

> During the week, I go to school in the mornings. When I return home at noon, I help my family with housework first and then eat lunch. I live with my four sisters and my mother. We all help each other.

MULTI-LEVEL OPTIONS *Elements of Literature*

Newcomer Have students draw the ingredients in the recipe for Kaymakli Kayasi. Then have them write a number on each picture to show the order the ingredient is added in the recipe.

Beginning Have students make a number of drawings that show ingredients and steps in the recipe for Kaymakli Kayasi. Help students label their drawings with the nouns for ingredients and action verbs for the numbered steps. Ask students to read aloud their verb labels and act out each step.

Intermediate Have students complete the steps in the recipe for Kaymakli Kayasi. If possible, have the class make the recipe. If that is not possible, have pairs of students work together. One student reads the recipe while the other mimes the steps.

Advanced Have students rewrite the recipe for Kaymakli Kayasi into the numbered steps chart on p. 51. Instruct pairs to use the same format to create a variation of the recipe. For example, students might create a variation that uses dried apple slices filled with peanut butter.

Listen, Speak, Interact

Distinguish Fact from Opinion

A **fact** is true information. An **opinion** is what someone thinks or believes. In "Turkish Delight," Hamdiye gives facts and opinions. Can you tell the difference? Here is an example:

Fact:　　I am 13 years old.
Opinion:　I am a clever person.

1. With a partner, reread or listen to the audio recording of paragraphs 1, 2, and 3 of the selection.

Facts	Opinions

2. List facts and opinions in a chart like the one here.
3. Compare your list with another set of partners.
4. Share your list with the class.

Elements of Literature

Instructions

Authors use **instructions** to list the steps in doing something. The recipe in "Turkish Delight" gives instructions. It explains the steps needed to make an apricot dessert.

Recipes include a list of ingredients, or food items needed to make a recipe. Then the recipe explains what to do with the ingredients. People often write these instructions in a numbered list.

1. Reread the recipe for Cream-filled Apricots.
2. Rewrite the instructions in paragraph 8. Give each step a number starting with 1.
3. Use the list shown to help you organize the steps.

Steps

1.
2.
3.
4.
5.
6.
7.
8.

Activity Book
p. 27

Student
CD-ROM

⬤ ✕	**Content Connection**
÷ ▲	*Math*

Point out that the directions they have written for the Kaymakli Kayisi recipe makes eight pieces. Ask students to calculate how much of each ingredient they would need if they were going to make enough for each person in their class to have one of the treats.

Learning Styles
Interpersonal

Point out that in "Turkish Delight," Hamdiye states opinions about herself. *Ask: What are your opinions about her? What facts from the selection support your opinions?* Have students create a Character Trait Web. Have them place the girl's name in the center. On each branch of the web, ask them to write an opinion about her. At the end of each branch, have them draw a box and write a fact from the selection that supports the opinion. Have them share their webs in pairs.

Listen, Speak, Interact

Distinguish Fact from Opinion

1. **Identify facts and opinions** Have students work in pairs. Remind them that facts can be proven and that opinions show what people think or feel.
2. **Newcomers** Reread paragraph 1 with this group. Ask them to find facts, such as where Hamdiye lives or how she looks. (Dargeçit, Turkey; black hair, dark skin) Ask them to find opinions that tell what she thinks about herself. (reflective, clever)

Elements of Literature

Instructions

1. **Use personal experience** Have students work in pairs to create a recipe for a lunch they can make, such as a peanut butter and jelly sandwich or a salad. Tell them to list the ingredients. Then have them create a set of directions that include numbered steps.
2. **Multi-level options** See MULTI-LEVEL OPTIONS on p. 50.

Answers

1. Soak apricot halves in water for two hours to soften them.
2. Mix water, sugar, and lemon juice in a pan and bring to a fast boil over medium heat.
3. Carefully add the apricots using a spoon and cook for 5 minutes.
4. Turn off heat.
5. Scoop the apricots from the pan and arrange on a plate.
6. Let cool.
7. Dab some whipped cream on each apricot.
8. Sprinkle with chopped almonds.

✓ ASSESS

Have students write 2 facts and 2 opinions from the story.

Word Study

Recognize Root Words and the Suffix -ish

Recognize roots and suffixes Write on the board: *British, Irish, Spanish.* Tell students that the suffix *-ish* is often used to describe both nationalities and languages. Point out that the countries usually have similar roots. Then ask them to identify the countries. (Britain, Ireland, Spain)

Answers

1. childish — like a child; English — having to do with England; foolish — like a fool; reddish — like the color red

Grammar Focus

Use the Verb *To Be* with Complements

Identify Parts of Speech Help students identify one or two sentences with the verb *to be* and complements from paragraph 1. Then have students work in pairs to complete the exercise.

Answer

Example: I am 13 years old. "am" = a form of *to be,* "13 years old" = complement

ASSESS

Direct students to paragraph 3. Have them write forms of *to be* and their complements.

Word Study

Recognize Root Words and the Suffix -ish

Many English words are made by combining a **root word** and a **suffix.** A *root word* is a word or part of a word that can be used to make other words. A *suffix* is an ending. The suffix *-ish* means "like" or "having to do with." The word *Turkish* means "having to do with Turkey."

Words	Definitions
childish	having to do with England
English	like the color red
foolish	like a child
reddish	like a fool

1. Work with a partner. On a piece of paper, match each word with its correct definition.
2. Check your answers with another pair of students.
3. Write sentences using three of the words.
4. Write the words and their definitions in your Personal Dictionary.

Personal Dictionary   Activity Book p. 28   Student CD-ROM

Grammar Focus

Use the Verb *To Be* with Complements

A **complement** describes or renames the subject of a sentence. A complement can be a noun, a pronoun, or an adjective. Complements can follow a form of the verb *to be.* Forms of *to be* include *am, is,* and *are.*

Look at these sentences. The underlined words are complements.

The dogs **are** big and brown.

She **is** my sister.

I **am** older.

1. Read paragraphs 1, 2, and 3 of "Turkish Delight." On a piece of paper, write two sentences that include a form of *to be* and a complement.
2. Circle the *to be* forms and underline the complements.
3. Write two sentences of your own using a form of *to be* and a complement. Be sure to use the correct forms of *to be* and to spell these forms correctly.

Activity Book pp. 29–30   Student Handbook   Student CD-ROM

52   Unit 1 Traditions and Cultures

MULTI-LEVEL OPTIONS *From Reading to Writing*

Newcomer Have students draw an illustration of themselves and their family. Ask them to show an action picture of the family doing various activities in their home. Help students label the people and activities.

Beginning On the upper two-thirds of a sheet of art paper, have students draw themselves and their families engaged in activities in their home. On the lower third, help them copy and complete the cloze letter on p. 53.

Intermediate Have students create a timeline of their family's activities on a typical day. Tell them to write transition words and phrases, such as *in the morning, then, after lunch,* above each timeline entry. Have students use the organizers to compose their letters. Remind them to use first-person pronouns.

Advanced After students have completed first drafts of their letters, have them meet in peer response groups. Ask responders to note any adjectives ending in the suffix *-ish* and any *to be* verbs with complements that writers used in describing themselves and their families.

From Reading to Writing

Write a Personal Narrative

Write a letter to a new pen pal. Your letter will be a personal narrative that tells about you. Write one paragraph.

1. Describe yourself and your family. Include details about how old you are, what you look like, your daily activities, where you live, and what you like to do.
2. Use the first-person pronouns *I, me, we,* and *us.*
3. Use time words to show order.

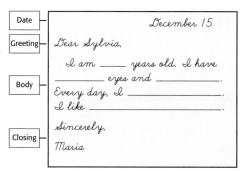

Date
Greeting
Body
Closing

December 15

Dear Sylvia,

I am _____ years old. I have _____ eyes and _____.

Every day, I _____.

I like _____.

Sincerely,

Maria

Activity Book
p. 31

Student Handbook

Across Content Areas

Design a Turkish Rug

People who make rugs are **weavers.** Weavers make **designs** in the cloth. A design can be a shape or a picture.

Sometimes weavers use **symbols** as their designs. A symbol is something that stands for something else. For example, a flying bird might be a symbol of freedom.

In "Turkish Delight," Hamdiye describes a kind of Turkish rug called a *kilim.* Turkish weavers make colorful designs in the rugs. These designs are often symbols.

The picture shows two common symbols found on Turkish rugs.

1. On a piece of paper, design a "Turkish rug." Draw symbols that you would weave on a Turkish rug.

2. Share your design with a small group. Explain what each symbol means and why you chose it.

Activity Book
p. 32

Chapter 4 Turkish Delight **53**

From Reading to Writing

Write a Personal Narrative

1. **Pre-writing** Students can "tell" their letter to a partner before writing it down. Direct partners to ask questions to clarify details. Clarify the meaning of *pen pal.*
2. **Write a letter** Remind students of the transition words they studied: *after, during, then.* Remind them to use the format for a friendly letter in the text.
3. **Multi-level options** See MULTI-LEVEL OPTIONS on p. 52.

Across Content Areas: The Arts

Design a Turkish Rug

1. **Define and clarify** Ask students for examples of symbols they know, such as a country's flag or the school mascot. Then have students choose colors and draw their rug designs.
2. **Explain symbols** Students can share their designs in small groups and explain the meanings of symbols they've included. Display the designs and hold a gallery walk.

 **ASSESS**

Have students write three characteristics of a personal narrative.

Reteach and Reassess

Text Structure Have students make a two-column chart with the headings *First-Person Pronouns* and *Personal Details.* Ask students to reread the selection to find three examples for each heading.

Reading Strategy Ask pairs who have lived in different countries to meet and share about their families and traditions. Have pairs use a Venn diagram to compare and contrast families.

Elements of Literature Ask students to write a list of materials and numbered steps for something they know how to make.

Reassess Have students write a letter home from their imaginary trip to Turkey. Ask them to include facts and opinions about the country. Remind them to use first-person pronouns.

Chapter Materials

Activity Book: *pp. 33–40*
Audio: *Unit 1, Chapter 5; CD 1, Track 6*
Student Handbook
Student CD-ROM: *Unit 1, Chapter 5*
Teacher Resource Book: *Lesson Plan, Teacher Resources, Reading Summary, Activity Book Answer Key*
Teacher Resource CD-ROM
Assessment Program: *Quiz, pp. 15–16; Teacher and Student Resources, pp. 115–144*
Assessment CD-ROM
Transparencies
The Heinle Newbury House Dictionary/CD-ROM
Web site: http://visions.heinle.com

Sadako and the Thousand Paper Cranes

an excerpt from a novel based on a true story by Eleanor Coerr

Objectives

Reading Identify cause and effect as you read historical fiction.

Listening and Speaking Perform a dialogue.

Grammar Recognize possessive nouns.

Writing Write a fictional narrative.

Content Math: Learn geometric shapes and vocabulary.

Objectives

Preview Read the objectives aloud. *Ask: Which objective is new for you?*

Use Prior Knowledge

Describe a Sickness

Relate to personal experience Have students think about a time when they were sick. *Ask: What's the worst thing about being sick?* Tell students to draw and label pictures about their experiences with sickness.

Answers
Examples: **2.** tired, body aches, hot, cold, sad, bored, lonely

Use Prior Knowledge

Describe a Sickness

In "Sadako and the Thousand Paper Cranes," the main character is named Sadako. She is in the hospital because she is very sick. She feels sad and lonely. Her family and friends come to visit her, and they cheer her up.

1. Think about a time when you or someone you know was very sick.
2. With a partner, write words that describe being sick. Use a web like the one shown. How does a sick person's body feel? What emotions and thoughts does a sick person have?

3. Draw pictures to go with your web of words. Show how a person looks when he or she feels sick, sad, or lonely.

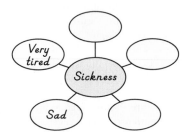

MULTI-LEVEL OPTIONS *Build Vocabulary*

Newcomer Show students how to create cluster diagrams for the setting words: *hospital, nurse, visiting hours, shot, sick.* Have them make quick sketches to represent these things on the branches of the map. Point to each item, say the word for it, and have students repeat it.

Beginning Have students work in pairs. Give each pair 8 index cards. Tell them to draw pictures illustrating *hospital, nurse, shot,* and *sick* on 4 cards. Help them write the words for the pictures on the other cards. Have partners spread out the cards and take turns matching a word card to each picture card.

Intermediate After students have created a sentence for each word, challenge them to create sentences that include two or more of the words.

Advanced Have students think of a synonym or related term for as many of the words as possible. (hospital-clinic, shot-needle, sick-ill, nurse-RN)

Build Background

Radiation Sickness

In 1945, during World War II, the United States dropped two atom bombs on the Japanese cities of Hiroshima and Nagasaki. The bombs spread radiation— harmful energy waves that come from atom bombs. Radiation made people very sick. They felt very weak and had trouble fighting germs. This reading tells a story about Sadako Sasaki. She was a Japanese girl who had radiation sickness.

Content Connection

Japan is a nation of islands. It is in the Pacific Ocean near the east coast of China.

Build Vocabulary

Identify Words About Setting

The **setting** of a story is its time and place. One way to learn new words is to relate them to a setting where they are used. The setting for "Sadako and the Thousand Paper Cranes" is a hospital. Work with a small group to learn words that relate to the setting of hospitals.

1. Read the words in the box.

nurse	shot	sick
hospital	visiting	hours

2. Work with your group to figure out what each word means. Use a dictionary if necessary. Write the meanings in your Personal Dictionary.

3. Write a sentence for each word.

Personal Dictionary

The Heinle Newbury House Dictionary

Activity Book *p. 33*

Student CD-ROM

Chapter 5 Sadako and the Thousand Paper Cranes **55**

Content Connection
Science

Learning Styles
Kinesthetic

Build Vocabulary Provide books and book-marked Web sites about medical inventions and discoveries. Have students use information from these sources to make a timeline of pictures or phrases identifying at least six medical innovations. Have students note which were discovered before the setting of the story (1950s) and which came later.

Build Background Provide additional background for understanding the story by introducing the concept of origami. Simple designs can be found on the Internet with key words: *origami* or *paper-folding games.* Give students an opportunity to create an origami design.

Build Background

Radiation Sickness

Teacher Resource Book: *Web, p. 37*

1. **Use personal knowledge** *Ask: What do you know about Japan? Can you find it on the map?* Have students brainstorm all the words that come to mind when they think of Japan. Write down the words in a web on the board.

2. **Connect to theme** *Say: The theme of this unit is traditions and cultures. How do you think Japanese culture has changed since 1945?*

3. **Content Connection** Ask students to use an atlas to find the names of the four main islands of Japan. (Honshu, Hokkaido, Kyushu, and Shikoku)

Build Vocabulary

Identify Words About Setting

Teacher Resource Book: *Personal Dictionary, p. 63*

1. **Extend your vocabulary** Have students work in groups to expand their vocabulary lists to include general hospital terms (emergency rooms, operations) and hospital workers (doctor, aide, receptionist). Have them sort their lists into people, places, and things.

2. **Reading selection vocabulary** You may want to introduce the glossed words in the reading selection before students begin reading. Key words: *shot, tacks, thread, courage, statue.* Instruct students to write the words with correct spelling and their definitions in their Personal Dictionaries. Have them pronounce each word and divide it into syllables.

3. **Multi-level options** See MULTI-LEVEL OPTIONS on p. 54.

ASSESS

Have students write six words related to hospitals or being sick.

Text Structure

Novel Based on a True Story

Review genre Direct students to the chart of a novel's features. *Say: We read "Coyote." That was fiction. Did it have a setting, characters, and a plot, too?* (yes) *Was it based on a true story?* (no)

Reading Strategy

Identify Cause and Effect

1. **Teacher think aloud** *Say: I was late today Why? Because I overslept. The word* because *gives the reason, so the effect, or result, was "I was late."* Then ask students to give their own examples of cause and effect.
2. **Multi-level options** See MULTI-LEVEL OPTIONS below.

Have students write a definition of historical fiction.

Text Structure

Novel Based on a True Story

The reading selection is taken from a book called *Sadako and the Thousand Paper Cranes.* A story that fills a book is a **novel.** This is a special kind of novel. It is a novel based on a true story. The author did not make up the whole story. The story really happened, but it did not happen exactly the way the author wrote it.

We can also say that this story is **historical fiction.** In historical fiction, the author makes up some or all of the story. Look at the distinguishing features of this genre.

Historical Fiction	
Setting	the time and place of a story; some are made up
Characters	the people; some are made up
Plot	what happens in the story Beginning ↓ Middle ↓ End

Pay attention to and analyze the setting, the characters, and the plot as you read.

Student CD-ROM

Reading Strategy

Identify Cause and Effect

The reason something happens is its **cause.** The event that happens is an **effect.** As you read the selection, think about why the events in the story happen.

1. One way to find a cause and an effect is to ask a question and then answer it. Use the word *because* in your answer to connect the cause and the effect.
2. Read these sentences:

    She got sick.
    She was in Hiroshima when the bomb fell.

Why did she get sick?
She got sick *because* she was in Hiroshima when the bomb fell.
   the cause = being in Hiroshima
   the effect = getting sick

3. Make a chart like this. As you read the selection, write causes and effects.

Causes	Effects
She was in the hospital.	She didn't hear her mother making breakfast.

Student CD-ROM

56 Unit 1 Traditions and Cultures

MULTI-LEVEL OPTIONS *Reading Strategy*

Newcomer Introduce the concept of cause and effect by miming a cough. *Ask: Why? Say: Because* and mime sickness. From time to time in reading the story, point to aspects of the illustrations and *ask: Why?* Have students say, "Because . . ." and point to or act out the cause.

Beginning Give students cards with the words *cause* and *effect* on them. *Say: I dropped the chalk. It broke.* Have students hold up the card to show which sentence tells a cause and which tells an effect. As you read the story, ask whether certain details tell causes or effects. Have students use their cards to respond.

Intermediate Have students work in pairs. Tell them to take turns asking each other *Why* questions about story characters and actions, then respond with *Because* statements.

Advanced Have students consider the cause and effect relationship related to the author's purpose. *Ask: Why do you think the author wrote this story? What effect did the story have on you?*

SADAKO AND THE THOUSAND PAPER CRANES

an excerpt from a novel based on a true story
by Eleanor Coerr

57

Cultural Connection

Ask students to look at the pictures of cranes on p. 57 and in other resources. Have them discuss why they think many cultures have chosen cranes to stand for good luck, good health, and peace.

Learning Styles
Natural

Ask students to examine the cranes in the picture on p. 57. Then have them focus on the paper crane in the illustration. *Ask: How did the creator of the paper crane make it resemble a real crane?*

Reading Selection Materials

Audio: *Unit 1, Chapter 5; CD 1, Track 6*
Teacher Resource Book: *Reading Summary, pp. 73–74*
Transparencies: *#3, Reading Summary*

Suggestions for Using Reading Summary

- Introduce new vocabulary or cognates.
- Cut the summary into strips, or jumble the sentences on an overhead transparency. Students put the sentences in order.
- Practice the reading strategy.
- Students read aloud or with a partner.
- Students paraphrase the summary.
- Students do a cloze activity.
- Students create a visual or graphic organizer, such as a timeline or storyboard, to illustrate the summary.
- Students paraphrase the summary.

Preview the Selection

1. **Discuss medium and message** *Say: Photos, painting, and sculpture are different mediums for art. What medium is this? What do you see in the artwork? What is different about the crane in the middle?* (It's folded paper.)
2. **Discuss symbolism in art** *Say: Flying birds sometimes symbolize freedom. In the United States, the eagle stands for freedom. In Japan, the crane traditionally symbolizes long life.* Ask students if they know any other bird symbols. (dove: peace)
3. **Connect** Remind students that the unit theme is *traditions and cultures.* Ask students to predict some traditions that will be described in this story.

Read the Selection

1. **Choral reading** Play the audio of the Prologue. *Say: A prologue is a short introduction. It gives the background and the setting. What is the setting?* (a hospital in Hiroshima in 1955) *Who is the main character?* (Sadako Sasaki, a 12-year-old girl) Have students read the prologue together aloud.

2. **Relate to personal experience** *Ask: When was the last time you were sick? How do you feel emotionally when you're sick? Bored? Sad? Can you make a cause-and-effect statement? When I'm sick I feel . . . because . . . .*

Sample Answer to Guide Question
Sadako hopes that yesterday was a bad dream because she doesn't want to be sick.

See Teacher Edition pp. 434–436 for a list of English-Spanish cognates in the reading selection.

Audio
CD 1. Tr. 6

Prologue

This excerpt is set in a hospital room in Hiroshima, Japan. It is around 1955—ten years after the atom bomb was dropped on the city. The main character is a 12-year-old girl named Sadako Sasaki. She becomes sick and is taken to the hospital. There Sadako learns that she has leukemia, which is a sickness of the blood. Her sickness is caused by being around the radiation that the bomb left behind.

The Golden Crane

Identify Cause and Effect

What causes Sadako to hope that yesterday was a bad dream?

1   The next morning Sadako woke up slowly. She listened for the familiar sounds of her mother making breakfast, but there were only the new and different sounds of a hospital. Sadako sighed. She had hoped that yesterday was just a bad dream. It was even more real when Nurse Yasunaga came in to give her a **shot.**

2   "Getting shots is part of being in the hospital," the **plump** nurse said briskly. "You'll get used to it."

shot   the use of a needle to put medicine into a vein   **plump**   full and round in shape

58   Unit 1   Traditions and Cultures

MULTI-LEVEL OPTIONS *Read the Selection*

Newcomer Play the audio. As the class listens, use facial expressions and gestures to reinforce meaning. *Ask: Is the girl sick?* (yes) *Is she at home?* (no) *Is she happy?* (no) *Does a friend bring a surprise?* (yes)

Beginning Read the story aloud. Support meaning by pointing to parts of the illustration. *Ask: Where is the girl?* (hospital) *Where does she want to go?* (home) *Who comes to see her?* (a friend) *What gift does the friend bring?* (a paper bird)

Intermediate Read the Prologue aloud. Then have students do a paired reading. *Ask: What is the matter with Sadako?* (She is sick.) *What does she probably miss by being in the hospital?* (family, friends, school) *How does Chizuko try to make Sadako feel better?* (by bringing her a gift)

Advanced Have students do a paired reading. *Ask: What is a clue that Sadako may be in the hospital a long time?* (The nurse says she will get used to shots.) *Predict Chizuko's answer to Sadako's question at the end of the page.* (Making birds will help her forget she feels bad.)

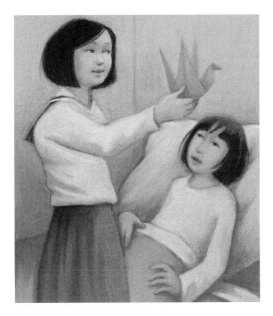

Read the Selection

1. **Shared reading** Play the audio. Have students join in by taking turns reading aloud. Assign narrator and dialogue parts.

2. **Read for information** Divide the class into small groups. Write these question words on the board: *Who, What, Where, When, How, Why.* Have students write one or two information questions about the story. Then have them exchange questions and answer them.

3. **Read aloud for understanding** Divide the class into groups of three. *Say: Each person takes the role of Sadako, Chizuko, or the narrator. Practice reading paragraphs 3–7 aloud; then change roles.*

4. **Identify cause and effect** Read the guide question and give students time to think about their answers. Then elicit answers and write them on the board.

5. **Multi-level options** See MULTI-LEVEL OPTIONS on p. 58.

Sample Answer to Guide Question
She wants the sickness to be over so she can go home.

Identify Cause and Effect

Why does Sadako want the sickness to be over?

---

3   "I just want the sickness to be over with," Sadako said unhappily, "so I can go home."

4   That afternoon Chizuko was Sadako's first visitor. She smiled **mysteriously** as she held something behind her back. "Shut your eyes," she said. While Sadako squinted her eyes tightly shut, Chizuko put some pieces of paper and scissors on the bed. "Now you can look," she said.

5   "What is it?" Sadako asked, staring at the paper.

6   Chizuko was pleased with herself. "I've figured out a way for you to get well," she said proudly. "Watch!" She cut a piece of gold paper into a large square. In a short time she had folded it over and over into a beautiful crane.

7   Sadako was **puzzled.** "But how can that paper bird make me well?"

---

mysteriously   in a secret way   **puzzled**   confused, not understanding

Chapter 5 Sadako and the Thousand Paper Cranes   **59**

 Spelling

Adverbs ending in *-ly*

Direct students to the first sentence in paragraph 1. *Ask: What word tells* how *Sadako woke up?* (slowly) Have students mime waking up slowly. Point out the *-ly* ending of the word *slowly. Say: Adverbs, or words that tell* how *something is done, often end with* -ly.

Apply Have students work in pairs to locate *-ly* adverbs and the verbs they modify in paragraphs 2, 3, 4, and 6. (said briskly, said unhappily, smiled mysteriously, said proudly) Have students say the dialogue or act out the actions using voice, facial expressions, and gestures to show the meanings of the adverbs.

Read the Selection

1. **Summarize** *Ask: Do you remember the three features of historical fiction?* (setting, characters, and plot) *What do we know so far about the setting?* (It's in a hospital in Hiroshima, 1955.) Continue with questions about characters and plot.
2. **Silent reading** Play the audio. Then give students time to read the page silently.

Sample Answer to Guide Question
The gods will grant her wish and make her healthy.

Identify Cause and Effect

What does the old story say will happen if someone folds one thousand cranes?

---

8   "Don't you remember that old story about the crane?" Chizuko asked. "It's supposed to live for a thousand years. If a sick person folds one thousand paper cranes, the gods will **grant** her wish and make her healthy again." She handed the crane to Sadako. "Here's your first one."

9   Sadako's eyes filled with tears. How kind of Chizuko to bring a good luck charm! Especially when her friend didn't really believe in such things. Sadako took the golden crane and made a wish. The funniest little feeling came over her when she touched the bird. It must be a good **omen.**

10   "Thank you, Chizuko **chan,**" she whispered. "I'll never never part with it."

11   When she began to work with the paper, Sadako discovered that folding a crane wasn't as easy as it looked. With Chizuko's help she learned how to do the difficult parts. After making ten birds, Sadako lined them up on the table beside the golden crane. Some were a bit **lopsided,** but it was a beginning.

grant   give or allow what is asked for
omen   a sign of something that is going to happen in the future

chan   a Japanese suffix added to the end of a name to show affection
lopsided   with one side much larger or heavier than the other

60   Unit 1   Traditions and Cultures

MULTI-LEVEL OPTIONS *Read the Selection*

Newcomer *Ask: Did Sadako have to make many cranes?* (yes) *Did she think the cranes would make her well?* (yes) *Did Sadako cry because she was sad?* (no) *Did her brother help her make cranes?* (no)

Beginning *Ask: How many cranes does Sadako have to make altogether?* (a thousand) *Was it easy or hard to make the cranes at first?* (hard) *Where did Sadako's brother put the cranes?* (hung them from the ceiling)

Intermediate *Ask: Why did Sadako think the cranes would make her well?* (because of an old folktale) *How did Sadako learn to make the cranes?* (Her friend showed her.) *How do you know that Sadako's brother wanted her to be well?* (because he offered to help by hanging the birds)

Advanced *Ask: Why did Sadako's eyes fill with tears?* (She was happy to have a good friend.) *Why did Sadako's eyes twinkle with mischief?* (She knew her brother would be surprised at the number of cranes.) *What do you predict Masahiro's response will be? Why?* (He will hang the birds because he cares about his sister.)

Identify Cause and Effect

How does the golden crane make Sadako feel?

12   "Now I have only nine hundred and ninety to make," Sadako said. With the golden crane nearby she felt safe and lucky. Why, in a few weeks she would be able to finish the thousand. Then she would be strong enough to go home.

13   That evening Masahiro brought Sadako's homework from school. When he saw the cranes, he said, "There isn't enough room on that small table to show off your birds. "I'll hang them from the ceiling for you."

14   Sadako was smiling all over. "Do you promise to hang every crane I make?" she asked.

15   Masahiro promised.

16   "That's fine!" Sadako said, her eyes **twinkling** with **mischief.** "Then you'll hang the whole thousand?"

17   "A thousand!" Her brother groaned. "You're joking!"

18   Sadako told him the story of the cranes.

---

twinkling shining

mischief   small, irritating acts or behavior, usually by children

Chapter 5 Sadako and the Thousand Paper Cranes   **61**

1. **Use art to preview** *Say: Look at the picture. Who do you think is visiting her? What does he think about the cranes?*
2. **Paired reading** Play the audio. Have students read to each other in pairs. They can also practice reading the dialogue parts on pp. 60–61.
3. **Relate to personal experience** *Ask: Have you ever felt that something was an omen? Do you ever carry a good luck charm?*
4. **Identify cause and effect** Read the guide question and give students time to think about their answers. Elicit answers and write them on the board.
5. **Multi-level options** See MULTI-LEVEL OPTIONS on p. 60.

Sample Answer to Guide Question
The crane makes her feel safe and lucky.

Punctuation

Apostrophes with contractions

Direct students to the first sentence of paragraph 9. *Ask: Whose eyes filled with tears?* (Sadako's) Point to the apostrophe and the -s. *Say: This punctuation mark, an apostrophe, and an -s show that something belongs to someone.* Point out the word *didn't* in the next sentence. *Say: An apostrophe can also show that two words have been put together and a letter left out to make a short form.* Write *did not* on the board. Cross out the *o* and replace it with an apostrophe. Write: *didn't.*

Apply Ask students to find another possessive noun in paragraph 11 and tell what it means. (Chizuko's) Help students to find the other contractions on pp. 60–61. (don't, it's, here's, I'll, wasn't, isn't, that's, you'll, you're) Make a classroom chart showing the contractions and the words that form them.

Read the Selection

1. **Use art to preview** *Say: Look at the picture. What is her brother doing? How does that make Sadako feel?*

2. **Find text features** Direct students to paragraph 20. *Ask: Do you see a different sort of text here? What genre is it?* (poetry) *How do you know?* (It has stanzas.) Tell students that this form of poetry is Japanese haiku.

3. **Shared reading** Play the audio. Then have students join in by taking turns reading aloud.

4. **Identify cause and effect** Read the guide question, and give students time to think about their answers. Then elicit answers and write them on the board.

Sample Answer to Guide Question
It was the most difficult to make.

19   Masahiro ran a hand through his straight black hair. "You tricked me!" he said with a **grin.** "But I'll do it anyhow." He borrowed some **thread** and **tacks** from Nurse Yasunaga and hung the first ten cranes. The golden crane stayed in its place of honor on the table.

20   After supper Mrs. Sasaki brought Mitsue and Eiji to the hospital. Everyone was surprised to see the birds. They reminded Mrs. Sasaki of a famous old poem:

> Out of colored paper, cranes
> come flying into
> our house.

Identify Cause and Effect

Why did Mrs. Sasaki choose the tiniest crane?

21   Mitsue and Eiji liked the golden crane best. But Mrs. Sasaki chose the tiniest one made of fancy green paper with pink **parasols** on it. "This is my choice," she said, "because small ones are the most difficult to make."

---

grin a big smile   **tacks** small sharp nails
thread a twisted fiber, such as cotton, wool, and so on   **parasols** light umbrellas used as protection from the sun

62 Unit 1 Traditions and Cultures

MULTI-LEVEL OPTIONS *Read the Selection*

Newcomer *Ask: Did Sadako's brother hang the golden crane?* (no) *Did Sadako's mother visit her in the hospital?* (yes) *Was her mother surprised to see the cranes?* (yes) *Did Sadako get well?* (no)

Beginning *Ask: Who visited Sadako next?* (mother) *Which crane did she like best?* (the tiniest one) *How many cranes did Sadako make?* (644) *What helps people remember Sadako today?* (statue)

Intermediate *Ask: How were Chizuko and Masahiro alike?* (Both wanted to help Sadako.) *How did the cranes help Sadako after the visitors left?* (They gave her courage when she was lonely.) *Why do people remember Sadako today?* (because she was a brave girl)

Advanced *Ask: How did making cranes help Sadako even though they did not make her well?* (They gave her hope and happiness in her last days.) *Why does it make sense that there is a statue of Sadako in the Peace Park?* (because Sadako's story reminds us how important it is to work for peace)

22 After visiting hours it was lonely in the hospital room. So lonely that Sadako folded more cranes to keep up her **courage.**

23 Eleven . . . I wish I'd get better. Twelve . . . I wish I'd get better . . .

Epilogue

Sadako continues to make cranes even though her sickness causes her to feel weak. After she makes 644 cranes, Sadako dies. People all over Japan learn about Sadako Sasaki's experience. As a result, a statue of her is built in the Peace Park of Hiroshima. People from all over the world visit the statue. They leave paper cranes to remember Sadako and to promote peace.

courage   the ability and strength to face difficulties

About the Author   Eleanor Coerr (born 1922)

Eleanor Coerr was born and grew up in Canada. She loved to write as a young girl. Coerr eventually became a reporter. She traveled a lot. She visited the Peace Park in Hiroshima. She decided to write a book about Sadako. Eleanor Coerr wrote, "Sometimes one book can change an author's life. *Sadako and the Thousand Paper Cranes* . . . has been that book for me . . . It has moved thousands of children around the world to fold cranes as wishes for peace."

► How do you think Eleanor Coerr felt about Sadako and her life? What makes you think that?

Chapter 5   Sadako and the Thousand Paper Cranes   **63**

A Capitalization

Titles

Say: Titles for people begin with capital letters. Find the title of someone who works in the hospital in paragraph 19. (Nurse) *Ask: Why is the N capitalized?* (because *Nurse* is a title) *Say: Abbreviations, short forms, for titles also begin with capitals. What word in paragraph 20 is a title for Sadako's mother?* (Mrs.) *How does it start?* (with a capital *M*)

Evaluate Your Reading Strategy

Identify Cause and Effect *Say: You have practiced an important reading strategy. Now you can decide how well you have done. Does this statement describe how you read?*

I ask questions as I read to find the causes of events. Identifying causes and effects helps me understand better when I read.

Read the Selection

1. **Shared reading** Play the audio. Point out that the epilogue tells what happens after the end of the text. Have students join in by taking turns reading aloud.
2. **Express opinions** On the board, write: *How did you feel at the end of the story? Is there a message of hope in the story? Did you like this story? Why?* Give students time to think about their answers. Then discuss as a class.
3. **Multi-level options** See MULTI-LEVEL OPTIONS on p. 62.

About the Author

Evaluate information about the author Read the biography. *Ask: How do you think Eleanor Coerr's life as a reporter helped her write this novel?* Remind students they can find the complete novel in the library.

Across Selections

Literary genres *Say: "Sadako and the Thousand Paper Cranes" has features from several genres. Can you name them?* (narration, dialogue, poem, folktale) *Ask: What is the point of view of this selection?* (third person) *What other reading have we done with third-person point of view?* ("Coyote") Have students work in pairs to examine other similarities between these two selections.

Spelling, Punctuation, Capitalization

After the Reading Comprehension section, students will practice spelling, punctuation, and capitalization in the Activity Book.

Beyond the Reading

Reading Comprehension

Question-Answer Relationships

Sample Answers

1. She's in a hospital in Hiroshima.
2. She brings paper and scissors.
3. Sadako's were a bit lopsided.
4. They want her to feel better; they love her. Sadako also loves her visitors. They make her happy.
5. It is important to have hope and courage. It is important to do something for the future. You can have a big effect on other people.
6. The author feels sad for her, but admires her. This makes me feel sad for Sadako too.
7. It makes the story more powerful. It informs readers about history.
8. I think Sadako was really sick and people made paper cranes for her. I don't think she really had a friend named Chizuko.
9. Where did the author get her information? Who was the real Sadako?
10. The way the illustrator drew the characters helps me understand their feelings better. The illustrator also drew the characters and scenes like they were real and made the story seem true.

Build Reading Fluency

Adjust Your Reading Rate for Quotations

Demonstrate to the students how you change your rate of reading depending on the purpose and type of reading material.

Reading Comprehension

Question-Answer Relationships (QAR)

"Right There" Questions

1. **Recall Facts** Where is Sadako?
2. **Recall Facts** What does Chizuko bring to Sadako?

"Think and Search" Questions

3. **Compare and Contrast** How are Sadako's cranes different from the golden crane that Chizuko makes?
4. **Analyze Character Relationships** How do you think Sadako's visitors feel about her? How do you think Sadako feels about her visitors?
5. **Summarize Text** How would you summarize the important ideas in the selection?

"Author and You" Questions

6. **Understand Tone** How do you think the author feels about Sadako? How does this affect how you feel about her?

7. **Analyze Text Types** Why do you think the author chose to base the story on a true event?
8. **Analyze Text Types** What events in the story do you think are historically correct? What events do you think are fiction? Explain.

"On Your Own" Questions

9. **Form Questions** What questions would you research about the background of the story?
10. **Evaluate** How does the illustrator's choice of style, elements of art, and method of drawing help you to understand and gather more meaning from the text?

Activity Book
p. 34

Student
CD-ROM

Build Reading Fluency

Adjust Your Reading Rate for Quotations

Reading quotations (what characters say) helps you learn to adjust your reading rate. You must pause and read with expression. Learning to read with expression makes others want to listen.

Reread the conversation between Sadako and Chizuko. Look for the quotation marks (" . . . ").

1. With a partner, take turns rereading aloud paragraphs 4–7 on page 59.
2. Read the quotations with expression.
3. Pause after each quotation.
4. Choose the quotation you like best.
5. Read aloud with expression to the class.

64 Unit 1 Traditions and Cultures

MULTI-LEVEL OPTIONS *Elements of Literature*

Newcomer On the board, draw a face with a speech balloon labeled *say*, a stick figure running labeled *do*, and a heart labeled *feel*. Point to an illustration of Sadako. Then point to each drawing and give an example from the story that tells something about the main character. Invite students to imitate your modeling.

Beginning Have students make a cluster diagram with the following branches: *Sadako's words, Sadako's actions, Sadako's feelings.* Work with students to find an example of each in the story. Have students draw the examples they find and write a short label for each drawing.

Intermediate Have students create three-column charts in their Reading Logs. Tell them to head the columns: *Words, Actions, Feelings.* Ask students to place examples from the story in each column. Have them use these notes to write a short summary describing the main character.

Advanced Remind students that the selection is an excerpt from a novel. Tell them to write questions they have about the main character that might have been answered in other parts of the book. Have students check out the book from the library to answer their questions.

Listen, Speak, Interact

Perform a Dialogue

In fiction, characters often say things to each other. This is called **dialogue.** You can find dialogue on the page because it has **quotation marks** (" . . . ") around the words the characters say.

> "Getting shots is part of being in the hospital," the plump nurse said briskly.

1. With a partner, find some dialogue in the story that you like. Copy several lines.
2. Be sure to put quotation marks around what the characters say.

3. Listen to the audio recording of the selection to help you distinguish and produce the intonation (changing voice level) of the words you use.
4. Practice saying the dialogue to each other. Speak clearly and slowly.
5. Say only the words in quotation marks. Don't read things like "he said" and "she said."
6. Present your dialogue to the class. Be sure to use effective rate, volume, pitch, and tone.

Elements of Literature

Understand Characterization

Characterization is the way an author creates a character. Eleanor Coerr describes what Sadako says, does, and feels to tell you what the main character is like. Read this sentence from the selection:

> Sadako was puzzled.

The sentence tells you how Sadako feels.

> Sadako's eyes filled with tears.

This sentence shows what Sadako does. (She cries.) The word *tears* also provides clues about how Sadako feels.

The author also tells you how other characters in the story act toward Sadako.

This gives you more information about the main character. For example, Chizuko makes Sadako a crane to cheer her up. This tells you that the main character is loved and cared for by others.

1. Find a description in the story that provides information about Sadako.
2. Then find a description about another character that also helps you learn about the main character.
3. Write these descriptions in your Reading Log. Explain what they tell you about Sadako.

Reading Log   Activity Book p. 35   Student CD-ROM

Chapter 5 Sadako and the Thousand Paper Cranes **65**

Listen, Speak, Interact

Perform a Dialogue

1. **Understand directions** Have students work in pairs to read the exercise and directions. Tell them to locate and select quotations to complete the activity.
2. **Newcomers** Arrange newcomers in pairs with intermediate students. Monitor them as they select and practice their dialogues.

Elements of Literature

Understand Characterization

▎Teacher Resource Book: *Reading Log, p. 64*

1. **Paraphrase** Take turns with students reading the explanation. Then have small groups work to paraphrase the steps for performing their dialogues.
2. **Collaborate to write** Have students work in pairs to write a description of a character. Tell them to record their descriptions in their Reading Logs.
3. **Multi-level options** See MULTI-LEVEL OPTIONS on p. 64.

✓ ASSESS

Say: Name three characters from the story. Tell me one or two adjectives to describe each one.

Content Connection
The Arts

Point out that actors in movies deliver their dialogue with expression to help the audience understand and enjoy the story. Point out that background music can also be an important part of a performance. Engage students in discussing the parts of the selection they read and deciding what types of music would be appropriate for each. Students may suggest particular pieces of music or describe the tempo and mood they would recommend.

Learning Styles
Mathematical

Use directions in a book to demonstrate how to make an origami bird. Have partners work together. One will make the piece; the other will record the time it takes. Help the class figure out the average time to make the bird. Then engage the class in figuring out how long it would take to make one thousand. Have students discuss what the results of their experiment suggest about Sadako's character.

Beyond the Reading

Word Study

Recognize Adjectives Ending in *-ed*

Identify Adjectives Write on the board: *Sadako was _____-ed. Her brother was _____-ed.* Have students work in pairs to complete these sentences with adjectives ending in *-ed*. (tired, surprised, amused, tricked)

Answers
Paragraph 7: puzzled
Paragraph 20: surprised

Grammar Focus

Recognize Possessive Nouns

Apply Work in small groups. Ask students to put one item they own, such as a key, book, or hat, in the middle of the group. Have students take turns picking up an item, saying who it belongs to, and returning it to its owner. Remind students to use possessive nouns.

Answers
1. Sadako's, Chizuko's, Sadako's
2. Sadako's eyes, Chizuko's help, Sadako's homework

ASSESS

Have students write two sentences with possessive nouns.

Word Study

Recognize Adjectives Ending in *-ed*

Adjectives are words that describe a person, a place, or a thing. Some adjectives can be made from verbs by adding *-ed* to the simple form of the verb. A simple form of a verb is the verb without any endings.

Chizuko was pleas**ed** with herself.

Simple Form of Verb	+ed	Adjective
pleas~~e~~	+ ed	pleased

Notice that if the simple form of a verb ends in an *e*, you drop the *e* before you add *-ed*.

Find two more examples of adjectives ending in *-ed* in the reading. Write them in your Personal Dictionary. Look in paragraphs 7 and 20.

Personal Dictionary   Activity Book p. 36   Student CD-ROM

Grammar Focus

Recognize Possessive Nouns

A **possessive noun** is a noun that shows who has or possesses something. The author uses possessive nouns to show things that Sadako has.

That afternoon Chizuko was <u>Sadako**'s**</u> first visitor.

The word *Sadako* is a singular noun. A **singular noun** is a noun that stands for only one person or thing. To make a singular noun possessive, add *'s*.

1. Find two more examples of singular possessive nouns in the selection. Look in paragraphs 9, 11, and 13.
2. Explain what the character has in each example.

3. Look around the classroom. Identify three things that three different people have. On a piece of paper, write possessive nouns to describe what each person has. For example:

My teacher's desk is brown.

David's backpack is very large.

Activity Book pp. 37–38   Student Handbook   Student CD-ROM

66   Unit 1 Traditions and Cultures

MULTI-LEVEL OPTIONS *From Reading to Writing*

Newcomer Create a language experience story. First, help them select a time you have studied in social studies. Instruct them to draw their ideas on a storyboard to plan the characters, setting, and events. When the plan is finished, have students use it to act out their story.

Beginning Have students look at an illustration in their social studies text or another resource that shows a time in history with which they are familiar. Help them record words and phrases on a storyboard to plan a story based on the picture. Use the storyboard to create a Language Experience Story with students.

Intermediate Have pairs meet to read aloud their completed stories to each other. Tell responders to ask any questions they have about the main character. Have partners work together to decide how including more dialogue and details about actions and feelings might answer these questions.

Advanced Have students use social studies texts, library books, and bookmarked Internet sources to research the time periods they choose. Point out that including factual details related to clothing, food, transportation, and events of the times will make their stories seem more realistic.

From Reading to Writing

Write a Fictional Narrative

Write a three-paragraph fictional narrative set in a special time in history. You can choose a story that you have read about, or you can make it up.

1. Describe the setting—the time and place of your story.
2. Use characterization to tell readers about your characters.
3. Put your events in chronological order. Clearly connect the events by using words to show what happens next, such as *soon, next,* and *finally.*
4. Include dialogue with quotation marks.

```
                                    Title
  ○   ┌─1─┬──────────────────────────────────────────┐
      │   │ Setting: time and place                  │
      │   │ Characters: the people in the story      │
      │   │ Problem: what the people have to do      │
      └───┴──────────────────────────────────────────┘

  ○   ┌─2─┬──────────────────────────────────────────┐
      │   │ Plot: what happens                       │
      └───┴──────────────────────────────────────────┘

  ○   ┌─3─┬──────────────────────────────────────────┐
      │   │ Conclusion: how the problem is           │
      │   │ resolved; how the characters change      │
      └───┴──────────────────────────────────────────┘
```

Activity Book
p. 39

Student
Handbook

Across Content Areas

Learn Geometric Shapes and Vocabulary

The art of making different figures from paper is called **origami**. If you unfold one of these figures, you will see that the folds make many different **geometric** shapes. Geometry is a type of math in which you study shapes, lines, and angles.

The following sentences show how geometry relates to origami. Complete each sentence with one of these words.

| triangle △ |
| square □ |
| **diagonal**—a line connecting opposite corners of a square or a rectangle |
| **symmetrical**—the same on both sides |

1. A _____ piece of paper is six inches long and six inches wide.
2. Connect the two opposite corners of the square and press to fold the paper. A _____ with three sides is formed.
3. Unfold the paper. The shapes on both sides of the fold are the same size and shape. They are _____ .
4. The line connecting one corner to the opposite corner is a _____ .

Activity Book
p. 40

Chapter 5 Sadako and the Thousand Paper Cranes **67**

From Reading to Writing

Write a Fictional Narrative

1. **Pre-writing** Have students describe their story's setting, plot, and characters in pairs. Partners can ask questions to clarify information.
2. **Use chronological order** Have students briefly write the events in their story in a numbered list. Then have them add time words to indicate chronological order.
3. **Peer editing** Have students check each other's stories for clarity, punctuation, and capitalization.
4. **Multi-level options** See MULTI-LEVEL OPTIONS on p. 66.

Across Content Areas: Math

Learn Geometric Shapes and Vocabulary

Learn math terms Have students create a geometry display by drawing or making the shapes from colored paper. Have them group the shapes and create titles for each group.

Answers
1. square 2. triangle 3. symmetrical 4. diagonal

✓ ASSESS

Have students draw and label two geometric shapes.

Reteach and Reassess

Text Structure Have students review the features chart on p. 56. Discuss with students which story details were most likely true and which were made up.

Reading Strategy Have students write or act out cause-and-effect statements summarizing the main events of the selection. Ask them to use the pattern: _____ because _____.

Elements of Literature Have students create a Character Traits Web for Sadako. Ask them to draw or write her traits on the branches. Then have students code the traits to indicate whether they were revealed through one or more of the following: her words, actions, feelings, or through others.

Reassess Have students use Reader's Theater to summarize the selection.

Materials

Student Handbook
CNN Video: *Unit 1*
Teacher Resource Book: *Lesson Plan, p. 6;*
  Teacher Resources, pp. 35–64; Video Script,
  pp. 161–162; Video Worksheet, p. 173;
  School-Home Connection, pp. 119–125
Teacher Resource CD-ROM
Assessment Program: *Unit 1 Test, pp. 17–22;*
  Teacher and Student Resources,
  pp. 115–144
Assessment CD-ROM
Transparencies
The Heinle Newbury House Dictionary/CD-ROM
Heinle Reading Library: *The Legend of Sleepy*
  Hollow
Web site: http://visions.heinle.com

Listening and Speaking Workshop

Present a Narrative About Your Favorite Holiday

Step 1: Use a chart to get organized.
Have students copy the chart onto a piece of paper.

Step 2: Answer questions.
Have students fill in charts with notes and drawings.

Listening and Speaking Workshop

Present a Narrative About Your Favorite Holiday

> **Topic**
>
> Tell a story about the most fun you have had on a holiday. Describe the setting (the time and place), the characters (the people), and the events in the order in which they happened.

Step 1: Use a chart to get organized.

Make notes or draw pictures as you plan your story.

Holiday: _____	Notes and Pictures
Setting Place Time of day and year	
Characters	
Events What happened? Was there a problem? What was the solution?	
Ending How did you feel? Why was it a good time?	

Step 2: Answer questions.

1. Where did the holiday take place?
2. Who was with you?
3. What happened to make it fun? Describe the specific events in order. What feelings did you have?

Step 3: Think of an opening that will get the audience's attention.

1. Ask a question.
2. Say something funny.
3. Make an interesting statement.

Step 4: Use visuals.

Make some visuals to make your presentation more interesting. You can use a poster, some pictures, or a computer presentation.

Step 5: Practice telling your story to a partner.

1. Use your chart to help you.
2. Use your visuals.
3. Use the information from the checklists to revise your presentation.

Step 6: Present.

1. Speak loudly enough for everyone to hear. Speak slowly.
2. Use gestures (movements of your body).
3. Be expressive. For example, use your voice to show excitement.

MULTI-LEVEL OPTIONS *Listening and Speaking Workshop*

Newcomer Help students use pictures to complete their charts. Then have them use their charts to act out their holiday stories for small groups.

Beginning Have students use words and pictures to fill out their charts. Ask them to meet in small groups to present their stories using the notes on their charts. Have listeners ask follow-up questions of the storytellers.

Intermediate Provide time for students to get peer responses to their notes. Ask the responders to question any details they don't understand, especially in the "Events" section. Ask students to add details to their charts before presenting their stories to the class.

Advanced After their notes are complete, discuss the importance of expressive delivery of their stories. Have students consider using different voices or sound effects to enhance the presentation. Provide rehearsal time before asking students to present their stories to the class.

Active Listening Checklist

1. I liked _____ because _____
_____ .

2. I want to know more about _____ .

3. I thought the opening was interesting / not interesting.

4. You spoke confidently and knew the subject well. Yes / No

5. I understood the major ideas of your story.

6. I needed you to clarify _____ .

Speaking Checklist

1. Did you speak too slowly, too fast, or just right?

2. Did you speak loudly enough for the audience to hear you?

3. Did you use visuals to make the story more interesting?

4. Did you clarify ideas with examples?

5. Did you look at the audience?

Student Handbook

Viewing Workshop

View and Think

Compare and Contrast Cultures

In this unit you read about people who were part of different cultures. A **culture** is a group of people who share something in common. For example, people who live in the same area and have the same traditions are part of the same culture.

1. Go to a library and borrow a video about a culture that is different from yours.

2. Before you view the video, prepare some questions. For example:
   a. What is the land like where the people live?
   b. What kind of work do many of the people do?
   c. What traditions do the people practice?
   d. What is the food like?

3. View the video and find out if your questions were answered. What other things did you learn from the video?

4. Think about your culture. Compare and contrast your culture with the culture on the video.

Further Viewing

Watch the *Visions* CNN Video for Unit 1. Do the Video Worksheet.

CNN Video

 Content Connection
Math

Have students conduct a survey among family members, friends, and classmates to determine what holidays are the most fun. Have students use bar graphs to display the results of their studies.

Learning Styles
Visual

Have small groups create artifacts showing what they learned about a particular place, its people, and its culture. For example, students who learned about the Yanomami of the rain forest might make a model of a round community house, bring in a plantain, and so on. Display the artifacts around your classroom. Provide time for a gallery walk so that students can view each other's work and ask questions.

Step 3: Think of an opening that will get the audience's attention.
Model an interesting opening. *Ask: Do you know anyone whose birthday is Jan. 1? Everyone around the world celebrates my birthday. Being born on a holiday is not always great.*

Step 4: Use visuals.
Help students organize the visuals they select. Have students indicate in their notes where a visual should be presented.

Step 5: Practice telling your story to a partner.
Have students work in pairs. Remind them to take time at the end of each story to fill in their checklists.

Step 6: Present.
Have students analyze the checklist responses and make notes about changes and adjustments to their oral presentations. Invite another class or parents to see the presentations.

 **ASSESS**

Say: Name three good ways to start a story. (a question, a funny comment, an interesting statement)

Portfolio

Students may choose to record or videotape their speeches to place in their portfolios.

Viewing Workshop

View and Think

Teacher Resource Book: *Venn Diagram, p. 35*

1. **Use resources** *Ask: How can you find a video in the library? What kinds of videos will show different cultures?* (travel videos, folktales) Remind them that a reference librarian can help locate videos quickly.

2. **Prepare for viewing** Review questions and have each student add a question of his/her own.

3. **Use a graphic organizer** Instruct students to use a Venn diagram to compare and contrast the cultures. Have them make notes of other things they learn from the video.

Writer's Workshop

Write a Personal Narrative About a Trip

Teacher think aloud Before beginning, go over the narrative chart carefully with students. Then *say: I took several trips last year. I think my trip to Florida was the most interesting. I collected beautiful shells in the Gulf of Mexico.*

Step 1: Write a draft.

Have students think of a working title for their narrative, so that they are clear about the topic. Then have them write a numbered list of 3–5 things that happened and a list of the characters. Instruct students to use these notes as they start their drafts.

Step 2: Revise your draft.

Have students use the checklist in the box to make sure they have made revisions and have followed instructions. Refer to the Narrative Checklist in the Student Handbook.

Writer's Workshop

Write a Personal Narrative About a Trip

Prompt

A personal narrative tells a story about something you did. Tell about a trip you took. Where did you go? What happened? How did you feel about the trip? What made it interesting?

Narrative Chart

Beginning
- Get the reader's interest.
- Say what you are going to write about.
- Describe the characters.
- Describe the setting (time and place).

↓

Middle
- Tell what happened.
- Use details and descriptions.
- Use dialogue with quotation marks.

↓

End
- How did you feel at the end?
- Did you learn anything?
- Would you take this trip again?

Step 1: Write a draft.

1. Begin with a strong opening. Use a question or some dialogue that will interest the reader.
2. Write a sentence to introduce the topic (what you are going to write about).

3. Put all the events in chronological order. Blend paragraphs into larger chunks of writing. Use transition words like *first, then,* and *next.*
4. Use a dictionary or other reference materials to help you with spelling and meaning.

Step 2: Revise your draft.

Carefully reread your draft and make sure that you did these things.

Content and Organization
1. You thought about your audience and your purpose for writing.
2. You used details to make the story exciting.
3. You used dialogue with quotation marks.
4. You wrote a beginning, a middle, and an end.
5. You wrote a title for your story.

Sentence Construction
6. You wrote clearly and used different kinds of sentences.

Usage
7. You used strong descriptive words and correct grammar.

MULTI-LEVEL OPTIONS *Writer's Workshop*

Newcomer Have students use a comic strip format. Ask them to show their destination and the people traveling in the first frame. Tell students to develop a sequence of three or more frames showing what happened on the trip. Have them finish with a frame showing how the travelers felt.

Beginning Provide sentence starters for students to use in creating their stories. These may include: *I went to _____ with _____. The first thing that happened was _____. Then _____. At last _____. One thing I learned was _____.*

Intermediate Demonstrate how to use a three-column chart to plan the middle of a personal narrative. In the left column, have students list events in time order. In the middle column, have them list sensory details related to each event. In the right column, have them list related dialogue.

Advanced After students have completed first drafts, have them set aside their writing. Tell them to look at examples of personal narratives in books and magazines. Discuss the techniques authors used to introduce these narratives. Then ask students to return to their drafts and revise their opening paragraphs.

Step 3: Peer edit.

1. Ask a partner to read your story.
2. Ask your partner how you can make your narrative better.
3. Revise your narrative if necessary. Add, elaborate, delete, combine, or rearrange text to make your story clearer.

Step 4: Proofread and finish.

1. Proofread (carefully read) your story to check for mechanics: correct spelling, punctuation, and capitalization.
2. If possible, type your story on a computer. Check for mechanics using the computer software.
3. If your narrative is more than one page long, number the pages.
4. Make a title page that includes your name and the title.
5. Exchange papers with a partner. Proofread each other's story to be sure that the edits make sense.

Step 5: Publish.

1. If you are writing on a computer, choose a font (kind of type) for your narrative. You can also use a border to decorate your narrative.
2. If you are writing by hand, make a final copy in your best handwriting.
3. You can add pictures or drawings to your narrative if you wish.
4. Create a class collection of the stories. Create a table of contents to organize the stories.
   a. Analyze your classmates' published works as models for writing. Review them for their strengths and weaknesses.
   b. Set your goals as a writer based on your writing and the writing of your classmates.

The Heinle
Newbury House
Dictionary

Student
Handbook

Step 3: Peer edit.

Have peer editors ask at least two questions about their partner's story and point out at least two things the editors feel are especially good. Refer to the EQS sheet in the Student Handbook.

Step 4: Proofread and finish.

Show students how to check their papers so that all sentences have an initial capital letter. Then tell them to check for final punctuation. Finally, have them check for spelling. Refer to the Peer Editing and Editor's Checklists in the Student Handbook.

Step 5: Publish.

Give students plenty of time for this final step. Tell them to make their stories attractive so others will want to read them. Allow time for students to read each other's stories.

ASSESS

Ask students to identify three things to check when proofreading a story.

Portfolio

Students may choose to include their writing in their portfolios.

Community Connection

Point out that not all trips have to be to faraway places. Ask students to identify places in their own communities that are interesting to visit, such as historic landmarks or factories making unusual products. Ask students to draw or write about a real or imaginary visit to one of these places.

Learning Styles
Linguistic

Point out that part of writing a good story is writing dialogue that sounds natural for the characters. *Say: Let us begin our journey. Let's start our trip. Which sounds more natural for someone your age?* Ask students to meet in pairs to check the dialogue in each other's narratives to be sure it sounds natural.

Projects

Project 1: Create a Poster About a New Tradition

1. **Use resources** Discuss with students how they can find out this information about their town or city. In smaller towns, they may need to talk with a town librarian or historian.
2. **Compose a letter** Have pairs collaborate to write a letter to a city or town official to suggest their new tradition. Tell pairs to organize the letter into an introduction, a body, and a conclusion. Then have pairs give feedback to another pair and revise their letters.

Project 2: Give a Cross-Cultural Presentation

1. **Define a topic** Have students form groups and choose two cultures to work with. Help them narrow down their topic to one characteristic. For example, *say: If you want to compare foods in different cultures, pick just one meal or one type of food (snacks, party food) to compare.*
2. **Research** Have students brainstorm where they can find more information. Help them plan what kinds of visuals or objects to use and how to obtain them.

Portfolio

Students may choose to include their projects in their portfolios.

Projects

These projects will help you learn more about the theme of the unit—traditions and cultures. Ask your teacher for help if you need it.

Project 1: Create a Poster About a New Tradition

Create a new tradition based on an important event in your city or town.

1. Learn more about your city or town. Read Internet sites or books you find in the library. Find a fact that tells about an important event in the history of your community. For example, when was it founded?
2. Brainstorm ways to celebrate that event each year. On what date should it be celebrated? List activities people can do to celebrate the tradition.
3. Describe your new tradition on a piece of posterboard. Include the event that will be remembered, the date of the tradition, and special activities to celebrate it.
4. Arrange the information in a way that is easy for people to read. You may include pictures with captions.
5. Use capitalization and punctuation that will clarify and enhance your information.

> **PUBLIC LIBRARY DAY**
>
> Come CELEBRATE our public library's anniversary—75 years!
>
> Poetry readings!
>
> Free cookies and juice!
>
> Wednesday, November 15, from 10–4.

Project 2: Give a Cross-Cultural Presentation

In a group of three, find out about the differences between two cultures.

1. In your group, choose two cultures.
2. Cultures have many different characteristics. Choose three from the list below.

> **Examples of Characteristics**
> Food
> Holidays
> Traditional clothing
> How people greet each other
> How people feel about family

3. Research (find out about) the three characteristics you chose for your two cultures. You can:
   a. Use the Internet. Use the keyword "cultures" or, for example, "Chinese culture."
   b. Use reference books.
   c. Interview people from each of the cultures you chose.
4. As you find information, look for pictures, objects, and other visuals to use in your presentation.
5. Write a report to organize the information you found. List the sources that were used, such as books or websites.
6. Present your results to the class. Explain the differences between the two cultures. Act out what people do. Use visuals.

MULTI-LEVEL OPTIONS *Projects*

Newcomer Have students use art materials to create simple costumes or props to use as they present information about holidays from two cultures.

Beginning Have students look in books, download data from the Internet, or draw pictures to illustrate similarities and differences between the two cultures they choose. Ask them to point out key features and tell whether they are the same or different.

Intermediate Have students work in groups of three to present their information as an interview role-play. One student is the reporter and the other two students each represent a different culture. Have students write interview questions about the information they have learned.

Advanced Have groups present their findings as letters between two pen pals from different cultures. Instruct groups to compose a series of letters with each telling about an aspect of one of the cultures. In presenting the information, one group member can act as moderator and introduce the other two who will take turns reading the letters.

Further Reading

Here is a list of books about the theme of traditions and cultures. Pick one or more of them. Notice how you read at a different rate or speed depending on the type of text. Write your thoughts and feelings about what you read in your Reading Log. Take notes about your answers to these questions. Then discuss your answers with a partner.

1. What new cultural traditions did you read about?
2. Are the traditions you read about similar to the ones of your family?
3. How are cultures the same? How are they different?

Sadako and the Thousand Paper Cranes
by Eleanor Coerr, Penguin USA, 2002. Sadako is sick with leukemia because of the atom bomb that was dropped on Hiroshima during World War II. A friend reminds Sadako of the Japanese legend that says if a sick person folds one thousand cranes, she will become healthy again.

Native American Games and Stories
by James and Joseph Bruchac, Fulcrum Publishing, 2000. Learn how to play authentic Native American games and the stories of their origins. Instructions are included on how to make the necessary equipment.

Fiesta Femenina: Celebrating Women in Mexican Folktale
by Mary-Joan Gerson, Barefoot Books, Inc., 2001. This book tells eight Mexican folktales from a variety of different cultures. Read folklore from the ancient Maya and Aztec as well as stories of Euro-Mexican origin.

Culture and Customs of Costa Rica
by Chalene Helmuth, Greenwood Publishing Group, Inc., 2000. Take a journey through the history of Costa Rica from its discovery by Christopher Columbus in 1502 to its establishment as one of the most progressive Central American countries.

China: The Culture
by Bobbie Kalman, Crabtree Publishing Co., 2001. This book explores Chinese culture. Read about how a potato print and abacus are used. Discover traditional Chinese performing arts, festivals, and foods.

Texas Traditions: The Culture of the Lone Star State, Vol. 1
by Robyn Montana Turner, Little, Brown & Co., 1996. Texas is truly a multicultural state. This book offers a glimpse into the various cultures that have made Texas the unique place it is today.

Homeless Bird
by Gloria Whelan, HarperCollins Children's Books, 2001. In this book, thirteen-year-old Koly has an arranged marriage, as dictated by Indian custom. She is soon widowed and abandoned by her husband's family. But she discovers the courage to survive on her own.

 Companion Web site

 Reading Log

 Heinle Reading Library The Legend of Sleepy Hollow

Apply and Expand   **73**

Further Reading

1. **Find resources** Find out who has a library card and which public library is closest to them. Ask them what kinds of things they like to do in the library. (read magazines, browse, etc.)
2. **Use the library** Have students find out which of the titles listed are not available at their local library. Then have them ask a librarian to make an inter-library loan.

▮ Assessment Program: *Unit 1 Test, pp. 17–22*

Heinle Reading Library

The Legend of Sleepy Hollow and Rip Van Winkle by Washington Irving
In a specially adapted version by Jack Kelly

The folks of the valley are a superstitious lot, believing in witches and goblins and ghosts and things they can't see, as much as they believe in the real world around them. This leads to some mighty adventures for some wonderful characters like Ichabod Crane, Rip Van Winkle, Brom Bones, and a host of others. Thrill to the tales of the Headless Horseman, the long night's sleep that lasted 20 years, and the most surprising ending to any treasure hunt ever.

Visions Companion Site

http://visions.heinle.com
For additional student activities and teacher resources, see the Visions Companion Web site.

Unit Materials

Activity Book: *pp. 41–80*
Audio: *Unit 2; CD 1, Tracks 7–11*
Student Handbook
Student CD-ROM: *Unit 2*
CNN Video: *Unit 2*
Teacher Resource Book: *Lesson Plans, Teacher Resources, Reading Summaries, School-Home Connection, Video Script, Video Worksheet, Activity Book Answer Key*
Teacher Resource CD-ROM
Assessment Program: *Quizzes and Test, pp. 23–38; Teacher and Student Resources, pp. 115–144*
Assessment CD-ROM
Transparencies
The Heinle Newbury House Dictionary/CD-ROM
More Grammar Practice workbook
Heinle Reading Library: *Aesop's Fables*
Web site: http://visions.heinle.com

Visions Staff Development Handbook

Refer to the Visions Staff Development Handbook for more teacher support.

Unit Theme: Environment

Clarify the theme word Discuss the meaning of *environment*. Have students look it up in a dictionary. *Ask: What is the environment like around our school? Write two sentences that describe the school's environment. Remember to write the word* environment *with correct spelling in the sentences.*

Unit Preview: Table of Contents

1. **Use the table of contents to locate information** *Ask: How many different genres are listed?* (5) *Name them.* (poem, interview, fable, novel, nonfiction)
2. **Connect** *Ask: Which titles interest you?*

UNIT 2

Environment

74

UNIT OBJECTIVES

Reading
Describe images as you read a poem • Distinguish facts from opinions as you read an interview • Identify main idea and details as you read a fable • Draw conclusions as you read narrative fiction • Outline information to understand reading as you read an informational text

Listening and Speaking
Act out a poem • Role-play an interview • Perform a skit • Interpret nonverbal communication • Recall details

Tiger in a Tropical Storm (Surprise!), Henri Rousseau, oil painting. 1891.

View the Picture

1. Describe the environment that you see in this painting.
2. How would you describe the environment where you live?

In this unit, you will read selections about different types of environments and the living things in them. You will read and learn how to recognize a poem, a fable, an interview, a fiction story, and an informational article. You will practice writing each of these forms.

75

View the Picture

1. **Art background** Henri Rousseau (1844–1910), a French post-Impressionist, is known for his imaginative and fantastic jungle scenes and wild beasts. In this painting, Rousseau used a translucent varnish-like material on top of the painting to help capture movement of the strong wind and lashing rain.

2. **Art interpretation** *Ask: Is this a real or imaginary place?* (imaginary) *How does the artist's use of oils make the image seem to move?* (It creates curved lines that seem to show movement.) *How do the colors, shapes, and lines in this painting tell a story?* (The colors, shapes, and lines of the jungle plants are similar to those of the tiger's stripes and body position. This tells the story that the tiger is trying to hide by camouflaging itself. The tiger wants to surprise someone or something. That's why "surprise" is part of the title of the painting.)

   a. **Speculate** *Say: The artist spent his life working in a customs office in Paris. He had never been abroad, but he spent time in the botanical gardens in Paris. Where did he get the ideas for this jungle scene?*

   b. **Use personal experience** *Ask: Do you like art about animals?* Have students describe other images of animals they know and like.

   c. **Connect to theme** *Say: The theme of this unit is* environment. *How would you describe the environment of this painting?*

Grammar
Identify the simple present tense • Identify and punctuate questions • Identify object pronouns • Recognize and use comparative adjectives • Identify the subject and verb of a sentence

Writing
Write a poem about the environment • Write a personal narrative • Write a fable • Write narrative fiction • Write an informational report

Content
Science: Learn about types of climate • The Arts: Design a mural • Science: Learn about conservation • Science: Learn about plants • Social Studies: Read pie charts

CHAPTER 1

Here Is the Southwestern Desert

a poem
by Madeleine Dunphy

Into the Reading

Objectives

Reading Describe images as you read a poem.

Listening and Speaking Act out a poem.

Grammar Identify the simple present tense.

Writing Write a poem about the environment.

Content Science: Learn about types of climate.

Chapter Materials

Activity Book: *pp. 41–48*
Audio: *Unit 2, Chapter 1; CD 1, Track 7*
Student Handbook
Student CD-ROM: *Unit 2, Chapter 1*
Teacher Resource Book: *Lesson Plan, Teacher Resources, Reading Summary, Activity Book Answer Key*
Teacher Resource CD-ROM
Assessment Program: *Quiz, pp. 23–24; Teacher and Student Resources, pp. 115–144*
Assessment CD-ROM
Transparencies
The Heinle Newbury House Dictionary/CD-ROM
More Grammar Practice Workbook
Web site: http://visions.heinle.com

Objectives

Preview Read the objectives aloud. *Ask: Is there an objective you already know?*

Use Prior Knowledge

Describe Images of a Desert

Share experiences Ask students to share experiences visiting a desert. *Ask: What did it feel like? What did you see? How was it different from the climate here?* Then have students visualize desert images in their minds.

Answers

Examples: **1.** See: cactus, sand; Hear: wind, birds; Smell/taste: dry air; Touch: hot rocks, prickly cactus.

Use Prior Knowledge

Describe Images of a Desert

The reading selection in this chapter describes the desert of the southwestern United States. A desert is a dry region with little or no rain.

1. Close your eyes and suppose you are in the desert. What images (pictures) come to your mind? What do you see, hear, smell, taste, and touch in the desert?
2. In the ovals of the web, write words that relate to your images and ideas of the desert. If you wish, you may add extra ovals to the web.

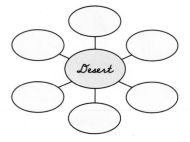

Desert

76 Unit 2 Environment

MULTI-LEVEL OPTIONS *Build Vocabulary*

Newcomer Have students illustrate the sentences. Then help them write the sentences on their drawings.

Beginning Have students work in pairs to act out the sentences. Then have them write the definitions in their Personal Dictionaries.

Intermediate Ask students to work in pairs to find synonyms for each underlined word. Have them add the words and synonyms to their Personal Dictionaries.

Advanced Have students write a sentence for each underlined word. Tell them to include context clues to the meanings of the target words.

Build Background

The Southwestern Desert

The *southwestern desert* refers to the desert regions in Arizona, New Mexico, Texas, Oklahoma, California, Nevada, and Utah. Some of these deserts extend into Mexico.

Content Connection
Some well-known southwestern deserts are the Mojave, the Sonoran, and the Chihuahuan Deserts.

Build Vocabulary

Use Context to Understand Vocabulary

The **context** of a word is the other words around it. You can use the context to help you understand new words.

1. Read the sentences below. The underlined words are from the reading selection.

   a. The bird perches on the tree.
   b. The bird spies on the worm.
   c. The sun blazes on the tree.
   d. The dog unearths the bone.

2. Now read these definitions. Match the definitions with the underlined words in the sentences. Use the context to help you decide which definition is correct.

   a. to dig up
   b. to land and rest on something
   c. to burn strongly
   d. to see after looking around

3. Write the words and their definitions in your Personal Dictionary.

Personal Dictionary   The Heinle Newbury House Dictionary   Activity Book *p. 41*   Student CD-ROM

Chapter 1   Here Is the Southwestern Desert   **77**

Content Connection
Science

Build Vocabulary Divide the class into four groups. Assign each group to work with one of the vocabulary words. Ask groups to create pictures or phrases showing other ways the words can be used to describe parts of nature. (squirrel *perches* on a fence, fire *blazes* through the forest) Provide time for groups to share their work with the class.

Learning Styles
Natural

Build Background Assign each of three groups to use books, Web sites, and pictures to make a profile of one of the following deserts: Mojave, Sonoran, or Chihuahuan. Have students find out the high, low, and average temperatures, amount of rainfall, and types of plants and animals. Provide time for groups to present their findings. Ask students to use what they learned to add to their Prior Knowledge webs.

Build Background

The Southwestern Desert

1. **Use a map** Read the description. Have students point to the places on the map as you name them.
2. **Content Connection** The North American Desert, which includes the Southwestern Desert and deserts in Northern Mexico, is approximately 500,000 square miles.

Build Vocabulary

Use Context to Understand Vocabulary

Teacher Resource Book: *Personal Dictionary, p. 63*

1. **Teacher think aloud** Write on the board: *I forgot to water the plant all week. It was parched.* Say: *I know that plants dry out when they aren't watered. I can guess that parched means dry or needing water. I can guess the meaning of words from their context.*
2. **Pair work** Have students work in pairs to match the words and definitions.
3. **Reading selection vocabulary** You may want to introduce the glossed words in the reading selection before students begin reading. Key words: *cactus, shelter, hawk, lizard, pounce.* Instruct students to write the words with correct spelling and their definitions in their Personal Dictionaries. Have them pronounce each word and divide it into syllables.
4. **Multi-level options** See MULTI-LEVEL OPTIONS on p. 76.

Answers
2. perches-b; spies-d; blazes-c; unearths-a

 **ASSESS**

Ask: What is the environment like in the desert?

Text Structure

A Poem

1. **Review** *Ask: What poems have we already read?* ("Family Photo" and "Thanksgiving") *What features of a poem have we already learned?* (experiences, images, stanzas, rhyme, rhythm, strong language)
2. **Locate derivation** Have students locate the derivation of *repetition* in the glossary in the Student Handbook or other sources, such as online or CD-ROM dictionaries.
3. **Recognize features** *Say: Repetition is often used in music. Usually there is a chorus, which is repeated after each verse. Repetition is often used in poetry, too. It gives a rhythm to the poem.*

Reading Strategy

Describe Images

1. **Describe images** *Say: When you think of the desert, what animals do you imagine? What plants do you imagine?*
2. **Use resources** If possible, have students look up *desert* in reference materials to locate pictures of desert plants and animals.
3. **Multi-level options** See MULTI-LEVEL OPTIONS below.

ASSESS

Have students define *repetition*.

Text Structure

A Poem

In this chapter, you will read the poem "Here Is the Southwestern Desert." This poem includes the features shown in the chart.

As you read the poem, notice how all of the stanzas repeat lines from the previous stanzas. Think about the following questions as you read:

1. What lines are repeated in each stanza?
2. What lines are added to each stanza?

Poem	
Repetition	the repeating of an idea, a phrase, or a sentence
Stanzas	groups of lines used to separate ideas

Student
CD-ROM

Reading Strategy

Describe Images

Writers often use words that help readers create **images** (pictures) in their minds. Poetry often has many images in it.

In "Here Is the Southwestern Desert," the author describes animals, plants, and other parts of the environment. In each stanza, she adds new images.

As you read or listen to the audio recording of the poem, close your eyes from time to time. Describe the images that you see to the class in your own words. Use the images you form to help you understand the meanings of new words.

Listen carefully to the images described by your classmates. What effect do they have on you?

Student
CD-ROM

78 Unit 2 Environment

MULTI-LEVEL OPTIONS *Reading Strategy*

Newcomer Have students close their eyes and make a mental image of a place in nature where they have been. Ask them to open their eyes and draw the image.

Beginning Have students choose a place in nature. Ask them to close their eyes and imagine the sights, sounds, smells, tastes, and textures of the place. Then tell them to open their eyes and use different colored markers or crayons to list words describing the images they formed in their minds.

Intermediate Ask students to close their eyes and form a mental image of a favorite place in nature. Have students list phrases that describe their mental pictures. Suggest that students start each phrase with a capital letter to make the list look like a poem. Have them draw borders around their free verse poems.

Advanced Ask students to listen carefully as you read aloud a detailed description of a natural environment. Then ask students to draw the environment in as much detail as possible. Reread the piece slowly having students identify words and phrases that inspired various parts of their drawings.

Here Is the
SOUTHWESTERN DESERT

a poem by Madeleine Dunphy

79

Reading Selection Materials

Audio: *Unit 2, Chapter 1; CD 1, Track 7*
Teacher Resource Book: *Reading Summary,*
   pp. 75–76
Transparencies: *#4, Reading Summary*

Suggestions for Using Reading Summary

- Introduce new vocabulary or cognates.
- Cut the summary into strips, or jumble the sentences on an overhead transparency. Students put the sentences in order.
- Practice the reading strategy.
- Students read aloud or with a partner.
- Students paraphrase the summary.
- Students do a cloze activity.
- Students create a visual or graphic organizer, such as a timeline or storyboard, to illustrate the summary.
- Students paraphrase the summary.

Preview the Selection

1. **Interpret the image** Have students look at the art. *Ask: How does this desert look different from what you imagine? What is similar? What colors are used in the painting? Are the colors warm or cool colors?*
2. **Identify medium and style** *Ask: What medium is this picture?* (oil painting) *Is this a realistic style or impressionistic style?* (impressionistic)
3. **Connect** *Ask: What does this environment remind you of?*

Community Connection

Work with the class to create a Venn diagram comparing their community with a desert community. Have them use the information that they have gathered so far, the picture on p. 79, and their prior knowledge to compare and contrast climate, landforms, wildlife, and inhabitants.

Teacher Resource Book: *Venn Diagram, p. 35*

Learning Styles
Intrapersonal

Have students use the information they have learned about deserts so far and the picture on this page. *Ask: How would you feel visiting a desert?* Ask students to write journal entries that tell what it might be like to experience the climate, vegetation, and wildlife in a desert setting. Have them write what they would like and not like about this environment.

Read the Selection

1. **Identify text structure** *Ask: What line is repeated here?* (Here is the southwestern desert.) *What do you notice about the length of each stanza?* (Each one is longer; each one builds on the one before.)
2. **Choral reading** Play the audio. Then have small groups do choral readings of different stanzas.
3. **Illustrate vocabulary** Ask for volunteers to draw a cactus, a hawk, and a lizard on the board.

Sample Answer to Guide Question
I imagine that the cactus is big and green and it's near a rock.

See Teacher Edition pp. 434–436 for a list of English-Spanish cognates in the reading selection.

Audio
CD 1. Tr. 7

Describe Images

What is your image of the cactus? Is it big or small? What color is it? Where is it?

1   Here is the southwestern desert.

2   Here is the **cactus**
that is covered with **spines**
and can live without rain
for a very long time.
Here is the southwestern desert.

3   Here is the **hawk**
that perches on the cactus
that is covered with spines
and can live without rain
for a very long time.
Here is the southwestern desert.

4   Here is the **lizard**
who is spied by the hawk
that perches on the cactus
that is covered with spines
and can live without rain
for a very long time.
Here is the southwestern desert.

cactus   a plant that grows in the desert and has sharp needles
spines   sharp, pointy needles on a cactus
hawk   a large bird that hunts animals for food
lizard   a reptile with four legs

80   Unit 2 Environment

MULTI-LEVEL OPTIONS *Read the Selection*

Newcomer Play the audio. Have students point to each stanza as the lines are read. *Ask: Is this poem about a desert?* (yes) *Is there a plant in the desert?* (yes) *Does the plant need a lot of rain?* (no) *Are there animals in the desert?* (yes)

Beginning Play the audio. Then read the poem aloud and invite students to chime in when they can. *Ask: What place does the poem tell about?* (desert) *What is the weather there like?* (dry) *What plants grow there?* (cactus, trees) *What animals are in the desert?* (hawk, lizard, roadrunner)

Intermediate Play the audio. Then have students do a paired reading of the poem. *Ask: What happens if you touch the plant in this poem?* (You get pricked by a spine.) *How does the cactus stay alive in the desert?* (It doesn't need much water.) *How does the climate described in this poem make you feel?* (dry, thirsty)

Advanced Have students read the poem silently then reread it aloud chorally. *Ask: What must the cactus, hawk, and lizard have in common?* (They can live without a lot of water.) *Why is the roadrunner under the tree?* (because of its shade)

1. **Use the illustration** *Say: This is a roadrunner, and this is a lizard. What are they doing? Why is the roadrunner chasing the lizard?*
2. **Choral reading** Play the audio. Then divide the class in half. Have each half read alternate stanzas with you.
3. **Describe images** Discuss the guide question and have students describe their images. Remind them that there is no right or wrong answer.
4. **Identify features of a poem** *Say: Rhymes are often one feature of a poem, but this poem doesn't have regular rhymes. Are there any rhyming words in it?* (spines, time)
5. **Multi-level options** See MULTI-LEVEL OPTIONS on p. 80.

Sample Answer to Guide Question
I imagine that the lizard and the roadrunner are running very fast and are pretty far apart.

Describe Images

What is your image of the roadrunner and the lizard? Are they running fast or slowly? Is the roadrunner close to the lizard, or are they far apart?

---

5   Here is the **roadrunner**
that chases the lizard
who is spied by the hawk
that perches on the cactus
that is covered with spines
and can live without rain
for a very long time.
Here is the southwestern desert.

6   Here is the tree,
which **shelters** the roadrunner
that chases the lizard
who is spied by the hawk
that perches on the cactus
that is covered with spines
and can live without rain
for a very long time.
Here is the southwestern desert.

---

roadrunner   a type of bird that can run very quickly and lives in the desert

shelters   provides protection

Chapter 1   Here Is the Southwestern Desert   **81**

 Spelling

desert/dessert

On the board, draw a sketch of sand, a cactus, and a blazing sun. Draw an ice cream cone. *Say: The spelling of some words is very similar. It is easy to get them mixed up.* Write *desert* under the first picture and *dessert* under the other. Point out that the only difference is the number of *-s's*. Challenge students to come up with a memory device to help them remember the difference. (You want more dessert; there

are more *s's* in this word.) Point out the differences in pronunciation.

   Apply   Write on the board:

A cactus grows in the _____.
My favorite _____ *is apple pie.*
Fruit makes a healthy _____.
A _____ *is a hot, dry place.*

Have students choose the correct word to complete each.

Read the Selection

1. **Use art to preview** Have students look at the art on pp. 82 and 83. Ask questions to help students identify the sun, bobcat, badger, and squirrel. *Ask: How do you think the bobcat feels lying in the sun? Is the squirrel surprised to see the badger?*

2. **Choral reading** Divide the class into two groups. Have each group read aloud alternate lines. Direct both groups to read the last line of each stanza.

3. **Describe mental images** Discuss the guide questions. Have students close their eyes to imagine.

Sample Answer to Guide Question
I imagine that the sun is very bright and the bobcat is very lazy. The day is beautiful, and the bobcat feels great.

7   Here is the sun
    that **blazes** on the tree,
    which shelters the roadrunner
    that chases the lizard
    who is spied by the hawk
    that perches on the cactus
    that is covered with spines
    and can live without rain
    for a very long time.
    Here is the southwestern desert.

Describe Images

What is your image of the sun and the bobcat? What is the day like? Do you think the bobcat feels good?

8   Here is the **bobcat**
    who **basks** in the sun
    that blazes on the tree,
    which shelters the roadrunner
    that chases the lizard
    who is spied by the hawk
    that perches on the cactus
    that is covered with spines
    and can live without rain
    for a very long time.
    Here is the southwestern desert.

blazes   burns strongly

basks   enjoys the sun while sitting or lying down

bobcat   a wild cat that lives in North America and has a short tail and brown fur with spots

82   Unit 2 Environment

MULTI-LEVEL OPTIONS *Read the Selection*

Newcomer *Ask: Is the sun out?* (yes) *Is a bobcat lying in the sun?* (yes) *Was the squirrel in the ground?* (yes) *Was the badger in the ground?* (no)

Beginning *Ask: What is the sun shining on?* (the tree) *What is lying in the sun?* (the bobcat) *What part of his body does the badger use?* (his nose) *Where was the squirrel?* (in the ground)

Intermediate *Ask: How did the badger discover that the bobcat was nearby?* (He smelled him.) *How did the badger discover the squirrel?* (He found him when he was digging a hole.)

Advanced *Ask: Which animal is probably the hottest and which is the coolest? Why?* (The bobcat is hottest because he is basking in the sun; the squirrel is coolest because he was underground.) *What have you noticed about the pattern of the poem?* (The poet adds something new in each stanza and then repeats what came before.)

9   Here is the **badger**
that smells the bobcat
who basks in the sun
that blazes on the tree,
which shelters the roadrunner
that chases the lizard
who is spied by the hawk
that perches on the cactus
that is covered with spines
and can live without rain
for a very long time.
Here is the southwestern desert.

Describe Images

What is your image of the squirrel and the badger? What is the badger doing? Where is the squirrel? Is the squirrel frightened?

10   Here is the squirrel
who is **unearthed** by the badger
that smells the bobcat
who basks in the sun
that blazes on the tree,
which shelters the roadrunner
that chases the lizard
who is spied by the hawk
that perches on the cactus
that is covered with spines
and can live without rain
for a very long time.
Here is the southwestern desert.

---

badger   an animal that digs and lives in the ground   **unearthed**   uncovered

Chapter 1   Here Is the Southwestern Desert   **83**

Read the Selection

1. **Shared reading** Play the audio. Have students join in for the verbs and last line of each stanza.
2. **Multi-level options** See MULTI-LEVEL OPTIONS on p. 82.

Sample Answer to Guide Question
I imagine the badger smelling the air while digging out the squirrel. The squirrel is in the hole and is surprised.

 Spelling

Long vowel sounds and the -ed suffix

Long Vowels *Say: Words that have a long vowel sound usually follow two patterns. The first pattern is vowel-consonant + silent e. The second pattern is two vowels together.* Have students locate *blaze* and *rain* in stanza 7. Ask them to find other words with long vowels sounds in stanza 7. (chases, spines, time, tree)

   -ed suffix Show students how to accurately spell the inflection that changes verbs to the simple past tense. Write on the board: *unearth + ed. Say: We can show that an action happened in the past by adding -ed to most verbs.* Write: *spy.* Demonstrate dropping the *-y* and adding *-ied* as you *say: When a verb ends in* -y, *you have to drop the* -y *and add* -ied *to show past tense.* Ask students to find the past tense of spy in stanza 7. (spied)

Read the Selection

1. **Shared reading** Play the audio. Then read the poem aloud and have students join in when they can.
2. **Determine the purpose for listening** *Ask: What animals are added to the poem?* Then have students close their books as you play the audio. (coyote, snake) *Ask: What was your purpose for listening?* (to identify new information in the poem)
3. **Describe images** With books still closed, discuss the guide questions and have students describe their images.

Sample Answer to Guide Question
The coyote moves very slowly; then it pounces quickly.

Describe Images

What is your image of the coyote? Does it move quickly or slowly?

11   Here is the **coyote**
    that **pounces** on the squirrel
    who is unearthed by the badger
    that smells the bobcat
    who basks in the sun
    that blazes on the tree,
    which shelters the roadrunner
    that chases the lizard
    who is spied by the hawk
    that perches on the cactus
    that is covered with spines
    and can live without rain
    for a very long time.
    Here is the southwestern desert.

---

coyote   a type of wolf that is similar to a dog and lives in parts of North America

pounces   attacks by jumping quickly on something

84   **Unit 2** Environment

MULTI-LEVEL OPTIONS *Read the Selection*

Newcomer *Ask: Is a coyote in the desert?* (yes) *Does the coyote jump on the bobcat?* (no) *Does the snake unearth the coyote?* (no)

Beginning *Ask: Does pounce mean jump on?* (yes) *Who pounces on the squirrel?* (coyote) *How do you think the squirrel feels?* (surprised) *What sound does the snake make?* (hiss)

Intermediate *Ask: What do the coyote and squirrel have in common?* (Both have another animal chasing them.) *What is the coyote likely to do when it hears the snake's hiss?* (run away from it)

Advanced *Ask: How do you think the coyote feels when the snake hisses? Why?* (scared, because a hiss is a dangerous sound) *How do you predict the poet will end the poem?* (Maybe she will have a human come to the desert.)

Describe Images

What is your image of the snake? How big is it? Is it lying flat on the ground, or is its head raised? What sound does it make?

12   Here is the snake
that **hisses** at the coyote
that pounces on the squirrel
who is unearthed by the badger
that smells the bobcat
who basks in the sun
that blazes on the tree,
which shelters the roadrunner
that chases the lizard
who is spied by the hawk
that perches on the cactus
that is covered with spines
and can live without rain
for a very long time.
Here is the southwestern desert.

---

hisses   makes a low, soft sound

Chapter 1   Here Is the Southwestern Desert   **85**

Read the Selection

1. **Choral reading**   Read the poem aloud. Then have students read the stanzas with you.
2. **Identify a pattern in a poem**   *Ask: What is the pattern in the poem?* (A new animal is presented, then the whole poem repeats.) *Why do the stanzas keep getting longer?* (A new animal is added to the beginning of each stanza.)
3. **Multi-level options**   See MULTI-LEVEL OPTIONS on p. 84.

Sample Answer to Guide Question
The snake is very long; its head is curled up and it's hissing.

 Spelling

***ou* sound**

Write on the board and say: *pounce*. Have students find *pounce* in stanza 11. *Say: One way to spell the sound* /au/ *is* ou. Tell students to find another word in the last line of stanza 11 with the *ou* sound. (southwestern) Write the word on the board and underline the *ou*.

Apply   Make a two-column chart on the board. Head each column with one of the following words: *found, out.* Have students suggest words that rhyme with the headings of each column. (hound, pound, sound; shout, pout, scout) Write these words under the headings. Underline the *ou* in each.

Read the Selection

1. **Shared reading** Play the audio. Then read the poem aloud. Have students join in for the last word of each line and the last line of each stanza.

2. **Listening for rhythm** *Say: Poetry carries its own rhythm. Listen to the entire poem and listen for the rhythm.* Students can listen with eyes closed or while reading along in the book.

3. **Describe images** Have students describe their own images of the poem.

Sample Answer to Guide Question
The hare is sitting on a rock and is very frightened.

Describe Images

What is your image of the hare? Where is it? Do you think it is frightened?

13   Here is the **hare**
who hears the snake
that hisses at the coyote
that pounces on the squirrel
who is unearthed by the badger
that smells the bobcat
who basks in the sun
that blazes on the tree,
which shelters the roadrunner
that chases the lizard
who is spied by the hawk
that perches on the cactus
that is covered with spines
and can live without rain
for a very long time.
Here is the southwestern desert.

---

hare   an animal like a large rabbit

86   Unit 2 Environment

MULTI-LEVEL OPTIONS *Read the Selection*

Newcomer *Ask: Did the hare make a noise?* (no) *Did the snake make a noise?* (yes) *Does the hare eat the cactus?* (yes) *Is the cactus important to every creature in the desert?* (yes)

Beginning *Ask: What animal hears the snake?* (hare) *What sound does the snake make?* (hiss) *What food does the hare eat?* (cactus) *What plant is important to every creature in the desert?* (cactus)

Intermediate *Ask: What senses are mentioned in the poem?* (the sound of a snake, feeling of the sun, sight of the animals, smell of the bobcat, and touch of the cactus spines) *What do you notice about the way the poet begins stanza 2 and stanza 14?* (They are the same.)

Advanced *Ask: What pattern did the poet use?* (She added a new idea to each stanza. Then she repeated all the events described in the earlier stanzas.) *Why could you call this poem a circle poem?* (because it started and ended with the same thing—the cactus)

Describe Images

What is your image of the hare and the cactus? What is the hare doing to the cactus?

14 Here is the cactus
that is food for the hare
who hears the snake
that hisses at the coyote
that pounces on the squirrel
who is unearthed by the badger
that smells the bobcat
who basks in the sun
that blazes on the tree,
which shelters the roadrunner
that chases the lizard
who is spied by the hawk
that perches on the cactus
that is covered with spines
and can live without rain
for a very long time.
Here is the southwestern desert.

About the Author

Madeleine Dunphy (born 1962)

Madeleine Dunphy travels a lot to write her books. She goes to many faraway and interesting places, such as The Democratic Republic of Congo, the Amazon Rain Forest, Peru, Cambodia, and Australia. Dunphy also taught environmental studies in Thailand.

➤ How do you think Madeleine Dunphy's travels and experience helped her write "Here Is the Southwestern Desert"?

Chapter 1 Here Is the Southwestern Desert **87**

A Capitalization

First word in a sentence

Say: The first word of a sentence always begins with a capital letter. Read the long sentence in stanza 13. (Here is the hare . . .) *Read the short sentence.* (Here is the southwestern desert.) *How could you tell where each sentence began?* (capital letter)

Evaluate Your Reading Strategy

Describe Images *Say: You have practiced an important reading strategy. Now you can decide how well you have done. Does this statement describe how you read?*

When I read a poem, I stop and describe images to myself. This helps me understand and enjoy the poem.

Read the Selection

1. **Paired reading** Have students practice reading the entire poem in pairs. Ask them to use rhythm and feeling while they read.
2. **Multi-level options** See MULTI-LEVEL OPTIONS on p. 86.

Sample Answer to Guide Question
The hare is nibbling at the cactus.

About the Author

1. **Analyze facts** Have students do a paired reading of the biography. *Ask: Where did Madeleine Dunphy travel?* (The Democratic Republic of Congo, the Amazon Rain Forest, Peru, Cambodia, and Australia) *Where has she taught?* (Thailand) *Why would an environmental studies instructor write a poem like "Here Is the Southwestern Desert"?* (It shows the interdependence of all living things in a natural environment.)
2. **Use a map** Have students use a map to locate the countries Madeleine Dunphy has visited or worked in.

Across Selections

Teacher Resource Book: *Venn Diagram, p. 35*

Have students work in pairs to compare the text features of this poem with "Thanksgiving." Ask them to examine rhyme, repetition, words that show the five senses, and length of stanzas. Have them record their comparisons in a Venn diagram.

Spelling, Punctuation, Capitalization

After the Reading Comprehension section, students will practice spelling, punctuation, and capitalization in the Activity Book.

Beyond the Reading

Reading Comprehension

Question-Answer Relationships

Sample Answers

1. a cactus
2. a hare, snake, coyote, squirrel, badger, bobcat, roadrunner, lizard, and hawk
3. a cactus and tree
4. rainy weather
5. runs fast
6. They hunt and eat other animals.
7. It is a dry, hot place, but there are lots of animals. There are not many plants.
8. I live in a climate that is sunny, but it is not as hot as the desert. We get more rain, too, so we have lots of grass and plants.
9. People depend on other people for food, services, and shelter.
10. This poem has a cycle just like the food chain. Every animal and plant in the poem depends on another animal or plant, just like in the food chain.

Build Reading Fluency

Echo Read Aloud

Model reading aloud with expression. Read one line at a time. Ask the class to read (echo) the same line you just read before going on to the next line or sentence.

Reading Comprehension

Question-Answer Relationships (QAR)

"Right There" Questions

1. **Recall Facts** What plant is covered with spines?
2. **Recall Facts** What animals are named in the poem?
3. **Recall Facts** What plants are named in the poem?

"Think and Search" Questions

4. **Draw Conclusions** What type of weather does the desert *not* have for a long time?
5. **Use Context Clues** What do you think the roadrunner does well?

"Author and You" Questions

6. **Make Inferences** How do you think the animals in the poem get food?

7. **Describe** Based on what you learned from the poem, how would you describe the desert?

"On Your Own" Questions

8. **Compare** How does the desert compare with the environment you live in?
9. **Explain** How do people depend on each other?
10. **Connect Ideas** How does this poem connect to what you learned about the food chain on page 25?

Activity Book p. 42   Student CD-ROM

Build Reading Fluency

Echo Read Aloud

Effective readers learn to read with feeling. Echo reading helps you read with feeling and expression. Your teacher reads a line. Then the class reads (echoes) the same line aloud. Turn to page 80.

1. Listen to your teacher read.
2. Read the same line aloud with expression.
3. Continue listening and reading.

MULTI-LEVEL OPTIONS *Elements of Literature*

Newcomer Make a matrix. Label the columns: *Thanksgiving/Here is the Southwestern Desert*. Label the rows: *a poem/rhyming words/free verse/2 lines,/5+ lines*. Help students compare and contrast the two poems by checking off the features of each. *Ask: Do all poems rhyme?* (no) *Are all poems the same length?* (no)

Beginning Make a matrix. Label the columns: *Thanksgiving/Here is the Southwestern Desert*. Label the rows: *poem/rhyming words/free verse/stanzas: same/stanzas: different*. Have pairs work together to check off the features. *Say: Contrast the rhyming and length in the poems.* (rhymes/free verse; short stanzas, increasingly long stanzas)

Intermediate Have students reread the "Family Photo" on p. 5 and "Thanksgiving" on p. 31. Ask them to identify how the stanzas and rhymes of these poems are similar to and different from "Here is the Southwestern Desert." Tell students to record their answers on a Venn diagram.

Advanced Have students use a three-column chart to compare and contrast "Family Photo" (p. 5), "Thanksgiving" (p. 31) and "Here is the Southwestern Desert." Have students review and fill in the features of poetry (rhymes, stanzas, repetition, etc.) they have learned. Have them share their charts with a partner.

Listen, Speak, Interact

Act Out a Poem

The poem "Here Is the Southwestern Desert" includes many action verbs. Work in a small group to act out a part of the poem.

1. Choose a series of lines from the poem.
2. Identify the action that each person in the group will demonstrate.
3. As a group, act out the actions for the class. Do not use words. Use movements only.

4. Ask the class to guess which lines of the poem you are demonstrating.
5. Discuss your presentation. Talk about how acting out part of the poem helped you understand and remember it better.

Elements of Literature

Recognize Free Verse

Poems sometimes have rhyming words at the ends of the lines. Rhyming words end with the same sounds. For example, the words *hill* and *Jill* rhyme in these lines:

Jack and *Jill*
went up the *hill*.

Free verse is a type of poetry that does not use rhyming words. The stanzas of a free verse poem can also be made up of a different number of lines.

With a partner, study how free verse is used in "Here Is the Southwestern Desert."

1. Notice how the number of lines changes in each stanza. Why did the writer add more lines to each stanza?
2. Read a few lines of the poem to your partner. Then listen as your partner reads aloud a few lines.
3. Note how the last words of each line do not rhyme. Discuss why you think the writer didn't use rhyming words. Write your conclusion in your Reading Log.

Reading Log   Activity Book *p. 43*   Student CD-ROM

Chapter 1 Here Is the Southwestern Desert   **89**

Listen, Speak, Interact

Act Out a Poem

1. **Identify action verbs** Divide the class into small groups. Ask them to identify the action verb in stanza 3. (perches) Point out that each group must find the action verbs first. Then have groups select and practice performing one stanza.

2. **Newcomers** Review the art for each stanza of the poem. Have students choose an animal and act out its movements or sounds. Ask other students to brainstorm words to describe the actions.

Elements of Literature

Recognize Free Verse

1. **Recognize free verse** Ask a volunteer to read the explanation. Have students review "Family Photo" (p. 5) and "Thanksgiving" (p. 29). *Ask: Which poem is written in free verse?* ("Family Photo") Have students work in pairs to complete the exercise.

2. **Multi-level options** See MULTI-LEVEL OPTIONS on p. 88.

Answers

Examples: **1.** The poet added more lines as she added more animals. **3.** The poet has more freedom to choose words when they don't rhyme. The repetition creates its own rhythm, which is what rhyming words also do.

 ASSESS

Ask: What are two things you like about this poem?

Cultural Connection

Divide your class into groups. Give each group several examples of a type of poetry associated with a particular country or culture, such as haiku and limericks. Have groups list qualities of these types of poetry. Provide time for groups to present their findings and compare and contrast them with the results of other groups.

Learning Styles
Musical

Suggest that another way to respond to poetry is musically. If possible, provide a collection of hand instruments such as bongos, recorders, tambourines, and triangles. Ask small groups to create musical responses to the rhythm of the poem. For example, they may beat out the rhythm or use a different sound to represent each animal. If musical instruments are not available, have students improvise with classroom objects.

Word Study

Recognize Word Origins

Identify word origins Help students think of English words that are from other languages. There are many food words, for example, lasagna, tofu, burrito. Spell these words on the board. Have students copy the words into their Personal Dictionaries.

Grammar Focus

Identify the Simple Present Tense

1. **Use simple present tense** Write on the board: *(chase) Roadrunners* _____ *lizards. A coyote* _____ *a squirrel.* Have students work together to complete the sentences.

2. **Discuss irregular verbs** *Say: Verbs that don't follow this rule are called "irregular verbs." The verbs* be, have, do, *and* go *are irregular.* Teach students the simple present form of these verbs. (be: am, is, are; have: have, has; do: do, does; go: go, goes) *Say: The third person singular forms for these irregular verbs are different.* (is, has, does, goes)

Answers
1. basks, blazes, shelters, chases, perches

ASSESS

Write on the board: 1. *snake/hiss/lizard* 2. *bobcats/bask/sun.* Have students write simple present tense sentences.

Word Study

Recognize Word Origins

Many words in English are influenced by other cultures and languages. "Here Is the Southwestern Desert" uses words whose origins are Greek, Old English, and Nahuatl, a Native American language.

1. Reread stanza 13. Find the words *cactus, hare,* and *coyote.*
2. Read the chart to learn what languages these words come from.
3. Do you know of any other English words that come from other cultures and languages? If so, share these with the class.

Word	Language	Root Word
cactus	Greek	kaktos
hare	Old English	hara
coyote	Nahuatl	coyotl

Activity Book
p. 44

Student
CD-ROM

Grammar Focus

Identify the Simple Present Tense

Use the **simple present tense** to say that something happens regularly or that it is generally true. The simple present tense has two forms.

I <u>like</u> to bask in the sun.

The bobcat <u>like**s**</u> to bask in the sun.

When the subject of a simple present tense verb is **third person singular** (*he, she,* or *it*), you must add an *-s* to the verb.

1. Reread stanza 8 of the poem. Find the simple present tense verbs.
2. Write three sentences that tell what you do every day. Capitalize and punctuate each sentence correctly to make its meaning clear.

	Singular (just one)	**Plural (more than one)**
First Person	I <u>like</u> the sun.	We <u>like</u> the sun.
Second Person	You <u>like</u> the sun.	You <u>like</u> the sun.
Third Person	She <u>like**s**</u> the sun. He <u>like**s**</u> the sun. It <u>like**s**</u> the sun.	They <u>like</u> the sun.

Note: When the verb ends in *ss, sh, ch, x,* or *z,* add **-es:** perch—perch**es**

Activity Book
pp. 45–46

Student
Handbook

Student
CD-ROM

90 Unit 2 Environment

MULTI-LEVEL OPTIONS *From Reading to Writing*

Newcomer Create a free verse group poem. Brainstorm and list environmental topics. Have the group choose one. Then have students make cluster maps with key words about the sights, sounds, tastes, and textures associated with this place in nature. Help students develop sentences from their key words.

Beginning Ask each student to draw a picture of an environment that is the subject of his/her poem. Then have students generate a list of words and phrases describing that environment. Finally, help students decide on a sequence in which to present these descriptions to form a free verse poem.

Intermediate Have students select an environment other than the desert as the subject of their free verse poem. Suggest that they use stanzas 2 and 3 as a model for their work.

Advanced After students have completed their poems, invite them to audiotape dramatic readings. Have them include music or sound effects.

From Reading to Writing

Write a Poem About the Environment

"Here Is the Southwestern Desert" is a poem about the environment. Write your own poem about the environment. Use the poetry features you learned.

1. Brainstorm ideas using a web like the one shown.
2. Include at least two stanzas that have different numbers of lines.
3. Repeat at least one line in each stanza.
4. Use the simple present tense.
5. Illustrate your poem.

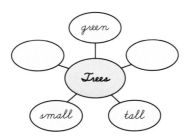

6. Read your poem to the class or to a partner. Speak slowly, clearly, and with expression.

Activity Book   Student
p. 47   Handbook

Across Content Areas

Learn About Types of Climate

A **climate** is the kind of weather that a place or region has. Here are four types of climates:

A **desert climate** is hot and dry.

In a **tropical climate,** the weather is hot all year. During part of the year, it rains a lot. During the rest of the year, it doesn't rain much.

Regions with **continental climates** usually have four seasons. It can be very hot in the summer and very cold in the winter.

An **arctic climate** has very long, cold winters. Summers are short and not warm.

Work with a partner. Choose the correct words to complete these sentences.

1. Alaska has ____ .
   a. an arctic climate
   b. a continental climate
2. Much of Arizona has ____ .
   a. a desert climate
   b. a continental climate
3. Hawaii has ____ .
   a. a continental climate
   b. a tropical climate

Work with a partner to create a record of temperatures in your community for one week. Organize the record according to days of the week. Revise it as you correct spelling mistakes.

Activity Book
p. 48

From Reading to Writing

Write a Poem About the Environment

1. **Follow directions** Read the instructions for the activity. Then brainstorm and list different environmental subjects.
2. **Pair work** After students have worked on their poems, have them exchange papers and give each other feedback. Remind them to check for the correct forms of the present simple tense.
3. **Read poetry aloud** Have students practice reading their poems to a partner. Then ask volunteers to read their poems to the class.
4. **Multi-level options** See MULTI-LEVEL OPTIONS on p. 90.

Across Content Areas: Science

Learn About Types of Climate

Infer meaning from context Ask students to give their own definitions of the bold-faced words, using information from the context.

Answers
1. a 2. a 3. b

✓ ASSESS

Have students describe two different types of climate.

Reteach and Reassess

Text Structure Show students several poems. Have them identify the number of stanzas and lines per stanza as well as determining whether the poet uses rhyme or repetition.

Reading Strategy Have students close their eyes and listen as you read a short, descriptive poem about nature to the class. Ask students to draw the images the poem made in their minds. Have students share their drawings.

Elements of Literature Ask students to create a diagram to show the form of "Here Is the Southwestern Desert." For example, students may draw triangles of increasing size.

Reassess Read aloud a poem about nature. Let students interpret its meaning by acting it out or by drawing an image.

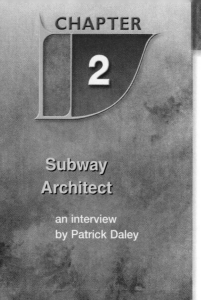

CHAPTER

2

Subway
Architect

an interview
by Patrick Daley

Into the Reading

Chapter Materials

Activity Book: *pp. 49–56*
Audio: *Unit 2, Chapter 2; CD 1, Track 8*
Student Handbook
Student CD-ROM: *Unit 2, Chapter 2*
Teacher Resource Book: *Lesson Plan, Teacher
    Resources, Reading Summary, Activity Book
    Answer Key*
Teacher Resource CD-ROM
Assessment Program: *Quiz, pp. 25–26; Teacher
    and Student Resources, pp. 115–144*
Assessment CD-ROM
Transparencies
The Heinle Newbury House Dictionary/CD-ROM
Web site: http://visions.heinle.com

Objectives

Preview Read the objectives aloud. *Ask: What
is the difference between a fact and an opinion?*

Use Prior Knowledge

Identify Different Types of
Transportation

Use a graphic organizer Have students fill in
their Word Wheels. Then list on the board all the
different kinds of transportation in students'
Word Wheels.

Objectives

Reading Distinguish facts from opinions
as you read an interview.

Listening and Speaking Role-play an
interview.

Grammar Identify and punctuate
questions.

Writing Write a personal narrative.

Content The Arts: Design a mural.

Use Prior Knowledge

Identify Different Types of Transportation

A subway is a train system that runs
below the ground. Many large cities have
a subway. People ride the subway to get
from one place in a city to another or to
travel to towns near the city. Have you
ever ridden on a subway?

1. On a piece of paper, draw a Word
   Wheel like the one here.
2. Think about the ways you can travel
   around your city or town.
3. Write your ideas in the wheel.

4. Compare your wheel with a partner's.
   Which types of transportation do you
   use? When do you use them?

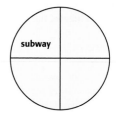

subway

MULTI-LEVEL OPTIONS *Build Vocabulary*

Newcomer Write *subway* on a
note card. Point to the word and
look confused. Then turn to the
picture on p. 95. Point to the
subway train in the picture. Show
understanding with your facial
expression. Draw a quick sketch
of a subway train on the back of
the card. Help students use cards
as they read.

Beginning Draw two sides of
a note card on the board. Write
subway on one card face. Have
students work in pairs to find a
definition in paragraph 1 on p. 92.
Record their definitions on back of
the second card face. Distribute
cards. Have them use *subway* on
their first card. Help students use
additional cards as they read.

Intermediate Draw two sides
of a note card on the board. Write
boroughs on one card face. Have
students work in pairs to infer the
meaning from information at the
top of p. 93. Record a definition on
back of the second card face.
Have them use *boroughs* on their
first card. Monitor students' note-
taking as they read.

Advanced Have students use
the note card technique to
examine the meanings of *borough*
and *architect* on p. 93. Monitor
students' note-taking as they
read.

Build Background

New York City

New York City is located in the southeastern part of New York state. It has the largest population of any city in the United States. New York City is made up of five areas called *boroughs*. The five boroughs are: Manhattan, Brooklyn, Queens, the Bronx, and Staten Island.

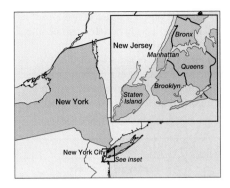

Content Connection

New York City grew quickly in the late 1800s and the streets became very crowded. To solve this problem, the city constructed its first subway system in 1904.

Build Vocabulary

Take Notes as You Read

You can use note cards while reading to **take notes** on words you do not understand.

1. As you read "Subway Architect," identify any words you do not understand as you read the text.
2. Write each word on one side of a note card. Use one card for each word.
3. As you continue to read, you may understand some of the words you wrote down earlier. Write those meanings on the other sides of the note cards.
4. When you finish reading, review your note cards. Ask your teacher or use a dictionary to find the meanings of any words you still do not understand. Write those definitions on the note cards.
5. Exchange note cards with a partner. Test each other as a way to review and memorize words.

The Heinle Newbury House Dictionary   Activity Book p. 49   Student CD-ROM

Content Connection
Technology

Build Vocabulary Have small groups of students use books or Internet sources to read about maglev (magnetically levitated) trains. Ask students to use the note card technique to develop an understanding of any unfamiliar words.

Learning Styles
Mathematical

Build Background Write this information about New York subways on the board:

Borough	Miles of Track
Manhattan	71
Queens	42
Bronx	33
Brooklyn	84
Total	230

Have students calculate the percentage of track in each borough and make a pie chart to show the results. (M.—30.9%; Q.—18.3%; Bx.—14.3%; Bklyn.—36.5%)

Build Background

New York City

1. **Relate to personal experience** *Ask: Have you ever been to New York City? What is New York City famous for?*
2. **Use a map** Have students point to the places on the map as you name them.
3. **Content Connection** The first subway in the U.S. opened in New York City in 1904.

Build Vocabulary

Take Notes as You Read

Teacher Resource Book: *Personal Dictionary, p. 63*

1. **Practice the strategy** Distribute index cards or paper cut into card size. Have students silently reread the paragraph about New York City at the top of the page. *Ask: What is a new word for you? Look it up in the dictionary and write down the definition on your note card. Spell the word correctly and divide it into syllables.*
2. **Reading selection vocabulary** You may want to introduce the glossed words in the reading selection before students begin reading. Key words: *architect, station, challenge, project, bumps, elderly, proud.* Instruct students to write the words with correct spelling and their definitions in their Personal Dictionaries. Have them pronounce each word and divide it into syllables.
3. **Multi-level options** See MULTI-LEVEL OPTIONS on p. 92.

✓ ASSESS

Tell students to brainstorm a word list about New York City. Have them read their lists to the class.

Text Structure

Interview

1. **Relate to personal experience** *Say: We are going to read an interview. Where do you find interviews?* (magazines, newspapers, radio, TV) *Who have you heard being interviewed?*
2. **Multi-level options** See MULTI-LEVEL OPTIONS below.

Reading Strategy

Distinguish Facts from Opinions

Define and clarify *Say: Tell me four things about transportation in our area.* Record students' answers. Then have students identify which are facts and which are opinions.

ASSESS

Have students give one fact and one opinion about their favorite form of transportation.

Text Structure

Interview

An **interview** is a series of questions and answers, usually between two people. The **interviewer** asks the questions, and the **interviewee** answers them. The interview usually gives information about the interviewee's life, experiences, or opinions. The interview you will read is made up of the following features:

Interview	
Questions	asked by the interviewer Each question is labeled Q.
Answers	information given by the interviewee Each answer is labeled A.

The selection also includes an **introduction.** The introduction explains what the interview is about.

1. Before you read, look at how the interview is organized.
2. Pause after reading the introduction (paragraphs 1–3). What do you think you will learn in this interview?
3. After you have read the interview, write in your Reading Log what you learned about the person interviewed.

Reading Log   Student CD-ROM

Reading Strategy

Distinguish Facts from Opinions

Facts explain information that is true. **Opinions** tell what someone thinks about something. An opinion cannot be proven to be true or false.

Look at the following examples of fact and opinion.

Fact: There is a subway in New York City.

Opinion: The subway is the best way to travel.

1. Look for examples of facts and opinions as you read "Subway Architect."
2. Think about how you can tell the difference between a fact and an opinion. For example, opinions might start with words like "I think . . ."

Student CD-ROM

MULTI-LEVEL OPTIONS *Text Structure*

Newcomer Write on the board: *Question* and *Answer. Say: I will interview you.* Point to *Question. Ask: Did you take a ride on a subway?* When a volunteer answers, point to *Answer.* Continue the interview with additional yes/no questions about subways. *(Do you like to ride the subway? Is it fast? Is it fun?)*

Beginning Write *Question* and *Answer* on separate cards. Hold up the question card. *Ask: What is a subway like?* Give the answer card to a student to answer. Continue interviewing students about subways. When they are ready, pass the question card to students.

Intermediate Have students work in small groups. Give groups six cards with one of the following on each: *Who? What? When? Why? Where? Answer.* Have a student select a *Wh-* card and ask an interview question about subways. Any student in the group can take the *Answer* card to respond. Continue until all have had a turn.

Advanced Have students use a KWL Chart in their Logs. *Say: List what you know about subways under* Know. *Write questions you want to ask a subway designer under* Want to Know. Tell them that they will list what they learn from "Subway Architect" under *Learn.*

SUBWAY ARCHITECT

an interview
by Patrick Daley

95

Reading Selection Materials

Audio: *Unit 2, Chapter 2; CD 1, Track 8*
Teacher Resource Book: *Reading Summary,*
pp. 77–78
Transparencies: #4, *Reading Summary*

Suggestions for Using
Reading Summary

- Introduce new vocabulary or cognates.
- Cut the summary into strips, or jumble the sentences on an overhead transparency. Students put the sentences in order.
- Practice the reading strategy.
- Students read aloud or with a partner.
- Students paraphrase the summary.
- Students do a cloze activity.
- Students create a visual or graphic organizer, such as a timeline or storyboard, to illustrate the summary.
- Students paraphrase the summary.

Preview the Selection

1. **Interpret the image** Have students look at the photo. *Ask: What do you see in the photo? How can you tell the train is moving?*
2. **Discuss message of medium** *Ask: What feeling do you get from this photograph?* (a busy, bustling feeling) *Look at the painting on p. 75. Do you see any similarities?* (the vertical and horizontal lines, light and shadow) *Do you get the same feeling from each picture?*
3. **Connect** *Say: The theme of this unit is the environment. What kind of environment is this?* (urban) *Can you tell anything about the climate or the animals there?* (not much) *What do you think this environment would look like if you could see a larger picture?*

Content Connection
The Arts

Learning Styles
Interpersonal

Have students look at the picture on p. 95. *Ask: What qualities is the photographer trying to show about a subway train?* (speed, city travel, movement) Have students look at photos, drawings, and paintings of types of transportation. Repeat the question about what the photographer or artist is trying to communicate. Have students use these visuals to compare and contrast other types of transportation with subway travel.

Say: Subways connect people. Have students work in pairs to prepare a web to show these connections. First, have students draw a subway train in the center of a page. Then have them draw tracks branching out from the train. At the end of every branch, have students draw or write people or things with which a subway may connect its riders. (family, friends, workplaces, stores, entertainment, doctors)

▌Teacher Resource Book: *Web, p. 37*

Read the Selection

1. **Identify text structure** *Say: This is the introduction to the interview. How many paragraphs are there?* (3)
2. **Shared reading** Play the audio. Ask three volunteers to read one paragraph each.
3. **Distinguish facts from opinions** Have students work in pairs. Have them decide if the introduction is primarily fact or opinion. (fact)

Sample Answer to Guide Question
Facts include: A subway is a system of trains that runs underground. New York City has one of the busiest subways in the world. Millions of people ride it each day. It's about 100 years old.

See Teacher Edition pp. 434–436 for a list of English-Spanish cognates in the reading selection.

Audio
CD 1, Tr. 8

1 Do you like to ride trains or subways? Got any ideas for building a better train or subway **station?** Could you handle hanging out underground?

2 If so, you might want to check out Jorge Ramos's job. Jorge spends a lot of time under the streets of New York City. That's because he's fixing part of the subway.

3 A subway is a system of trains that run underground. New York City has one of the busiest subways in the world. Millions of people ride it each day. And it's about 100 years old! So, how do you improve something so big, busy, and old? Let's find out!

Distinguish Facts from Opinions

Name a fact that appears in this paragraph.

station a place where people using the subway arrive and depart

---

MULTI-LEVEL OPTIONS *Read the Selection*

Newcomer Play the audio. Then reread the selection with gestures and drawings to reinforce meanings of key words. *Ask: Is Mr. Ramos a subway worker?* (yes) *Is his job to build a new subway?* (no) *Is his job to make an old subway better?* (yes) *Does he like riding the subway?* (yes)

Beginning Play the audio. Then do a paired reading. *Ask: Where did Jorge Ramos grow up?* (Colombia, South America) *What did he like to do as a boy?* (draw) *What did he become interested in?* (subways) *How does he feel about subways?* (He loves them.)

Intermediate Read the Reading Summary aloud. Have students do a paired reading. *Ask: Why does the introduction say Mr. Ramos spends time under the streets?* (He plans subway stations.) *How do you think his hobby as a boy helps him in his job?* (He learned to draw buildings and structures.)

Advanced Have students read the selection silently. *Ask: Why might Mr. Ramos think subways are the best way to travel?* (Riders do not have to buy cars and fuel or worry about traffic.) *Do you think Mr. Ramos cares more about people or things? Why?* (people; because he talks a lot about making things easier and safer for people)

4 **Q:** First, there's one question that I have to ask. . . .

5 **A:** Wait! I know what the question is. And the answer is YES! I do ride the subway. It's fast. It's fun. It's the best way to get around. I love being in a subway train!

6 **Q:** Okay. So what kind of work does an **architect** like you do?

7 **A:** I draw plans for buildings, homes, and even subway stations.

8 **Q:** Have you always liked to draw?

9 **A:** Yes. I grew up in Colombia, in South America. As a boy, I drew pictures of the beautiful buildings in my country. I thought some day I would draw pictures for magazines and books. But when I moved to the United States, I became interested in subway stations.

10 **Q:** Really? Why are you so interested in subway stations?

11 **A:** It's a big **challenge** to design a space that millions of people use each day. It's got to be easy for people to figure out where they're going. And the space must be easy for people to move around in. You don't want them bumping into each other or **plowing** each other down! Also, the space has to look good, and be safe.

> **Distinguish Facts from Opinions**
>
> What is Jorge Ramos's opinion about riding the subway?

---

architect a person who designs buildings and other structures

challenge a situation that tests someone's abilities

plowing crashing into

Chapter 2 Subway Architect **97**

Read the Selection

1. **Summarize** Play the audio. *Say: Close your books. What was Jorge Ramos's opinion about riding the subway?* Write all student answers on the board. Don't correct their answers.

2. **Read for specific information** Have students open their books and reread the passage to check their answers to the question.

3. **Paired reading** Have students practice in pairs, taking the part of the interviewer or Jorge Ramos.

4. **Take notes** Give students time to make vocabulary cards for words they don't understand. Have them help each other write definitions or look up words in a dictionary.

5. **Multi-level options** See MULTI-LEVEL OPTIONS on p. 96.

Sample Answer to Guide Question
He thinks it is fast, fun, and the best way to get around.

 Spelling

It's vs. *its*

Write on the board and *say: it's. Ask: What punctuation do you see in this word?* (an apostrophe) *Say: Let's figure out what the word means.* Have students find *it's* in paragraph 3. Remind them that an apostrophe can show that two words have been joined together. The apostrophe stands for a letter that was left out. *Ask: What does it's mean in this sentence?* (it is) Have students find other examples of *it's* in paragraphs 5 and 11. Write *its* on the board.

Say: This word doesn't have an apostrophe, so no letters are missing. Write: *The subway train runs on its track. Ask: What does its show in this sentence?* (possession or belonging to)

Apply Have pairs of students work together to write one sentence using *it's* and one using *its*. Provide time for class sharing.

Read the Selection

1. **Shared reading** Play the audio. Ask pairs of students to join in for different sections of the interview.

2. **Check comprehension** Ask questions to check general comprehension. *Ask: What's the first thing he does when he starts a project?* (He has a neighborhood meeting.) *Does everyone want the same thing in the station?* (no) *What's the next step after the meeting?* (to meet with builders and subway workers)

Sample Answer to Guide Question
He is asking for a fact.

---

12 **Q:** Tell me about the **project** you're working on right now.

13 **A:** We are fixing up a subway station in a part of New York City called Queens.

> **Distinguish Facts from Opinions**
>
> In paragraph 14, is the interviewer asking for a fact or an opinion?

14 **Q:** What's the first thing you did to get that project started?

15 **A:** I had a big meeting. I asked people from the neighborhood how they thought their subway station could be improved.

16 **Q:** What was that meeting like?

17 **A:** It was loud! Everyone had an opinion. In fact, you'd be surprised how many opinions there were at that meeting.

18 **Q:** Oh **yeah?** Like what?

19 **A:** Some people wanted a bigger station. Some people thought the station was too big. Some people wanted the station to be cleaner. Some wanted it to be safer. Some people thought that the station needed **murals** and other kinds of art.

---

project a specific task
yeah a slang term for "yes"

murals large paintings done on walls

98 Unit 2 Environment

MULTI-LEVEL OPTIONS *Read the Selection*

Newcomer *Ask: Is Mr. Ramos working on a subway station in Brooklyn?* (no) *Did he have a meeting about it?* (yes) *Was the meeting quiet?* (no) *Is building a station easy?* (no)

Beginning *Ask: What is Mr. Ramos working on fixing up?* (subway station) *Whose ideas did he get first?* (people in the neighborhood) *Whose ideas did he get second?* (builders) *When can't workers work on the subway?* (during the day, in winter)

Intermediate *Ask: What does Mr. Ramos do before the building starts?* (He gets ideas from riders and builders.) *Can Mr. Ramos use all the ideas he gets? Explain.* (No. Some people want opposite things.) *Why can't workers work on the subway during the day?* (because people need to use the subway to get to work and school)

Advanced *Ask: Why do you think that Mr. Ramos's meetings with riders are loud?* (because subways are important to the riders; they have strong feelings about their station.) *What do you think Mr. Ramos does with all the ideas he collects?* (He probably uses as many as he can, but sometimes he must make choices between opposite ideas.)

20 **Q:** Did you start building the station right after the meeting?

21 **A:** No. I began planning *how* to build it. I met with builders. I met with people who work for the subway system. Then I took my plans back to the neighborhood.

22 **Q:** Why would you go back to another meeting? The first one sounded **awful**!

23 **A:** Well, it wasn't really so awful—just noisy and busy. Plus, I really want people in the neighborhood to be a part of the planning. After all, it really is *their* subway station.

24 **Q:** After all of that, the building part must be easy, right?

25 **A:** Are you kidding? Working on a subway station is never easy. Here's why: We can't close the subway station during the day. So we have to work late at night. Also, we can't work in bad weather. So forget about getting much done in the winter.

> **Distinguish Facts from Opinions**
>
> Find one fact and one opinion in paragraph 25.

---

awful   very bad

Chapter 2 Subway Architect   **99**

Read the Selection

1. **Paired reading** Have students practice reading the interview in pairs. After they have practiced, invite several pairs to read for the class.
2. **Take notes** Give students time to make vocabulary cards for words they don't understand. Have them help each other write definitions or use a dictionary.
3. **Multi-level options** See MULTI-LEVEL OPTIONS on p. 98.

Sample Answer to Guide Question
Facts: They can't close the subway during the day, so they have to work at night. They can't work in bad weather. Opinion: Working on a subway station is never easy.

❜ Punctuation

Italics for emphasis

Read paragraph 21 aloud. Ask students what they noticed about your reading of the word *how*. (You said it stronger than the rest of the words.) **Ask:** *How did I know the writer wanted me to say it that way?* (The print is different.) **Say:** *That kind of print is called* italics. *It is used to tell a reader that a word is especially important and should be stressed.*

Apply Write on the board the following sentences using a different print for the words in italics:

I am not riding on the subway.

I need you to get off the train *now*.

Subway trains can go *fast*.

Have student volunteers read aloud the sentences. Remind them to emphasize the italicized words.

Read the Selection

1. **Shared reading** Play the audio. Then ask pairs of students to join in for different sections of the interview.
2. **Listen for information** Write on the board: *How does he test out subway signs? What is an artist doing for the subway?* Have students close their books as they listen to the audio for the entire interview. Then discuss their answers. Students can check their books.

Sample Answer to Guide Question
I think it is a fact because it is a law.

26 **Q:** What's left to do at the station you're building now?

27 **A:** I have to make sure that the subway signs are clear and helpful. So I'll test them first. I'll make **a bunch** of paper signs. Then I'll go to the station and tape them up. I'll pretend that I am a visitor. Can I find my way around? Or do I get lost? I'll take a lot of notes about what happens. After that test, I'll make changes to the signs. Then the paper signs will be made into real signs.

28 **Q:** What else have you done to help visitors in the station?

29 **A:** There is a law that says we must put **ramps** and elevators in all stations. That way, **elderly** people and people in wheelchairs can ride the subway. Next to the tracks where the trains come, we paint the floor with a special paint. The paint has tiny **bumps** in it. The bumps let blind people know when they are standing too close to the train tracks.

> **Distinguish Facts from Opinions**
>
> Do you think the first sentence of this answer is a fact or an opinion? Why do you think so?

---

a bunch many
ramps walkways that go between two levels of a building or a train

elderly old
bumps rounded, raised pieces of something

100 Unit 2 Environment

MULTI-LEVEL OPTIONS *Read the Selection*

Newcomer *Ask: Is work on the station finished?* (no) *Does Mr. Ramos still have to make signs?* (yes) *Will there be art in the station?* (yes)

Beginning *Ask: What does Mr. Ramos still have to make for the station?* (signs) *Who do the bumps near the track help?* (blind people) *What will help make the station look nice?* (art) *How does Mr. Ramos want subway employees to feel about the station?* (proud)

Intermediate *Ask: How does Mr. Ramos check the signs for the station?* (He tries out paper signs before he makes the real signs.) *Why does Mr. Ramos use special paint with bumps to let blind people know where the track is?* (because they cannot see signs that warn of danger) *What does Mr. Ramos's last answer show?* (He cares about his work.)

Advanced *Say: Give an example of the kind of note Mr. Ramos might write about a sign.* (People get confused about which way to go. Add an arrow.) *How are paragraphs 11 and 33 alike?* (They both show that Mr. Ramos cares a lot about subway stations working well for people.)

30 **Q:** Is there anything else left to do?

31 **A:** Yes. A **sculptor** is making art to hang on the walls. When that's done, the city **inspector** will come. She will decide whether the station is ready for all riders.

32 **Q:** What do you want people to say about the new station?

33 **A:** I want subway **employees** to say, "I'm **proud** I work here." I want visitors to say, "What a nice station." I want people in the neighborhood to say, "I love this station!" Building a good subway station is my gift to the neighborhood.

> **Distinguish Facts from Opinions**
>
> Is Jorge Ramos expressing facts or opinions in paragraph 33?

---

sculptor an artist who shapes objects from stone, metal, or other substances

inspector a person who looks at something closely

employees people who work for a person, business, government, or other organization

proud pleased, satisfied with someone's success

About the Author ⟩ Patrick Daley

Patrick Daley has written books for students. One of these books includes debate topics (topics to argue for or against something). Daley used to work as the editor of a magazine. He was also the publisher of a reading program students can use to improve their reading skills.

➤ Why do you think Patrick Daley wrote an interview about a subway architect? To explain? To entertain? To influence?

Chapter 2 Subway Architect **101**

 Spelling

Schwa sound and r-controlled vowels

Review vowel sounds. Have students identify the vowels in *rat* and *rate*. (short, long) *Say: Not all vowels are long or short.* Write *about* on the board. Have them use a dictionary to see how the *a* is marked. Explain that this is called a *schwa* sound. Also, explain that vowels followed by *-r* are pronounced in special ways. Have students use this knowledge to recognize other words with the same sounds in paragraph 31. (art, done, come, sculptor, inspector, whether, riders)

Evaluate Your Reading Strategy

Distinguish Facts from Opinions *Say: You have practiced an important reading strategy. Now you can decide how well you have done. Does this statement describe how you read?*

> When I read, I can tell the difference between facts and opinions. When I distinguish between facts and opinions, I understand the ideas in the text better.

Read the Selection

1. **Paired reading** Have students complete the reading in pairs with one student playing the interviewer and the other Jorge Ramos.
2. **Take notes** Give students time to make vocabulary cards for new words. Have them help each other write definitions or use a dictionary.
3. **Multi-level options** See MULTI-LEVEL OPTIONS on p. 100.

Sample Answer to Guide Question
He is stating his hopes and opinions.

About the Author

1. **Analyze facts** Read the paragraph aloud. *Ask: Who does the author write books for?* (students) *What other kinds of work has he done?* (editing, publishing)
2. **Discuss author's intention** Discuss the guide question. *Ask: Is "Subway Architect" a narrative or an interview?* (an interview) *Is it fiction or non-fiction?* (non-fiction) *Imagine this same information written in a narrative. Which would you prefer reading? Why?*

Across Selections

Discuss text structure Direct students to "Turkish Delight." (p. 45) Tell students that both "Turkish Delight" and the "Subway Architect" give information about a person's life and work. Have students work in pairs to make a matrix with headings: "interview" and "personal narrative." Ask them to write these features down the left-hand column: First-person point of view (narrative); Question/Answer format (interview); Personal details (both); Uses pronouns I, me, us (both); Gives facts (both). Instruct students to check off the features under the correct column.

Spelling, Punctuation, Capitalization

After the Reading Comprehension section, students will practice spelling, punctuation, and capitalization in the Activity Book.

Beyond the Reading

Reading Comprehension

Question-Answer Relationships

Sample Answers

1. He draws plans for buildings, homes, and subway stations.
2. He had a meeting with people in the neighborhood.
3. They can't work on the subway station during the day or in bad weather.
4. He planned how to build it, met with the builders, met with subway workers, and took his plans back to the neighborhood.
5. I think he does pay attention to other people's opinions, because he has a lot of meetings to ask for people's opinions, and he makes changes in his plans.
6. I knew the subway took people to school and work. I didn't know building subway stations was so hard.
7. How many subway stations are in New York City? How fast are the subway trains? How many people can fit inside one subway car?
8. What kind of education do you need to become an architect? How much do they pay?
9. What is the most popular college major for architects? What is the average salary of architects in New York City?

Build Reading Fluency

Repeated Reading

Assessment Program: *Reading Fluency, Chart, p. 116*

As students read aloud, time the reading and count the number of incorrectly pronounced words. Record results in the Reading Fluency Chart.

Reading Comprehension

Question-Answer Relationships (QAR)

"Right There" Questions

1. **Recall Facts** What kinds of things does Jorge Ramos do as an architect?
2. **Recall Facts** What was the first thing Jorge Ramos did to start his project in Queens?
3. **Recall Facts** Why isn't working on a subway station easy, according to Jorge Ramos?

"Think and Search" Question

4. **Identify Steps in a Process** Look at paragraph 21. Name the four steps that Jorge Ramos took to build a subway station.

"Author and You" Question

5. **Recognize Character Traits** Do you think Jorge Ramos is a person who pays attention to other people's opinions? Why?

"On Your Own" Questions

6. **Use Prior Knowledge** What did you know about the subway before reading the interview? What did you learn?
7. **Raise Questions** What unanswered questions do you have after reading the selection? How would you look for the answers to your questions?
8. **Ask Questions** What questions do you have about different jobs? How could you do an interview to find the answers?
9. **Revise Questions** Discuss two of your questions with your teacher. How could you revise your questions to make them clearer?

Activity Book
p. 50

Student
CD-ROM

Build Reading Fluency

Repeated Reading

Repeated reading can help increase your reading rate and build confidence. Each time you reread you improve your reading. Turn to page 98. Your teacher or partner will time your rereading for six minutes.

1. With a partner, one read the questions, the other read the answers aloud.
2. Stop after six minutes.

102 Unit 2 Environment

MULTI-LEVEL OPTIONS *Elements of Literature*

Newcomer *Ask: Why did Mr. Ramos pick his job? What does he like about it?* Have students point to and act out things that Jorge Ramos likes about his job. (drawing, people, subways, buildings)

Beginning Have pairs create Character Trait Webs to show the parts of Mr. Ramos's job that he likes. Ask them to draw a face representing Mr. Ramos. Then tell pairs to make branches out from the face and draw and label parts of Mr. Ramos's job that he likes. (drawing, people, subways, buildings)

Intermediate Work with students to identify aspects of the job that motivated Jorge Ramos to become an architect. Ask students if they would be attracted to the same career. Have them explain why or why not.

Advanced After students have written about Jorge Ramos's motivation, *say: Mr. Ramos loves his work, but there are difficult parts to every job. What parts of being an architect might he not like as well as others?* (not being able to meet everyone's needs; having an inspector tell him things that must be redone)

Listen, Speak, Interact

Role-Play an Interview

With a partner, role-play an interview between Jorge Ramos and the interviewer.

1. Decide who will role-play Jorge Ramos and who will role-play the interviewer.
2. If you are the interviewer:
   a. Make a list of five new questions to ask Jorge Ramos.
   b. Base your questions on what you learned from the selection.
3. If you are Jorge Ramos:
   a. Answer the questions the way Jorge Ramos might answer them.
   b. Combine your personal knowledge with what you learned from the text to respond.
4. Perform your role play for the class. Be sure to look at each other as you act out the interview. Speak clearly so that the audience believes you.
5. Evaluate your classmates' role plays for content and delivery. Were your classmates believable?

Elements of Literature

Understand Character Motivation

Characters in literature can be real, like Jorge Ramos, or they can be made up. But all characters have **motivation.** Motivation is the reasons characters act the way they do.

1. Reread paragraphs 8–11.
2. What do you think motivated Jorge Ramos to be an architect? In your Reading Log, write two or three sentences to express your ideas.
3. Choose a character from a reading in Unit 1. Compare and contrast that character's motivation with Jorge Ramos's motivation.
4. Share your ideas with a partner.

Reading Log   Activity Book p. 51   Student CD-ROM

 Content Connection
Social Studies

Say: One reason people pick their jobs is because of what they like to do. Another reason is the place where the person lives. Assign small groups to use books and online resources to find out about the climate, geography, resources, and needs of a particular area. Have students list jobs these conditions might motivate a person to select.

Learning Styles
Visual

Before performing their interviews, have students collaborate on creating visual aids that the student playing Jorge Ramos can show the interviewer. These may be drawings or diagrams of subway station plans, sample signs, or facts and figures related to subway use.

Listen, Speak, Interact

Role-Play an Interview

1. **Brainstorm** Have students work in groups to brainstorm and list questions for their interviews.
2. **Compose an interview form** Ask groups to create a form for their interview. Have them organize the form into questions and answers. Have pairs of students practice the interview using the form. Students should revise the form if necessary.
3. **Newcomers** Work with these students to write questions the whole group can practice. Then pair them with intermediate or advanced students to role-play an interview.
4. **Present a dramatization** Have students perform their role-plays for the class. After each presentation, ask the class what they liked about the presentation.

Elements of Literature

Understand Character Motivation

1. **Discuss motivation** Have students discuss different jobs they would like to do. Ask them to explain what about a particular job is interesting to them. Ask them why they think they would be good at that job.
2. **Multi-level options** See MULTI-LEVEL OPTIONS on p. 102.

Answers

Example: Jorge Ramos liked to draw pictures and buildings; he loves traveling by subway; he likes the challenge of designing a station that works well, looks good, and is safe.

 **ASSESS**

Have students discuss a definition for motivation. Ask them to give examples of what motivates them in their lives.

Word Study

Learn About the Prefix *Sub-*

Teacher Resource Book: *Personal Dictionary, p. 63*

1. **Identify word prefixes** Read the explanation and the chart. Have students work in pairs to complete the activity.
2. **Use a dictionary** Have students find other familiar words beginning with *sub-* in the dictionary. They can add these to their Personal Dictionaries.

Answers

Sample answers: Subfreezing—below freezing; submarine—a ship that moves under water; subtitle—words under a picture

Grammar Focus

Identify and Punctuate Questions

Identify questions Have students create posters for the classroom that show the different clues that identify a question. Display the posters for students' reference.

Answers

1. What; a question mark 2. Why, What

ASSESS

Have students write three questions about subways. Instruct them to use three different question words.

Word Study

Learn About the Prefix *Sub-*

A **prefix** is a group of letters added to the beginning of a word. It changes the word's meaning. For example, the word *subway* has the prefix *sub-*. The prefix *sub-* means "below" or "under."

1. Copy the chart in your Personal Dictionary.
2. With a partner, discuss the meaning of the root word. Then try to guess the meanings of the words with *sub-*.
3. Use a dictionary to check your work.

Prefix	Word	New Word	Meaning
sub-	way	subway	train system that runs underground
sub-	freezing	subfreezing	
sub-	marine	submarine	
sub-	title	subtitle	

4. Find other words in the dictionary with the prefix *sub-*. Write two sentences with the words. Be sure to spell the root words and prefix correctly.

Personal Dictionary   The Heinle Newbury House Dictionary   Activity Book p. 52   Student CD-ROM

Grammar Focus

Identify and Punctuate Questions

In this chapter you learned that an interview includes **questions.** The questions in the reading selection are easy to find because the letter *Q* is placed before them. However, there are other ways to identify questions.

The punctuation at the end of a question is a **question mark.**

How are you**?**

Many questions begin with **question words:** *Who, What, When, Where, Why,* and *How.*

<u>Where</u> are you going?

<u>What</u> is your name?

1. Reread paragraph 16.
   a. What is the question word?
   b. Identify the punctuation used at the end of the question.
2. Reread paragraphs 22 and 28. Identify the question words.

Activity Book pp. 53–54   Student Handbook   Student CD-ROM

104   Unit 2 Environment

MULTI-LEVEL OPTIONS *From Reading to Writing*

Newcomer Have students make posters to show their hobbies. On the left side, they can draw themselves involved in their hobbies (sorting stamps, carving wood). On the right side, have the group brainstorm a list of words that describe their feelings (curious, excited, challenged) about the hobby. Have students write key words on their posters.

Beginning Ask students to bring in examples, photographs, or drawings of their hobbies. Instruct them to use index cards to create captions for these items. Then have them share in small groups.

Intermediate Have students plan a Hobby Fair. Ask them to create displays to exhibit with their paragraphs. Invite another class to visit the displays and have your students answer their questions.

Advanced Have students compose journal entries after completing their paragraphs. Instruct them to explore how their personality and environment motivated them to pursue this hobby.

From Reading to Writing

Write a Personal Narrative

Jorge Ramos says that he liked to draw when he was a boy. Drawing was his hobby. A hobby is an activity that you enjoy doing often. Write three paragraphs about one of your hobbies.

1. Make notes to help you organize the following information:
   a. **Facts:** Information about your hobby.
   b. **Opinions:** Why you enjoy this hobby.
2. Use the information in your notes to help you write your paragraphs.
3. Remember to capitalize the first word of each sentence. Remember to indent your paragraphs.

My Hobby

 Beginning
Give facts about your hobby.

 Middle
Describe how you learned your hobby.

 End
Tell why you enjoy your hobby.

Activity Book
p. 55

Student
Handbook

Across Content Areas

Design a Mural

In "Subway Architect," you learned that some subway stations have **murals**—large paintings on walls. Suppose that it is your job to create a mural for a new subway or bus station.

1. Think of a design that shows something about the neighborhood where the station is located.
2. Draw the plan for your mural on a piece of paper. Use colored pencils, markers, or paint.

3. Write an explanation that tells how the mural relates to your neighborhood.
4. Work with a partner to write a news story about your mural. Organize your ideas in a logical order. Revise the story to correct spelling and grammar mistakes. Read your news story to the class.

Activity Book
p. 56

Reteach and Reassess

Text Structure Display an interview from a magazine. Have students compare the features of this interview with "Subway Architect."

Reading Strategy Have students write or draw three facts they learned about subways. Ask them to write their opinions of subways and share reasons.

Elements of Literature Have students work in pairs for a role-play. One student is a subway rider. The other is a reporter. Have the interviewer ask why the subway rider is

motivated to take the subway rather than use other types of transportation.

Reassess Have pairs interview each other about their hobbies. First, give partners time to briefly introduce their hobbies. Then allow time for each student to generate three to five questions to ask about the partner's hobby. Finally, have students interview each other.

From Reading to Writing

Write a Personal Narrative

1. **Teacher think aloud** Draw the chart. *Say: I've been collecting stamps for 10 years. Why do I like it so much? Well, I learned a lot about new nations in Africa and Europe through my collection. I like knowing about places I hear about on the news. I enjoy trading stamps with other collectors, too.* Demonstrate how to use your ideas to complete the chart.
2. **Write about facts and opinions** Have students work independently to draft and write their paragraphs. Ask volunteers to read their paragraphs to the class.
3. **Check spelling** Remind students to check their spelling in their final drafts. Tell them to use a spell check program or a dictionary for words they are not sure about.
4. **Multi-level options** See MULTI-LEVEL OPTIONS on p. 104.

Across Content Areas: The Arts

Design a Mural

1. **Relate to personal experience** *Ask: Have you ever seen a mural? Where? What did it look like? Are there any murals in our school or community?*
2. **Design a mural** Students can work in groups to pick a topic and design their murals. Display the designs in the classroom.

 **ASSESS**

Have students write a fact and an opinion about mural designs.

CHAPTER 3

Into the Reading

Why the Rooster Crows at Sunrise

a fable
by Lynette Dyer Vuong

Chapter Materials

Activity Book: *pp. 57–64*
Audio: *Unit 2, Chapter 3; CD 1, Track 9*
Student Handbook
Student CD-ROM: *Unit 2, Chapter 3*
Teacher Resource Book: *Lesson Plan, Teacher Resources, Reading Summary, Activity Book Answer Key*
Teacher Resource CD-ROM
Assessment Program: *Quiz, pp. 27–28; Teacher and Student Resources, pp. 115–144*
Assessment CD-ROM
Transparencies
The Heinle Newbury House Dictionary/CD-ROM
Web site: http://visions.heinle.com

Objectives

Preview Read the objectives aloud. *Ask: What objectives do you think you will be most interested in learning?*

Use Prior Knowledge

Talk About the Importance of the Sun

1. **Brainstorm** Have students brainstorm in small groups. Have one student record the ideas.
2. **Speculate** *Ask: What would life be like without the sun?*

Use Prior Knowledge

Talk About the Importance of the Sun

With a partner, talk about the importance of the sun. Think about this question:

How does the sun help us?

1. Make a list of ideas on a piece of paper. For example: The sun gives us heat.
2. Share your ideas with the class.
3. Talk about what the world would be like without the sun.

The Sun
1. The sun gives us heat.

MULTI-LEVEL OPTIONS *Build Vocabulary*

Newcomer Write on the board: *We are starving to death because we can't see to find food. Say: We are starving.* Then act out each of the context words. Have students explain the meaning of the sentence with a drawing in their Personal Dictionaries.

Teacher Resource Book: *Personal Dictionary, p. 63*

Beginning Have students act out the meaning of the sentence: *We are starving to death because we can't see to find food.* Then have them put the information about the sentence in their Personal Dictionaries.

Intermediate Have students work in pairs to write a definition of *starving*. Tell them to use a dictionary to check its meaning and add it to their Personal Dictionary.

Advanced To expand their vocabulary, have students look up *starving* in a thesaurus. Ask them to identify any other words that the author could have used to convey the same meaning. Have them add a synonym to their Personal Dictionary

Build Background

Oral Tradition

The reading selection in this chapter is a modern version of an old Vietnamese story. Parts of the story have been passed down from parents to children. Telling stories in this way is called the **oral tradition.**

Storytelling is an important tradition in many cultures. The stories often teach children important ideas and values.

CHINA
MYANMAR
LAOS
South China Sea
THAILAND
CAMBODIA → VIETNAM

Content Connection
Vietnam is a country in Southeast Asia. It has a tropical climate.

Build Vocabulary

Understand Words in Context

Context is the information that surrounds a word. You can use context to help you understand new words.

We are **starving** to <u>death</u> because we <u>can't</u> see to <u>find food</u>.

1. Read or listen to the selection. Use context to help you learn the meanings of new words.

2. Complete a chart like the one here in your Personal Dictionary.

Word	Context Words	What I Think Word Means	Dictionary Definition
starving	death can't find food	very hungry	to feel pain or die from lack of food

Personal Dictionary — The Heinle Newbury House Dictionary

Activity Book p. 57 — Student CD-ROM

Home Connection

Build Vocabulary Ask students to write sentences that use one word from another language. Engage the class in figuring out the meaning of the word from context.

Learning Styles
Linguistic

Build Background Invite students to act out or tell a traditional story they know. Have students discuss what lesson might be learned from the tale. Ask them if the characters, setting, or events are similar to other stories they know.

Build Background

Oral Tradition

1. **Use a map** Have students locate Vietnam on a world map or globe. Have them identify other countries that border Vietnam.

2. **Review** *Ask: What genre was "Coyote"?* (folktale) *A folktale is a story told aloud. It's also part of an oral tradition.*

3. **Content Connection** Vietnam has lush tropical rain forests, with animals such as elephants, deer, bears, tigers, leopards, and monkeys.

Build Vocabulary

Understand Words in Context

Teacher Resource Book: *Personal Dictionary, p. 63*

1. **Use a strategy** Have students look at the first paragraph of Build Background at the top of the page. *Ask: What words help us understand what oral tradition means?* (telling stories; passed down from parents to children)

2. **Reading selection vocabulary** You may want to introduce the glossed words in the reading selection before students begin reading. Key words: *respect, polluted, atmosphere, shivered, pleaded, bargain.* Instruct students to write the words with correct spelling and their definitions in their Personal Dictionaries. Have them pronounce each word and divide it into syllables.

3. **Multi-level options** See MULTI-LEVEL OPTIONS on p. 106.

ASSESS

Have students write a question about Vietnam. Then have them exchange papers with a partner and answer the question.

Text Structure

Fable

Locate derivation Have students locate the derivation of *personification* in the glossary in the Student Handbook or other sources, such as online or CD-ROM dictionaries. Ask students to record the meaning and derivation in their Reading Logs.

Reading Strategy

Identify Main Idea and Details

Teacher Resource Book: *Web, p. 37*

1. **Use a graphic organizer** Have students create a classification web with the middle circle labeled "main idea" and other circles extending from it labeled "details." Tell students they will use their web as they read the story.
2. **Multi-level options** See MULTI-LEVEL OPTIONS below.

Answers

1. Details: housewives hung laundry in front of her face; people dumped garbage under her nose; people burned wood and trash.
2. Long ago people didn't respect the sun, so her father carried her away.

ASSESS

Have students write three features of a fable. (personification, plot, moral)

Text Structure

Fable

In this chapter you will read or listen to the audio recording of the **fable** "Why the Rooster Crows at Sunrise." A fable is a short narrative that teaches a lesson. The distinguishing features of a fable are listed in the chart. Look for the features as you read or listen to "Why the Rooster Crows at Sunrise."

Fable	
Personification	the characters are animals that act like humans
Plot	what happens in the story Beginning ↓ Middle ↓ End
Moral	a lesson taught in a fable

Student
CD-ROM

1. With a partner, talk about a fable you know. What country or region does it come from? Did you learn it by the oral tradition? Does it have a moral? What is it?
2. With a partner, compare and contrast the features of "Why the Rooster Crows at Sunrise" to fables you have heard from other regions and cultures.

Reading Strategy

Identify Main Idea and Details

When you read a story, it is important to understand the **main idea.** The main idea is the most important idea. **Details**—examples, explanations, and events—tell us more about the main idea.

1. Read paragraph 1 of "Why the Rooster Crows at Sunrise." Find three details about how the people treated the sun.

2. What do you think the main idea of this paragraph is?
3. As you read this fable, look for details that help you identify main ideas.

Student
CD-ROM

108 Unit 2 Environment

MULTI-LEVEL OPTIONS *Reading Strategy*

Newcomer Have small groups prepare a Main Idea Table with a horizontal rectangle (the tabletop) and three legs. Then play the audio of paragraph 1. Have different students draw the paragraph's main idea in the tabletop and a supporting detail on each leg.

Beginning Have students work in pairs to draw a Main Idea Table. Read paragraph 1 aloud. Have students write or draw the paragraph's main idea in the tabletop and a supporting detail on each leg.

Intermediate Have students work in pairs to create a Main Idea Table to use with paragraph 1.

Advanced Have students create a Main Idea Table to use as they read paragraph 1.

Why the Rooster
Crows at Sunrise

a fable by Lynette Dyer Vuong

109

Reading Selection Materials

Audio Unit 2, Chapter 3; CD 1, Track 9
Teacher Resource Book: *Reading Summary,*
    pp. 79–80
Transparencies: #5, *Reading Summary*

Suggestions for Using
Reading Summary

- Introduce new vocabulary or cognates.
- Cut the summary into strips, or jumble the sentences on an overhead transparency. Students put the sentences in order.
- Practice the reading strategy.
- Students read aloud or with a partner.
- Students paraphrase the summary.
- Students do a cloze activity.
- Students create a visual or graphic organizer, such as a timeline or storyboard, to illustrate the summary.
- Students paraphrase the summary.

Preview the Selection

1. **Interpret the image** Have students look at the photo. *Ask: What animal do you see?* (a rooster) *What time of day do you think it is?* (morning)
2. **Connect** *Ask: Have you ever seen a rooster? What kind of sound do they make? When do they make this sound? Where might you see a rooster?*

Content Connection
Science

Tell students that animals in fables have some qualities of the actual creatures, as well as some human qualities. Ask them to use pictures, books, and online resources to learn factual information about roosters and their habits. Have students take notes to share with the class. Ask them to save their findings to use in comparing the rooster in the fable with actual roosters.

Learning Styles
Intrapersonal

Ask students to explore their feelings about sunrises. Have them draw or write journal entries about any sunrises they have seen. Ask them to describe how they felt or think they would have felt as they watched the sun come up over the horizon. Have them include in their entries any thoughts they have about why sunrise is an important time of the day for many people.

Read the Selection

1. **Shared reading** Play the audio. Then ask volunteers to join in for several sentences each.
2. **Paraphrase the main idea** Ask students to work in pairs. Have them reread paragraph 1. Have them discuss and paraphrase the main idea. (The sun's father took her away from the polluted earth).
3. **Compare and contrast story with visuals** *Ask: How is the illustration similar to the story?* (shows some of the same events, such as the sun shining, people burning wood, smoke choking the sun) *How are they different?* (The story has more information, such as what characters actually said and other details. The illustration shows characters' feelings and facial expressions, such as the person burning wood.)

Sample Answer to Guide Question
Jade Emperor moved the sun to a safe place away from pollution that would poison her.

See Teacher Edition pp. 434–436 for a list of English-Spanish cognates in the reading selection.

Audio
CD 1, Tr. 9

1 Long ago the sun lived close to the earth. She spent her days just above the treetops, shining down on the fields and houses below. But as day followed day, she grew more and more unhappy with her **lot.** The people who owed her their light and warmth neither gave her thanks nor showed her any **respect.** Housewives hung their laundry in front of her face and dumped their garbage right under her nose. Men and women alike burned wood and trash, choking her with the smoke, until one day her father, Ngoc Hoang—Jade **Emperor,** the king of heaven—took **pity** on her and carried her away from the **polluted atmosphere.**

2 "The people don't deserve you," Jade Emperor said as he set her down in a safe place on the other side of the Eastern Sea. "If I had left you there, they would have poisoned you with their **filth.**"

3 Now day was no different from night. People **shivered** in their houses and could not recognize each other even when they stood side by side.

Identify Main Idea and Details

Find the main idea in paragraph 2.

lot condition in life	**polluted** made dirty
respect thoughtful concern about the importance of something	**atmosphere** the air above Earth
Emperor a title for a ruler	**filth** dirt and garbage
pity the feeling of sorrow or sympathy caused by the suffering or hardships of others	**shivered** shook in the body from cold

110 Unit 2 Environment

MULTI-LEVEL OPTIONS *Read the Selection*

Newcomer Play the audio. Point to relevant parts of the illustrations as the story is being told. *Ask: Were people good to the sun?* (no) *Did the sun go away?* (yes) *Were people unhappy?* (yes) *Did the animals make a plan to get the sun back?* (yes)

Beginning Play the audio. Then do a paired reading. *Ask: How did the sun feel about the way people treated her?* (unhappy) *Where did she go?* (across the Eastern Sea) *Who decided to help get the sun back?* (the rooster, duck, and bluebird)

Intermediate Have students do a paired reading. *Ask: How did people treat the sun?* (They were ungrateful and disrespectful.) *How did the Emperor solve the problem?* (He took her away.) *How did people react? Why?* (They were upset because they missed her warmth and light.) *How did the animals react?* (They went to talk to the sun.)

Advanced Have students read the selection silently. *Ask: Why do you think people treated the sun as they did?* (They thought she would always be there.) *What is another effect people might have felt from the sun being gone?* (no seasons) *How did the animals show a spirit of cooperation?* (Each figured out how he or she could help with the plan.)

Read the Selection

1. **Summarize** Play the audio. *Ask: What was happening to the sun when the fable started?* (People were polluting the air and were not showing respect.) *What did Jade Emperor do?* (He took her to the other side of the sea.) *What happened when there was no sun?* (It was dark; people and animals could not find food.) *What did some animals decide to do?* (They decided to persuade the sun to return.) *Can you summarize the fable so far?*

2. **Choral reading** Divide the class into two groups. Have the groups read alternate paragraphs aloud as you lead.

3. **Identify details** Have students answer the guide question. Then have volunteers find the details relating to the main idea. Write the details on the board.

4. **Multi-level options** See MULTI-LEVEL OPTIONS on p. 110.

Sample Answer to Guide Question
Main idea: The rooster, duck, and bluebird decide to go and talk with the sun in person. Details: The rooster will appeal to her in person; he will do the talking. The bluebird will lead the way. The duck will carry the rooster on his back.

Identify Main Idea and Details

What is the main idea of paragraphs 5 to 10? What are the details that helped you find the main idea?

4   In the forest the animals could not see to hunt, and day by day they grew hungrier. At last they gathered to discuss the situation.

5   The rooster spoke first. "If only we could go to the sun and **appeal** to her in person, perhaps she would take pity on us and give us a little light."

6   The duck nodded. "We could try. If only we knew where to find her."

7   "I've heard she lives across the Eastern Sea," the bluebird **chirped**. "I'd be willing to lead you there if you'd do the talking."

8   "I'd do the talking," the rooster offered, "if I had a way to get there. But you know I can't swim. How could I get across the Eastern Sea?"

9   The duck smiled. "On my back, of course. No one's a better swimmer than I am."

---

appeal ask for help   **chirped** made a high, short, sharp sound

Chapter 3 Why the Rooster Crows at Sunrise **111**

 Punctuation

Quotation marks for dialogue

Call attention to the first sentence in paragraph 7. *Say: You can tell this sentence is dialogue because it has quotation marks around it. Dialogue is the exact words a character says.* Ask a volunteer to find and read aloud the rest of the dialogue in paragraph 7.

   Apply Have students work in pairs to find two more examples of dialogue in paragraphs 4–10. Tell them to practice and

present their dialogues. Remind them that they should only say the words inside the quotation marks.

Read the Selection

1. **Shared reading** Play the audio. Have volunteers join in to read the parts of narrator, sun, rooster, duck, and bluebird. Remind students to read with expression.

2. **Check comprehension** Ask questions to check general comprehension. *Ask: Why doesn't the sun want to come back?* (She had to leave for her health; the air was very polluted.) *What does the sun agree to do?* (She agrees to shine for a few hours every day.)

3. **Identify main idea and details** Discuss the guide questions in small groups. Have students report their answers to the class.

Sample Answer to Guide Question

Main Idea: She doesn't want to go back because her life was in danger. Details: She had to leave for her health's sake and because of the polluted atmosphere.

10   The three friends set off at once, the bluebird leading the way and the rooster riding on the duck's back. At last they reached the other side of the sea, where they found the sun **taking her ease.**

11   "Please come back, sister sun," they begged as they told her of the **plight** the world was in. "Come back and stay with us the way you did before."

> **Identify Main Idea and Details**
>
> What is the main idea of paragraph 12? What details tell you this?

12   But the sun shook her head. "How can you ask me to come back? You know I had to leave for my health's sake. Why, my very life was in danger in that polluted atmosphere."

13   "We are starving to death because we can't see to find food. Won't you take pity on us and give us a little light before we all die?" the rooster **pleaded.**

14   The sun was silent for a long moment. Finally she **sighed.** "I know you must be **desperate,** or you wouldn't have come all this way to see me." She sighed again. "I can't live with you as I used to; but if you'll call me when you need light, I'll come and shine for you for a few hours."

---

taking her ease   relaxing, being comfortable
plight   a difficult situation
pleaded   requested urgently

sighed   let out air from the mouth from emotion or being tired
desperate   in immediate, very strong need

112   Unit 2   Environment

MULTI-LEVEL OPTIONS *Read the Selection*

Newcomer *Ask: Did the sun agree to shine all the time?* (no) *Did she agree to shine some every day?* (yes) *Did the rooster agree to wake the sun in the morning?* (yes) *Did everyone do what he or she promised?* (yes)

Beginning *Ask: When did the sun agree to shine?* (a few hours a day) *Who agreed to wake her?* (rooster) *Who agreed to help?* (bluebird) *How do you think everyone felt at the end of the story?* (happy)

Intermediate *Ask: How did the sun feel at first about coming back? Why?* (She didn't want to return because of the pollution.) *How did the sun's solution take care of herself and others?* (She shines enough to help them but not to hurt herself.) *How does the end of the story show something that really happens?* (Roosters really crow in the morning.)

Advanced *Ask: When the sun agreed to shine for a few hours, what did she mean?* (that she would shine during the day and leave at night) *What part of this story reflects modern times? Explain.* (We still harm nature sometimes by polluting the environment.)

15   The rooster nodded eagerly. "My voice is loud, so I'll do the calling. When you hear me **crowing,** you'll know it's time to wake up and get ready to cross the sea."

16   "I can help too." The bluebird stepped forward. "My voice may not be as loud as brother rooster's; but once he wakes you, you'll be able to hear me, and you'll know it's time to leave your home and start your journey."

17   The sun agreed. And from then on, the sun, the rooster, and the bluebird have kept their **bargain.** When the rooster crows, the sun knows it's time to get ready for her day's work; and just as the birds begin their chirping, she appears over the eastern **horizon.**

Identify Main Idea and Details

What is the main idea of this fable?

---

crowing making a loud cry
bargain an agreement

horizon the place in one's view where the earth's surface forms a line with the sky

---

About the Author

Lynette Dyer Vuong (born 1938)

Lynette Dyer Vuong grew up in the state of Michigan. When she was seven years old, she discovered her love of writing. She began to write about adventures in ancient lands. After high school, she lived in Vietnam for 13 years. While in Vietnam, Dyer Vuong spent much time in bookstores exploring Vietnamese stories. The fable "Why the Rooster Crows at Sunrise" is a story she adapted from the original. It is included in a collection of other stories from Vietnam.

➤ Why do you think the author wrote "Why the Rooster Crows at Sunrise"? To inform? To entertain? To teach?

Chapter 3 Why the Rooster Crows at Sunrise   **113**

Read the Selection

1. **Use verbal and non-verbal cuing strategies** *Say: A story is more interesting when we can imagine how a character says something or what they do while they talk. Look at paragraph 12. 'The sun shook her head.'* Model shaking your head "No." Locate the other quotations and model how they can be said and acted out. *(pleaded, sighed, nodded, stepped forward)* Ask volunteers to read paragraphs 11–16 with expression.
2. **Multi-level options** See MULTI-LEVEL OPTIONS on p. 112.

Sample Answer to Guide Question
Nature is important to people and we should treat it with respect.

About the Author

1. **Analyze facts** Read the paragraph aloud. *Ask: Where did the author grow up?* (Michigan) *When did she live in Vietnam?* (after high school) *How long did she live there?* (13 years)
2. **Discuss author's intention** Discuss why the author wrote the fable.

Across Selections

▌ Teacher Resource Book: *Venn Diagram, p. 35*

Use a graphic organizer Have students use a Venn diagram to compare and contrast the folktale *"Coyote"* with this fable. (Compare: stories passed down through generations; told orally; animals are personified; the setting is in nature. Main contrast: A fable has a moral.)

Spelling, Punctuation, Capitalization

After the Reading Comprehension section, students will practice spelling, punctuation, and capitalization in the Activity Book.

❜ Punctuation

Semicolons

Direct students to the third sentence in paragraph 16. *Say: The mark after* rooster's *is a semicolon. Are the parts of the sentence before and after the semicolon both complete thoughts?* (yes) *What mark could have been used instead?* (period) Point out that *but* does not start with a capital letter. Tell students that two related and complete ideas can be joined with a semicolon. Ask students to find another example in paragraph 17. (work;)

Evaluate Your Reading Strategy

Identify Main Idea and Details *Say: You have practiced an important reading strategy. Now you can decide how well you have done. Does this statement describe how you read?*

When I read, I look for the main idea. When I recognize important details, I can understand the main idea better.

Beyond the Reading

Reading Comprehension

Question-Answer Relationships

Sample Answers
1. The sun lived close to the earth.
2. The sun's father took her to a safe place, the other side of the Eastern Sea.
3. the rooster, duck, and bluebird
4. because people didn't give her thanks or respect; because pollution was hurting her health
5. The sun agreed to return to earth a few hours a day; the rooster agreed to crow to wake her up; and the bluebird agreed to sing so she would know when to start her journey.
6. They learned that they needed the sun for light, heat, and food; they learned that they needed to treat nature with respect.
7. Perhaps people were more careful about polluting the atmosphere.
8. Illustrations can show things that are imaginary, but photos can only show things that are real. Since the fable includes some things that are imaginary, such as the sun and animals acting like people, illustrations were used. The realistic style and the expressions on the characters' faces help me to visualize the story and understand it better.
9. People tell fables to understand and explain the natural world.

Build Reading Fluency

Read Silently

Assessment Program: *Reading Fluency Chart, p. 116*

When students have completed the reading fluency activity, record their progress in the Reading Fluency Chart.

Reading Comprehension

Question-Answer Relationships (QAR)

"Right There" Questions
1. **Recall Facts** Where did the sun live long ago?
2. **Recall Facts** Where did the sun's father take her?
3. **Recall Facts** What characters gathered to discuss their problem of not having daylight?

"Think and Search" Questions
4. **Analyze Causes and Effects** Why did the sun's father take her away from the earth?
5. **Summarize** Summarize the bargain that the rooster, the duck, and the bluebird made with the sun.

"Author and You" Questions
6. **Identify the Main Idea** What lesson do you think the characters learned after the sun left?

7. **Draw Conclusions** How do you think life on the earth changed after the sun agreed to shine for a few hours?
8. **Analyze Illustrations** Why do you think illustrations are used with the fable instead of photos? How do the style (look and feel) and elements (parts) of the illustrations add to the effect of the fable?

"On Your Own" Question
9. **Make Inferences** Why do you think people tell fables such as "Why the Rooster Crows at Sunrise"?

Activity Book
p. 58

Student
CD-ROM

Build Reading Fluency

Read Silently

Reading silently is good practice. It helps you learn to read faster. An effective reader reads silently for longer periods of time.

1. Listen to the audio recording of paragraph 1, page 110.
2. Listen to the chunks of words as you follow along.
3. Reread paragraph 1 silently two times.
4. Your teacher will time your second reading.
5. Raise your hand when you are done.
6. Record your timing.

MULTI-LEVEL OPTIONS *Elements of Literature*

Newcomer Ask volunteers to act out the actions of one of the animal characters in the fable. Have the class determine which character is being portrayed.

Beginning Have students look through picture books that include fanciful animal characters. Have them identify realistic and human qualities of these creatures.

Intermediate Ask students to use one of the animals or the sun as the subject of their diagrams. When this task is complete, have students reread paragraphs 1 and 2. *Say: The author doesn't tell much about Jade Emperor. What do you think the sun's father looks like? What real life and personified qualities do you imagine him having?*

Advanced Discuss other animals, such as an owl or a group of fireflies, that could be added to the story. Have students brainstorm how these characters might be personified.

Listen, Speak, Interact

Perform a Skit

Imagine that the sun stopped rising in our world today. Create a three-minute **skit** (a short play) about the world without the sun.

1. With two or three other students, brainstorm an idea.
2. Write your skit. Include speaking roles for everyone in the group.
3. Practice your skit. You may use props or costumes.
4. Present your skit to the class.
5. Evaluate each skit. Could you hear all the speakers? Was the skit believable?

Elements of Literature

Review Personification

In this chapter, you learned that **personification** is one feature of a fable. A writer using personification gives human thoughts, feelings, and actions to animals or things.

1. Review the fable. How is each character like a human?
2. How is each character *not* like a human?
3. Copy the chart in your Reading Log. Choose one character from the fable. In the left column, write how the character is like a human. In the right column, write how the character is not like a human.

Fable Character: _____	
Like a Human	**Not Like a Human**

Reading Log   Activity Book   Student
                   p. 59   CD-ROM

Chapter 3 Why the Rooster Crows at Sunrise   **115**

Content Connection
Science

Have students review some modern challenges related to the environment. For instance, they may study simple explanations and diagrams concerning the destruction of the ozone layer or the greenhouse effect in science texts or other nonfiction resources.

Learning Styles
Musical

Point out that many songs for young children personify animals. Ask students to list songs that they know or heard when they were young that personify animals. ("The Ants Go Marching," "Baa Baa Black Sheep," "A Frog Went A-Courtin' ") Have students identify the personified traits.

UNIT 2 • CHAPTER 3
Beyond the Reading

Listen, Speak, Interact

Perform a Skit

1. **Group work** Have students write a script of their skits. Instruct them to include directions for using props, moving around, or speaking with special emphasis.
2. **Present a dramatization** Have students perform their skits for the class. Ask them to use props or create background scenery. After each skit, ask the class what they liked about it.
3. **Newcomers** Help this group create a script for a section of the fable. Assign students various roles. Then play the audio as they read aloud and act out their parts.

Elements of Literature

Review Personification

1. **Find examples** Direct students to paragraph 1. Have them identify phrases that personify the sun or her father. (spent her days; she grew unhappy; in front of her face/took pity on her; he carried her away) Then have students choose their characters and work in groups to complete the chart.
2. **Multi-level options** See MULTI-LEVEL OPTIONS on p. 114.

Answers
1. The sun can talk, move like a human, and reason. The rooster, duck, and bluebird can all talk with each other.
2. They are not like humans because they still can make animal sounds, and they don't really do human things like hang laundry, burn wood, pollute the environment, etc.

ASSESS

Have students explain how one of the animals in the story is personified.

Chapter 3 / Beyond the Reading   **115**

Word Study

Learn About Words with Multiple Meanings

1. **Locate pronunciation** Have students locate the pronunciation of *homonym* in the glossary in the Student Handbook or other sources, such as online or CD-ROM dictionaries.
2. **Identify homonyms** Have students add other homonyms from the story to their Personal Dictionaries. (paragraph 6—duck; paragraph 13—light; paragraph 14—long)

Answers
2. lot (one's condition in life; fate), safe (free from harm; protected)

Grammar Focus

Identify Object Pronouns

Identify object pronouns Point out that object pronouns are never the subject of sentences. Explain that subject pronouns have object pronoun forms. (I/me, she/her, we/us) *You* and *it* keep the same form.

Answers
1. Jade Emperor took *her* away.
2. In the end, the sun helped *them.*

ASSESS

Have students find three object pronouns in paragraphs 13 and 14 (me, us, you).

Word Study

Learn About Words with Multiple Meanings

Homonyms are words that are pronounced the same and may be spelled the same, but they have different meanings.

> The duck smiled, "On my **back,** of course."

> "Come **back** and stay with us the way you did before."

1. With a partner, reread paragraphs 1 and 2. Find the words *lot* and *safe.*
2. In a dictionary, find the definition that goes with the word as it is used.

Paragraph	Homonyms	Meanings
9	back	the top of an animal
1	lot	
2	safe	

3. Copy the chart in your Personal Dictionary. Write the meanings.

Personal Dictionary

The Heinle Newbury House Dictionary

Activity Book p. 60

Student CD-ROM

Grammar Focus

Identify Object Pronouns

You know that nouns and pronouns can be used as subjects of sentences. The subject pronouns are *I, you, he, she, it, we,* and *they.*

Noun	**Pronoun**
The animals went to the sun.	They asked her to come back.

Many sentences also have **objects.** The subject of a sentence does something to the object.

Subject	**Object**
The people choked	the sun with smoke.

Pronouns can also be used as **objects** in sentences. The object pronouns are *me, you, him, her, it, us,* and *them.*

Subject	**Object**
The people choked	her with smoke.

Use object pronouns in place of the underlined nouns below. Choose the appropriate pronouns and spell them correctly.

1. Jade Emperor took his daughter away.
2. In the end, the sun helped the animals.

Activity Book pp. 61–62

Student Handbook

Student CD-ROM

116 Unit 2 Environment

MULTI-LEVEL OPTIONS *From Reading to Writing*

Newcomer Have students decide on a lesson to teach. Then tell them to agree on characters and a setting. Finally, help them brainstorm a sequence of events that lead to the lesson. Tell students to create pictures for the beginning, middle, and end of their fable.

Beginning Use the planning diagram to create a class language experience fable. Write the lesson the students wish the fable to teach. Record words and phrases in the character boxes to describe the human qualities of animal characters. Use a list of numbered events to show how the fable will develop. Then have students do a choral reading of their fable.

Intermediate After each fable is presented to the class, ask the audience to summarize the lesson they learned. Have the writers state whether the summaries reflect what they intended the lesson of the story to be.

Advanced After groups have created first drafts, ask each group to meet with another for peer response. Have groups react to characters, setting, plot, and moral. Then have responders identify sentences containing object pronouns and check each instance to be sure the correct pronoun has been used.

From Reading to Writing

Write a Fable

In a small group, write a fable. Your fable should teach a lesson, or a moral; for example, "Studying is important" or "We should take care of Earth."

1. Copy the diagram below to help you get started. Use it to organize your ideas.

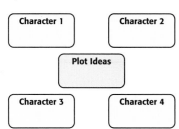

2. Create characters that act like humans. Use pronouns and object pronouns correctly in your fable to tell about your characters.
3. Think of main ideas and give details to explain them.
4. Be sure your fable has a beginning, a middle, and an end.
5. Draw a picture for your fable.
6. Capitalize and punctuate your fable correctly to strengthen its meaning.
7. Review and edit your fable to publish and share with your class and others.

Activity Book   Student
p. 63   Handbook

Across Content Areas

Learn About Conservation

Conservation is the protection of the environment. Look at these words related to *conservation.*

1. To **conserve** the environment is to protect it from pollution.
2. A person who works to conserve the environment is a **conservationist.**
3. **Conservation** is the act of protecting the environment.

Complete these sentences with *conserve, conservationist,* and *conservation.*

People still pollute the environment. A _____ tells people how they can help the environment. For example, people can _____ the environment by not throwing their garbage on the ground. _____ is important because we need a clean, healthy place to live.

Activity Book
p. 64

Reteach and Reassess

Text Structure Read one of Aesop's fables or another fable to students. Have them use a chart such as the one on p. 108 to identify the features of the fable.

Reading Strategy Have students use their responses to guide questions on main idea and details to draw or write a summary of the fable in this chapter.

Elements of Literature Instruct students to draw or describe a personification of something from nature other than an animal.

For example, students may focus on the wind, the moon, or a tree.

Reassess Have students write a short paragraph that shows the personification of an animal or other part of nature. Have them include a sentence of dialogue and remind them to use quotation marks.

From Reading to Writing

Write a Fable

1. **Use prior knowledge** *Ask: Do you know any fables with animals that you could tell the class?*
2. **Brainstorm** Together with the class, think of a lesson or moral for a fable, a simple plot, and some characters. Discuss different possibilities for the story.
3. **Write a fable** Have students copy the diagram and fill it in with ideas for the fable. It can be similar to or different from the class fable. After students have written their stories and illustrated them, have them read their stories to the class.
4. **Multi-level options** See MULTI-LEVEL OPTIONS on p. 116.

Across Content Areas: Science

Learn About Conservation

1. **Define terms** Have a student read the explanation and sentences. Ask them to copy and complete the sentences.
2. **Make a conservation poster** Have small groups brainstorm a list of ways to conserve the classroom, school, or community environment. Make a poster of students' suggestions. Display the poster in the classroom or school.

Answers
conservationist, conserve, Conservation

 **ASSESS**

Have students write a definition of a fable.

CHAPTER
4

Gonzalo

an excerpt from a novel
by Paul Fleischman

Chapter Materials

Activity Book: *pp. 65–72*
Audio: *Unit 2, Chapter 4; CD 1, Track 10*
Student Handbook
Student CD-ROM: *Unit 2, Chapter 4*
Teacher Resource Book: *Lesson Plan, Teacher Resources, Reading Summary, Activity Book Answer Key*
Teacher Resource CD-ROM
Assessment Program: *Quiz, pp. 29–30; Teacher and Student Resources, pp. 115–144*
Assessment CD-ROM
Transparencies
The Heinle Newbury House Dictionary/CD-ROM
Web site: http://visions.heinle.com

Objectives

Preview Have students read the objectives in pairs. *Ask: What objectives do you know something about?*

Use Prior Knowledge

Discuss Learning a New Language

Connect to personal experience Do you learn any English by watching TV? What helps you learn conversation? What helps you learn vocabulary?

Answers
2. *Examples:* take a class, study from a book, spend time with speakers of the language, listen to songs, read magazines, etc.

Objectives

Reading Draw conclusions as you read narrative fiction.

Listening and Speaking Interpret nonverbal communication.

Grammar Recognize and use comparative adjectives.

Writing Write narrative fiction.

Content Science: Learn about plants.

Use Prior Knowledge

Discuss Learning a New Language

In this chapter's reading selection, the main character learns English by watching television. How else can people learn a new language?

1. With a partner, copy the chart on a piece of paper.
2. List your ideas in your chart. Circle the idea that you think is best.
3. Share your ideas with the class.

How to Learn a New Language
1. watch television

118   Unit 2   Environment

MULTI-LEVEL OPTIONS *Build Vocabulary*

Newcomer Have students draw a rectangle divided in half with a vertical line. Tell them to copy the word *janitor* on the left. After you have acted out and discussed the meaning of the word, have students illustrate its meaning on the right. Instruct students to use this format for other words from the selection.

Beginning Have students make Word Rectangles divided into thirds. Instruct them to use these to record vocabulary from the selection, drawings to help them remember meanings, and synonyms for the words.

Intermediate After students have created several Word Squares, have pairs use them to play a game. One student will select two Word Squares from his/her partner's Personal Dictionary. The owner of the dictionary must use both words in a meaningful sentence.

Advanced Have students change the first box heading of their word square from *Word* to *Word/Synonym*. Direct students to add a synonym each time they create a word square.

Build Background

Guatemala

The characters in "Gonzalo" come from Guatemala, a country in Central America. Spanish is the official language of Guatemala, but native people speak about 20 different languages. Many Guatemalans are farmers. They grow sugarcane, cotton, coffee, corn, and bananas.

Content Connection

The Mayan people make up about half the population of Guatemala. Their culture is over 1,500 years old.

Build Vocabulary

Use Word Squares to Remember Meanings

Making **word squares** can help you remember the meanings of new words. Look at this example:

Word	Symbol
equation	2 + 2 = 4
Meaning	**Sentence**
math statement that says two amounts are equal	I am learning about equations in math.

1. Create two word squares. Fill in the squares for the underlined words in these sentences.
   a. He could not sit out in the plaza.
   b. He was the janitor at my school.
2. Use a dictionary to find the meanings.
3. As you read "Gonzalo," make word squares for other words that you want to remember.

The Heinle Newbury House Dictionary | Activity Book p. 65 | Student CD-ROM

Chapter 4 Gonzalo **119**

Community Connection

Build Vocabulary Work with students to make a two-column chart headed *Gonzalo's Community* and *Our Community*. Have students preview the glossed words. Work with them to list setting words, such as *gateway, bodega, pawnshop, manhole,* and *plaza* under *Gonzalo's Community*. Discuss which words may also describe things that are in their community and have them write *no* or *yes* with an example.

Learning Styles
Visual

Build Background Tell students that about one-half of Guatemalans have Mayan Indian ancestors and the other half are from mixed Spanish and Native American backgrounds. Have students use pictures, books, and the Internet to learn about the languages, dress, and way of life of both groups. Tell students to create diagrams or illustrations showing similarities and differences. Display the results for students to use as they read.

Build Background

Guatemala

1. **Use prior knowledge** *Ask: Do you know what sugarcane is? Cotton? What kind of climate do you think they have in Guatemala?* (hot, tropical)
2. **Use a map** Have students point to the countries in Central America on the map as you name them.
3. **Content Connection** Guatemala was the center of the ancient Mayan civilization, and many pyramids and monuments have been excavated there.

Build Vocabulary

Use Word Squares to Remember Meanings

Teacher Resource Book: *Personal Dictionary, p. 63*

1. **Use a dictionary** Have students look up the two definitions and read them to the class.
2. **Reading selection vocabulary** You may want to introduce the glossed words in the reading selection before students begin reading. Key words: *kindergartner, landlady, mumbles, wandered, baby-sit, fainted, enemies.* Instruct students to write the words with correct spelling and their definitions in their Personal Dictionaries. Have them pronounce each word and divide it into syllables.
3. **Multi-level options** See MULTI-LEVEL OPTIONS on p. 118.

Answers
Examples: **a.** plaza/picture of a town center/city square or open area/There are many plazas in Mexican towns. **b.** janitor/picture of a broom/person who cleans public areas/Our school janitors work hard.

 **ASSESS**

Say: Write two ways you are learning English.

Text Structure

Narrative Fiction

1. **Make a chart** Have students make a four-column chart headed *details, plot, main problem, solution* and fill it in as they read.
2. **Locate derivation** Have students locate the derivation of *narrator* in the glossary in the Student Handbook or other sources, such as online or CD-ROM dictionaries.

Reading Strategy

Draw Conclusions

1. **Draw conclusions** Direct students to the map on p. 119. Ask them to work in pairs to draw a conclusion about the countries or bodies of water on the map. (Belize and El Salvador are the only Central American countries that do not touch both the Pacific Ocean and the Caribbean Sea. Nicaragua is the largest Central American country.)
2. **Multi-level options** See MULTI-LEVEL OPTIONS below.

ASSESS

Write on the board: *I went to bed late last night. I got up at 5 A.M.* **Ask:** *What conclusion can you draw?* (I didn't sleep very much last night; I am very tired and sleepy today.)

Text Structure

Narrative Fiction

"Gonzalo" is an example of **narrative fiction.** The chart shows the features of narrative fiction.

As you read "Gonzalo," identify the point of view. Also, look for and analyze the story's details, plot, main problem, and how the characters resolve it.

Narrative Fiction	
Structure	has a beginning, a middle, and an end
Narrator's Point of View	first person—narrator is a person in the story
	third person—narrator is not a person in the story
Details	gives information about characters and events to help readers connect with the story
Plot	events in the story
Problem and Solution	tells how characters resolve a problem

Student CD-ROM

Reading Strategy

Draw Conclusions

You **draw conclusions** when you decide that something is true, or not true, after thinking carefully about all the facts. For example:

You read: Guatemala and Belize are the only countries in Central America that have a border with Mexico.

Conclusion: El Salvador does not have a border with Mexico.

Drawing conclusions will help you understand and remember what you read.

As you read or listen to "Gonzalo," use information in the text to draw conclusions about the characters. Compare your conclusions with a partner.

Student CD-ROM

120 Unit 2 Environment

MULTI-LEVEL OPTIONS *Reading Strategy*

Newcomer Engage students in drawing conclusions about everyday situations. Look uncomfortable, fan yourself with a piece of paper, and open the window. Use gestures as you *ask: Do I feel hot?* (yes) Get out a paper and pencil and sit down at a desk. *Ask: What will I do?* (write)

Beginning Have students practice the skill of drawing conclusions before applying the skill to the story. Pick up a student's homework. Look at it and smile. Pat the student on the back. *Ask: What kind of work is this?* (good) *How do you know?* Tell students to use clues to decide about story events.

Intermediate Tell students that they can draw conclusions from what they read *and* from what they see. Preview the picture on p. 121. *Ask: What conclusion can you draw about the boy and the man?* (They are related; they know each other well.) Tell students that they will have a chance to draw other conclusions about the boy from the text.

Advanced Have students draw four wheels with hubs and spokes. Ask them to write one of the following above each wheel: *boy, father, mother, uncle.* Tell students to jot down clues to the traits and motivation of each character on the spokes as they read. Then ask them to write conclusions about the characters in the hubs.

GONZALO

an excerpt from a novel
by Paul Fleischman

121

Reading Selection Materials

Audio: *Unit 2, Chapter 4; CD 1, Track 10*
Teacher Resource Book: *Reading Summary,*
pp. 81–82
Transparencies: #5, *Reading Summary*

Suggestions for Using
Reading Summary

• Introduce new vocabulary or cognates.
• Cut the summary into strips, or jumble the
  sentences on an overhead transparency.
  Students put the sentences in order.
• Practice the reading strategy.
• Students read aloud or with a partner.
• Students paraphrase the summary.
• Students do a cloze activity.
• Students create a visual or graphic
  organizer, such as a timeline or storyboard,
  to illustrate the summary.
• Students paraphrase the summary.

Preview the Selection

1. **Interpret the image** Have students look at
   the illustration. *Ask: Who do you think these
   people are? Where are they going? Do you
   think the older man knows the way? What
   culture do you think they could be from?*
2. **Discuss message of medium** *Ask: Is this
   a very realistic illustration? What kinds of
   colors are used? What feelings do those
   colors give you?*
3. **Connect** Remind students that the theme of
   this unit is the environment. *Ask: Is this an
   urban or country environment? What kind of
   climate does it have? How is it similar to or
   different from our environment?*

 **Home
Connection**

Have students interview family members
about their memories of coming to this
country. Suggest questions such as: *What
seemed the strangest to you? What was the
most exciting? What was the hardest thing to
learn? Who helped you? What was the most
helpful thing anyone did?* Provide time for
students to share responses.

Learning Styles
Natural

Take a walk around the schoolyard or the
surrounding neighborhood. *Ask: What things
seemed strange or confusing to you at first?
What might seem that way to someone else
coming to our community from another
country?* If it is not possible to take a walk in
the neighborhood, have students draw a
map of the area and use it to point out
things that might be unfamiliar to a
newcomer.

Read the Selection

1. **Read a prologue** Remind students they read prologues for "Coyote" and "Sadako and the Thousand Paper Cranes." Ask them the purpose of a prologue. (to introduce a selection)

2. **Reciprocal reading** Play the audio. Have students each write one or two questions. Then have students read aloud in groups and ask each other questions as they read.

3. **Recognize style** *Say: Gonzalo has a sense of humor; he's funny. Can you find some funny things he says?* (It's Garcia's Equation. Cartoons make you smart. His English was worse than a kindergartner's.)

4. **Relate to personal experience** *Ask: Do you have any adult relatives who have a hard time speaking English? Why is it hard for them to learn?*

Sample Answer to Guide Question
He worked all day with people who spoke Spanish; he had no chance to hear or speak English.

See Teacher Edition pp. 434–436 for a list of English-Spanish cognates in the reading selection.

Audio
CD 1, Tr. 10

Prologue

The narrator of the story is named Gonzalo Garcia. He lives in a Spanish-speaking neighborhood in a city in the United States.

1   The older you are, the younger you get when you move to the United States.

2   They don't teach you that equation in school. Big Brain, Mr. Smoltz, my eighth-grade math teacher, hasn't even heard of it. It's not in *Gateway to Algebra*. It's Garcia's Equation. I'm the Garcia.

3   Two years after my father and I moved here from Guatemala I could speak English. I learned it on the playground and watching lots of TV. Don't believe what people say—cartoons make you *smart*. But my father, he worked all day in a kitchen with **Mexicans** and **Salvadorans**. His English was worse than a **kindergartner's**. He would only buy food at the *bodega* down the block.

> **Draw Conclusions**
>
> Why was the father's English "worse than a kindergartner's"?

gateway a passage, something that helps you reach a goal
algebra a form of math
Mexicans people from the country of Mexico
Salvadorans people from the country of El Salvador

kindergartner a four- or five-year-old child in kindergarten, or classes before the first grade of school
bodega a store where the owners speak Spanish

122   Unit 2   Environment

MULTI-LEVEL OPTIONS *Read the Selection*

Newcomer Read the story aloud. Use facial expressions and gestures to aid student comprehension. *Ask: Was Gonzalo born in the United States?* (no) *Did he learn English fast when he moved here?* (yes) *Did adults in his family learn fast?* (no)

Beginning Read the Reading Summary. Then read the story aloud. *Ask: Where is the Gonzalo's homeland?* (Guatemala) *When did he come to the United States?* (two years ago) *Who in the family learned English fast?* (Gonzalo) *Who learned slowly?* (his father and uncle)

Intermediate Have students do a paired reading. *Ask: How did Gonzalo learn English?* (from TV and friends) *What did his father do when he needed to speak English and couldn't?* (He had his son talk to people for him.) *What did Tio Juan do when he needed to speak English and couldn't?* (He stayed home and talked to himself.)

Advanced Have students read silently. *Ask: Why did the boy learn English faster than his father?* (He spent time with people who spoke English. His father worked with people who spoke Spanish.) *What does the first sentence on p. 122 mean?* (The adults had to rely on Gonzalo the way children usually rely on adults.)

Outside of there he lowered his eyes and tried to get by on **mumbles** and smiles. He didn't want strangers to hear his mistakes. So he used me to make phone calls and to talk to the **landlady** and to buy things in stores where you had to use English. He got younger. I got older.

4   Then my younger brothers and mother and **Tío** Juan, her uncle, came north and joined us. Tío Juan was the oldest man in his **pueblo.** But here he became a little baby. He'd been a farmer, but here he couldn't work. He couldn't sit out in the plaza and talk—there *aren't* any plazas here, and if you sit out in public some gang driving by might use you for **target practice.** He couldn't understand TV. So he **wandered** around the apartment all day, in and out of rooms, talking to himself, just like a kid in **diapers.**

> ### Draw Conclusions
>
> What conclusion can you make about Tío Juan? What information helped you draw this conclusion?

---

mumbles   quiet and unclear words

landlady   a woman who owns a building where people rent apartments

tío   the Spanish word for "uncle"

pueblo   the Spanish word for "village"

target practice   when people practice shooting at something

wandered   walked around without trying to get someplace

diapers   what babies wear to cover the area between the legs

Chapter 4   Gonzalo   **123**

Read the Selection

1. **Silent reading** Read or play the audio. Then give students time to read it silently.
2. **Point of view** Ask: *Who is telling the story?* (Gonzalo) *What is the point of view?* (first person)
3. **Identify characters** Ask: *Who are the main characters in the story so far?* (Gonzalo, his father, and Tío Juan) *Who are the other people in Gonzalo's family?* (his mother and younger brothers)
4. **Multi-level options** See MULTI-LEVEL OPTIONS on p. 122.

Sample Answer to Guide Question
He used to be respected ("oldest man in his pueblo"). He wasn't happy here because he had no place to go and no one to talk with. ("wandered around the apartment . . . talking to himself")

A Capitalization

Titles of people and books, names of countries, peoples, languages

Say: Titles of people begin with capital letters. Have students find *Mr. Smoltz* in paragraph 2. *Ask: Why is the -m capitalized?* (title) *Important words in titles of books also begin with capitals. Which words are capitalized in Gonzalo's math book in paragraph 2?* (Gateway, Algebra) *The names of countries, people who live in them, and the languages they speak also begin with capitals.* Point out *United States* (paragraph 1), *Mexican,* and *English* (paragraph 3).

Apply Write on the board: *mr. garcia spoke spanish in guatemala. Now he lives in the united states with mrs. garcia. The book, beginning english, can help tio juan learn a new language.*

Instruct students to rewrite these sentences with the proper capitalization. Have them share their answers in pairs.

Read the Selection

1. **Shared reading** Play the audio. Then have volunteers join in for sections of the story.
2. **Check comprehension** Assign paragraphs 5, 6, and 7 to three different groups. Write on the board: *Who, What, Where, How, Why.* *Say: Write 3 or 4 questions about your paragraph.* Then have students pass their questions to another group and answer each other's questions.

Sample Answer to Guide Question

His pueblo probably didn't have a beauty parlor. Tío Juan stared as if he had never seen a woman with a drier over her head before.

Draw Conclusions

What conclusion can you make about the number of beauty parlors in Tío Juan's pueblo? How do you know?

5   One morning he wandered outside and down the street. My mother **practically fainted.** He doesn't speak Spanish, just an Indian language. I finally found him standing in front of the **beauty parlor,** staring through the glass at a woman with a **drier** over her head. He must have wondered what weird planet he'd moved to. I led him home, holding his hand, the way you would with a three-year-old. Since then I'm supposed to **baby-sit** him after school.

6   One afternoon I was watching TV, getting smart on *The Brady Bunch.* Suddenly I looked up. He was gone. I checked the halls on all five floors of the apartment house. I ran to the street. He wasn't in the *bodega* or the **pawnshop.** I called his name, imagining my mother's face when she found out he'd fallen through a **manhole** or been run over. I turned the corner, looking for the white

---

practically nearly, almost
fainted fell over unconscious
beauty parlor a place to get your hair cut and fingernails polished
drier a machine that sits over your head and dries your hair
baby-sit watch a child while the parents are away

The Brady Bunch a U.S. television show popular in the 1970s
pawnshop a business that lends people money in exchange for holding their personal valuables for a short time
manhole a hole in the street used to reach water pipes and telephone wires

124   Unit 2 Environment

MULTI-LEVEL OPTIONS *Read the Selection*

Newcomer *Ask: Was Gonzalo watching television?* (yes) *Did he know that his uncle went out?* (no) *Was Gonzalo worried about his uncle?* (yes) *Was the uncle in a garden?* (yes)

Beginning *Ask: Who went out when Gonzalo was watching television?* (his uncle) *Where did he look for his uncle?* (in the bodega and in the pawnshop) *What helped Gonzalo find his uncle?* (his uncle's hat) *Where was the uncle?* (in a vacant lot)

Intermediate *Ask: How did Tío Juan leave the apartment without Gonzalo knowing it?* (Gonzalo was watching TV.) *How did he try to find his uncle? How did he find him?* (He looked in many places. Finally, he saw his uncle's white hat.) *What do you think Tío Juan would like to do?* (grow some plants)

Advanced *Ask: How do you think Tío Juan was feeling in his new country? Why?* (lonely and frustrated because he could not talk to people outside his family or do the things he was used to doing) *What do you think will happen next? Why?* (Tío Juan will grow plants in the garden. He knows how to do this because he was a farmer.)

straw hat he always wore. Two blocks down I **spotted** it. I **flew** down the sidewalk and found him standing in front of a **vacant** lot, making gestures to a man with a shovel.

7   I took his hand, but he pulled me through the trash and into the lot. I recognized the man with the shovel—he was the janitor at my old school. He had a little garden planted. Different **shades** of green leaves were coming up in rows. Tío Juan was smiling and trying to tell him something. The man couldn't understand him and finally went back to digging. I turned Tío Juan around and led him home.

> ### Draw Conclusions
>
> What is Tío Juan trying to tell the man with the shovel? What information in the text helped you draw this conclusion?

spotted saw
flew ran very quickly
vacant empty

shades colors that are only slightly different from a basic one

Chapter 4 Gonzalo **125**

Read the Selection

1. **Paired reading** Have students read aloud in pairs.
2. **Relate to personal experience** *Ask: Do you sometimes have to help an adult who can't speak English? Do you ever have to baby-sit? Have you ever had an emergency while baby-sitting?*
3. **Multi-level options** See MULTI-LEVEL OPTIONS on p. 124.

Sample Answer to Guide Question
He's trying to tell him about farming. "Tío Juan was smiling and trying to tell him something."

 ### Punctuation

Italics

Remind students that they learned in Unit 1 that they can use italics to show which words to stress. *Say: Italics are also used for titles of shows and titles of books.* Have students find the italicized words in the first sentence in paragraph 6. *Ask: Why is* The Brady Bunch *in italics?* (It's the name of a television show.) Have students locate the other use of italics in this paragraph. *(bodega) Say: It is italicized because it is a word from a language other than English.*

Point out that when they are using a computer, they should use italics to show titles of shows and words from other languages. When writing by hand, they should underline.

Apply Direct students to paragraph 2. Have them find the title of a book that is italicized. *(Gateway to Algebra)*

Read the Selection

1. **Listen for information** Write on the board:
   What did Tío Juan tell Gonzalo's mother about? (about the vacant lot and the garden) *What did Tío Juan do at the garden?* (studied the sun and soil, turned the soil) Have students close their books. Play the audio. Then discuss their answers.

2. **Shared reading** Read the text aloud and have students join in when they can.

3. **Discuss motivation** *Ask: Why do you think Gonzalo didn't want anyone to see him helping his uncle?* (He would be embarrassed.) *Why do you think Gonzalo helped his uncle?* (He saw that his uncle was happy and interested in the garden; he wanted to learn from him.)

Sample Answer to Guide Question
She wanted Tío Juan to be able to plant. She asked Gonzalo to take Tío Juan back to the garden.

> **Draw Conclusions**
>
> Why does Gonzalo's mother buy a trowel and seeds? What information in the text helped you draw this conclusion?

8   That night he told my mother all about it. She was the only one who could understand him. When she got home from work the next day she asked me to take him back there. I did. He studied the sun. Then the soil. He felt it, then smelled it, then actually tasted it. He chose a spot not too far from the sidewalk. Where my mother changed busses she'd gone into a store and bought him a **trowel** and four packets of seeds. I cleared the trash, he **turned the soil.** I wished we were farther from the street and I was praying that none of my friends or girlfriends or **enemies** saw me. Tío Juan didn't even notice people—he was **totally wrapped up** in the work.

---

trowel   a small tool used to dig up soil
turned the soil   plowed

enemies   people who wish you harm
totally wrapped up   completely focused on

MULTI-LEVEL OPTIONS *Read the Selection*

Newcomer *Ask: Did Tío Juan buy some seeds?* (no) *Did mother buy seeds for Tío Juan?* (yes) *Did mother plant the seeds?* (no) *Was Tío Juan happy at the end of the story?* (yes)

Beginning *Ask: Whom did Tío Juan talk to about the garden?* (mother) *What did mother buy for Tío Juan?* (seeds) *Who helped him plant them?* (Gonzalo) *How did Tío Juan feel at the end of the story?* (happy)

Intermediate *Ask: What kind of seeds do you think mother bought Tío Juan? Why?* (vegetable seeds because the boy says his uncle knows about growing food) *How did Tío Juan and Gonzalo get the ground ready for planting?* (cleaned up trash, turned the soil, made ditches, sprinkled in the seeds)

Advanced *Ask: Why didn't Gonzalo want his friends to see him?* (They might think that it was strange that he was cleaning up a dirty lot. They might think his uncle was strange.) *What does the last sentence mean?* (Tío Juan did not have to rely on others; he could do important work even if he didn't speak English.)

**Draw
Conclusions**

Draw a conclusion
about how planting
a garden changes
Tío Juan "from a
baby back into
a man."

9 He showed me exactly how far apart the rows should be and how deep. He couldn't read the words on the seed packets, but he knew from the pictures what seeds were inside. He poured them into his hand and smiled. He seemed to recognize them, like old friends. Watching him carefully **sprinkling** them into the **troughs** he'd made, I realized that I didn't know anything about growing food and that he knew everything. I stared at his busy fingers, then his eyes. They were focused, not faraway or confused. He'd changed from a baby back into a man.

sprinkling dropping lightly and in small amounts   **troughs** long and narrow ditches

About the Author

Paul Fleischman (born 1952)

Paul Fleischman lives in Monterey, California. The story you read is part of the novel *Seedfolks*. Fleischman created the character Gonzalo from his experience as a volunteer in an English as a Second Language middle school class. He decided to write *Seedfolks* after learning that gardening can help people who feel isolated and lonely. He believes that community gardening joins people together and gives them a sense of accomplishment.

➤ If you could ask Paul Fleischman a question about this story, what would it be?

Chapter 4 Gonzalo **127**

Read the Selection

1. **Use word squares** Provide time for students to complete word squares for new vocabulary in the story.
2. **Silent reading** Have students reread the story silently.
3. **Multi-level options** See MULTI-LEVEL OPTIONS on p. 126.

Sample Answer to Guide Question
He knew about gardening and farming, and so he became a knowledgeable adult. In the garden, he could be independent and didn't have to depend on others like a child.

About the Author

Analyze facts *Ask: What is* Seedfolks*?* (a novel he wrote) *Where did he volunteer?* (in an ESL middle school class) *Why does he think community gardening is good?* (It joins people together and gives them a sense of accomplishment.)

Across Selections

Say: We have read other narrative stories. ("Birthday Barbecue" p. 8; "Turkish Delight" p. 46; "Sadako and the Thousand Paper Cranes" p. 58) *Ask: Which story has been your favorite? Why did you like it?* Then have students identify the point of view of each narrative. Create a point of view two-column chart for the class. Label the two columns *1st person* and *3rd person*. Have students record the titles of their readings under the correct column.

Spelling, Punctuation, Capitalization

After the Reading Comprehension section, students will practice spelling, punctuation, and capitalization in the Activity Book.

 Spelling

I before e

On the board, write: *friends.* Have students spell the word aloud. *Say: People have trouble remembering whether the -i or the -e comes first in this word. Some people remember this spelling rule with a jingle:* -i before -e except after c.

Apply Have students go on a word search to find examples (believe, lie) and exceptions (their, weird). Put the words on a chart and display it in the classroom.

Evaluate Your Reading Strategy

Draw Conclusions *Say: You have practiced an important reading strategy. Now you can decide how well you have done. Does this statement describe how you read?*

As I read, I draw conclusions by thinking about the facts. When I draw conclusions, it helps me understand the characters' actions.

Beyond the Reading

Reading Comprehension

Question-Answer Relationships

Sample Answers

1. He learned English on the playground and from watching TV.
2. He was a farmer.
3. He couldn't communicate and couldn't go anywhere by himself, so he became like a child.
4. She was worried that he would get hurt or lost.
5. She bought him a trowel and seeds so he could plant things and farm again.
6. The seeds are familiar to him; they remind him of his old life.
7. It makes you independent and confident.
8. At the beginning, the mood is a little negative. The mood becomes hopeful and positive when his uncle begins gardening and Gonzalo begins to respect him. The change of mood emphasizes the change in Gonzalo's view of his uncle from a "baby" to an adult.
9. I have had to speak with people for my relatives because they only know a little English.
10. The theme crosses cultures by showing that it is always difficult for people to move to a new country and learn a new language. It connects cultures by showing that some things are the same everywhere in the world, such as growing food or plants.

Build Reading Fluency

Audio CD Reading Practice

Explain that reading silently while listening to the audio helps improve reading fluency. Remind them to keep their eyes on the words. Repeat the audio as needed.

Reading Comprehension

Question-Answer Relationships (QAR)

"Right There" Questions

1. **Recall Facts** How does Gonzalo say he learned English?
2. **Recall Facts** What was Tío Juan's job in Guatemala?

"Think and Search" Question

3. **Identify the Main Idea** How does Tío Juan grow younger when he comes to the United States?

"Author and You" Questions

4. **Draw Conclusions** Why was Gonzalo's mother so frightened when Tío Juan left the house alone?
5. **Describe** How does Gonzalo's mother solve Tío Juan's problem?
6. **Make Inferences** Why does the author describe the seeds as Tío Juan's "old friends"?

"On Your Own" Questions

7. **Discuss** How might learning to live in a new place make a person "older"?
8. **Identify Mood** What is the mood of the narrator at the beginning of the story? Does the mood change from the beginning to the end of the story? Does it contribute to the effect of the text?
9. **Compare Experiences** Have you or your classmates had similar experiences to Gonzalo's? Describe these experiences.
10. **Connect** How does the theme (the general message) of "Gonzalo" cross cultures? How does it connect cultures?

Activity Book p. 66   Student CD-ROM

Build Reading Fluency

Audio CD Reading Practice

Listening to the Audio CD of "Gonzalo" is good reading practice. It helps you to become a fluent reader. Turn to page 122.

1. Listen to the Audio CD for "Gonzalo."

2. Follow along in your student book, page 122.
3. Listen to the phrases, pauses, and expression of the reader.

128 Unit 2 Environment

MULTI-LEVEL OPTIONS *Elements of Literature*

Newcomer Have students draw an illustration to show what Gonzalo thought of Tío Juan for most of the story. Then ask students to illustrate what Gonzalo thought of his uncle at the end. *Ask: What did Gonzalo learn?*

Beginning Have students list words that Gonzalo might have used to describe his uncle for most of the story. (baby, not smart) Then ask them to list words to tell what he might have said about his uncle at the end. (smart, talented) Have students compare the lists and tell what Gonzalo learned.

Intermediate After students reread paragraph 9, have them reread the last sentences of paragraphs 4 and 5. Ask if they think Gonzalo would still talk about his uncle this way. Have pairs of students role-play Gonzalo telling a friend about his uncle at the end of the story. After these activities, students may write in their Reading Log.

Advanced Once students have determined what Gonzalo learned and have written a statement telling the theme in their logs, *ask: How can you apply the theme of this story to real life?* (I should realize that everyone I meet has some special gift, even if I don't see it right away.)

Listen, Speak, Interact

Interpret Nonverbal Communication

Verbal communication uses words. When people communicate without using words, it is **nonverbal communication.**

In the reading selection, Gonzalo does not speak the same language as Tío Juan. How might a person communicate with someone who speaks another language?

1. With a partner, think of a simple activity that you can express without using words. An example is asking for something to eat.

2. Decide how you will express your activity nonverbally.

3. Present your activity to the class.

4. Ask the class to guess your activity.

5. When you don't understand something, how can you ask the person to help you? What verbal and nonverbal language can you use?

Elements of Literature

Discuss the Theme

The **theme** is the general message that the author wants you to get from the story. A theme is often not stated directly. You figure it out as you read.

Sometimes the theme in a reading is a lesson about life. The characters in the story give you clues (details that help you understand) to the theme through their words and actions.

1. With a partner, reread paragraph 9 of "Gonzalo."

2. What did Gonzalo learn from Tío Juan?

3. What do you think the theme of the story is?

4. Write your interpretation of the theme in your Reading Log. Also write some of the details that helped you understand the theme.

5. Does the theme connect to the reading selections in Chapters 1, 2, and 3? Explain.

Reading Log   Activity Book p. 67   Student CD-ROM

Chapter 4   Gonzalo   **129**

Listen, Speak, Interact

Interpret Nonverbal Communication

1. **Clarify terms** Model a nonverbal action for the class to guess. (making a phone call, pouring a cup of coffee, or unlocking a door)

2. **Newcomers** Pair up newcomers with intermediates for this activity. Have pairs create and perform a nonverbal role-play. Ask other students to guess the action. Then have the pairs write a sentence together describing the action. Have newcomers write the sentences in their Reading Logs.

3. **Identify nonverbal cues** Have all pairs mime their role-plays. Then *ask: What did people do to make it easy to guess? How important are facial expressions?*

Elements of Literature

Discuss the Theme

1. **Compare and contrast** Have students write words and phrases that show how Gonzalo sees Tío Juan at the beginning of the reading (like a kid in diapers) and the end of the story (busy fingers). Have small groups use their examples to discuss what Gonzalo learned.

2. **Multi-level options** See MULTI-LEVEL OPTIONS on p. 128.

Answers
2. He learned about planting seeds.
3. and 4. *Possible answers:* The theme points out that it is difficult to be in an unfamiliar environment because people become may helpless like children.
5. The theme of all four reading selections is that our environment is important and can affect us in different ways.

 **ASSESS**

Say: Demonstrate two examples of nonverbal communication.

 Content Connection
The Arts

Point out that songs may also have themes. Provide an opportunity for students to listen to ballads, folk songs, or other music that tells a story to identify lessons or messages the songwriter was trying to communicate.

Learning Styles
Kinesthetic

Tell students that entire languages have been built around nonverbal communication. Introduce students to American Sign Language used by hearing impaired people. Present books on sign language from your school or community library. Give students a chance to learn some of the signs and use them with classmates.

Word Study

Using the Dictionary

Use other sources Point out to students that word origins are usually found in large dictionaries. Word meanings, pronunciations, and origins are also found in other sources, such as online or CD-ROM dictionaries.

Answers
1. They show pronunciation.
2. Latin; "broad street"
3. four; the first definition

Grammar Focus

Recognize and Use Comparative Adjectives

Use comparative adjectives Write on the board: *smart, intelligent, little, tall, short, difficult.* Have students work in pairs. Instruct each pair to say the comparative forms of the adjectives and use them in sentences.

Answers
1. older, younger
2. *Example:* I am happier than my pet fish. I am more talkative than my mother.

ASSESS

Have students write the comparative forms of: *long, comfortable, tall.*

Word Study

Using the Dictionary

Look up the word **plaza** (paragraph 4) in a large dictionary. You will find an entry like this:

> **pla•za** /ˈplɑ-zə, ˈplæ-/ *n* [Sp, fr. L *platea* broad street—more at PLACE] (1683)
> **1a:** a public square in a city or town **b:** an open area usually located near urban buildings and often featuring walkways, trees and shrubs, places to sit, and sometimes shops **2:** a place on a thoroughfare (as a turnpike) at which all traffic must temporarily stop (as to pay tolls) **3:** an area adjacent to an expressway which has service facilities (as a restaurant, service station, and rest rooms) **4:** SHOPPING CENTER

1. What do the first symbols mean? Use them to pronounce the word. Your teacher will help you.
2. Where did the word come from (word origin)? Do you know what the word means in its original language?
3. How many meanings does the word have? Which meaning fits the use of **plaza** in paragraph 4?
4. Do the same activity with the following words from the reading.
   a. equation (paragraph 2)
   b. kindergartner (paragraph 3)
   c. weird (paragraph 5)

Activity Book
p. 68

Student
CD-ROM

Grammar Focus

Recognize and Use Comparative Adjectives

Adjectives describe nouns—people, places, and things.

Tío Juan is an <u>old</u> man.

Sometimes authors use adjectives to compare people, places, or things. This makes their writing more vivid.

Tío Juan is 70. My grandfather is 75. My grandfather is old**er** than Tío Juan.

Older is the **comparative form** of the adjective *old*. Add -*er* to a short adjective to make a comparative form.

Tío Juan's garden is beautiful. It is **more beautiful** than my garden.

Use *more* for long adjectives like *beautiful*.

1. Find two examples of comparative adjectives in "Gonzalo." Look in paragraph 1.
2. Write two sentences using the comparative form of adjectives.

Activity Book
pp. 69–70

Student
Handbook

Student
CD-ROM

130 Unit 2 Environment

MULTI-LEVEL OPTIONS *From Reading to Writing*

Newcomer Help each student create an idea for a character and determine what that character will learn. Then have students create a storyboard to show the steps the character goes through in learning.

Beginning Provide a story frame like this one for students to use in creating a beginning, a middle, and an ending for their story.

_____ wanted to learn _____. First, he/she _____. Next, he/she _____. Then he/she _____. In the end, _____ felt _____.

Intermediate *Ask: What makes people want to learn? What keeps them trying when it is difficult? Writers of stories about characters who learn something must make the characters seem real.* Have students create Character Webs to show traits their characters will have and how these may be shown.

Advanced Have each student identify a theme to communicate through his or her story. Ask students to pre-write some ways that the theme may be woven into their narratives. Have peer responders meet to provide feedback.

From Reading to Writing

Write Narrative Fiction

In "Gonzalo," the main character learns English after moving to the United States. Write a story about a fictional character (someone you make up) who needs to learn how to do something.

1. Choose a title for your story.
2. Make sure your story has a beginning, a middle, and an end.
3. Include details that tell how the person resolves his or her problem about how to do something.
4. Use comparative adjectives to show how the person changes.

Title

○ **Beginning**
Who is the person? What does he or she need to learn?

○ **Middle**
How did he or she learn it?

○ **End**
How does he or she change?

Activity Book
p. 71

Student Handbook

Across Content Areas

Learn about Plants

Three main parts of plants are the **roots, leaves,** and **stems.**

Roots go down into the soil. They take water and **nutrients** (things that make the plant grow) from the soil.

Leaves have many shapes. They are usually, but not always, green. Leaves make energy for the plant.

Stems hold up the leaves.

On a piece of paper, complete the labels. Write one of these words:

roots	stem	leaf

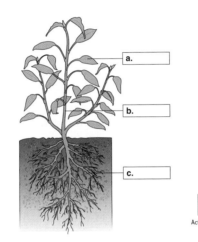

a.

b.

c.

Activity Book
p. 72

Chapter 4 Gonzalo **131**

From Reading to Writing

Write Narrative Fiction

1. **Brainstorm ideas** Brainstorm and record ideas about things people can learn. (the value of helping others, how to deal with siblings, how to play soccer) Help students choose an idea. Ask questions about characters to help students focus on important details.
2. **Proofread writing** Have students carefully check that their stories have the four features listed. *Ask: What else should you check for when you proofread?* (spelling, capitalization, punctuation) *Say: Be sure to spell words correctly in the final draft.*
3. **Share narratives** Ask volunteers to read their stories to the class.
4. **Multi-level options** See MULTI-LEVEL OPTIONS on p. 130.

Across Content Areas: Science

Learn About Plants

Relate to personal experience *Ask: Do you or does someone you know have a garden? What do you grow? Can you describe the stems and leaves of a plant you know?*

Answer
Top to bottom: leaf, stem, roots

 **ASSESS**

Have students write three sentences that compare the character in their narrative to Gonzalo. Remind them to use comparative adjectives.

Reteach and Reassess

Text Structure Have students use the narratives they wrote. Ask them to make a chart like the one on p. 120 to identify the features in their stories.

Reading Strategy Reread "About the Author" with students. Ask them to draw conclusions about Paul Fleischman.

Elements of Literature Have students read the responses they wrote to the theme of "Gonzalo" in their Reading Logs. *Ask: What other stories do you know with a similar theme?*

Reassess Ask students to return to the chart on page 120. Have them use it to think how they could develop a sequel to "Gonzalo." Instruct students to tell the story from the point of view of Mrs. Garcia. Tell them to write about a problem she might have. Help students identify possible themes.

CHAPTER
5

Rain Forest
Creatures

an excerpt from a
nonfiction book
by Will Osborne
and Mary Pope Osborne

Into the Reading

Chapter Materials

Activity Book: *pp. 73–80*
Audio: *Unit 2, Chapter 5; CD 1, Track 11*
Student Handbook
Student CD-ROM: *Unit 2, Chapter 5*
Teacher Resource Book: *Lesson Plan, Teacher Resources, Reading Summary, Activity Book Answer Key*
Teacher Resource CD-ROM
Assessment Program: *Quiz, pp. 31–32; Teacher and Student Resources, pp. 115–144*
Assessment CD-ROM
Transparencies
The Heinle Newbury House Dictionary/CD-ROM
Web site: http://visions.heinle.com

Objectives

Preview Read the objectives aloud. *Ask: What objective is new for you?*

Use Prior Knowledge

Describe Your Image of a Rain Forest

Share images *Ask: What do you imagine a rain forest looks like? What kinds of plants and animals live there? What are some things you would* not *find in a rain forest?* Have students discuss their ideas about rain forests.

Objectives

Reading Outline information to understand reading as you read an informational text.

Listening and Speaking Recall details.

Grammar Identify the subject and verb of a sentence.

Writing Write an informational report.

Content Social Studies: Read pie charts.

Use Prior Knowledge

Describe Your Image of a Rain Forest

A forest is an area covered by trees. In a rain forest, it rains a lot. There are often very large rivers. Rain forests are the home of millions of different kinds of plants and animals.

1. You are taking a walk in a rain forest. What do you see? What do you hear? What do you feel? What can you smell?
2. Fill in the chart with some ideas and then describe your images to your partner.

3. Are your ideas of what you will find in a rain forest correct? Use the Internet to check your answers. (Search for the words *rain forest*.)

A Walk in a Rain Forest				
	See	**Hear**	**Feel**	**Smell**
Animals	*snakes*			
Plants				*flowers*
Other things in nature			*It's hot!*	

MULTI-LEVEL OPTIONS *Build Vocabulary*

Newcomer Use books or Internet sites about rain forests to show pictures illustrating the vocabulary words. Say the word as you point to each picture. Then say the word and ask students to point to the appropriate picture. Ask students to draw the meanings of these words in their Personal Dictionaries.

Beginning Have students write words or phrases in their Personal Dictionaries to help them remember the meaning of each word. Also, ask them to draw small sketches by the words in their Personal Dictionaries.

Intermediate Tell students that in addition to definitions, examples can also help them recall the meanings of words. As they enter each of the four words in their Personal Dictionaries, ask them to identify an example of the concept as well.

Advanced Have students work in pairs to create a Word Wheel for each of the four words. Use individual Word Wheels to create a class Word Wheel for each word.

Build Background

The Amazon Rain Forest

The Amazon Rain Forest is the largest rain forest in the world. It is located in South America and covers about 25 percent of the continent— about 2.3 million square miles. Most of the rain forest is located in the country of Brazil. Scientists are constantly discovering new species in this huge natural environment.

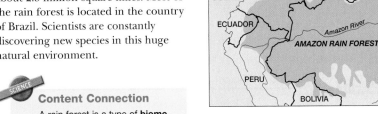

Caribbean Sea · ATLANTIC OCEAN · GUYANA · SURINAME · VENEZUELA · FRENCH GUIANA · PACIFIC OCEAN · COLOMBIA · ECUADOR · Amazon River · AMAZON RAIN FOREST · PERU · BRAZIL · BOLIVIA

Content Connection

A rain forest is a type of **biome.** A biome is a very large environment that has a specific climate as well as certain plants and animals.

Build Vocabulary

Use Text Features

Some nonfiction texts include **text features** that help the reader identify vocabulary words. Look at the following vocabulary words. In the selection, they appear in italics, a different kind of type in which the letters slant to the right. *This sentence is in italics.*

predators
camouflage
prey
nocturnal

1. Write the four words in your Personal Dictionary.
2. As you read, stop when you find each of these words.
3. Write the definition that you find in the text next to the word listed in your Personal Dictionary.
4. Write your own sentences using these vocabulary words.

Personal Dictionary

The Heinle Newbury House Dictionary

Activity Book p. 73

Student CD-ROM

Chapter 5 Rain Forest Creatures **133**

Community Connection

Build Vocabulary Ask students to draw a picture of a place in their community, such as a field, park, or woods, where animals are found. Have them show and label any predators, prey, or animals that use camouflage or nocturnal animals who live there.

Learning Styles
Musical

Build Background Play an audiotape of sounds of the rain forest or log on to a Web site that plays sounds of the rain forest. (Search for key words: *sounds, rain forest.*) Have students listen to the audio and identify the sounds they hear.

Build Background

The Amazon Rain Forest

1. **Use a map** Have students identify the countries on the map. Ask them to find the longest river. (the Amazon) Ask if any students have lived in or visited these countries or the rain forest.
2. **Content Connection** The Amazon River is 3900 miles from the source to the mouth. It is the second longest river in the world after the Nile.

Build Vocabulary

Use Text Features

Teacher Resource Book: *Personal Dictionary, p. 63*

1. **Learn strategies** Have students write the words and definitions in their Personal Dictionaries. They can write sentences after they read.
2. **Reading selection vocabulary** You may want to introduce the glossed words in the reading selection before students begin reading. Key words: *creatures, twinkle, foot, raid.* Instruct students to write the words with correct spelling and their definitions in their Personal Dictionaries. Have them pronounce each word and divide it into syllables.
3. **Multi-level options** See MULTI-LEVEL OPTIONS on p. 132.

✓ ASSESS

Tell students to brainstorm as many words as they can about the rain forest. Have them read their lists to the class.

Text Structure

Informational Text

1. **Relate to personal experience** *Ask: In what classes do you read informational texts?* (science, math, social studies, health) *Can you show me some headings and captions in one of your textbooks?*

2. **Multi-level options** See MULTI-LEVEL OPTIONS below.

Reading Strategy

Outline Information to Understand Reading

1. **Clarify and understand** *Say: We use Roman numerals for the main sections of an outline. The Romans developed this system of numbers in ancient times.* Write on the board: *I, II, III, IV, V. Ask: Can you guess the next Roman numeral?* (VI)

2. **Model using an outline** Demonstrate filling in the outline by starting with a blank form and having volunteers suggest the title and the sections for Roman numeral I. Monitor students as they create individual outline forms to use as they read.

Answers
B. Protection; **3.** Scare predators away;
II. Night Creatures; **2.** Fireflies; **3.** Click beetles

ASSESS

Ask: What is an informational text?

Text Structure

Informational Text

The reading in this chapter is an **informational text.** Informational texts explain and give information about a topic. In an informational text, authors call our attention to information in a few ways.

As you read each section of "Rain Forest Creatures," look at the headings and captions.

Informational Text	
Headings	titles for separate sections of text; printed in large, bold type
Captions	words that explain a picture

Student
CD-ROM

Reading Strategy

Outline Information to Understand Reading

Making an **outline** of an informational text helps you remember what you read. Look at the outline here.

1. Copy the outline and complete it as you read or listen to the audio recording of "Rain Forest Creatures."

2. Use the headings in the text as the main topics. Then add details. This outline goes to paragraph 9. Finish it on your own.

Student
CD-ROM

The title of the reading

Rain Forest Creatures

Main topic- **I.** Predators and Protection
Subtopic —— **A.** Predators
First detail —— 1. Predators kill other
for subtopic   animals
Second —— 2. Prey—killed and eaten
detail for   **B.** _____
subtopic
                  1. Camouflage—colors
                     help animals blend in
                  2. Staying still
                  3. _____
           II. _____
                  A. Definition: A nocturnal
                     creature that comes out
                     only at night
                  B. Examples
                     1. Bats
                     2. _____
                     3. _____

MULTI-LEVEL OPTIONS *Text Structure*

Newcomer Help students preview the illustrations in "Rain Forest Creatures." Then preview the headings with students. Act out the meaning of each heading. *Ask: Is this about rain forests?* (yes) *Is it about animals in the rain forest?* (yes) *Is it about plants?* (no)

Beginning Preview illustrations, headings, and captions with students. Then *ask: Where would we find facts about animals that swim?* (Water Creatures) *Where can we see how animals hide?* (photo on p. 136) *Where can we find out about animals that come out at night?* (Night Creatures)

Intermediate Have students preview the headings, illustrations, and captions in the selection and make predictions about what kinds of questions may be answered in each section. Ask students to write two questions for each section. Have them revisit these after reading to see whether the questions were answered.

Advanced Have students preview the selection to see what features the authors used. Then ask students to browse through books and magazines to see other kinds of features that nonfiction authors use. (graphs, charts, maps, organizers) After reading, *ask: What other features might have been useful in this selection?*

Rain Forest Creatures

an excerpt from a nonfiction book by
Will Osborne and Mary Pope Osborne

135

Reading Selection Materials

Audio: *Unit 2, Chapter 5; CD 1, Track 11*
Teacher Resource Book: *Reading Summary,*
  pp. 83–84
Transparencies: #6, *Reading Summary*

Suggestions for Using Reading Summary

- Introduce new vocabulary or cognates.
- Cut the summary into strips, or jumble the sentences on an overhead transparency. Students put the sentences in order.
- Practice the reading strategy.
- Students read aloud or with a partner.
- Students paraphrase the summary.
- Students do a cloze activity.
- Students create a visual or graphic organizer, such as a timeline or storyboard, to illustrate the summary.
- Students paraphrase the summary.

Preview the Selection

1. **Interpret the image** Have students look at the photo. *Ask: What animals do you see? What colors do you see? Do you often see these colors in your environment?*
2. **Use art to speculate** *Ask: What does this photo suggest you may learn in this selection? What would you like to learn about the rain forest?* Help students formulate questions and write them on the board.
3. **Connect** *Ask: How would you describe this environment?* (It's very hot and very wet. There are lots of plants and animals.)

 Content Connection
The Arts

Learning Styles
Intrapersonal

Say: Look carefully at this picture of a rain forest. If this were a scene in a movie, what kind of music do you think would be playing in the background? Why? (mysterious, because there are so many strange and unusual plants and animals; fast, because there is so much activity)

Say: Put yourself in this picture. Imagine that you are walking in a rain forest. Ask students to write or draw their ideas about the following questions: *How do you think you would feel? Why?* (amazed at the beautiful trees and plants; a little scared of the animals that are so different than the ones in my community; sad that some people destroy the rain forest)

Read the Selection

1. **Recognize features** *Ask: Can you find a heading?* (Predators and Protection) *Where do you usually find captions?* (under the photo) *What words are in italics?* (predators, prey, camouflage)

2. **Paired reading** Pair newcomers with advanced students and beginning students with intermediates for a paired reading.

3. **Discuss a photo** *Ask: What kind of animal is this?* (frog) *Why is it hiding?* (for protection) *What is its predator?* (snakes, large birds) *Is this a good camouflage? Why?* (Yes. The colors blend in with the plant.)

Sample Answer to Guide Question
Predators and Protection. It is the first Roman numeral heading.

See Teacher Edition pp. 434–436 for a list of English-Spanish cognates in the reading selection.

---

1 They **creep** and **crawl**! They **flit** and fly! They **growl** and **howl**! The world's rain forests are alive with millions of animals, bugs, and birds.

Predators and Protection

2 Most rain forest animals depend on other animals for food. Animals that kill and eat other animals are called *predators*. The animals that predators kill are called their *prey*.

Many rain forest **creatures** have 3 special ways of protecting themselves from predators. Some have colors that help them blend with their natural surroundings. This kind of protection is called *camouflage* (KAM-uh-flahzh).

Some creatures fool predators by 4 looking like plants. If they stay very still, predators will leave them alone—because they won't see them!

> **Outline Information to Understand Reading**
>
> What is the heading for this section? Where is it on your outline?

Audio
CD 1, Tr. 11

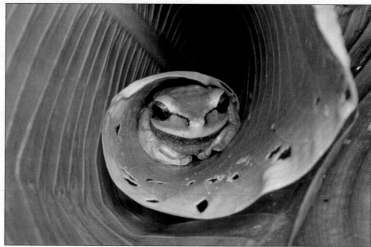

Tree frog in leaf

creep move slowly	**growl** make a low sound in anger
crawl move slowly and close to the ground	**howl** cry loudly
flit move quickly	**creatures** living beings

136 Unit 2 Environment

MULTI-LEVEL OPTIONS *Read the Selection*

Newcomer Play the audio. Point to relevant pictures and have students identify key words in the captions. *Ask: Are there many animals in the rain forest?* (yes) *Do some animals eat others?* (yes) *Do some animals hide from each other?* (yes) *Do all the animals come out at night?* (no)

Beginning Read the Reading Summary. Then do a paired reading. *Ask: What do predators eat?* (other animals) *What helps some animals hide from others?* (their color) *When do nocturnal creatures come out?* (at night)

Intermediate Have students do a paired reading. *Ask: How are predators and prey related?* (Predators eat prey.) *How does camouflage help animals?* (It helps them hide from predators.) *How are the eyes of nocturnal animals different from those of other animals?* (Their eyes are bigger to help them see better at night.)

Advanced Have students read silently. *Ask: For which kinds of animals might camouflage be most important? Why?* (Small or slow ones because it would be harder for them to get away from predators.) *What senses help nocturnal animals move around and stay safe?* (sight, smell)

Night monkeys

5 Some creatures scare predators away by looking bigger and scarier than they really are. Many moths and butterflies have marks on their wings that look like big eyes. When these creatures open their wings, predators think the eyes belong to a creature that might eat *them!*

> **Outline Information to Understand Reading**
>
> The detail in this paragraph is "scare predators away." Write this detail in your outline.

Night Creatures

6 The rain forest is just as alive at night as it is during the day. Many creatures come out only after the sun has gone down. They are called *nocturnal* (nok-TUR-nul) creatures.

7 Many nocturnal creatures have very large eyes. Their big eyes let in more light and help them see in the **moonlit** forest.

---

nocturnal active at night

moonlit given light from the moon

Chapter 5 Rain Forest Creatures **137**

Read the Selection

1. **Reciprocal reading** Play the audio. Divide students into small groups. Assign each group member a paragraph to read aloud. Write on the board: *What, When, Where, Why, How.* Have students use these words to ask their group questions about their paragraphs.
2. **Use an outline** Remind students to fill in the information for *B* and *3* in their outlines.
3. **Multi-level options** See MULTI-LEVEL OPTIONS on p. 136.

Sample Answer to Guide Question
B. 3. Scare predators away.

⟨,⟩ Punctuation

Exclamation points

Say: Exclamation points are used to show strong feelings, such as surprise, anger, or excitement. Find the sentences that end in exclamation points in paragraph 1. Ask a volunteer to read the sentences expressively.
Ask: What feeling do you think the authors wanted to express? (excitement) *Why do you think they started the selection in this way?* (to get readers interested in what they have to say)

Apply Have students find two other sentences that end in exclamation points in paragraphs 4 and 5. Ask students to write their own exclamatory sentence telling one exciting or surprising fact about rain forest creatures.

Read the Selection

1. **Preview vocabulary** Write on the board: *bat, insect, crocodile, ant.* **Ask:** *Can anyone draw a picture of one of these? What do you know about these insects and animals?*
2. **Shared reading** Play the audio. Have volunteers join in for different paragraphs.
3. **Check comprehension** *Ask: What kind of animal is a bat?* (nocturnal) *What senses does a bat use?* (smell and sound/hearing) *What other nocturnal creatures are discussed?* (fireflies and click beetles) *What water creatures are mentioned?* (fish, snakes, crocodiles, lizards)

Sample Answer to Guide Question
B. 2. fireflies 3. click beetles

Crocodile

8   Bats are common nocturnal creatures. There are hundreds of different kinds of bats in the world's rain forests. Many bats have a strong sense of smell that helps them find fruits and flowers in the dark. Others use sound to find and capture insects and to find their way in the night.

9   At night, rain forest trees **twinkle** with fireflies and click beetles. Scientists think insects like these "talk" to each other with their flashing lights.

Water Creatures

10   Rivers run through most of the rain forests of the world. Thousands of different kinds of fish live in these rivers. Snakes, crocodiles, and lizards **slither** and sleep on the banks.

Army Ants

11   Army ants have painful **stingers.** They **raid** the rain forest floor in large **swarms,** searching for food.

> **Outline Information to Understand Reading**
>
> Add the creatures mentioned in paragraph 9 to your outline.

twinkle   shine
slither   move by sliding and turning
stingers   pointed body parts that are used to stab

raid   attack suddenly
swarms   large numbers of insects that move in groups

138   Unit 2 Environment

MULTI-LEVEL OPTIONS *Read the Selection*

Newcomer *Ask: Are there bats in the rain forest?* (yes) *Do bats use taste to find food?* (no) *Are rain forests dry?* (no) *Do army ants kill people?* (no)

Beginning *Ask: What senses do bats use to find food?* (smell and sound) *What creatures flash lights?* (fireflies, click beetles) *Where do crocodiles and snakes live?* (near rivers) *What might an army ant do to people?* (sting them)

Intermediate *Ask: How do bats find and capture food?* (They use their senses of smell and sound.) *How do army ants travel?* (They march in large groups.) *How do army ants probably kill their prey?* (by stinging them to death)

Advanced *Ask: Why do the authors put quotation marks around the word* talk *in paragraph 9?* (to show that the insects communicate but not using words like humans) *Why do you think army ants travel in large swarms?* (so they can capture larger creatures)

12 A swarm of marching army ants travels a **foot** every minute. Sometimes there are more than a million ants in the swarm!

Outline Information to Understand Reading

Which details about army ants will you include in your outline?

foot 12 inches, or about 30.5 centimeters

13 Army ants catch and kill spiders and insects. Sometimes they also kill small animals that can't get out of their way.

14 Army ants don't eat people. But you still wouldn't want to be in their path. A sting from an army ant really hurts!

About the Authors

Mary Pope Osborne and Will Osborne

Mary Pope Osborne has lived a life of adventure. She grew up in a military family and moved frequently. She enjoyed living in many different places. Pope Osborne continued to love change as an adult. After graduating from college, she held a variety of jobs that included working as an actress, a waitress, a travel consultant, a medical assistant, and a children's book editor. She met her husband, the coauthor of "Rain Forest Creatures," at a play in which he performed.

➤ Why do you think the authors wrote about the rain forest? Was it to entertain, to influence, or to express an opinion?

Chapter 5 Rain Forest Creatures **139**

 Spelling

Consonant before -le

On the board, write: twin<u>kle</u>. *Say: When words end with a consonant + -le, those letters are pronounced as a separate syllable. Find and say another word in paragraph 9 that ends in consonant -le.* (beetles)

Apply Have students find two more examples in "Gonzalo" on page 123. (mumble, little)

Evaluate Your Reading Strategy

Outline Information to Understand Reading *Say: You have practiced an important reading strategy. Now you can decide how well you have done. Does this statement describe how you read?*

When I read informational text, I use an outline to organize important information. Outlining information helps me understand and remember better.

Read the Selection

1. **Choral reading** Have students do a choral reading. Ask one or two student to "lead" the reading in front of the class.
2. **Use an outline** Remind students to complete their outlines. *Ask: What are the headings on page 138?* (Water Creatures, Army Ants) *Where would we put this in your outline?* (Numerals III and IV) Help students complete examples and details.
3. **Multi-level options** See MULTI-LEVEL OPTIONS on p. 138.

Sample Answer to Guide Question
Search for food on rain forest floor; travel in armies; catch and kill spiders and insects.

About the Author

Analyze facts *Ask: Why did Mary Pope Osborne move often as a child?* (Her father was in the military.) *Who did she write "Rain Forest Creatures" with?* (her husband)

Across Selections

Discuss text structure *Say: In "Subway Architect" we also learned information about a new subject. Both readings explain and inform, but they are different in many more ways. Can you think of other ways the two informational readings are different?* (narrative/interview, point of view, setting, tone, style) *Share your ideas with a partner.*

Spelling, Punctuation, Capitalization

After the Reading Comprehension section, students will practice spelling, punctuation, and capitalization in the Activity Book.

Beyond the Reading

Reading Comprehension

Question-Answer Relationships

Sample Answers

1. It means protection to help blend into their natural surroundings.
2. at night
3. spiders, insects, and sometimes small animals
4. It shows that they travel in large numbers on foot, like an army.
5. bats and army ants: Bats eat fruits, flowers, and insects. Army ants also eat insects, but they don't eat flowers or fruit.
6. No, they must have poor eyesight because they depend on hearing and smell instead of sight.
7. Colors might include green, yellow, and brown because these are the colors of plants and trees.
8. Answers will vary.
9. They want us to learn about creatures in the rain forest.
10. Yes, I think it is important because the animals need the environment to live in.

Build Reading Fluency

Adjust Your Reading Rate to Scan

Explain that students need to adjust their reading to quickly scan the text to locate key words. Have them read the question then quickly scan to find the answer and identify key words.

Reading Comprehension

Question-Answer Relationships (QAR)

"Right There" Questions

1. **Recall Facts** What does *camouflage* mean?
2. **Recall Facts** When do nocturnal creatures come out?
3. **Recall Facts** What animals do army ants eat for food?

"Think and Search" Questions

4. **Describe** How does the word *army* describe what army ants are like?
5. **Compare and Contrast** Choose two animals described in the article and tell how they are similar and different.

"Author and You" Questions

6. **Draw Conclusions** Do you think bats have good eyesight? Explain your answer.

7. **Make Inferences** The writers explain that rain forest creatures have colors that help them blend with their natural surroundings. What do you think some of these colors are? Why?

"On Your Own" Questions

8. **Explain** If you could be a rain forest creature, which one would you like to be? Explain your answer.
9. **Understand Author's Purpose** What do the authors want you to learn in this article?
10. **Discuss** Do you think that it is important to protect the rain forest? Why or why not?

Activity Book
p. 74

Student
CD-ROM

Build Reading Fluency

Adjust Your Reading Rate to Scan

When you scan, you adjust your reading rate to read fast. **Scanning** means looking quickly at the text for key words to help you answer a question. Work with a partner. Read aloud key words as you look for information. Write your answers on a piece of paper.

1. What is a predator?
2. What size eyes do nocturnal creatures have?
3. Name two creatures that live on the water banks.
4. What creatures make the rain forest trees twinkle?
5. Why do army ants kill?

MULTI-LEVEL OPTIONS *Elements of Literature*

Newcomer Read the captions aloud. Have students act out their meanings. Tell them to create their own picture or image of the rainforest. Help them write captions and share them in groups.

Beginning Look at and discuss each picture and its caption with students. Then have them create their own phrase or sentence approximation to restate the caption in simpler language.

Intermediate Ask students to create their own visual for this reading. Tell them to use their imagination or look for images in books or on the Internet. Then have them describe the visual in their own words.

Advanced *Say: Pictures and captions usually show something that was said in the text or add related information that was not in the text. How would authors decide which type to use?* (Show something from text if ideas are difficult. Add details if space is limited.)

Listen, Speak, Interact

Recall Details

Play a game where the goal is to remember the most details and content from the reading vocabulary.

1. First, write seven questions and answers for "Rain Forest Creatures." An example is, "What rain forest creature has a strong sense of smell?" (Answer: a bat)
2. Write each question and answer on a note card. Make sure to use vocabulary from the selection.
3. Then, meet with a partner. Take turns asking each other questions. Do not look in your books.
4. Keep score by giving one point for each correct answer. If you and your partner both wrote the same question and answer, you both automatically get one point.
5. When you finish, add up the points to find out who won the game.

Elements of Literature

Examine Visual Features

In this chapter, you learned that the purpose of an informational text is to explain something. This type of writing often includes **visuals** with **captions** to help the reader understand the text.

1. Look at the pictures on each page of the selection.
2. Read each caption. Think about how the captions help you understand the picture as well as the text.
3. Think of two more pictures that you would like to add to the selection.
4. Draw a diagram like this one. Write the page number for each picture. Draw the pictures in the boxes.
5. Write a caption that explains each picture and supports the text.

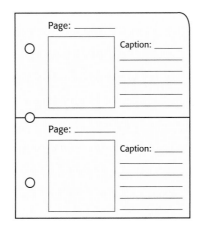

Page: _____
Caption: _____

Page: _____
Caption: _____

 Activity Book p. 75

 Student CD-ROM

Chapter 5 Rain Forest Creatures **141**

Listen, Speak, Interact

Recall Details

1. **Pair work** Monitor students as they write their questions. After students have worked with one partner, they can change partners and do additional questions.
2. **Newcomers** Work separately with these students if possible. Help them write questions. They can ask questions in groups.

Elements of Literature

Examine Visual Features

1. **Discuss visuals** Talk about what other visuals they would like to include. Have students find pictures of rain forest creatures in books or on the Internet to provide ideas for their drawings.
2. **Multi-level options** See MULTI-LEVEL OPTIONS on p. 140.

 **ASSESS**

Ask: How can an outline help you recall details?

 Content Connection
Math

Have pairs of students use books and Web sites to gather statistical information about rain forests. For example, a student might find the number of bird, reptile, and mammal species that live in the Amazon Rain Forest. Ask students to use a graph or table to create a visual feature that could be included in an article on the Amazon Rain Forest.

Learning Styles
Visual

Have small groups create board games reviewing facts about animals in the rain forest. For example, a group may draw a path of squares with an animal illustration in each and a set of question cards about those animals. Tell students to make up rules for how players will proceed around the board and what it will take to win. Have groups try out their games and then explain them to the class.

Word Study

Learn Word Origins

Discuss word origins *Ask: What words do you know that English has borrowed from another language? Are they spelled differently? Do they have the same meaning?*

Answers

collage-d; group-b; dialogue-e; role-f; souvenir-a; genre-c

Grammar Focus

Identify the Subject and Verb of a Sentence

Identify parts of speech Write on the board: *Go to school by bus. We by 8 A.M.* Have students identify the missing parts. (subject, verb) Have students rewrite the sentences correctly. Ask volunteers to read their suggestions.

Answers

1. not complete; I saw many animals in the rain forest. Subject (I), verb (saw)
2. not complete; It is hot and rainy there. Subject (It), verb (is)
3. complete; subject (bats), verb (are)

ASSESS

Have students copy two sentences from the reading and underline the subject and verb.

Word Study

Learn Word Origins

Many English words come from other languages and cultures. For example, the word *camouflage* is a French word that has become a part of the English language.

English has been borrowing words from French for over a thousand years. Sometimes the spelling in English has changed a little from the original French word.

1. In your Personal Dictionary, copy the list of other English words that come from French.
2. Match each word with the correct definition listed in the right-hand column. Use a dictionary to help you.

English Words from French	Definitions
collage	**a.** an object that is bought to remember a place
group	
dialogue	**b.** people that have something in common
role	
souvenir	**c.** type of writing
genre	**d.** different pictures placed together
	e. a talk between two people
	f. the part one has in a group

Personal Dictionary · The Heinle Newbury House Dictionary · Activity Book p. 76 · Student CD-ROM

Grammar Focus

Identify the Subject and Verb of a Sentence

The **subject** of a sentence is the word or phrase that performs the action indicated by the **verb.** Every complete sentence has a subject and a verb. Note the underlined subject and the circled verb in this sentence from paragraph 9:

At night, rain forest trees (twinkle) with fireflies and click beetles.

1. Write five sentences from the selection on a piece of paper.

2. Underline the subject of the sentence. Then circle the verb.
3. Decide if the following sentences are complete or not. If not, add a subject or a verb to make them complete.
   a. Many animals in the rain forest.
   b. Is hot and rainy there.
   c. Bats are nocturnal creatures.

Activity Book pp. 77–78 · Student Handbook · Student CD-ROM

MULTI-LEVEL OPTIONS *From Reading to Writing*

Newcomer Have students work in groups to create informational drawings or three-dimensional models of a place in the community. For example, students may present two parts of an amusement park. Tell them to show who goes to the places and what they do. Help students write labels for the activities shown.

Beginning Write a language experience story. Have students choose a location to be the topic of their report. Create a simple map of the place with students. On the map, write labels and phrases to note the parts of the location and the kinds of activities done in each part. Help students use the notes to write their group report.

Intermediate After students have written first drafts, have pairs meet for peer response. Ask responders to check for subjects and verbs in each sentence. Have responders help each other refine the visual features which can be added to the reports.

Advanced Remind students that reports should not be a list of facts. Point out that adding examples, statistics, and stories to their reports can make them interesting as well as informative. Ask students to use one or more of these techniques.

From Reading to Writing

Write an Informational Report

Write an informational report that explains something about a place in your community.

1. Write the report in the third person (use the pronouns *he, she, it,* and *they,* not *I* and *we*) and the present tense. Remember that a sentence must have a subject and a verb.
2. Include two or more separate sections. Write a heading for each section. The headings should provide clues about the main idea of each section.
3. Draw one or two pictures for the report. Add captions that explain what the pictures show.

Activities at Summer Park

○ Summer Park has something for everyone.

Swimming

○ There are two pools and one lake.

Team Sports

○

Activity Book
p. 79

Student
Handbook

Across Content Areas

Read Pie Charts

Earth's rain forests are disappearing. The **pie charts** here show the change from 1950 to 2002. Each circle represents Earth's land surface.

1. Which color shows the rain forests?
2. Which color shows other kinds of land on Earth?
3. Which statement is true, **a** or **b**?
   a. The rain forests were bigger in 1950 than in 2002.
   b. The rain forests were smaller in 1950 than in 2002.

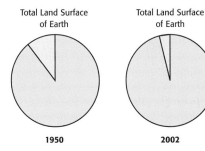

Total Land Surface
of Earth

Total Land Surface
of Earth

1950

2002

☐ Rain Forests
☐ Other Land

Activity Book
p. 80

Chapter 5 Rain Forest Creatures **143**

From Reading to Writing

Write an Informational Report

1. **Identify audience** *Ask: Who do you think might be interested in reading this?* (a newcomer or visitor) Remind students to include details to give their audience the most information possible.
2. **Proofread** After students have written their final drafts, have them trade papers and check the title, number of sections, capitalization, and that each sentence has a subject and verb.
3. **Multi-level options** See MULTI-LEVEL OPTIONS on p. 142.

Across Content Areas: Social Studies

Read Pie Charts

Relate to content areas *Say: You often find pie charts in social studies books. What other content books may have pie charts?* (math, science) *How do pie charts help show information?* (They provide a visual summary of data and numbers.)

Answers
1. green 2. orange 3. a

 **ASSESS**

Ask: What pronouns are used in an informational report? (he, she, it, they)

Reteach and Reassess

Text Structure Have students identify the informational text features in "Rain Forest Creatures." Discuss how the headings, pictures, and captions helped to make the writing clear and interesting.

Reading Strategy Have students review the outlines they created. Ask them to write a summary based on the outlines.

Elements of Literature Have students look at the visual features of a magazine or newspaper article. Ask them to identify the features and tell what they think the article will be about.

Reassess Have students make a cluster map. Tell them to write the title of the selection in the large circle, the most important three or four ideas they learned from the selection in the medium circles, and supporting details in the small circles.

Materials

Student Handbook
CNN Video: *Unit 2*
Teacher Resource Book: *Lesson Plan, p. 12;*
  Teacher Resources, pp. 35–64; Video Script,
  pp. 163–164; Video Worksheet, p. 174;
  School-Home Connection, pp. 126–132
Teacher Resource CD-ROM
Assessment Program: *Unit 2 Test, pp. 33–38;*
  Teacher and Student Resources, pp. 115–144
Assessment CD-ROM
Transparencies
The Heinle Newbury House Dictionary/CD-ROM
Heinle Reading Library: *Aesop's Fables*
Web site: http://visions.heinle.com

Listening and Speaking Workshop

Perform an Interview

Step 1: Prepare for your interview.
Using the rain forest as an example, help
students develop additional questions.

Step 2: Practice your questions as you get more information.
Have one pair of volunteers practice their
interview in front of the class. Give them
feedback on their questions, answers, eye
contact, speech, and posture.

UNIT 2 — Apply and Expand

Listening and Speaking Workshop

Perform an Interview

> **Topic**
>
> In Unit 2, you read selections about
> environments in a desert, a large city,
> and a rain forest. With a partner, write
> an interview and perform it in class.

Step 1: Prepare for your interview.

1. Decide who will be the
   interviewer—the one who asks
   questions—and who will be the
   interviewee—the one who answers
   the questions.
2. Make a list of questions and answers.
   Use what you learned from the
   readings in the unit to help you
   brainstorm. For example:
   a. What is your name?
   b. Where do you live?
   c. What's good about the
      environment where you live?
   d. What can you do to make it better?
3. Be prepared to revise (change) your
   questions as you get more
   information.

Step 2: Practice.

1. Use the "Interviewer's Guidelines."
2. If possible, record your interview so
   you can evaluate your work.
3. Speak clearly and look at each other.
4. Sit up straight and listen to the
   other person.

> **Interviewer's Guidelines**
>
> 1. Listen for important words and
>   phrases.
> 2. If the interviewee has difficulty
>   answering a question, consider
>   changing it.
> 3. Be polite.
>   a. Don't interrupt the interviewee.
>   b. Thank the interviewee for doing
>   the interview with you.

5. If you don't understand or need to
   revise your questions:
   Interviewer: Ask politely for more
   details.
   Interviewee: Ask the interviewer to
   repeat a question or to restate it (say
   it in different words).
6. After the interview:
   a. The interviewer summarizes
      (states in his or her own words)
      the interviewee's answers.
   b. The interviewee checks the
      interviewer's summary. If you
      made a recording, use it to help
      you check.

**Step 3: Present your interview to the
class or another audience.**

1. Tell the interview topic.
2. Conduct your interview using the
   questions and answers that you
   practiced above.

144 **Unit 2** Environment

MULTI-LEVEL OPTIONS *Listening and Speaking Workshop*

Newcomer Work with students
to create simple interview
questions and answers. Use facial
expressions and gestures to
clarify meaning. After the
questions and answers have been
prepared and reviewed, act as the
interviewer. Ask one question of
each student in the group.

Beginning Help each student
to create an interview question on
a slip of paper. Have pairs meet to
share their questions and write an
answer to each on another slip of
paper. Ask students to add
drawings to the slips to help them
recall the questions and answers.
Provide time for the group to
rehearse together before they
perform.

Intermediate Discuss with
students the importance of
avoiding questions that can be
answered *yes* or *no*. Ask them to
include some questions that ask
how, what if, and *why.*

Advanced Have students
watch a televised interview at
home or in school to determine
what kinds of behaviors set
interviewees at ease. Also, have
them notice what kinds of
questions result in interesting
discussions. Ask students to use
what they learn to make their own
interviews more effective.

Step 4: Evaluate your classmates' interviews.

1. Use the Active Listening Checklist to evaluate your classmates' interviews.
2. Create other items to add to the Active Listening Checklist.

Student Handbook

> ✓ **Active Listening Checklist**
>
> 1. I liked _____ because _____ .
> 2. I want to know more about _____ .
> 3. I understood the major ideas of your interview. Yes / No
> 4. The interviewer spoke confidently and knew the subject well. Yes / No
> 5. I understood the purpose of the interview. Yes / No

Viewing Workshop

View, Compare, and Contrast

Respond to Media

In Unit 2 you read the poem "Here Is the Southwestern Desert." Compare this poem with a rhyming tale entitled "Bringing the Rain to Kapiti Plain."

1. Rent a video of "Bringing the Rain to Kapiti Plain" or borrow one from your school library.
2. Watch the video with a partner.
3. Discuss with your partner how the video and the poem "Here Is the Southwestern Desert" are similar and different.
4. Use a chart like the one shown to record your responses.
5. Discuss with your class how reading the poem affects how you feel about deserts. Discuss how viewing the video affects how you feel about Kapiti Plain.

> *Here Is the Southwestern Desert*
> *Bringing the Rain to Kapiti Plain*
>
> | *Alike:* | *Different:* |
> | --- | --- |

6. Discuss with the class which media form (print or video) is more influential and informative.
   a. Explain with examples what you liked or disliked about each.
   b. Explain if you think the purpose of both versions is to inform, entertain, or persuade.

Further Viewing

Watch the *Visions* CNN Video for Unit 2. Do the Video Worksheet.

CNN Video

Step 3: Present your interview to the class or another audience.
Design, create, and distribute invitations to family, administrators, students, or other classes. Remind students to include dates and times of the presentations.

Step 4: Evaluate your classmates' interviews.
Model completing the Active Listening Checklist based on the volunteer presentation in Step 2. Discuss polite ways to give feedback.

ASSESS

Ask: *Which question got the most interesting answer? What question word was used?*

Portfolio

Students may choose to record or videotape their speeches to place in their portfolios.

Viewing Workshop

View, Compare, and Contrast

1. **Review text features** Have students reread "Here is the Southwestern Desert" on p. 80. Tell them to list the features of this poem. (stanzas, little rhyming, each stanza builds on the next, repetition)
2. **Use a graphic organizer** Have students discuss their completed comparison charts with another pair.

Content Connection **The Arts**	Learning Styles **Natural**

Compile a master list of the suggestions students made in their interviews about improving their local environment. Ask groups to create a collage showing ways to care for the local environment. Have them hang their art in places such as the school foyer, cafeteria, halls, and media center to help increase awareness.

Point out that both "Here is the Southwestern Desert" and "Bringing the Rain to Kapiti Plain" tell about things found in certain environments. Take students outside and ask them to collect some things from nature that are common in their environment. (Remind students not to do anything that could harm the environment, such as breaking branches off bushes.) Ask students to make attractive displays of the items.

Writer's Workshop

Write Rules

Step 1: Get ideas for your rules.
Ask: Does our school have any rules for the bus? Where could we find the rules? What rules do you follow when you walk to school?

Step 2: Organize your rules.
Ask: Can you explain why you think this is the most important rule?

Step 3: Write a draft of your guide.
Have students work in pairs to explain the reasons their rules are important before writing their drafts. You may want to give students the option of choosing another form of writing for rules, such as a poem, a letter, or a presentation.

Writer's Workshop

Write Rules

Prompt

Following rules about safety can make your neighborhood a better place to live. Write a guide that tells about rules that would help a person in your neighborhood.

Step 1: Get ideas for your rules.
1. With a partner, brainstorm ideas for rules. Use the Cluster Map.
2. Use resources to help you find rules. Go to the library to research information about safety rules, or look on the Internet (search word: *safety*).
3. Use graphic features, such as pictures and signs, to help you locate information. Also, use headings. They often tell about important ideas.

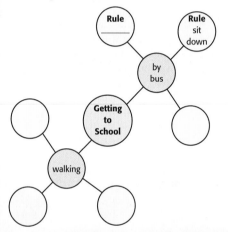

Step 2: Organize your rules.
1. Evaluate your research. Make sure the information you found is useful.
2. Summarize information about the rules you found on a piece of paper. Use your own words.
3. Choose three of the most important rules. Organize them in order, with the most important one first.
4. Use the three rules to complete the outline in the model below. This outline in the next step will also help you to summarize and organize information.

Step 3: Write a draft of your guide.
1. Think of a title for your rules.
2. Write a paragraph that explains why you are writing this list of rules. This is the introduction.
3. Write a heading for your rules.
4. Write your three rules in a numbered list (1, 2, 3). Start each rule on a new line.

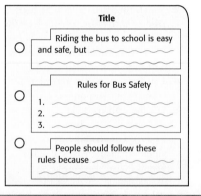

MULTI-LEVEL OPTIONS *Writer's Workshop*

Newcomer Introduce international symbols, such as the one showing that it is okay for people to cross a street, and a bike with a slash showing bike riding is not allowed. Have each student create two signs: one showing behavior that is okay and one with a slash showing something that is not okay.

Beginning Have students write their safety rules in the form of a picture book for primary grade students. Have them create detailed pictures and include phrases telling what is and is not safe to do.

Intermediate Have students turn their rules into a safety pamphlet for upper elementary students. Ask them to think about appropriate words and explanations for this age group. Suggest that they may want to use headings to make specific information easier to find.

Advanced After writing a first draft, ask pairs to meet. Have them discuss how they could use their guides as part of a safety lesson for upper elementary students. As they discuss their plans, tell them to look for places where more details or examples are needed.

5. You can explain a rule if you think your audience needs more information.
6. After your list of rules, write a final paragraph to explain why following these rules are good for people. This is the conclusion.
7. Use reference sources, such as a dictionary or grammar guide, to help you clearly write your paragraph.

Step 4: Revise the draft of your guide.

Carefully reread your draft and make sure you did the following:

1. You thought about your audience and your purpose for writing.
2. You wrote a paragraph of introduction and a paragraph of conclusion.
3. You used a heading for your rules. You put them in a numbered list.
4. You used reference sources to help you clarify ideas and revise text.
5. You used a resource, such as your Student Handbook, to help you revise your guide.

Step 5: Get peer editing.

1. Ask a partner to read your guide.
2. Ask your partner how you can make your guide better.
3. Revise your guide if necessary.

Step 6: Proofread and finish.

1. Use reference sources to proofread your guide. Check for mechanics: correct spelling, punctuation, and grammar.
2. If possible, type your story on a computer and check for mechanics.
3. Review your guide to make sure the rules are clearly written.

Step 7: Publish your guide.

1. Add visuals and captions that will help your audience understand.
2. If you wrote your guide on a computer, choose a font that you like. You can choose one font for your opening and closing paragraphs, and another one for your rules.
3. If you are writing by hand, make a final copy in your best handwriting.
4. With other students, post your guides on a bulletin board in the classroom or in the school so that other people can read them. If possible, post them on the Internet.
5. Take your guide home and share it with your family members.

The Heinle Newbury House Dictionary

Student Handbook

Step 4: Revise the draft of your guide.
Remind students to look back to their idea map and make sure they have included all their rules in the order from most to least important. Remind students to use a title at the beginning of the guide.

Step 5: Get peer editing.
Have each student give a partner at least two suggestions. Remind students to praise the strong points in the writing, too.

Step 6: Proofread and finish.
Point out that rules do not have a stated subject because the subject is understood. (*Sit down while the bus is moving.*)

Step 7: Publish your guide.
Compile students' work into a class safety guide. Make it available in the class library.

ASSESS

Ask: What part of your guide are you the most proud of? What was the hardest part of this project?

Portfolio

Students may choose to include their writing in their portfolios.

Cultural Connection

Remind students that in addition to rules for safety, it is also important to follow rules of good behavior. Explain that each culture has its own rules about manners. Ask students to share some of the rules for good behavior from other cultures. Select a few of these rules for students to follow for the rest of the day.

Learning Styles
Kinesthetic

After students have completed writing rules, small groups may meet to create short skits. The performances should show what could happen if one of the rules in their guides is broken and what would happen if it were obeyed. If possible, videotape each group's performance and ask the school media specialist to place the tape in the media center to be viewed by other students.

UNIT 2
Apply and Expand

Projects

Project 1: Make a Poster of a Special Environment

1. **Brainstorm** Suggest additional environments, like a hotel, a shopping mall, or a day care center.
2. **Design posters** Remind students to plan the design of their poster. Have them identify the main idea of the poster, the title, and artwork that supports the main idea.

Project 2: Prepare and Present a News Report

1. **Brainstorm topics** Have students brainstorm ideas for their report. Tell them to list parts of the environment, such as air, water, trees, or buildings, and things that might harm them.
2. **Provide a model** Show students a television news report from a local news channel. Tell students to pay attention to the type of speech, tone of voice, posture, and dress of the reporters.
3. **Collaborate with others** Have students complete the project in pairs or small groups.
4. **Practice and present** Have students practice their presentations with a partner before giving them to the class.

Portfolio

Students may choose to include their projects in their portfolios.

Projects

The following projects will help you expand what you learned about environments.

Project 1: Make a Poster of a Special Environment

Research an environment made by people.

1. Think of some special environments not in nature where people might live or work; for example, a submarine, a spacecraft, and a zoo.
2. Choose one special environment to learn more about. Make a list of questions about the place:
   a. What happens in the environment?
   b. What does a person (or animal) need to live there?
   c. What are the good and bad things about the environment?
   d. How can it be better?
3. Use your school library to research information about the environment. Record the answers to your questions and other facts on note cards. Write the answers in complete sentences.
4. Use headings, tables of contents, and graphic features (maps, pictures, charts). Use these text features to locate and organize information.
5. Ask your teacher or librarian to help you interpret information in the graphic features.
6. Revise your questions as you get information. Ask your school librarian to help you find the answers to additional questions.

7. Present the results of your research on a poster. Include pictures that relate to the environment. Include lists and charts to organize and summarize facts you learned about the environment.

Project 2: Prepare and Present a News Report

What is your community doing to protect the environment? Prepare a news report to discuss this issue.

1. Work with a partner to create questions to research. Ask your teacher or the librarian to help you.
2. Use multiple resources, such as newspapers and the Internet, to find answers to your questions.
3. If possible, interview the mayor or someone in charge of protecting the community's resources.
4. Organize your research and compose a news report.
5. Be sure to clarify and support your ideas with evidence, elaborations, and examples.
6. Edit your report and revise it to make it accurate.
7. Use a computer to write your report.
8. Pretend that you are speaking on television or on radio. Think about your audience. Adjust your word choice, diction (way of speaking), style, and usage to your audience.
9. Practice your news report.
10. Present your news report to the class or as a school announcement.

MULTI-LEVEL OPTIONS *Projects*

Newcomer Have students make detailed drawings on their posters of the environment they chose. Help them label the people who live or work there and significant words in the environment.

Beginning Have students complete their posters. Then have them make labels with a word or phrase related to a person, place, or thing shown on their poster on each card.

Intermediate Encourage students to select an environment related to a particular career that interests them. Have students role-play being a person involved in that profession as they present their posters. Invite them to bring in or make models of items that would be used in the environment.

Advanced Have students focus on the school environment. They might interview the principal or other school officials about what goes into planning a school. As an extension of their poster, encourage them to make suggestions to solve some problems or to make the environment better.

Further Reading

The following is a list of books that examine the theme of the environment. Chose one or more of them. Write your thoughts and feelings about what you read in your Reading Log. Answer the following questions:

1. How do humans affect the environment? How can humans protect the environment?
2. How are the environments you read about the same or different from the one you live in?
3. Can you connect the issues in the books you read to those of the reading selections in this unit?

Seedfolks
by Paul Fleischman, HarperCollins Children's Books, 1997. In this book by award-winning author Paul Fleischman, a story is told by thirteen different characters about a vacant lot in Cleveland, Ohio, that the community turns into a garden.

Lostman's River
by Cynthia C. DeFelice, William Morrow & Co., 1995. In 1906, Tyler and his family move from New York City to the Florida Everglades. Once there, Tyler discovers hunters who threaten the ecosystem of the Everglades. He fights to protect the Everglades and the animals that live there.

John Muir: Young Naturalist
by Montrew Dunham and Al Fiorentino, Simon & Schuster Children's, 1998. This is the biography of the "father of the conservation movement" in the United States. John Muir worked with President Theodore Roosevelt to establish the National Parks Service and create Yosemite National Park.

How Cities Work: Open Your Eyes to the Wonders of the Urban Environment
by Preston Gralla, DIANE Publishing Co., 1999. This book explains how the water, gas, and electric systems operate to keep cities functioning.

Environments of the Western Hemisphere
by John C. Gold, Twenty-First Century Books, 1997. This books discusses the different environments of North and South America. The book highlights the successes and failures of the people who have settled the land in the Western Hemisphere.

Song of the Trees, Vol. 1
by Mildred D. Taylor, Dial Books for Young Readers, 1976. Award-winning author Mildred Taylor writes about an African-American family in the southern United States during the Great Depression. The family tries to save the forest on their land from being cut down.

Weather and Sky: Explore the Extreme Forces of the Earth and Harsh Environment of Space
by Tim Walker and Chris Oxlade, Advantage Publishers Group, 2000. This book discusses the mysteries of natural disasters and space. Explore the planets and comets. Read about the devastation caused by typhoons and tornadoes.

Companion Web site

Reading Log

Heinle Reading Library Aesop's Fables

Further Reading

Sharing resources Have students bring books about the environment that interest them. Ask them to look for new books about the environment in the library. Put the books in a special area of the classroom where students can browse and read the materials.

▌ Assessment Program: *Unit 2 Test, pp. 33–38*

Heinle Reading Library

Aesop's Fables

Here are not only the Tortoise and the Hare, and the Grasshopper and the Ant, but dozens more of the delightful creatures that have been entertaining and instructing people for thousands of years. The storyteller Aesop lived in ancient Greece, far away from us in time and distance. But his clever little stories have as much meaning for us today as they did when he first told them so long ago. . . .

Visions Companion Site

http://visions.heinle.com
For additional student activities and teacher resources, see the Visions Companion Web site.

UNIT 3

Conflict and Cooperation

Unit Materials

Activity Book: *pp. 81–120*
Audio: *Unit 3; CD 1, Tracks 12–16*
Student Handbook
Student CD-ROM: *Unit 3*
CNN Video: *Unit 3*
Teacher Resource Book: *Lesson Plans, Teacher Resources, Reading Summaries, School-Home Connection, Video Script, Video Worksheet, Activity Book Answer Key*
Teacher Resource CD-ROM
Assessment Program: *Quizzes, Test, and Mid-Book Exam, pp. 39–60; Teacher and Student Resources, pp. 115–144*
Assessment CD-ROM
Transparencies
The Heinle Newbury House Dictionary/CD-ROM
More Grammar Practice workbook
Heinle Reading Library: *Dr. Jekyll and Mr. Hyde*
Web site: http://visions.heinle.com

Visions Staff Development Handbook

Refer to the Visions Staff Development Handbook for more teacher support.

Unit Theme: Conflict and Cooperation

Clarify the theme words *Say: A conflict can be a fight, like a war, a disagreement between friends, or a struggle inside us. Can you give an example of a conflict?*

Unit Preview: Table of Contents

1. **Use the table of contents to make predictions** *Ask: Which titles do you think are based on true stories? Why? What genres will we read?* (song, play, diary entry, personal narrative, informational text)
2. **Connect** *Ask: Which genre in this unit do you like best?*

150

UNIT OBJECTIVES

Reading
Make inferences as you read song lyrics • Recognize sequence of events as you read an excerpt from a diary • Analyze cause and effect as you read a play • Summarize to recall ideas as you read a personal narrative • Identify main idea and details as you read an informational text

Listening and Speaking
Practice intonation • Role-play a persuasive conversation • Talk about values • Summarize and paraphrase • Talk about dealing with stress

Martin Luther King Jr. memorial, in Selma, Alabama.

View the Picture

1. Describe what you see.
2. Why do you think someone made a statue of Martin Luther King Jr.?

In this unit, you will read about conflict and cooperation. You will explore this theme by reading a song, a diary entry, a play, an excerpt from a personal narrative, and an informational text. You will also practice writing these forms.

151

View the Picture

1. **Art background** Tell students that this bronze bust welcomes visitors to the historic Brown Chapel in Selma, Alabama. It was dedicated to Dr. Martin Luther King Jr. in 1979. Fourteen years earlier, King tried to lead a voting-rights march from Selma to the state capital in Montgomery. The marchers were stopped with tear gas, beatings, and arrests before they reached their goal, but the event resulted in a national outpouring of support for the civil rights movement. Within five months, President Lyndon B. Johnson had signed the Voting Rights Act of 1965 into law, protecting the voting rights of all citizens equally.

2. **Art interpretation** *Ask: Do you think Dr. Martin Luther King Jr. is a good subject for the theme of this unit? How does he represent conflict and cooperation?*

   a. **Use personal experience** *Ask: What do you know about Dr. King and the protests he led in the 1960s? Have you seen any other memorials, such as the Lincoln Memorial or the Washington Monument?*

   b. **Connect to theme** *Say: The theme of this unit is* conflict and cooperation. *How does the subject of this bust represent the theme?*

ASSESS

Have students draw an image of conflict or cooperation and write a caption for the drawing.

Grammar

Talk about the future using *will* and *shall* • Use verbs with infinitives • Use compound sentences with *and* • Use *could* and *couldn't* • Recognize complex sentences with *if*

Writing

Write lyrics for a song about the future • Write your opinion • Write a summary • Write to solve a problem • Write an informational text

Content

The Arts: Learn about types of songs • Social Studies: Learn the points of the compass • Science: Classify fruits and vegetables • Language Arts: Learn about graphic features • Language Arts: Learn different meanings of *conflict*

We Shall
Overcome

a traditional song

Chapter Materials

Activity Book: *pp. 81–88*
Audio: *Unit 3, Chapter 1; CD 1, Track 12*
Student Handbook
Student CD-ROM: *Unit 3, Chapter 1*
Teacher Resource Book: *Lesson Plan, Teacher
    Resources, Reading Summary, Activity Book
    Answer Key*
Teacher Resource CD-ROM
Assessment Program: *Quiz, pp. 39–40; Teacher
    and Student Resources, pp. 115–144*
Assessment CD-ROM
Transparencies
The Heinle Newbury House Dictionary/CD-ROM
Web site: http://visions.heinle.com

Objectives

Reading Make inferences as you read
song lyrics.

Listening and Speaking Practice
intonation.

Grammar Talk about the future using *will*
and *shall*.

Writing Write lyrics for a song about
the future.

Content The Arts: Learn about types
of songs.

Objectives

Preview *Ask: Which objective is the most
interesting to you? Why?*

Use Prior Knowledge

Share and Compare Traditional Songs

Connect to personal experience *Say: We all
learn songs when we are growing up. For
example, "Row, Row, Row Your Boat" and "I've
Been Working on the Railroad" are both
traditional songs. Can you sing these songs?
Can you sing any traditional songs in another
language?*

Use Prior Knowledge

Share and Compare Traditional Songs

   Traditional songs are songs that are
passed down from generation to
generation. People usually learn
traditional songs in school or from their
families.

1. With a partner, talk about or sing
    some traditional songs that you
    know from your culture or region.
    a. What is the title, or name, of
        the song?
    b. What is the song about?
    c. How does the language in
        the song reflect the culture
        or region?

Name of Student	Title of Song	What Song Is About
Julio	Mi Escuelita	a school

2. Copy the chart on a piece of paper.
    Write information about the songs.
3. Share your chart with the rest of
    the class.

MULTI-LEVEL OPTIONS *Build Vocabulary*

Newcomer Write on the board:
peace, fights. Have students look
at pictures in nonfiction and
historical fiction books concerning
various times in history. Have
students point to pictures of
people interacting peacefully
(meeting, helping each other,
shaking hands) and ones showing
battles and conflicts.

Beginning After discussing the
words with students, assign them
to work in pairs. Give each pair a
word card with one of the words
on it. Ask them to create a simple
skit showing the meaning of the
word on their card. Provide time
for students to share their skits
with the class.

Intermediate Have students
work in pairs to predict how the
vocabulary words will be used in
a selection about the civil rights
movement.

Advanced Have students
consider how the vocabulary
words are related. Ask them to
create diagrams showing the
relationship between two or more
of the words. Tell them to select
colors, lines, shapes, and
placements that will show how
the words connect. Have students
present and explain their
diagrams.

Build Background

The Civil Rights Movement

African-Americans did not always have the same rights as other Americans. For example, in many places, African-Americans had to sit in the back of public buses or trains. In the 1950s and 1960s, many people worked to get equal rights for all Americans. This is called the Civil Rights movement. People participated in marches, or long walks, to protest and push for change. During the marches, they sang songs about freedom. Freedom means that you can speak and act without being stopped. One famous freedom song is "We Shall Overcome."

Content Connection

In 1965, about 25,000 people marched into Montgomery, Alabama, to show they wanted equal rights for all Americans.

Build Vocabulary

Learn Words About Freedom

"We Shall Overcome" uses words that help you understand freedom.

We shall live in peace.

Peace is a part of freedom. Peace is a time without war.

1. Copy the chart in your Personal Dictionary.
2. With a partner, read the definitions.
3. Complete the chart with the words listed below.

| justice | right | democracy |

Word	Definition
	a type of government where people vote for the representatives who make laws
	carrying out and applying laws in a way that is fair
	freedom or permission to do something by law

Personal Dictionary   The Heinle Newbury House Dictionary   Activity Book p. 81   Student CD-ROM

Chapter 1 We Shall Overcome   **153**

Content Connection
Social Studies

Build Background Have students look at photographs from the civil rights era in juvenile and young adult nonfiction books. Ask them to create a list of actions people took to correct unfair practices. (marching, speaking, signing petitions, conducting sit-ins, writing articles and songs)

Learning Styles
Visual

Build Vocabulary Remind students that they learned in "Sadako and the Thousand Paper Cranes" (Unit 1) that the crane is a symbol of peace. Ask students to use the Internet and other resources to find as many symbols of peace from around the world as possible. (dove, hand sign, Chinese alphabet character for peace, rainbow ribbon, peace sign)

Build Background

The Civil Rights Movement

1. **Build background** Write *discrimination* on the board. Have students look it up in a dictionary. *Say: During the 1950s and 1960s, there was a lot of discrimination against African-Americans. They could not go to the same schools, eat in the same restaurants, or attend the same theaters as other Americans. Do you know anything about the civil rights movement?*

2. **Content Connection** Dr. Martin Luther King Jr. (1929–1968) was an African-American minister and civil rights leader who led many marches and demonstrations, first in the South and later nationwide.

Build Vocabulary

Teacher Resource Book: *Personal Dictionary, p. 63*

Learn Words About Freedom

1. **Use vocabulary** *Ask: What countries are democracies? What rights do you have in the United States? What rights do citizens of other countries have? Courts try to apply justice to situations of law. Is justice always possible?*

2. **Reading selection vocabulary** You may want to introduce the glossed words in the reading selection before students begin reading. Key words: *overcome, dignity.* Instruct students to write the words with correct spelling and their definitions in their Personal Dictionaries. Have them pronounce each word and divide it into syllables.

3. **Multi-level options** See MULTI-LEVEL OPTIONS on p. 152.

Answers
Chart top to bottom: democracy, justice, right.

ASSESS

Say: Write four words related to the civil rights movement.

Text Structure

Song Lyrics

1. **Recognize features** *Say: A song is like a poem. What are groups of lines called in a poem?* (stanzas) *Do poems have lines that are repeated?* (sometimes) *Do songs have rhyming words?* (sometimes)

2. **Relate to personal experience** *Ask: Do you know the lyrics of your favorite songs? What makes them good?* Have volunteers share lines from their favorite songs.

Reading Strategy

Make Inferences

1. **Teacher think aloud** *Say: I went to a store last night. When I looked inside the store, I saw that it was dark inside. I know that stores turn off their lights when they are closed. I can infer that the store had already closed.*

2. **Use a glossary** Have students locate the meaning and derivation of *inference* in the glossary in their Student Handbook.

3. **Multi-level options** See MULTI-LEVEL OPTIONS below.

ASSESS

Have students tell you the meaning of lyrics, verses, and refrain.

Text Structure

Song Lyrics

The reading selection in this chapter is a **song**. A song has words called **lyrics** that are set to music. The chart shows some features of lyrics that are used in "We Shall Overcome."

As you read, listen to, or sing "We Shall Overcome," look for these features.

♫ Song Lyrics ♫	
Verses	groups of lines
Refrain	lines repeated at the end of each verse
Direction	a word or words that tell how to sing the song

Student
CD-ROM

Reading Strategy

Make Inferences

When you **make inferences,** you use information in the text and what you already know to make a guess. For example, you hear a song about a person who wants to live in the mountains. You might make the inference that the person likes the mountains.

Writers do not always say everything directly. If you make inferences as you read, you will understand more of what the writer is saying.

1. As you read or listen to "We Shall Overcome," make inferences about the people who sing the song. Write your inferences on a piece of paper.

2. Compare your inferences with a partner. Did you both hear the same message?

Student
CD-ROM

MULTI-LEVEL OPTIONS *Reading Strategy*

Newcomer Help students make inferences about the picture on p. 155. *Ask: Do the people want to change something?* (yes) *Do they want others to know how they feel?* (yes) *Are they fighting?* (no)

Beginning Direct students to the picture on p. 155. Ask them to make some guesses about what is happening. *Ask: What are the people doing?* (letting others know their feelings; marching for a cause) *How are they doing this?* (peacefully)

Intermediate Have pairs of students work together to make inferences about the picture on p. 155. As they share their ideas, ask if information in the picture led them to make each inference. (The people want to bring attention to the problem. They are marching peacefully. They are singing, not fighting.)

Advanced Tell students that people who write books select their words and illustrations carefully so readers can make certain inferences. *Ask: What are some inferences you think the writer wanted you to make?* (People of all ages and races worked for better treatment of African-Americans.)

WE SHALL OVERCOME

a traditional song

155

Reading Selection Materials

Audio: *Unit 3, Chapter 1; CD 1, Track 12*
Teacher Resource Book: *Reading Summary, pp. 85–86*
Transparencies: #7, *Reading Summary*

Suggestions for Using Reading Summary

- Introduce new vocabulary or cognates.
- Cut the summary into strips, or jumble the sentences on an overhead transparency. Students put the sentences in order.
- Practice the reading strategy.
- Students read aloud or with a partner.
- Students paraphrase the summary.
- Students do a cloze activity.
- Students create a visual or graphic organizer, such as a timeline or storyboard, to illustrate the summary.
- Students paraphrase the summary.

Preview the Selection

1. **Interpret the image** Have students look at the photograph. *Say: This is a picture of folk singer Pete Seeger singing on the steps of the New York State Capitol Building during a civil rights demonstration. Why do you think he is singing here? What kind of music do you think he is playing? Do you think his music has a message? What might the message be?*
2. **Connect to theme** *Say: In times of conflict, people often use music to express their feelings and opinions. What songs or music groups do you know that have a message? What is the message? Is music a good way to spread a message?*

Community Connection

Have students identify some situations or problems in their community that citizens are working to change or solve. Ask them to describe any actions that people in the community have taken to let others know their feelings about the issues. (pamphlets, meetings, petitions, news reports)

Learning Styles
Linguistic

Point out that demonstrators who are trying to convince others to make changes often carry signs with slogans, or short phrases. Given what they learned about the civil rights movement from p. 153, ask students to write slogans that demonstrators could have used to share their feelings.

Read the Selection

1. **Choral reading** Play the audio. Play the audio again and have students sing along.
2. **Identify text features** Remind students that the prologue and the photograph provide background information for the song. *Ask: How many verses are there?* (5) *What is the refrain?* (Oh, deep in my heart I do believe . . . someday.) *What other parts are repeated?* (In each verse, the first line is repeated three times.)
3. **Relate to personal experience** *Ask: Have you ever heard or sung this song before? When?*

Sample Answer to Guide Question
They want to overcome discrimination and inequality.

See Teacher Edition pp. 434–436 for a list of English-Spanish cognates in the reading selection.

Audio
CD 1, Tr. 12

Prologue

"We **Shall Overcome**" is a song about peace and justice. The words come from a song that was written in 1901. The song has gone through many changes.

People sang "We Shall Overcome" during marches of the **Civil Rights** movement in the 1960s in the United States. Now people all over the world sing it when they are fighting for their civil rights.

With dignity

Make Inferences

What do the people singing the song want to overcome?

shall will	**civil rights** the rights of each citizen
overcome fight against something successfully	**dignity** pride in oneself

156 Unit 3 Conflict and Cooperation

MULTI-LEVEL OPTIONS *Read the Selection*

Newcomer Play the audio. *Ask: Is the song about peace?* (yes) *Do people singing this song want to be free?* (yes) *Does the song talk about being rich?* (no) *Are the people singing this song alone?* (no)

Beginning Play the audio. *Ask: What do people who sing this song want?* (peace, freedom) *When do they think they will get what they want?* (someday)

Intermediate Play the audio. Then have students sing it. *Ask: How long ago was the song written?* (over 100 years ago) *How do the singers describe the world they want?* (as a free, peaceful world) *How does stanza 5 say that the singers will get what they want?* (by working together)

Advanced Have students sing the song. *Ask: Why do you think civil rights demonstrators used this song even though it was old?* (It expressed their feelings.) *What can you infer from the last two lines of each stanza?* (People think that change doesn't happen fast.)

2   **We'll** walk hand in hand,
     We'll walk hand in hand,
     We'll walk hand in hand someday.
     Oh, deep in my heart I do believe
     we'll walk hand in hand someday.

3   We shall live in peace,
     We shall live in peace,
     We shall live in peace someday.
     Oh, deep in my heart I do believe
     we shall live in peace someday.

4   We shall all be free,
     We shall all be free,
     We shall all be free someday.
     Oh, deep in my heart I do believe
     we shall all be free someday.

5   We are not alone,
     We are not alone,
     We are not alone someday.
     Oh, deep in my heart I do believe
     we are not alone someday.

> **Make Inferences**
>
> Why do the people who are singing say they are not alone? Explain your answer.

We'll We will

Chapter 1 We Shall Overcome   **157**

Read the Selection

1. **Shared reading** Divide the class into five groups. Read or sing the selection aloud. Have each group join in for one of the verses.
2. **Make inferences** *Say: In stanza 2, the song says, "We'll walk hand in hand." Who does "we" refer to? Why do you think so? Who does "we" refer to in stanza 5?*
3. **Multi-level options** See MULTI-LEVEL OPTIONS on p. 156.

Sample Answer to Guide Question
They don't feel alone because they know that other people in other places are also struggling for their civil rights.

Across Selections

▮ Teacher Resource Book: *Venn Diagram, p. 35*

Say: A song and a poem share several features. Look at "We Shall Overcome" and "Here Is the Southwestern Desert" (p. 80). Have students work in pairs to create a Venn diagram that compares and contrasts the features. (Song: directions, verses; poem: stanzas; both: refrain/repetition)

Spelling, Punctuation, Capitalization

After the Reading Comprehension section, students will practice spelling, punctuation, and capitalization in the Activity Book.

Punctuation

Comma between city and state

Direct students to the "Content Connection" box on p. 153. Ask them to find *Montgomery, Alabama*. **Ask:** *What mark is between the city, Montgomery, and the state, Alabama?* (a comma) *Yes, a comma is used between a city and state.* On the board, write the name of your city and state. Ask students to tell you how to punctuate it.

   Apply Have students name cities and states they have visited. Write these on the board and have students punctuate them.

Evaluate Your Reading Strategy

Make Inferences *Say: You have practiced an important reading strategy. Now you can decide how well you have done. Does this statement describe how you read?*

> When I read, I make inferences. Making inferences helps me understand the message of what I am reading.

Reading Comprehension

Question-Answer Relationships

Sample Answers

1. We Shall Overcome
2. 1901
3. hand in hand
4. If you sing with dignity, you show pride. They want people to stand up for their rights and freedom.
5. No. That is why they are marching.
6. directions for singing, musical notes, a refrain, verses
7. It made me believe in the words of the song. It gave me hope and strength to face difficulties and challenges.
8. When people sing together, it makes them feel unified and lifts their spirits. It could help them believe in themselves.

Build Reading Fluency

Adjust Your Reading Rate to Memorize

Demonstrate to students that reading to memorize means adjusting your reading to be slow with stops to review your progress.

Reading Comprehension

Question-Answer Relationships (QAR)

"Right There" Questions

1. **Recall Facts** What is the title of the song?
2. **Recall Facts** When was the song written?
3. **Recall Facts** According to the song, how will people walk someday?

"Think and Search" Questions

4. **Make Inferences** Why is there a direction to sing the song "with dignity"?
5. **Make Inferences** Are the people singing the song living in peace?

"Author and You" Question

6. **Understand Features** List three features that tell you the reading selection is a song.

"On Your Own" Questions

7. **Describe Effects** What effect did listening to the song and lyrics have on you?
8. **Explain** Do you think singing a song like this helps people reach their goals? Explain your answer.

Activity Book
p. 82

Student
CD-ROM

Build Reading Fluency

Adjust Your Reading Rate to Memorize

One purpose of reading is to memorize. You must adjust your reading rate to read slowly. You need to read, think, and reread to remember. Reading a song can give you excellent practice in reading to memorize.

1. Listen to the audio recording of "We Shall Overcome."
2. In small groups, read or sing each line slowly on pages 156–157.
3. Practice memorizing the song.
4. In small groups, present the song to the class.

MULTI-LEVEL OPTIONS *Elements of Literature*

Newcomer Play the audio. Ask students to beat out gently the rhythm of the words on their desks each time they hear lines that are repeated.

Beginning Remind students that songwriters repeat some lines to show that the ideas are very important. Stanza by stanza, rehearse the repeated lines with students. Then sing the song or play the audio. Ask students to join in with strong, expressive voices on the repetitive lines.

Intermediate Have students look through songbooks or poetry anthologies to find other examples of repetition. Ask them to compare and contrast examples they find with the pattern of repetition in "We Shall Overcome."

Advanced Have students reread "Here Is the Southwestern Desert" in Unit 2. Have them compare and contrast the type of repetition used in the poem with the repetition in "We Shall Overcome." Discuss the author's purpose for repetition in each case.

Listen, Speak, Interact

Practice Intonation

When you sing a song, your voice goes up and down. When you speak, your voice also goes up and down. This is called **intonation.**

In English, statements have intonation like this. Listen as your teacher demonstrates how this intonation sounds:

We shall overcome.

1. Work with a partner. Take turns reading a verse from "We Shall Overcome." Follow the intonation for statements as you read.
2. Compare your intonation with your partner's. Did your voices go up and down on the same words?
3. Compare your reading of the lyrics with the way they are sung on the audio recording.

Elements of Literature

Recognize Repetition

"We Shall Overcome" uses **repetition.** Repetition is saying the same thing more than once. You repeat something when you want to say it more strongly. Repetition helps the people singing the song show that they feel strongly about the song's message.

1. Copy this chart in your Reading Log.
2. Reread "We Shall Overcome," or listen to the audio recording again.
3. In your chart, write the line from each verse that is repeated.
4. Think about why the people singing these verses might feel strongly about the lines that are repeated.
5. Compare the lyrics of the song to the poems you read in Unit 1. How are they the same? How are they different?

Verse	Repeated Line
Verse 1	We shall overcome
Verse 2	
Verse 3	
Verse 4	
Verse 5	

Reading Log   Activity Book p. 83   Student CD-ROM

Cultural Connection

Have students point up or down to indicate when your voice goes up and down during your demonstration of intonation. Point out that some languages have intonation and some do not. Then ask student volunteers to say a few sentences in another language. Have other students point up or down if they hear the speaker's voice go up or down.

Learning Styles
Kinesthetic

Divide the class into five groups. Assign each group a stanza. Instruct group members to use American Sign Language dictionaries from the library or make up hand and body movements for the repetitive lines in each stanza. Have groups rehearse signing their stanzas. Provide time for students to perform for another class.

Listen, Speak, Interact

Practice Intonation

1. **Model intonation** Write on the board: *Where are you going? To town.* Draw intonation lines and have students practice the rising and falling voice pattern.
2. **Choral reading** Model the intonation pattern shown in the text and have students repeat. Read one verse of the song. Then have students read it with you to practice intonation.
3. **Newcomers** Show the rising and falling intonation pattern with your hand as you say the lines. Have students repeat after you and use their own hand gestures. Then have them say the lines individually with their own gestures.

Elements of Literature

Recognize Repetition

1. **Discuss genre features** Remind students that poems also use repetition, such as in "Here Is the Southwestern Desert." Point out that the refrain is repeated after each verse and that this is a form of repetition.
2. **Use a glossary** Have students locate the meaning and derivation of *repetition* in the glossary in their Student Handbook.
3. **Multi-level options** See MULTI-LEVEL OPTIONS on p. 158.

Answers

3. Verse 2: We'll walk hand in hand. Verse 3: We shall live in peace. Verse 4: We shall all be free. Verse 5: We are not alone.
4. *Possible answer:* Repeating the lines gives them more importance. The lines that are repeated are asking for human rights.
5. *Possible answers:* Similarities: groups of lines (stanzas in all three poems), rhyme ("Thanksgiving"), rhythm ("Thanksgiving"), repetition ("Here Is the Southwestern Desert"). Differences: strong language ("Thanksgiving"), images ("Family Photo"), experiences ("Family Photo").

ASSESS

Have groups of students each sing a verse from the song or read it with proper intonation.

Word Study

Recognize Homographs

1. **Define and clarify** Have students repeat examples after you, distinguishing the pronunciation between the homographs.
2. **Clarify meaning and usage** Have students use a print, online, or CD-ROM dictionary or thesaurus to clarify the meaning and usage of the new words.

Answers

Bass (rhymes with *class*): a type of fish; *bass* (sounds like *base*): a low singing voice. *Tear* (rhymes with *air*): to rip; *tear* (rhymes with *fear*): a drop of salty liquid from the eye. *Lead* (rhymes with *seed*): to go first; *lead* (rhymes with *head*): a soft metal.

Grammar Focus

Talk About the Future Using *Will* and *Shall*

Compare tenses Write on the board: *I am going to buy a ticket tomorrow. I will buy a ticket tomorrow.* Explain that the meaning is almost the same. Show the contraction *we'll.* Point out that the negative contraction of *will* is *won't.*

Answer

We'll walk hand in hand.

ASSESS

Say: Write two sentences about something you promise to do tomorrow. Use the verb will.

Word Study

Recognize Homographs

The English language contains some words that are spelled the same but have different pronunciations and meanings. These words are called **homographs.** Look at these examples of homographs:

> We shall <u>live</u> in peace. (verse 3)

> We heard a <u>live</u> concert on the radio.

In the first sentence, the word *live* means "to be alive." This word is pronounced with a short *i* as in *sit.*

In the second sentence, the word *live* means "a performance that is heard as it is happening." This word is pronounced with a long *i* as in *line.*

1. Copy these homographs in your Personal Dictionary.

bass/bass	tear/tear	lead/lead

2. Use a dictionary to check the pronunciations and meanings of the words.
3. With a partner, practice pronouncing the words.
4. Write the definitions in your Personal Dictionary.

Personal Dictionary   The Heinle Newbury House Dictionary   Activity Book p. 84   Student CD-ROM

Grammar Focus

Talk About the Future Using *Will* and *Shall*

The **future tense** tells about things that are going to happen. The words *will* and *shall* show future tense.

Will is used more often. It describes an activity that you predict or promise to do in the future.

> We **will** go to the zoo tomorrow.

Will can be made into a contraction (shortened words).

> We'**ll** go to the zoo tomorrow.

Shall is rarely used today to talk about the future, but it can be used to make a suggestion.

> Shall we leave now?

Reread verse 2 of "We Shall Overcome." On a piece of paper, write a sentence that uses *will.*

Activity Book pp. 85–86   Student Handbook   Student CD-ROM

160   Unit 3   Conflict and Cooperation

MULTI-LEVEL OPTIONS *From Reading to Writing*

Newcomer Have students listen to pieces of instrumental music. Invite students to select pieces that express how they would like to feel in the future. Ask students to create drawings of their future hopes and wishes. Help them create captions. Invite students to play their music and show their drawings.

Beginning Have students use the song "We Shall Overcome" as a model. As a class, help them keep the rhythm and pattern of the song, but have them change the endings of the lines to tell about their *own* future wishes. Have students sing the song they create.

Intermediate If students have difficulty matching a familiar song to the lyrics they write, provide an alternative. Have them listen to various pieces of instrumental music and select one to play as they read their lyrics as a poem.

Advanced In addition to considering lyrics and melody, ask students to think about the kinds of instruments that would be most appropriate for their songs. Ask them to justify their choice. (loud drums, tubas, and trumpets, because I have big plans; a single recorder, because I know I have to make my own dreams come true)

From Reading to Writing

Write Lyrics for a Song About the Future

Write lyrics for a song about what you will do in the future.

1. Choose a topic to write about.
2. Give your song a title.
3. Follow the structure of a song. Give a direction about how to sing the song. Write one verse. Use repetition.
4. Use *will* to tell about what you think will happen to you.
5. You can think of a song that you know and match your lyrics to the music and intonation of that song.
6. Choose a style (how the song is written) and a voice (how the song sounds) that best fit your topic and audience.

We Will Laugh	
direction:	*happily*
verse:	*I will laugh with my family,*
	I will laugh with my friends,
	I will laugh with my neighbors.
	Oh, we will all laugh together.

7. Perform your song. As you listen to your classmates, recognize the structure and intonation of their song.

Activity Book
p. 87

Student
Handbook

Across Content Areas

Learn About Types of Songs

Here are some types of songs:

lullaby a song that you sing to a child to help him or her fall asleep

anthem a song that shows admiration or respect for something

ballad a song that tells a story

hymn a religious song

Complete each of the following sentences with the correct type of song.

1. The old man sang a ____ about how a famous princess saved her country.
2. We looked at the flag as we sang the national ____ .
3. We sang a ____ at church.
4. The baby cried and cried until his mother sang a ____ .

In a small group, write a letter to a favorite songwriter. Tell this person why you like his or her songs. Organize your letter into paragraphs. Revise it for spelling and grammar.

Activity Book
p. 88

Chapter 1 Chapter 1 We Shall Overcome **161**

From Reading to Writing

Write Lyrics for a Song About the Future

1. **Teacher think aloud** Read the instructions for the activity and the example. *Say: I'm going to write about next weekend. I will call my friends. I will go to a party. I will . . .*
2. **Share lyrics** Direct students to create their songs in small groups. Have groups read or sing their lyrics to the class.
3. **Multi-level options** See MULTI-LEVEL OPTIONS on p. 160.

Across Content Areas: The Arts

Learn About Types of Songs

Relate to personal experience *Ask: Does anyone know a lullaby to sing for us?* Have students give examples of the different kinds of songs.

Answers
1. ballad 2. anthem 3. hymn 4. lullaby

✓ ASSESS

Have students give a definition of *lyrics* and *verse*.

Reteach and Reassess

Text Structure Have students look at selections in a music book. Ask them to see how many of the features described on p. 154 they can find. Have them note any other features that were not included on the chart.

Reading Strategy Play or share the lyrics from another song from the civil rights era, such as "If I Had a Hammer" by Peter, Paul, and Mary. Ask students to make inferences about the feelings and beliefs of the people who wrote the song.

Elements of Literature Read a poem or song that includes repetition. Have students chart the pattern of the repetition.

Reassess Share with students the lyrics of a patriotic song from a Web site or songbook. Pick one that includes repetition, such as "You're a Grand Old Flag." Have students identify repetition and make inferences about the ideas expressed.

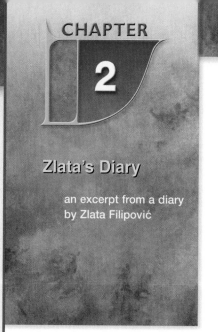

CHAPTER
2

Zlata's Diary

an excerpt from a diary
by Zlata Filipović

Into the Reading

Objectives

Reading Recognize sequence of events as you read an excerpt from a diary.

Listening and Speaking Role-play a persuasive conversation.

Grammar Use verbs with infinitives.

Writing Write your opinion.

Content Social Studies: Learn the points of the compass.

Chapter Materials

Activity Book: *pp. 89–96*
Audio: *Unit 3, Chapter 2; CD 1, Track 13*
Student Handbook
Student CD-ROM: *Unit 3, Chapter 2*
Teacher Resource Book: *Lesson Plan, Teacher Resources, Reading Summary, Activity Book Answer Key*
Teacher Resource CD-ROM
Assessment Program: *Quiz, pp. 41–42; Teacher and Student Resources, pp. 115–144*
Assessment CD-ROM
Transparencies
The Heinle Newbury House Dictionary/CD-ROM
Web site: http://visions.heinle.com

Objectives

Preview Read the objectives. *Ask: Do you know what a diary is? Have you ever kept a diary?*

Use Prior Knowledge

Discuss Your Feelings About Experiences

Connect to personal experience *Say: The selection in this chapter is a diary. People write about their feelings in a diary. You can write about what makes you happy, sad, scared, or angry. Use one of your experiences to model filling in the chart on the board.*

Use Prior Knowledge

Discuss Your Feelings About Experiences

Think about experiences in your life that made you feel happy, sad, scared, or angry.

1. On a piece of paper, make a chart like the one here. Write some of your experiences in the chart. How did each experience make you feel?
2. Share your chart with a partner.

Experience	How I Felt
I moved to a new city.	sad

Examples of Experiences

I got an A in math.

My cat ran away.

I broke my arm.

Examples of Feelings

happy   hopeful

sad   brave

scared   angry

162   Unit 3 Conflict and Cooperation

MULTI-LEVEL OPTIONS *Build Vocabulary*

Newcomer Hug yourself and shiver. *Say: cold.* Wipe your brow and fan yourself. *Say: hot.* Demonstrate a few other opposites. Then smile broadly and *say: happy.* Point to students to indicate that they should demonstrate the opposite, *sad.* Have students draw illustrations of opposites in their Personal Dictionaries.

Beginning Give pairs of students ten paper slips. Have a student write a word, such as *tall,* on a slip and draw an illustration. Tell the student's partner to write and draw the opposite on another slip. Have students create additional opposite pairs. Then instruct them to mix up the slips and rematch them.

Intermediate Have students match the antonyms. Then tell them to find and record one synonym for each word. Have them write a sentence for each synonym and share it with a partner.

Advanced As students read the selection, ask them to select one of the glossed words on each page. Ask them to write these words, along with their antonyms, in their Personal Dictionaries.

Build Background

Bosnia and Herzegovina

Bosnia and Herzegovina is a country in Eastern Europe. Its capital city is Sarajevo. Bosnia and Herzegovina was once part of the country of Yugoslavia. In 1992, Bosnia and Herzegovina broke away from Yugoslavia to form a new country. This began years of war between different groups of people in the area.

In 1995, the groups agreed to stop fighting. Today, the government of the country is working to make it strong.

Content Connection

Bosnia and Herzegovina is on the Balkan Peninsula in southeastern Europe. A **peninsula** is a body of land surrounded by water on three sides.

Build Vocabulary

Find Antonyms in a Thesaurus

Antonyms are words that have opposite meanings; for example, *night/day, happy/sad, good/bad.*

Read the words and definitions. Match each word with its antonym. Check your answers in a dictionary or a **thesaurus.** A thesaurus is a book that gives synonyms and antonyms. You can also find a thesaurus on the Internet. Do a search for *thesaurus.*

Words and Definitions	Antonyms
war fighting	create
destroy ruin	combine
separate move apart	wonderful
terrible very bad	peace

The Heinle Newbury House Dictionary   Activity Book p. 89   Student CD-ROM

Chapter 2 Zlata's Diary **163**

Content Connection
Technology

Build Vocabulary In addition to introducing students to Internet thesauruses, show them how to use the thesaurus built into the word processing software your students use. Show them how to look up words while they are writing. Brainstorm with students about times when a thesaurus may be helpful to a writer.

Learning Styles
Visual

Build Background Tell students that they can learn about the people and places of a country by looking at its artwork. Bookmark web sites (search using keywords: Bosnia, art) and provide books for students to browse through. *Ask: What can you tell about Bosnia and Herzegovina from its art?*

Build Background

Bosnia and Herzegovina

1. **Use a map** Have students locate Bosnia and Herzegovina on a globe or map. Ask them to also find Italy, France, and Germany.
2. **Use prior knowledge** *Ask: What other countries have had wars recently?*
3. **Content Connection** Bosnia and Herzegovina has a diverse population of Serbs, Bosnian Muslims, and Croats.

Build Vocabulary

Teacher Resource Book: *Personal Dictionary, p. 63*

Find Antonyms in a Thesaurus

1. **Define and clarify** On the board, write: *tall, quiet, expensive, hot. Ask: What's the opposite of tall?* Continue with other words. Explain that antonyms are opposite words.
2. **Locate pronunciation** Have students locate the pronunciation of *thesaurus* in the glossary in their Student Handbook or other sources, such as online or CD-ROM dictionaries.
3. **Use a thesaurus** Model using a thesaurus. Explain that a thesaurus is like a dictionary, but it lists similar words or synonyms. Some thesauruses also give antonyms.
4. **Reading selection vocabulary** You may want to introduce the glossed words in the reading selection before students begin reading. Key words: *natural, packed, guilty, whispering, unhappiness, wondering, explosions.* Instruct students to write the words with correct spelling and their definitions in their Personal Dictionaries. Have them pronounce each word and divide it into syllables.
5. **Multi-level options** See MULTI-LEVEL OPTIONS on p. 162.

Answers
war-peace; destroy-create; separate-combine; terrible-wonderful

 **ASSESS**

Say: Give the antonyms for these words: loud, young, together. (quiet, old, alone)

Text Structure

Diary

Recognize text features Read over the features of a diary and point out similarities to other genres. *Say: A diary has entries like a book has chapters. Direct address is similar to the voice or person an author uses. The informal writing is like some song lyrics.*

Reading Strategy

Recognize Sequence of Events

1. **Identify sequence** Have students skim the diary for dates. Then ask them to pick one date to enter on a timeline. (For example, the entry for April 14 on p. 167.) Do it together as a class.
2. **Multi-level options** See MULTI-LEVEL OPTIONS below.

Answers

Sample timeline for April 14, p. 167: People are leaving Sarajevo. Keka and Braco came this morning. They are in the kitchen with her parents. Keka and her mother are crying.

ASSESS

Have students give a sequence of four events from their morning today.

Text Structure

Diary

"Zlata's Diary" is an excerpt from the **diary** of Zlata Filipović, a 12-year-old girl. A diary is a book with blank pages in which you write your experiences and thoughts every day. As you read, look for the features of a diary.

Student
CD-ROM

Diary	
Structure	A diary is divided into sections called entries. There is an entry for each day the author writes. Each entry includes the date and important events.
Personal Experiences	A diary includes the most important events, feelings, and thoughts of each day. A diary entry can be very personal because the diary is not meant to be read by anyone else.
Direct Address	Many writers "speak" to their diary. They give their diary a name and use the pronoun *you*. Zlata names her diary *Mimmy*.
Informal Writing	A diary sometimes uses everyday language that may not be grammatically correct, such as incomplete sentences.

Reading Strategy

Recognize Sequence of Events

The **sequence of events** is the order in which events happen. It can help you remember what you read. It can also help you find information in a text. This timeline lists a sequence of events.

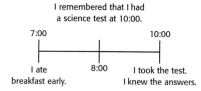

1. As you read or listen to the audio recording of "Zlata's Diary," identify the dates of each diary entry.
2. Transition words and phrases such as *today* and *right now* can help you understand the order of events.
3. Organize the ideas on a timeline. Show the sequence of events for one of the diary entries in the selection.

Student
CD-ROM

164 Unit 3 Conflict and Cooperation

MULTI-LEVEL OPTIONS *Reading Strategy*

Newcomer Have students draw a timeline and write times in three hour intervals from the time they get up until when they go to bed. Ask them to draw under each time what they did the previous day at those times.

Beginning Give each student slips of paper. Ask them to draw five things they did the previous day. Have students lay out the slips horizontally in time order to form a timeline. Have them choose one of the following words to write on each slip: *first, second, in the morning, at noon, at night, soon, then, later, next, last.*

Intermediate Have each student identify a familiar folktale or other short story. Ask students to use a timeline to recall the sequence of events in the story.

Advanced *Say: People who write diaries sometimes move back and forth in time. They may tell about something they are feeling at the time they are writing but then write about an event that happened earlier. When a writer goes back in time, it is called a flashback. Find examples as you read.*

Zlata's Diary

an excerpt from a diary
by Zlata Filipović

165

Reading Selection Materials

Audio: *Unit 3, Chapter 2; CD 1, Track 13*
Teacher Resource Book: *Reading Summary,*
  pp. 87–88
Transparencies: *#7, Reading Summary*

Suggestions for Using
Reading Summary

- Introduce new vocabulary or cognates.
- Cut the summary into strips, or jumble the sentences on an overhead transparency. Students put the sentences in order.
- Practice the reading strategy.
- Students read aloud or with a partner.
- Students paraphrase the summary.
- Students do a cloze activity.
- Students create a visual or graphic organizer, such as a timeline or storyboard, to illustrate the summary.
- Students paraphrase the summary.

Preview the Selection

1. **Interpret the image** Have students look at the photo. *Ask: How old do you think this girl is? How would you describe her expression—happy, sad? What is she holding?*
2. **Connect** *Ask: How do you think this diary will connect with the unit theme* conflict and cooperation?

Home Connection

Have students meet in pairs. Ask them to talk about how they feel about the idea of keeping a diary. *Ask: How could a diary be helpful to a person? What might inspire a person to keep a diary? What kinds of things could someone write about in a diary?*

Learning Styles
Interpersonal

Have students study the picture of Zlata. *Ask: What things do you think the girl in the picture has in common with you and your friends? Look closely at the girl's expression and body language. How do you think she is feeling? Why do you think that?* Have students discuss questions in small groups.

Read the Selection

1. **Do a break-in reading** Play the audio. Then have one student read aloud until another student wants to "break in." The second student reads a sentence along with the first one as a cue he/she is breaking in. At the end of that sentence, the first student stops reading and the second one continues until another student wants to break in. Monitor to ensure each student has a turn. Ask a volunteer to start with the prologue.

2. **Discuss tone** *Ask: What is the tone, or feeling, of this letter? Is she sad, angry, hopeful, hopeless? Explain why you think so and find support in the diary.*

3. **Explore the facts** Give students a few minutes to write one or two questions about the diary entry. Then have students ask the class their questions.

Sample Answer to Guide Question
April 12, 1992. She wrote, "I keep thinking about the march I joined today."

See Teacher Edition pp. 434–436 for a list of English-Spanish cognates in the reading selection.

Audio
CD 1. Tr. 13

Prologue

When Zlata Filipović began her diary, she was living in Sarajevo, the capital city of Bosnia and Herzegovina. As Zlata writes, enemy armies are surrounding Sarajevo and attacking the city from the hills with bombs and guns.

Zlata named her diary "Mimmy," which was the name of a pet fish she once had. Keka, Braco, Mirna, Bojana, Verica, Oga, Martina, Matea, and Dejan are the names of her friends and family members.

Zlata and her father walk through the streets of Sarajevo.

Recognize Sequence of Events

On what date did Zlata join the peace march? How do you know?

1   *Sunday, April 12, 1992*
Dear Mimmy,

The new sections of town—Dobrinja, Mojmilo, Vojničko polje—are being badly **shelled.** Everything is being destroyed, burned, the people are in **shelters.** Here in the middle of town, where we live, it's different. It's quiet. People go out. It was a nice warm spring day today. We went out too. Vaso Miškin Street was full of people, children. It looked like a **peace march.** People came out to be together, they don't want war. They want to live and enjoy themselves the way they used to. That's only **natural,** isn't it? Who likes or wants war, when it's the worst thing in the world?

2   I keep thinking about the march I joined today. It's bigger and stronger than war. That's why it will win. The people must be the ones to win, not the war, because war has nothing to do with **humanity.** War is something **inhuman.**

Zlata

---

shelled   shot at by bullets and bombs
shelters   rooms or buildings where people hide from attacks
peace march   when a group of people walk together and demand peace

natural   normal
humanity   human beings as a group
inhuman   cruel; without kindness for other people

166   Unit 3   Conflict and Cooperation

MULTI-LEVEL OPTIONS *Read the Selection*

Newcomer Play the audio. Use facial expressions and gestures to reinforce meaning. *Ask: Was there war near Zlata's city?* (yes) *Was there war in Zlata's neighborhood?* (no) *Are people afraid war will come?* (yes)

Beginning Read the selection aloud. *Ask: What is happening near where Zlata lives?* (a war) *What are people doing to stay out of the war?* (leaving the city)

Intermediate Have students do a paired reading. Then *ask: How is life in the new parts of Zlata's town?* (There is war in the new parts; her neighborhood is peaceful.) *What is causing people to leave the city?* (They want to leave before fighting breaks out where they live.)

Advanced Have students read silently. *Ask: Why does Zlata write in a diary?* (to express her feelings about what is happening around her) *What do you think Zlata is afraid will happen to her family?* (She is afraid all or part of her family will have to leave the city.)

Zlata puts her arms around her parents.

Read the Selection

1. **Paired reading** Play the audio. Then have students practice reading the selection in pairs.
2. **Identify sequence** *Ask: How many days later is this entry from the first one?* (2 days) *What has happened between then and now?* (Many families and people started leaving Sarajevo.) *Who came to visit this morning?* (Keka and Braco)
3. **Contrast tone** *Ask: How would you compare the tone of this entry with the one before?* (It is much sadder.) *Why do you think that is?* (She sees many people leaving, and her mother and father don't know what to do; Keka and her mother are crying.)
4. **Multi-level options** See MULTI-LEVEL OPTIONS on p. 166.

Sample Answer to Guide Question
She saw sad pictures on TV. Keka and Braco came over.

Recognize Sequence of Events

Name two events that happened on April 14 before Zlata began writing.

3

Tuesday, April 14, 1992

Dear Mimmy,

People are leaving Sarajevo. The airport, train and bus stations are **packed.** I saw sad pictures on TV of people **parting.** Families, friends separating. Some are leaving, others staying. It's so sad. Why? These people and children aren't **guilty** of anything. Keka and Braco came early this morning. They're in the kitchen with Mommy and Daddy, **whispering.** Keka and Mommy are crying. I don't think they know what to do—whether to stay or to go. Neither way is good.

Zlata

---

packed crowded, or filled, with people
parting leaving

guilty having done something wrong
whispering speaking in a soft, quiet voice

Chapter 2 Zlata's Diary **167**

---

9 Punctuation

Commas in dates

Direct students to the date for the diary entry on p. 166. *Ask: What punctuation mark separates the day from the month and the date from the year?* (comma) Write on the board: *Tuesday April 14 1992. Ask: Where should I put commas?* (after *Tuesday* and after *14 hr*) Have students look at p. 167 to see if they are correct.

Apply Put today's date on the board. Also list dates of some upcoming school events and holidays. Ask students to copy these dates and punctuate them.

Read the Selection

1. **Silent reading** Play the audio. Then give students time to read the entry silently. Have them answer the guide question individually.

2. **Identify characters** Ask students to dictate the names and spelling of all the people mentioned in this entry as a volunteer writes them on the board. For each character, have students speculate about who the person is: a friend, a relative, a family friend, or a neighbor. In some cases, it may not be clear. Ask students to give reasons for their answers.

Sample Answer to Guide Question
1. Mirna spent forty-eight hours in the shelter.
2. Zlata spoke to Mirna on the phone.
3. Mommy is crying.

4

Wednesday, April 15, 1992

Dear Mimmy,

There has been **terrible gunfire** in Mokjmilo [a part of Sarajevo]. Mirna spent a whole forty-eight hours in the shelter. I talked to her on the phone, but not for long because she had to go back down to the shelter. I **feel sorry for** her.

5 Bojana and Verica are going to England. Oga is going to Italy. And worst of all, Martina and Matea have already left. They went to Ohrid [a lakeside town in Macedonia]. Keka is crying, Braco is crying and Mommy is crying. She's on the phone right now, and she's crying. And "those boys" up there in the hills keep shooting at us. I just heard that Dejan had left too.

OOOHHHHH! Why war?!

Love you, Mimmy,
Zlata

> **Recognize Sequence of Events**
>
> List these events in the order that they happened: Mommy is crying, Mirna spent forty-eight hours in the shelter, Zlata spoke to Mirna on the phone.

Zlata writes about her hopes and fears in her diary.

---

terrible very bad, very frightening
gunfire a shooting of guns

feel sorry for pity, feel bad for someone

MULTI-LEVEL OPTIONS *Read the Selection*

Newcomer *Ask: Is the fighting near Zlata's city?* (yes) *Is everyone sad and worried?* (yes) *Are Zlata's friends leaving the city?* (yes)

Beginning *Ask: What has come to Zlata's city?* (war) *What are Zlata's friends doing?* (leaving) *How is everyone feeling?* (sad, scared)

Intermediate *Ask: How are people trying to stay safe?* (hiding in shelters and leaving the city) *Why is Zlata's mother constantly in tears?* (She is afraid that her family will have to split up.) *How does Zlata feel about her suitcase being packed?* (scared that this means she will be leaving town soon)

Advanced *Ask: What does Zlata mean when she writes, "Why war?"* (that she doesn't understand why people use war as a way to solve problems when it causes so much pain to innocent people) *Is Zlata really angry with Martina, Matea, and Dejan? Explain.* (No, she is upset with the war for causing so much sadness and uncertainty.)

Recognize Sequence of Events

What does Zlata learn about Martina, Matea, and Dejan on April 16? How is this information different from what she learned on April 15?

6

Thursday, April 16, 1992

Dear Mimmy,

Martina, Matea and Dejan didn't leave, after all. That's really not fair! Yes, of course it is, they mustn't go. But it isn't fair because we all **cried our eyes out** and in the end they didn't leave. There are not enough buses, trains or planes for all the people that want to get out of here.

Love you,
Zlata

7

Saturday, April 18, 1992

Dear Mimmy,

There's shooting, **shells** are falling. This really is WAR. Mommy and Daddy are worried, they sit up until late at night, talking. They're **wondering** what to do, but it's hard to know. Whether to leave and split up, or stay here together. Keka wants to take me to Ohrid. Mommy can't make up her mind—she's **constantly in tears.** She tries to hide it from me, but I see everything. I see that things aren't good here. There's no peace. War has suddenly entered our town, our homes, our thoughts, our lives. It's terrible.

It's also terrible that Mommy has **packed** my suitcase.

Love,
Zlata

---

cried our eyes out cried for a long time
shells bullets
wondering wishing to know

constantly happening all the time
in tears crying
packed put objects in a container in order to move them

Chapter 2 Zlata's Diary **169**

Read the Selection

1. **Paired reading** Play the audio. Then have students do a partner read aloud.
2. **Share feelings about the selection** Ask students questions to help them express their feelings about the diary entries. *Ask: Have you ever been in a frightening situation? Have there been times when the adults around you were also afraid? How did that make you feel? What helps you feel brave or strong? Have you ever had to say goodbye to many friends at the same time?* Allow students who are comfortable talking about their feelings to share them with the class.
3. **Multi-level options** See MULTI-LEVEL OPTIONS on p. 168.

Sample Answer to Guide Question
She learns that they didn't leave after all. She thought they went to Ohrid.

 ## Spelling

There, they're, their

On the board, write: *there, they're,* and *their.* Tell students these words are homophones (words that sound the same but have different spellings and meanings). Contrast with homographs from Word Study in Chapter 1. Point to *there* and *say:* There *tells you the place or that something exists or is.* There *is gunfire.* Point to *their* and *say:* Their *answers the question* who owns it? *It means belonging to them.* Zlata's friends are leaving their *homes.* Point to *they're* and *say:*

They're *is a contraction for* they are. *It tells who is doing something. Mommy and Daddy are talking.* They're *wondering what to do.*

Apply Write on the board: _____ *thinking about leaving the city. It is hard to leave* _____ *friends.* _____ *is so much to do to get ready.* Have students complete each. (They're, their, There)

Read the Selection

1. **Shared reading** Play the audio. Divide the class into two groups. Have groups join in for alternate sentences.
2. **Discuss conflict** *Say: Zlata doesn't know whether to stay or go. Why does she want to go?* (to escape the war) *If she leaves, who might have to stay behind?* (her parents and grandparents) *Why do you think she decides to stay?* (She wants to stay together with her family.)
3. **Multi-level options** See MULTI-LEVEL OPTIONS below.

Sample Answer to Guide Question
She will tell Keka that you have to be brave and stay with those you love and those who love you.

8

Monday, April 20, 1992

Dear Mimmy,

War is no joke, it seems. It destroys, kills, burns, separates, brings **unhappiness.** Terrible shells fell today on Baščaršija, the old town center. Terrible **explosions.** We went down into the **cellar,** the cold, dark, **revolting** cellar. And ours isn't even all that safe. Mommy, Daddy and I just stood there, holding on to one another in a corner that looked safe. Standing there in the dark, in the warmth of my parents' arms, I thought about leaving Sarajevo. Everybody is thinking about it, and so am I. I couldn't **bear** to go alone, to leave behind Mommy and Daddy, Grandma and Granddad. And going with just Mommy isn't any good either. The best would be for all three of us to go. But Daddy can't. So I've decided we should stay here together. Tomorrow I'll tell Keka that you have to be brave and stay with those you love and those who love you. I can't leave my parents, and I don't like the other idea of leaving my father behind alone either.

Your Zlata

> ### Recognize Sequence of Events
> According to Zlata, what event will happen tomorrow?

Zlata must carry jugs of water home because there is no running water.

---

unhappiness sadness
explosions blasts from bombs
cellar the space below ground level under a building

revolting making someone feel sick; unpleasant; disgusting
bear deal with without suffering or complaining

170 Unit 3 Conflict and Cooperation

MULTI-LEVEL OPTIONS *Read the Selection*

Newcomer *Ask: Did Zlata's family hide in the cellar?* (yes) *Did they feel safe?* (no) *Does Zlata want to leave?* (no) *Is Zlata a real person?* (yes) *Does she still live in Bosnia?* (no)

Beginning *Ask: What does Zlata think of war?* (terrible) *Where does her family hide?* (cellar) *What does Zlata think the family should do?* (stay in the city) *What was Zlata's diary made into?* (book) *Where does she live now?* (Paris, France)

Intermediate *Ask: How does Zlata feel about war? Why?* (It is terrible; it harms people and places.) *Did Zlata think the family should stay or leave? Why?* (stay, so they could all be together) *How did Zlata use her experience to help others?* (She shared her diary and helps children who have experienced war.)

Advanced *Ask: Why do you think Zlata kept a diary during the war?* (to have a place to express her feelings about the terrible things that were happening) *People say that there is some good in everything. How does this apply to Zlata's experiences?* (She uses her experiences to help others affected by war.)

About the Author

Zlata Filipović (born 1980)

Zlata Filipović began writing her diary in 1991, when Sarajevo was still at peace. Zlata's life and her diary changed when the war began. Instead of writing about friends, sports, music, and school, she began to write about daily life during war. She could no longer go to school, there was very little to eat, and a group of her friends was killed in a park. In 1993, Zlata's diary was published, and the world learned about the young girl's fears and hopes. That same year, Zlata and her parents moved to Paris, France. After she moved, Zlata worked to help other children affected by war.

➤ Why do you think Zlata Filipović continued to write in her diary after the war began? What challenges did she face?

About the Author

Analyze facts Tell students that Zlata started writing her diary when she was 11 years old. When the war started, her diary became a personal record of the attack on Sarajevo. *Ask: What year did Zlata start writing her diary?* (in 1991) *When was her diary published?* (in 1993) *When did she move to Paris with her parents?* (in 1993)

Across Selections

Say: We often read about war in the newspaper or in history books. How is reading a diary about war different? Do you think a diary is a good way to communicate about war? What things does a newspaper or textbook include about war that you might not read in a diary?

Spelling, Punctuation, Capitalization

After the Reading Comprehension section, students will practice spelling, punctuation, and capitalization in the Activity Book.

Chapter 2 Zlata's Diary **171**

A Capitalization

Evaluate Your Reading Strategy

Letter greetings and closings

Ask students to look at p. 170. *Say:* Dear Mimmy *is the greeting in this letter. How is it capitalized?* (*Dear* begins with a capital.) Your Zlata *is the letter's closing. What do you notice about how it is capitalized?* (*Your* begins with a capital.)

Apply Have students look back at the other entries in this selection to see more examples of greetings and closings.

Recognize Sequence of Events *Say: You have practiced an important reading strategy. Now you can decide how well you have done. Does this statement describe how you read?*

As I read a diary, I look for dates and phrases that tell me when events happened. When I know the sequence of events, I can recall facts better.

Reading Comprehension

Question-Answer Relationships

Sample Answers

1. Sarajevo
2. She learns that people are leaving the city.
3. They are discussing what to do, and they are very worried.
4. They go down into the cellar.
5. Keka wants to take her to Ohrid. Zlata decides to stay with her family.
6. People came together and showed that they wanted to live, not have war. She says that the people are bigger and stronger than war and that they must be the ones to win over war.
7. Before, the bombing was in the new sections of town and her section was peaceful. On April 20, her neighborhood was bombed.
8. Maybe she doesn't want Zlata to worry.
9. Yes. It's important to stay with your family.
10. I'd tell her not to worry and that things will get better. I try to think about positive things.
11. When I visited another country by myself, I was afraid and didn't want to leave my family, either.
12. I would want my family to be together whether we stayed or left.

Build Reading Fluency

Reading Silently

Assessment Program: *Reading Fluency Chart, p. 116*

When students have completed the reading fluency activity, record their progress in the Reading Fluency Chart.

Beyond the Reading

Reading Comprehension

Question-Answer Relationships (QAR)

"Right There" Questions

1. **Recall Facts** Where does Zlata live?
2. **Recall Facts** What does Zlata learn from watching TV?
3. **Recall Facts** Why do Zlata's parents stay up late?
4. **Recall Facts** What does Zlata's family do when there are explosions near where they live?

"Think and Search" Questions

5. **Summarize** How does Keka want to help Zlata? What does Zlata finally decide about Keka's plan?
6. **Analyze Cause and Effect** Why does the "peace march" on April 12 make Zlata feel hopeful?
7. **Compare and Contrast** Why is the part of Sarajevo where Zlata lives safer on April 12 than it is on April 20?

"Author and You" Questions

8. **Draw Conclusions** Why do you think Zlata's mother tries to hide how she feels from Zlata?
9. **Make Judgments** Do you think Zlata makes the right decision about staying in Sarajevo? Why or why not?

"On Your Own" Questions

10. **Respond** If you were Zlata's friend, what advice would you give her to help her feel brave? How do you stay brave when you are scared?
11. **Compare Your Experiences** Have you had any experiences that made you feel the way Zlata does in these diary entries? Tell about them.
12. **Reflect** What do you think you would do if you were in Zlata's situation?

Activity Book
p. 90

Student
CD-ROM

Build Reading Fluency

Reading Silently

Reading silently for longer periods of time helps you become a better reader. It helps you learn to read faster.

1. Listen to the audio recording of "Zlata's Diary."
2. Listen to the chunks of words as you follow along.
3. Reread the diary entry on page 167 silently two times.
4. Your teacher will time your second reading.
5. Raise your hand when you are finished.
6. Record your timing.

172 Unit 3 Conflict and Cooperation

MULTI-LEVEL OPTIONS *Elements of Literature*

Newcomer Have students look at the photographs again and recall the part of the selection associated with each photo. Ask students to use facial expressions to indicate the tone for each of these parts of the story.

Beginning Make cards with one of the following words on each: *sad, scared, brave, worried, angry.* Draw a face on each to show the meaning of the word. One by one, show the cards to students. Ask them to point to or act out parts of the story that relate to each tone word.

Intermediate After students have determined the tone of each sentence, ask them to read the sentences aloud. Tell students to use the appropriate tone of voice to show the attitude the writer intended to communicate.

Advanced Remind students that the selection is written in the first person. *Say: If someone wrote about Zlata, the writer would have put Zlata's words in quotes. Think about ways that could be written. For example,* write: *"That's why it will win,"* Zlata declared forcefully. Have students choose a sentence and rewrite it in the third person.

Listen, Speak, Interact

Role-Play a Persuasive Conversation

When you want someone to do something, you can talk to the person and give reasons why it's a good idea to do it. A conversation like this is a **persuasive conversation.**

Keka wants to take Zlata away from Sarajevo, but Zlata decides to stay.

1. With a partner, reread paragraph 8. List Zlata's reasons for wanting to stay in Sarajevo.

2. Brainstorm a list of reasons why Zlata should leave Sarajevo.
3. One of you is Zlata, and the other is Keka. Role-play a conversation. Keka will try to persuade Zlata to leave Sarajevo. Zlata will explain why she wants to stay. How does your conversation end?
4. Share your role play with the class.

Elements of Literature

Identify Tone

Tone is the writer's attitude (way of thinking and feeling) toward the subject and characters. An author's tone may be hopeful, sad, angry, scared, confident, or brave. A text may have more than one tone.

Words and phrases show an author's tone. For example, Zlata writes, "Families, friends separating. Some are leaving, others staying." Her tone here is sad—people who love each other are separating.

1. With a partner, read these sentences from "Zlata's Diary":
   a. I keep thinking about the march . . . It's bigger and stronger than war. That's why it will win.
   b. OOOHHHHH! Why war?!

c. War has suddenly entered our town . . . It's terrible.
   d. Tomorrow I'll tell Keka that you have to be brave and stay with those you love . . .
2. Talk to a partner about the tone that the sentences show. Sometimes more than one tone is possible.
3. Discuss your answers with another pair of students. Are your answers the same?

Activity Book
p. 91

Student
CD-ROM

Content Connection
The Arts

Tell students that artists communicate their attitudes about subjects just as writers do. Have small groups look through books of fine art. Ask them to select several paintings to discuss with their groups. Tell them to decide what tone the artist was trying to communicate with each and how he or she used shapes, lines, and colors to convey that tone.

Learning Styles
Kinesthetic

Point out that people do not try to persuade others merely with their words. Explain that facial expressions and gestures can also help persuade people. Have students identify examples of persuasive body language. (eye contact, sincere expression, firm stance, strong arm motions) Ask them to be aware of body language as they role-play the parts of Zlata and Keka.

Listen, Speak, Interact

Role-Play a Persuasive Conversation

1. **Teacher think aloud** *Say: When I want to persuade my family to see a movie, I try to give them good reasons. I might tell them that the star is a good actor or that it's the kind of action movie they like. I know that giving reasons helps persuade people to do things.*

2. **Newcomers** Write a 2-column chart labeled: *Zlata's reasons to stay* and *Keka's reasons to go.* Help students formulate ideas to fill in the chart. Role-play the conversation several times, taking different roles.

3. **Perform a role-play** Ask volunteers to perform their role-plays for the class. After each one, ask students what was persuasive about the argument.

4. **Analyze speaker's credibility** After practicing their role plays, have students analyze the credibility of their partners. *Ask: Did your partner act like the character? Was she believable? Did you trust his/her words? Why or why not? What suggestions would you give your partner to be more credible?* (example: be more confident, use stronger emotion, and so on)

Elements of Literature

Identify Tone

1. **Use a chart** Have students work in pairs to make a chart with columns labeled: *happy, sad, angry, hopeful, scared,* and *brave.* Ask them to find phrases from Zlata's diary that show each feeling. Have them record the phrases on their charts.

2. **Multi-level options** See MULTI-LEVEL OPTIONS on p. 172.

Answers
Possible answers: **1.a.** hopeful **b.** mad, angry
c. frightened **d.** confident, brave

 **ASSESS**

Ask: What would you do in Zlata's situation? Write two sentences giving reasons.

Word Study

Form Contractions

Review homophones Write on the board: *you're* and *your*. **Ask:** *What kind of words are these?* (homophones) *How do you know?* (same pronunciation but different spellings and meanings) *What other homophones did we learn?* (there, their, they're) *Which is a contraction of* you are? (you're) *How do you know?* (apostrophe) *What does* your *mean?* (It's a possessive pronoun meaning *belongs to you*.)

Answers
2. **a.** They're in the kitchen with Mommy and Daddy.
   b. She's on the phone right now.

Grammar Focus

Use Verbs with Infinitives

Use verbs with infinitives Have students write their sentences on the board and circle the infinitives.

Answers
2. **a.** want (verb), to live (infinitive) **b.** had (verb), to go (infinitive) **c.** tried (verb), to hide (infinitive) **d.** have (verb), to be (infinitive)

ASSESS

On the board, write: *you're* and *your*. Have students complete the sentences:
Is that _____ dog?
_____ taking it for a walk, aren't you?

Word Study

Form Contractions

We use **contractions** to put two words together to make a shorter word. A contraction always includes an **apostrophe** (’). Here are some common contractions:

First Word	Second Word	Contraction
I +	am ⇒	I'm
they +	are ⇒	they're
you +	are ⇒	you're
it +	is ⇒	it's
does +	not ⇒	doesn't

People often use contractions when they speak English and when they write informally. "Zlata's Diary" contains many contractions because it is written as if Zlata were speaking to a friend.

1. Copy the chart in your Personal Dictionary. Add other contractions as you learn them.
2. Read these sentences.
   a. They are in the kitchen with Mommy and Daddy.
   b. She is on the phone right now.
3. On a piece of paper, rewrite the sentences. Use contractions for the underlined words.

Personal Dictionary   The Heinle Newbury House Dictionary   Activity Book p. 92   Student CD-ROM

Grammar Focus

Use Verbs with Infinitives

An **infinitive** is made up of the word *to* plus the simple form of a verb. For example, *to go* and *to be* are infinitives.

Many verbs can be followed by an infinitive. Look at this example:

I want to eat dinner.

Want is the verb. *To eat* is the infinitive.

1. Copy the following sentences on a piece of paper.
   a. They want to live.
   b. She had to go back down.
   c. She tried to hide it.
   d. You have to be brave.
2. Circle each verb. Underline each infinitive.
3. Write three sentences of your own that include a verb and an infinitive. Choose from these verbs: *try, want, decide, begin, hope*. Write your own infinitives.

Activity Book pp. 93–94   Student Handbook   Student CD-ROM

174   Unit 3 Conflict and Cooperation

MULTI-LEVEL OPTIONS *From Reading to Writing*

Newcomer Have students express a general opinion about "Zlata's Diary." Have them draw a thumbs-up or a thumbs-down symbol at the tops of their papers. Ask students to draw the reason they would or not tell someone else to read the selection.

Beginning Have students state an opinion about whether they would recommend the selection. Have them make a two-column chart labeled *plus* and *minus*. Ask them to indicate with words or phrases what they did or did not like. Have them circle the side with the most supportive details. Help students summarize their opinions of the piece.

Intermediate Have students support their opinion statements with examples from the text and their prior knowledge. (*Example:* Zlata tells about "terrible gunfire." From seeing a story about war on television, I think this is a good description of one scary thing about war.)

Advanced Provide an opportunity for students to develop a more detailed and complex response. *Say: You may feel that, in some ways, "Zlata's Diary" gives a good idea of life during war and, in some ways, it does not. Feel free to include both responses in your writing. Be sure to provide clear support for both opinions.*

From Reading to Writing

Write Your Opinion

Your opinion is what you believe about something. Study the writings and details of "Zlata's Diary." Write a paragraph that explains your opinion of the diary.

1. What is your opinion? Do you think "Zlata's Diary" gives readers a good idea of life during a war? Use this as the first sentence in your paragraph.
2. Support your opinion with details from the text. For example, Zlata tells about "terrible gunfire." This detail shows that many people are in danger during a war.
3. Indent your paragraph.

> *I think "Zlata's Diary"* _____
>
> *Zlata Filipović writes about* _____
>
> *This detail shows* _____

4. Use contractions to make shorter words in your paragraph. Be sure to include the apostrophe in each contraction.

Activity Book
p. 95

Student
Handbook

Across Content Areas

Learn the Points of the Compass

Look at this map. Find the **compass rose.** The compass rose tells you the directions.

N = north	NW = northwest
S = south	SW = southwest
E = east	NE = northeast
W = west	SW = southeast

With a partner, make up five sentences like this: *Romania is north of Bulgaria.* Read your sentences to another pair of students.

Activity Book
p. 96

From Reading to Writing

Write Your Opinion

1. **Use language signals** Provide students with words that signal opinions, such as *agree, believe, disagree, feel, suppose,* and *think.*
2. **Check details** Have students carefully check that their opinions are supported by details from the text.
3. **Multi-level options** See MULTI-LEVEL OPTIONS on p. 174.

Across Content Areas: Social Studies

Learn the Points of the Compass

Use a map Direct students to a state map. Have them make up directional sentences from their city to other cities in the state.

Answers

Examples: Slovenia is northwest of Bosnia-Herzegovina. Yugoslavia is southwest of Romania. Austria is north of Slovenia. Hungary is east of Austria. Romania is southeast of Hungary

✓ ASSESS

Have students describe where their state is compared to the Mississippi River.

Reteach and Reassess

Text Structure Write on the board: *structure, personal experience, direct address, informal writing.* Have students give an example of each from "Zlata's Diary." *Ask: Are there any features Zlata could have left out and still had her diary work as a good place to record her ideas?* (direct address) *What else could Zlata put in her diary?* (drawings, photographs, quotes)

Reading Strategy Have students make a sequence chart to show the main events of the selection.

Elements of Literature Have students identify the tone of "We Shall Overcome" and defend their response with examples.

Reassess Have students create a journal entry to tell about a previous school day. Before writing, have them decide the tone they want to communicate.

CHAPTER 3

The Peach Boy

a play
by Suzanne Barchers

Into the Reading

Chapter Materials

Activity Book: *pp. 97–104*
Audio: *Unit 3, Chapter 3; CD 1, Track 14*
Student Handbook
Student CD-ROM: *Unit 3 Chapter 3*
Teacher Resource Book: *Lesson Plan, Teacher Resources, Reading Summary, Activity Book Answer Key*
Teacher Resource CD-ROM
Assessment Program: *Quiz, pp. 43–44; Teacher and Student Resources, pp. 115–144*
Assessment CD-ROM
Transparencies
The Heinle Newbury House Dictionary/CD-ROM
Web site: http://visions.heinle.com

Objectives

Preview Have pairs read the objectives. *Ask: What objectives do you know something about?*

Use Prior Knowledge

Discuss Cooperation

1. **Teacher think aloud** *Say: When I play on a team, everyone plays together to win the game. How do we do that? I guess we cooperate and help each other. We can be nice about mistakes. We can make suggestions to each other.*

2. **Relate to personal experience** Ask students to share some of their goals. Have others suggest ways of cooperating that will help them reach their goals.

Objectives

Reading Analyze cause and effect as you read a play.

Listening and Speaking Talk about values.

Grammar Use compound sentences with *and*.

Writing Write a summary.

Content Science: Classify fruits and vegetables.

Use Prior Knowledge

Discuss Cooperation

A goal is something that you want for the future; for example, to go to college is a goal. Cooperation is working together to reach a goal.

1. Work with a partner. Make a chart like the one here on a piece of paper.

2. Read the goals in the chart. Discuss with your partner how you can cooperate with other people to reach each goal.

3. Write your ideas in the chart.

My Goals	How Cooperating with Other People Can Help Me Reach My Goals
I want to get a good grade on my test.	I can ask my teacher questions. I can study with a partner.
I want to learn another language.	
I want to do something to improve my community.	

176 Unit 3 Conflict and Cooperation

MULTI-LEVEL OPTIONS *Build Vocabulary*

Newcomer Provide magazines or have students draw pictures for each word.

Beginning Ask students to draw a scene that includes all of the items in the vocabulary list. Have them label each item in their illustrations.

Intermediate After students have written a definition for each word, ask them to choose one of the words and make a word web to explore it further. Have them include related words, synonyms, a sentence using the word, and feelings and experiences the word brings to mind for them.

Advanced Have students list proper noun examples for as many of the vocabulary words as possible. (*Example:* river— Amazon River)

Build Background

Japanese Folktales

"The Peach Boy" is a play based on a popular **folktale** from Japan. A folktale is a story that is passed down from generation to generation. Folktales often tell about things that are important to a certain culture.

The main character in "The Peach Boy" is a Japanese hero named Momotaro. Many Japanese folktales tell about Momotaro's exciting adventures. In these adventures, Momotaro often fights monsters or people who do wrong.

 Content Connection

The name *Momotaro* contains the Japanese word *Momo*. *Momo* means "peach." A peach is a type of fruit. In Japanese folktales, eating peaches allows people to live forever.

Build Vocabulary

Define Words Related to Nature

The reading selection includes words related to things in nature. Some of these things are types of land, bodies of water, or plants. Look at these words from the selection:

| stream | mountains | forest |
| peach | river | pine tree |

1. Copy the chart in your Personal Dictionary.
2. Write the correct nature word for each definition. Use the nature words from the list.
3. Use a dictionary to look up any words you do not know.

Nature Word	Meaning
river	a large body of water that moves in one direction
	a juicy, round fruit with a large seed inside it
	a tall, straight tree with sharp leaves called needles
	a small flowing body of water
	an area of land with many trees
	tall forms of land and rock higher than hills

Personal Dictionary · The Heinle Newbury House Dictionary · Activity Book p. 97 · Student CD-ROM

Chapter 3 The Peach Boy **177**

 Content Connection
The Arts

Build Vocabulary Ask students to look through books of landscapes to see how artists have depicted streams, mountains, rivers, and forests. Tell them to suggest words to describe these landforms in the paintings and drawings they find. (*Example:* rushing, wild river) Have them list words that name other things from nature shown in the picture. (*Examples:* branches, squirrels, hills)

Learning Styles
Linguistic

Build Background Be sure students understand why, in the Japanese culture, Momotaro is a good name for a brave, adventurous story hero. Have students share names of main characters from folktales they have read from various cultures and regions. Engage students in discussing whether those characters' names had special meanings. *Ask: What do you think would be a good name for a folktale hero from your culture?*

Build Background

Japanese Folktales

1. **Use prior knowledge** *Ask: Do you know any folktales with monsters or "bad people" in them?* (Jack and the Beanstalk, Beauty and the Beast, Cinderella) *Can you summarize the folktale?*
2. **Use a map** Have students locate Japan on the map. Ask them to share information they know about Japan.
3. **Content Connection** In the 3rd and 4th centuries A.D., Japan borrowed the Chinese writing system of ideograph characters. Chinese *kanji* is an important part of Japanese writing today.

Build Vocabulary

Teacher Resource Book: *Personal Dictionary, p. 63*

Define Words Related to Nature

1. **Brainstorm** Have students work in pairs to find synonyms or related words for the boxed vocabulary. (river: waterway; stream: creek; mountains: peaks, hills; forest: woods; peach: fruit; pine tree: fir) Have students share their words to create a classroom word map.
2. **Use other sources** In addition to a print dictionary, have students use an online or CD-ROM dictionary to locate the meanings of unfamiliar words.
3. **Reading selection vocabulary** You may want to introduce the glossed words in the reading selection before students begin reading. Key words: *floating, delighted, favor, journey, hurried, treasures.* Instruct students to write the words with correct spelling and their definitions in their Personal Dictionaries. Have them pronounce each word and divide it into syllables.
4. **Multi-level options** See MULTI-LEVEL OPTIONS on p. 176.

Answers
Chart top to bottom: river, peach, pine tree, stream, forest, mountains

 **ASSESS**

Have students write two sentences using words related to nature.

Text Structure

Play

1. **Relate to personal experience** *Ask: Have you ever been to a play? Have you seen any plays at school? What was the play about?*
2. **Recognize features** Have students define: *play, characters, narrator, dialogue.*

Reading Strategy

Analyze Cause and Effect

1. **Identify cause and effect** Have students give their own examples of cause and effect. *Say: You studied hard for a test. What was the effect?* (did well on the test) *Your friend gave you a small present. What was the cause?* (Today is your birthday.)
2. **Multi-level options** See MULTI-LEVEL OPTIONS below.

Answers

2. **a.** cause: Saleem studied for the test. effect: Saleem got an "A" on the test. **b.** cause: Monica forgot to put gas in the car. effect: The car ran out of gas. **c.** cause: Many people moved to the town. effect: The traffic got very bad.

ASSESS

Write on the board: *Cause: I didn't hear the doorbell.* Have students write a sentence that shows an effect.

Text Structure

Play

"The Peach Boy" is a **play.** In a play, actors speak in front of an audience. They pretend to be characters in the play. Look at the features of a play listed in the chart.

As you read "The Peach Boy," find out who the characters are. Pay attention to their actions. How do the characters cooperate in the play?

Play	
Characters	people in a drama
Narrator	a person who tells about the characters and events (not all plays have narrators)
Dialogue	the words each character says

Student CD-ROM

Reading Strategy

Analyze Cause and Effect

Authors sometimes use **cause and effect** to organize their story. A **cause** is the reason why an event happens. An **effect** is an event that happens as a result of a cause. Readers analyze cause and effect to understand why events happen in a story. Look at this example:

> The strong winds <u>caused</u> the tree to fall over.

> **Cause:** There were strong winds.
> **Effect:** The tree fell over.

1. Read the pairs of sentences in the chart. One shows a cause, and one shows an effect.
2. For each pair, decide which sentence shows the cause and which shows the effect.

a.	Saleem got an "A" on the test. Saleem studied for the test.
b.	Monica forgot to put gas in the car. The car ran out of gas.
c.	The traffic got very bad. Many people moved to the town.

3. Look for causes and effects as you read "The Peach Boy."
4. With a partner, perform a scene that contains one of the causes and effects that you found in the play.

Student CD-ROM

MULTI-LEVEL OPTIONS *Reading Strategy*

Newcomer Mime eating. *Ask: Why?* (hungry) Mime sleeping. *Ask: Cause?* (tired) Invite students to mime actions. Ask the class to act out or tell the cause.

Beginning Straighten up papers and books on your desk. *Say: My desk looks better. What caused it to look better? I cleaned it up.* Point to various things in the classroom, such as a broken piece of chalk. *Ask: What caused this?* (It fell.) Have them answer in a word or phrase.

Intermediate Have students work in pairs to make a two-column chart labeled *cause* and *effect.* Tell them to list on the right some things that happen in nature. (Birds fly south.) On the left, have them list a cause for each. (Winter comes.) Tell students to put arrows from the causes to the effects.

Advanced Have students review "Zlata's Diary" (p. 166). Have them list as many causes and effects from the story as possible. (Cause: Bombing near the city. Effect: People started to leave.)

The PEACH BOY

a play by Suzanne Barchers

179

Reading Selection Materials

Audio: *Unit 3, Chapter 3; CD 1, Track 14*
Teacher Resource Book: *Reading Summary, pp. 89–90*
Transparencies: *#8, Reading Summary*

Suggestions for Using Reading Summary

- Introduce new vocabulary or cognates.
- Cut the summary into strips, or jumble the sentences on an overhead transparency. Students put the sentences in order.
- Practice the reading strategy.
- Students read aloud or with a partner.
- Students paraphrase the summary.
- Students do a cloze activity.
- Students create a visual or graphic organizer, such as a timeline or storyboard, to illustrate the summary.
- Students paraphrase the summary.

Preview the Selection

1. **Interpret the image** *Ask: How can you tell this painting is about a good harvest?* (Everything is big and ripe. All the peaches look delicious.) *Why do you think this illustration was chosen for the selection?* (The play is entitled "The Peach Boy" and the illustration is about peaches.)
2. **Connect** *Ask: Do you like peaches? Do they grow in our area? Where are they grown in the United States?*

Content Connection
Science

Assign pairs of students to find out more about peaches. Ask them to use encyclopedias or online resources to learn how and where peaches grow, the size and types of peach trees, the needs of the plant, and diseases and insects that affect them. Challenge students to find an interesting way to share the peach facts they discover.

Learning Styles
Natural

If possible, bring in fresh peaches for students to feel, smell, and taste. (If not, have students look at the picture on p. 179.) Ask students what season this painting is about (late summer, early fall) and how they know. Ask them to share experiences they have had related to peaches. (*Examples:* Peaches make me feel happy and excited because my grandmother makes great peach pie. They make me feel free because they remind me of afternoon snacks in the summer.)

Read the Selection

1. **Use illustrations** Direct students to the drawings. Ask them to guess when the story takes place. Have them give reasons for their answers. Then ask them to predict what will happen in this story.
2. **Choral reading** Play the audio. Then divide the class into four groups and assign each group a role. Have students read the parts chorally with you. Then reassign roles and reread the selection.

Sample Answer to Guide Question
She sees a peach and thinks that if she can pull it in, she will enjoy a beautiful peach.

See Teacher Edition pp. 434–436 for a list of English-Spanish cognates in the reading selection.

Audio
CD 1. Tr. 14

1 **Narrator:** Long ago there lived an old man and old woman in a village in Japan. They were **fine** people, but they had no children. One day they were eating their breakfast.

2 **Man:** What are you doing today, my wife?

3 **Woman:** I am going to the stream to **scrub** clothes. What are you going to do, my husband?

4 **Man:** I am off to the mountains to cut some **firewood** for the stove.

5 **Narrator:** The man went to the mountains and the woman went to the stream. When the woman began to scrub her clothes, she noticed something strange **floating** in the river. A big, ripe peach was floating right to her.

6 **Woman:** This is my lucky day! I'll pull the peach to me with this stick. What a fine big peach this is! Wait until my husband sees it.

> **Analyze Cause and Effect**
>
> What caused the woman to say, "This is my lucky day!"?

fine excellent	**firewood** wood used to start a fire or to keep it burning
scrub wash by rubbing hard	**floating** resting or moving on the top of water or other liquid

180 Unit 3 Conflict and Cooperation

MULTI-LEVEL OPTIONS *Read the Selection*

Newcomer Play the audio. Play it again and have students join in when they can. *Ask: Did the man and woman have children?* (no) *Did the woman go to the mountains?* (no) *Did the woman find a stick?* (no) *Did she find a peach?* (yes) *Was there a surprise in the peach?* (yes) *Did the man eat the peach?* (no)

Beginning Play the audio. Then assign students various roles. Play the audio again and have students read their roles along with the audio. *Ask: Why did the woman go to the stream?* (scrub clothes) *What did she find at the river?* (peach) *Who wants to eat the peach?* (the man) *What was inside the peach?* (boy)

Intermediate Have students do a read aloud in small groups. *Ask: What was the woman doing when she saw the peach?* (washing clothes in the river) *Why was the woman excited?* (She wanted to share the peach with her husband.) *How did the man and woman first know there was a boy inside the peach?* (They heard his voice.)

Advanced Assign roles to students and have them read their parts aloud. *Ask: Contrast the woman's reaction and the man's reaction to the peach?* (She thought the peach was good luck. He was excited about eating it.) *How do you think the couple will react to the boy? Why?* (They will be surprised to find a boy in the peach but pleased to have a child.)

7   **Narrator:** The old woman could hardly wait for her husband to come home.

8   **Woman:** Husband, come quickly. Come see what I have found!

9   **Man:** What is it, wife? Is something the matter?

10   **Woman:** Look at this peach! Isn't it the finest you have ever seen?

11   **Man:** How did you buy a peach like this?

12   **Narrator:** The old woman told him how it came floating down the stream.

13   **Man:** This is a **fine piece of fortune.** I have worked hard today. This will make a wonderful dinner for me.

14   **Narrator:** Just as the old man was about to cut the peach with his knife, he heard a voice.

15   **Momotaro:** Please don't cut me.

16   **Man: My goodness!** What is this I hear?

17   **Narrator:** Suddenly the peach split in half, and a little boy jumped out.

18   **Man and Woman: Goodness gracious!**

> **Analyze Cause and Effect**
>
> What caused the little boy to jump out of the peach?

---

fine piece of fortune   good luck
My goodness!   a phrase that shows surprise

Goodness gracious!   a phrase that shows surprise

Chapter 3   The Peach Boy   **181**

Read the Selection

1. **Use the illustration** *Ask: What is the man about to do?* (cut open the peach) *What will happen when he cuts it open?* (A little boy will jump out.)
2. **Choral reading** Play the audio. Then divide the class into four groups and assign each group a role and a group leader. Have each group read the parts chorally with its leader.
3. **Discuss genre** *Say: In most folktales, things in nature have special powers, such as talking. What has special powers in this story?* (the peach)
4. **Dramatize** Have three volunteers dramatize the play up to this point. Ask them to use non-verbal cues to help create the scene, such as acting out eating breakfast and scrubbing clothes.
5. **Multi-level options** See MULTI-LEVEL OPTIONS on p. 180.

Sample Answer to Guide Question
The little boy jumped out of the peach because the peach split in half.

Punctuation

Colon

Ask students to look at p. 180. *Say: Why did the writer put the words* narrator, man, *and* woman *on the left of the lines?* (To show who is talking) *Look at the punctuation mark after each name. It is called a* colon. *Colons are always used to separate the name of the speaker from what he or she says in a play.*

Read the Selection

1. **Shared reading** Play the audio. Then have volunteers join in for different parts.
2. **Analyze cause and effect** Write on the board: *Why does the boy ask his mother to make some cakes?* (He wants to go on a journey.) *Why is the boy going to the Island of the Ogres?* (He wants to do some good of his own.) Have students work in small groups to write answers to the questions.

Sample Answer to Guide Question
The land will be free of ogres; people's belongings will be returned to them; people will live without fear.

19 **Narrator:** The little boy ate one half of the peach and then ate the other half. The old man and woman decided to call him Momotaro, meaning Boy of the Peach. They were **delighted** to have a child and took great care of him. He quickly grew into a fine young man. One day he asked his mother for a **favor.**

20 **Momotaro:** Mother, please make me some cakes.

21 **Woman:** Why, my son?

22 **Momotaro:** You have been very good to me. It is time I did some good of my own. I need the cakes for my **journey.**

23 **Woman:** But son, where are you going?

> **Analyze Cause and Effect**
>
> What effects does Momotaro think his journey will have?

24 **Momotaro:** To the **Island** of the **Ogres.** They have stolen from many people. I hope to free the land of those creatures and return the **belongings** to the people. Then they can live without fear.

25 **Man:** That is a fine idea. I wish you well.

26 **Narrator:** Momotaro's mother made him the cakes. Soon he was ready to leave.

27 **Man and Woman:** Good-bye, son. **Take care.**

28 **Momotaro:** Don't worry, my dear parents. I will be back soon.

---

delighted very happy
favor a helpful act
journey a long trip
island a piece of land completely surrounded by water

ogres giants in folktales who eat people
belongings things people own
take care an expression that means "be careful"

182 Unit 3 Conflict and Cooperation

MULTI-LEVEL OPTIONS *Read the Selection*

Newcomer *Did the boy take a trip?* (yes) *Did the man and woman go with him?* (no) *Did the boy go on the trip to get rid of mean ogres?* (yes) *Does a horse help the boy?* (no)

Beginning *Where is the boy going?* (the Island of the Ogres) *What did the boy take on his trip?* (cakes) *Who did the boy want to stop from being mean?* (ogres) *Who wanted to help the boy?* (a dog)

Intermediate *How did the man and woman probably feel about the boy's trip?* (They were sad to see him leave, but they knew why he had to go.) *What can you tell about the boy from his actions? Explain.* (He was brave because he was willing to try to get rid of mean ogres.) *How could a dog help?* (help the boy fight the ogres)

Advanced *Why didn't the boy stay in his nice home?* (He had a good life and wanted others to have one also.) *Why do you think the dog offered to help?* (He thought the trip sounded like an adventure.) *What do you predict will happen next?* (The boy will meet another animal who wants to help.)

29 **Narrator:** Momotaro **hurried** away. He was **anxious** to get to the Island of the Ogres. He was walking through the forest when he began to feel hungry. He sat under a pine tree and **unwrapped** his cakes. Suddenly he saw a huge dog **slinking** toward him. The dog spoke to him.

30 **Dog:** Momotaro, what do you have that smells so good?

31 **Momotaro:** I have a cake my mother made for me this morning.

32 **Dog:** If you give me one of your cakes, I will come with you to the Island of the Ogres. I can help you there.

33 **Momotaro:** You are **welcome** to the cake. I **appreciate** your offer of help.

> **Analyze Cause and Effect**
>
> The dog says he will go with Momotaro. Is this a cause or an effect?

---

hurried moved quickly	**slinking** walking as if afraid or guilty
anxious wanting to do something, impatient	**welcome** given permission
unwrapped took the cover off of, opened	**appreciate** be thankful for

Chapter 3 The Peach Boy   **183**

Read the Selection

1. **Use the illustration** Have students look at the illustration. *Ask: How old do you think the boy is now?* (16 to 18 years old) *Do you think he is wealthy?* (no) *Why not?* (His clothes are simple.) *Is this his dog?* (no)

2. **Shared reading** Play the audio. Then have volunteers join in for different parts.

3. **Dramatize** Have three volunteers dramatize the play up to this point. Ask them to use non-verbal cues to help create the scene.

4. **Multi-level options** See MULTI-LEVEL OPTIONS on p. 182.

Sample Answer to Guide Question
An effect.

 Spelling

Silent *w* before *r*

Ask: What sounds do you hear in the word unwrap? (u-n-r-a-p) Remind students that some words are not spelled the way they sound. *Say: Some words have silent letters. Unwrap is an example.* Have students locate the word in paragraph 29. *Ask: What letter is silent?* (w)

Apply *Say: The words I am going to list have silent w's. Write each as I say it:* wrap, wrong, write, wreath, wrinkle. *Circle the silent* w.

Read the Selection

1. **Choral reading** Play the audio. Then do a choral reading with students. Invite volunteers to "lead" different pages by reading the narrator's part.

2. **Discuss motivation** *Ask: Do you think Momotaro wants to be a hero and become famous, or do you think he really wants to help people on the island? Why do you think so?* (I think he really wants to help people because he welcomes the animals' help. If he just wanted to be a hero, he might have tried to do it by himself.)

Sample Answer to Guide Question
He wanted the monkey and the pheasant to help him. After he gave them the cakes, they offered to come with him.

34 Narrator: Momotaro and the dog continued on their way. Suddenly something jumped in front of Momotaro. It was a monkey.

35 Monkey: Momotaro! I hear you are going to the Island of the Ogres. I would like to go with you to help.

36 Dog: Who needs a monkey? I am going to help Momotaro!

37 Momotaro: There is no need to argue. You may both come. Here is a cake for you, monkey friend.

Analyze Cause and Effect

What do you think caused Momotaro to give cakes to the monkey and the pheasant? Look in the next paragraph and find the effect.

38 Narrator: The three continued on their journey. Suddenly they were stopped by a large **pheasant.** The dog **leaped** at it, but the pheasant fought back. Momotaro stopped the fight. He gave the pheasant a cake.

39 Pheasant: Thank you, Momotaro. I would like to go with you to the Island of the Ogres. I think I can be of help to you.

40 Narrator: The four of them continued down the path, **chatting** and becoming friends. Soon they came to the sea. Momotaro found a boat, and they climbed in it. They came to the island, where the ogres' **castle** was surrounded by high walls and a big gate. Momotaro studied the castle and explained his plan to his friends.

---

pheasant a large, colorful bird with a long tail
leaped jumped

chatting talking in a friendly way
castle a large building with thick walls to guard against attack

184 Unit 3 Conflict and Cooperation

MULTI-LEVEL OPTIONS *Read the Selection*

Newcomer *Ask: Did a turkey want to come with the boy?* (no) *Did all the animals want to help?* (yes) *Did the boy beat the ogres by himself?* (no) *Did the boy keep all the treasures?* (no)

Beginning *Ask: What animals helped the boy?* (dog, monkey, pheasant) *Who lost the fight?* (ogres) *What did the boy find after the fight?* (treasures) *To whom did he give them?* (their owners)

Intermediate *Ask: How did the animals help Momotaro?* (They fought the ogres with him.) *How did the boy fix the wrong that the ogres had done?* (He returned stolen treasures to their owners.) *How do you think the man and woman felt at the end?* (proud and happy to have their boy back)

Advanced *Ask: How must the animals and boy have felt when they got to the island?* (afraid of the giants but determined to win) *What must the owners of the treasures have felt about the boy? Why?* (They probably felt he was brave because he had done what they could not. Also, they probably thought he was fair and kind to help them.)

41 **Momotaro:** Pheasant, you fly over the castle gate and **peck** at the ogres. Monkey, climb over the wall and **pinch** the ogres. The dog and I will break the bars and come to help when possible.

42 **Narrator:** The pheasant flew over the gate and pecked at the ogres. The monkey climbed over the wall and pinched the ogres. Momotaro and the dog broke the bars and fought hard and long. Soon all the ogres were either dead or taken prisoner.

43 **Momotaro:** Now, my friends. Let us look at their **treasures.**

Analyze Cause and Effect

What was the effect of Momotaro's plan?

44 **Narrator:** There were many jewels and fine **goods.** Momotaro returned the stolen goods to the owners and told the people they need never fear the ogres again. There were many riches left for Momotaro and his friends. He returned home to the old man and woman. They were very happy to see him, and they all lived happily for many years.

---

peck hit with a sharp object, such as a bird's beak
pinch squeeze between the finger and thumb

treasures riches
goods items that can be bought and sold

About the Author

Suzanne Barchers (born 1946)

Suzanne Barchers has worked as a teacher, a writer, and an editor. She has written books about teaching language arts. Barchers has also written many books for young people about history and folktales.

➤ Why do you think Suzanne Barchers wanted to retell this story about Momotaro? To entertain, to inform, or to persuade?

Chapter 3 The Peach Boy **185**

Punctuation

Comma for direct address

Have students reread paragraph 41. *Ask: Who is Momotaro talking to in the first sentence?* (Pheasant) *What mark is after the bird's name?* (comma) *A comma is used to separate the person being talked to from what is being told to that person. Find another example in this paragraph.* (Monkey, climb . . .)

Apply *Say: Write a sentence Momotaro could have used to tell dog what to do.* (Dog, break the bars with me.)

Evaluate Your Reading Strategy

Analyze Cause and Effect *Say: You have practiced an important reading strategy. Now you can decide how well you have done. Does this statement describe how you read?*

> I look for causes and effects as I read. Finding causes and effects helps me understand why events in a text happen.

Read the Selection

1. **Dramatize the story** Have students do a choral reading of the whole play while seven volunteers mime the roles. Individuals or small groups of students can read each part. Give students time to practice. Invite parents or another class to view the performance.
2. **Multi-level options** See MULTI-LEVEL OPTIONS on p. 184.

Sample Answer to Guide Question
There were several effects: he returned the riches to the people and they didn't have to fear the ogres again; he and his friends returned home with riches; the old man and woman were happy to see him.

About the Author

Analyze facts *Ask: What different jobs has the author had?* (teacher, writer, editor) *What is the author interested in writing about?* (history and folktales)

Across Selections

Teacher Resource Book: *Venn Diagram, p. 35*

Say: Another folktale we read was "Coyote" (p. 17). Let's compare and contrast the two folktales. Draw a Venn diagram on the board. Discuss similarities and differences. Have students fill in the diagram. Possible similarities are: animals have human qualities; unreal things happen. Possible differences are: "Coyote" is a poem and explains creation of earth; "The Peach Boy" teaches values.

Spelling, Punctuation, Capitalization

After the Reading Comprehension section, students will practice spelling, punctuation, and capitalization in the Activity Book.

Beyond the Reading

Reading Comprehension

Question-Answer Relationships

Sample Answers

1. in a village in Japan
2. Boy of the Peach
3. a dog, a monkey, and a pheasant
4. the dog
5. he realizes that they could help him
6. They want to help because Momotaro gave them cakes. Maybe they didn't like the ogres and wanted to live without fear, too.
7. My cousin helped me learn to ride a bicycle. I thought I'd never learn, but she practiced with me every day for a week until I finally could do it.
8. I don't think he would have been able to fight the ogres by himself because he had no weapons; he was just one against many, and the ogres had a castle surrounded by high walls and a big gate.

Build Reading Fluency

Read Aloud to Engage Listeners

Model reading aloud with expression. Remind students to keep their eyes on the words as they read. This will help them with phrasing, intonation, and pronunciation.

Reading Comprehension

Question-Answer Relationships (QAR)

"Right There" Questions

1. **Recall Facts** Where do the old man and the old woman live?
2. **Explain** What does "Momotaro" mean?
3. **Recall Facts** Who goes with Momotaro to the Island of the Ogres?

"Think and Search" Question

4. **Recognize Sequence of Events** Which character is the first to join Momotaro on his journey?

"Author and You" Questions

5. **Understand Character Motivation** Why do you think Momotaro allows the three animals to join him on his journey?

6. **Make an Inference** Why do you think the dog, the pheasant, and the monkey want to help Momotaro fight the ogres?

"On Your Own" Questions

7. **Relate Your Experiences** Can you remember a time when your friends or family helped you to reach a goal? What happened?
8. **Present an Opinion** Do you think Momotaro would have been able to fight the ogres if the dog, the pheasant, and the monkey had not helped him? Why or why not?

Activity Book   Student
p. 98   CD-ROM

Build Reading Fluency

Read Aloud to Engage Listeners

Practicing reading aloud helps increase your fluency and expression. Learning to read with expression makes others want to listen to you.

1. Listen to the audio recording of "The Peach Boy."
2. Turn to page 180 and follow along.
3. Pay attention to phrasing and expression.

4. With a partner, read aloud the paragraphs three times.
5. Select your favorite paragraph.
6. Read in front of the class with expression.

186 Unit 3 Conflict and Cooperation

MULTI-LEVEL OPTIONS *Elements of Literature*

Newcomer *Say: The people who owned the jewels had a problem.* Tell half the group to draw the problem. Have the other half draw how the problem was resolved. Have students who drew the problem pair with students who drew the resolution. Invite students to share their illustrations with each other.

Beginning Brainstorm a list of problems in the play. Then have students make drawings to show the resolution of each problem. Help them write a short caption for each picture.

Intermediate Direct students to complete their charts. Ask them to meet in small groups and think of ideas for alternate resolutions. Have each group develop a short script based on one of the alternate resolutions.

Advanced Have students create a Storyboard for another adventure involving Momotaro. Ask them to decide on a problem and plan out the steps to a resolution. Invite students to use the map to develop a story.

Listen, Speak, Interact

Talk About Values

In Build Background you learned that "The Peach Boy" is based on a folktale from Japan. Folktales often show a culture's values—things that are important to people. For example, a value of the culture in the United States is being able to take care of yourself.

1. With a partner, talk about the values you think the selection shows.
2. Use details from the selection to help you. For example, Momotaro's parents are very happy when he

becomes their son. This detail shows that family is probably important in Japanese culture.

3. Write your ideas on a piece of paper.
4. Share your notes with the class. Listen carefully as your classmates also share their ideas. What evidence do your classmates share to support their opinions?
5. With your partner, perform a scene in "The Peach Boy" that illustrates your ideas.

Elements of Literature

Recognize Problems and Resolutions

A play often includes **problems and resolutions**—ways that problems are corrected. Authors use problems and resolutions to create interesting stories in their plays. Look at this problem and resolution from the reading selection:

Problem: Momotaro needs food for his journey.

Resolution: His mother makes some cakes for him.

1. Read the problems from the selection listed in the chart. Copy the chart in your Reading Log.
2. With a partner, talk about the author's resolution for each problem.

Problem	Author's Resolution
The ogres have stolen from many people.	
The dog and the pheasant fight each other.	
It is difficult to get into the ogres' castle. It has high walls and a big gate.	

3. Write each resolution in your chart.
4. Perform a dramatic interpretation of your resolution to the class.

Reading Log   Activity Book   Student
                    p. 99   CD-ROM

Chapter 3 The Peach Boy **187**

Listen, Speak, Interact

Talk About Values

1. **Clarify terms** *Say: Each family has different values, or things that are important to them. For example, in my family, respectful communication is a value. Can you give me your own examples?* (We help each other; older children help take care of younger ones.)
2. **Newcomers** Do this exercise together with newcomers. Write on the board: _____ *is important in my culture. I know this because* _____. Help students complete the sentences.

Answers
1. and 2. *Possible answers:* He values cooperation because he breaks up fights between the animals, and he also shows the animals how to work together towards a goal.

Elements of Literature

Recognize Problems and Resolutions

1. **Analyze cause and effect** Have students work in groups. Ask them to discuss how figuring out a solution to a problem is a lot like understanding cause and effect.
2. **Multi-level options** See MULTI-LEVEL OPTIONS on p. 186.

Answers
Resolutions: He will return their treasures; Momotaro broke up the fight; Momotaro came up with a plan.

 **ASSESS**

Have students write two values that are important to them and give examples.

Word Study

Identify Homophones

1. **Review homophones** Write on the board: *it's, there, your.* Tell students to write a homophone for each word. (its; their, they're; you're) Then have them write sentences using all the homophones.

2. **Use a resource to find correct spellings** *Say: Using the correct homophone can be tricky sometimes. When you're not sure which to use, look up the word in a dictionary.* Have students look up: *to/two/too, won/one, metal/medal.*

Answers
1. c 2. a 3. b

Grammar Focus

Use Compound Sentences With *and*

Use *and* in compound sentences Have pairs write compound sentences using *and.*

Answers
1. Suddenly the peach split in half. . . Momotaro found a boat. . .
2. a. The dog asked for a cake, and Momotaro gave him one. b. The pheasant flew over the gate, and the monkey climbed over the wall.

ASSESS

Have students define *compound sentence.*

Word Study

Identify Homophones

Some words in the English language sound the same but have different spellings and meanings. These words are called **homophones.** Look at these examples of homophones from the selection:

> Come <u>see</u> what I have found! (paragraph 8)

> Soon they came to the <u>sea</u>. (paragraph 40)

See and *sea* are homophones. They are pronounced the same, but they mean different things. *See* means "look at," and *sea* means "a large body of water." The two words also have different spellings.

Look at the homophones and definitions below. Match the homophones with the correct set of definitions. Ask another student or your teacher if you need help.

1. flour / flower
2. ant / aunt
3. ate / eight

a. an insect / a mother's sister
b. the past tense of eat / a number
c. grain used for baking / a plant

The Heinle Newbury House Dictionary   Activity Book p. 100   Student CD-ROM

Grammar Focus

Use Compound Sentences With *and*

A **compound sentence** is two complete sentences joined by a conjunction such as *and.* Conjunctions are words that join parts of sentences.

When you join two complete sentences with *and,* use a comma before *and.*

Two Sentences	The man went to the mountains. The woman went to the stream.
Compound Sentence	The man went to the mountains, **and** the woman went to the stream.

1. Find two more compound sentences with *and* in the reading. Look in paragraphs 17 and 40.
2. On a piece of paper, combine the sentences below using *and.* Don't forget to use a comma before *and.*
   a. The dog asked for a cake. Momotaro gave him one.
   b. The pheasant flew over the gate. The monkey climbed over the wall.

Activity Book pp. 101–102   Student Handbook   Student CD-ROM

188 Unit 3 Conflict and Cooperation

MULTI-LEVEL OPTIONS *From Reading to Writing*

Newcomer Write *beginning, middle,* and *end* on separate pieces of paper. Instruct students to draw an illustration to show what happened in each part of the play.

Beginning Have students create a comic strip summary of the play. Ask them to include three to four frames showing the most important events. Tell them to include speech balloons. Help them find dialogue from the play for the speech balloons.

Intermediate Remind students that they should focus on causes and effects as they read the story. Suggest that they base their summaries on the most important details that support the theme of the story.

Advanced Remind students of the importance of sentence variety in their writing. When peer response groups meet, have them pay special attention to opportunities for writers to combine some of their simple sentences into compound sentences.

From Reading to Writing

Write a Summary

A **summary** gives the most important information of a reading. Write a short summary of "The Peach Boy" that is only one paragraph long.

1. Reread or listen to the audio recording of "The Peach Boy" to summarize.
2. Begin your summary by stating in one sentence what "The Peach Boy" is about. This sentence tells the **theme** (main idea) of the reading.

3. Then write sentences that explain the most important ideas of the beginning, the middle, and the end of the play. Write one or two sentences for each part of the play.
4. Make sure each sentence has a subject and a verb. Each verb must agree with its subject.

Activity Book
p. 103

Student
Handbook

Across Content Areas

Classify Fruits and Vegetables

Sometimes, everyday language is different from language used in science. Here are the scientific definitions of *fruits* and *vegetables*.

Fruits are plants and have seeds inside. A fruit may contain one or more seeds. For example, a peach contains one large seed. An orange has many seeds.

Vegetables are also plants, but they do not have seeds inside them. Many foods that people call vegetables are called fruits in scientific language. For example, some people call a cucumber a vegetable. However, there are seeds inside a cucumber, so in science it is a fruit.

1. Look at these fruits and vegetables:

apple	spinach	tomato
carrot	watermelon	broccoli

2. Copy the chart below.

Fruits	Vegetables

3. Write each word from the list above in the correct column of your chart. Use the scientific definitions.

Activity Book
p. 104

Reteach and Reassess

Text Structure *Say: Imagine you are going to write a play. Set up a page with the features you will need. When you finish, check the diagram on p. 178 to see if you need to add anything.*

Reading Strategy Have students create cause and effect charts by drawing two columns of boxes. Have students fill in causes from the play on the left and effects on the right. Tell them to connect related causes and effects with arrows.

Elements of Literature Help students recall "Why the Rooster Crows at Sunrise" (p. 110) or another familiar story. Have students use a diagram similar to the one on p. 187 to tell about the problem and resolution and suggest an alternate solution.

Reassess Read aloud a folktale. Have small groups use the Reader's Theater approach to turn the story into a play.

From Reading to Writing

Write a Summary

1. **Write collaboratively** Write in outline form: *The Peach Boy is about _____. I. Beginning, A., B.; II. Middle, A., B.; III. End, A., B.* Ask questions to help students write a summary. Have volunteers write the notes on the board. Then have students work together to compose an oral summary. Instruct students to write their summaries individually.
2. **Proofread writing** Have students carefully check that their summaries have the first word of the paragraph indented, correct capitalization, and correct punctuation.
4. **Multi-level options** See MULTI-LEVEL OPTIONS on p. 188.

Across Content Areas: Science

Classify Fruits and Vegetables

Brainstorm a list Divide the class into two groups, one for fruit and one for vegetables. Have each group choose a person to write words on the board. Give each group 5 minutes to write as many fruits and vegetables as they can. When the time is up, have them check the lists according to the scientific definition of fruits and vegetables. Also have students check for correct spelling.

Answers
Fruits: apple, watermelon, tomato. Vegetables: carrot, spinach, broccoli.

ASSESS

Have students describe in their own words the difference between a fruit and a vegetable.

Talking in the New Land

an excerpt from
a personal narrative
by Edite Cunhã

Chapter Materials

Activity Book: *pp. 105–112*
Audio: *Unit 3, Chapter 4; CD 1, Track 15*
Student Handbook
Student CD-ROM: *Unit 3, Chapter 4*
Teacher Resource Book: *Lesson Plan, Teacher Resources, Reading Summary, Activity Book Answer Key*
Teacher Resource CD-ROM
Assessment Program: *Quiz, pp. 45–46; Teacher and Student Resources, pp. 115–144*
Assessment CD-ROM
Transparencies
The Heinle Newbury House Dictionary/CD-ROM
Web site: http://visions.heinle.com

Objectives

Preview *Ask: Can you explain how to summarize?*

Use Prior Knowledge

Share Feelings About Speaking in Different Situations

Connect to personal experience *Ask: What adults do you talk to outside your family? Do you ever have to speak English for someone else?*

Objectives

Reading Summarize to recall ideas as you read a personal narrative.

Listening and Speaking Summarize and paraphrase.

Grammar Use *could* and *couldn't*.

Writing Write to solve a problem.

Content Language Arts: Learn about graphic features.

Use Prior Knowledge

Share Feelings About Speaking in Different Situations

In the reading selection, the main character's father does not speak English. The character must speak English for him.

1. Suppose you had to do the things listed below because a family member did not speak English.
   a. Talk to a doctor about giving medicine to your brother.
   b. Tell a man that your father doesn't want to talk to him.
   c. Thank a woman for helping your mother.
   d. Talk to a man about a car that your mother is buying.

2. Make a chart like the one here.
3. Think about how you would feel about doing each thing listed.
4. Write each situation from the list in the chart. Write the sentence in the column that tells how you would feel.

Happy ☺	Scared 😖	Angry ☹

MULTI-LEVEL OPTIONS *Build Vocabulary*

Newcomer *Say: Some words mean the same thing.* Draw on the board two happy faces. Point to one. *Say: happy.* Write *happy* under the face. Point to the other. *Say: glad.* Write *glad* under the face. Follow the same procedure with faces showing the following emotions: *sad/unhappy, mad/angry, scared/afraid.*

Beginning Have students copy the following in a column on their papers: *surprised, scared, happy, mad.* Tell them to copy the following beside the first column: *glad, afraid, angry, shocked.* Have them draw a face next to each word to show its meaning. Ask students to connect similar faces (synonym pairs) with lines.

Intermediate Instruct students to use a thesaurus to find additional synonyms for *thick* and *fragrant.* Ask them to write two sentences using each synonym. Have them read their sentences in pairs.

Advanced Ask each student to write a descriptive paragraph about something in the classroom, such as an aquarium, a library corner, or a bulletin board display. Tell students to exchange papers with a partner and use a thesaurus to find synonyms for at least three of the descriptive words in each paragraph.

Build Background

Portugal

Portugal is a country in southwestern Europe. It is on the Atlantic Ocean, and some people there fish for a living. Many people work in factories, making things like clothing and paper products. Others grow crops such as grapes, olives, and tomatoes. People in Portugal speak Portuguese.

Content Connection

During the 1400s and 1500s, Portuguese explorers traveled to many parts of the world. These explorers were some of the first Europeans to visit Africa, Asia, and South America.

Build Vocabulary

Use Synonyms to Find Meaning

A **synonym** is a word that has a similar meaning to another word.

I could see a <u>slim</u>, <u>slender</u> lady dressed in brown.

Slim and *slender* are synonyms. *Slim* means "thin." *Slender* also means "thin."

1. Read these sentences. The two synonyms in each sentence are underlined.
   a. The lawn is covered with a <u>thick</u>, <u>dense</u> row of tall bushes.
   b. I hid in the <u>fragrant</u>, <u>sweet-smelling</u> shade of the bushes.

2. Decide which word to use in these sentences, *dense* or *sweet-smelling*. Use context clues in the sentences in #1.
   a. The crowd of students in the gym was _____ .
   b. The rose was _____ .

3. Check your answers in a dictionary or synonym finder.

The Heinle Newbury House Dictionary   Activity Book *p. 105*   Student CD-ROM

Chapter 4 Talking in the New Land   **191**

Content Connection
Math

Build Vocabulary Give students a list of mathematics terms, such as *fraction, sum, divide, multiply, subtract, length, square, equal*. Ask students to work in pairs to make up sentences for three of the words. Have students find synonyms for the target words in a print or electronic thesaurus and decide whether any of the synonyms could be used to replace the word in their sentence.

Learning Styles
Linguistic

Build Background Write several Portuguese words on the board: *livro* (book), *senhora* (lady), *mãe* (mother), *pai* (father), *escola* (school). Have Spanish-speaking students say the Spanish equivalent or have students look up the words in a translation dictionary or online dictionary. (libro, señora, madre, padre, escuela) Have students note similarities. Ask students for equivalents in other languages they know.

Build Background

Portugal

1. **Use a map** Have students point to places on the map as you name them. *Ask: What country is east of Portugal?* (Spain) *What ocean is Portugal on?* (the Atlantic Ocean) *Does Morocco border Portugal?* (no)

2. **Use inference** *Ask: What crops are grown in Portugal?* (grapes, olives, and tomatoes) *What type of climate do they have, and why do you think so?* (warm but not tropical climate; those crops need warm weather.)

3. **Content Connection** Vasco de Gama was a famous Portuguese explorer. He was the first European to sail to India (1497–1498).

Build Vocabulary

Teacher Resource Book: *Personal Dictionary, p. 63*

Use Synonyms to Find Meaning

1. **Use reference materials** Point out to students that a thesaurus is a good place to find synonyms.

2. **Clarify usage** *Say:* Thick *and* dense *are very close in meaning, but sometimes it's more appropriate to use one rather than the other. Reference aids often give information about when to use a particular word.* Have students look up the synonyms in a dictionary, thesaurus, and online or CD-ROM dictionary and thesaurus to clarify usage.

3. **Reading selection vocabulary** You may want to introduce the glossed words in the reading selection before students begin reading. Key words: *shadow, worry, escape, disappear, interrupt, ignore, trust*. Instruct students to write the words with correct spelling and their definitions in their Personal Dictionaries. Have them pronounce each word and divide it into syllables.

4. **Multi-level options** See MULTI-LEVEL OPTIONS on p. 190.

Answers
2. a. dense b. sweet-smelling

 **ASSESS**

Have students find synonyms for three glossed words.

Text Structure

Personal Narrative

Compare genre features *Say: We just read the play, "The Peach Boy." (p. 179) Does a play have characters and events like a narrative?* (yes) *Does this play use a first-person point of view?* (No, there is a narrator who has a third person point of view.)

Reading Strategy

Summarize to Recall Ideas

1. **Define and clarify** Have a volunteer read the explanation and summary. *Ask: In which other classes can you use the strategy of summarizing?*
2. **Multi-level options** See MULTI-LEVEL OPTIONS below.

ASSESS

Have pairs of students define a personal narrative in their own words.

Text Structure

Personal Narrative

"Talking in the New Land" is a **personal narrative.** A personal narrative is a story about real events that happened to the author. Look at the features of a personal narrative in the chart.

As you read, think about the events and problems in the selection. Have you had similar experiences?

Personal Narrative	
Characters	real people in the author's life
Events and Problems	events and problems in the author's life
First-Person Point of View	the pronouns *I, me, we,* and *us*

Student CD-ROM

Reading Strategy

Summarize to Recall Ideas

When you **summarize** a reading selection or part of a reading selection, you give only the most important events or ideas. Writing summaries can help you recall the ideas in a selection. Read this paragraph and its summary.

> Pablo's family members don't speak much English, but Pablo does. They often ask him to translate for them. He often goes to the mall with his mother to help her shop. He makes telephone calls for his father. Once his grandfather got into a car accident, and Pablo had to explain it to the police.

Summary: Pablo translates often for his parents.

As you read or listen to the audio recording of "Talking in the New Land," summarize the paragraphs.

Student CD-ROM

192 Unit 3 Conflict and Cooperation

MULTI-LEVEL OPTIONS *Reading Strategy*

Newcomer Read aloud the summary about Pablo on p. 192. Sketch on the board activities that Pablo does. Then draw Pablo talking without showing the context. Summarize by saying: *Pablo talks for his parents.*

Beginning Tell events related to your commute to school. For example, *say: Here is what happened on my way to school. There were many cars on the street. There were many trucks, too. My car was behind a slow bus. I had to stop at many red lights.* Ask students to summarize your story. (It was hard to get to school.)

Intermediate Have students work in small groups. Ask each student to write a paragraph about his or her trip to school. On separate slips of paper, have students summarize their writing. Instruct students to mix up the summaries. After each student reads his or her paragraph, have the group find the matching summary.

Advanced Find a summary of a familiar book, such as "Sadako and the Thousand Paper Cranes" (p. 58) or "Gonzalo" (p. 122), in a catalog or at an online bookstore. Have students read the summary and evaluate whether it is a good one based on the information about summaries on p. 192.

Talking in the New Land

an excerpt from a personal narrative
by Edite Cunhã

193

Reading Selection Materials

Audio: *Unit 3, Chapter 4; CD 1, Track 15*
Teacher Resource Book: *Reading Summary,*
pp. 91–92
Transparencies: #8, *Reading Summary*

Suggestions for Using Reading Summary

- Introduce new vocabulary or cognates.
- Cut the summary into strips, or jumble the sentences on an overhead transparency. Students put the sentences in order.
- Practice the reading strategy.
- Students read aloud or with a partner.
- Students paraphrase the summary.
- Students do a cloze activity.
- Students create a visual or graphic organizer, such as a timeline or storyboard, to illustrate the summary.
- Students paraphrase the summary.

Preview the Selection

1. **Interpret the image** Have students look at the illustration. Write on the board: *How, Where, What, Why.* Have two volunteers ask the class questions about the illustration using the question words.
2. **Discuss message of medium** *Ask: Is this a very realistic illustration? What feeling do you get from the illustration?*
3. **Connect** *Ask: How is this scene similar to where you live? How is it different? If you painted a picture of your neighborhood, what would you include in it?*

 Home Connection

Learning Styles
Linguistic

Ask: What chore have you had to do at home or in school that you don't like to do? Why don't you like to do it? Do you find it hard? Are you afraid you won't do it well? What could you do it make it more enjoyable?

Ask students to share experiences they have had translating, telling someone what an idea in one language means in another. Have students work in small groups to identify what a person has to know and what kinds of skills they must have to translate. (knowledge of both languages, good listening skills, ability to act out meanings, patience)

Read the Selection

1. **Do a Quaker reading** Play the audio. Then tell students to put a check in pencil at the start and end of passages they especially like. Give them a few minutes to do this. Then have them read their passages aloud. The order is unimportant. Point out that they can repeat sections other students have read aloud. Make sure everyone participates.

2. **Check comprehension** *Ask: How did she feel about her house?* (She liked it.) *How do you know?* (She says it was paradise.) *What does she mean when she says that a shadow fell over her days in paragraph 2?* (The shadow is speaking English for her father.) *Does her brother ever have to translate?* (no) *Why does the woman call their house?* (She wants to get her dishes from their cellar.)

Sample Answer to Guide Question
When she was nine, Edite moved to a house that she liked very much.

See Teacher Edition pp. 434–436 for a list of English-Spanish cognates in the reading selection.

Audio
CD 1. Tr. 15

Prologue
Edite Cunhã was born in Portugal. She moved to Massachusetts when she was seven years old. She began learning English in her new school. When this selection begins, Edite can speak English very well.

> **Summarize to Recall Ideas**
>
> Summarize paragraph 1 in writing.

1   When I was nine, **Pai** went to an **auction** and bought a big house on Tremont Street. We moved in the spring. The lawn at the side of the house dipped downward in a gentle slope and was covered with a thick, dense row of tall lilac bushes. I soon discovered that I could crawl between the bushes and hide from my brothers in the fragrant, sweet-smelling shade. It was **paradise.**

2   I was mostly wild and joyful on Tremont Street. But **now and then** there was a **shadow** that fell over my days.

3   "Oh, *Ediiiite! Ediiiite!*" Since Pai didn't speak English very well, he always called me, without the least bit of warning, to be his voice. He expected me to drop whatever I was doing to take care of something. Pai never called my brother, Carlos. No, Carlos never had to do anything but play! Recently, I'd had to talk on the telephone to a woman who wanted some old dishes. The dishes, along with a lot of old furniture and junk, had been in the house when we moved in. They were in the **cellar,** stacked in cardboard boxes and covered with dust. The woman called many times, wanting to speak with Pai.

Pai Portuguese for *Pa,* an informal word for *father*

auction a sale in which items are sold to the person who offers the most money

paradise a place where everything is beautiful and peaceful

now and then sometimes, once in a while

shadow the dark shape formed when something blocks the sun or other light

cellar the space below ground level under a building

194 Unit 3 Conflict and Cooperation

MULTI-LEVEL OPTIONS *Read the Selection*

Newcomer Play the audio. *Ask: Does Edite speak English?* (yes) *Does her father speak English?* (no) *Does Edite help her father by speaking for him?* (yes) *Does she like to do this?* (no) *Did her father sometimes ask Carlos to translate?* (no)

Beginning Read the Reading Summary. *Ask: What languages does Edite speak?* (Portuguese and English) *Who does not want to talk to English speakers?* (her father) *Who speaks English for Edite's father?* (Edite) *How does she feel about doing this?* (unhappy)

Intermediate Read aloud the story. *Ask: How does Edite's father manage without speaking English?* (He gets Edite to translate for him.) *How does Edite feel about helping in this way?* (She doesn't like it.) *How does she try to get out of helping? Does it work?* (She pretends not to hear when her father calls her; it doesn't work.)

Advanced Have students read silently. *Ask: Why doesn't Edite like to translate for her father?* (It is uncomfortable and hard to do. She also feels angry that her brother does not have to help.) *Why do you think Pai has Edite translate and not Carlos?* (Maybe Carlos does not speak as well as Edite does.)

4 "My father can't speak English," I would say. "He says to tell you that the dishes are in our house and they belong to us." But she did not seem to understand. Every few days she would call.

Summarize to Recall Ideas

Summarize paragraph 5 orally.

5 "Oh, *Ediiiite!*" Pai's voice **echoed** through the empty rooms. I wanted to pretend I had not heard it when it had that tone. But I couldn't **escape.** I couldn't disappear into thin air as I wished to do at such times.

6 "*Ediiiite!*" Yes, that tone was certainly there. Pai was calling me to do something only I could do. What was it now? Did I have to talk to the **insurance company**? They were always using words I couldn't understand: **premium** and **dividend.** That made me nervous.

7 "Please wait. I call my daughter," Pai was saying. He was talking to someone, someone in the house. Who could it be?

8 "Oh, *Ediiiite!*"

9 "*Que ééé?*"

10 "*Come over here and talk to this lady.*" *

* Words in italic type are translations of words spoken in Portuguese.

---

echoed   repeated because sounds bounced off walls or hard surfaces

escape   get away

insurance company   a company that will pay for a loss or an accident in exchange for regular payments

premium   the regular payment for an insurance policy

dividend   money that an insurance company makes and gives to a person who has an insurance policy

Que ééé?   "What iiiis (is) it?" in Portuguese

Chapter 4   Talking in the New Land   **195**

---

th Spelling

Abbreviations of addresses

Ask students to find the name of Edite's street in paragraph 1. Write on the board: *Tremont St.* Underline *St. Say: This is a short way to write* street. *It is an abbreviation.* Write on the board and introduce other abbreviations, such as *Rd., Hwy.,* and *Ave.* (road, highway, avenue) Have students guess their meaning and write the meaning under the abbreviation.

Apply   Write on the board the names of some streets, roads, highways, and avenues in your community. Have students copy the names using abbreviations.

Read the Selection

1. **Shared reading** Play the audio. Have volunteers join in for different sections of the story.

2. **Analyze characters** Model skimming for clues about how Edite feels about the situation. Write key words and phrases on the board, such as *reluctantly, helplessly,* and *My stomach turned over.* **Ask:** *How does Edite feel about the situation?* (unwilling and unable to help, nervous, impatient) *Why do you think she feels this way?* Then have students find two words or phrases that describe how Pai feels (Pai's face hardened. Pai was getting angry.)

Sample Answer to Guide Question
A lady came to talk to Pai about getting back some dishes.

> **Summarize to Recall Ideas**
>
> Summarize paragraph 11 in writing.

11   **Reluctantly,** I walked through the empty rooms toward the kitchen. Through the kitchen door I could see a slim lady dressed in brown standing at the top of the stairs. She had on high-heeled shoes and was holding a brown purse. As soon as Pai saw me he said to me, "*See what she wants.*"

12   The lady had dark hair that was very smooth. The ends of it flipped up in a way that I liked.

13   "Hello. I'm the lady who called about the dishes."

14   I stared at her without a word. My stomach **turned over.**

15   "*What did she say?*" Pai wanted to know.

16   "*She says she's the lady who wants the dishes.*"

17   Pai's face **hardened** some.

18   "*Tell her she's wasting her time. We're not giving them to her. Didn't you already tell her that on the telephone?*"

19   I nodded, standing **helplessly** between them.

---

reluctantly with hesitation

turned over felt funny

hardened looked hard

helplessly in an unprotected way

196 Unit 3 Conflict and Cooperation

MULTI-LEVEL OPTIONS *Read the Selection*

Newcomer *Does a lady come to visit Edite's father?* (yes) *Does she want her dishes back?* (yes) *Does Edite's father want to give the dishes to the lady?* (no)

Beginning *Ask: Who comes to visit?* (a lady) *What does she want?* (her dishes) *What does Edite's father say?* (no) *How does Edite feel?* (upset, helpless, angry)

Intermediate *Ask: How does the lady think she can get her dishes back?* (by talking to Pai in person) *How does Pai feel about her visit?* (It makes him angry.) *What do you think will happen next?* (The lady will try to talk Pai into giving back the dishes.) *How does Edite feel?* (stuck in the middle of the argument)

Advanced *Ask: Why does the lady come to the house?* (She probably thinks she can be more convincing in person.) *Why do you think the woman wants the dishes so badly?* (Maybe the dishes are special or valuable.)

20 "*Well, tell her again.*" Pai was getting angry. I wanted to **disappear.**

21 "My father says he can't give you the dishes," I said to the lady. She **clutched** her purse and leaned a little forward.

22 "Yes, you told me that on the phone. But I wanted to come **in person** and speak with your father because it's very important to me that—"

23 "My father can't speak English," I **interrupted** her. Why didn't she just go away?

24 "Yes, I understand that. But I wanted to see him." She looked at Pai, who was standing in the doorway to the kitchen holding his **hammer.** The kitchen was up one step from the porch. Pai was a small man, but he looked kind of scary staring down at us like that.

25 "*What is she saying?*"

26 "*She says she wanted to talk to you about getting her dishes.*"

> **Summarize to Recall Ideas**
>
> Summarize paragraph 24 in writing.

---

disappear go out of sight
clutched held tightly with the hands
in person physically present, face-to-face

interrupted started talking in the middle of someone else talking
hammer a tool with a handle and a metal head used for pounding

Chapter 4 Talking in the New Land   **197**

---

1. **Use illustrations** Direct students to the illustration. *What is the artist showing in this illustration? How does each person in the picture feel?*
2. **Silent reading** Give students time to read silently. Have them write words or phrases that show how Edite feels. (I wanted to disappear. He looked kind of scary.)
3. **Multi-level options** See MULTI-LEVEL OPTIONS on p. 196.

Sample Answer to Guide Question
The lady wants to speak to Pai, but Pai does not want to speak to her.

❜ Punctuation

Italics for words from other languages

Say: Italics can be used to show that words in a story have been translated from another language. Direct students to paragraph 15.
Say: This line is in English. Who said it? (Pai) *What language does he speak?* (Portuguese) *Paragraph 16 is Edite's answer. In what language did she answer Pai?* (Portuguese) *Since many people who read this story don't understand Portuguese, these lines are translated into English.*

Apply To be sure students understand, have them identify other examples of lines that were translated from Portuguese in this narrative.

Read the Selection

1. **Use art to predict** *Ask: Who is this person?* (the mother) *Do you think she will agree with the father, or will she want to give the dishes back? Why do you think so?*
2. **Paired reading** Play the audio. Then have students read aloud in pairs.

Sample Answer to Guide Question
Pai says everything in the house now belongs to him.

27   *"Tell her the dishes are ours. They were in the house. We bought the house and everything in it. Tell her the lawyer said so."*

28   The lady was looking at me **hopefully.**

29   "My father says the dishes are ours because we bought the house and the lawyer said everything in the house is ours now."

30   "Yes, I know that, but I was away when the house was being sold. I didn't know . . ."

31   There were **footsteps** on the stairs behind her. It was **Mãe** coming up from the second floor to find out what was going on. The lady moved away from the door to let Mãe in.

32   *"This is my wife,"* Pai said to the lady. The lady said hello to Mãe, who smiled and nodded her head. She looked at me, then at Pai in a **questioning** way.

Summarize to Recall Ideas
Summarize paragraph 27 orally.

---

hopefully in a way that shows hope
footsteps sounds of feet moving on a surface

Mãe Portuguese for *Ma*, an informal word for *mother*
questioning looking as if you have a question

198   Unit 3   Conflict and Cooperation

MULTI-LEVEL OPTIONS *Read the Selection*

Newcomer *Ask: Did the dishes belong to the lady's grandmother?* (yes) *Does she want them very much?* (yes) *Does Edite's mother want to give the dishes back to the lady?* (yes) *Does Edite's father feel better?* (no)

Beginning *Ask: Who came home?* (Edite's mother) *To whom did the dishes belong long ago?* (the lady's grandmother) *Does Edite's mother want to give the lady the dishes?* (yes) *How does Edite's father act?* (angry, stubborn)

Intermediate *Ask: How does the lady try to convince Edite's father?* (She explains that the dishes are special because they belonged to her grandmother.) *How does Edite's mother feel?* (She wants to give them back.) *What do you think Pai will say? How do you know?* (He will still say, "No." He is angry.)

Advanced *Ask: Why do you think Mãe wants to give the dishes back?* (She feels sorry for the woman and thinks it is right to give back the dishes.) *With whom is Pai angry? Why?* (He is angry with Mãe because she disagrees with him. He is angry with the woman because he does not believe her story.)

33   *"It's the lady who wants our dishes,"* Pai explained.

34   Mãe looked at her again and smiled, but I could tell she was a little **worried.**

35   We stood there in kind of a funny circle; the lady looked at each of us **in turn** and took a deep breath.

36   "I didn't know," she continued, "that the dishes were in the house. I was away. They are very important to me. They **belonged** to my grandmother. I'd really like to get them back." She spoke this while looking back and forth between Mãe and Pai. Then she looked down at me, leaning forward again. "Will you tell your parents, please?"

37   I spoke in a hurry to get the words out.

38   *"She said she didn't know the dishes were in the house because she was away. They were her grandmother's dishes, and she wants them back."* I felt deep **sorrow** at the thought of the lady returning home to find her grandmother's dishes sold.

39   *"We don't need all those dishes. Let's give them to her,"* Mãe said in her calm way. I felt **relieved.** We could give the lady the dishes and she would go away. But Pai got angry.

> **Summarize to Recall Ideas**
>
> Summarize paragraphs 38 and 39.

---

worried   feeling that something bad might happen
in turn   in order
belonged   were the property of; were owned by

sorrow   sadness
relieved   freed from bad feelings or worry

Chapter 4 Talking in the New Land   **199**

Read the Selection

1. **Analyze feelings** Have a volunteer read paragraph 38. *Say: Edite feels differently about the lady now. What tells us that?* (I felt deep sorrow.) *Why do you think she feels differently?* (She is beginning to understand why the dishes are important and perhaps can imagine how the lady feels.)

2. **Quaker dialogue** Have students select a portion of dialogue to read aloud to the class. Remind them to read with feeling and that they can read lines in any order and that lines can be read by more than one student. Monitor that all students participate.

3. **Multi-level options** See MULTI-LEVEL OPTIONS on p. 198.

Sample Answer to Guide Question
Edite translated that the lady explained that she was away when the house was sold. The mother thinks they should give back her grandmother's dishes.

---

th **Spelling**

Silent *gh* before *t*

Ask: What consonant sounds do you hear in bought*?* (b, t) *Yes, they are the only consonants that make sounds in the word. The word has other consonants in it, though.* Have students locate *bought* in paragraph 29. *Ask: Which consonants are silent?* (gh) *What letter is after the* gh*?* (t) Ask students to find another example of a word that has silent *gh* before *t* in paragraph 38. (thought)

Apply Tell students that you are going to say some words that have silent *gh* before *t*. Ask them to try to write the words: *brought, fought.*

Read the Selection

1. **Shared reading** Play the audio. Have students take turns reading parts of the selection aloud.

2. **Describe character's feelings** Direct students to the illustration on p. 200. *Ask: How do you think Edite feels? Why do you think she feels that way?* (Everyone wants something different, and she is in the middle.)

3. **Summarize** Have students work in pairs to write a summary of paragraphs 41 and 42. Then have volunteers read their summaries aloud. Discuss their similarities and differences. Point out that there are usually several ways to say the same thing.

Sample Answer to Guide Question
Edite explains to Pai in a frustrated voice why the lady wants the dishes and needs them. Pai thinks she's saying that to trick him.

Summarize to Recall Ideas

Summarize paragraphs 41 and 42 in writing.

---

40   *"I already said what I had to say. The dishes are ours. That is all."*

41   *"Pai, she said she didn't know. They were her grandmother's dishes. She needs to have them."* I was speaking wildly and loud now. The lady looked at me questioningly, but I didn't want to speak to her again.

42   *"She's only saying that to trick us. If she wanted those dishes she should have taken them out before the house was sold. Tell her we are not **fools**. Tell her to forget it. She can go away. Tell her not to call or come here again."*

43   "What is he saying?" The lady was looking at me again.

44   I **ignored** her. I felt sorry for Pai for always feeling that people were trying to trick him. I wanted him to **trust** people. I wanted the lady to have her grandmother's dishes. I closed my eyes and **willed** myself away.

fools people who make silly mistakes	**willed** tried to control something by using the power of your mind
ignored paid no attention to; did not listen to	
trust believe, feel that someone is honest	

MULTI-LEVEL OPTIONS *Read the Selection*

Newcomer *Ask: Does Pai change his mind?* (no) *Does Pai believe the woman?* (no) *Is Edite upset?* (yes) *Do you think Pai will ever change his mind?* (yes or no)

Beginning *Ask: Who wants the lady to have the dishes?* (Mãe and Edite) *Who does not want her to have the dishes?* (Pai) *What does Pai think the lady is trying to do?* (trick him) *What is Edite doing at the end of the story?* (yelling and crying)

Intermediate *Ask: How does Pai feel about the woman?* (He thinks she is trying to trick him or cheat him.) *How does Edite feel about her father?* (She feels angry at him, but she also feels sorry for him.) *How do you think the woman feels?* (very frustrated and sad that she could not change Pai's mind)

Advanced *Ask: Why doesn't Edite tell the lady what Pai said?* (She doesn't want to hurt her.) *What may be causing Pai to be mistrustful?* (Maybe he's frustrated because he can't tell for himself what people are saying.) *Predict what happens. Explain.* (When she's calmer, Edite talks to Pai about trusting people.)

45   *"Tell her what I said!"* Pai yelled.

46   *"Pai, just give her the dishes! They were her grandmother's dishes!"* My voice **cracked** as I yelled back at him. Tears were rising in my eyes.

47   I hated Pai for being so **stubborn.** I hated the lady for not taking the dishes before the house was sold. And I hated myself for having learned English.

Summarize to Recall Ideas

Summarize paragraph 47.

---

cracked   sounded uneven

stubborn   not wanting to change one's mind

About the Author

Edite Cunhã (born 1953)

Edite Cunhã started writing as a young teenager. She writes poetry and fiction. She now works as a teacher, an artist, and a writer. Cunhã says, "Writing for me is essential. It is like breath. It does not matter if my work is published or not. I must do it to feel alive at home in the world."

➤ What questions would you ask Edite Cunhã? How does her experience compare to that of Gonzalo in Unit 2, Chapter 4?

A   Capitalization

Family members' names

Point out the lower case *g* in *grandmother* and the capital *P* in *Pai* in paragraph 41. *Say: Both are words for family members, but one is capitalized and one is not. Pai is the name Edite calls her father. It must be capitalized. Grandmother is not the name the lady calls her grandmother.*

Apply List common and proper nouns for students' relatives. Have students tell which to capitalize. (Mom, cousin, Tio Luis)

Evaluate Your Reading Strategy

Summarize to Recall Ideas *Say: You have practiced an important reading strategy. Now you can decide how well you have done. Does this statement describe how you read?*

> After I read a paragraph, I summarize the most important events or ideas. Summarizing helps me remember these important ideas.

Read the Selection

1. **Dramatize the selection** Have students work in groups to dramatize different parts of the selection. Provide time to practice. Then have students perform for the class.

2. **Shared reading** Play the audio. Have students take turns reading parts of the selection aloud.

3. **Multi-level options** See MULTI-LEVEL OPTIONS on p. 200.

Sample Answer to Guide Question
Edite feels inner conflict. She is angry with others for putting her in this terrible situation. She is angry with herself for knowing English.

About the Author

Discuss author motivation *Ask: Why do you think the author wrote this story?* (She wanted to show what it was like to be caught in the middle of two cultures.)

Across Selections

Say: We read part of a novel about Gonzalo. (p. 122) *How was he like Edite?* (They both spoke English better than their families.) Ask students to compare and contrast Gonazalo's and Edite's reactions to family members who didn't speak English. (Gonzalo was frustrated, worried, and annoyed at his great uncle; Edite was angry with her father. Gonzalo's story had a happier ending. Both children had to act like an adult for an older person.)

Spelling, Punctuation, Capitalization

After the Reading Comprehension section, students will practice spelling, punctuation, and capitalization in the Activity Book.

Beyond the Reading

Reading Comprehension

Question-Answer Relationships

Sample Answers
1. Tremont Street
2. Carlos
3. translate for him
4. She wants to get her dishes back.
5. They should give them to the lady because they don't need them.
6. No, because he doesn't want to listen to the lady. He thinks she is trying to trick him and that she is lying.
7. Yes, because she wants to give her the plates; she believes the dishes belonged to the woman's grandmother.
8. He wants to keep the dishes because they are in his house. He doesn't want anyone to trick him out of something.
9. Yes. I think Edite and her mother will persuade her father that the woman is honest.
10. In both readings, there are adults who have problems because they can't speak English. Both readings have main characters who are children who do speak English and who help family members who don't speak it. They are different because Edite and her father can communicate in Portuguese. Gonzalo can't communicate with his uncle in a shared language.

Build Reading Fluency

Rapid Word Recognition

Rapid word recognition is an excellent activity for students who struggle with irregular spelling patterns. Time students for 1 minute as they read the words in the squares aloud.

Reading Comprehension

Question-Answer Relationships (QAR)

"Right There" Questions
1. **Recall Facts** On which street does Edite live?
2. **Recall Facts** What is Edite's brother's name?

"Think and Search" Questions
3. **Identify Theme** What does Edite often have to do for her father?
4. **Understand Plot** Why does the lady dressed in brown go to Edite's home?
5. **Explain** What does Edite's mother say they should do with the dishes?

"Author and You" Questions
6. **Recognize Character Traits** Do you think Edite's father is being fair to the lady? Why or why not?

7. **Make Inferences** Do you think Edite's mother feels bad for the lady? Explain.
8. **Make Inferences** Why do you think Edite's father wants to keep the dishes? Because he really likes them? Or is there another reason?

"On Your Own" Questions
9. **Predict** Do you think the lady will get her dishes back? Why do you think so?
10. **Connect Themes** Connect the theme of "Talking in the New Land" to "Gonzalo" (Unit 2, Chapter 4). How are the readings the same? How are they different?

Activity Book p. 106   Student CD-ROM

Build Reading Fluency

Rapid Word Recognition

Rapidly recognizing words helps increase your reading rate. It is an important characteristic of effective readers.

1. Review the words in the box.
2. Read the words aloud for one minute. Your teacher will time you.

3. Count how many words you read.
4. Record your results.

bought	thick	gentle	lawn	gentle	bought
house	lawn	thick	gentle	lawn	gentle
lawn	slope	house	bought	slope	house
gentle	gentle	lawn	house	bought	slope

MULTI-LEVEL OPTIONS *Elements of Literature*

Newcomer Draw an angry face, a questioning face, and a worried face on stick-on notes. Have students place these on the appropriate characters in the story illustrations. (angry: Pai and Edite, questioning: lady, worried: Mãe)

Beginning Review words for traits, motivations, and behaviors of characters in the selection. (angry, sad, confused, worried, upset) Have students point to characters in the story illustrations and say a word to express a trait or behavior demonstrated by that character.

Intermediate Have students work in groups. Assign each group a character. Have groups identify examples from the text of their character's trait, motivation, and point of view.

Advanced Have students make a three-column chart for each of the following characters: Pai, Mãe, the lady, Edite. Have students head the columns: *Traits, Motivation,* and *Point of View.* Tell students to use the charts to analyze each character.

Listen, Speak, Interact

Summarize and Paraphrase

Notice the difference between a **summary** and a **paraphrase:**

Summary	Paraphrase
You give only the most important information.	You say in your own words what another person says.

1. With a partner, reread paragraphs 13, 15, and 16 aloud.
2. Paraphrase each paragraph. Say what Edite said *in your own words.*
3. Choose a paragraph in the reading selection that you like. Summarize it in writing and give it to your partner.
4. Ask your partner: Did I include the most important information?

Elements of Literature

Analyze Characters

In "Talking in the New Land," Edite Cunhã describes the characters' **traits, motivations,** and **points of view.**

1. Read the meanings of the terms and then answer the questions to analyze the characters.

Term	Definition
trait	how characters look and behave
motivation	why characters do things
point of view	the characters' opinions and beliefs, likes, and dislikes

a. Reread paragraphs 18, 39, and 47. What do you learn about Pai's character traits?
b. In paragraph 36, what is the lady's point of view about the dishes?
c. Reread paragraph 39. What is Mãe's point of view about the lady and her dishes?
d. In paragraph 42, what is Pai's motivation for being so angry?

2. Share your answers with the class.

Activity Book   Student
p. 107   CD-ROM

Chapter 4 Talking in the New Land   **203**

Content Connection
Social Studies

Read aloud to students a paragraph about Portugal from a book, encyclopedia, or Web site. Ask students to tell in their own words the important details of what you read. Record these on the board. Then work with the class to create a summary of the most important information.

Learning Styles
Interpersonal

Have students use what they learned about character analysis to brainstorm words describing the kind of person they believe Edite to be. Then play a game of *What If.* Divide the class into teams of four or five. *Say: What if a friend told Edite that he had lost an important family photograph? How would she feel? Why?* (She would feel sorry for the friend because she is a caring person who doesn't like to see others unhappy.) Present other situations.

Listen, Speak, Interact

Summarize and Paraphrase

1. **Pair work** Have students compile their paragraphs for the paraphrasing exercise in a book for the class library. Remind them to organize the paragraphs in sequence.
2. **Newcomers** Work separately with these students. Choose one paragraph. Have students first identify the most important information. Then have them paraphrase orally, without looking at the book. Write down their ideas. Then help students organize their ideas into a group paragraph.

Answers
2. *Example:* Hi. I'm the person who phoned about the dishes.

Elements of Literature

Analyze Characters

1. **Brainstorm** Brainstorm lists of traits people exhibit, both good and bad. Have students work in pairs to organize the list into a chart labeled *admire/don't like.* Then have them discuss which characters in selections they have read have shown those traits.
2. **Multi-level options** See MULTI-LEVEL OPTIONS on p. 202.

Answers
2. **a.** He's stubborn. **b.** She believes the dishes are hers. **c.** She believes the woman and thinks they should give her the dishes. **d.** He thinks the woman is trying to trick them and make him look foolish.

 **ASSESS**

Have students write a short description of one of the characters.

Word Study

Learn the Prefix *Dis-*

Use vocabulary in context *Ask: Which characters in the story disagree? (Pai and the woman; Pai and Mãe; Edite and Pai) Which character disbelieves the woman? (Pai) Who feels discomfort because of Pai's behavior? (Edite)*

Answers

2. disagree—have a different idea about; disbelieve—not believe someone or something; discomfort—a feeling of not being comfortable.

Grammar Focus

Use *Could* and *Couldn't*

Review use of *could* and *couldn't* Write on the board: *When I was very young, I could/couldn't _____. Yesterday, I couldn't _____.* Have students make up sentences using the words.

Answers

1. I soon discovered that I could crawl . . .
2. She couldn't escape. She couldn't disappear.

ASSESS

Have students write two sentences using *could* and *couldn't*.

Word Study

Learn the Prefix *Dis-*

A **prefix** is a group of letters added to the beginning of a word. A prefix changes the meaning of the word. The prefix *dis-* often changes a word to its opposite.

appear be seen

disappear stop being seen

1. Read the words in the first box. Notice the prefix and the root word.
2. Match each word with the correct definition.
3. Write a sentence for each word. Be sure to spell the prefix correctly.

Words	Definitions
disagree	a feeling of not being comfortable
disbelieve	have a different idea about
discomfort	not believe someone or something

The Heinle Newbury House Dictionary   Activity Book p. 108   Student CD-ROM

Grammar Focus

Use *Could* and *Couldn't*

Could is the past form of *can*. We use *could* to describe past abilities (things you were able to do). If you were able to do something yesterday, then you *could* do it. If you were not able to do something yesterday, then you *could not* do it.

Sometimes writers join *could* and *not* into a contraction. A contraction is a word formed by joining two words. The contraction for *could not* is *couldn't*. Notice that the apostrophe takes the place of the "o" in *not*.

I <u>could</u> answer the question because I read the book.

I <u>couldn't</u> answer the question because I did not read the book.

1. Reread paragraph 1 of the selection. Find a sentence that uses *could* to show something a character was able to do.
2. Reread paragraph 5. Write a sentence that uses *couldn't* to show something a character was not able to do.
3. Write two sentences of your own— one with *could,* one with *couldn't.*

Activity Book pp. 109–110   Student Handbook   Student CD-ROM

MULTI-LEVEL OPTIONS *From Reading to Writing*

Newcomer Have students draw what they think will happen next. Then have them act out the ideas in their pictures.

Beginning Have students draw what they think will happen next. Help them write captions to tell about each character's feelings and actions.

Intermediate Suggest that students refer back to the work they did in Elements of Literature to be sure the words, actions, and thoughts of the characters in their paragraphs match the character traits, motivations, and points of view they identified.

Advanced Challenge students to write a fully developed ending to the story using as many paragraphs as necessary.

From Reading to Writing

Write to Solve a Problem

Write an ending to solve Edite's problem. Write one paragraph.

1. Choose one of these endings.
   a. Edite tells the lady that she cannot have her dishes.
   b. Edite tells the lady that she can have her dishes.
2. Give two reasons why Edite says this.

3. As you write, picture that you are Edite. Use first-person pronouns (*I, me, we,* and *us*).
4. Make sure you use correct capitalization and punctuation to strengthen your ending.

Activity Book
p. 111

Student
Handbook

Across Content Areas

Learn About Graphic Features

Reread paragraph 10 on page 195, and the footnote at the bottom of the page. The footnote explains the use of italic type—type that is slanted *like this.* Italic type is one **graphic feature.** There are others.

Graphic Feature	Example	Why Used
font	This is one font. *This is another font.*	to give readers different feelings
boldface	**This sentence is in boldface.**	to call attention to important words
bullets	• There is a bullet before this sentence.	to make lists easier to read

1. Read the following sentences. Decide which graphic feature is shown.
   a. Scientists look at **cells** to learn about our bodies.
   b. Make these changes to the report:
      • Indent paragraphs.
      • Fix spelling mistakes.
   c. *You are invited to my party!*
2. Work with a partner. Suppose you have a business where you make cards. Create an order form with graphic features.
3. Organize your form to include features and examples. Use a computer to help you.
4. Revise the form for clarity and neatness.

Activity Book
p. 112

From Reading to Writing

Write To Solve a Problem

1. **Collaborate with a partner** Brainstorm ideas for possible endings. Pair students who want to write similar endings. Have students plan the plot, character traits and motivations, and point of view before writing.
2. **Share narratives** Ask volunteers to read their story endings to the class.
3. **Multi-level options** See MULTI-LEVEL OPTIONS on p. 204.

Answers
2. *Examples:* **a.** She does what her father tells her to do. **b.** She does what she wants to do and what she thinks is right.

Across Content Areas: Language Arts

Learn About Graphic Features

Relate to personal experience *Ask: Do you see these typographical features in other textbooks?* Have students point out examples of each of the three features in another textbook.

Answers
1. **a.** boldface **b.** bullets **c.** font

ASSESS

Have students look at the boldfaced words on p. 194. *Ask: Why are those words in boldface?* (to make them stand out; to give them special emphasis)

Reteach and Reassess

Text Structure Ask students to think of something that has happened to them. Have them create a Storyboard to show the people who would be part of the story and the events they would tell if they wanted to share the event as a personal narrative. Students may draw or write on the Storyboard.

Reading Strategy Have students draw a picture or write a paragraph to summarize the story told in "Talking in the New Land."

Elements of Literature Ask students to select a character from a familiar book or television show. Have them draw or write about that character's looks, behaviors, motivation, and beliefs.

Reassess Read aloud a paragraph to students. Have them paraphrase the details and then summarize the main idea.

CHAPTER 5

Into the Reading

Plain Talk About Handling Stress

an informational text
by Louis E. Kopolow, M.D.

Chapter Materials

Activity Book: *pp. 113–120*
Audio: *Unit 3, Chapter 5; CD 1, Track 16*
Student Handbook
Student CD-ROM: *Unit 3, Chapter 5*
Teacher Resource Book: *Lesson Plan, Teacher Resources, Reading Summary, Activity Book Answer Key*
Teacher Resource CD-ROM
Assessment Program: *Quiz, pp. 47–48; Teacher and Student Resources, pp. 115–144*
Assessment CD-ROM
Transparencies
The Heinle Newbury House Dictionary/CD-ROM
Web site: http://visions.heinle.com

Objectives

Preview Have students read the objectives in pairs. *Ask: Which objectives are new for you?*

Use Prior Knowledge

Identify Ideas about Stress

Connect to personal experience *Say: Sometimes I feel stress about commuting to work because there is so much traffic. What makes you feel stressed? What is the most stressful part of your life right now?*

Answers
1. *Sample answers:* **a.** F **b.** T **c.** T **d.** T

Objectives

Reading Identify main idea and details as you read an informational text.

Listening and Speaking Talk about dealing with stress.

Grammar Recognize complex sentences with *if*.

Writing Write an informational text.

Content Language Arts: Learn different meanings of *conflict*.

Use Prior Knowledge

Identify Ideas About Stress

Most people feel stress sometime in their lives. Stress is a feeling of difficulty. For example, you might feel stress when you have too much homework. What do you know about stress?

1. Write these statements on a piece of paper. Write *T* if you think the statement is true. Write *F* if you think the statement is false. There are no right or wrong answers.
   ____ **a.** Stress is always bad.
   ____ **b.** Some stress can be good.
   ____ **c.** Stress can make you ill.
   ____ **d.** Stress can help you get work done.

2. Compare your answers with a partner's.
3. Talk about your answers with the class.

206 Unit 3 Conflict and Cooperation

MULTI-LEVEL OPTIONS *Build Vocabulary*

Newcomer Mime the meaning of *challenge*. For example, act out lifting a heavy object and *say: challenge, hard job*. Have students act out other things that are challenging for them, such as hitting a baseball or hiking.

Beginning Have students make the chart from p. 207 large enough so that they can place small drawings next to each word to remind them of the meanings.

Intermediate Ask students to add a column to the chart from p. 207. Have them add the heading "Personal Example." Tell students to write something in the column that is a challenge for them, requires mental effort, makes them tense, and so on.

Advanced Remind students of the work they have done with cause and effect (Chapter 3). Point out that stress is usually an effect of something that has happened. Have students write cause and effect statements that use some of the vocabulary words. (*Example:* I feel tension when I am late.)

Build Background

Stress and the Body

Too much stress can affect how people feel and think. For example, it can make people feel angry or sad. Too much stress can also affect the body. When people feel stress, their hearts often beat faster. Their muscles can become tense (tight). Many people get headaches from stress. They may not be able to concentrate (focus). Too much stress can cause people to get sick more often.

Content Connection

People can talk to friends, their family, or psychologists to deal with stress. Psychologists are trained to help people with problems.

Build Vocabulary

Learn Words Related to Stress in Context

The selection includes words related to stress. Here are some of these words:

Words Related to Stress	Meaning
challenge	a difficult job
mental	related to the mind
tension	a state of stress or nervousness
distress	emotional pain or suffering
physical	related to the body

Work with a partner. Copy the chart in your Personal Dictionary. Then complete the following sentences with words from the chart. Take turns reading the sentences aloud.

1. Running and playing tennis are ——— activities.
2. Learning to play the guitar is a ——— . It can be difficult.
3. Juan is very smart. He has strong ——— abilities.
4. Kim felt ——— because her dog died.
5. Today is the big test. The students feel a lot of ——— .

Personal Dictionary   Activity Book p. 113   Student CD-ROM

Chapter 5 Plain Talk About Handling Stress **207**

Content Connection
The Arts

Build Background Point out that some people listen to music when they feel stressed. Certain kinds of music can help people relax. Play excerpts of five types of music for students, such as classical, country, rap, jazz, meditation. Ask them to rate each piece from one to ten with ten being the most relaxing. Have students talk about what makes certain music relaxing for them.

Learning Styles
Mathematical

Build Background *Say: Your pulse shows how fast your heart is beating.* Demonstrate how to find a wrist pulse. Have students count their beats for six seconds. *Ask: What do we need to do to figure out the pulse for a minute?* (multiply by 10) In a serious voice, *say: Now each of you will give a speech to the class.* Have students calculate their pulses again. *Ask: Is anyone's higher? Why do you think that is?* (stress at the idea of giving a speech)

Build Background

Stress and the Body

1. **Relate to personal experience** *Say: When we feel stress, it can affect how we feel physically. For example, sometimes I get a headache when I'm stressed. Do you notice any physical effects of stress?*
2. **Content Connection** Explain to students that other physical ailments sometimes caused by stress include weight loss, back pain, asthma, stomach ulcers, and high blood pressure.

Build Vocabulary

Teacher Resource Book: *Personal Dictionary, p. 63*

Learn Words Related to Stress in Context

1. **Apply new vocabulary** Have students work in small groups to make up their own sentences using the words related to stress. Ask them to share their sentences with the class.
2. **Reading selection vocabulary** You may want to introduce the glossed words in the reading selection before students begin reading. Key words: *cope, improve, relax, schedule, break, routine, impossible.* Instruct students to write the words with correct spelling and their definitions in their Personal Dictionaries. Have them pronounce each word and divide it into syllables.
3. **Multi-level options** See MULTI-LEVEL OPTIONS on p. 206.

Answers
1. physical 2. challenge 3. mental 4. distress
5. tension

ASSESS

Say: Give an example of a stressful situation.

Text Structure

Informational Text

1. **Identify text features** Have students look at pp. 212 and 213. Ask them to identify the four headings. (Try physical activity. Share your stress. Know your limits. Take care of yourself.)
2. **Multi-level options** See MULTI-LEVEL OPTIONS below.

Reading Strategy

Identify Main Idea and Details

Find the main idea and details Have students read paragraph 5 on p. 212. Ask a volunteer to read the first and last sentence of the paragraph. *Ask: How could we state the main idea of this paragraph?* (Physical activity helps you release pressure when you feel stressed.) *What are some of the examples given?* (running, walking, playing tennis, working in a garden)

✔ ASSESS

Have students identify the two main headings on this page. (Text Structure, Reading Strategy)

Text Structure

Informational Text

An **informational text** gives facts and examples about a topic. "Plain Talk about Handling Stress" gives information about stress. Look at the features of an informational text in the chart.

As you read, notice how facts and examples help you understand the selection.

Informational Text	
Topic	what the text is about
Headings	titles used to organize information
Facts and Examples	details about the topic

Student
CD-ROM

Reading Strategy

Identify Main Idea and Details

The **main idea** is the most important idea in a reading. The **details** include all the information that helps you understand the main idea. Read this paragraph:

Exciting Mexico!
Mexico is an exciting place to live or visit. You can see different plants and animals. You can also see historic buildings.

Main Idea	Details
Mexico is an exciting place to live or visit.	You can see different plants and animals. You can also see historic buildings.

The details explain why Mexico is exciting.

Follow these tips to find the main idea and details in the selection:

1. Read each heading. Then read the first and last sentences of each paragraph. The main idea is usually found in one of these places.
2. The middle sentences are usually details. Ask yourself, "How do the details help me understand the main idea?"

Student
CD-ROM

MULTI-LEVEL OPTIONS *Text Structure*

Newcomer Give each student a nonfiction book from your classroom or school library. Have students look at the covers and then browse through the pages. Ask questions such as: *Which is about dogs? Which shows a mountain?* Have students hold up the appropriate books to answer your questions.

Beginning Give each student a nonfiction library book. Provide time for students to browse through the books. Give each student a card on which to write a word that tells the topic of the book. Then have them write a few words or phrases that tell information that may be found in it.

Intermediate Have students look through their social studies text or another nonfiction book with you. Have them identify topics, headings, facts, and examples.

Advanced Give each student a nonfiction book. Ask students to identify the topics of their books from the titles and covers. Have students list three questions they want to know about their topic. Ask them to browse through the book, looking at headings and skimming sections to see if the book is likely to answer their questions.

Plain Talk About

Handling Stress

an informational text
by Louis E. Kopolow, M.D.

209

Reading Selection Materials

Audio: *Unit 3, Chapter 5; CD 1, Track 16*
Teacher Resource Book: *Reading Summary,*
  pp. 93–94
Transparencies: #9, *Reading Summary*

Suggestions for Using Reading Summary

- Introduce new vocabulary or cognates.
- Cut the summary into strips, or jumble the sentences on an overhead transparency. Students put the sentences in order.
- Practice the reading strategy.
- Students read aloud or with a partner.
- Students paraphrase the summary.
- Students do a cloze activity.
- Students create a visual or graphic organizer, such as a timeline or storyboard, to illustrate the summary.
- Students paraphrase the summary.

Preview the Selection

1. **Interpret the image** Have students look at the photo. Give students a few minutes to write down what they think the person is thinking about. Then have volunteers share their ideas.
2. **Discuss message of medium** *Ask: Why is a photograph a good way to illustrate the theme of stress? What kind of photograph would you take to show stress?*
3. **Connect** *Ask: Do you ever feel like this? What do you do when you are stressed?*

Cultural Connection

Say: People in all cultures have stress. The reasons people feel stressed may be different in different places and times. Ask students to recall "We Shall Overcome," "Zlata's Diary," and "Talking in the New Land." *Ask: What caused stress in each?* (unfair treatment, war, language differences) Invite students to tell other examples of things that cause people to feel stress in different parts of the world.

Learning Styles
Intrapersonal

Have students draw or write a journal entry about what they do to lower their stress. Tell students to see how many of the tips they use are mentioned in the article. Ask them to notice any new ideas they might want to try in the future.

Read the Selection

1. **Shared reading** Play the audio. Then have pairs or groups of students take turns joining in for different parts of the selection. Go through the pages twice so that all students have a chance to read.

2. **Identify main idea and details** Ask a volunteer to read the first and last sentences of paragraph 1. *Ask: Which sentence is the main idea?* (the first one) *What are some details about the main idea?* (Without stress, life is dull. Stress adds flavor, challenge, and opportunity.)

Sample Answer to Guide Question
It is the small things that cause stress in our daily lives.

See Teacher Edition pp. 434–436 for a list of English-Spanish cognates in the reading selection.

1   You need stress in your life! Does that surprise you? Perhaps so, but it is quite true. Without stress, life would be **dull** and unexciting. Stress adds **flavor,** challenge, and **opportunity** to life. Too much stress, however, can seriously affect your physical and mental **well-being.** A major challenge in this stress-filled world of today is to learn how to **cope** with stress so that it does not become too much.

2   What kinds of things can cause too much stress in our lives? We often think of major **crises** such as natural disasters, war, and death as main sources of stress. These are, of course, stressful events. However, according to psychologist Wayne Weiten, on a day-to-day basis, it is the small things that cause stress: waiting in line, having car trouble, getting stuck in a **traffic jam,** having too many things to do in a **limited** time.

> **Identify Main Idea and Details**
>
> What is the main idea of paragraph 2?

Audio
CD 1. Tr. 16

dull   boring
flavor   an exciting quality
opportunity   a chance to advance or meet a goal
well-being   the condition of your body and mind
cope   face difficulties and try to overcome them

crises   emergencies
traffic jam   cars and trucks blocking the road and causing delays
limited   having only a certain amount of something

210   Unit 3   Conflict and Cooperation

MULTI-LEVEL OPTIONS *Read the Selection*

Newcomer Discuss how the picture shows stress. Play the audio. *Ask: Can stress be good for you?* (yes) *Can stress be bad for you, too?* (yes) *Do only big problems cause stress?* (no) *Can you do some things to help with stress?* (yes)

Beginning Do a paired reading. *Ask: How can stress be helpful?* (It makes life exciting; it adds flavor and challenge.) *What parts of you can stress harm?* (body, mind) *What is a little thing that can make people stressed?* (waiting in line) *Can you get rid of all, some, or none of your stress?* (some)

Intermediate Have students do a paired reading. *Ask: How can stress be helpful?* (by making you feel excited to do things) *How can stress be harmful?* (by hurting your body or upsetting your mind) *How will the writer help you with stress?* (by telling ways to reduce it)

Advanced Have students read silently. *Ask: Would studying for a test be harmful or helpful stress? Why?* (helpful if it gives you energy to learn; harmful if you got so upset it made you sick) *What would an earthquake and spilling your milk have in common?* (Both can cause stress but in different amounts.)

Reacting to Stress

3 While you can't live completely free of stress and distress, you can **prevent** some distress as well as **minimize** its **impact.** By recognizing the early signs of distress and then doing something about them, you can **improve** the quality of your life and perhaps even live longer.

> **Identify Main Idea and Details**
>
> What is the main idea of paragraph 3?

Helping Yourself

4 When stress does occur, it is important to recognize and deal with it. Here are some suggestions for ways to handle stress. As you begin to understand more about how stress affects you as an individual, you will come up with your own ideas of helping to **ease** the tensions.

---

prevent stop from happening
minimize lessen
impact effect

improve make better
ease make less difficult

Read the Selection

1. **Relate to personal experience** *Ask: What is a major stress in your life right now? What are some minor stresses?* Model answering the questions and then have volunteers answer.
2. **Silent reading** Have students reread silently.
3. **Group work** Have each group write three questions about the page. Then have groups exchange and answer questions.
4. **Multi-level options** See MULTI-LEVEL OPTIONS on p. 210.

Sample Answer to Guide Question
You can prevent some of the harmful effects of stress.

 Punctuation

Colon to introduce a list

Call attention to the sentence in paragraph 2 that starts *However, according to . . . Ask: What punctuation mark is used in the middle of this sentence?* (colon) *What is after the colon?* (list of stressful events) *We learned in Chapter 3 that colons are used to show dialogue in plays. Colons are also used to introduce a list of words or phrases.*

Apply Ask students to copy the following and complete it with a colon and a list or a series of drawings. Write: *These things make me feel stressed* ____, ____, *and* ____.

Read the Selection

1. **Choral reading** Play the audio. Then have students join in with you when they can as you reread aloud.

2. **Relate to personal experience** Write on the board: *What kinds of physical activity help you when you are stressed? How do you feel afterwards? When you feel stress, who do you like to talk with?* Then have students discuss the questions in groups.

Sample Answer to Guide Question
Physical exercise relieves that "up tight" feeling; it relaxes you; it turns frowns into smiles; body and mind work together.

---

5 **Try physical activity.**

When you are nervous, angry, or upset, **release** the **pressure** through exercise or physical activity. Running, walking, playing tennis, or working in your garden are just some of the activities you might try. Physical exercise will relieve that "up tight" feeling, **relax** you, and turn the **frowns** into smiles. Remember, your body and your mind work together.

> ### Identify Main Idea and Details
>
> Here is the main idea of paragraph 5: Physical activity can help lower stress. What details support this main idea?

Share your stress. **6**

It helps to talk to someone about your concerns and worries. Perhaps a friend, family member, teacher, or **counselor** can help you see your problem in a different light. If you feel your problem is serious, you might seek **professional** help from a psychologist, **psychiatrist, social worker,** or mental health counselor. Knowing when to ask for help may **avoid** more serious problems later.

---

release let something go
pressure tension; a feeling of being pushed to do things
relax stop being nervous, tense, or angry
frowns when you pull the eyebrows down and make your mouth tight; usually shows anger or sadness

counselor someone who gives advice
professional related to a job
psychiatrist a doctor who treats mental problems
social worker a person who works with others to help make their lives better
avoid stay away from

212 **Unit 3** Conflict and Cooperation

MULTI-LEVEL OPTIONS *Read the Selection*

Newcomer *Ask: Will exercising help with stress?* (yes) *Should you talk about your stress?* (yes) *Can you always make things better?* (no) *Do good food and sleep help with stress?* (yes)

Beginning *Ask: What is one thing you can do outdoors to help with stress?* (run) *Who is a person you can talk to about stress?* (friend, family) *Who is one person who can help with big, serious problems?* (psychologist) *What can you do to take care of yourself?* (get enough sleep, eat healthy food)

Intermediate *Ask: How can exercise help with stress?* (It helps your muscles relax. That helps your mind feel more relaxed.) *How can talking to someone help?* (Another person may help you think of a solution you did not see.) *How can getting enough sleep help?* (If you are rested, you can think better and handle problems better.)

Advanced *Would playing ball or playing a board game probably be better if you are stressed? Why?* (playing ball because it would help your body relax and that would help your mind) *Why is it a good idea to let go of stress when the big team game gets rained out?* (because you can't do anything about weather)

7 **Know your limits.**

If a problem is beyond your control and cannot be changed at the moment, don't fight the situation. Learn to accept what it is—for now—until such time when you can change it.

Identify Main Idea and Details

How does the section heading of this paragraph relate to the main idea?

Take care of yourself. **8**

You are special. Get enough rest and eat well. If you are **irritable** and **tense** from **lack** of sleep or if you are not eating correctly, you will have less ability to deal with stressful situations. If stress **repeatedly** keeps you from sleeping, you should ask your doctor for help.

irritable   easily bothered by things
tense   nervous, jumpy

lack   not enough of something
repeatedly   over and over again

Chapter 5 Plain Talk About Handling Stress   **213**

Read the Selection

1. **Shared reading** Play the audio. Have students join in when they can.
2. **Give examples** *Say: It's important to know what you can change and what you can't. For example, I really don't like taking the bus, but it's not something I can change. Instead of getting stressed about the bus, I need to accept it and not fight it. Can you give some examples of things that aren't in your control to change?*
3. **Paraphrase** Have students close their books. Write the four headings from pp. 212 and 213 on the board. Then have students paraphrase in writing the information under each heading. Have them share their paragraphs in pairs.
4. **Multi-level options** See MULTI-LEVEL OPTIONS on p. 212.

Sample Answer to Guide Question
To know your limits means to know what is beyond your control and to accept what you cannot change.

th Spelling

Ph → /f/ and silent *p*

Say: Let's learn about an interesting spelling of a sound. What consonant sound do you hear at the beginning of the word physical*?* (f) *Look at the heading in paragraph 5 to see what letters make the /f/ sound.* (ph) Challenge students to remember the animal that went with Momotaro, the dog, and the monkey in "The Peach Boy." Write on the board: *pheasant*. *Ask: What sound is at the beginning of the word?* (f) *What letters make the sound?* (ph)

Say: Here is another interesting spelling. Direct students to paragraph 6 and the word *psychologist*. Say the word aloud. *Ask: What is the first sound you hear in the word?* (s) *What about the* p*?* (silent) Ask students to point out another word in that paragraph that begins with a silent *p*. (psychiatrist) Pronounce it for students.

Read the Selection

1. **Discuss the photo** *Ask: What is this person doing?* (reading to small children) *Where do you think they are?* (in a library or classroom) *He must be volunteering to do this. Do you volunteer to do anything in your school, community, or other organization?*

2. **Paired reading** Play the audio. Then have students read alternate paragraphs aloud with a partner.

3. **Relate to personal experience** *Ask: What kinds of volunteer work can someone your age do? If you already volunteer, can you explain how you feel afterwards? Do you think it helps relieve your stress a little?*

Sample Answer to Guide Question
You will feel better if you get involved with others. If you are a participant, then you are involved with other people.

9   **Make time for fun.**
   Schedule time for both work and **recreation.** Play can be just as important to your well-being as work; you need a **break** from your daily **routine** to just relax and have fun.

10   **Be a participant.**
   One way to keep from getting bored, sad, and lonely is to go where it's all happening. Sitting alone can make you feel **frustrated.** Instead of feeling sorry for yourself, get involved and become a participant. Offer your services in neighborhood or **volunteer** organizations. Help yourself by helping other people. Get involved in the world and the people around you, and you'll find they will be **attracted** to you. You will be on your way to making new friends and enjoying new activities.

> **Identify Main Idea and Details**
>
> What is the main idea of paragraph 10? How does the section heading help you identify the main idea?

---

schedule   plan activities by date and time
recreation   fun things to do
break   a change from something usual
routine   a series of things someone does regularly

participant   a person who takes part in something
frustrated   feeling bothered by something
volunteer   when people help other people for no pay
attracted   interested in

MULTI-LEVEL OPTIONS *Read the Selection*

Newcomer *Is having fun important?* (yes) *Should you be by yourself if you are upset?* (no) *Will helping others make you feel better?* (yes) *Should you try to do all your work at the same time?* (no)

Beginning *What two things are important to have in your day?* (work, play) *What can you do if you are feeling lonely and sad?* (help others) *What can you make if you have lots to do?* (make a list of tasks)

Intermediate *How can playing be helpful?* (It gives you time away from stress.) *How can helping others lower your stress?* (It lets you focus on others instead of on your worries. It helps you meet new friends to do fun things with.) *How can lists help?* (They help you focus on each task so you don't feel that the job is so big; it helps you figure out the order of tasks.)

Advanced *What is the purpose of recess?* (So students can let go of the stress of working hard in class.) *What if you play alone indoors because you are stressed at all the litter in your neighborhood park? How could you reduce your stress?* (Organize a group of friends to clean up. It will help solve the problem and get you out with people.)

11 Check off your tasks.

Trying to take care of everything at once can seem **overwhelming,** and, as a result, you may not **accomplish** anything. Instead, make a list of what tasks you have to do, then do one at a time, **checking them off** as they're completed. Give **priority** to the most important ones and do those first.

Must you always be right? 12

Do other people upset you—particularly when they don't do things your way? Try **cooperation** instead of **confrontation;** it's better than fighting and always being "right." A little **give and take** on both sides will **reduce** the **strain** and make you both feel more comfortable.

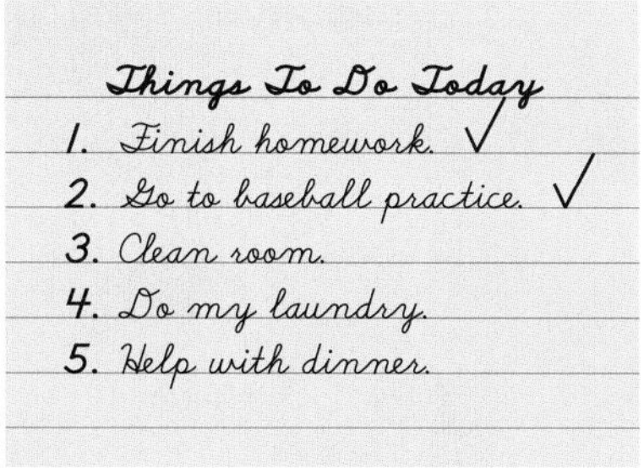

Identify Main Idea and Details

What is the main idea of paragraph 11?

Things To Do Today
1. *Finish homework.* ✓
2. *Go to baseball practice.* ✓
3. *Clean room.*
4. *Do my laundry.*
5. *Help with dinner.*

---

overwhelming   too much for you to deal with

accomplish   finish, complete

checking them off   putting a check next to the tasks with a pen or pencil

priority   the tasks that are the most important and require attention

cooperation   the act of working with someone toward the same goal

confrontation   the act of facing something difficult or dangerous

give and take   when people on both sides of a conflict listen to each other and accept some of each other's ideas

reduce   lessen

strain   difficulty

Chapter 5   Plain Talk About Handling Stress   **215**

, Punctuation

Quotation marks

Say: One way to use quotation marks is to show the exact words of a speaker. Here is another way to use quotation marks.

Direct students to paragraph 12 and the sentence that starts: *Try cooperation. . . .* Point out the word *right* in quotation marks. *Say: In this sentence, quotation marks around* right *show that the word is used in a special way. The author does not mean that the person he is talking about really is* right. *The person just* thinks *he or she is.* Direct

students to paragraph 5. *Say: Notice that* up tight *is in quotation marks. The words are used in a special way. The writer isn't really talking about something being tight. The words are slang for feeling stressed.*

Apply Write on the board: *Everyone is stressed out sometimes. No one has a perfect life.* Have students copy the sentences and insert quotation marks. ("stressed out," "perfect")

Read the Selection

1. **Reciprocal reading** Play the audio. Divide students into small groups. Have students read a paragraph aloud and ask questions about the paragraph to their group.

2. **Visualize a scene** Have students close their eyes for a few minutes. *Say: Try to imagine a very relaxing place. Imagine sitting on the beach, lying in the grass looking at the clouds, or sitting by a lake. Imagine what you see. How do you feel?* After a few minutes, have students open their eyes. Ask them to share the scene they imagined and how it made them feel.

Sample Answer to Guide Question
Sometimes a change of scenery can make you feel more peaceful. Details include: mental scenes, reading, playing music.

---

13   **It's OK to cry.**

A good cry can be a healthy way to bring **relief** to your **anxiety,** and it might even prevent a headache or other physical **consequence.** Take some deep breaths; they also release tension.

14   **Create a quiet scene.**

You can't always run away, but you can "dream the **impossible** dream." A quiet country scene painted mentally, or on a **canvas,** can take you out of the **turmoil** of a stressful situation. Change the scene by reading a good book or playing beautiful music to create a sense of peace and **tranquility.**

> **Identify Main Idea and Details**
>
> What is the main idea of paragraph 14? Which details support the main idea?

---

relief the taking away or lessening of pain
anxiety worry, nervous fear about what will happen in the future
consequence result
impossible not able to be done

canvas cloth stretched over a wooden frame for painting pictures
turmoil disorder, chaos, often with mental suffering
tranquility peace, calmness

216   **Unit 3** Conflict and Cooperation

MULTI-LEVEL OPTIONS *Read the Selection*

Newcomer *Ask: Is crying bad for stress?* (no) *Does taking deep breaths help with stress?* (yes) *Can art and music help with stress?* (yes) *Is winning always the most important thing in life?* (no)

Beginning *Ask: What can a good cry stop from happening?* (headache) *What is one thing that can make you feel more peaceful?* (reading, music, art, relaxation) *What do you need to learn to do to become less stressed?* (relax)

Intermediate *Ask: What do crying and breathing deeply have in common?* (Both release stress and may prevent headaches.) *How can art, music, and books help with stress?* (They help you "escape" from it in your mind.) *Why is it important to learn how to relax?* (People who know how to relax do not let stress harm them.)

Advanced *Ask: Why shouldn't people be embarrassed about crying?* (crying releases harmful stress) *What might be smart to do after studying for an hour? Why?* (Stop and listen to a CD to clear your mind before studying some more.) *What does* just *being without striving* mean? (It is okay to relax without doing anything sometimes.)

15 The Art of Relaxation

   The best strategy for avoiding stress is to learn how to relax. Unfortunately, many people try to relax at the same **pace** that they lead the rest of their lives. For a while, **tune out** your worries about time, **productivity,** and "doing right." You will find **satisfaction** in just *being*, without **striving.** Find activities that give you pleasure and that are good for your mental and physical well-being. Forget about always winning. Focus on relaxation, enjoyment, and health. Whatever method works for you, be good to yourself. If you don't let stress get **out of hand,** you can actually make it work for you instead of against you.

> **Identify Main Idea and Details**
>
> What is the main idea of paragraph 15? Which details support the main idea?

---

pace   speed of an activity

tune out   ignore, not pay attention to

productivity   how much a person can do in a certain time

satisfaction   pleasure because of having enough

striving   working hard for something

out of hand   out of control

About the Author — Louis E. Kopolow, M.D.

   Louis E. Kopolow is a psychiatrist. He is also a college teacher. He teaches others who want to be psychiatrists. Kopolow also runs counseling centers for men in Washington, D.C. These centers help men deal with questions, stress, and problems in their lives.

➤ Why do you think Louis E. Kopolow wrote "Plain Talk About Handling Stress"? To teach you how to handle stress? To teach you how to avoid stress? Explain.

Chapter 5   Plain Talk About Handling Stress   **217**

A   Capitalization

Headings

Remind students that they discussed the capitalization of book titles (Unit 2). *Ask: What is the rule?* (Capitalize the first word and other important words.) *We use the same rule for headings.* Direct students to the heading on p. 217. *Ask: Why are* the, art, *and* relaxation *capitalized?* (first word, important words)

Evaluate Your Reading Strategy

Identify Main Idea and Details   *Say: You have practiced an important reading strategy. Now you can decide how well you have done. Does this statement describe how you read?*

> When I read, I look for the main idea. When I recognize important details, I can understand the main idea better.

Read the Selection

1. **Do a Quaker reading**   Play the audio. Then tell students to prepare passages they especially like. Have students read the passages aloud in any order. Remind students they can repeat. Monitor that everyone participates.
2. **Multi-level options**   See MULTI-LEVEL OPTIONS on p. 216.

Sample Answer to Guide Question
The best way to avoid stress is to learn how to relax. Details include: tune out worries, find pastimes that give you pleasure, learn to relax.

About the Author

Explain the author's background   *Say: An author usually needs special training or education to write an informational text. What is this author's background?* (He is a psychiatrist and a college teacher. He runs counseling centers.)

Across Selections

Say: We read another informational text, "Rain Forest Creatures" (p. 131). Which text was more interesting to you? Which one was more closely related to your personal life?

Spelling, Punctuation, Capitalization

After the Reading Comprehension section, students will practice spelling, punctuation, and capitalization in the Activity Book.

Beyond the Reading

Reading Comprehension

Question-Answer Relationships

Sample Answers

1. yes
2. to learn how to relax
3. Stress adds flavor, challenge, and opportunity to life.
4. waiting in line, getting stuck in traffic, having too many things to do
5. make a list of tasks, prioritize your tasks, and check off tasks as you complete them
6. b. Dealing with stress can help you have a better life.
7. Learning the art of relaxation. You can do it any time and any place. It can help you enjoy life more.
8. I let other people have their own opinions, and I don't always try to prove I'm right.
9. Similarities: factual information, bold face section headings, gives advice (a recipe). Differences: "Turkish Delight": written in first person, includes author's opinions, includes a recipe. "Plain Talk About Handling Stress": more detailed, addressed to audience (you), longer with more sections, no recipe.

Build Reading Fluency

Adjust Your Reading Rate to Scan

Explain that students need to adjust their reading to quickly scan the text to locate key words. Have them read the question then quickly scan to find the answer and identify key words.

Reading Comprehension

Question-Answer Relationships (QAR)

"Right There" Questions

1. **Recall Facts** According to the author, do we need some stress in our lives?
2. **Recall Facts** What does the author say is the best strategy for avoiding stress?

"Think and Search" Questions

3. **Identify** Name two ways that stress can be good for you.
4. **Identify** Name three things that can cause stress on a day-to-day basis.
5. **Identify Steps in a Process** The author tells how to deal with having too many tasks. What steps does the author suggest?

"Author and You" Questions

6. **Identify the Main Idea** Which of these sentences is the main idea of the selection?

   a. Crying can help you release tension.
   b. Dealing with stress can help you have a better life.
   c. All stress is bad.

7. **Paraphrase** Explain one of the author's suggestions for handling stress. Use your own words.

"On Your Own" Questions

8. **Connect to Your Experiences** How do you handle stress in your life?
9. **Find Similarities and Differences Across Texts** Look up "Turkish Delight" in the table of contents of this book. Reread that selection. How is its text structure the same as or different from this chapter?

Activity Book p. 114   Student CD-ROM

Build Reading Fluency

Adjust Your Reading Rate to Scan

When you scan, you adjust your reading rate to read fast. Scanning means glancing at the text for key words to help you answer questions. Work with a partner. Read aloud key words as you look for information. Write your answers on a piece of paper.

1. What is one way to handle stress?
2. Who are three people you can share your stress with?
3. What is one way you can take care of yourself?
4. What is the title of the paragraph on "fun"?
5. What is the title of the paragraph about priorities?

MULTI-LEVEL OPTIONS *Elements of Literature*

Newcomer Show a simple nonfiction book with headings. State the main topic of the book, such as *transportation*. Point to the heading of a main section, such as *Air Travel*. Put your hands far apart. *Say: big idea.* Point to subheadings, such as *Jets, Helicopters, Gliders.* Put your hands closer together. *Say: smaller ideas.*

Beginning Give groups a set of cards with one of the following words on each: *birds, canaries, collies, dogs, parrots, pets, poodles.* Have students decide which is the topic (pets), which are general headings (dogs, birds), and which are specific headings (canaries, collies, parrots, poodles).

Intermediate Demonstrate using headings to form a web. *Say: Put the topic in the center. Use general headings as main branches of your web. Specific headings can branch off of main branches. List details under the specific headings.* Have students use this technique to web the information on pp. 211–213.

Advanced Remind students that they used an outline to note ideas from "Rain Forest Creatures" (p. 136). Discuss how the headings in this article can be used to build a study outline. *Say: Look at p. 134 to note how Roman numerals, capital letters, and numbers were used. Then outline the selection you have just read.*

Listen, Speak, Interact

Talk About Dealing with Stress

The selection suggests ways to deal with stress. How can you use these suggestions in a real-life situation?

1. Work with a small group.
2. Choose a stressful situation that you have experienced.
3. List ways that you could deal with the stressful situation. Use paragraphs 5–14 of the selection to help you.

Examples of Stressful Situations
You have too many things that you have to do.
You have just had an argument with your best friend.
You are waiting in a very long line at the store.

4. Think of ways you could act out dramatically the stressful situation and ways to deal with it.
5. Share your presentation with the class. Make sure to use words from the selection in your presentation.

Elements of Literature

Use Headings to Find Information

Informational texts often have **headings**—titles that come before a section or paragraph. Headings tell readers where to find information in a text.

"Plain Talk About Handling Stress" has two kinds of headings. One kind is general and appears before a group of paragraphs. The other kind is more specific and appears before one paragraph. Both kinds are in boldface.

Helping Yourself (page 211)

Try physical activity. (page 212)

On a piece of paper, match the information with the head that you would use to find it.

Information You Want to Find

1. How can I help others?
2. How can I lower my stress?
3. How can I relax?
4. Who can I talk to about stress?

Heads

a. Helping Yourself
b. The Art of Relaxation
c. Be a participant.
d. Share your stress.

Activity Book
p. 115

Student
CD-ROM

Content Connection
Technology

Say: Headings are not just used in nonfiction books. They are an important part of Web sites, too. Bookmark a few Web sites that have general and specific headings. Have pairs of students visit the sites and discuss the following questions: *How are general and specific headings shown? Is color, font, or movement used to make the headings stand out? Do the headings help or make it harder to understand the information?*

Learning Styles
Natural

Point out that many people find that being in nature makes them feel less stressed. Ask students to write descriptions of or draw places in nature that are soothing to them. Invite students to share their descriptions and drawings with classmates.

Listen, Speak, Interact

Talk About Dealing with Stress

1. **Group discussion** Have students divide themselves into three groups, one for each of the stressful situations in the chart. Have groups develop a role-play that shows the stressful situation. Then tell them to develop an alternative role-play that shows a good way to deal with it.
2. **Collaborate to compose record** *Ask: How do you handle stress?* Have students collaborate to compose a record of different techniques they use. Students should organize the record logically. Have them work together to revise the final record to publish.
3. **Newcomers** Work separately with these students. Have them create a series of comic book frames about one of the situations. Have them start by showing the stressful situation. Then have pairs create illustrations that show different ways to reduce the stress.

Elements of Literature

Use Headings to Find Information

1. **Examine the text** Ask students to identify the number of general headings (3) and specific headings (10) in "Plain Talk about Handling Stress." Ask them to decide which headings give details and examples. (specific headings)
2. **Multi-level options** See MULTI-LEVEL OPTIONS on p. 218.

Answers
1. c 2. a 3. b 4. d

ASSESS

Have students list four ways they deal with stress.

Word Study

Locate Meanings, Pronunciations, and Origins of Words

1. **Understand the influence of languages and cultures** Point out that the Greek language and culture have influenced the spelling of some words in English. *Ask: Why do so many English words come from Greek words?* (Greek was a common language of education for many years. When new ideas and technologies were invented, often a Greek term was used to name the idea.)

Answers
Psychiatry—the branch of medicine that cures mental diseases. Physical—f; Greek

Grammar Focus

Recognize Complex Sentences with *If*

Pairwork In pairs, have students check for correct punctuation of their sentences.

Answers

1. If you feel your problem is serious (dependent clause), *you might seek help . . . counselor* (independent clause). If stress repeatedly keeps you from sleeping (dependent clause), *you should . . . for help* (independent clause). If you don't let stress get out of hand (dependent clause), *you can actually . . . you* (independent clause).

ASSESS

Have students write a complex sentence with *if.*

Word Study

Locate Meanings, Pronunciations, and Origins of Words

A large dictionary gives information about words. It gives the **meaning,** the **pronunciation,** and the **origin**—the languages that a word comes from. Read these dictionary entries.

> **psy•chi•a•try** /sə'kaɪətri/ the branch of medicine that cures mental diseases [Greek *psukhē,* soul]
>
> **phys•i•cal** /'fɪzɪkəl/ of or related to the body [Greek *phusikē,* of nature]

1. Copy and complete the chart in your Personal Dictionary.

Word	The First Sound	Meaning	Derivation
psychiatry	s		Greek
physical		of or related to the body	

2. Write a sentence for each word. Check to make sure you spell every syllable in the word correctly.

Personal Dictionary   Activity Book p. 116   Student CD-ROM

Grammar Focus

Recognize Complex Sentences with *If*

A clause is a group of words with a subject and a verb. **Complex sentences** have two types of **clauses.**

1. **An independent clause** can stand on its own as a sentence.
2. **A dependent clause** cannot stand on its own as a sentence. It must be used with an independent clause.

Dependent Clause	Independent Clause
If you are irritable,	you will have less ability to deal with stressful situations.

This sentence is a **conditional sentence.** Conditional sentences have a dependent clause that begins with *if* and ends with a comma.

1. Look at paragraphs 6, 8, and 15 of the selection. Find and copy three conditional sentences.
2. Underline the dependent clauses. Circle the independent clauses.
3. Write your own conditional sentence with *if.* Use correct punctuation.

Activity Book pp. 117–118   Student Handbook   Student CD-ROM

MULTI-LEVEL OPTIONS *From Reading to Writing*

Newcomer Direct students to the comic book series they made for the Listen, Speak, Interact activity on p. 219. Work with them to create statements for word bubbles that they can paste onto the comic book pages.

Beginning Provide a framed paragraph for students to use in structuring their ideas. *Do you ever feel upset about _____? First, you can _____. You can also _____. Another idea is to _____. These ideas may help others because _____.*

Intermediate Remind students that an informational text includes facts and examples (p. 208). Point out that Dr. Kopolow does not just tell readers that exercise is important, but he gives examples. (running, walking, playing tennis) Tell students to include examples in their paragraphs.

Advanced Have students reread paragraph 2. Point out that the writer did not just use his own ideas, but he included ideas of others. Suggest that students include some information they learned from the selection in their own writing. Remind them to give credit to the author whenever they include another's ideas.

From Reading to Writing

Write an Informational Text

Write three paragraphs to solve how to deal with a stressful situation.

1. Paragraph 1: Include a **thesis statement.** (Tell readers what the text is about.)
2. Paragraph 2: Include details that support your thesis statement.
3. Paragraph 3: Write a conclusion. Tell how your ideas can help readers.
4. Use the pronoun *you* to speak directly to your readers.

5. Use a dictionary and grammar guide to help with your writing.
6. Use resources, like the Internet or library books on your topic, to help you gather information. Be sure to cite your resources.

Activity Book
p. 119

Student
Handbook

Across Content Areas

Learn Different Meanings of *Conflict*

Stressful situations often involve a conflict. The word *conflict* can mean different things. Look at these definitions:

---

con•flict /ˈkɑnˌflɪkt/ *n.* [Latin: *conflictus* collision] **1** a difference, disagreement *There is a conflict between what you are saying and what the contract says.* **2** an argument *The two men had a conflict over who would run the company.* **3** a war *World War I was an armed conflict among many nations of the world.*

---

1. Use the dictionary entry to pronounce *conflict*.
2. What is the origin of the word *conflict*?

3. Copy the following sentences. Match each one with the correct definition of *conflict*. Write *Definition 1, Definition 2,* or *Definition 3*.
   a. Giselle and Ali had a conflict over who would wash the car.
   b. Many people were killed in the conflict between the two armies.
   c. There was a conflict between the report in the newspaper and the report on the radio.

Activity Book
p. 120

Reteach and Reassess

Text Structure Have students make two-column charts. Instruct them to label the left columns: *Topic/Headings/Facts* and *Examples.* In the right column, tell them to give examples of each element from a chapter in their science or social studies textbook.

Reading Strategy *Say: You identified main ideas of paragraphs as you read. Now, create a Main Idea Table showing the main idea and key details of the* entire *selection.*

Elements of Literature Have pairs of students play a game. *Say: Take turns*

stating an idea from the selection. Your partner will use the headings to find the idea. You may time each other to see what the record time is.

Reassess Read aloud a short informational piece on a topic of interest to students. Then ask them to identify the main idea and details. They may use a web or an outline to record their responses.

From Reading to Writing

Write an Informational Text

1. **Analyze published example as a model for writing** Have students review the reading and analyze the organization and format. *Ask: What do you like about the reading? What aspects will you model when writing your informational text?*
2. **Write a thesis statement** Have students return to their role-play groups for Listen, Speak, Interact. Have members draft thesis statements individually and share them with the group.
3. **Write in complete sentences of varying types** Have students check to make sure all their sentences are complete. Have them identify simple, compound, and complex sentences and check the punctuation of dependent clauses.
4. **Revise a draft** Have students check their drafts and rewrite their paragraphs as needed.
5. **Multi-level options** See MULTI-LEVEL OPTIONS on p. 220.

Across Content Areas: Language Arts

Learn Different Meanings of *Conflict*

1. **Discuss parts of speech** *Ask: What part of speech is* conflict *in this dictionary entry?* (noun) *Can it also be used as a different part of speech?* (yes, verb) Have students look up the definition of the verb *conflict* in a print or electronic dictionary. Ask them to write a sentence using the verb. Point out that some words can have definitions that are different parts of speech.
2. **Use a dictionary** Have students look up the pronunciation of *conflict* when it is used as a verb. Point out that the second syllable is stressed when it is used as a verb.

Answers
3. **a.** Definition 2 **b.** Definition 3 **c.** Definition 1

 **ASSESS**

Have students write a sentence using the word *conflict* as a noun.

Materials

Student Handbook
CNN Video: *Unit 3*
Teacher Resource Book: *Lesson Plan, p 18;*
   Teacher Resources, pp. 35–64;
   Video Script, pp. 165–166; Video
   Worksheet, p. 175; School-Home
   Connection, pp. 133–139
Teacher Resource CD-ROM
Assessment Program: *Unit 3 Test and Mid-Book*
   Exam, pp. 49–60; Teacher and Student
   Resources, pp. 115–144
Assessment CD-ROM
Transparencies
The Heinle Newbury House Dictionary/CD-ROM
Heinle Reading Library: *Dr. Jekyll and Mr. Hyde*
Web site: http://visions.heinle.com

Listening and Speaking Workshop

Literary Response: Report your Favorite Selection

Step 1: Choose your favorite selection.
Direct students to the table of contents on p. 150. Have them find and skim their favorite selection.

Step 2: Brainstorm a list.
Have students organize themselves into groups for each selection. Instruct them to discuss the questions together before writing their own notes.

Listening and Speaking Workshop

Literary Response: Report Your Favorite Selection

> **Topic**
>
> Choose the reading selection that you enjoyed the most in this unit. Prepare a report to share with the class that explains why you liked the selection.

Step 1: Choose your favorite selection.

1. List information about the selection on a note card like the one here. Include the title, the author, the genre, and the topic. The genre tells what type of literature the selection is. The topic tells what the selection is about.
2. If you do not remember the genre of the selection, look at the Table of Contents for Unit 3 on page 150. The genre is listed below the title.

> *My Favorite Selection*
> Title: *The Peach Boy* _____
> Author: _____
> Genre: _____
> Topic: _____

Step 2: Brainstorm a list.

List reasons why you liked the selection. Use the following questions to help you.

1. Did the selection include an exciting or interesting plot?
2. As you read, did you see pictures in your mind?
3. Did the reading make you think about your own experiences?
4. Did you learn something that you did not know before?

Step 3: Prepare your report.

Choose three of the reasons from Step 2 to present. Make a note card about each one. Write an example to support your reason.

> *Reason #1*
> *The plot was funny.*
> *Ex: Momotaro jumped out of a peach!*

Step 4: Practice your report.

Practice your report with a friend or family member.

1. Use your note cards to help you remember what to say.
2. Begin by telling the title, author, genre, and topic of the selection.
3. Ask your friend or family member to evaluate your report by using the Active Listening Checklist.

MULTI-LEVEL OPTIONS *Listening and Speaking Workshop*

Newcomer Have each student copy the title of his or her favorite selection on unlined paper. Tell each student to create an illustration that shows a favorite character or event or an interesting idea they learned from the selection. Have students who picked the same selection meet to share their drawings.

Beginning Have students copy the title of their favorite selection on a piece of paper. Tell them to fold their paper into thirds and make a drawing in each part to show reasons why they liked the selection. Instruct them to write labels for characters, objects, and events in their drawings. Ask students to share their drawings and read their labels.

Intermediate Remind students of the importance of delivering their reports expressively. Discuss how not only their words, but also their tone of voice, facial expression, and body language can communicate their enthusiasm for the piece they selected and make the audience want to listen.

Advanced After giving their reports, have students who chose the same selection meet. Ask them to brainstorm a list of books individuals in the group have read that are similar to the selected piece. Post this list so that students may use it as a resource when they are looking for library books.

Active Listening Checklist

1. The report made me want to read _____ because _____.
2. The report did not make me want to read _____ because _____.
3. I want to know more about _____.
4. I understood the main ideas of your report. Yes / No

Speaking Checklist

1. Did I speak too fast, too slow, or just right?
2. Did I speak loud enough for the class to hear me?
3. Did I look at the class as I spoke?
4. Did I use examples from the selection to support my reasons?

Step 5: Present your report to the class.

1. Use the responses to the Active Listening Checklist to revise your report.

2. Present your report to the class.
3. When you are finished, use the Speaking Checklist to evaluate your report.

Student Handbook

Viewing Workshop

View, Compare, and Contrast

Learn About the Civil Rights Movement

In Unit 3, you read the lyrics to the song "We Shall Overcome." You learned that many people sang this song at civil rights meetings.

1. Borrow two videos of documentaries about the Civil Rights movement from the library. A documentary is a film or television program based on facts or events in history.
2. Compare and contrast the documentaries. Look for ways the makers of the documentaries represent the Civil Rights movement. How are the points of view and ideas alike? How are they different? Use a Venn Diagram to organize your ideas.

3. Is "We Shall Overcome" played or sung during either documentary? How did learning more about the Civil Rights movement help you understand why people often sang this song? Do you think the purpose of this video was to inform, entertain, or persuade?
4. How do the makers of these documentaries represent the meaning of the Civil Rights movement?

Further Viewing

Watch the *Visions* CNN Video for Unit 3. Do the Video Worksheet.

CNN Video

Step 3: Prepare your report.
Have a volunteer give you a reason from his or her list. Write it on the board. Then have the class turn to the reading text and help find an example to support the reason.

Step 4: Practice your report.
Remind students to ask a friend or family member to complete the Active Listening Checklist. Help students review the checklist carefully.

Step 5: Present your report to the class.
Ask students to talk about what they did well and how they can improve their presentations. Have students identify and analyze persuasive techniques. After each presentation, *ask: Did this presentation persuade you to like the selection? What details convinced you?*

ASSESS

Have students write a sentence about how they could improve their reports.

Portfolio

Students may choose to record or videotape their speeches to place in their portfolios.

Viewing Workshop

View, Compare, Contrast

1. **Evaluate a video** On the board, write: *What was the most surprising image in the video? Were any other songs sung during the video?* Have students discuss these answers in groups after watching the video.
2. **Reflect on what you learned** Have students write a list of what they have learned about the civil rights movement from watching the video. Have them share their observations.

Content Connection
The Arts

Suggest that songs can be *seen* as well as heard. Have students recall times they have seen songs signed with sign language or accompanied by dance steps. Have small groups work together to create gestures for "We Shall Overcome." Give each group a chance to perform for the class. Ask the audience to tell how the addition of the motions affected their understanding of and feelings about the content of song.

Learning Styles
Intrapersonal

Point out that people can be attracted to certain pieces of writing because the author's ideas remind them of something in their past. Another reason a reader can like a piece of writing is because it gives them a new idea that they can use in their day-to-day lives. Have students write about whether they were attracted to the piece of literature they selected for either of these reasons.

Writer's Workshop

Response to Literature: Write a Review of Literature

Write a review Read and discuss the prompt. If there is a school newspaper, discuss whether or not it has reviews of literature.

Step 1: Evaluate a selection.
Have students meet with others who are reviewing the same selection. Tell them to discuss the strengths and weaknesses. Have students take notes on their own charts.

Step 2: Write a draft.
Review the elements of a literature review. Have students select the most interesting or convincing strengths and weaknesses to write about. Ask them to point out specific paragraphs in the text to provide examples.

Writer's Workshop

Response to Literature: Write a Review of Literature

Writing Prompt

The editor of the school newspaper has asked students to send in reviews of literature. A review tells about the strengths (good things) and weaknesses (bad things) of a reading. Choose a selection from this unit and write a review to send to the newspaper.

Step 1: Evaluate a selection.

Decide which selection from this unit you will review.

1. Reread the selection in your book. Write a short summary of the selection on a piece of paper.
2. Use a chart like the one here to list the strengths and weaknesses of the selection. Think about why the selection is (or is not) a good piece of literature. Then think about how the selection might be improved.

Step 2: Write a draft.

Your review should be three paragraphs long. Include an introduction, a body, and a conclusion. Write your review on a computer, if possible. Use reference materials to help you correctly write your review.

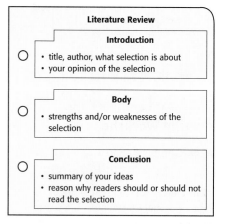

Literature Review

Introduction
- title, author, what selection is about
- your opinion of the selection

Body
- strengths and/or weaknesses of the selection

Conclusion
- summary of your ideas
- reason why readers should or should not read the selection

Step 3: Revise your work.

1. Reread your draft. Revise your work using your responses to these questions:
   a. Did I state my opinion clearly?
   b. Did I support my opinion by listing the strengths and weaknesses of the selection?
   c. Did I clearly summarize why people should or should not read the selection?
   d. Did I indent my paragraphs?

MULTI-LEVEL OPTIONS *Writer's Workshop*

Newcomer Have students agree on a selection. Write the title on the board. Elicit students' likes and dislikes about the piece. Record their ideas in words and phrases on a two-column chart. Have students make a final copy on paper. Work with students to submit the chart for use as a visual in the school newspaper.

Beginning Have students turn the notes on their charts into a review using the following sentence starters. *I read _____ by _____. I think it was _____. One thing I liked about it was _____. One thing I did not like was _____. I think people would (would not) like this selection because it _____.*

Intermediate After students have written a first draft, *say: You can strengthen your reviews by quoting ideas from the selection. Don't just say the author included vivid description. Give an example of a descriptive sentence from the piece. Remember to use quotation marks when you quote from the selection.*

Advanced On the board, write: *"Everyone would like this story." Say: This is probably untrue. It is unlikely that everyone would like it. Think carefully about who would and would not like the selection. For example, you might write: People who like realistic stories would not like "The Peach Boy." Readers who like fantasy tales would love it.*

2. Make sure your ideas are clear.
   a. Elaborate (explain) any difficult words or phrases.
   b. Delete (remove) any text that is repeated.
   c. Rearrange sentences so that your ideas follow a logical order.
   d. Combine sentences with words like *and, but, because, if,* or *when.*
3. With a partner, read each other's work. Then discuss how your reviews can be improved. Use what you learned to make revisions.

Step 4: Edit and proofread.

1. Read your review carefully to make sure that you have used correct spelling, punctuation, and grammar. Choose appropriate reference materials to help you.
   a. Use a dictionary to check the spelling of words.
   b. If you wrote your review on a computer, run the checks for spelling, punctuation, and grammar.
2. Use your Student Handbook as a resource to check your writing.

Step 5: Publish.

Prepare your review to send to the editor of the school newspaper.

1. If you wrote your review on a computer, choose a font that is easy to read. A font is a style of type. If you wrote the review by hand, make sure your handwriting is neat and clear.

2. Put your review in an envelope. Address the review to: Editor of the School Newspaper. Add the name and address of your school.
3. Write your name and address in the upper left corner of the envelope.

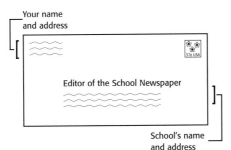

Your name and address

Editor of the School Newspaper

School's name and address

4. Make a bulletin board to publish the reviews written by the class. Put reviews of the same reading together. Analyze the reviews by comparing and contrasting them. Evaluate them for their strengths and weaknesses.
5. Set goals as a writer based on your writing and the writing of your classmates.

The Heinle Newbury House Dictionary

Student Handbook

Step 3: Revise your work.
Clarify and explain the questions as needed. Have students underline sentences in the draft where they stated their opinion.

Step 4: Edit and proofread.
Review punctuation. You may want to have students focus on specific editing and proofreading points.

Step 5: Publish.
Point out that students are publishing for a *general* audience. Explain that they should not assume the audience has read the selection. Remind them to provide sufficient information on the selection and use appropriate language.

ASSESS

Have students choose the review they thought was the best and write why they liked it.

Portfolio

Students may choose to include their writing in their portfolios.

Content Connection
Technology

Bookmark online bookstore examples of effective and ineffective reviews of children's books. If possible, include reviews of books from which some of the selections in this unit were taken. Discuss which reviews are clear, interesting, and helpful, and which are not and why.

Learning Styles
Interpersonal

Ask each student to select a partner in the class to work with. Specify one of the five selections in this unit for the partners to focus upon. Have each student complete the following statement about his or her partner: *I predict (name of partner) did/did not like (title of selection) because* _____. After students have finished writing, have them share their sentences with their partners to find out if their predictions were accurate.

Projects

Project 1: Create a Storyboard

Brainstorm ideas Create a list on the board of different conflicts they could illustrate. Point out any conflicts that may not work well with a storyboard. Have students brainstorm posters and visual displays for their storyboards.

Project 2: Present a Radio Program

1. **Relate to personal experience** *Ask: Do you ever listen to radio programs or television talk shows? What's the name of the show, and what do they talk about? What do you like about it?*

2. **Role-play a radio show** If students have difficulty role-playing the radio station worker, give them the option of having two "hosts" for their radio show. Tell them that each one may offer similar or different advice to the caller.

3. **Analyze speaker's credibility** After performing their role plays, have students analyze the credibility of their partner. *Ask: How well did your partner act out his/her role? Was she believable? Did you trust his/her words? Why or why not? What suggestions would you give your partner to be more credible?* (example: be more confident, use stronger emotion, and so on)

Portfolio

Students may choose to include their projects in their portfolios.

Projects

Project 1: Create a Storyboard

In Unit 3, you learned about different conflicts people can have. Create a storyboard. Show a conflict you know about and a solution for the conflict.

1. Choose a conflict from the unit or make one up.
2. On a piece of paper, draw four boxes like the ones shown. Number them in order.
3. In the first box, draw a conflict between two people. You may include dialogue, if you wish.
4. In the remaining boxes, show how the people solve their problems.

Project 2: Present a Radio Program

In this unit, you learned about stress. A person in a stressful situation may ask for help about how to handle it. There are radio programs that talk about how to handle stress. People telephone the radio station to ask for help with stress.

1. Work with a partner. List three stressful situations.
2. Brainstorm ways to handle the stressful situation. Refer to Chapter 5 if you need to.
3. Complete a chart like the one shown.
4. Take turns role-playing a situation in which one person calls a radio station to ask for help with a stressful situation. Another person should role-play the part of the radio station worker who helps the caller handle the stress.
5. Share your role play with others in the class.

Stressful Situation	Ways to Handle Stress

MULTI-LEVEL OPTIONS *Projects*

Newcomer Use a language experience approach to create a class storyboard. Include words and short phrases in speech balloons. Have students act out the events in each frame as you read the dialogue.

Beginning Choose a conflict with the group. Have students work in pairs. Give each pair four pieces of paper on which to create their storyboards. Then have each pair meet with another pair. Have the pairs take turns mixing up their four papers and asking the other pair to figure out the proper order to tell about the conflict.

Intermediate Have students work in pairs to create their storyboards. After pairs have completed their illustrations and dialogue, have them show the drawings and read the dialogue expressively to the class.

Advanced Have students use their storyboards as prewriting planners for creating a short play. Have students refer back to "The Peach Boy" to recall the structure for this kind of writing.

Further Reading

Here is a list of books about the themes of conflict and cooperation. Read one or more of them. Write your thoughts and feelings about what you read in your Reading Log. Take notes about your answers to these questions:

1. What kinds of conflicts are presented in the books you read?
2. How do the characters deal with the conflicts they are faced with?
3. What did you learn about handling conflicts from what you read?

Zlata's Diary: A Child's Life in Sarajevo
by Zlata Filipović, Christina Pribichevich-Zoric (translator), and Janine Di Giovanni (introduction), Penguin USA, 1995. Zlata's world changes from that of a normal teenager to one where she is dealing with the reality of war. She writes about her feelings and the hardships that her family experiences because of the war in Sarajevo.

Conflict Resolution: Communication, Cooperation, Compromise
by Robert Wandberg, Capstone Press, 2000. This book talks about the types, causes, and results of conflicts in the life of teenagers. It also discusses how to resolve the various types of conflicts.

Hoops
by Walter Dean Myers, Laurel Leaf, 1983. At 17, Lonnie Jackson is on his way to becoming a professional basketball player. His coach tries to teach Lonnie how to deal with the pressures of being a great player.

Soldier's Heart: Being the Story of the Enlistment and Due Service of the Boy Charley Goddard in the First Minnesota Volunteers
by Gary Paulsen, Delacorte Press, 1998. Charley Goddard lies about his age to enlist as a soldier during the Civil War. Fighting in the war turns out not to be the adventure he thought it would be.

Over the Wall
by John H. Ritter, Penguin Putnam Books for Young Readers, 2000. Tyler does not know how to control his temper. During the summer, he spends time with his cousins in New York where he learns how to use his love of baseball to better deal with his anger.

Breaking the Chains of the Ancient Warriors: Tests of Wisdom for Young Martial Artists
by Terrence Webster-Doyle, Atrium Society Education for Peace Publications, 1996. This is a collection of stories about the tests of wisdom. The tests of wisdom include humility, peaceful conflict resolution, love, strength, and honor.

Companion Web site

Reading Log

Heinle Reading Library
Dr. Jekyll and Mr. Hyde

Further Reading

1. **Identify conflicts** Have pairs of students choose one title and read the summary together. Ask them to discuss and predict what conflicts are likely to be in the story.

2. **Respond to literature** After reading a book, have students give an oral report. Instruct them to follow the organization presented on p. 224 for the review.

Assessment Program: *Unit 3 Test, and Mid-Book Exam, pp. 49–60*

Heinle Reading Library

The Strange Case of Dr. Jekyll and Mr. Hyde
by Robert Louis Stevenson
In a specially adapted version
by Mitsu Yamamoto

Dr. Jekyll is a kind and respected man. His friends cannot understand his companionship with the wicked, mysterious Mr. Hyde, who seems to have come from nowhere and yet has a terrible hold on the doctor. Even as Hyde commits crimes that shock all of London, no one can guess how—or why—the two men are so close. Only at the very end of this gripping tale is the incredible truth revealed.

Visions Companion Site

http://visions.heinle.com
For additional student activities and teacher resources, see the Visions Companion Web site.

Unit Materials

Activity Book: *pp. 121–152*
Audio: *Unit 4; CD 2, Tracks 1–6*
Student Handbook
Student CD-ROM: *Unit 4*
CNN Video: *Unit 4*
Teacher Resource Book: *Lesson Plans, Teacher Resources, Reading Summaries, School-Home Connection, Video Script, Video Worksheet, Activity Book Answer Key*
Teacher Resource CD-ROM
Assessment Program: *Quizzes and Test, pp. 61–74; Teacher and Student Resources, pp. 115–144*
Assessment CD-ROM
Transparencies
The Heinle Newbury House Dictionary/CD-ROM
More Grammar Practice workbook
Heinle Reading Library: *The Red Badge of Courage*
Web site: http://visions.heinle.com

Visions Staff Development Handbook

Refer to the Visions Staff Development Handbook for more teacher support.

Unit Theme: Heroes

Clarify the theme word *Say: A hero is someone who is brave or does something great. For example, a volunteer can be a hero; a sports star can be a hero. Who are some people you think are heroes?*

Unit Preview: Table of Contents

1. **Use the table of contents to make predictions** Read the chapter titles and authors of the reading selections. *Ask: What are the genres in this unit?* (legend, biography, speech, and poetry)
2. **Connect** *Ask: Do you know anything about Roberto Clemente or Nelson Mandela?*

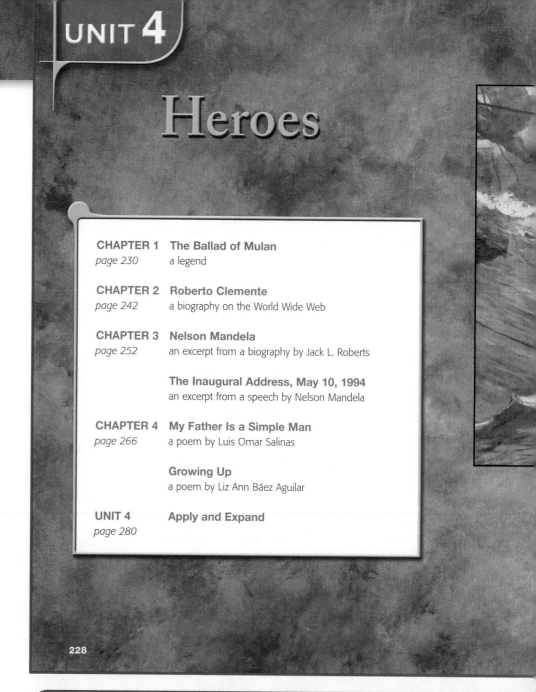

Heroes

228

UNIT OBJECTIVES

Reading
Make predictions as you read a legend • Use chronological order to recall and locate information in a biography • Draw inferences as you read a biography and a speech • Compare and contrast as you read two poems

Listening and Speaking
Develop a character • Discuss learning from a person's example • Create and present dialogue • Discuss jobs

The Life Line, Winslow Homer, oil on canvas. 1884.

View the Picture

1. Do you think the person in this picture is a hero? Use details from the picture to explain.
2. Who in your life do you think is a hero? Why?

In this unit, you will read a legend, two biographies, a speech, and two poems about heroes. You will learn about the different ways that people can be heroes. You will also learn the elements of these writing forms and how to write them yourself.

229

Grammar
Use prepositional phrases • Identify prepositional phrases of time • Recognize commands with *let* • Recognize reported speech

Writing
Write a legend • Write a biography • Write a persuasive speech • Write a poem

Content
Social Studies: Use map features to read a map • Science: Learn about earthquakes • Social Studies: Read a timeline • Social Studies: Read advertisements for jobs

View the Picture

1. **Art background** Winslow Homer (1836–1910) was trained as a lithographer whose most famous contributions to *Harper's Weekly* were scenes of the Civil War. In his later works, such as this oil painting, he often used the sea as a dramatic setting for themes of man's heroic struggle against the forces of nature.

2. **Art interpretation** Have students discuss what is happening in this scene. (A shipwrecked sailor is being pulled by another sailor from a dangerous-looking sea by thin ropes and pulleys.)

   a. **Explore and describe shapes and color** Ask students to discuss why Homer put splashes of red against browns, grays, and a white sea (to highlight the danger the men are in; life against death). Point out that the lines created by the ropes and pulleys don't seem to be attached to anything. *Ask: Do the ropes look safe? What might happen to both the victim and the rescuer?*

   b. **Interpret the painting** *Ask: How would you feel being saved in this way? How does the artist make you feel the movement and danger of the waves?*

   c. **Connect to the theme** Point out that the theme of this unit is *heroes*. Ask students if they or anyone they know has ever rescued people from danger.

ASSESS

Have students do a drawing of someone they think is a hero and write a caption for the drawing.

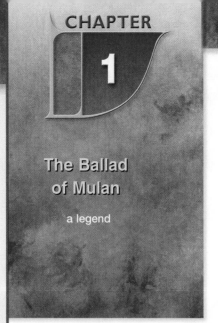

CHAPTER 1

Into the Reading

The Ballad of Mulan

a legend

Chapter Materials

Activity Book: *pp. 121–128*
Audio: *Unit 4, Chapter 1; CD 2, Track 1*
Student Handbook
Student CD-ROM: *Unit 4, Chapter 1*
Teacher Resource Book: *Lesson Plan, Teacher Resources, Reading Summary, Activity Book Answer Key*
Teacher Resource CD-ROM
Assessment Program: *Quiz, pp. 61–62; Teacher and Student Resources, pp. 115–144*
Assessment CD-ROM
Transparencies
The Heinle Newbury House Dictionary/CD-ROM
Web site: http://visions.heinle.com

Objectives

Preview Have a student read the objectives.
Ask: Which objective do you already know something about?

Use Prior Knowledge

Discuss Heroes

Brainstorm Brainstorm and list words that students think makes someone a hero. For example, *brave, strong, thinks about others, generous.*

Use Prior Knowledge

Discuss Heroes

A hero is a person who is very brave or who does something great. For example, a firefighter who saves people from a burning building is a hero.

1. Think of two people who you think are heroes.
2. With a group, discuss what you think makes someone a hero. Think about different ways that a person can be a hero.
3. On a piece of paper, write your ideas in a web like this one.
4. Draw a picture of a hero performing an act. Tell the class why the person is a hero.

230 Unit 4 Heroes

MULTI-LEVEL OPTIONS *Build Vocabulary*

Newcomer Have several students march in place. *Say: troops.* Have others march toward them. *Say: invaders.* Make a crown shape with your hands. Put it on your head. *Say: emperor.*

Beginning Make word cards for the vocabulary and for the following: *story, sad, soldiers, king, attacker, suffer.* Hold up matching cards and act out the meanings. Mix up the cards and display them where students can see them. Have volunteers match words with similar meanings.

Intermediate Have students discuss the vocabulary words. Ask them to tell how they know the word or the context in which they have heard it. *(Example:* My uncle plays songs on his guitar. Some of them are called ballads. Some tell sad or sorrowful stories.)

Advanced Have students use suffixes and root words to help decipher the meanings of the vocabulary. *(Examples:* sorrowful – sorrow/ful, emperor – empire, invaders – invade) Have them add those words to their Personal Dictionaries.

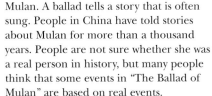

Build Background

Early China

"The Ballad of Mulan" takes place in China at some time between the years 386 and 534. During this time, China's rulers fought wars against armies from nearby lands. There were also many wars among the Chinese people.

"The Ballad of Mulan" describes the brave actions of a Chinese girl named Mulan. A ballad tells a story that is often sung. People in China have told stories about Mulan for more than a thousand years. People are not sure whether she was a real person in history, but many people think that some events in "The Ballad of Mulan" are based on real events.

Content Connection

For thousands of years, China was ruled by different groups of families known as dynasties. The leaders of these Chinese dynasties were called emperors.

Build Vocabulary

Evaluate Your Understanding of Words

You can use a dictionary to find the meanings and pronunciations of new words. Look at this dictionary entry.

> **bal•lad** /ˈbæləd/ n. frml. a poem or song that tells a story with simple words

1. Write these words in your Personal Dictionary.

ballad	sorrowful	troops
emperor	invaders	endure

2. Write the meanings of the words you know.
3. After you read "The Ballad of Mulan," write the meanings of the words you learned.
4. Use a dictionary to look up the meanings and pronunciations of the words you did not understand. Write down the definitions.

Personal Dictionary   The Heinle Newbury House Dictionary   Activity Book p. 121   Student CD-ROM

Chapter 1 The Ballad of Mulan **231**

Content Connection
Social Studies

Build Vocabulary Divide the class into small groups. Give each group a supply of stick-on notes with one of the vocabulary words written on it. Also, give each group a social studies text or world history book. *Say: Search for pictures that show as many of the vocabulary words as possible. Mark the pictures with the stick-ons.* For example, students may find a map showing the invasion of one country by another or a painting of the hardships early colonists endured.

Learning Styles
Visual

Build Background *Ask: What do you know about Mulan so far?* (girl, Chinese, lived a very long time ago, brave actions related to a war) *Say: Draw a picture of how you imagine her from what you know.*

Build Background

Early China

1. **Locate information on a map** Have students locate China on a map or globe. *Ask: What other countries are near China?* (Korea, Japan, India) *What kind of climate do you think China has?* (mostly temperate) *Why? What else do you know about China?*

2. **Content Connection** The earliest reliable historical evidence of ancient Chinese dynasties is of the Shang Dynasty, believed to have existed from 1994 to 1766 B.C.

Build Vocabulary

Teacher Resource Book: *Personal Dictionary, p. 63*

Evaluate Your Understanding of Words

1. **Use prior knowledge** Have students share what they already know about the vocabulary. *Ask: Which word has a suffix?* (sorrowful) *What does the suffix mean?* (full of)

2. **Use other sources** Have students locate the meanings and pronunciations of unfamiliar words in print, online, or CD-ROM dictionaries.

3. **Reading selection vocabulary** You may want to introduce the glossed words in the reading selection before students begin reading. Key words: *invaders, troops, fierce, victorious, astonished, glory.* Instruct students to write the words with correct spelling and their definitions in their Personal Dictionaries. Have them pronounce each word and divide it into syllables.

4. **Multi-level options** See MULTI-LEVEL OPTIONS on p. 230.

 **ASSESS**

Have the class write a definition of *hero* in their own words and give a few examples.

Text Structure

Legend

1. **Compare features of a legend and a fable**
   Say: We read "The Peach Boy," a fable. A fable is similar to a legend. Look at the features of a legend. What is similar? (main character, exaggeration, values) *What is different?* (In fables, events are not based on real events; animals are given human qualities.)

2. **Multi-level options** See MULTI-LEVEL OPTIONS below.

Reading Strategy

Make Predictions

Use illustrations to make predictions Direct students to the illustrations. Have students give details to support their predictions. *Ask:* (p. 234) *What does Mulan's facial expression tell you?* (She is worried.) (p. 235) *Do you think the other fighters know that she is a woman?* (no) (p. 236) *Why do you think Mulan is at the Emperor's palace?* (to receive an award) (p. 237) *Why isn't Mulan wearing her armor anymore?* (She has returned home.)

ASSESS

Say: Have students write a prediction about tomorrow's weather.

Text Structure

Legend

"The Ballad of Mulan" is a **legend.** A legend is a made-up story that has been passed down from generation to generation. A generation is a group of people that are about the same age.

As you read or listen to "The Ballad of Mulan," note how Mulan's actions show that caring for your parents is an important value.

Student
CD-ROM

Legend	
Main Character	The legend is usually about a hero, who was often a real person in history.
Events	The legend's events are usually based on real events in history, but parts of the story are often made up.
Exaggeration	The qualities and actions of the hero are often exaggerated (shown as greater than they really were). This is done to show, for example, how strong, honest, or good the hero was.
Values	Legends teach values (ideas about what is important and right).

Reading Strategy

Make Predictions

When you **make predictions,** you use information or pictures in a text to guess what might happen next. As you continue to read, you may need to change your predictions.

1. Read the title of the selection on page 233. Then look at the pictures on pages 234–237. What predictions can you make about what the selection is about? Who is the most important character? What clues helped you make your predictions? Write your answers on a piece of paper.

2. As you read each paragraph of "The Ballad of Mulan," ask yourself, "What do I think will happen next?" After you read new clues, check if your prediction is correct.

3. As you continue to read, write down predictions about how the story will end. When you finish reading, compare your predictions with what really happened.

Reading Log

Student
CD-ROM

232 Unit 4 Heroes

MULTI-LEVEL OPTIONS *Text Structure*

Newcomer Remind students that a hero does important or brave things. Divide the class into pairs and give each pair a book of legends from the school library. Have each pair find an illustration of a hero in one of the legends. Have them use the illustration to determine something important or brave the hero did.

Beginning Show students a thick book. *Say: This book is (number) inches thick.* Then tell students you are going to exaggerate. *Say: This book is as thick as a mattress.* Make other factual and exaggerated statements about classroom items. Have students give true or exaggerated replies.

Intermediate Have students tell the titles of any legends they have heard or read. Ask them to give the name of the main character and describe one thing he or she does.

Advanced Ask students to discuss a legend they know in groups. Have them give an example of each feature on the chart from the legend. Ask them to include their examples as a new column to the chart on p. 232.

THE BALLAD OF

Mulan

a legend

233

Reading Selection Materials

Audio: *Unit 4, Chapter 1; CD 2, Track 1*
Teacher Resource Book: *Reading Summary,
    pp. 95–96*
Transparencies: #9, *Reading Summary*

Suggestions for Using
Reading Summary

- Introduce new vocabulary or cognates.
- Cut the summary into strips, or jumble the
  sentences on an overhead transparency.
  Students put the sentences in order.
- Practice the reading strategy.
- Students read aloud or with a partner.
- Students paraphrase the summary.
- Students do a cloze activity.
- Students create a visual or graphic
  organizer, such as a timeline or storyboard,
  to illustrate the summary.
- Students paraphrase the summary.

Preview the Selection

1. **Use an illustration to predict** Tell students
   that the illustration relates to the legend they
   will read. Have them describe the illustration
   and make predictions about the story.
2. **Connect** Remind students that the unit
   theme is *heroes.* Ask them how the picture
   might relate to the theme.

**Community
Connection**

Tell students to look at the setting in the
picture very carefully. Ask them to list or
draw all the ways this setting is different
from their own community.

Learning Styles
Intrapersonal

Ask students to list or draw things they do to
care for and help their families. *Ask: Which
of these are things that a young Chinese girl
long ago could have done?* Have them circle
their responses. Tell them that they will read
a story about a girl who did something very
unusual to help her family.

Read the Selection

1. **Use illustrations to compare and contrast**
Direct students to the illustrations. Tell your students they are two views of Mulan. *Ask: What differences do you see?* (with her mother/alone, working on a loom/riding a horse, in female clothing/in armor)

2. **Choral reading** Divide the class into two groups. Have each group read alternate paragraphs with you. Do it twice so that each group reads both parts.

3. **Discuss feelings** *Ask: How would you feel if your father or brother had to go to war?*

Sample Answer to Guide Question
She will try to take her father's place.

See Teacher Edition pp. 434–436 for a list of English-Spanish cognates in the reading selection.

Audio
CD 2. Tr. 1

1 Long ago, in a village in northern China, there lived a girl named Mulan. One day, she sat at her **loom** weaving cloth. *Click-clack! Click-clack!* went the loom.

2 Suddenly, the sound of weaving changed to **sorrowful** sighs. "What troubles you?" her mother asked.

3 "Nothing, Mother," Mulan softly replied.

4 Her mother asked her again and again, until Mulan finally said, "There is news of war."

5 "**Invaders** are attacking. The Emperor is calling for **troops.** Last night, I saw the **draft** poster and twelve **scrolls** of names in the market. Father's name is on every one."

Make Predictions

How do you think Mulan will try to help her father?

6 "But Father is old and **frail,**" Mulan sighed. "How can he fight? He has no grown son and I have no elder brother."

7 "I will go to the markets. I shall buy a saddle and a horse. I must fight in Father's place."

8 From the eastern market Mulan bought a horse, and from the western market, a saddle. From the southern market she bought a **bridle,** and from the northern market, a whip.

---

loom a machine for weaving thread into cloth	**scrolls** rolls of paper or other material on which to write
sorrowful very sad	
invaders people who enter a place by force	**frail** weak
troops groups of soldiers	**bridle** straps on a horse's head to control it
draft a call to fight in the military	

234 Unit 4 Heroes

MULTI-LEVEL OPTIONS *Read the Selection*

Newcomer Play the audio and point to relevant parts of the illustrations. *Ask: Is Mulan a young girl?* (yes) *Is her father supposed to go to war?* (yes) *Does Mulan go instead of him?* (yes) *Was her trip easy?* (no)

Beginning Read the Reading Summary aloud. *Ask: Who is Mulan?* (a girl) *What is happening?* (war) *Who was supposed to go and fight?* (her father) *Who went in his place?* (Mulan)

Intermediate Have students do a reciprocal reading. *Ask: Why was Mulan worried about the war?* (She was afraid her father would have to fight.) *Why couldn't her father go?* (He was old and weak.) *How did Mulan decide to solve the problem?* (by going to war instead of her father)

Advanced Have students read silently. *Ask: What do Mulan's actions show about her? Explain.* (caring and brave because she was willing to go to war for her father even though she would be in danger) *What does paragraph 10 show about Mulan's feelings?* (She probably missed her family.)

9   At dawn Mulan dressed in her **armor** and bid a sad **farewell** to her father, mother, sister, and brother. Then she **mounted** her horse and rode off with the soldiers.

10   By nightfall she was camped by the bank of the Yellow River. She thought she heard her mother calling her name.

11   But it was only the sound of the river crying.

12   At sunrise Mulan took leave of the Yellow River. At **dusk** she reached the **peak** of Black Mountain.

13   In the darkness she longed to hear her father's voice but heard only the **neighing** of enemy horses far away.

14   Mulan rode ten thousand miles to fight a hundred battles. She crossed peaks and **passes** like a bird in flight.

15   Nights at the camp were **harsh** and cold, but Mulan endured every hardship. Knowing her father was safe warmed her heart.

16   The war dragged on. **Fierce** battles **ravaged** the land. One after another, noble generals lost their lives.

Make Predictions

Do you think Mulan will be a good soldier? Which text clues helped you make your prediction?

armor covering worn by soldiers to protect the body	**neighing** loud, high sounds made by horses
farewell good-bye	**passes** openings that you can travel through
mounted climbed on	**harsh** unpleasant, rough
dusk the time after the sun sets and before the dark of night	**fierce** violent, wild
peak the pointed top of a mountain	**ravaged** destroyed, ruined

Chapter 1   The Ballad of Mulan   **235**

Read the Selection

1. **Paired reading** Play the audio. Then have students reread in pairs.

2. **Make a timeline** Have students help you write a timeline. On the board, write: *1. Mulan hears about the war.* **Ask:** *What does Mulan decide to do?* (She decides to go in her father's place.) *What does she do to get ready?* (She buys a horse, saddle, bridle, and whip.) *What does she do next?* Have students write the events in the timeline. Continue asking questions to elicit the sequence of events.

3. **Identify exaggeration** *Say: Mulan's actions are exaggerated in the legend. Where in the story can you find exaggeration?* (Mulan rode ten thousand miles to fight a hundred battles.)

4. **Understand imagery** *Say: Sometimes a story has images, or words that help create pictures in your mind, to make it more interesting. For example, I could say, "My brother runs like a rabbit." Can you find an example of imagery on this page?* (She crossed peaks and passes like a bird in flight.) Explain that a bird can travel quickly over difficult terrain.

5. **Multi-level options** See MULTI-LEVEL OPTIONS on p. 234.

Sample Answer to Guide Question
The text says that she "endured every hardship" and "rode ten thousand miles to fight a hundred battles."

---

9   **Punctuation**

Italics, hyphen, and exclamation point

Direct students' attention to paragraph 1. Have them find *Click-clack!* **Ask:** *What three things make this word look different from the others in the paragraph?* (italics, hyphen, exclamation point) Remind students that they have already learned that italics can be used to show special words. *Ask: Why is this word special?* (It is a word for a sound.) *Say: We have also learned that exclamation points show feeling or surprise. By using an exclamation point here, the writer probably* wanted to show that the sharp noise of the loom was the only sound in a quiet room. We have not talked about hyphens yet in any of these units. A hyphen is a little line that can connect the parts of a two-part word. Some compound words, such as click-clack, are joined with hyphens.

Read the Selection

1. **Shared reading** Play the audio. Have students join in when they can.
2. **Speculate** *Ask: Do you think the Emperor knows that Mulan is a woman? Why or why not? How do you think the role of women in ancient China was different from today?*

Sample Answer to Guide Question
Mulan will ask to see her family. She always thought about her father when she was away.

17 Mulan's skill and courage won her respect and **rank.** After ten years, she returned as a great general, **triumphant** and **victorious!**

18 The Emperor **summoned** Mulan to the High Palace. He praised her for her bravery and leadership in battle.

19 The Court would **bestow** many great **titles** upon her. Mulan would be **showered** with gifts of gold.

20 "Worthy General, you may have your heart's desire," the Emperor said.

21 "I have no need for honors or gold," Mulan replied.

22 "All I ask for is a swift camel to take me back home." The Emperor sent a troop to **escort** Mulan on her trip.

23 In town, the news of Mulan's return created great excitement. Holding each other, her proud parents walked to the village gate to welcome her.

> **Make Predictions**
>
> What do you think Mulan will ask the Emperor to give her? Why do you think this?

rank a high position in the army	**bestow** give formally
triumphant having won victory or success	**titles** high social positions
victorious triumphant	**showered** gave a lot of something
summoned called or sent for	**escort** lead, guide

236 Unit 4 Heroes

MULTI-LEVEL OPTIONS *Read the Selection*

Newcomer *Ask: Was Mulan a brave soldier?* (yes) *Did the ruler want to give her a gift?* (yes) *Did she want gold?* (no) *Were other soldiers surprised when they learned that Mulan was a woman?* (yes)

Beginning *Ask: Who asked Mulan to come to the palace?* (the Emperor) *What did he want to give her for her bravery?* (riches) *What did she want?* (to go home) *How did people feel when they learned that a woman had been a soldier?* (surprised)

Intermediate *Ask: Why did the Emperor offer gifts to Mulan?* (to thank her for the good job she had done) *What did her answer show about her?* (She did not want praise or riches.) *Explain why Mulan's comrades were so surprised.* (They fought beside her for 10 years and didn't know she was a woman.)

Advanced *Ask: What does paragraph 28 mean?* (Example: In emergencies, it's what you do, not who you are, that's important.) *Compare and contrast this story with "Zlata's Diary."* (Both told about feelings and actions of a girl during war. Zlata stayed with her family; Mulan became a soldier.)

24　Waiting at home, Mulan's sister **beautified** herself. Her brother sharpened his knife to prepare a pig and sheep for the feast in Mulan's honor.

25　Home at last! Mulan threw open her bedroom door and smiled. She removed her armor and changed into one of her favorite dresses.

26　What a surprise it was when Mulan appeared at the door! Her **comrades** were **astonished** and amazed. "How is this possible?" they asked.

27　"How could we have fought side by side with you for ten years and not known you were a woman!"

28　Mulan replied, "They say the male rabbit likes to hop and leap, while the female rabbit prefers to sit still. But in times of danger, when the two rabbits **scurry** by, who can tell male from female?"

29　Mulan's **glory** spread through the land. And to this day, we sing of this brave woman who loved her family and served her country, asking for nothing in return.

Make Predictions

What do you think amazes the soldiers?

beautified　made pretty	**scurry**　run quickly, often in fear
comrades　close friends or people who work with you	**glory**　great honor or fame
astonished　very surprised	

Chapter 1　The Ballad of Mulan　**237**

---

th Spelling

Silent *k* in *kn*

Ask: What is the first sound you hear in the word known*?* (n) *Find the word in paragraph 27 to see the first letter. Yes,* k. *The* k *is silent.*

　Apply Write the following on the board. Have students complete the sentences with *kn-* words.

Tie a _____ in the rope. (knot)
I scraped my _____ when I fell. (knee)
Cut your meat with a _____. (knife)
_____ on the door. (Knock)

Evaluate Your Reading Strategy

Make Predictions *Say: You have practiced an important reading strategy. Now you can decide how well you have done. Does this statement describe how you read?*

> When I read, I use my knowledge of what has happened to make predictions about what will happen next. Making predictions gets me involved in the story and makes reading more enjoyable.

Read the Selection

1. **Silent reading** Read the rest of the story. Then give students time to reread silently.
2. **Dramatize the legend** Assign the following parts to volunteers: a narrator, Mulan, several comrades, and Mulan's parents, sister, and brother. Have the narrator read, while the characters act out paragraphs 23–29. The soldiers and Mulan should speak their lines. Go through the scene again, so that another group can act it out. Remind them to exaggerate their actions.
3. **Multi-level options** See MULTI-LEVEL OPTIONS on p. 236.

Sample Answer to Guide Question
They are amazed that the person who fought so bravely beside them is a woman.

Across Selections

Say: "Mulan" is a legend, a story that is passed down from generation to generation. We also read "The Peach Boy," a story passed down as well. Have students turn to "The Peach Boy" on page 179. *Ask: Is "The Peach Boy" a legend?* (No, it's a folktale.) *What's the difference between a legend and a folktale?* (A legend is about a real person and is based on real events. A folktale is a fictional story that has values that are important to a culture.)

Spelling, Punctuation, Capitalization

After the Reading Comprehension section, students will practice spelling, punctuation, and capitalization in the Activity Book.

Beyond the Reading

Reading Comprehension

Question-Answer Relationships

Sample Answers

1. She is a girl who lives in a village in northern China.
2. Because her father is too old and she doesn't have an older brother, she goes so her father will be safe.
3. She buys a horse from the eastern market, a saddle from the western market, a bridle from the southern market, and a whip from the northern market.
4. 10 years
5. She felt sad, but she was determined to go.
6. They are proud and happy.
7. She fought for her family and for her father, not for gold or riches. She felt it was her duty.
8. She wanted to show that she was a woman.
9. courageous, brave, honorable, strong, honest, devoted to family
10. Mulan was a hero, and there are many stories that can be told about her adventures. She demonstrated many good values in her actions.
11. Answers will vary.

Build Reading Fluency

Repeated Reading

Assessment Program: *Reading Fluency Chart, p. 116*

As students read aloud, time the reading and count the number of incorrectly pronounced words. Record results in the Reading Fluency Chart.

Reading Comprehension

Question-Answer Relationships (QAR)

"Right There" Questions

1. **Recall Facts** Who is Mulan?
2. **Recall Facts** Why does Mulan take her father's place in the army?
3. **Recall Facts** Where does Mulan buy what she needs to fight in her father's place?
4. **Recall Facts** How long is Mulan away from her home?

"Think and Search" Questions

5. **Evaluate Evidence** How does Mulan feel about leaving her home?
6. **Summarize** How does Mulan's family feel about her coming home?

"Author and You" Questions

7. **Analyze Characters** Why do you think Mulan refused the honors and gold that the Emperor offered her?

8. **Make Inferences** Why do you think Mulan changed into one of her favorite dresses when she returned home?

"On Your Own" Questions

9. **Describe Character** What three words would you use to describe Mulan? Why did you choose these words?
10. **Understand Genre Features** Why do you think people still tell legends about Mulan?
11. **Compare Oral Traditions** What other legends or ballads do you know? What regions or cultures are they from? Compare them to "The Ballad of Mulan."

Activity Book   Student
p. 122   CD-ROM

Build Reading Fluency

Repeating Reading

Repeated reading helps increase your reading rate and builds confidence. Each time you reread you improve your reading fluency.

1. Turn to page 234.
2. Your teacher or partner will time you for six minutes.
3. With a partner, take turns reading each paragraph aloud.
4. Stop after six minutes.

238   Unit 4   Heroes

MULTI-LEVEL OPTIONS *Elements of Literature*

Newcomer Ask students to fold a page in half vertically. Have them draw the main character on one half of the paper and the minor ones on the other half. One by one, point to each of the characters. Have volunteers act out something that character did in the story.

Beginning Prepare students to make their charts. Write each of the following on separate cards: *Mulan, Emperor, mother, father, brother, sister, comrades.* Ask volunteers to select one of the cards and say *main character* or *minor character.* Have students act out or use short phrases to describe something the character did.

Intermediate Ask students to identify the character traits of the main and minor characters. Tell them to use the events they have cited in their charts as clues to the traits of the characters. Have students add a third column to their charts, headed *Traits,* where they can list these qualities.

Advanced After students have created their charts, tell them to complete a chart for a reading selection in a previous unit, such as "Sadako and the Thousand Paper Cranes." Ask them to compare and contrast the number and involvement of the minor characters.

Listen, Speak, Interact

Develop a Character

You learned earlier that characters in legends are often based on real people. Many of these real people did something great or had great qualities.

1. Work with a partner to think of a new character for a legend. Base your character on a real person. This real person can be someone who lived long ago or someone who is alive today.

2. Discuss what your character did and his or her important qualities—honesty and strength, for example.

3. Write down your ideas on a piece of paper. Then draw a picture of your character or create a song about your character.

4. Tell or sing your legend for the class.

Elements of Literature

Determine Main and Minor Characters

The **main character** is the most important character in a story. Most of a story is about what the main character feels and does.

Minor characters are less important characters. They often speak with the main character and take part in some events in the story.

1. In your Reading Log, complete a chart like the one shown.

2. Write the names of the main character and three minor characters.

3. Describe one event for each character.

Character	Event
Main Character	
Minor Character: The Emperor	He sends a troop to help Mulan return home.
Minor Character	
Minor Character	

Reading Log   Activity Book p. 123   Student CD-ROM

Content Connection
The Arts

Point out that different writers and artists can tell the same story with their own special touch. Borrow a film or a different print version of the story of Mulan from the public library. Show or read part of it to students. Have them discuss whether the same main and minor characters are present and whether they are portrayed as they were in "The Ballad of Mulan."

Learning Styles
Natural

Explain that many early American legends were about people who overcame dangers of nature as they settled the West. Share some examples of heroic characters, such as John Henry, Johnny Appleseed, and Davy Crockett. Suggest that some students may want to create modern legends about heroes who work in nature, such as forest rangers or environmentalists.

Listen, Speak, Interact

Develop a Character

1. **Determine purpose for listening** *Ask: Why are you listening to your classmates' presentations? What is the purpose—to gain information, to solve a problem, or to enjoy and appreciate?*

2. **Recognize character traits** Have students work in small groups to create their new character and his/her traits. Students can each draw a picture of the character doing something that shows a particular trait. For example, a superhero shows his strength by carrying five people from a burning house. Have volunteers explain their characters to the class.

3. **Newcomers** Help students think of jobs that often require heroic acts, like a firefighter, a police officer, or an EMT. Have them draw people doing one of those jobs. Help them write key words for their drawings.

Elements of Literature

Determine Main and Minor Characters

1. **Identify minor characters** Have students skim the story and make a list on the board of all the minor characters.

2. **Multi-level options** See MULTI-LEVEL OPTIONS on p. 238.

Answers

Possible answers: Main character: Mulan—went to war in place of her father. Minor characters: Sister—She beautified herself for Mulan's return. Brother—He sharpened his knife to prepare for the feast. Emperor—He praised Mulan for her bravery.

✓ ASSESS

Have students write two sentences describing one of the characters from the legend.

Word Study

Use the Suffix -ly to Form Adverbs

1. **Review suffixes** Remind students that they studied the suffix -ful. Have them find a word with -ful in paragraph 2. (sorrowful)
2. **Use the suffix -ly** Write on the board: happy, careful, week. Have students add -ly and give definitions.
3. **Use a resource to find correct spelling** Remind students that spelling may change when adding suffixes. Have students use a resource to find the correct spelling.
4. **Use adverbs for vivid and precise writing** Model vivid and precise writing by using adverbs.

Answers
softly—soft (root word), in a soft manner; quietly—quiet (root word), in a quiet manner

Grammar Focus

Use Prepositional Phrases

Clarify and define Write on the board: We are in the classroom. Have students identify the subject, verb, and prepositional phrase.

Answers
paragraph 7: to the markets, in Father's place; 15: at the camp; 23: in town, to the village gate; 24: at home, for the feast.

ASSESS

Say: Write two sentences using prepositional phrases.

Word Study

Use the Suffix -ly to Form Adverbs

A **suffix** is a group of letters that is added to the end of a word. A suffix changes the meaning of a word.

The suffix -ly means "in a certain manner." The word *suddenly* in paragraph 2 of the selection means "in a sudden, or unexpected, manner." *Suddenly* is an adverb. Adverbs usually tell how, when, or where something happens.

1. In your Personal Dictionary, complete a chart like the one here.
2. Write the root word and the suffix for each -ly word. Then write what you think each -ly word means.
3. Use a dictionary to check your definitions.

Root Word	Suffix	-ly Word	Definition
sudden +	-ly ⇒	suddenly	in a sudden manner
		softly	
		quietly	

4. Write a sentence of your own for each -ly word in the chart. Be sure to spell the root words and suffix correctly.

Personal Dictionary   The Heinle Newbury House Dictionary   Activity Book p. 124   Student CD-ROM

Grammar Focus

Use Prepositional Phrases

Prepositions are words like *in, at, on, over, by, under, through, over, with.* A **prepositional phrase** is a group of words that starts with a preposition and contains a noun or a pronoun as its object. Look at these prepositional phrases. The prepositions are in bold type, and the objects are underlined.

in a <u>village</u>   **at** her <u>loom</u>

Prepositional phrases can answer the questions "Where?" or "When?" Writers often use them to describe settings.

1. Find the prepositional phrases in paragraphs 7, 15, 23, and 24. Write them on a piece of paper. Circle the prepositions and underline the objects.
2. Share your work with a partner.
3. Together, write three prepositional phrases that describe the setting of your classroom, for example: "There is a map on the wall."

Activity Book pp. 125–126   Student Handbook   Student CD-ROM

240   Unit 4   Heroes

MULTI-LEVEL OPTIONS *From Reading to Writing*

Newcomer Help students identify a value that is important to them, such as treating everyone with kindness. *Say: Draw a hero for your legend. Draw three pictures showing how the hero did something great.* Provide time for sharing with partners.

Beginning Create a class role-play featuring a person who students learned about in a social studies unit. Help them identify a value important to that person. Work with students to create a role-play showing an event related to the value they identified. Help them decide how to exaggerate the hero's actions.

Intermediate Have students use books, encyclopedias, and online sources to learn about their heroes before writing their legends. Suggest that they make two-column charts headed *Facts* and *Exaggerations* listing real life facts about their heroes and ideas for exaggerating these facts in their legends.

Advanced Point out that careful development of the hero is a key to writing an effective legend. *Say: Readers will learn about the hero of your legend through what he or she says, does, thinks, and feels. Minor characters' actions toward the main character also help readers know the main character.*

From Reading to Writing

Write a Legend

"The Ballad of Mulan" teaches several important values. One of them is that people should love and care for their parents.

Write a short legend that teaches a value that is important to you. Base your legend on a real person from history who did something great. Parts of your legend may be made up.

1. Think of a hero from history who did something great. This hero will be your main character.

2. Decide what value this hero's actions show, such as honesty or working hard to reach a goal. You can exaggerate the hero's actions.

3. Write your legend with a clear beginning, a middle, and an end. Use transition words like *then*, *next*, *soon*, and *finally* to organize your ideas.

4. Use prepositional phrases to make your writing clear.

Activity Book
p. 127

Student
Handbook

Across Content Areas

Use Map Features to Read a Map

Maps often include features to help you read them. One of these features is a **compass rose,** which shows **direction.** Another feature is a chart to show **distance** (how far apart things are). Maps may also include charts that explain map **symbols.** Map symbols, such as stars and lines, may stand for capital cities and rivers.

Use the map of China to answer the questions.

1. What is the capital city of China?
2. Name the rivers shown on the map.
3. About how many miles is the city of Lanzhou from the city of Beijing?

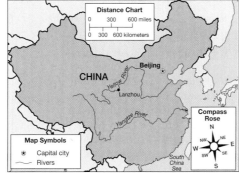

Distance Chart
0   300   600 miles
0   300   600 kilometers

CHINA

Beijing

Lanzhou

Yellow River

Yangtze River

Compass Rose
N
NW   NE
W   E
SW   SE
S

Map Symbols
 Capital city
~ Rivers

South China Sea

Activity Book
p. 128

Chapter 1   The Ballad of Mulan   **241**

Reteach and Reassess

Text Structure Read a short legend aloud. Have students fill out a chart like the one at the top of p. 232 to identify the features of the legend.

Reading Strategy Have students predict the kinds of activities they will do in Chapter 2 based on the activities they have done in previous units. (vocabulary, reading, writing)

Elements of Literature Have students list or draw the main and minor characters in the legends they wrote in this unit.

Reassess Have students recall what happened at the end of the selection they read. Ask them to write or draw a prediction of what Mulan would likely do next. Tell students to be sure their predictions take into account the kind of person Mulan is.

From Reading to Writing

Write a Legend

1. **Brainstorm** Brainstorm with students a list of famous people they could write about and why they are heroic. Have the class choose one person to write about. Discuss what value his/her actions showed.

2. **Use adverbs to make writing vivid and precise** Model the use of adverbs to make writing vivid and precise. Add adverbs to student sentences and write them on the board.

3. **Story round robin** Going around the room, compose a story orally with each person adding a sentence. Start the story with *Once upon a time . . .* The purpose is to get ideas and a story line.

4. **Collaborative writing** Have students work in pairs or small groups to write their legends. When they are finished, they should proofread and illustrate their stories and display them in the room.

5. **Multi-level options** See MULTI-LEVEL OPTIONS on p. 240.

Across Content Areas: Social Studies

Use Map Features to Read a Map

Locate information on a map *Ask: What information can we get from this map?* (compass directions, rivers, distances, cities, capital city, the ocean)

Answers
1. Beijing 2. Yangtze, Yellow 3. about 700 miles

 **ASSESS**

Have students list features of a legend.

CHAPTER 2

Into the Reading

Roberto Clemente

a biography
on the
World Wide Web

Chapter Materials

Activity Book: *pp. 129–136*
Audio: *Unit 4, Chapter 2; CD 2, Track 2*
Student Handbook
Student CD-ROM: *Unit 4, Chapter 2*
Teacher Resource Book: *Lesson Plan, Teacher Resources, Reading Summary, Activity Book Answer Key*
Teacher Resource CD-ROM
Assessment Program: *Quiz, pp. 63–64; Teacher and Student Resources, pp. 115–144*
Assessment CD-ROM
Transparencies
The Heinle Newbury House Dictionary/CD-ROM
Web site: http://visions.heinle.com

Objectives

Preview Have a student read the objectives. *Ask: Have you ever read a biography, the true story of someone's life? Who was it about?*

Use Prior Knowledge

Discuss Sports Heroes

1. **Clarify terms** Write on the board: *Sports star; sports hero.* **Ask:** *What is the difference between a sports star and a sports hero? A sports star is a talented player. A sports hero is a sports star who has done something brave or helpful.*
2. **Compare lists** Have a volunteer write the heroes' names on the board. Decide who is the most popular.

Objectives

Reading Use chronological order to recall and locate information in a biography.

Listening and Speaking Discuss learning from a person's example.

Grammar Identify prepositional phrases of time.

Writing Write a biography.

Content Science: Learn about earthquakes.

Use Prior Knowledge

Discuss Sports Heroes

Sports heroes are great athletes. What do you know about sports heroes?

1. With a partner, make a chart like the one here.
2. List the names of two or three sports heroes that you know about.
3. List what you know about each sports hero. For example, list the sports hero's team, what sport the person plays, or what awards the person has won.
4. Compare your list with other groups' lists. Which sports heroes are listed most often?

Sports Heroes	Facts I Know
Michael Jordan	He used to play basketball for the Chicago Bulls.

MULTI-LEVEL OPTIONS *Build Vocabulary*

Newcomer Explore students' prior knowledge of baseball vocabulary. Have each student draw at least one person, object, and action related to the sport. Help students label these illustrations. Save their work to refer to as you explain baseball concepts during the reading of the biography.

Beginning Relate the vocabulary for this selection to sports teams in the school or community. For example, you might help students see that the World Series is like a championship game the students play in intramural sports or a community recreation program.

Intermediate Have students work in groups. Be sure each group has at least one student who is knowledgeable about baseball. Have the groups work together to compose sentences about their city's team (or the team closest to their city) and players on that team. Tell them to use the vocabulary words in their sentences.

Advanced Have pairs of students look through the sports page of a newspaper to see how many of the vocabulary terms they can find in the articles.

Build Background

Puerto Rico

Puerto Rico is an island in the Caribbean Sea, southeast of Florida. Puerto Rico is part of the United States, but it is not a state. It is a commonwealth. Puerto Ricans are United States citizens.

Content Connection

There are many islands in the Caribbean. Most are independent countries, like Haiti, The Dominican Republic, Cuba, and Antigua. Some of the languages spoken are Spanish, French, Dutch, and Creole.

This means that they are free to move to and from the United States. Spanish is the main language of Puerto Rico.

Build Vocabulary

Recognize Baseball Terms

"Roberto Clemente" includes many baseball terms that may be unfamiliar to you.

1. Use this chart as you read the selection.
2. Copy the words and meanings that interest you in your Personal Dictionary.

Personal Dictionary

The Heinle Newbury House Dictionary

Activity Book p. 129

Student CD-ROM

Baseball Terms	
Term	**Meaning**
Major League Baseball	professional baseball in the United States
National League	a group of teams that are part of Major League Baseball
American League	a group of teams that are part of Major League Baseball
World Series	games played between the best National League and American League teams
MVP	Most Valuable Player; an award

Cultural Connection

Build Vocabulary Ask students to identify their favorite sports team here or in another country. Have them teach the class a few sports-related words from another language.

Learning Styles
Linguistic

Build Background Ask any students who have visited or lived in Puerto Rico to share descriptions of its climate, land, plants, and festivals. If none of your students is from there, use books to provide additional background. Tell students that Puerto Rico means *rich port* in Spanish. Ask each student to contribute a picture or a word to a class collage that shows why Puerto Rico can be described as a rich port. Suggest that students use colors that they think communicate the feeling of the island.

Build Background

Puerto Rico

Teacher Resource Book: *Web, p. 37*

1. **Use prior knowledge** Draw a web on the board and have students tell you facts they know about Puerto Rico. Then have them see what new information they can learn from the text.
2. **Provide background information** *Say: Puerto Rico was claimed by Christopher Columbus in 1493. It was a Spanish possession until the U.S. gained control in 1898. It became a commonwealth on July 25, 1952.*
3. **Content Connection** Point out that the language spoken in a region often reflects its history. Explain that Spanish, French, and Dutch are spoken in many islands of the Caribbean because Spain, France, and Holland once ruled over those regions. *Ask: Why do we speak English in America?* (because the English once ruled over this region)

Build Vocabulary

Teacher Resource Book: *Personal Dictionary, p. 63*

Recognize Baseball Terms

1. **Use prior knowledge** *Ask: What do you know about baseball? What special terms do you know?* Have volunteers go to the board to write words they know. Invite students to explain or demonstrate meanings.
2. **Reading selection vocabulary** You may want to introduce the glossed words in the reading selection before students begin reading. Key words: *heritage, tragic, determined, unfortunately.* Instruct students to write the words with correct spelling and their definitions in their Personal Dictionaries. Have them pronounce each word and divide it into syllables.
3. **Multi-level options** See MULTI-LEVEL OPTIONS on p. 242.

ASSESS

Say: Write three things you know about Puerto Rico.

Text Structure

Biography

1. **Recognize features** Bring in some biographies for students to look at. Have them look at the table of contents and see if dates or special events are listed. Remind them that a biography is based on a true story.
2. **Multi-level options** See MULTI-LEVEL OPTIONS below.

Reading Strategy

Use Chronological Order to Recall and Locate Information

Use chronological order *Say: Think about the order of events in "Mulan." First, Mulan heard the news of war. What did she do next? And then? And after that? If we remember things in chronological order, it is easier to remember what happened.*

Answers

To be completed after students have read the text.
1955—joined the Pittsburgh Pirates; 1964—married Vera Cristina Zabola in Puerto Rico; Dec. 31, 1972—died in a plane crash

 **ASSESS**

Have students write a chronology of four events using *first, next,* and *then.*

Text Structure

Biography

"Roberto Clemente" is a **biography.** A biography is the true story of someone's life written by another person.

As you read, look for the features of a biography listed in the chart. Think about the events in Roberto Clemente's life. Do you admire what he did?

Biography	
Dates	important dates in the person's life
Events	important things that happened in the person's life
Other People	people who were important in the person's life
Order of Events	usually begins with events that happened early in the person's life; usually ends with events that happened at the end of the person's life

Student CD-ROM

Reading Strategy

Use Chronological Order to Recall and Locate Information

Chronological order is the order in which events happen. Knowing when an event happened can help you find it in a text. It can also help you remember what you have read.

1. As you read "Roberto Clemente," take notes on important events and dates. Look for key words such as *first, next, then,* and *today* that help you keep track of the chronology.
2. When you finish the selection, use your notes to complete a chart like the one here. Write the events in the order in which they happened. Write the date next to the event if a date is given.

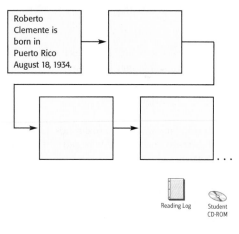

Reading Log   Student CD-ROM

244   Unit 4   Heroes

Roberto Clemente

a biography on the
World Wide Web

245

Reading Selection Materials

Audio: *Unit 4, Chapter 2; CD 2, Track 2*
Teacher Resource Book: *Reading Summary,*
  pp. 97–98
Transparencies: #10, *Reading Summary*

Suggestions for Using
Reading Summary

- Introduce new vocabulary or cognates.
- Cut the summary into strips, or jumble the sentences on an overhead transparency. Students put the sentences in order.
- Practice the reading strategy.
- Students read aloud or with a partner.
- Students paraphrase the summary.
- Students do a cloze activity.
- Students create a visual or graphic organizer, such as a timeline or storyboard, to illustrate the summary.
- Students paraphrase the summary.

Preview the Selection

1. **Interpret the image** Have students look at the photo. *Ask: How old do you think Clemente is in this photo? Close your eyes for a minute, and imagine you are in this stadium. What sounds do you hear?* (the crowd, the bat hitting the ball, the referee yelling)
2. **Connect to theme** Remind students that the unit theme is *heroes*. *Ask: How can a baseball player become a hero? What could a baseball player do that is heroic? What have other sports stars done that you think is heroic?*

 Content Connection
Math

Tell students that Roberto Clemente had a great batting average. Explain that a batting average is figured by dividing the number of hits a player gets by the *at-bats* (number of time he/she tried). Clemente hit the ball 3000 times. He was at bat 9454 times. Have students figure out his batting average. (.317) Have them find information about other batters or use made-up data to practice figuring out batting averages.

Learning Styles
Kinesthetic

Tell students that this biography is about a baseball player. Explain that he was a *batter* and a *fielder*. Ask for other baseball positions (pitcher, catcher, outfielder). Have students who have played baseball act out the positions in slow motion. Invite all the students to imitate the model they have seen.

Read the Selection

1. **Listen for information** *Say: Listen to the text, and write down the dates you hear.* With books closed, have students listen as you play the audio. Have students tell you the dates and any other information they heard.
2. **Paired reading** Have students take turns reading the text aloud with a partner.
3. **Use chronology** Have students copy the timeline from p. 244 and fill in the second and third boxes.
4. **Relate to personal experience** Ask students about current players they know. *Ask: Who played in the World Series last year? Do you know which team was from the National League? Which players are often Most Valuable Players (MVPs) in games?*

Sample Answer to Guide Question
He joined the Pittsburgh Pirates.

See Teacher Edition pp. 434–436 for a list of English-Spanish cognates in the reading selection.

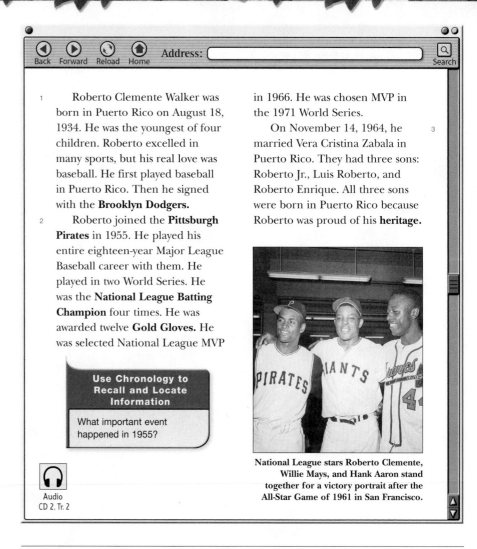

Address:

1 Roberto Clemente Walker was born in Puerto Rico on August 18, 1934. He was the youngest of four children. Roberto excelled in many sports, but his real love was baseball. He first played baseball in Puerto Rico. Then he signed with the **Brooklyn Dodgers.**

2 Roberto joined the **Pittsburgh Pirates** in 1955. He played his entire eighteen-year Major League Baseball career with them. He played in two World Series. He was the **National League Batting Champion** four times. He was awarded twelve **Gold Gloves.** He was selected National League MVP in 1966. He was chosen MVP in the 1971 World Series.

3 On November 14, 1964, he married Vera Cristina Zabala in Puerto Rico. They had three sons: Roberto Jr., Luis Roberto, and Roberto Enrique. All three sons were born in Puerto Rico because Roberto was proud of his **heritage.**

> **Use Chronology to Recall and Locate Information**
>
> What important event happened in 1955?

Audio
CD 2. Tr. 2

National League stars Roberto Clemente, Willie Mays, and Hank Aaron stand together for a victory portrait after the All-Star Game of 1961 in San Francisco.

Brooklyn Dodgers a professional baseball team that now plays in Los Angeles
Pittsburgh Pirates a professional baseball team
National League Batting Champion the National League player who hits the most balls in a season

Gold Glove an award given to the best players who play in the field and catch the ball
heritage beliefs, history, and traditions

246 Unit 4 Heroes

MULTI-LEVEL OPTIONS *Read the Selection*

Newcomer Play the audio. Use gestures and facial expressions to reinforce meaning. *Ask: Was Roberto Clemente from Puerto Rico?* (yes) *Was he a great football player?* (no) *Did he win many awards?* (yes) *Did he die trying to help others?* (yes)

Beginning Read aloud the selection. *Ask: Where was Roberto Clemente born?* (Puerto Rico) *What was his favorite sport?* (baseball) *What is one award he won?* (Gold Glove) *What was he trying to do when he died in a plane crash?* (help people)

Intermediate Have students do a partner read aloud. *Ask: How did Roberto Clemente win so many awards?* (He was an excellent player.) *How did he show his feelings about Puerto Rico?* (He made sure his sons were born there so that they would be Puerto Rican, too.) *How did he die?* (He was on his way to help earthquake victims, and his plane crashed.)

Advanced Have students read silently. *Ask: How do you think being famous affected Clemente? Explain.* (It did not make him conceited. He used his fame to help others, such as the earthquake victims he was trying to help when he died.) *What does paragraph 6 mean?* (that his family is probably helping others as he did)

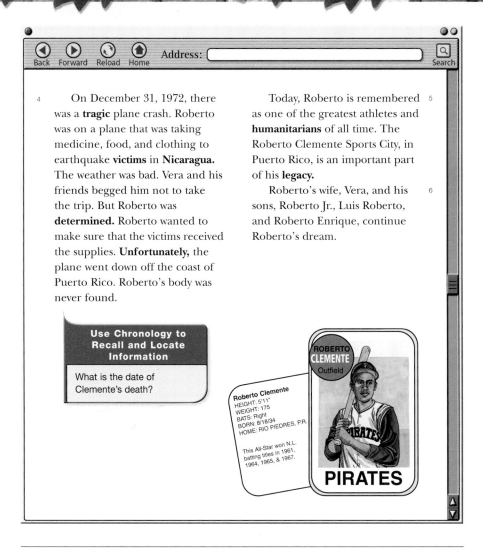

On December 31, 1972, there was a **tragic** plane crash. Roberto was on a plane that was taking medicine, food, and clothing to earthquake **victims** in **Nicaragua.** The weather was bad. Vera and his friends begged him not to take the trip. But Roberto was **determined.** Roberto wanted to make sure that the victims received the supplies. **Unfortunately,** the plane went down off the coast of Puerto Rico. Roberto's body was never found.

Today, Roberto is remembered as one of the greatest athletes and **humanitarians** of all time. The Roberto Clemente Sports City, in Puerto Rico, is an important part of his **legacy.**

Roberto's wife, Vera, and his sons, Roberto Jr., Luis Roberto, and Roberto Enrique, continue Roberto's dream.

Use Chronology to Recall and Locate Information

What is the date of Clemente's death?

ROBERTO CLEMENTE Outfield

Roberto Clemente
HEIGHT: 5'11"
WEIGHT: 175
BATS: Right
BORN: 8/18/34
HOME: RIO PIEDRES, P.R.

This All-Star won N.L. batting titles in 1961, 1964, 1965, & 1967.

PIRATES

---

tragic very sad, having to do with a disaster
victims people who have been harmed or hurt
Nicaragua a country in Central America
determined really wanted to (do something)

unfortunately sadly
humanitarians people who do good for others
legacy something passed on to another generation

Chapter 2 Roberto Clemente **247**

 Spelling

Abbreviations

Say: We have learned in other units that words for places and measurements can be shortened into abbreviations. This biography has some abbreviations, too. Find the short way to write Most Valuable Player *in paragraph 2.* (MVP) *Most abbreviations have periods, but some do not.*

Apply *Say: Find an abbreviation for* junior *in paragraph 3.* (Jr.)

Evaluate Your Reading Strategy

Use Chronological Order to Recall and Locate Information *Say: You have practiced an important reading strategy. Now you can decide how well you have done. Does this statement describe how you read?*

When I read, I look for words such as *first* or *next* to help me determine chronological order. This helps me to recall what happened. It also helps me locate information in a reading.

Read the Selection

1. **Reciprocal reading** Have volunteers read the page aloud. On the board, write: *Who, What, Where, When, How, Why.* Have volunteers use these words to ask the class questions about information on the page.

2. **Use text features** Direct students to the text. *Ask: Is this information from a book or a magazine?* (neither, from the Internet) *How do you know?* (the "toolbar" at the top of the page) *Do you go online to find information for school? Give an example.*

3. **Use chronology** Have students finish their timelines.

4. **Relate to personal experience** *Say: Roberto Clemente was helping earthquake victims. Have any of you ever been in an earthquake? An earthquake is a natural disaster. What other natural disasters are there?* (tornado, fire, flood, blizzard, hurricane) *What do people do to help victims? Have you ever volunteered for something like this?*

5. **Multi-level options** See MULTI-LEVEL OPTIONS on p. 246.

Sample Answer to Guide Question
December 31, 1972

Across Selections

Teacher Resource Book: *Two-Column Chart, p. 44*

Have students work in groups to make a two-column chart. *Say: Mulan and Roberto Clemente are different kinds of heroes. List all the differences you can.* (a legend/a real person; lived in different times and were different genders; Mulan fought in a war./Clemente was a baseball star and a humanitarian.) Have students share their lists with another group.

Spelling, Punctuation, Capitalization

After the Reading Comprehension section, students will practice spelling, punctuation, and capitalization in the Activity Book.

Beyond the Reading

Reading Comprehension

Question-Answer Relationships

Sample Answers

1. 12
2. He was going to Nicaragua.
3. the Brooklyn Dodgers
4. National League Batting Champion, Gold Glove, National League Most Valuable Player, World Series Most Valuable Player
5. He played professional baseball for 18 years and won many awards.
6. He did many good things for people who needed help.
7. after
8. athletic, determined, caring
9. The weather was bad, and they were afraid the plane might crash.
10. Yes. Many people admire sports stars and want to be like them. It's important for them to be a good model to people. One way to be a good model is by helping people in need.

Build Reading Fluency

Reading Chunks of Words

Explain that reading chunks of underlined words helps improve reading fluency. Ask students to listen as you model reading chunks before they practice with a partner.

Reading Comprehension

Question-Answer Relationships (QAR)

"Right There" Questions

1. **Recall Facts** How many Gold Gloves did Clemente win?
2. **Recall Facts** Where was Clemente going when his plane crashed?

"Think and Search" Questions

3. **Understand Sequence of Events** Which U.S. baseball team did Clemente join first?
4. **Identify** Which awards did Clemente receive for his skills in baseball?
5. **Recognize Character Traits** Why is Clemente thought of as a great athlete?
6. **Recognize Character Traits** Why is Clemente thought of as a great humanitarian?

7. **Use Chronology to Recall Information** Did Clemente get married before or after joining the Pittsburgh Pirates? Use your knowledge of the chronology to find the answer.

"Author and You" Questions

8. **Describe** What three words would you use to describe Clemente?
9. **Draw Conclusions** Why do you think Clemente's wife and friends did not want him to fly to Nicaragua?

"On Your Own" Question

10. **Support Opinions** Do you think that it is important for sports stars to help people in need? Explain your answer.

Activity Book
p. 130

Build Reading Fluency

Reading Chunks of Words

Reading chunks or phrases of words is an important characteristic of fluent readers. It helps you stop reading word by word.

1. With a partner, take turns reading aloud the underlined chunks of words.
2. Read aloud two times each.

> On December 31, 1972, there was a tragic plane crash. Roberto was on a plane that was taking medicine, food, and clothing to earthquake victims in Nicaragua. The weather was bad. Vera and his friends begged him not to take the trip. But Roberto was determined.

248 Unit 4 Heroes

MULTI-LEVEL OPTIONS *Elements of Literature*

Newcomer Write the following on each of four softballs: *I, he, she, they.* Gently toss one of the balls to a student. Have him or her say a short sentence starting with the word on the ball while pointing to the subject of the sentence. (*Examples:* Pointing to oneself, *I am standing.* Pointing to a boy, *He is sitting.*)

Beginning Mime hitting a baseball with a bat. Then point to yourself. *Say: I hit the ball.* Point to a student and have her mime hitting a ball. *Say: She hit the ball.* Continue the same procedure with sentences about other actions you and students act out. Ask students to chime in on the pronouns.

Intermediate Have students work in pairs. Ask students to write a few sentences about themselves in the first person. Have them exchange papers and rewrite the sentences in the third person.

Advanced Introduce the concept of autobiographies. Have students look up the meaning of this word if they do not know it. *Ask: From what point of view would an autobiography be written?* (first-person) *How might the facts and opinions in an autobiography differ from those in a biography?*

Listen, Speak, Interact

Discuss Learning from a Person's Example

When you learn from a person's example, you try to act like that person.

1. With a small group, list reasons why Roberto Clemente is a hero. Ask these questions:
   a. Which of his actions make him a sports hero?
   b. Which other actions, besides his sports skills, make him a hero?

2. Discuss how people could learn from Clemente's example. List your answers to the following questions:
   a. Which of his actions do you think people should imitate (copy)?
   b. Why do you think so?
   c. What can people do to help others in need?

3. Present your answers to the class.

Elements of Literature

Recognize Third-Person Point of View

Point of view is the relationship of a narrator to a story. Biographies are usually told from the **third-person point of view.** This means that the writer describes the actions and feelings of other people, not his or her own actions and feelings.

Look back at the following readings. Are they told from first-person or third-person point of view? Talk about your ideas with a partner.

1. "Coyote," page 18
2. "Thanksgiving," page 30
3. "Sadako and the Thousand Paper Cranes," page 58
4. "Gonzalo," page 122

Point of View		
	First Person	**Third Person**
Who Is the Narrator?	someone in the story	someone not in the story
Pronouns Used	I, me, we, us	he, him, she, her, it, they, them
What the Narrator Describes	his or her own actions and feelings	other people's actions and feelings
Examples	I played baseball.	He played in two World Series.

Activity Book
p. 131

Student
CD-ROM

Chapter 2 Roberto Clemente **249**

Content Connection
The Arts

Tell students that songs may also be written from a first- or third-person point of view. Ask students to sing some songs they know. Have students tell the point of view of each. Ask them to identify pronouns that provided clues to the point of view of the songs.

Learning Styles
Interpersonal

Suggest that people are thought of as heroes not just for *what* they do but also because of *why* they do these things. Ask students to work in pairs to find hints in the biography, as well as using their own prior knowledge, to discuss possible reasons for Roberto Clemente's actions.

Listen, Speak, Interact

Discuss Learning from a Person's Example

1. **Discuss baseball terms** *Say: Clemente won the Most Valuable Player Award many times. What makes a person an MVP? Is it their individual performance? Is it their teamwork? What about the Gold Glove Award? Players use their gloves to catch balls. Who earns a Gold Glove Award?* (a good field catcher; someone who makes important plays)

2. **Newcomers** Work with these students to reread paragraph 4. Help them choose and illustrate one event in the paragraph that shows why Clemente was a hero.

Answers
Possible answers:
1. **a.** excellent batting, playing on the field, a team player; **b.** He was proud of his heritage, and he used his influence to help others.
2. **a.** I think people should follow his example of helping others.

Elements of Literature

Recognize Third-Person Point of View

1. **Discuss point of view** Have students turn to the table of contents for Unit 1 (p. 2). For each selection have students discuss whether it is the first-person or third-person point of view. They may need to look at the text to refresh their memories.

2. **Multi-level options** See MULTI-LEVEL OPTIONS on p. 248.

✓ ASSESS

Have students identify the point of view in "Gonzalo" (p. 121) (first-person) and "The Peach Boy" (p. 179) (third-person).

Word Study

Understand the Prefix *un-*

Form words using the prefix *un-* Write on the board: *able, attractive, clear, comfortable, healthy.* Have students add the prefix *un-* and give the new meanings. Have students make up sentences with the words.

Answers
unsafe—dangerous; uncooked—raw; unhappy—sad

Grammar Focus

Identify Prepositional Phrases of Time

Use prepositions with time Write on the board: *We start the school week _____ Monday. We don't go to school _____ July. We celebrate Thanksgiving _____ the 4ᵗʰ Thursday of November.* Have students complete the sentences. *Ask: What is the rule for using* on *or* in *with time expressions?* (Use *on* with day of the week and date. Use *in* with the year or the month.)

Answers
paragraph 2: in 1955; in 1966; paragraph 3: on November 14, 1964; paragraph 4: on December 31, 1972

 **ASSESS**

Have students form small groups and brainstorm as many words as they can that begin with the prefix *un-*.

Word Study

Understand the Prefix *un-*

A **prefix** is a group of letters that is added to the beginning of a word. A prefix changes the meaning of a word.

> Unfortunately, the plane went down off the coast of Puerto Rico.

The word *unfortunately* has the prefix *un-*. In this word, *un-* means "not." This prefix is added to the word *fortunately*, which means "happily." ***Un**fortunately* means "not happily," or "sadly."

1. Copy the chart in your Personal Dictionary.

New Word	Meaning
unsafe	
uncooked	
unhappy	

2. Write these words in the correct box.

raw	sad	dangerous

3. Write a sentence for each new word. Be sure to spell the prefix correctly.

Personal Dictionary   The Heinle Newbury House Dictionary   Activity Book p. 132   Student CD-ROM

Grammar Focus

Identify Prepositional Phrases of Time

Some prepositional phrases answer the question "When?"

> I was born on January 1, 1992.

The prepositional phrase *on January 1, 1992* tells *when* I was born.

Look at the chart to see how the author uses prepositions to show time.

1. Find prepositional phrases of time in paragraphs 2–4 of the selection.
2. Write two original sentences that have these prepositions.

Activity Book pp. 133–134   Student Handbook   Student CD-ROM

Prepositional Phrases of Time		
	When to Use	**Example**
on	when describing an event on a day of the week or a date that includes a month, day, and year	The game was <u>on</u> Saturday. Clemente was born <u>on</u> August 18, 1934.
in	when describing an event that happened in a certain year or month	Roberto joined the Pittsburgh Pirates <u>in</u> 1955. He got married <u>in</u> November.

MULTI-LEVEL OPTIONS *From Reading to Writing*

Newcomer Show a picture from a book or Web site of a coat of arms. *Say: This is a coat of arms. It shows important things about a family or person.* Have students create a coat of arms to show the important things about the life of the subject they have chosen.

Beginning Have students create a timeline to display the life events of their subject. Ask them to record important dates and to write words and phrases under each to show what happened to the person at those times.

Intermediate Have students read their biographies slowly to peer responders. Tell responders to listen carefully to see if they can follow the time order. Have responders recommend places where transition words or prepositional phrases might make the writing clearer.

Advanced Suggest that students add quotes by the subject (or by others about the subject) to add interest to their biographies. Remind them to clearly identify the speaker and use quotation marks properly.

From Reading to Writing

Write a Biography

Write a biography of someone you know, such as a friend or family member. Write three to five paragraphs.

1. Ask the person these questions to write your biography.
   a. When were you born? Where were you born?
   b. Name two important events that happened in your life. When did each of these events happen?
   c. Name two things that you like to do today.
2. Use the dates to organize events in the order that they happened. Use prepositional phrases of time.
3. Write in the third-person point of view.
4. Use possessive nouns when telling about something the person owns.

Activity Book
p. 135

Student
Handbook

Across Content Areas

Learn About Earthquakes

Earthquakes happen when huge rocks move or break deep inside Earth. During an earthquake, the ground shakes. This shaking is caused by **seismic waves.** Seismic waves are the energy that is released from the breaking of rocks.

A scientist who studies earthquakes is called a **seismologist.** Seismologists use a **seismograph**—a machine that notes how much the ground moves during an earthquake. A number based on a scale called the **Richter Scale** tells how strong an earthquake is.

1. On a piece of paper, write *T* if you think a statement is true. Write *F* if you think a statement is false.
   a. To learn about earthquakes, you could speak with a seismologist.

Seismograph

   b. Seismographs cause earthquakes.
   c. Seismic waves form before rocks break inside Earth.
2. Write a record of three earthquakes that have happened. Use references to research the information. Organize your record to show dates and location. Revise your record for spelling.

Activity Book
p. 136

Chapter 2 Roberto Clemente **251**

Reteach and Reassess

Text Structure Have students make charts like the one on the top of p. 244 for the biographies they wrote.

Reading Strategy Have students recall several events from the school year so far. Ask them to use a diagram like the one on p. 244 to organize drawings or descriptions of the events in time order.

Elements of Literature Read a one-paragraph biography from the students' Social Studies curriculum. Have them identify and explain the point of view.

Reassess Write several first-person sentences about yourself on the board. Have students use the ideas to write a short third-person paragraph about you.

From Reading to Writing

Write a Biography

1. **Model interviewing** Ask for a volunteer to be interviewed by the class. As students ask questions, have one student write the answers on the board. Remind students to ask for details about the important events. For example: *Where did it happen? Who else was there? Why was this an important event for you?*
2. **Collaborate on a biography** Use the notes about the student. Write his/her biography as students dictate it. Help students check for errors. Have them write their own biographies. Give them guidelines for giving feedback. Write on the board: *What was the most interesting sentence? What else would you like to learn about this person? What did you like about this biography?*
3. **Multi-level options** See MULTI-LEVEL OPTIONS on p. 250.

Across Content Areas: Science

Learn About Earthquakes

1. **Use prior knowledge** *Ask:* What states sometimes have earthquakes? (California, Washington, Alaska) *What countries have earthquakes?* (Mexico, Nicaragua, Turkey, China, Japan)
2. **Study word roots** *Say:* Graph *is a Greek root meaning* write. *A seismograph "writes" or records an earthquake.* Write these words and have students discuss and look up meanings: *phonograph, photograph, autograph, cardiograph.*

Answers
1. a. T b. F c. F

 **ASSESS**

Have students name two facts that usually are found in a biography.

CHAPTER 3

Into the Reading

Chapter Materials

Activity Book: *pp. 137–144*
Audio: *Unit 4, Chapter 3; CD 2, Tracks 3–4*
Student Handbook
Student CD-ROM: *Unit 4, Chapter 3*
Teacher Resource Book: *Lesson Plan, Teacher
Resources, Reading Summary, Activity Book
Answer Key*
Teacher Resource CD-ROM
Assessment Program: *Quiz, pp. 65–66; Teacher
and Student Resources, pp. 115–144*
Assessment CD-ROM
Transparencies
The Heinle Newbury House Dictionary/CD-ROM
Web site: http://visions.heinle.com

Objectives

Preview Read the objectives. *Ask: Where do
you sometimes hear speeches? What kinds of
people often give speeches?*

Use Prior Knowledge

Discuss Freedom

Connect to personal experience *Say: In some
countries, people do not have the same
freedom to say things in public. For example, in
China, people are sometimes afraid of criticizing
the government in public. How is the freedom to
say what you want important to you?*

Nelson Mandela
an excerpt from a biography
by Jack L. Roberts

The Inaugural
Address,
May 10, 1994

an excerpt from a speech
by Nelson Mandela

Objectives

Reading Draw inferences as you read a
biography and a speech.

Listening and Speaking Create and
present dialogue.

Grammar Recognize commands with *let*.

Writing Write a persuasive speech.

Content Social Studies: Read a timeline.

Use Prior Knowledge

Discuss Freedom

When people have freedom, they are
able to do or say certain things without
being afraid. For example, people in the
United States have freedom of speech—
they can say or write what they want.
What other examples of freedom can
people have?

1. With a partner, complete a web like
the one here on a piece of paper.
2. Brainstorm examples of freedom
that you have. List these in your
web. You may add more circles
if needed.

3. With another pair of students,
discuss what your lives would be like
if someone took your freedom away.

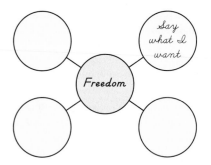

MULTI-LEVEL OPTIONS *Build Vocabulary*

Newcomer *Say: Some words
have more than one meaning.*
Draw on the board a person
running. Write and *say: can run.*
Underline *can.* Draw on the board
a can of food. Write and *say: can
of soup.* Underline *can.* Work
through the words *well* and *rest* in
the same way.

Beginning Have pairs make
two word cards for each of the
following: *can, well,* and *rest.*
Have students draw pictures to
remind them of the meanings.
Instruct pairs to spread out the
cards and take turns doing an
action related to one of the words,
such as opening a can. The
partner then picks up the
matching card.

Intermediate Have students
write two sentences for each
word. Ask them to use a different
meaning of the word in each
sentence. (*Example:* I *can* write a
song. There is only one *can* of
tomatoes left.)

Advanced Tell students to
write one sentence for each word.
Challenge them to use both
meanings within each sentence.
(*Example:* I *can* use a small *can* of
cherries as a topping for my ice
cream.)

Build Background

Apartheid

For many years, the government of South Africa practiced **apartheid.** This kept white people and black people separate from each other. Under apartheid, black South Africans had few freedoms. They could not go to the same schools as white South Africans. They could not live in the same neighborhoods. They were not allowed to vote or take part in government.

Content Connection
The country of South Africa is located at the southern tip of Africa.

Nelson Mandela worked for many years to end apartheid. Apartheid finally ended in 1991. In 1994, all people in South Africa were able to vote for the president of the country. They chose Nelson Mandela as their president.

Build Vocabulary

Infer Meanings of Homonyms

Homonyms are words that sound the same and are often spelled the same, but have different meanings. Look at these homonyms:

can: meaning "be able to"

can: meaning "a metal container for food"

Use context clues in each sentence to choose the correct definition of each word. Write the word and definition in your Personal Dictionary.

1. We know it <u>well</u> that we cannot achieve success alone.
   a. a water hole made in the ground
   b. in a complete way, fully

2. We thank all the people in this country and the <u>rest</u> of the world.
   a. sleep, not work
   b. what is left over

Personal Dictionary | The Heinle Newbury House Dictionary | Activity Book p. 137 | Student CD-ROM

Content Connection
Social Studies

Build Background Show a map of South Africa. Have students note its location and what bodies of water and land border it. Help students find Umtata, where Nelson Mandela was born; Pretoria, where Mandela attended the University of South Africa; and the Bashee River, mentioned in the selection.

Learning Styles
Linguistic

Build Vocabulary Have students explore the following homonyms: *bark* (tree covering, dog's sound), *pitcher* (baseball player, container), *scale* (tool for weighing, part of a fish). Have them write the words in ways that show their meanings. For example, a student might draw a tree and write *bark* close by, then draw a dog barking.

Build Background

Apartheid

1. **Use a map** Have students locate South Africa on a globe or map. Have them identify the capital (Johannesburg) and countries on South Africa's border. (Namibia, Botswana, Zimbabwe, Mozambique, Swaziland)
2. **Compare** *Ask: How was the situation in South Africa similar to the situation in the U.S. in the 1950s and 1960s?* Explain that the term *apartheid* applies to the political system in South Africa that legally separated people of different races.
3. **Content Connection** South Africa is often called the cradle of civilization because it is where archaeologists discovered 2.5 million-year-old fossils of the earliest human ancestors, as well as 100,000-year-old remains of modern man.

Build Vocabulary

Teacher Resource Book: *Personal Dictionary, p. 63*

Infer Meanings of Homonyms

1. **Use a dictionary** Write on the board: *There is <u>still</u> no easy road to freedom.* Have students look up *still* in the dictionary. Ask them to choose the definition used in this sentence.
2. **Clarify meanings** Have students clarify the meanings of the homonyms using print, online, or CD-ROM dictionaries.
3. **Reading selection vocabulary** You may want to introduce the glossed words in the reading selections before students begin reading. Key words: *justice, racial equality, politician, dedicate, sacrifice, reality, united.* Instruct students to write the words with correct spelling and their definitions in their Personal Dictionaries. Have them pronounce each word and divide it into syllables.
4. **Multi-level options** See MULTI-LEVEL OPTIONS on p. 252.

Answers
1. b 2. b

 **ASSESS**

Say: Write two sentences about South Africa.

Text Structure

Biography and Speech

Review features of a biography *Say: We are going to read a biography of Nelson Mandela. What are some features of a biography that you remember?* (based on true story of someone's life; events, dates, chronological order; written in third-person)

Reading Strategy

Draw Inferences

1. **Draw inferences** Reread paragraph 3 of Roberto Clemente (p. 246). *Ask: Do you think he was proud to be Puerto Rican? What facts do you know? Did he give all of his sons Spanish names? What does this tell you? These are inferences we draw from the information and what we know.*
2. **Multi-level options** See MULTI-LEVEL OPTIONS below.

Answer

1. We can infer that they were poor.

ASSESS

Have students give three features of a speech.

Text Structure

Biography and Speech

"Nelson Mandela" is a **biography.** Remember, a biography is the true story of someone's life written by another person.

"The Inaugural Address, May 10, 1994" is a **speech.** A speech is spoken aloud to a group of people. People may write down the speech to remember it and so that others can read it. A good speech often has the features shown in the chart.

As you read or listen, notice how both the biography and the speech give you information about what Nelson Mandela is like.

Speech	
First-Person Pronouns	pronouns *we* and *us* to show that the speaker feels the same as the people listening
Repetition	repeated words in some sentences in order to make an idea clear
Simple Sentences	short sentences that are easy to understand
Strong Ending	a sentence that makes people feel a certain way, such as happy or excited

Student CD-ROM

Reading Strategy

Draw Inferences

When you **draw inferences,** you use information in a text and what you already know to understand what you read.

Draw inferences as you read the selections.

1. Read the first sentence of the biography. What inference can you draw about Rolihlahla's family?
2. Use a chart like the one here to continue making inferences as you read both selections.

Text Information	What I Know	Inference I Can Draw
The family lives in a hut.	Rich families don't live in huts.	The family is probably poor.

Reading Log   Student CD-ROM

MULTI-LEVEL OPTIONS *Reading Strategy*

Newcomer Have students look at the picture on p. 255. Tell students to use what they know to figure out answers to your questions. *Ask: Is this man Nelson Mandela?* (yes) *Is he a young man?* (no) *Does he seem happy?* (no)

Beginning Direct students to the portrait and titles on p. 255. *Ask: Who is this man?* (Nelson Mandela) *Does he look joyful or not?* (No, he looks sad, thoughtful, or worried.)

Intermediate Ask students to look at the picture and read the titles on p. 255. *Ask: What can you infer about the portrait?* (It's probably Nelson Mandela.) *What can you infer from the title of the speech?* (It was his first speech as president.)

Advanced Have students study the photograph on p. 255. Ask them to jot down their thoughts about the man. Have them tell their partners what they inferred about Nelson Mandela from his portrait.

NELSON MANDELA

an excerpt from a biography
by Jack L. Roberts

THE INAUGURAL ADDRESS
May 10, 1994

an excerpt from a speech
by Nelson Mandela

255

Reading Selection Materials

Audio: *Unit 4, Chapter 3; CD 2, Track 3*
Teacher Resource Book: *Reading Summary,*
    pp. 99–100
Transparencies: #11, *Reading Summary*

Suggestions for Using
Reading Summary

- Introduce new vocabulary or cognates.
- Cut the summary into strips, or jumble the sentences on an overhead transparency. Students put the sentences in order.
- Practice the reading strategy.
- Students read aloud or with a partner.
- Students paraphrase the summary.
- Students do a cloze activity.
- Students create a visual or graphic organizer, such as a timeline or storyboard, to illustrate the summary.
- Students paraphrase the summary.

Preview the Selections

1. **Interpret the image** Have students look at the photo. *Ask: How old do you think Nelson Mandela is in this photo? How would you describe his expression?*
2. **Connect** *Say: Nelson Mandela and Roberto Clemente are both called heroes. In what ways do you think that Nelson Mandela might be a different type of hero?* (He was a political leader and organizer. He devoted his entire life to the struggle.)

Home
Connection

Learning Styles
Intrapersonal

Point out that people say that you can tell a lot about a person by looking at his or her eyes. *Ask: What can you tell about Nelson Mandela from looking at his eyes?* (*Example:* He looks kind but strong and serious.) *Whom in your family does he remind you of? Why?* (*Example:* His eyes remind me of my Grandma. She had a difficult time coming to this country, but she is still kind and loving and always helps others.)

Say: In Build Background, you learned that Nelson Mandela worked to end unfair separation of white and black people. In the selections, you will learn how hard he worked. Think of a problem in our community or world that you care about deeply. Draw or write what you might be willing to do, now or in the future, to help solve that problem.

Read the Selection

1. **Choral reading** Play the audio. Divide the class into two groups. Have each group read the paragraphs with you chorally. Then have pairs read sentences with you chorally.

2. **Identify characters** *Ask: Who is the main character?* (Rolihlahla) *Who are the minor characters?* (his father and the paramount chief)

3. **Analyze facts** Give students a few minutes to write one or two questions about p. 256. Then have students ask the class their questions.

Sample Answer to Guide Question
We can infer that Rolihlahla's father will ask the paramount chief to take care of his son Rolihlahla.

See Teacher Edition pp. 434–436 for a list of English-Spanish cognates in the reading selection.

Audio
CD 2. Tr. 3

Nelson Mandela
an excerpt from a biography by Jack L. Roberts

1   *Twelve-year-old Rolihlahla* stood silently by his father's side in their tiny **thatched hut** near the Bashee River. The young tribal prince knew that this was an important day.

2   Rolihlahla's father was a poor but respected chief of the Tembu, one of many black African groups in the southeastern part of South Africa. But now this proud chief was sick, and certain he would die soon. So he had asked the **paramount** chief of the Tembu tribe to come to his family *kraal,* or farm.

> **Draw Inferences**
>
> What inference can you draw about what might happen to Rolihlahla?

South African kraal

---

thatched with a roof of straw or leaves
hut a very small, plain home

paramount the highest ranking or most important

256 Unit 4 Heroes

MULTI-LEVEL OPTIONS *Read the Selection*

Newcomer Play the audio. *Ask: Was the boy's father well?* (no) *Was Rolihlahla the sick man's son?* (yes) *Did the man ask the tribe's chief to take care of his son?* (yes) *Did the son care about other people?* (yes)

Beginning Read aloud the selection to students. *Ask: How old was Rolihlahla?* (12) *What was the matter with the boy's father?* (very sick) *Whom did the father ask to take care of the boy?* (chief) *What kind of boy was Rolihlahla?* (helpful)

Intermediate Have students do a paired reading. *Ask: How do you think the boy felt? Why?* (sad that his father was so sick) *How do you think the father felt? Why?* (worried about how the boy would grow up without him) *How do you think the boy is related to Nelson Mandela?* (The boy is Mandela.)

Advanced Have students read aloud to partners. *Ask: Why did the author start with this story?* (to show the difficulties of Mandela's early life and hint at his future greatness) *What is the biggest hint that Mandela will become more than a chief?* (Paragraph 4 gives a clue that he will help the whole nation.)

3   The dying man wanted to make sure that Rolihlahla, his only son, would have a good education. He wanted to make sure that Rolihlahla would be **raised** to become a future chief of the Tembu.

4   Rolihlahla's father spoke softly to the paramount chief, asking him to take Rolihlahla to raise. "I am giving you this servant, Rolihlahla," he said.

"I want you to make him what you would like him to be." Then he proudly added, "I can say from the way he speaks to his sisters and friends that his **inclination** is to help the nation."

> **Draw Inferences**
>
> What inference can you draw about the work that Rolihlahla will do?

---

raised   taught during his childhood   **inclination**   a natural liking for something

Chapter 3   Nelson Mandela *and* The Inaugural Address, May 10, 1994   **257**

Read the Selection

1. **Paired reading**   Play the audio for pp. 256 and 257. Then have students read it aloud in pairs.
2. **Discuss motivation**   *Ask: Why has the father called the chief? Why does the father think it is especially important that Rolihlahla get a good education?*
3. **Paraphrase**   Have students tell what has happened so far in their own words. Remind them that there might be several ways to paraphrase the story so far. (*Possible paraphrase:* Rolihlahla's father is offering him as a servant to the paramount chief so that he can get a good education.)
4. **Multi-level options**   See MULTI-LEVEL OPTIONS on p. 256.

Sample Answer to Guide Question
I would infer that he would do any kind of work the chief asked of him because the father says he is giving him "this servant."

 Spelling

***Ew* for long /u/**

Have students look at the word *knew* in the last sentence of paragraph 1. *Ask: What letters make the* u *sound?* (ew) Tell students to jot down the word *knew* on a piece of paper and underline the *ew.*

   Apply   Tell students that you are going to say two other words that have the long /u/ spelled *ew.* Ask them to write the words under *knew* in their Reading Logs. *Say: few, blew. Say: Now that you know the letters* ew *form the long /u/ sound, find other examples*

of words with the long /u/ spelled this way as you read the rest of the biography and the speech. When you find them, write the words in your Reading Logs and pronounce them. (*grew* in paragraph 6 of the biography, *new* in paragraph 5 of the speech)

Read the Selection

1. **Reciprocal reading** Play the audio. Then have a student read paragraph 5. *Ask: What was his father's prediction?* (that his inclination was to help the nation) *Now, ask questions to the class.* After the student has asked one or two questions about the paragraph, have a volunteer read the next paragraph. Have the student ask the class questions about the paragraph in the same way. Follow the same procedure for paragraph 7.

2. **Relate to prior knowledge** Write on the board: *civil rights leader, patriot, prince, politician, prisoner, president. Ask: Can you give me names of other people who are civil rights leaders?* Discuss with students other well-known people who match these titles.

Sample Answer to Guide Question
I can infer that he was in prison because he led a struggle for justice.

5   Sadly, Rolihlahla's father did not live to see his **prediction** come true. But **fortunately** for millions of people in South Africa and throughout the world, Rolihlahla's inclination was, **indeed,** to help the nation.

6   The young boy grew up to become better known throughout the world as Nelson Mandela, **civil rights leader** and hero to millions. He grew up to lead the struggle for **justice** and **racial equality** in South Africa. He became a **beloved** South African **patriot** whose struggle for freedom never weakened **despite** some twenty-seven years behind prison walls.

Draw Inferences

What inference can you draw about why Mandela was in prison?

prediction a statement about what will happen in the future	**justice** laws carried out fairly
fortunately luckily	**racial equality** when people of all races are treated the same
indeed truly	**beloved** very loved
civil rights leader a leader who works to gain equal rights for all citizens	**patriot** a person who is proud of his or her country
	despite even though

258   Unit 4   Heroes

MULTI-LEVEL OPTIONS *Read the Selection*

Newcomer *Is Rolihlahla the same person as Nelson Mandela?* (yes) *Did he work to help people to be free?* (yes) *Was it an easy job?* (no) *Did he become president of his country?* (yes)

Beginning *What is Rolihlahla's other name?* (Nelson Mandela) *What did he work for?* (freedom) *How long did he go to prison for his work?* (27 years) *What did he do in 1994?* (became president of South Africa)

Intermediate *Do you think Mandela's father would have been proud of him? Why?* (yes, because he spent his life being a leader and helping others) *What was Mandela's goal his whole life?* (to end the unfair way people were treated in South Africa)

Advanced *Why was Nelson Mandela able to accomplish such great things?* (He had one goal, and he focused on it no matter how hard the task.) *Mandela was president until 1999. What do you think he has been doing since then? Why?* (speaking and writing about justice and peace because these are the things he cares about)

7   At various times during his life, Nelson Mandela has been a prince, a **politician,** and a prisoner. And on May 10, 1994, he became president of South Africa.

8   Through it all, he has been **committed** to one goal for himself and the millions of black South Africans:

Nelson Mandela has always been a man **determined** to be free.

> **Draw Inferences**
>
> What inference can you draw about what Mandela is like? Write three words that you think describe him.

politician a person who tries to get elected in government

committed determined to do something

determined set on doing something

About the Author | **Jack L. Roberts**

Jack L. Roberts has written many biographies about well-known and important people. In addition to his book about Nelson Mandela, Roberts has also written about Bill Clinton and Booker T. Washington.

➤ Do you think Jack L. Roberts wrote a biography of Nelson Mandela to describe Mandela as a person or to describe apartheid in South Africa? Explain.

Chapter 3 Nelson Mandela *and* The Inaugural Address, May 10, 1994 **259**

Punctuation

Hyphens in numbers

Say: In Chapter 1, you learned that small lines called hyphens are sometimes used to connect the parts of two-part words. Find a two-part word in paragraph 6 that has a hyphen. Yes, twenty-seven *has a hyphen. When we spell out two-part numbers, we use hyphens to join the parts.*

Apply Play a riddle game with students. *Say: I am the number of days in January. What am I?* (thirty-one) *I am 100 minus 1.*

What am I? (ninety-nine) When students respond, write their answer on the board and ask them how to punctuate it.

Read the Selection

1. **Paired reading** Play the audio for pp. 258 and 259. Then have students practice reading aloud in pairs.
2. **Multi-level options** See MULTI-LEVEL OPTIONS on p. 258.

Sample Answer to Guide Question
I can infer that he is committed, determined, and selfless.

About the Author

Discuss author motivation *Ask: Why do you think this author likes to write biographies about well-known leaders?* (Perhaps because he thinks that people can learn from reading about their lives or because it teaches people about history.) *Do you think this author likes to do research? Why?* (Yes. To write a biography, you have to do research to find all the facts about a person's life.)

Answer
Possible answer: Both. I think that the author wrote to describe Mandela the person and how he became such an important leader, but he also wrote to teach people about apartheid. Mandela and apartheid cannot really be separated.

Read the Selection

1. **Compare communication in different forms** Have students read the speech silently. Then have students close their books. Play the audio. *Ask: How was it different listening to the speech rather than reading it?* Discuss features of the speech that add to the impact: rhythm (including pauses) and intonation of the speaker, emotion in his voice, use of repetition, including the audience with first person, and phrases like *let there be.*

2. **Identify text features** Have students look at the speech and identify these elements: first-person pronouns, repetition, simple sentences. Have them copy the chart from p. 254 and fill in examples for each feature.

Sample Answer to Guide Question
We can infer that these people had many difficulties (*sacrificed in many ways*) and many died (*surrendered their lives*).

See Teacher Edition pp. 434–436 for a list of English-Spanish cognates in the reading selection.

Audio
CD 2, Tr. 4

The Inaugural Address, May 10, 1994
an excerpt from a speech by Nelson Mandela

1 . . . We **dedicate** this day to all the heroes and heroines in this country and the rest of the world who **sacrificed** in many ways and **surrendered** their lives so that we could be free.

> **Draw Inferences**
> What inferences can you draw about what happened to many of these "heroes and heroines"?

2 Their dreams have become **reality.** Freedom is their reward . . .

3 We understand it still that there is no easy road to freedom.

4 We know it well that none of us acting alone can achieve success.

5 We must therefore act together as a **united** people, for national **reconciliation,** for nation building, for the birth of a new world.

6 Let there be justice for all.

7 Let there be peace for all.

8 Let there be work, bread, water and salt for all.

9 Let each know that for each the body, the mind and the soul have been freed to **fulfill** themselves . . .

10 Let freedom **reign** . . .

11 God bless Africa! . . .

inaugural address a speech given by a new president on the day that he or she takes office
dedicate name in honor of someone or something
sacrificed gave up something important for a special purpose
surrendered gave up

reality what is real
united joined together
reconciliation an agreement made after an argument or fight
fulfill satisfy, make happy
reign rule, be everywhere

260 Unit 4 Heroes

MULTI-LEVEL OPTIONS *Read the Selection*

Newcomer Play the audio. *Ask: Is Mandela thanking people who worked for freedom?* (yes) *Does he want people to work together?* (yes) *Does he think it is easy to win freedom?* (no) *Does he want everyone to be free?* (yes)

Beginning Read the Reading Summary aloud. Play the audio. *Ask: What do people have to do to become free?* (work together) *What is something Mandela wants for everyone?* (justice, fair treatment)

Intermediate Play the audio. Then have students read the speech chorally. *Ask: When was this speech given?* (when Mandela became president) *How does Mandela think people can gain freedom?* (by working together) *How would he like to see the world?* (as a peaceful, fair place where everyone has what he or she needs)

Advanced Play the audio. Then have students do an expressive choral reading. *Ask: How do you think Mandela felt giving this speech? Why?* (hopeful and determined because he is expecting more hard work ahead of him) *What is the main idea he tried to get across?* (that he needs everyone to work with him to make things better)

Nelson Mandela accepting the Nobel Peace Prize.

Read the Selection

1. **Practice oration** Have students practice reading the speech to each other, imitating the speaking style used in the speech. Then invite volunteers to give the speech to the class. Tell them to imagine speaking to a very large crowd.
2. **Multi-level options** See MULTI-LEVEL OPTIONS on p. 260.

About the Author

Use chronological order Have students work in groups to write a timeline of the important events in Mandela's life. Remind them that putting events in chronological order makes it easier to recall the important events.

Answer
Possible answer: It was more important to ask people to work together, because there is still a lot to do, and it can only be done by uniting.

Across Selections

Say: Although Roberto Clemente and Nelson Mandela are different kinds of heroes, they have some similarities. How are they similar? What kinds of personal risks did they take for what they believed in? (They both spent time helping others; they both did what was important, even though they put themselves in danger; they both made sacrifices for what they thought was important. Clemente gave up his life, and Mandela gave up years of freedom while he was in jail.)

Spelling, Punctuation, Capitalization

After the Reading Comprehension section, students will practice spelling, punctuation, and capitalization in the Activity Book.

About the Author

Nelson Mandela (born 1918)

Nelson Rolihlahla Mandela was born in a village in South Africa on July 18, 1918. After the death of his father, Mandela was raised by a leading tribal chief. In 1942, Mandela earned a law degree from the University of South Africa. In 1944, he joined the African National Congress (ANC), a group that worked against South Africa's apartheid laws.

In 1962, the South African government put Mandela in prison because of his work to end apartheid. He spent about 27 years in prison and was finally released on February 11, 1990. In 1993, Mandela won the Nobel Peace Prize, an award given each year for a great achievement in bringing about peace in the world. In 1994 Mandela was elected president of South Africa. He was president until 1999 and worked to bring white and black South Africans together.

➤ What do you think was more important to Nelson Mandela when he wrote his inaugural address: thanking the people who worked to end apartheid or asking the South African people to work together?

Chapter 3 Nelson Mandela *and* The Inaugural Address, May 10, 1994 **261**

 Punctuation

Evaluate Your Reading Strategy

Ellipses

Tell students that when three dots appear in a row, it is called an *ellipsis*. Tell students it is a punctuation mark that means something has been left out of what a person has said. Direct students to the first sentence in paragraph 1. *Ask: What do you see at the beginning?* (an ellipsis) *What does that tell you about the speech?* (There was a part of the speech before the first sentence shown on this page.) Have students find other examples in paragraphs 2, 9, 10, and 11.

Make Inferences *Say: You have practiced an important reading strategy. Now you can decide how well you have done. Does this statement describe how you read?*

When I read, I make inferences. Making inferences helps me understand the message of what I am reading.

Beyond the Reading

Reading Comprehension

Question-Answer Relationships

Sample Answers

1. He wanted him to have a good education and to be raised to become a future chief.
2. He will help the nation.
3. He became a civil rights leader.
4. He wishes for justice, peace, work, bread, water, salt, and the freedom for people to fulfill themselves.
5. The author thinks that Nelson Mandela was one of the most important people in the struggle against apartheid and that he made many sacrifices for this freedom.
6. These are people in South Africa and in the rest of the world who have worked for civil rights and freedom.
7. I would be excited and hopeful about the future.
8. He is a hero because he worked his whole life for freedom and equality. He put himself in danger to help all South Africans.
9. brave, heroic, a strong leader

Build Reading Fluency

Echo Read Aloud

Model reading aloud with expression. Read one line at a time. Ask the class to read (echo) the same line you just read before going on to the next line or sentence.

Reading Comprehension

Question-Answer Relationships (QAR)

"Right There" Questions

1. **Recall Facts** In "Nelson Mandela," what did Rolihlahla's father want for his son?
2. **Recall Facts** In "Nelson Mandela," what does Rolihlahla's father say the boy will do?

"Think and Search" Questions

3. **Draw Conclusions** In "Nelson Mandela," how does Rolihlahla "help the nation" when he grows up?
4. **Identify** In "The Inaugural Address, May 10, 1994," what things does Mandela wish for all South African people?

"Author and You" Questions

5. **Understand Author's Perspective** How do you think the author of "Nelson Mandela" feels about Mandela? Explain.

6. **Draw Inferences** Reread paragraph 1 of "The Inaugural Address, May 10, 1994." Who do you think these "heroes and heroines" are?
7. **Understand Author's Perspective** Suppose you are Nelson Mandela giving his inaugural speech. Describe your feelings and hopes for the future of South Africa.

"On Your Own" Questions

8. **Explain** Do you think that Nelson Mandela is a hero? Explain.
9. **Describe Character Traits** What three words best describe Nelson Mandela? Why do you think so?

Activity Book
p. 138

Student
CD-ROM

Build Reading Fluency

Echo Read Aloud

Effective readers learn to read with feeling. Echo reading helps you read with feeling and expression. Your teacher reads a line. Then the class reads (echoes) the same line aloud. Turn to page 260.

1. Listen to your teacher read.
2. Read the same line aloud with expression.
3. Continue listening and reading.

MULTI-LEVEL OPTIONS *Elements of Literature*

Newcomer *Say: We must keep our room neat. It is a big job. I need every one of you to help. Every single person can help. Please work with me to do this big job.* Then repeat the speech with facial expressions and gestures to reinforce key words and repeated ideas. Have students raise their hands to signal key words and repetition.

Beginning Make this speech: *We must keep our room neat. It is a big job. I need every one of you to help. Every single person can help. Please work with me to do this big job.* Then hand out copies of the speech. Help students find and circle key words. Have them underline repetitive ideas.

Intermediate Ask students to work in pairs to prepare a dramatic reading. One student can rehearse paragraphs 1–2 while the other prepares to deliver paragraphs 6–11. Ask students to emphasize strong words and repeated ideas with their voices.

Advanced Ask students to work in pairs taking on the roles of speechmaker and coach. The speechmaker can read the speech expressively. The coach can provide feedback and additional suggestions concerning words and ideas to reinforce with tone of voice. Have students tape the delivery and listen to it.

Listen, Speak, Interact

Create and Present Dialogue

Sometimes a biography has **dialogue**— what people in a text say to each other.

Even though a biography describes events that really happened, the dialogue does not always show *exactly* what the people said. Many events in a biography happened a long time ago, and people often cannot remember everything they said. The writer may write dialogue to show what the people possibly said.

1. With a partner, reread or listen to paragraph 4 of "Nelson Mandela." Rolihlahla's father tells the chief what he wants him to do. Discuss the father's perspective.

2. What do you think the chief said? Create four to six lines of dialogue for him and for the father.
3. Practice your dialogue with your partner. One of you is the chief, the other is the father.
4. Read your dialogue for the class. Act out your speech with expression. When you read, read only the words in quotation marks (" ").

Activity Book
p. 139

Elements of Literature

Analyze Style in a Speech

Style is the way writers use language. In Nelson Mandela's speech, some elements of his style are word choice, sentence length, and repetition. This speech has an inspiring style—it makes the listener want to take action.

1. Reread or listen to paragraphs 1 and 2. Find strong words in the paragraphs that make the audience pay attention. What effect do these words have on you?

2. Reread paragraphs 3 and 4. Read closely to find the repetition. What effect do you think the repetition has on the listener?
3. What other elements of style do you notice? How long are the sentences? What effect does this have?

Student
CD-ROM

Content Connection
Social Studies

Bring in a short biography about Nelson Mandela or another person who fought for freedom. Have students examine some of the quotes with you. Ask students to identify a quote that they think is exactly what the person said, such as one from a speech or a meeting. Have them identify one that may not have been the person's exact words. Ask each student to choose one example of dialogue to present to the class.

Learning Styles
Kinesthetic

Suggest that nonverbal language also adds to or takes away from the message of a speech. Have students watch a videotape of someone delivering a speech. Tell students to note how the person stands and the gestures he or she uses. Have students choose parts of Mandela's speech and deliver it using gestures and a stance they feel strengthens the message.

Listen, Speak, Interact

Create and Present Dialogue

1. **Collaborate** Have students suggest things that the father and the chief could say to each other. Encourage them to expand. For example, they could start with the father thanking the chief for coming to see him; the chief could ask about his health. Then have students write their dialogues in pairs.
2. **Newcomers** Pair newcomers with intermediates and have them create a dialogue together. The intermediates can write the dialogue and the newcomers can copy it in their Reading Logs.
3. **Perform a role-play** Ask volunteers to perform their role-plays for the class.

Elements of Literature

Analyze Style in a Speech

1. **Pair work** Have students alternate rereading each paragraph while the other listens and notes strong words and repetitions.
2. **Multi-level options** See MULTI-LEVEL OPTIONS on p. 262.

Answers

1. Strong words: *heroes and heroines, sacrificed, surrendered, reality, freedom.* These words make me want to join him in his fight for freedom.
2. Repetition: *We understand (know) it still (well) that . . .* Repetition helps the listener remember what was said.
3. Sentence length: The sentences are short. It makes the speech easy to understand and remember.

ASSESS

Ask: What did Mandela's father tell him before the chief arrived? Have students make up a short dialogue between Mandela and his father.

Word Study

Identify the Suffix -ion

Expand vocabulary Have students brainstorm other words ending with the suffix -ion. Write them on the board. Provide students with prompts: *participate, elect, medicate, locate.*

Answers
educate—education—knowledge learned in school; predict—prediction—a statement about what will happen in the future

Grammar Focus

Recognize Commands with *Let*

1. **Write commands with *let*** Have students read their commands with expression. Have students write another statement, exchange papers with a partner, use the statements to write commands with *let*.
2. **Use contractions** Write on the board: *Let us close our books.* **Ask:** *Does anyone know how we can combine words in this sentence to make it shorter?* (use a contraction for *let us*) *What is the contraction for* let us*?* (let's)

Answers
1. Let every town be safe. 2. Let the air in the cities be clean. 3. Let every worker have a good-paying job.

ASSESS

Have students write three words ending with the suffix *-ion*.

Word Study

Identify the Suffix -ion

A **suffix** is a group of letters that is added to the end of a word. A suffix changes the meaning of a root word.

The suffix *-ion* usually changes verbs into nouns. Here the verb is the root word.

protect + -ion → protection

verb + suffix → noun

1. Complete a chart like the one here in your Personal Dictionary. Write the correct verb and suffix for each *-ion* word.

Verb	Suffix	*-ion* Word	Meaning
protect +	-ion ⇒	protection	action taken against harm
		education	
		prediction	

2. Use the verb to write what you think is the meaning of each *-ion* word. Be sure to spell the root word and suffix correctly. If the verb ends in *-e,* drop the *-e* before you add *-ion.*
3. Check your definitions of the *-ion* words in a dictionary.

Personal Dictionary   The Heinle Newbury House Dictionary   Activity Book p. 140   Student CD-ROM

Grammar Focus

Recognize Commands with *Let*

The verb *let* can be used to express a command or a strong desire. Nelson Mandela wants there to be peace, so he says, "Let there be peace."

Here are some more examples.

Let all children have a good education.

Let them all go to college.

Let there be jobs for them when they graduate.

Here are some ideas that you might use in a speech. On a piece of paper, restate them using *let*.

1. Every town should be safe.
2. The air in the cities should be clean.
3. Every worker should have a good-paying job.

Activity Book pp. 141–142   Student Handbook   Student CD-ROM

264 Unit 4 Heroes

MULTI-LEVEL OPTIONS *From Reading to Writing*

Newcomer Have students draw a pair of "before" and "after" sketches of changes they would make to improve their classroom. Provide time for students to share their drawings and ideas.

Beginning Provide a framework for students to use in preparing their speech. *Thank you for _____. We should work together to _____. Let's make our class _____. Our class is _____.*

Intermediate Point out that people want to hear specific ideas when they listen to a speech. Ask students to support general thoughts in their speeches with specific examples and suggestions. (*Example:* Let's make our classroom a good place to study in. We can set up quiet zones to work alone and meeting places for quiet talk.)

Advanced Have students review what they learned about powerful words and the impact of repetition. Tell students to underline the most important ideas in their first drafts. Then ask them to check a thesaurus to see if they can find stronger word choices. Also, tell them to consider repeating key phrases.

From Reading to Writing

Write a Persuasive Speech

Imagine that your classmates just elected you as class president. Write a short speech in which you describe how you want to improve your school. Write your speech so that it is appropriate for classmates.

1. Thank your classmates for electing you.
2. Write two sentences using *we* or *us* to persuade your classmates to work together.
3. Include three sentences that use *let* as a command to explain how your school should be.
4. End your speech by saying something great about your school, such as "Our school is the best!"
5. Read your speech aloud to your classmates. Use gestures and tone of voice to show meaning and to make your speech appropriate for your classmates.
6. If possible, use presentation software for your speech. Include visuals to support your statements to improve your school.

Activity Book
p. 143

Student
Handbook

Across Content Areas

Read a Timeline

Read the timeline of events in the life of Nelson Mandela.

1. What is the total number of years that the timeline shows?
2. How many years after Mandela helped form the ANCYL did he become president of the ANCYL?
3. What happened in 1990?
4. How long was Mandela in prison?

Activity Book
p. 144

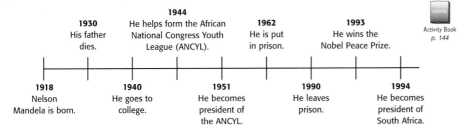

1930 His father dies.

1944 He helps form the African National Congress Youth League (ANCYL).

1962 He is put in prison.

1993 He wins the Nobel Peace Prize.

1918 Nelson Mandela is born.

1940 He goes to college.

1951 He becomes president of the ANCYL.

1990 He leaves prison.

1994 He becomes president of South Africa.

From Reading to Writing

Write a Persuasive Speech

1. **Brainstorm** Have students brainstorm a list of improvements for the classroom or school.
2. **Respond to speeches** After students have given their speeches, have them talk about which speeches they especially liked and why they liked them. Point out the importance of presentation and delivery of a speech.
3. **Analyze persuasive techniques** After students have listened to their classmates' speeches, have them analyze the persuasive techniques used. *Ask: What was the purpose of the speeches?* (persuade) *What techniques did the speakers use to persuade the audience?* Have pairs list techniques. *Ask: What effect did the speeches have on you? Did they cause you to change your beliefs? Why or why not?*
4. **Multi-level options** See MULTI-LEVEL OPTIONS on p. 264.

Across Content Areas: Social Studies

Read a Timeline

Discuss application to content area classes
Ask: What other classes can you use a timeline in? Have you used one recently? Explain.

Answers
1. 76 years 2. 7 years 3. He left prison. 4. 28 years

 **ASSESS**

In small groups, have students write three sentences with *let* to describe improvements they would like to make to their town or city.

Reteach and Reassess

Text Structure Have students review the information about endings on the chart at the top of p. 254. *Ask: What feelings do you think Mandela wanted people to have at the end of his speech? Do you think they had those feelings? Explain.*

Reading Strategy Ask pairs to tell each other the titles of books they have read and liked. Have students make inferences about their partners based on the kinds of books they enjoy.

Elements of Literature Play an audio or videotape of a portion of a political speech. Ask students to identify strong words and repetition.

Reassess Have students draw or write facts about a person who was famous in the past or is well known now for doing something for others. Ask students to draft a one-paragraph speech that person might give if asked to talk about something important to him or her.

CHAPTER 4

Into the Reading

Chapter Materials

Activity Book: *pp. 145–152*
Audio: *Unit 4, Chapter 4; CD 2, Tracks 5–6*
Student Handbook
Student CD-ROM: *Unit 4, Chapter 4*
Teacher Resource Book: *Lesson Plan, Teacher
    Resources, Reading Summary, Activity Book
    Answer Key*
Teacher Resource CD-ROM
Assessment Program: *Quiz, pp. 67–68; Teacher
    and Student Resources, pp. 115–144*
Assessment CD-ROM
Transparencies
The Heinle Newbury House Dictionary/CD-ROM
Web site: http://visions.heinle.com

Objectives

Preview Read the objectives. *Ask: What
do you already know about jobs and job
advertisements?*

Use Prior Knowledge

Discuss Role Models

1. **Teacher think aloud** *Say: I have several
   role models I can think of.* Name them and
   draw a web. Talk about one of the people,
   recording the reasons you admire him/her in
   the outer branches.
2. **Brainstorm** Have students brainstorm and
   discuss role models in small groups. Then
   students can complete their webs
   individually.

My Father Is a Simple Man

a poem
by Luis Omar Salinas

Growing Up

a poem
by Liz Ann Báez Aguilar

Objectives

Reading Compare and contrast as you
read two poems.

Listening and Speaking Discuss jobs.

Grammar Recognize reported speech.

Writing Write a poem.

Content Social Studies: Read
advertisements for jobs.

Use Prior Knowledge

Discuss Role Models

Role models are people whom we want
to be like. For example, a good teacher
may be a role model for someone who
wants to be a teacher.

1. Brainstorm role models in your life.
   List them on a piece of paper.
2. Choose one role model from your
   list. Complete a web like the one
   here. In the middle circle, write the
   name of the role model. In the outer
   circles, write at least three reasons
   why this person is your role model.
   Add as many circles as you need.
3. Discuss your role model with a
   small group.

266   Unit 4   Heroes

MULTI-LEVEL OPTIONS *Build Vocabulary*

Newcomer Help students
write *scholar* in the *word*
box. Have them draw a picture of a
scholar in the *sentence* box.
Provide more concrete words,
such as *father* or *chef,* for this
group to use to complete word
squares.

Beginning Help students
identify a synonym for each
vocabulary word. (scholar—
teacher, perpetual—not ending,
architect—builder) Ask them to
write these words instead of
definitions in the *meaning* box.

Intermediate After students
have created their word squares,
ask them to share their word
squares in small groups. Instruct
each group to choose the symbol
that best represents each of the
three words. Then have groups
share with the entire class.
Students may revise their symbols
based on the groups' ideas.

Advanced Have students work
in pairs. Tell them to determine
the relationship between the
vocabulary words and the words'
symbols. (*Example: Scholars* write
books; *scholars* graduate from
universities.)

Build Background

Mexican-American Authors

In this chapter, you will read two poems by Mexican-American poets. Some Mexican-Americans write poetry, fiction, essays, and plays about their cultural experiences.

They write about growing up, their family, and Mexican-American traditions. Many of these writings mix the English and Spanish languages.

 Content Connection

Before the mid-1800s, Mexico owned large parts of land in what is now the United States. When these places became part of the United States, many Mexican people became United States citizens.

Build Vocabulary

Use Word Squares to Remember Meaning

Using word squares can help you remember the meanings of new words.

1. Listen as your teacher discusses these words.

scholar   perpetual   architect

2. In your Personal Dictionary, complete a word square for each word.
3. Write the word in the **word** box.
4. Use a dictionary or glossary to write the **meaning**.
5. Draw a **symbol** to remember the word.
6. Write a sentence with the word in the **sentence** box.

Word	Symbol
Meaning	**Sentence**

Personal Dictionary   The Heinle Newbury House Dictionary   Activity Book p. 145   Student CD-ROM

Chapter 4 My Father Is a Simple Man *and* Growing Up   **267**

 Cultural Connection

Build Background Present some other books of poetry by Mexican-American poets or about Mexican-American traditions. Examples include *My Name is Jorge: On Both Sides of the River* by Jane Medina and *Canto Familiar* by Gary Soto. Have students look at the illustrations and skim the text to learn about Mexican-American customs and traditions.

Learning Styles *Musical*

Build Vocabulary Explain that word squares help students use their sense of sight to remember words and meanings. Suggest that some students remember better by using their sense of hearing. Challenge students to think of ways to remember the meanings of the vocabulary words using their sense of hearing. For example, they may chant *scholar—school*, say *perpetual* stringing out the word to show it means ongoing, or make up a rap for the word *architect*.

Build Background

Mexican-American Authors

1. **Use prior knowledge** If you have students of Mexican-American backgrounds in your class, have them share knowledge about their culture. *Ask: Have you read any stories or poems by Mexican-American authors? Did the author use any Spanish? Do you know other Mexican-American authors?*

2. **Content Connection** According to Census 2000, there are more than 20 million residents of Mexican origin in the U.S. Mexican-Americans make up 58% of the nation's Latino population.

Build Vocabulary

Use Word Squares to Remember Meaning

Teacher Resource Book: *Word Squares, p. 41; Personal Dictionary, p. 63*

1. **Use a graphic organizer** Help students brainstorm symbols for *scholar,* such as a pair of glasses, a book, or a graduation cap. Follow the same procedure for *perpetual* and *architect.*

2. **Reading selection vocabulary** You may want to introduce the glossed words in the reading selections before students begin reading. Key words: *convince, patience, punishing, applause, chef.* Instruct students to write the words with correct spelling and their definitions in their Personal Dictionaries. Have them pronounce each word and divide it into syllables.

3. **Multi-level options** See MULTI-LEVEL OPTIONS on p. 266.

 **ASSESS**

Say: Write two sentences using perpetual, scholar, *and* architect.

Text Structure

Poem

Compare features After going over the chart of features, have students look briefly at the two poems (pp. 270 and 274). *Ask: Which poem has longer stanzas?* ("My Father Is a Simple Man") *Do the poems have rhyming words?* (no) *Why does the author use italics for some stanzas in "Growing Up? "* (to show a different speaker)

Reading Strategy

Compare and Contrast

1. **Compare and contrast components of art** Direct students to the art on p. 269. Ask them to compare and contrast the two figures.
2. **Multi-level options** See MULTI-LEVEL OPTIONS below.

Answers

Possible answers: **1.** The poems are about families growing up. One is written by a son; the other is by a daughter. **2.** Similarities: They both have first-person point of view, simple language, and no rhyming. Differences: "Growing Up" is shorter, has a response from the mother, and uses some Spanish.

ASSESS

Have students list four features of a poem.

Text Structure

Poem

"My Father Is a Simple Man" and "Growing Up" are **poems.** Look at the features of these poems in the chart.

Poems can look very different from one another. As you read, notice how the punctuation and lengths of sentences are different in each poem.

Poem	
Content	The poet describes his or her thoughts, feelings, or experiences.
First-Person Pronouns	The poet often uses *I, we, me,* and *us* to show his or her ideas.
Images	Details help readers form pictures in their minds.
Stanzas	The poem is separated into groups of lines called stanzas.

Student
CD-ROM

Reading Strategy

Compare and Contrast

When you **compare,** you notice how two things are alike. When you **contrast,** you notice how two things are different. You can compare and contrast two poems.

1. Read the titles of both poems. What do you think the poems are about? How do you think the poems are alike? How do you think they are different?
2. Look at the picture on page 270 and read the first sentence of the poem. Now look at the picture on page 274 and read the first four lines. How are the two poems alike? How are they different?

3. Use a Venn Diagram like the one here to help you compare and contrast as you read each selection.
4. Use comparative adjectives when possible.

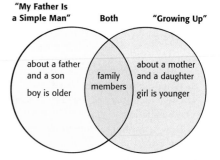

"My Father Is a Simple Man" — Both — "Growing Up"

about a father and a son

boy is older

family members

about a mother and a daughter

girl is younger

Student
CD-ROM

MULTI-LEVEL OPTIONS *Reading Strategy*

Newcomer Have groups look through illustrated books on Mexico and the United States. Give groups several colors of stick-ons. Have students find illustrations of similarities between the two countries and mark these with the same color stick-ons. Have students mark differences with different colored stick-ons.

Beginning Have students look at a map that shows Mexico and the United States. Have them use a Venn diagram to record words and phrases about geographic similarities and differences between the countries. (*Example:* Mexico – smaller; the United States – larger; both – Gulf of Mexico)

Intermediate Have students add information about the features and forms of the poems to the Venn diagrams.

Advanced Have students look through some books of poetry by a single poet. Ask them to identify similarities and differences in the forms of the poems the person has written.

My Father Is a Simple Man

a poem
by Luis Omar Salinas

Growing Up

a poem
by Liz Ann Báez Aguilar

269

Reading Selection Materials

Audio: *Unit 4, Chapter 4; CD 2, Tracks 5–6*
Teacher Resource Book: *Reading Summary,*
    pp. 101–102
Transparencies: #11, *Reading Summary*

Suggestions for Using
Reading Summary

- Introduce new vocabulary or cognates.
- Cut the summary into strips, or jumble the sentences on an overhead transparency. Students put the sentences in order.
- Practice the reading strategy.
- Students read aloud or with a partner.
- Students paraphrase the summary.
- Students do a cloze activity.
- Students create a visual or graphic organizer, such as a timeline or storyboard, to illustrate the summary.
- Students paraphrase the summary.

Preview the Selections

1. **Interpret the image** Have students look at the illustration. *Ask: What do you think the relationship is between the two people?* (father and son) *How does this picture relate to the theme of heroes?*
2. **Connect to theme** *Say: Remember the theme for this unit is heroes. How can a parent be a hero? Do you ever think of your parents or grandparents as heroes?*

Content Connection
The Arts

Learning Styles
Linguistic

Invite students to examine the artwork on p. 269. *Ask: How do you think the people in the picture feel about each other? Why? What do you think the photographer was trying to show? Why do you think this photograph was included in this unit? Why do you think it was included in this chapter?*

Remind students that the theme of this unit is *heroes.* Tell them to look at the titles of the poems they will read. Based on the theme and the titles, ask students to brainstorm a list of words they think the poets may use in these works.

Read the Selection

1. **Choral reading** Play the audio. Repeat as students read along. Read stanzas 1 and 2 aloud. Have groups of students read with you.

2. **Discuss tone** *Ask: How do you think the author feels towards his father?* (He loves him.) *How would you describe the tone or feeling of the poem?* (patient, familiar or routine, warm towards his father)

3. **Relate to personal experience** *Ask: Do you ever walk somewhere with a parent or grandparent? Where do you walk? What do you sometimes talk about? Do you enjoy the walk? Why? How did you feel about walking with this person when you were a young child?*

Sample Answer to Guide Question
The father walks more slowly than the speaker.

See Teacher Edition pp. 434–436 for a list of English-Spanish cognates in the reading selection.

Audio
CD 2. Tr. 5

Compare and Contrast

Compare how the father walks with how the speaker of the poem walks.

My Father Is a Simple Man
a poem by Luis Omar Salinas

1. I walk to town with my father
to buy a newspaper. He walks slower
than I do so I must **slow up.**
The street is filled with children.

2. We argue about the price
of **pomegranates,** I **convince**
him it is the fruit of **scholars.**
He has taken me on this journey
and it's been **lifelong.**

slow up   move less quickly
pomegranates   round fruits with reddish skin and many juicy red seeds
convince   cause someone to believe that something is true

scholars   people who have learned much through study
lifelong   lasting your entire life

270   Unit 4   Heroes

MULTI-LEVEL OPTIONS   *Read the Selection*

Newcomer Play the audio. *Ask: Is the poem about a father?* (yes) *Is the father taking a drive with his son?* (no) *Does the father want the son to eat oranges?* (yes) *Does the father want the son to be healthy?* (yes)

Beginning Play the audio. *Ask: Who is with the father?* (his son) *Where are they?* (in town) *What are they doing?* (talking) *What does the father tell the son to eat?* (oranges)

Intermediate Have students read the poem chorally. *Ask: How do you think the father and son feel about each other? Explain.* (They get along well. They are having a good conversation.) *How does the father think eating oranges will affect the son?* (keep him healthy)

Advanced Have students do a paired reading. *Ask: When the poet says* We argue *in paragraph 2, does he mean the people are fighting? Explain.* (No, he just means that they have different feelings.) *What does paragraph 4 mean?* (The father likes living, but he is not afraid of dying.)

Read the Selection

1. **Shared reading** Divide the class into four groups. Play the audio. Have each group join in for one of the stanzas.
2. **Check comprehension** *Ask: Why does the father say that oranges are perpetual?* (because they have seeds which continue to produce more oranges) *Could you compare the seeds of an orange to the generations of a family?* (yes, because they both continue in a cycle) *Is the father afraid of death?* (no)
3. **Multi-level options** See MULTI-LEVEL OPTIONS on p. 270.

Sample Answer to Guide Question
The son says pomegranates are the fruit of scholars, meaning they make you smart; his father says oranges are perpetual, which means they give you life.

> **Compare and Contrast**
>
> Contrast what the poet says about pomegranates in stanza 2 with what he says about oranges in stanza 3.

3 He's sure I'll be healthy
   so long as I eat more oranges,
   and tells me the orange
   has seeds and so is **perpetual**;
   and we too will come back
   like the orange trees.

4 I ask him what he thinks
   about death and he says
   he will gladly face it when
   it comes but he won't jump
   out in front of a car.

---

perpetual   continuing forever

th Spelling

Ui for the long /u/ sound, ch for the /k/ sound

Ask: *What vowel sound do you hear in* fruit? (long /u/) *Look at the word* fruit *in paragraph 2 to see how it is spelled. Sometimes the long /u/ sound is spelled* ui. Remind students that *ew* is also used for the long /u/ sound. Then write *school* on the board. **Say:** *The letters* sch *sound like* sk. Have students find and pronounce a word in stanza 2 that starts with *sch* (scholars).

Apply Write the following sentence on the board. Ask students to complete it with a word that contains *ch* and one that contains *ui.*

The boy wore his new _____ to a special event at _____. (suit, school)

Read the Selection

1. **Listen for rhythm and intonation** Play the audio for the entire poem so that students hear the rhythm and intonation of the poem.
2. **Paired reading** Have students do a partner read aloud.
3. **Make inferences** Have students make inferences. *Ask: Do you think the author's father is well-educated?* (No. He only went to 6th grade.) *Do you think that the father is retired or is still working?* (retired; he *was* a worker and provider.) *Who do you think the father provided for?* (his family)
4. **Use a Venn diagram to compare and contrast** Draw a Venn diagram to help with the guide question. Because much is not said but implied in the poem, students will have to make additional inferences.

Sample Answer to Guide Question
Similarities: Both are patient, feel warmly toward each other, and respect each other. Differences: father - sixth-grade education, older, simpler, wise; son - a scholar, younger, perhaps not as "simple" as his father.

5   I'd gladly give my life
for this man with a sixth
grade education, whose kindness
and **patience** are **true** . . .

Compare and Contrast

Compare and contrast the father and the son.

---

6   The truth of it is, he's the scholar,
and when the **bitter-hard** reality
comes at me like a **punishing**
evil stranger, I can always
remember that here was a man
who was a worker and **provider,**
who learned the simple facts
in life and lived by them,
who held no **pretense.**

---

patience   the ability to bear pain or trouble while waiting for something
true   real, honest
bitter-hard   very difficult

punishing   having the quality of causing pain
provider   a person who supports his or her family
pretense   a reason or an act that hides the real reason for doing something

272   Unit 4   Heroes

MULTI-LEVEL OPTIONS *Read the Selection*

Newcomer *Ask: Did the father finish high school?* (no) *Does the son think his father is smart?* (yes) *Did the father work hard for his family?* (yes)

Beginning *Ask: How many years of school did the father have?* (six) *Does the son think his father is smart or not smart?* (smart) *What else does the boy think the father is?* (patient, honest) *What did the man do for his family?* (work hard)

Intermediate *Ask: How does the son think the father got smart?* (by learning from life) *In one sentence, summarize how the son feels about the father.* (He loves and admires him.) *What qualities of the father do you think the son would like to have?* (patience, kindness, honesty, hard work)

Advanced *Ask: How can you tell that the son loves his father?* (He says he would give his life for him; he talks about his father's good qualities.) *If the son were to plan a party for his father, do you think he would plan something simple or fancy? Explain.* (plain because his father is a simple, humble man)

Compare and Contrast

People often have large funerals for great or famous people. Contrast this with how the speaker thinks that people will act when his father dies.

7   And when he leaves without
benefit of **fanfare** or **applause**
I shall have learned what little
there is about greatness.

---

fanfare   a loud, showy introduction to an event

applause   hand clapping to show that you like something

About the Author

Luis Omar Salinas (born 1937)

Luis Omar Salinas was born in Robstown, Texas. He lived in Monterrey, Mexico, until he was four. After his mother died, Salinas moved to California with his uncle. He grew up and went to school in California. He studied and taught writing at California State University. Today, Salinas continues to write powerful poetry that describes Mexican-American life.

➤ Listen to the audio recording of the poem to appreciate the author's message. What does he tell you about the father? How is the father a hero?

Chapter 4   My Father Is a Simple Man *and* Growing Up   **273**

1. **Silent reading** Give students time to read silently, looking up words in the dictionary as needed.
2. **Discuss meaning** Read the last stanza aloud. *Ask: How would you paraphrase this, or say it in your own words?* You may want students to look at the two parts of the sentence and paraphrase each part. A possible paraphrase: The poet learned about greatness—what's really important in life—from his father, a man who will die quietly and humbly.
3. **Multi-level options** See MULTI-LEVEL OPTIONS on p. 272.

Sample Answer to Guide Question
The speaker thinks that there will not be much said or done for his father when he dies because true greatness isn't about having a large, fancy funeral.

About the Author

Analyze facts Have students form small groups and write several true-false questions about the author. Then groups can exchange and answer the questions.

Answers
Sample answer: The father is a hero because he worked hard and provided for his family; he was wise even though he didn't have much education; and he is not afraid of death.

  Punctuation

Commas to separate dependent adjective clauses

Write on the board: *The boy's father was smart, kind, and patient. Ask:* Why are there commas in this sentence? (to separate describing words in a series) Write on the board the following excerpt from the poem: *I can always remember that there was a man who was a worker and provider, who learned the simple facts in life and lived by them, who held no pretense.* Underline each clause with a separate line. *Ask: What do the*

underlined parts of the sentence do? (describe the father) *Yes, they are* clauses *that describe. What do the commas in this sentence do?* (separate the describing clauses)

   Apply Write: *I am glad to work with students who are smart who are hard working and who are fun to teach.* Ask students to tell you where to put commas. (after *smart* and after *working*)

Read the Selection

1. **Relate to personal experience** *Say: In this poem, the speaker asks her mother many questions. What kinds of questions did you ask your mother or father when you were young? What did you want to be when you were young? What do you want to be now?*

2. **Identify text features** *Ask: What is repeated in the poem?* (the question "What if I become" and "M'ija, you will") *What does "m'ija" mean in Spanish?* ("mi hija," or *my daughter*, an affectionate term)

3. **Choral reading** Play the audio. Then divide the class into two groups. Assign one group the daughter's lines and the other group the mother's lines. Have a volunteer lead each group.

Sample Answer to Guide Question
The form of this poem is question-and-answer between mother and daughter. "My father Is a Simple Man" is a poem in the first person.

See Teacher Edition pp. 434–436 for a list of English-Spanish cognates in the reading selection.

Audio
CD 2, Tr. 6

Growing Up
a poem by Liz Ann Báez Aguilar

Compare and Contrast

Compare and contrast the form of this poem with "My Father Is a Simple Man."

1 When I grow up,
I want to be a doctor.

2 **M'ija,** you will **patch** scraped knees
and wipe away children's tears.

3 But what if I become an **architect?**

4 *M'ija, you will build beautiful houses
where children will sing and play.*

5 And what if I become a teacher?

6 *M'ija, you will teach
your students to read every day.*

M'ija the Spanish term for "my daughter"   **architect** a person who designs buildings
patch fix or mend

274 Unit 4 Heroes

MULTI-LEVEL OPTIONS *Read the Selection*

Newcomer Play the audio. *Ask: Is the poem about a girl and her mother?* (yes) *Does the girl know what she wants to be when she grows up?* (no) *Does the girl think about being a teacher?* (yes) *Does the girl want to be like her mother?* (yes)

Beginning *To whom is the girl talking?* (her mother) *What is something she may want to be when she grows up?* (doctor, architect, teacher, or chef) *What kind of architect does her mother think the girl would be?* (a good one) *Who does the girl want to be like when she grows up?* (her mother)

Intermediate *How is the girl trying to figure out what to be when she grows up?* (by talking to her mother) *How does the mother feel about the girl's choices?* (that she will be good at whatever she does) *How does the girl feel about her mother?* (that she is good at everything)

Advanced *How can you tell that the mother has confidence in her daughter?* (No matter what the girl says she may do, the mother thinks she will be good at it.) *How does stanza 11 connect to the rest of the poem?* (The mother has all the skills the girl will need for any job.)

7   But what if I become a famous **chef?**

8   *M'ija, your* **arroz con pollo**
        will be eaten with **gozo.**

9   And Mami, what if I want to be like you someday?

10   *M'ija, why do you want to be like me?*

> **Compare and Contrast**
>
> In stanza 11, the poet compares Mami to a doctor, an architect, a teacher, and a chef. Explain how she does this.

11   Oh Mami, because you care for people, our house is built on love,
        you are wise, and your **spicy stew** tastes delicious.

---

chef   the leading cook in a restaurant
arroz con pollo   the Spanish term for "rice with chicken"

gozo   the Spanish term for "joy"
spicy   tasty, hot
stew   a thick soup of meat and vegetables

About the Author   Liz Ann Báez Aguilar

Liz Ann Báez Aguilar has written many poems and short stories. She enjoys doing community service. She sometimes visits sick people in the hospital. She also works with her church to take clothing and other things to orphanages in Mexico. (Orphanages are homes for children whose parents have died.) Aguilar currently teaches English at San Antonio College in Texas. She lives in San Antonio, Texas, where she was born.

➤ Based on "Growing Up," do you think Liz Ann Báez Aguilar believes that being a good mother is an important job? Explain.

 Spelling

Silent *t* before *ch*

Ask: What sounds do you hear in patch? (/p/, /a/, /ch/) *Yes, they are the sounds we hear in the word.* Patch *is spelled with a silent letter, though. Look at paragraph 2 to find out what it is.* (t)

    Apply On the board, write *match, sketch, hopscotch, pitch, hutch.* Ask volunteers to say the words. Then have students use the dictionary to find the meanings of any word they don't know.

Evaluate Your Reading Strategy

Compare and contrast *Say:* You have practiced an important reading strategy. Now you can decide how well you have done. Does this statement describe how you read?

> When I want to compare, I ask, "How are these two things the same?" When I want to contrast, I ask, "How are these two things different?" When I compare and contrast as I read, I understand more about the author's message.

Read the Selection

1. **Break-in reading** Have one student begin reading; then another student "breaks in" by reading to the end of a line with the first student. The first student stops reading, and the second continues until a third student "breaks in." Read the poem several times and monitor that everyone participates.
2. **Multi-level options** See MULTI-LEVEL OPTIONS on p. 274.

Sample Answer to Guide Question
The poet repeats the phrases describing the work of a doctor, an architect, a teacher, and a chef in order to show that Mami, as a loving mother, does them all.

About the Author

Reciprocal reading Have a student read the biography aloud. Invite volunteers to ask comprehension questions about the text.

Answer
Sample answer: The poet thinks it is important because she equates the mother's work with the work of professionals.

Across Selections

Say: These people are very different kinds of heroes from Nelson Mandela and Roberto Clemente. How are the father and mother in the poem heroic? (The father is simple but wise, patient, and truthful. The mother cares for her family with love.)

 **ASSESS**

Ask: Which poem did you like better? Why?

Spelling, Punctuation, Capitalization

After the Reading Comprehension section, students will practice spelling, punctuation, and capitalization in the Activity Book.

Beyond the Reading

Reading Comprehension

Question-Answer Relationships

Sample Answers

1. to buy a newspaper
2. He should eat more oranges.
3. 6th grade
4. Because her mother does the work of many.
5. doctor, architect, teacher, chef
6. a daughter and her mother
7. She uses Spanish words because her mother spoke Spanish to her.
8. wise, hard-working, simple; he respects his father.
9. wise, caring, loving
10. My father is great because he worked hard so his children could stay in school.

Build Reading Fluency

Audio CD Reading Practice

Explain that reading silently while listening to the audio helps improve reading fluency. Remind students to keep their eyes on the words. Repeat the audio as needed.

Reading Comprehension

Question-Answer Relationships (QAR)

"Right There" Questions

1. **Recall Facts** In "My Father Is a Simple Man," why does the speaker go to town with his father?
2. **Recall Facts** According to the father in "My Father Is a Simple Man," how will the speaker stay healthy?
3. **Recall Details** In "My Father Is a Simple Man," at which grade level did the father leave school?
4. **Summarize** Why does the daughter in "Growing Up" want to be like her mother?

"Think and Search" Questions

5. **Identify** What four jobs are mentioned in "Growing Up"?
6. **Draw Conclusions** Who are the two speakers in "Growing Up"?

"Author and You" Questions

7. **Understand Author's Perspective** Why do you think Liz Ann Báez Aguilar uses Spanish words in "Growing Up"?
8. **Recognize Character Traits** What three words do you think the speaker in "My Father Is a Simple Man" might use to describe his father? What does this say about their relationship?
9. **Recognize Character Traits** What three words do you think the daughter in "Growing Up" might use to describe her mother?

"On Your Own" Question

10. **Explain** Do you know someone you would call "great"? Why is that person "great"?

 Activity Book p. 146   Student CD-ROM

Build Reading Fluency

Audio CD Reading Practice

Listening to the Audio CD for "My Father Is a Simple Man" is good reading practice. It will help you to become a fluent reader.

1. Listen to the Audio CD.
2. Follow along in your book on page 270.
3. Listen to the phrases, pauses, and expression of the reader.
4. Reread with expression paragraphs 1 and 2.

MULTI-LEVEL OPTIONS *Elements of Literature*

Newcomer Have students also consider the imagery in "Growing Up." Reread paragraph 4 aloud. *Say: beautiful, children, sing, play.* Ask students to draw a picture of the kind of house the mother thinks the daughter will build.

Beginning Apply the concept of imagery to "Growing Up." Examine the mother's comments about the kind of houses she imagines her daughter will build if she becomes an architect. Have students draw an image of a house she might design. Ask them to label the places where they show the poet's ideas: *beautiful, children, singing, playing.*

Intermediate Ask each student to select a job from "Growing Up." Have students examine the mother's description of the girl doing that job. Ask students to jot down the key words in the description and then draw the images these words inspire.

Advanced Have students reread "Growing Up." Tell them to pay special attention to the mother's image of the girl doing each job. *Say: Write one more stanza for each job giving another image. (Example: M'ija, you will build lovely offices where people whistle while they work.)*

Listen, Speak, Interact

Discuss Jobs

"Growing Up" describes four different jobs: doctor, architect, teacher, chef. What do you know about these jobs?

1. The class will work in at least four groups. Each group is assigned one of the jobs described in "Growing Up."
2. With your group, answer the following questions about the job you were assigned. Many of these questions have more than one answer. List your answers on a piece of paper.

a. Describe the job. What do people who work this job do?
b. How do you think people learn to do this job?
c. Do you think that you would like this job? Why or why not?
3. Present your answers to the class. For the last question, each person in the group should present his or her own answer.

Elements of Literature

Recognize Imagery

Poets use **imagery** to help you form pictures in your mind as you read. We call these pictures **images.** Imagery can help you understand what a poet is describing, and it can also help you enjoy a poem.

In stanza 6 of "My Father Is a Simple Man," the poet uses the image of a "punishing, evil stranger." This image helps us understand that the poet is describing a bad and scary feeling.

1. With a partner, reread or listen to stanza 3 of "My Father Is a Simple Man." What images does the poet use? Compare answers with your partner.
2. Choose one image to draw in your Reading Log.
3. Discuss your drawing with a partner. How did this image help you understand what the poet describes?

Activity Book
p. 147

Student
CD-ROM

Listen, Speak, Interact

Discuss Jobs

1. **Group work** Have students group themselves according to which profession they want to discuss.
2. **Newcomers** Work with these students, discussing the questions about being a teacher. Write their answers in note form on the board, and have them copy.

Answers
Example: **2. a.** A doctor helps people who are sick or injured. **b.** college, medical school, and training in a hospital **c.** I would like to be a doctor. I love science, and I like to help people.

Elements of Literature

Recognize Imagery

1. **Share feelings about images** Invite volunteers to share their drawings with the class and explain how they relate to the poet's image.
2. **Multi-level options** See MULTI-LEVEL OPTIONS on p. 276.

Answer
1. Image—orange trees

✓ ASSESS

Have students identify an image they like in one of the poems.

Content Connection
Technology

Tell students that most jobs now involve use of some kind of technology. Have students use books, Web sites, and interviews to find out how technology is used in the job the group is investigating. Ask them to include this information in their answer to item 2a in Listen, Speak, Interact.

Learning Styles
Natural

Tell students that many poets use images from nature in their poetry. If possible, take students outdoors and ask them to focus on a plant, cloud formation, or other aspect of nature. Have them jot down words, phrases, and sketches that come to mind. If you are unable to take students outdoors, have them use pictures of outdoor scenes.

Word Study

Identify the Suffix -er

Use the suffix -er Write on the board: *paint, drive, bake, produce, manage, help.* Have students come to the board and add the suffix. Ask students to make up sentences using the words.

Answers

1. and 2. worker (a person who works), provider (a person who provides), teacher (a person who teaches)

Grammar Focus

Recognize Reported Speech

Write reported speech Have students write sentences about what someone in their family often says, using reported speech. Start by writing an example of your own. Have them share their sentences in groups.

Answers

1. a. My father always says (that) he wants to be healthy. **b.** Every morning, my mother says (that) she is going to make some stew.

ASSESS

Write on the board: *He says, "I'm sure you will be healthy as long as you eat more oranges."* Have students write it as reported speech. (He says he is sure (that) you will be healthy as long as you eat more oranges.)

Word Study

Identify the Suffix -er

The suffix *-er* can change verbs into nouns. The suffix *-er* means "a person who does something." For example, *writer* means "a person who writes."

If a verb ends in *-e*, you drop the *-e* before you add the suffix *-er*.

1. Find three examples of nouns that contain the suffix *-er* in the two poems. Look at stanza 6, line 6, of "My Father Is a Simple Man" and stanza 5 of "Growing Up."
2. Complete a chart like the one here in your Personal Dictionary. Use a dictionary to check your definitions.

Verb	Suffix	Noun	Definition
write +	-er ⇒	writer	a person who writes
+	-er ⇒		
+	-er ⇒		
+	-er ⇒		

3. Write a sentence of your own using each of the four words in the chart. Be sure to spell the root correctly.

Personal Dictionary · The Heinle Newbury House Dictionary · Activity Book p. 148 · Student CD-ROM

Grammar Focus

Recognize Reported Speech

Read these two sentences.

My father says, **"I won't jump out in front of a car."**

My father says that he won't jump out in front of a car.

The first sentence is **direct speech.** It gives the actual words that the person said. Direct speech uses quotation marks.

The second sentence is **reported speech.** Notice that *I won't jump* changes to *he won't jump.* Also, reported speech does not use quotation marks. You can use *that* before the reported speech, or you can leave it out.

My father says he won't jump out in front of a car.

1. Rewrite the examples of direct speech as reported speech. Be sure to use correct subject-verb agreement.
   a. My father always says, "I want to be healthy."
   b. Every morning, my mother says, "I am going to make some stew."

Activity Book pp. 149–150 · Student Handbook · Student CD-ROM

278   Unit 4 Heroes

MULTI-LEVEL OPTIONS *From Reading to Writing*

Newcomer Have students make a visual poem. Ask them to draw three boxes on unlined paper. Help them write the name of their role model in each box. Then tell them to draw an image in each box that shows why they admire that person.

Beginning Have students create three drawings showing reasons they admire the subject of their poem. Help them write words and phrases at the bottom of each drawing to express their feelings about the person.

Intermediate Have students look at how the poem "Growing Up" is displayed on the page and how it is illustrated. Give students paper on which to write their final copies and create illustrations that sum up the ideas in their poems. If possible, have students present their poems to the people they were written about.

Advanced Have students reread both poems in the last stanzas of each to see how the poets ended their works with memorable thoughts. Challenge students to add a fourth stanza to their work. Ask them to provide a summary thought or image that readers will remember.

From Reading to Writing

Write a Poem

Write a poem about the role model that you described in Use Prior Knowledge on page 266.

1. Use your web from Use Prior Knowledge. Choose information from three circles to write three sentences. Separate your sentences into three stanzas.

2. In each sentence, use imagery to help your readers form pictures in their minds.

3. Write a title for your poem that describes your role model.

4. Use your best handwriting and copy your poem on a nice piece of paper. Illustrate or decorate your poem.

5. Create a classroom collection of everyone's poems. Make a cover and a table of contents.

Activity Book   Student
p. 151   Handbook

Across Content Areas

Read Advertisements for Jobs

Ads (advertisements) for jobs use a lot of **abbreviations,** or shortened forms of words.

1. Match these job ad abbreviations with their full forms.

p/t	experience
f/t	full time
wknds	hour
hr	part time
exp	weekends

2. Read the job ads below and answer these questions.
   a. Which ad gives the hourly pay, "baggers" or "store assistant"?
   b. Which job is only part time?
   c. Which job is only on weekends?
   d. Which job requires experience?

> **BAGGERS** needed. P/t, f/t.
> $8.50/hr. Shop Here
> Supermarket. Apply 9 to 5,
> Mon. to Fri. 2435 Broadway.
>
> **STORE ASSISTANT,** Cosmo
> Garden Center. Retail exp
> required. P/t, wknds.
> Call 981-350-5555.

Activity Book
p. 152

UNIT 4 • CHAPTER 4
Beyond the Reading

From Reading to Writing

Write a Poem

1. **Identify a metaphor** *Say: A metaphor is an expression used to describe a person or thing by relating it to something with the same qualities. For example, here it says, "my teacher is a tree," because the teacher provides protection like a tree. Try to use other metaphors when you write your poems.*

2. **Share original poetry** Have volunteers read their poems to the class.

3. **Multi-level options** See MULTI-LEVEL OPTIONS on p. 278.

Across Content Areas: Social Studies

Read Advertisements for Jobs

Relate to personal experience *Ask: Do any of you have jobs? What is your job? What are your hours? Do you need experience for the job?* Have students share information about job experiences.

Answers
1. p/t—part time, f/t—full time, wknds—weekends, hr—hour, exp—experience. 2. a. baggers, b. store assistant, c. store assistant, d. store assistant

 **ASSESS**

Have students write an advertisement for a job they would like. Remind them to include information about pay, hours, and necessary experience.

Reteach and Reassess

Text Structure Have students review the features of poetry on p. 268. Ask students to use stick-on notes to mark examples of each of these features on one of the poems in this chapter.

Reading Strategy Have students work in pairs. Ask them to use a Venn diagram to compare the poems that each wrote for From Reading to Writing.

Elements of Literature Read aloud a descriptive stanza from a poem. Ask students to draw the image the poem brings to mind. Discuss with students which of the poet's words inspired their drawings.

Reassess Have small groups of students use the format from From Reading to Writing to create short poems about various jobs. Have students from two groups share their poems and compare and contrast the jobs they have described.

Materials

Student Handbook
CNN Video: *Unit 4*
Teacher Resource Book: *Lesson Plan, p. 23;
Teacher Resources, pp. 35–64; Video Script,
pp. 167–168; Video Worksheet, p. 176;
School-Home Connection, pp. 140–146*
Teacher Resource CD-ROM
Assessment Program: *Unit 4 Test, pp. 69–74;
Teacher and Student Resources,
pp. 115–144*
Assessment CD-ROM
Transparencies
The Heinle Newbury House Dictionary/CD-ROM
Heinle Reading Library: *The Red Badge of
Courage*
Web site: http://visions.heinle.com

Listening and Speaking Workshop

Give a Descriptive Presentation

Review features of a biography Introduce the workshop by explaining that students will be doing an oral biography. Review key features of a biography: third-person point of view, events, facts, and dates.

Step 1: Identify what you know about the person and ask questions. Suggest different people students could do presentations on: family members, neighbors, teachers, coaches. For students who want to work collaboratively, have them choose people from the school: teachers, principal, janitors.

Listening and Speaking Workshop

Give a Descriptive Presentation

> **Topic**
> Choose a person that you know very well and admire. Describe that person in a presentation to the class.

Step 1: Identify what you know about the person and ask questions.

On a note card, answer the following questions. If you do not know an answer, ask someone who might know. Revise your questions as needed. Write your answers in complete sentences. Use one card for each question and answer.

1. What is the person's name?
2. How do you know the person?
3. What does the person look like?
4. What is the person like? For example, *funny, smart,* and *kind.*
5. Where does the person live?
6. What are the person's hobbies?
7. What is some other information, such as the person's job or where the person goes to school?

Step 2: Organize your presentation.

1. On another note card, write an opening that will get your audience's attention. For example:
   a. Use a quote that the person said.
   b. Give your opinion about something the person does well.

2. On your note cards, write numbers in the order in which you will present the information.

> **3.** He is my father.
> **2.** His name is Carlos Sanchez.
> **1. Opening**
> The person who I am going to describe is the best cook in the world.

Step 3: Show pictures that describe what you will say. You may:

1. Draw a picture or bring in a photograph of the person.
2. Draw a picture that shows one of the person's favorite hobbies.

Step 4: Practice your presentation.

1. Practice your presentation in front of a partner. Use the tips in the Presentation Checklist.
2. Ask your partner to complete the Active Listening Checklist.
3. Revise the presentation as needed.
4. Give your presentation to the class.

Step 5: Give your presentation.

1. Give your presentation. If possible, record it on video. Then watch your presentation and note how you could improve.

MULTI-LEVEL OPTIONS *Listening and Speaking Workshop*

Newcomer Have each student write the name of his/her subject and the person's age. Have the student point on a map to the city where the person lives. Tell students to make paper masks to show how the subjects look. Ask students to role-play their subjects at work and play.

Beginning Have students draw pictures of their subject doing various activities. Help students choose and rehearse an introductory word to say before showing each picture (*home, work, hobby*). The word might also be the name of the subject.

Intermediate *Say: You need to manage holding your note cards and your pictures during your presentation. You need to do this without dropping anything or getting distracted. Take time to make a plan.* For instance, some students may choose to attach their pictures to the board or an easel and point to them. Others may ask for classmates to assist them.

Advanced Discuss Presentation Checklist points 1, 3, and 4. *Say: Your talks will be more natural if you speak conversationally instead of reading your note cards.* Have students mark key ideas on their note cards with highlighters. Have them rehearse looking at the cards, looking up, and speaking directly to their audience.

Presentation Checklist

1. Look at your audience. Do not just read from your note cards.

2. Speak slowly, clearly, and loudly enough for your audience to hear you.

3. Your sentences should sound natural, as if you were speaking to a group of friends.

4. If you forget what you want to say, use your note cards to remind you.

5. Hold up the pictures at the correct times.

6. When you finish, thank your audience for listening.

Active Listening Checklist

1. The opening was interesting: Yes / No

2. I could hear what you were saying: Yes / No

3. The order in which you presented the information made sense: Yes / No

4. The pictures were interesting. They helped show what you were describing: Yes / No

5. The most interesting thing I learned about the person you described was _____ .

Student
Handbook

Viewing Workshop

View and Think

Compare and Contrast Biographies

1. Find a biography of Roberto Clemente on the Internet. Search with the words "Roberto Clemente."

2. Compare and contrast the biography you find with the biography in Chapter 2.

3. Complete a Venn Diagram like the one here to compare and contrast the biographies.

4. Which biography do you think gave better or more information about Roberto Clemente? Explain. Write your answer in a short paragraph.

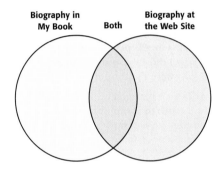

Biography in My Book | Both | Biography at the Web Site

Further Viewing

Watch the *Visions* CNN Video for Unit 2. Do the Video Worksheet.

CNN Video

Content Connection
Science

Suggest that students who have pets might prepare a descriptive presentation about their pets. Point out that since they cannot interview the subject, they will have to do research. Have students observe and take notes on their pets' characteristics, behaviors, and preferences. Tell students to look at or read books on animal behavior to learn more about why their pets may do some of the things they observed.

Learning Styles
Mathematical

Say: An important part of sports biographies is statistics, numbers that tell how well the person plays. Ask students to note any statistics in the biographies they read (runs batted in, stolen bases, and so on). Have students who are baseball fans explain unfamiliar terms to their classmates. Ask them to compare statistics in the two biographies to be sure they are consistent.

UNIT 4
Apply and Expand

Step 2: Organize your presentation. Discuss different openings that will get attention. Using one student's presentation as an example, brainstorm different possible quotes or opinions.

Show students how to support and clarify ideas. Remind them to use examples and elaboration. For example, when they describe a person's character, such as being honest, they should explain *how* he or she has shown herself to be honest.

Step 3: Show pictures that describe what you will say. Remind students that their pictures should be large enough for the class to see during the presentation.

Step 4: Practice your presentation. Review the Presentation Checklist. Model a brief, exaggerated, humorous presentation of the worst presentation behaviors, such as reading from note cards or speak softly and too quickly, so the students see what they should not do. When students practice, have them actually stand up to simulate presenting.

Step 5: Give your presentation in front of the class. Remind students to complete the Active Listening Checklist after listening.

ASSESS

Have students discuss what they found most challenging about giving an oral presentation and any tips they learned.

Portfolio

Students may choose to record or videotape their speeches to place in their portfolios.

Viewing Workshop

View and Think

1. **Research using the Internet** Have students work in pairs or small groups to research using the Internet.

2. **Compare and contrast information** Provide questions to help guide their comparisons. *Ask: What new information did you find on the Web? What information from the text is not mentioned in the book?*

Apply and Expand

Writer's Workshop

Write a Biography

Write a review Read and discuss the prompt. Have students think of other questions they would like to ask the person.

Step 1: Research the person. Have students plan where and when they will do the interview.

Step 2: Use a timeline to organize dates and events in the person's life. Have students explain their timelines in pairs.

Step 3: Write a draft. To help students check their drafts, have them go through with a highlighter or colored pencil and underline the descriptive adjectives and adverbs, time words, and past perfect verbs.

Writer's Workshop

Write a Biography

> **Prompt**
>
> Write a biography of a person you admire. Choose someone you want to know more about. It could be someone in history or a living person.

Your biography should be five paragraphs long. You may use the multiple resources available in your classroom or library, such as encyclopedias, biographies, reference books, and the Internet. Ask your teacher or librarian to help you.

Step 1: Research the person.

Write your questions about this person on note cards. Add to and revise your questions as you learn more information. Here are some questions you might use:

1. When and where was the person born?
2. What are three or four important events in this person's life?
3. When did these events happen?
4. Why were they important?

Write your research on your note cards. Be sure to paraphrase or summarize. Do *not* copy the research information word-for-word.

Step 2: Use a timeline to organize dates and events in the person's life.

Organize your note cards in chronological order. Then put the dates

and events on a timeline. You may add more dates to the timeline.

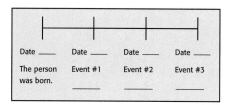

| Date ____ | Date ____ | Date ____ | Date ____ |
| The person was born. | Event #1 | Event #2 | Event #3 |

Step 3: Write a draft.

1. Use the biography outline on page 283. It will help you summarize and organize your information. If possible, write on a computer.
2. Begin with a strong opening. Use superlative adjectives (best, most, fastest, youngest) to clearly describe the person.
3. Use details to describe important events. Use adjectives and adverbs to describe important events and why you admire the person.
4. Use your timeline to put events in correct time order. Show differences in events by using time words, such as *first, then,* and *today,* as well as dates.
5. Use past tense verbs to show an event that already happened. For example, "He <u>won</u> the race."
6. Use past perfect verbs to show two different events that already happened; for example: "He <u>had won</u> the race last year."
7. Choose a title for your biography.

MULTI-LEVEL OPTIONS *Writer's Workshop*

Newcomer Have students create picture biographies. Then have them draw three key events from the person's life. Help students identify words describing qualities of the person to write on each picture. Show students how to bind the pages into a book for the class library.

Beginning Have students draw pictures based on their research. Help them write speech balloons to show what is happening in the pictures. Show students how to bind their biographies into books for the class library.

Intermediate Remind students what they have learned about imagery. Ask them not just to identify important events, but also to include imagery to make the writing clear and interesting. (*Example:* Tio Jorge saved a dog on a snowy night. *vs.* Tio Jorge rushed out of his house in a blizzard to rescue a dog trapped in thick, thorny bushes.)

Advanced When students read or listen to each other's biographies, ask them to take notes on the qualities that students respect in others. Have them write a summary paragraph telling about qualities that are generally admired by students in their class.

I. **Paragraph 1**
  A. Begin with a strong opening.
  B. Who is the person?
  C. When and where was the person born?

II. **Paragraph 2**
  A. Describe the first important event.
    1. What?
    2. When?
    3. Where?
    4. Why?

III. **Paragraph 3**
  A. Describe the first important event.
    1. What?
    2. When?
    3. Where?
    4. Why?

IV. **Paragraph 4**
  A. Describe the first important event.
    1. What?
    2. When?
    3. Where?
    4. Why?

V. **Paragraph 5**
  1. Tell the results of the event.
    1. What impact did the person have?
    2. Why is this person admired?

Step 4: Revise your draft.

1. Ask a partner to read your draft and then complete the Editor's Checklist on a piece of paper.
2. Discuss how you could improve your draft with your partner.
3. Make changes to improve your draft.

Step 5: Edit and proofread.

Use reference materials, such as a dictionary or grammar guide, to help you edit your biography. If you wrote your biography on a computer, run checks for spelling, punctuation, and grammar. Make changes if necessary. Remember to check paragraph indents.

Editor's Checklist

1. The biography has a strong opening.
  ____ Yes ____ No

2. The events are in correct time order. The writer uses transition words.
  ____ Yes ____ No

3. The writer includes details and adjectives.
  ____ Yes ____ No

4. The writer gives reasons for his or her opinions.
  ____ Yes ____ No

5. The writer uses a variety of sentence types: simple, compound, and complex.
  ____ Yes ____ No

Step 6: Publish your biography.

1. If you wrote your biography by hand, rewrite it in your best handwriting. If you wrote it on a computer, use a font and spacing that is easy to read.
2. Make a title page. Include the title and your name.
3. Draw a picture on the title page. The picture should describe something in the biography.
4. Make a copy of your biography for the person you wrote about. Ask if it describes him or her correctly.

The Heinle Newbury House Dictionary   Student Handbook

UNIT 4
Apply and Expand

Step 4: Revise your draft. Remind students to complete the Editor's Checklist after reading their partner's draft.

Step 5: Edit and proofread. Review how to write quotes in reported speech. Have students look at the explanation on p. 278 and check their drafts.

Step 6: Publish your biography. Have students give their biographies to a family member or a friend. Have students report back with what that person said about the biography or what they liked about it. Based on their feedback, have students refine their biographies for the specific audience they chose to share it with.

ASSESS

Have students list four things that should be included in a biography.

Portfolio

Students may choose to include their writing in their portfolios.

Community Connection

Tell students that there are people in each community who have made important contributions to it. Share information about people important to the history of your town, city, or state. Ask students to write paragraphs or draw pictures describing the contributions of those people.

Learning Styles
Intrapersonal

Ask students to think about what they would want someone who was writing a biography about them to say. Have students draft a paragraph or sketch an illustration describing some of their admirable qualities and accomplishments.

UNIT 4
Apply and Expand

Projects

Project 1: Interviews About Heroes

1. **Conduct interviews** Students can work in pairs. Help them decide how and when they will conduct the interviews. Arrange for students to interview another class.
2. **Draw conclusions** Provide phrases for drawing conclusions from their data. For example, write: *Several people think _____ is an important quality. More adults than young people think _____. Not many people think _____ is a hero.*
3. **Revise records** After students have listened to all the findings, have them revise their records in pairs.

Project 2: Be a Hero

1. **Research** Arrange a trip to the school or community library. Have students choose an area of interest before beginning their research.
2. **Interview a hero** In pairs, have students interview each other about their service project. Instruct them to use the interview questions from the Writer's Workshop to find out information about the person they are interviewing. Have students share their interviews with the class.

Portfolio

Students may choose to include their projects in their portfolios.

Projects

These projects will help you learn more about different types of heroes.

Project 1: Interviews About Heroes

Interview five people about their heroes.

1. Copy the Interview Organizer on a piece of paper or use a computer. Prepare questions to fill in the chart.
2. Choose five people of different ages to interview. List their answers.
3. Write a summary of your chart.
   a. Did anyone have the same heroes?
   b. Were most of the heroes famous people or everyday people?
   c. Did the interviewees list similar qualities for their heroes?
   d. Did they have similar or different reasons for picking their heroes?
   e. Draw some conclusions. For example: "Most people chose ordinary people as their heroes."
4. Report your findings to your class. Make a record of the heroes. Analyze the record of these interviews. How many different heroes were identified? What do all the heroes have in common? Organize the records into famous people and everyday people.

Project 2: Be a Hero

There are ways you can be a hero in your school and community.

1. Research areas in your school and community where help is needed. Some ideas might be: clean up a nearby park; read to first-graders in an elementary school; play cards with senior citizens at the nursing center. Your teacher and school librarian will have some ideas.
2. Pick a project you can do by yourself or with a partner.
3. Organize and carry out your service project. How many people are needed to do what you have decided? What tools will you need? Who do you need to talk with to arrange things?
4. After you finish your service project, report back to your class. What did you do? What did you learn? How did the people you helped feel about you? Were you their hero?
5. Write a news report of your service project. Send it to your school newspaper. Remember to answer the *Wh-* questions: *who, what, when, where, why,* and *how.* Try to persuade the newspaper audience to find a community service project to do.

Interview Organizer				
Person's Name	Who is your hero?	Why is this person your hero?	Is your hero a famous or an everyday person?	Three words that describe qualities of a hero

MULTI-LEVEL OPTIONS *Projects*

Newcomer Help students create a poster illustrating their service project. Instruct them to write a title for their poster and draw images of actions they performed and changes their service brought. Display posters in the classroom or school.

Beginning Have students work in pairs to draw a comic strip about their work as heroes. Tell students to include a beginning frame that shows a problem, middle frames that show steps they used in trying to solve it, and an ending that shows the solution.

Intermediate Have students create a design for a "superhero" costume that shows the work they did as a hero in the school or community. Have them present their costume designs to the class, explaining how the costume relates to the work they did.

Advanced Ask students to create stories starring themselves as "service superheroes." *Say: Think of a problem in your community. Decide how you could solve the problem. Create any powers you may need to solve the problem. Think about the steps needed. Think about what would happen in the end.*

Further Reading

Here is a list of books about heroes. Read one or more of them. Write your thoughts and feelings about what you read in your Reading Log. Answer these questions:

1. What makes the people heroes?
2. Which hero inspired you the most?

Pride of Puerto Rico:
The Life of Roberto Clemente
by Paul Robert Walker, Odyssey Classics, 1991. This book tells the life story of the legendary Pittsburgh Pirates right fielder, from his childhood to his tragic death.

Through My Eyes
by Ruby Bridges, Scholastic Trade, 1999. In this book, Ruby Bridges retells her experiences as the first African-American child to attend William Frantz Elementary School, a school for white children.

Heroes of the Day, Vol. 3
by Nancy Louis, ABDO Publishing Co., 2002. On September 11, 2001, real-life heroes saved many lives. This book describes the heroic actions of police officers, paramedics, emergency telephone operators, and ordinary citizens.

Women Warriors: Myths and Legends of Heroic Women
by Marianna Mayer, William Morrow & Co., 1999. This book contains 12 tales, folktales, and myths about female military leaders, warriors, goddesses, and other heroes.

Boys Who Rocked the World:
From King Tut to Tiger Woods
by Mattie Stepanek, Beyond Words Publishing Co., 2001. This book features the biographies of 30 boys who changed the world by the age of 20. The biographies include a wide range of people, from King Tut to Bill Gates.

Girls Who Rocked the World: Heroines from Sacajawea to Sheryl Swoopes
by Amelie Welden, Gareth Stevens, 1999. This book includes 35 biographies about girls who changed the world by the time they were 20 years old. The biographies include Anne Frank, Jane Goodall, and Joan of Arc.

B. Franklin, Printer
by David A. Adler, Holiday House, 2001. Printer, writer, scientist, inventor, patriot: everything Franklin did was marked by cheer, energy, and hard work. He organized the postal system and America's first subscription library. Now he is our favorite Founding Father.

Tallchief: America's Prima Ballerina
by Maria Tallchief with Rosemary Wells, Viking, 1999. Born with music in her body, Tallchief became the greatest American-born ballerina of her time, even though she didn't formally study ballet until age 18. This book details her growing-up years that inspired her dancing.

Companion Web site   Reading Log   Heinle Reading Library The Red Badge of Courage

---

UNIT 4
Apply and Expand

Further Reading

1. **Read summaries** Have volunteers read the summaries. Ask students which books would interest them and why.
2. **Locate resources** Ask volunteers to check titles out from the library and bring them to class. Students can read the books during free time or for a special assignment.

▪ Assessment Program: *Unit 4 Test, pp. 69–74*

Heinle Reading Library

The Red Badge of Courage by Stephen Crane In a specially adapted version by Malvina G. Vogel

The time is 1863. The setting, the Civil War, America's bloodiest conflict. Henry Fleming, a country boy on the Union side, is full of emotion as he and his fellow soldiers wait for their first battle to begin. Will Henry become the hero he dreams of being? Will he and his friends even survive the deadly fire of the enemy? And who is the enemy, but other American boys like himself? Fear and courage exist at the same time, as each man undergoes his own trial by fire, his own grasping for the red badge. . . .

Visions Companion Site

http://visions.heinle.com
For additional student activities and teacher resources, see the Visions Companion Web site.

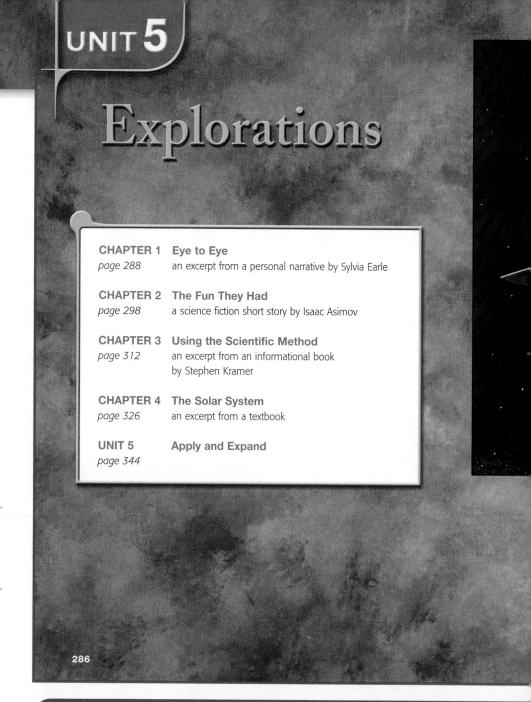

Unit Materials

Activity Book: *pp. 153–184*
Audio: *Unit 5; CD 2, Tracks 7–10*
Student Handbook
Student CD-ROM: *Unit 5*
CNN Video: *Unit 5*
Teacher Resource Book: *Lesson Plans, Teacher Resources, Reading Summaries, School-Home Connection, Video Script, Video Worksheet, Activity Book Answer Key*
Teacher Resource CD-ROM
Assessment Program: *Quizzes and Test, pp. 75–88; Teacher and Student Resources, pp. 115–144*
Assessment CD-ROM
Transparencies
The Heinle Newbury House Dictionary/CD-ROM
More Grammar Practice workbook
Heinle Reading Library: *The Invisible Man*
Web site: http://visions.heinle.com

Visions Staff Development Handbook

Refer to the Visions Staff Development Handbook for more teacher support.

Unit Theme: Explorations

▌ Teacher Resource Book: *Web, p. 37*

Clarify the theme word On the board, write: *explorations.* Ask students for related words and write them in a word web on the board.

Unit Preview: Table of Contents

1. **Use the table of contents to make predictions** Read the chapter titles and authors. *Ask: What are the genres in this unit?* (personal narrative, science fiction short story, informational book, textbook)
2. **Connect** *Ask: What are some popular science fiction movies?*

UNIT 5

Explorations

286

UNIT OBJECTIVES

Reading
Draw conclusions as you read a personal narrative ● Make inferences from text evidence as you read science fiction ● Recognize cause and effect relationships as you read an informational text ● Summarize information as you read an excerpt from a textbook

Listening and Speaking
Describe a place that you have explored ● Present advantages and disadvantages ● Use information to raise unanswered questions ● Paraphrase to recall information

Winged Shuttle Craft, Concept drawing by North American Rockwell Corporation.

View the Picture

1. What is this shuttle craft exploring?
2. Have you ever explored something? Have you explored a new part of your town? Have you read a new kind of book?

In this unit, you will read three nonfiction selections and one science fiction short story. Each reading focuses on an exploration. You will also learn the elements of these forms and how to write them yourself.

287

View the Picture

1. **Art background** Tell students that North American Rockwell created this concept for a winged shuttlecraft for NASA. It is designed to carry astronauts or cargo between Earth and distant space stations. *Ask: Do you think the artist is actually looking at this shuttlecraft or drew it from imagination? Why do scientists need illustrations like this "concept" when they are designing machines for space travel?*

2. **Art interpretation** *Ask: What place in this illustration draws your attention? What do you like about this art?*

   a. **Speculate about shape and form** Have students discuss the purposes of the different "wings" of the shuttle. For example, ask them why some are cylinders (storing supplies or fuel) or what the "dish" might be used for. (communication)

   b. **Explore and describe color** Point out that the sky is dark. Ask them to discuss where the light is coming from that illuminates the shuttle and Earth. Ask them if the colors and Earth seem realistic.

3. **Connect to theme** *Say: The theme of this unit is* exploration. *What difficulties do you think space explorers like ones who use these shuttles faced?*

ASSESS

Have students draw a picture of the inside of this space shuttle.

Grammar

Recognize and use the simple past tense
- Use dependent clauses with *because*
- Use *might* to show possibility • Identify superlative adjectives

Writing

Write a personal narrative • Write an ending to a science fiction short story
- Write an informational text • Outline an informational text

Content

Science: Identify types of scientists
- Science: Define Internet terms
- Science: Learn about sleep • Science: Compare planet orbits

CHAPTER 1

Eye to Eye

an excerpt from a
personal narrative
by Sylvia Earle

Into the Reading

Chapter Materials

Activity Book: *pp. 153–160*
Audio: *Unit 5, Chapter 1; CD 2, Track 7*
Student Handbook
Student CD-ROM: *Unit 5, Chapter 1*
Teacher Resource Book: *Lesson Plan, Teacher
    Resources, Reading Summary, Activity Book
    Answer Key*
Teacher Resource CD-ROM
Assessment Program: *Quiz, pp. 75–76; Teacher
    and Student Resources, pp. 115–144*
Assessment CD-ROM
Transparencies
The Heinle Newbury House Dictionary/CD-ROM
Web site: http://visions.heinle.com

Objectives

Preview Read the objectives aloud. *Ask: Which
objective do you already know something
about? What verb tenses have we already
learned?*

Use Prior Knowledge

Explore What You Know About Whales

Use prior knowledge Have students share
what they know about whales. On the board,
have students write what else they would like
to learn about whales.

Answers
1. F 2. T 3. T 4. F 5. F

Objectives

Reading Draw conclusions as you read a
personal narrative.

Listening and Speaking Describe a
place that you have explored.

Grammar Recognize and use the simple
past tense.

Writing Write a personal narrative.

Content Science: Identify types
of scientists.

Use Prior Knowledge

Explore What You Know About Whales

In "Eye to Eye," the author describes
whales. What do you know about whales?

Read each statement. On a piece of
paper, write *T* if you think the statement is
true and *F* if you think the statement is
false. Discuss your answers with a partner.
Check them with your teacher.

1. Whales are fish.
2. There are many kinds of whales.
3. Whales can swim very fast.
4. Whales do not make sounds.
5. Most whales live in the same place
   their whole life.

MULTI-LEVEL OPTIONS *Build Vocabulary*

Newcomer Draw or show
pictures of a dinner and a snack.
On the board, write: *main.* Point to
the dinner. *Say: main meal.* Then
write: *mane.* Show a picture of a
horse. Point to its mane. *Say:
horse's mane,* emphasizing the
vocabulary word. Use the same
procedure to introduce *sea/see*
and *wail/whale.*

Beginning Write the sentences
on the board with the vocabulary
words but not the definitions.
Read the sentences aloud. Mime
the meanings of the vocabulary
choices. Have students pick the
correct words and circle them on
the board.

Intermediate Have students
create an additional sentence for
each of the six words. Ask them to
read aloud their sentences and
have partners determine which
vocabulary word will complete
each.

Advanced Have students
create a descriptive paragraph
using as many of the vocabulary
words as possible. As they read
aloud their descriptions, have
classmates identify the spellings
of the vocabulary words used.

Build Background

Humpback Whales

Humpback whales live in all of the world's oceans. They usually grow to about 40 to 50 feet (12 to 15 meters) long. Humpback whales can sing. Their songs have many different sounds. Humpback whales in the same area may sing the same songs and, over time, make the same changes to their songs.

 Content Connection
Many scientists believe that humpback whales sing to communicate with one another.

Build Vocabulary

Use Context to Identify Correct Homophones

Homophones are words that are pronounced the same but have different meanings. Homophones may also have different spellings.

main most important

mane a long strip of hair on the neck of some animals

Choose the correct homophone for the following sentences. Use the **context**—nearby words or the sentence meaning. Use a dictionary to pronounce each homophone.

1. I called to _____ if the store was still open.
   a. **see** find out about something
   b. **sea** a body of salt water
2. The _____ lives in the ocean.
   a. **wail** a cry of sadness
   b. **whale** a very large mammal shaped like a fish

 The Heinle Newbury House Dictionary

 Activity Book p. 153

 Student CD-ROM

Chapter 1 Eye to Eye **289**

 **Content Connection**
Math

Build Background Help students understand the enormity of whales. Have students measure the length of the classroom and compare it to the length of a humpback. (40–50 feet) Tell students that the average humpback weighs 40 tons. Point out that an average pony weighs 600 pounds. Ask them to convert the whale's weight to pounds (80,000) and estimate how many times heavier a whale is than a pony (about 133 times).

Learning Styles
Kinesthetic

Build Vocabulary Divide the class into two teams. Tell students in each team to list phrases that include the vocabulary words, such as Main Street, main event, horse's mane, zebra's mane. Have students play charades. Each team will act out the phrases it has written. When the other team guesses the phrase, it must spell the vocabulary word.

Build Background

Humpback Whales

1. **Analyze facts** Have each student write two questions about the paragraph. Have them ask the questions in small groups.
2. **Content Connection** Whales are the only mammals on earth that spend their entire lives, from birth to death, in the water. They are also the only animals, besides elephants, with brains larger than humans.

Build Vocabulary

Use Context to Identify Correct Homophones

Teacher Resource Book: *Personal Dictionary,* p. 63

1. **Clarify terms** *Say: Homophones have the same sound but different meanings.* Write: *son, it's, two, your, eye, won, their. Ask: Do you know the homophones for these words?* (sun; its; too, to; you're; I; one; there, they're)
2. **Use a glossary** Have students locate the meaning and derivation of *homophone* in the glossary of their Student Handbook or other sources, such as online or CD-ROM dictionaries.
3. **Reading selection vocabulary** You may want to introduce the glossed words in the reading selection before students begin reading. Key words: *brakes, flippers, aid, record, vibrated, orchestra.* Instruct students to write the words with correct spelling and their definitions in their Personal Dictionaries. Have them pronounce each word and divide it into syllables.
4. **Multi-level options** See MULTI-LEVEL OPTIONS on p. 288.

Answers
1. a 2. b

 ASSESS

Write on the board: *main, mane, sea, see, wail, whale.* Have students say sentences with the homophones. Then have the class give the correct spelling of each.

Text Structure

Personal Narrative

1. **Review features of a personal narrative** *Say: "Talking in the New Land" (p. 194) and "Birthday Barbecue" (p. 8) are personal narratives. What are some features of a personal narrative?* (first person, based on real events)
2. **Multi-level options** See MULTI-LEVEL OPTIONS below.

Reading Strategy

Draw Conclusions

Draw conclusions Have students reread paragraph 1 of "Talking in the New Land." (p. 194) *Say: The author writes that she could hide from her brothers. What does your experience tell you about hiding? When do you hide from someone? So what conclusion could you draw about how the author feels about her brothers sometimes?* (They sometimes bother her or annoy her, so she likes to hide from them.)

ASSESS

Have students look up *conclusion* in the dictionary and select the best meaning for this usage.

Text Structure

Personal Narrative

"Eye to Eye" is a **personal narrative.** A personal narrative describes real events that happened to the author. It tells those events as a story. As you read the selection, look for the features of a personal narrative shown in the chart.

As you read "Eye to Eye," notice that you learn about humpback whales and the author's feelings about these whales.

Personal Narrative	
Events	what happens to the author
First-Person Pronouns	*I, me, we,* and *us*
Descriptive Language	sense words that help readers see and feel what happens
Details	information about what the author knows or learns

Student CD-ROM

Reading Strategy

Draw Conclusions

Authors do not always explain everything. Sometimes, you must **draw conclusions** to figure out what an author thinks or feels. To draw conclusions, use what the author writes and your experiences to determine what the author thinks or feels.

In Unit 4, you made inferences from what you read and your experiences. This is similar to drawing conclusions.

As you read "Eye to Eye," draw conclusions about the author, Sylvia Earle. Use a chart like this one. Write your conclusions in your Reading Log.

What the Author Writes	Your Experiences	Your Conclusion
As soon as I got home, I went to bed.	You know from your experiences that people go to bed when they are tired.	The author probably was tired.

MULTI-LEVEL OPTIONS *Text Structure*

Newcomer Have students bring in photographs of themselves showing an event such as a holiday, family party, or trip. Help students identify descriptive words they could use in telling stories about the events.

Beginning Have students bring in photos of themselves at family events. Help them paperclip their photos to pieces of colored construction paper to form a border. Ask students to write words and phrases in the border that relate to the stories that the photos tell.

Intermediate Have students bring in a photo of themselves and think about the story it tells. Have them create a web with a branch for sight, sound, taste, smell, and texture. Ask students to write descriptive language on the branches that they could use in telling the story of the photo.

Advanced Have students bring in photos of themselves. Ask them to meet in small groups to show the photos and tell the story behind each. Have students include descriptive language and interesting details in their comments.

Eye to Eye

an excerpt from a personal narrative
by Sylvia Earle

291

Reading Selection Materials

Audio: *Unit 5, Chapter 1; CD 2, Track 7*
Teacher Resource Book: *Reading Summary,*
pp. 103–104
Transparencies: *#12, Reading Summary*

Suggestions for Using Reading Summary

- Introduce new vocabulary or cognates.
- Cut the summary into strips, or jumble the sentences on an overhead transparency. Students put the sentences in order.
- Practice the reading strategy.
- Students read aloud or with a partner.
- Students paraphrase the summary.
- Students do a cloze activity.
- Students create a visual or graphic organizer, such as a timeline or storyboard, to illustrate the summary.
- Students paraphrase the summary.

Preview the Selection

1. **Interpret the image** Have students look at the photo. *Ask: What's the whale doing?* (jumping) *Can you see the flippers? The tail? Where do you think this photo might have been taken?*
2. **Connect to theme** *Say: We usually think of exploring new lands or exploring outer space. But people who study animals explore in a different way. They look for answers to questions we have about animals.*

Content Connection
Science

Learning Styles
Natural

In preparation for reading, have small groups of students use books, pictures, and Internet sites to find out more about humpback whales. Ask each group to summarize what it learns by making a diagram of a whale. Ask students to label parts, such as flippers, "hump," and skin colors.

Tell students that they will read about a scientist who took a trip to explore whales. Ask students to look at the picture on p. 291 and think about what kind of ship and tools a scientist might need for this type of exploration. Have them imagine what the trip to the whale's underwater home might be like. Tell students to draw or write journal entries that a scientist headed out to sea to explore whales might write.

Read the Selection

1. **Use a map** Have students look at the map and then locate Hawaii on a globe or world map. *Ask: What kind of climate does Hawaii have? Do you think the water is warm there?* Point out that Hawaii is on the same latitude as Central America and is near the equator, so it has a tropical climate.

2. **Shared reading** Read the selection aloud. Then have students take turns reading paragraphs with you. Ask questions to help students use and understand new vocabulary. *Ask: When do you use brakes?* (riding a bike) *Why are brakes important?* (so you don't crash into things) *What other animals have flippers?* (ducks, dolphins, seals)

3. **Pair work** Have students work together to write an answer to the guide question.

Sample Answer to Guide Question
She doesn't seem to be afraid or worried about her personal safety. She says, "It was too late to worry . . ."

See Teacher Edition pp. 434–436 for a list of English-Spanish cognates in the reading selection.

Audio
CD 2. Tr. 7

Prologue
Sylvia Earle is a scientist who studies ocean plants and animals. In "Eye to Eye," Earle is working with other scientists to study humpback whales. These scientists want to know more about the actions of these whales, such as why they sing and how they move underwater.

> **Draw Conclusions**
>
> How do you think Sylvia Earle feels as the whale swims toward her? Explain why you think so.

1 I was floating in clear, warm water along the coast of Maui, one of the Hawaiian Islands. Far below was the largest creature I had ever seen—a female humpback whale. She looked as big as a bus and was heading straight toward me. It was too late to worry about whether or not I was in her way or if whales have **brakes.**

2 A moment later her **grapefruit-size** eyes met mine. She **tilted** right, then left, as her 15-foot **flippers** and powerful tail **propelled** her past me far faster than humans can swim or run. I glanced at my own slip-on flippers, a wonderful **aid** for human feet underwater but no match for a whale's **built-in propulsion system . . .**

3 "Home" for whales is a place several thousand miles long, with the dining room at one end in cool, northern waters and the **nursery** at the other in the **tropics.**

The Hawaiian Islands

brakes tools that stop something	**aid** help, assistance
grapefruit-size something the size of a grapefruit, a large, round fruit	**built-in** having as part of something; something that cannot be removed
tilted leaned	**propulsion system** a system used to get an object to start moving and keep it moving
flippers wide, flat limbs on certain sea animals, used for swimming; objects that people wear on their feet to swim faster and more easily	**nursery** (in this reading) the place where young whales grow up
propelled moved something with force; thrust	**tropics** the hot region of Earth

292 Unit 5 Explorations

MULTI-LEVEL OPTIONS *Read the Selection*

Newcomer Play the audio. Then have students read the Reading Summary. *Ask: Is the scientist studying whales?* (yes) *Is the scientist in the water with the whales?* (yes) *Is she afraid of whales?* (no) *Does she want to hear the sounds whales make?* (yes)

Beginning Read aloud the selection. Then have students reread it in pairs. *Ask: What kind of whale is the scientist studying?* (humpback) *What do whales use to swim?* (flippers) *Where do whales swim when they leave the cold waters in the north?* (to Hawaii) *What does the scientist want to hear?* (whale songs)

Intermediate Have students read aloud in pairs. *Ask: How do you think the scientist feels about whales? Explain.* (She thinks they are amazing; she talks about interesting things they do.) *Why was it hard to record whale sounds?* (There were many sounds from all directions.)

Advanced Have students read silently. *Ask: What does the author mean when she talks about whales having brakes?* (She didn't know if the whale would crash into her.) *What does paragraph 3 mean?* (Whales swim over a big area, finding food in the cold areas and having babies in the warm areas.)

4   In Hawaii Al [Giddings, a photographer,] and I were in the nursery, trying to see if we could **record** the short **grunts** and **squeals associated** with certain whale behaviors . . .

5   It might seem easy, but when swimming underwater, it is almost impossible to determine the direction sounds are coming from. Often, many whales are **vocalizing** at once, and the sounds may travel many miles.

6   In the weeks that followed we heard whales singing day and night, and once while underwater, whalesong was so loud that the air spaces in my body **vibrated**—a feeling something like being next to a very loud drum or in the **midst** of an **orchestra** . . .

Draw Conclusions

Sylvia Earle listens to whale songs for weeks. What conclusions can you draw about her?

---

record   make a sound or video recording of something on a disk or tape
grunts   short, deep sounds, from the throat
squeals   high-pitched screams
associated   connected

vocalizing   speaking, singing
vibrated   shook
midst   the middle of a place or an activity
orchestra   a usually large group of musicians who play music on instruments, such as the violin and horns

---

About the Author

Sylvia Earle (born 1935)

As a child, Sylvia Earle loved nature and the ocean. When she grew up, Earle became a scientist. She studies plants and animals that live in the ocean. She has said, "I was swept off my feet by a wave when I was three and have been in love with the sea ever since . . . everywhere [there are] strange and wonderful forms of life that occur only underwater."

➤ Why do you think that Sylvia Earle wrote "Eye to Eye"? To teach people about humpback whales? Or to describe what it was like to study humpback whales? Explain.

Chapter 1   Eye to Eye   **293**

 Spelling

Oa for the long /o/ sound

Tell students that there are several ways to spell long /o/. *Ask: What are two words in paragraph 1 that have the long /o/ sound?* (floating, coast) *What vowels do you see in the middle of these words?* (oa) *Yes, oa is one way of spelling the long /o/ sound.*

Apply   On the board, write: *boat, toast, throat, foam, coat.* Have students draw sketches to show the meaning of each word.

Evaluate Your Reading Strategy

Draw Conclusions   *Say: You have practiced an important reading strategy. Now you can decide how well you have done. Does this statement describe how you read?*

In order to draw conclusions, I first read the text carefully. Then I ask myself, "What does the text tell me about the author?" Drawing conclusions helps me better understand what the author thinks and feels.

Read the Selection

1. **Paired reading**   Play the audio. Then have students read aloud with a partner.
2. **Identify facts**   Have students work in pairs to find facts in the text. (*Examples:* Humpback whales can have eyes the size of grapefruits and 15-foot flippers. They use their tails for propulsion. Their home is from the northern waters to the tropics.)
3. **Locate derivations using dictionaries**   Have students look at these glossed words and determine what words they are derived from: *propelled, associated, vocalizing, vibrated.* Have students check the derivations in a print, online, or CD-ROM dictionary.
4. **Multi-level options**   See MULTI-LEVEL OPTIONS on p. 292.

Sample Answer to Guide Question
She is patient and determined. She is a dedicated scientist.

About the Author

Discuss facts   Have students read aloud in small groups. Then tell them to write two factual questions about the author. Have groups exchange the questions and answer them.

Answer
Example: I think her main purpose was to describe what it was like studying whales because she talks about how she felt. She also includes a lot of information about whales, however, so her narrative is informative, too.

Across Selections

Compare genres   Direct students to "Rain Forest Creatures" on p. 135. *Ask: Is this an informational text or a personal narrative?* (personal narrative) *What is the point of view?* (first-person) *How is this selection similar to "Eye to Eye"?* (They both give factual information about animals.) *Which selection did you enjoy more, and why?*

Spelling, Punctuation, Capitalization

After the Reading Comprehension section, students will practice spelling, punctuation, and capitalization in the Activity Book.

Beyond the Reading

Reading Comprehension

Question-Answer Relationships

Sample Answers

1. Sylvia Earle
2. She was in the water off the coast of Maui, Hawaii.
3. It's hard to tell because she is underwater and many whales are vocalizing at once.
4. their 15-foot flippers and a powerful tail
5. slip-on flippers
6. They sound like being in the middle of an orchestra.
7. It would be interesting to go to tropical climates. The dangers in the ocean—from tides to sharks—would be scary.
8. What made you decide to specialize in studying whales?

Build Reading Fluency

Read Silently

| Assessment Program: *Reading Fluency Chart, p. 116*

When students have completed the reading fluency activity, record their progress in the Reading Fluency Chart.

Reading Comprehension

Question-Answer Relationships (QAR)

"Right There" Questions

1. **Recall Facts** Who is the author of "Eye to Eye"?
2. **Recall Details** Where is Earle when she first sees the female humpback whale?

"Think and Search" Questions

3. **Recognize Cause and Effect** Why is it often difficult for Earle to tell where whale sounds are coming from?
4. **Explain** Reread paragraph 2. What helps humpback whales swim faster than humans?
5. **Identify** What does Earle use to help her swim underwater?

"Author and You" Question

6. **Paraphrase** Reread paragraph 6. Using your own words, describe what the whale songs sound like to Earle.

"On Your Own" Questions

7. **Evaluate** What do you think would be interesting about being an ocean scientist? What would be scary?
8. **Understand Author's Perspective** What question would you like to ask the author?

Activity Book
p. 154

Student
CD-ROM

Build Reading Fluency

Read Silently

Reading silently is good practice. It helps you learn to read faster. An effective reader reads silently for increasing lengths of time.

1. Listen to the audio recording of paragraphs 1 and 2 on page 292.
2. Listen to the chunks of words as you follow along.
3. Reread paragraphs 1 and 2 silently two times.
4. Your teacher will time your second reading.
5. Raise your hand when you are done.
6. Record your timing.

MULTI-LEVEL OPTIONS *Elements of Literature*

Newcomer In the outer circles of their webs, have students draw pictures for the things being compared. Challenge students to think of other comparisons that could be used in place of *bus, grapefruits,* and *drum.* Ask them to add circles on the right and draw pictures for these ideas.

Beginning Have students think of additional comparisons related to humpback whales and create webs for them. (*Example:* whale/heavy/locomotive)

Intermediate Direct students to the picture on p. 291. Ask them to write three descriptive sentences about the whale using *like* or *as.*

Advanced Have students brainstorm words for emotions Sylvia Earle might have felt concerning her exploration. (curious, excited, amazed) Ask students to write sentences comparing her feelings about her adventure to other events, using *like* or *as.* (*Example:* As I jumped into the sea, I felt as excited as someone opening a gift.)

Listen, Speak, Interact

Describe a Place That You Have Explored

When you explore, you go somewhere new or do something to learn new things. What places have you explored?

1. On a piece of paper, brainstorm a list of places that you have explored; for example, a community park.
2. Choose one place on your list. Write a description of three things that you learned about this place.
3. In a small group, take turns describing the place that you explored. Ask and answer questions about each description.

Places That I Have Explored
• the park in my community
• Blue Beach
• a new store by my house
In the park in my community:
People play soccer in the park.
There's a statue of a horse.
There's a garden with roses.

Elements of Literature

Analyze Figurative Language

Sylvia Earle uses **figurative language** to help readers form images (pictures) in their minds.

One way to use figurative language is to use the words *like* or *as* to compare two things. This is called a *simile*.

<u>The whale</u> looked **as big as** <u>a bus</u>.

The author compares the size of the whale to a bus. It shows readers how big the whale is.

1. Write these sentences in your Reading Log.
   a. The whale's eyes were as large as grapefruits.
   b. The whale sounded like a loud, deep drum.
2. Complete a word web like the one shown. In the outer circles, write the two things that are being compared in each sentence. In the middle circle, write what quality describes the two things.

Activity Book p. 155   Student CD-ROM

Chapter 1 Eye to Eye   **295**

Content Connection
The Arts

Enter the key words *whale* and *song* into an Internet search engine. Choose a site with a description saying that visitors can listen to whale songs. Let students listen to several and then write sentences using *like* or *as* to compare the whale sounds to other sounds. (*Example:* The whale song sounded like a low siren.)

Learning Styles
Intrapersonal

Say: Think about what attracted you to explore the place you described in Listen, Speak, and Interact. Think of a friend or family member who might like that place, too. Write a sentence explaining who might like the place and why. (*Example:* My grandma might like to explore Blue Beach, too, because she collects seashells.)

Listen, Speak, Interact

Describe a Place That You Have Explored

1. **Provide a model** Describe a place that you have explored. For example, *say: When I was in New York City, I explored Central Park. I learned you can row a boat, ice skate, or visit a zoo there. There are concerts and plays in the summer.*
2. **Newcomers** Have students draw pictures of places they have explored. Help them write three descriptive words or phrases.

Elements of Literature

Analyze Figurative Language

1. **Use figurative language** Write on the board: *They had flippers as big as _____. The ocean water was as _____ as _____.* Have students work in pairs to complete the sentences with new figurative language. (*examples:* doors; warm/a bath)
2. **Interpret the literary device** Have students find other examples of figurative language in the reading. (Paragraph 6 — like being in the middle of an orchestra; Paragraph 3 — dining room at one end, nursery in the tropics)
3. **Multi-level options** See MULTI-LEVEL OPTIONS on p. 294.

Answers
2. a. eyes—large—grapefruits
   b. whale—sounded like—drum

✓ ASSESS

Have students write a sentence describing one feature of a whale using figurative language.

Word Study

Recognize Compound Adjectives

Use compound adjectives Write on the board: *Her grapefruit-size eyes met mine. Her eyes were grapefruit size.* Tell students that the compound adjectives in the reading only take a hyphen when they come *before* the noun.

Answers
2. a. grapefruit + size → grapefruit-size; about the size of a grapefruit **b.** fifteen + foot → fifteen-foot; having a length of fifteen feet **c.** slip + on → slip-on; able to slip on and off easily

Grammar Focus

Recognize and Use the Simple Past Tense

Review irregular verbs Divide the class into small groups and give them five minutes to list as many irregular past tense verbs as possible. When the time is up have each group write their list on the board. Compare and correct the lists.

Answers
followed, heard, was, vibrated

ASSESS

Say: Write two sentences about what you did yesterday.

Word Study

Recognize Compound Adjectives

Compound adjectives are adjectives that are made up of two or more words. Many compound adjectives contain a **hyphen** (-). You can often find the meaning of a compound adjective by looking at the words it contains.

The hour-long movie was very funny.

Hour-long contains *hour* and *long*. It means "lasting for an hour."

First Word	Second Word	Compound Adjective	Meaning
hour +	long ⇒	hour-long	lasting an hour
+	⇒		
+	⇒		
+	⇒		

1. Read these sentences.
  a. Her grapefruit-size eyes met mine.
  b. Her fifteen-foot flippers propelled her past me.
  c. I glanced at my own slip-on flippers.
2. In your Personal Dictionary, complete a chart like the one shown. Write the words that make up each of the compound adjectives.

Personal Dictionary   The Heinle Newbury House Dictionary   Activity Book p. 156   Student CD-ROM

Grammar Focus

Recognize and Use the Simple Past Tense

The **simple past tense** describes an action that began and ended in the past. Regular past tense verbs end in *-d* or *-ed*.

She tilt**ed** right, then left.

Some verbs are irregular. Their past tense forms are spelled differently. The verb *be* has two past tense forms.

Reread paragraph 6 of the selection and find the four past tense verbs in it.

Simple Form	Past Tense Form
go	went
meet	met
see	saw
hear	heard

Be: Past Tense Forms	
I/He/She	**was** at school yesterday.
You/We/They	**were** at school yesterday.

Activity Book pp. 157–158   Student Handbook   Student CD-ROM

296 Unit 5 Explorations

MULTI-LEVEL OPTIONS *From Reading to Writing*

Newcomer Ask students to write their stories in a storyboard. Have them draw the characters (themselves, the animals), the setting, and several of the qualities or actions of the animals. Have them show how they felt about seeing the animals. Provide time for sharing.

Beginning Have students create storyboards using words and phrases to tell about the animals, the setting, the sights, sounds, and smells related to the creatures, and their feelings about them. Provide time for pairs to share their storyboards.

Intermediate Have students make sensory webs to brainstorm descriptions of the sights, sounds, and smells related to the animals they are writing about. Tell students to include some of these ideas in their narratives.

Advanced Direct students to paragraph 3. *Say: This fact is not something that the writer saw on her trip. It is a fact she probably learned from a book.* Before students begin writing, ask them to read encyclopedia articles about their subjects. Suggest that they include a fact or two in their narratives.

From Reading to Writing

Write a Personal Narrative

On a piece of paper, draw a picture of an unusual animal. Then write a two-paragraph personal narrative about it.

1. Use the first-person pronouns *I, me, we,* and *us.* These pronouns show that you are describing what happened to you and what you saw.
2. Use figurative language. Compare the animal to something else.
3. Use comparative and superlative adjectives to describe great things about your animal. For example, your animal might be stronger than another animal, or it might be the strongest of a group.

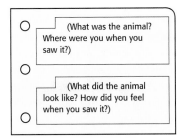

○ ⎡ (What was the animal? Where were you when you saw it?)

○ ⎡ (What did the animal look like? How did you feel when you saw it?)

○

4. Enter your draft on a computer. Use spell check to check your spelling.

Activity Book
p. 159

Student
Handbook

Across Content Areas

Identify Types of Scientists

Sylvia Earle is a **scientist**—a person who works in science. There are many different types of scientists. Here is a list of some types:

biologist	a person who studies living things
botanist	a person who studies plants and trees
zoologist	a person who studies animals
marine biologist	a person who studies things that live in the ocean

Work with a partner to write a job application form. Suppose this form would be used to hire one of these scientists for your town. Organize the form to include sections for name, address, and experience. Also include a section for a description of the job. Revise your form as you think of more needs for the community.

Activity Book
p. 160

Reteach and Reassess

Text Structure Have students review the chart on p. 290. Tell them to underline an example of each feature in the narratives they wrote or drew. Ask them to use a different color marker for each feature.

Reading Strategy Have students create a trait web with Sylvia Earle's name in the center. *Say: Draw branches coming out from the center. Put a circle at the end of each branch. Write a trait you think the author has in the circle. Write your reason for thinking she has that trait on the branch.*

Elements of Literature Have students use figurative language to describe an interesting tree, plant, or flower.

Reassess Have students review About the Author from *Plain Talk About Handling Stress* (p. 217). Help them recall the article and *ask: What conclusions can you draw about the author's thoughts and feelings?*

From Reading to Writing

Write a Personal Narrative

1. **Discuss unusual animals** Bring in pictures of unusual animals. Help students identify the animals and think of some descriptions using figurative language. For example, *This alligator's mouth is as dangerous as a knife.* Talk about where you might see these animals.
2. **Use various forms** Give students the option of *choosing* a form for their writing. They may choose to write a diary entry, a poem, a report, etc.
3. **Review selection** Have students review the reading selection in this chapter. Analyze the organization and technique the author uses. *Ask: What aspects of the reading will you model when you write your own personal narrative?*
4. **Multi-level options** See MULTI-LEVEL OPTIONS on p. 296.

Across Content Areas: Science

Identify Types of Scientists

1. **Refer to content classes** *Ask: What are you studying in science class? What type of scientist studies that topic?* Write on the board: chemist, physicist, metallurgist. *Ask: What do you think these scientists study?*
2. **Brainstorm a list** Have students brainstorm a list of qualifications for the job. Then instruct them to write questions about the qualifications. Tell students to include these questions on the job application.

 **ASSESS**

Have students list features of a personal narrative.

Chapter Materials

Activity Book: *pp. 161–168*
Audio: *Unit 5, Chapter 2; CD 2, Track 8*
Student Handbook
Student CD-ROM: *Unit 5, Chapter 2*
Teacher Resource Book: *Lesson Plan, Teacher Resources, Reading Summary, Activity Book Answer Key*
Teacher Resource CD-ROM
Assessment Program: *Quiz, pp. 77–78; Teacher and Student Resources, pp. 115–144*
Assessment CD-ROM
Transparencies
The Heinle Newbury House Dictionary/CD-ROM
Web site: http://visions.heinle.com

The Fun They Had

a science fiction short story by Isaac Asimov

Objectives

Reading Make inferences from text evidence as you read science fiction.

Listening and Speaking Present advantages and disadvantages.

Grammar Use dependent clauses with *because*.

Writing Write an ending to a science fiction short story.

Content Science: Define Internet terms.

Objectives

Preview Have a student read the objectives aloud. *Ask: Which objectives do you already know something about?*

Use Prior Knowledge

Compare and Contrast Schools

Group work Before students do their Venn diagrams, talk about schools they could compare. They could compare their school with another school in the area, with a private/public school, or with schools in other countries. After they have finished the group work, invite several students to put their diagrams on the board.

Use Prior Knowledge

Compare and Contrast Schools

Compare and contrast schools that you know about.

1. Work with a small group. Compare and contrast these topics:
   a. what the school buildings look like
   b. the number of students that go to the schools
   c. the subjects taught
   d. the ages of the students
2. On a separate piece of paper, complete a Venn Diagram like this one. Use the information from your discussion to complete the diagram with your group.
3. Discuss your Venn Diagram with the class.

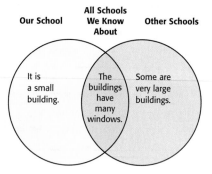

MULTI-LEVEL OPTIONS *Build Vocabulary*

Newcomer Write on the board: *1 run, 2 run.* Point to the first and mime jogging. Point to the second and mime operating a vacuum cleaner. Introduce two meanings of *funny* and *awfully* in the same manner.

Beginning Divide the class into groups of six. Give each student in each group a card with one of the vocabulary words on one side and its definition on the other. Say and act out sentences, such as *The milk smelled funny.* Have the student in each group who has the correct word and definition hold up the card.

Intermediate Ask students to use dictionaries to find as many additional meanings as they can for *run* and write sentences that reflect those meanings. (*Example:* Jan will *run* for class president.)

Advanced Have students explore some other multiple meaning words and make charts to show their meanings. For example, they may use dictionaries to look up: *sign, wound, mine,* and *fly.*

Build Background

Schooling in the United States

Schools in the United States have changed over the years. In the mid-1600s, people from England set up the first public schools paid for by the public. Many of the school buildings had only one room. Students of all ages learned together.

In the mid-1800s, many schools put children into grades. Each grade had its own room and teacher. Many states wrote laws saying that all children must go to school. Today, all children in the United States must go to school. They learn many different subjects.

Content Connection

In the United States, **public schools** are free for students and are paid for by people in the community and the government.

Build Vocabulary

Explore Multiple Meaning Words

Multiple meaning words are words that are spelled and pronounced the same but have different meanings. For example, *run* can mean "to move quickly on foot" or "to make a machine work."

I love to exercise. I <u>run</u> five miles a day.

You know from the first sentence that the person is talking about exercise. So, *run* in this sentence means "to move quickly on foot."

Decide which meaning the words have in these sentences.

1. The movie was very <u>funny</u>. I laughed until my sides hurt.
   a. causing laughter
   b. odd, strange
2. I liked the concert a lot. The last song was <u>awfully</u> good.
   a. badly, dreadfully
   b. very

The Heinle Newbury House Dictionary   Activity Book *p. 161*   Student CD-ROM

Chapter 2   The Fun They Had   **299**

Content Connection
Social Studies

Build Background Have small groups use books, pictures, and the Internet to find out about one-room schoolhouses. Ask students to summarize what they learn by drawing diagrams to show what was typically in one of those schools.

Learning Styles
Visual

Build Vocabulary Have pairs work together to create visual reminders of the meanings of the vocabulary words. For example, students could write the word *run* and draw running shoes on the bottoms of the letters and then write *run* sitting on the seat of a lawn mower.

Build Background

Schooling in the United States

1. **Identify facts** Have pairs of students write four informational (*wh-*) questions about "Schooling in the United States." Then join pairs to ask and answer the questions.
2. **Use personal experience** *Ask: What have your parents told you about schools when they were growing up? How were they different from our school?*
3. **Content Connection** In 1880, only 2.5% of American youth of high school age graduated from high school. About one hundred years later, in 1985, 77% of high school age youth graduated from high school.

Build Vocabulary

Explore Multiple Meaning Words

Teacher Resource Book: *Personal Dictionary, p. 63*

1. **Clarify meaning and usage** Tell students to look up *funny* and *awfully* in print, online, or CD-ROM thesauruses and dictionaries to clarify meaning and usage. Have them check their answers. Repeat for other multiple meaning words, such as *change* and *grade*.
2. **Reading selection vocabulary** You may want to introduce the glossed words in the reading selection before students begin reading. Key words: *waste, calculated, progress, satisfactory, centuries, adjusted.* Instruct students to write the words with correct spelling and their definitions in their Personal Dictionaries. Have them pronounce each word and divide it into syllables.
3. **Multi-level options** See MULTI-LEVEL OPTIONS on p. 298.

Answers
1. a 2. b

 **ASSESS**

Have students write two sentences using *funny* and using *awfully*.

Text Structure

Science Fiction

Relate to personal experience Brainstorm and record a list of science fiction movies. Have the class work in groups based on the movies they have seen. *Say: Discuss the setting, characters, and several scientific facts from the movie.* Then have volunteers report to the class.

Reading Strategy

Make Inferences from Text Evidence

1. **Define and clarify** Students may notice that drawing conclusions and making inferences are quite similar. Have them discuss what the differences are. Explain that a conclusion is a definite decision, based on facts, whereas an inference is drawn from opinions and "clues" in a text.
2. **Use a glossary** Have students locate the meaning and derivation of *inference* in the glossary of their Student Handbook or other sources, such as online or CD-ROM dictionaries.
3. **Multi-level options** See MULTI-LEVEL OPTIONS below.

 **ASSESS**

Have groups of students write their own definition of science fiction, giving an example.

Text Structure

Science Fiction

"The Fun They Had" is **science fiction.** Science fiction is a made-up story that is based on scientific facts (information from science that is true). Look for the features of science fiction in the chart.

In "The Fun They Had," the author describes how machines can change school. Think about which changes you think are good changes as you read. Also think about changes that might cause problems.

Science Fiction	
Setting	often takes place in the future, a time that has not happened yet
Characters	see the world differently from how people do today
Scientific Facts	machines and ways of life that the author imagines

Student CD-ROM

Reading Strategy

Make Inferences from Text Evidence

When you **make inferences from text evidence,** you use clues in a text. You also use your experience to understand a story better.

Suppose you are reading a story about a man who puts on a heavy coat, a hat, and boots. You can use these clues to make an inference that the story takes place in winter.

Use a chart like the one below as you read. This will help you make inferences.

Text Evidence	What I Know from My Experience	Inferences
The man puts on a heavy coat, a hat, and boots.	People wear this clothing when it is cold.	The story takes place in winter.

Student CD-ROM

MULTI-LEVEL OPTIONS *Reading Strategy*

Newcomer Ask students to look at the picture on page 301. Have them make some inferences. *Ask: Is this a place where people live?* (no) *Is it a place where people learn?* (yes) *Are people learning there now?* (no)

Beginning Have students make inferences about the picture on page 301. *Ask: What kind of building do you think this is?* (school) *Is it new or old?* (old) *What is it used for now?* (nothing)

Intermediate Have students work in pairs to make as many inferences as possible about the building in the picture. Tell them to be prepared to explain what led them to each inference.

Advanced Have students list inferences about the picture on page 301. After they have completed their lists, have students explain how their inferences connect to clues in the picture and to their prior experience.

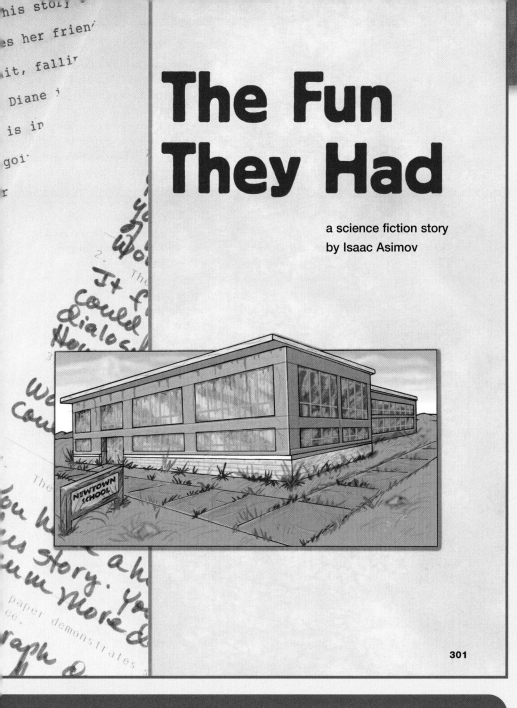

The Fun They Had

a science fiction story

by Isaac Asimov

NEWTOWN SCHOOL

301

Reading Selection Materials

Audio: *Unit 5, Chapter 2; CD 2, Track 8*
Teacher Resource Book: *Reading Summary,*
    pp. 105–106
Transparencies: #12, *Reading Summary*

Suggestions for Using
Reading Summary

- Introduce new vocabulary or cognates.
- Cut the summary into strips, or jumble the sentences on an overhead transparency. Students put the sentences in order.
- Practice the reading strategy.
- Students read aloud or with a partner.
- Students paraphrase the summary.
- Students do a cloze activity.
- Students create a visual or graphic organizer, such as a timeline or storyboard, to illustrate the summary.
- Students paraphrase the summary.

Preview the Selection

1. **Interpret the image** Have students look at the illustration. *Ask: How would you describe this school? How is it similar to or different from our school? What details has the artist added that give more impact to the illustration?*
2. **Connect to theme** *Say: The unit theme is* explorations. *How does science fiction relate to exploration?*

 Content Connection
Technology

Learning Styles
Intrapersonal

Ask students to name some types of technology in their school. (computers, overhead projectors, calculators) Tell students they will read a made-up story about how students may learn in the future. Have small groups meet to brainstorm kinds of technology that may be used in schools far in the future. (*Examples:* jet buses to whisk students home in seconds; robots to help teachers grade papers)

Tell students that in "The Fun They Had," they will find out how the main character feels about how she studies and learns. Ask students to draw or write journal entries telling what helps them learn and what makes it hard to learn.

Read the Selection

1. **Listen for information** Write on the board: *setting, characters.* Tell the students they will be listening for information as you play the audio. Write on the board or **ask:** *What is the setting? Where are the characters? Did you hear what year it is? Who are the characters? Who do you think the main character is? Why?*

2. **Choral reading** Divide the class into two groups and have each group read aloud alternate paragraphs with you. Do it twice so that each group reads both parts. Have students answer the information questions above.

3. **Summarize** Have the class summarize the story so far. Write the summary on the board.

4. **Relate to personal experience** *Ask: Have you ever found something really old in your house? What was it? Who did it belong to? How old was it? What is the oldest thing you have in your house?*

Sample Answer to Guide Question
I don't think they have ever read a book before because they are so curious about it. In paragraph 3, she says how funny it was.

See Teacher Edition pp. 434–436 for a list of English-Spanish cognates in the reading selection.

Audio
CD 2. Tr. 8

> **Make Inferences from Text Evidence**
>
> How often do you think Margie and Tommy read books? Why do you think so?

1   Margie even wrote about it that night in her diary. On the page headed May 17, 2157, she wrote, "Today Tommy found a real book!"

2   It was a very old book. Margie's grandfather once said that when he was a little boy *his* grandfather told him that there was a time when all stories were printed on paper.

3   They turned the pages, which were yellow and **crinkly**, and it was awfully funny to read words that stood still instead of moving the way they were supposed to—on a screen, you know. And then, when they turned back to the page before, it had the same words on it that it had had when they read it the first time.

4   "Gee," said Tommy, "what a **waste.** When you're through with the book, you just throw it away, I guess. Our television screen must have had a million books on it, and it's good for plenty more. I wouldn't throw it away."

5   "Same as mine," said Margie. She was eleven and hadn't seen as many textbooks as Tommy had. He was thirteen.

6   She said, "Where did you find it?"

7   "In my house." He pointed without looking, because he was busy reading. "In the **attic.**"

8   "What's it about?"

9   "School."

---

crinkly   formed into folds or thin lines
waste   a loss of something because it is not used well

attic   a space, often used for storage, under the roof of a house

302   Unit 5   Explorations

MULTI-LEVEL OPTIONS *Read the Selection*

Newcomer Play the audio. *Ask: Does the story take place in the future?* (yes) *Do the children in the story learn from books?* (no) *Do they learn from a teacher like yours?* (no) *Do they use learning machines?* (yes)

Beginning Have students listen as you read aloud. *Ask: When does the story take place?* (2157) *What does the boy find that is not used in 2157?* (book) *Who teaches the children?* (machine) *Does Margie like or dislike school?* (dislike)

Intermediate Have students do a paired reading. *Ask: Why are the children so interested in the book Tommy found?* (Books are not used in 2157.) *What is a mechanical teacher like?* (a computer) *What doesn't Margie like about school?* (She doesn't like the bad grades she has been getting; she doesn't like using the punch code.)

Advanced Have students do a paired reading. *Ask: What might make Margie like school better?* (learning from a real teacher) *How do you think Margie feels when the mechanical teacher sends back her marks on homework and tests? Why?* (sad, disappointed, and frustrated because she doesn't do well)

Make Inferences from Text Evidence

What inference can you make about how well Margie does in school? Which evidence did you use to make your inference?

10 Margie was **scornful.** "School? What's there to write about school? I hate school."

11 Margie always hated school, but now she hated it more than ever. The mechanical teacher had been giving her test after test in geography, and she had been doing worse and worse until her mother had shaken her head **sorrowfully** and sent for the County Inspector.

12 He was a round little man with a red face and a whole box of tools with dials and wires. He smiled at Margie and gave her an apple, then took the teacher apart. Margie had hoped he wouldn't know how to put it together again, but he knew how all right, and, after an hour or so, there it was again, large and black and ugly, with a big screen on which all the lessons were shown and the questions were asked. That wasn't so bad. The part Margie hated most was the **slot** where she had to put homework and test papers. She always had to write them out in a **punch code** they made her learn when she was six years old, and the mechanical teacher **calculated** the **mark in no time.**

scornful   showing dislike

sorrowfully   in a way that shows sadness

slot   a small opening, usually shaped like a rectangle

punch code   a way of showing information by making holes in a piece of paper; the paper is then read by machines

calculated   did math to figure something, such as a grade

mark   a grade, such as on a test

in no time   quickly, fast

Chapter 2 The Fun They Had   **303**

Read the Selection

1. **Paired reading** Play the audio. Then have students practice reading aloud in pairs.
2. **Check comprehension** Ask: *How does Margie feel about school?* (She hates it.) *What was wrong with her mechanical teacher?* (It gave her test after test, and she was doing worse and worse.) *Can you describe the mechanical teacher?* (It's large, black, and ugly, with a big screen. There is a slot to put in homework.)
3. **Multi-level options** See MULTI-LEVEL OPTIONS on p. 302.

Sample Answer to Guide Question
I can infer that she probably did an average job in school. She says she hates school; she was doing worse and worse in geography, but that was a problem with the mechanical teacher.

A Capitalization

Months

Direct students to paragraph 1. *Say: Find the name for a month.* (May) *What kind of letter begins the word?* (capital) *Yes, names for months of the year begin with capital letters.*

  Apply Ask students to tell you their favorite holidays. Make a list on the board. Have students identify the month each holiday is celebrated. Ask volunteers to write the month beside the holiday. Underline the first letter to call attention to the capital letter.

Read the Selection

1. **Shared reading** Play the audio. Then have students join in for different sections of the text aloud. You could also assign parts to students: narrator, the Inspector, Margie, and Tommy.

2. **Discuss characters** Write on the board: *knowledgeable, smart, curious, a know-it-all, bored with school.* Explain that a "know-it-all" is a person who acts like they know everything. *Ask: Which words would you use to describe Margie? What words would you use to describe Tommy?* Have students look up words in the dictionary as needed.

13   The Inspector had smiled after he was finished and patted Margie's head. He said to her mother, "It's not the little girl's fault, Mrs. Jones. I think the geography **sector** was **geared** a little too quick. Those things happen sometimes. I've slowed it up to an average ten-year level. Actually, the overall **pattern** of her **progress** is quite **satisfactory**." And he patted Margie's head again.

14   Margie was disappointed. She had been hoping they would take the teacher away altogether. They had once taken Tommy's teacher away for nearly a month because the history sector had **blanked out** completely.

15   So she said to Tommy, "Why would anyone write about school?"

16   Tommy looked at her with very **superior** eyes. "Because it's not our kind of school, stupid. This is the old kind of school that they had hundreds and hundreds of years ago." He added **loftily,** pronouncing the word carefully, "*Centuries* ago."

17   Margie was hurt. "Well, I don't know what kind of school they had all that time ago." She read the book over his shoulder for a while, then said, "Anyway, they had a teacher."

18   "Sure they had a teacher, but it wasn't a *regular* teacher. It was a man."

19   "A man? How could a man be a teacher?"

---

sector   a section, or part

geared   set up, prepared

pattern   a repeated set of events, characteristics, or features

progress   advancement, movement toward a goal

satisfactory   good enough, acceptable

blanked out   could not be seen

superior   giving the feeling that you are better than others

loftily   as if higher above, or better, than others

centuries   time periods of 100 years

304   Unit 5   Explorations

MULTI-LEVEL OPTIONS *Read the Selection*

Newcomer *Ask: Is the kind of school Tommy talks about like your school?* (yes) *Is the kind of teacher he talks about like yours?* (yes) *Does Margie think a person could be a good teacher?* (no) *Does Margie want to know more about the schools Tommy talks about?* (yes)

Beginning *Ask: Is Tommy telling Margie about a human teacher or a teaching machine?* (human) *Which kind of teacher does Margie think is smarter?* (machine) *What does Margie want to do?* (read the book) *What does her mother say she has to do?* (her lessons)

Intermediate *Ask: Why does Tommy talk to Margie the way he does in paragraph 16?* (because he knows about schools from before 2157 and she doesn't) *How do you think Margie feels about the schools Tommy describes? What is a clue to her feelings?* (She is curious; she wants to read about them.)

Advanced *Ask: Is Tommy's description of schools of the past true? Explain.* (Parts are true, such as human teachers; parts are not, such as students learning the same thing the same way and teachers just asking questions and giving homework.) *What will Tommy do now?* (study with his mechanical teacher)

Make Inferences from Text Evidence

Which text evidence could you use to make the inference that Margie thinks Tommy is smart?

20 "Well, he just told the boys and girls things and gave them homework and asked them questions."

21 "A man isn't smart enough."

22 "Sure he is. My father knows as much as my teacher."

23 "He can't. A man can't know as much as a teacher."

24 "He knows almost as much, I **betcha**."

25 Margie wasn't prepared to **dispute** that. She said, "I wouldn't want a strange man in my house to teach me."

26 Tommy screamed with laughter. "You don't know much, Margie. The teachers didn't live in the house. They had a special building and all the kids went there."

27 "And all the kids learned the same thing?"

28 "Sure, if they were the same age."

29 "But my mother says a teacher has to be **adjusted** to fit the mind of each boy and girl it teaches and that each kid has to be taught differently."

30 "Just the same, they didn't do it that way then. If you don't like it, you don't have to read the book."

31 "I didn't say I didn't like it," Margie said quickly. She wanted to read about those **funny** schools.

32 They weren't even half-finished when Margie's mother called, "Margie! School!"

33 Margie looked up. "Not yet, Mamma."

34 "Now!" said Mrs. Jones. "And it's probably time for Tommy, too."

---

betcha   informal pronunciation for "bet you," meaning that you think you are right and another person is wrong

dispute   argue against

adjusted   changed

funny   odd, strange

Chapter 2   The Fun They Had   **305**

Read the Selection

1. **Silent reading** Play the audio. Then give students time to read silently.

2. **Group work** Write on the board: *What does Margie learn about school that she didn't know before? What did she already know?* Have students work in groups to write answers to the questions. Then have students share their answers with the class.

3. **Multi-level options** See MULTI-LEVEL OPTIONS on p. 304.

Sample Answer to Guide Question

Evidence from the text: "She hadn't seen as many textbooks as Tommy had." "Tommy looked at her with very superior eyes." "Margie wasn't prepared to dispute that." Also, Margie asks him many questions.

---

th   **Spelling**

Gh for the /f/ sound

Ask: What sound do you hear at the end of enough? *(/f/) Look at paragraph 21 to see what letters make that sound in the word* enough. *(gh) Yes, gh is one way to spell the sound /f/.*

Apply Tell students that you are going to say some words and you want them to say an opposite. *Say:* smooth (rough), *cry* (laugh), *easy* (tough). Write the words on the board. Underline the *gh* in each.

Read the Selection

1. **Reciprocal reading** Play the audio. Then have volunteers read sections of the story and ask the class questions about it.

2. **Discuss feelings about a character's situation** Reread paragraphs 37 and 38. *Ask: How do you think Margie feels about learning with the mechanical teacher? How would you like to learn with a mechanical teacher? What would you like about it? What would you dislike about it?*

Sample Answer to Guide Question
The text shows that Margie is curious, wants to learn things, and wants to read more about the "funny schools."

> **Make Inferences from Text Evidence**
>
> What text evidence supports the inference that Margie could be a good student if she wanted to?

35   Margie said to Tommy, "Can I read the book some more with you after school?"

36   "Maybe," he said **nonchalantly.** He walked away **whistling,** the dusty old book **tucked** beneath his arm.

37   Margie went into the schoolroom. It was right next to her bedroom, and the mechanical teacher was on and waiting for her. It was always on at the same time every day except Saturday and Sunday, because her mother said little girls learned better if they learned at regular hours.

38   The screen was lit up, and it said, "Today's **arithmetic** lesson is on the addition of **proper fractions.** Please **insert** yesterday's homework in the **proper** slot."

39   Margie did so with a sigh. She was thinking about the old schools they had when her grandfather's grandfather was a little boy. All the kids from the whole neighborhood came, laughing and shouting in the schoolyard, sitting together in the same schoolroom, going home together at the end of the day. They learned the same things, so they could help one another on the homework and talk about it.

---

nonchalantly in a relaxed, carefree way

whistling making a musical sound by blowing air through the lips

tucked put beneath something else

arithmetic math dealing with addition, subtraction, multiplication, and division

proper fractions fractions (numbers smaller than whole numbers) in which the top number is smaller than the bottom number, for example ½

insert put something into something else

proper correct

306   Unit 5 Explorations

MULTI-LEVEL OPTIONS   *Read the Selection*

Newcomer *Ask: Is Margie's classroom in her house?* (yes) *Does she work on her lessons every day of the week?* (no) *Is her lesson about science?* (no) *Does Margie think it would be fun to go to a school like yours?* (yes)

Beginning *Ask: Where is Margie's classroom?* (in her house) *Are the days Margie goes to school the same as or different from yours?* (same) *What subject is Margie learning?* (math) *What does Margie think of the kind of school you go to?* (fun)

Intermediate *Ask: What are some ways Margie's school is like yours?* (She goes the same days; she learns math.) *How do you think Margie would feel about going to a school like yours? Why?* (excited because she says kids must have loved it, and she thought they had fun)

Advanced *Ask: Why do you think students learn in their homes in this story?* (because each has his or her own "teacher"; they don't have to go to a building or share a teacher like we do) *Do you think Margie would learn better in a school like yours? Explain.* (Yes, because she would be happier working with others.)

40   And the teachers were people . . .

41   The mechanical teacher was flashing on the screen:
"When we add the fractions ½ and ¼—"

42   Margie was thinking about how the kids must have loved
it in the old days. She was thinking about the fun they had.

Make Inferences from Text Evidence

What inference can you make about how Margie feels about going to school alone? Explain.

About the Author

Isaac Asimov (1920–1992)

Isaac Asimov was born in Russia. He moved to the United States as a young child. When he was 18, he sold his first science fiction story to a magazine. Later, Asimov studied science in college and became a college teacher. But his real love was writing. He wrote almost 500 books! Asimov once said, "All I do is write. I do practically nothing else . . . The longer I write, the easier it gets."

➤ Why do you think that Isaac Asimov wrote "The Fun They Had"? To explain his opinion? Or do you think he just wanted to write something that would be fun to read? If you could ask Isaac Asimov one question about this story, what would it be?

Chapter 2   The Fun They Had   **307**

th   Spelling

Silent *t* and silent *l*

Remind students that some words include silent letters. Direct students' attention to the word *whistling* in paragraph 36. Read the word aloud and ask students to repeat it. *Ask: What letter is silent?* (t) Next, tell students to find *half-finished* in paragraph 32. *Ask: What letter is silent?* (l) *Find another word with a silent* l *in paragraph 39.* (talk)

Evaluate Your Reading Strategy

Make Inferences from Text Evidence *Say: You have practiced an important reading strategy. Now you can decide how well you have done. Does this statement describe how you read?*

When I do not understand something in a story, I reread. I look again for text clues or evidence to help me make inferences. Making inferences helps me better understand story characters and events.

Read the Selection

1. **Paired reading** Read the rest of the story aloud. Then have students practice reading pp. 306 and 307 aloud to each other.
2. **Summarize** Have students work in pairs to summarize the story in two or three sentences. Have students read their summaries to the class and discuss any differences.
3. **Locate derivations using dictionaries** Have students look at these glossed words and determine what words they are derived from: *nonchalantly, whistling*. Have students check the derivations in a print, online, or CD-ROM dictionary.
4. **Multi-level options** See MULTI-LEVEL OPTIONS on p. 306.

Sample Answer to Guide Question
She doesn't like to go to school alone. She thinks that it was fun in the old days to go to school together, sit together in class, and help each other with homework.

About the Author

Analyze facts about the author

Identify facts Have students read the text about the author in pairs and write two true-false questions about the author. Then have students exchange questions and answer them.

Across Selections

Connect to unit theme Have students turn to About the Author in "Eye to Eye" (p. 293) and reread the text. *Ask: How is Sylvia Earle an explorer?* (She explores the world of whales.) *Isaac Asimov is also an explorer, but a different kind of explorer. What does he explore?* (what life might be like in the future)

Spelling, Punctuation, Capitalization

After the Reading Comprehension section, students will practice spelling, punctuation, and capitalization in the Activity Book.

Beyond the Reading

Reading Comprehension

Question-Answer Relationships

Sample Answers

1. a very old book
2. All stories were printed on paper.
3. her mechanical teacher
4. The teacher is a person; there is a special building that all of the kids go to; kids the same age learn the same things.
5. The mechanical teacher is different because it is not human; it grades papers very quickly. It is similar to real teachers because it gives homework, tests, and grades.
6. Tommy acted very superior to Margie and made fun of her questions.
7. to show what was good about old schools and what might be lost in the future
8. He didn't like the idea of mechanical teachers because he thought they were impersonal, would break down, and cause trouble to the students. The author uses the characters and plot to show how he feels about mechanical teachers.
9. She didn't like going to school alone or learning from a machine.
10. The illustrator shows the mechanical teacher as an unfriendly, impersonal machine. All the pictures help me better understand the story because they help me visualize what the author wrote about.
11. No, I like having a teacher.

Build Reading Fluency

Rapid Word Recognition

Rapid word recognition is an excellent activity for students who struggle with irregular spelling patterns. Time students for 1 minute as they read the words in the squares aloud.

Reading Comprehension

Question-Answer Relationships (QAR)

"Right There" Questions

1. **Recall Facts** What does Tommy find?
2. **Recall Details** What did Margie's grandfather tell her about books?
3. **Recall Details** What does the County Inspector fix at Margie's house?

"Think and Search" Questions

4. **Identify** Name three things that Margie learns about old schools.
5. **Compare and Contrast** How is Margie's mechanical teacher different from the teachers described in Tommy's book? How are the teachers similar?
6. **Recognize Character Traits** How did Tommy behave toward Margie? Was he kind to her? Did he make fun of her?

"Author and You" Questions

7. **Understand Plot** Why did someone write a book about old schools?

8. **Understand Author's Tone** From the tone of the story, do you think that Isaac Asimov liked the idea of mechanical teachers? Explain what effect this has on the text.
9. **Paraphrase** In your own words, tell what Margie's feelings were about school.

"On Your Own" Questions

10. **Evaluate** How does the illustrator show the mechanical teacher? Do all the pictures help you to better understand the story? Why or why not?
11. **Evaluate** Would you like to learn from a mechanical teacher? Why or why not?

Activity Book   Student
p. 162   CD-ROM

Build Reading Fluency

Rapid Word Recognition

Rapidly recognizing words helps increase your reading rate. It is an important characteristic of effective readers.

1. With a partner, review the words in the box.
2. Read the words aloud for one minute. Your teacher will time you.

wrote	through	once	page	once	wrote
diary	page	through	once	page	once
page	know	diary	wrote	know	diary
once	once	page	diary	wrote	know
know	diary	wrote	know	through	page

3. Count how many words you read in one minute.

MULTI-LEVEL OPTIONS *Elements of Literature*

Newcomer Have each student write 2157 at the top of a piece of art paper. Have students draw Margie studying. Ask them to include as much detail as possible in their illustrations. Provide time for students to share and compare their visions of the story setting.

Beginning Have students draw Margie and Tommy in the setting of the selection. Ask them to label items in the illustration.

Intermediate Ask students to discuss what kind of playground Margie and Tommy might have in their community in 2157. Ask them to think about the location of the playground, the types of equipment on it, and the types of games children might play in this setting.

Advanced Ask students to work in groups. Have each student write a detailed description of his/her vision of a different room in Margie's home. Have students share their descriptions and put all their ideas together to create a diagram of how the character's home might look.

Listen, Speak, Interact

Present Advantages and Disadvantages

What do you think about learning on a computer?

1. With a partner, make a list of advantages (things that are good) and disadvantages (things that are bad) about learning on a computer.

Learning on a Computer	
Advantages	Disadvantages
Computers are fun to learn on.	You can't talk to a computer as you can to a teacher.

2. Your teacher will lead a class discussion. As you present your ideas, your teacher will write them on the board.

3. As a class, choose three of the most important advantages and three of the most important disadvantages.

4. Now decide whether your advantages and disadvantages are facts (things that can be proven) or opinions (things that people think or believe).

Elements of Literature

Analyze Setting

Every story has a **setting.** Setting is the time and place of a story. In "The Fun They Had," the setting is an important part of the story. It puts the reader in a certain place and time. It shows how the characters' lives are different from people's lives today.

1. Work with a partner. Reread paragraphs 1, 32, and 37 and take notes on details that describe the setting. Answer these questions about the setting of "The Fun They Had." Write your answers in your Reading Log.

a. In what year does the story happen?

b. On what date does Tommy find the book?

c. Where are Tommy and Margie reading the book?

d. Where is Margie's schoolroom?

2. With a partner, discuss why the setting is important. How would this story be different if it were set in another time and place?

Reading Log   Activity Book p. 163   Student CD-ROM

Chapter 2   The Fun They Had   **309**

Listen, Speak, Interact

Present Advantages and Disadvantages

1. **Relate to prior experience** *Ask: How can you use a computer to learn? How have you used a computer to learn in the past?*

2. **Support and clarify** Have students support and clarify *facts* with evidence and examples. Have them support and clarify *opinions* with examples and elaboration.

3. **Newcomers** Reread with this group. Have them talk about the ways they use computers. Ask them to make a list or draw pictures of the ways computers are helpful to them.

Elements of Literature

Analyze Setting

Teacher Resource Book: *Reading Log, p. 64*

1. **Compare different settings** Have students compare the setting of another learning experience in "Why the Rooster Crows at Sunrise." (p. 110)

2. **Multi-level options** See MULTI-LEVEL OPTIONS on p. 308.

Answers

1. **a.** 2157   **b.** May 17   **c.** at Margie's house
   d. in a room next to her bedroom

Community Connection

Ask students to meet in small groups. Have each group select a setting in their community. Ask them to discuss and draw how that place might look in the year 2157. Have them tell how the place might be different, how it might be used, what kind of technology might be found there, and other aspects of their visions of the future in their community.

Learning Styles
Mathematical

After students have created their lists of advantages and disadvantages, help them compile two class circle graphs to show the percentages of each response.

Word Study

Use the Latin Root Words to Find Meaning

Use new vocabulary Have students make up sentences using *inspect, inspector, inspection*. Point out that the word *spectator and spectacles* come from the same root. Have students look up the words in the dictionary and use them in sentences.

Answers

2. a person who looks at something carefully; the act of looking carefully

Grammar Focus

Use Dependent Clauses with *Because*

Clarify and define Write on the board: *My brother isn't in school today. He is sick.* Have students identify the subject and verb in each sentence. Then have them join the sentences using *because.* Write the new sentence. Explain that *because he is sick* is now the dependent clause.

Answers

1. **a.** They took his teacher away because the history sector had blanked out. **b.** Margie's mother told her to go to sleep because it was very late.

ASSESS

In groups, have students write two sentences with dependent clauses with *because.*

Word Study

Use the Latin Root Words to Find Meaning

Root words are the words from which other words are made. Many English words are based on root words from other languages, such as Latin.

For example, the word *inspect* is based on the Latin root word *specere*. This word means "to look."

You can use this root word to help understand the word *inspect*. Do you see a word part from *specere* in *inspect*? *Inspect* means "to look at carefully."

1. Copy the chart in your Personal Dictionary. Each of the words comes from the word *specere*.

Specere	
Word	**Meaning**
inspect	to look at carefully
inspector	a person who _____
inspection	the act of _____

2. Use the meaning of *specere* to help you complete the definitions.
3. Check your answers in a dictionary.

Personal Dictionary   The Heinle Newbury House Dictionary   Activity Book p. 164   Student CD-ROM

Grammar Focus

Use Dependent Clauses with *Because*

A **clause** is part of a sentence. It has a subject and a verb. An **independent clause** can stand alone. A **dependent clause** cannot stand alone.

Writers often join two sentences with the word *because*. By adding *because*, a sentence becomes a dependent clause.

Independent Clause	**Dependent Clause**
Margie read the book,	because she wanted to learn about the past.

You use a comma before a dependent clause with *because*.

1. On a piece of paper, combine these sentences using *because*.
   a. They took his teacher away. The history sector had blanked out.
   b. Margie's mother told her to go to sleep. It was very late.
2. In each sentence, underline the independent clause one time and the dependent clause two times.
3. Write two sentences that have a dependent clause with *because*.

Activity Book pp. 165–166   Student Handbook   Student CD-ROM

310   Unit 5 Explorations

MULTI-LEVEL OPTIONS *From Reading to Writing*

Newcomer Have students act out what they think happens next. Provide art and craft materials for students to make simple props and to draw a backdrop on a large piece of paper.

Beginning Have students create storyboards to show what happens next to Margie. Ask them to write word or phrase captions for each frame. Provide time for students to share their ideas.

Intermediate Remind students that Margie is in her house at the end of the story. Point out that if the setting of the ending they are adding is different, they will need to provide a *transition* so that readers do not get confused. Provide an example: *The next day, Margie went to the Technology Supermarket.*

Advanced Point out that they learned in Text Structure that science fiction authors include scientific facts. Tell students to read nonfiction information about aspects of their setting before beginning to write. For example, if they are setting the story on another planet, they should read about that place.

From Reading to Writing

Write an Ending to a Science Fiction Short Story

"The Fun They Had" ends with Margie thinking about what it would be like to go to school with other children. Write a paragraph about what happens next.

1. Brainstorm ideas for your paragraph. Your ideas can include a scientific idea or a tool that changes how characters live. Here is an example: Margie might build a time machine and travel to the year 2008.

2. Decide which characters will be in your paragraph. Will you also make up a new character?

3. Decide the setting. Does it take place in Margie's house? On a different planet?

4. Include a dependent clause with *because*. Use correct punctuation.

5. Use nouns correctly to show how many people, places, and things.

6. Use progressive verbs to tell about actions that are happening.

Student
Handbook

Across Content Areas

Define Internet Terms

We use the Internet and the World Wide Web to learn about different topics. Here are some things to help you when looking for facts.

browser a tool that lets you visit sites on the Internet or World Wide Web

URL (uniform resource locator) the address of a Web page, such as http://www.heinle.visions.com

cursor an arrow or black line on a computer screen that shows where you are writing or clicking your mouse

links words or pictures on a Web page (usually underlined or a different color) that bring you to other pages when you click on them with your cursor

The picture below shows a Web page. Match the Internet terms with the information in the picture.

Activity Book
p. 168

Chapter 2 The Fun They Had **311**

Reteach and Reassess

Text Structure Have students draw or write a story map for a science fiction story. Tell them to include setting, main character, a problem, and a solution on their maps.

Reading Strategy Have each student exchange the story ending he or she wrote with a partner. Ask students to make an inference about the setting and main character of their partner's story.

Elements of Literature Ask students to describe how "The Fun They Had" would

have been different if the setting had been 1857.

Reassess Create a class list of inferences students can make about how learning today differs from learning in "The Fun They Had."

From Reading to Writing

Write an Ending to a Science Fiction Short Story

1. **Use illustrations to brainstorm** Have students make sketches and drawings of the ending and the setting as they brainstorm before writing. Point out that using illustrations can help them get different ideas.
2. **Collaborative writing** Have students work in pairs or small groups to write their endings. When they are finished, they should proofread their stories and display them in the room with illustrations if possible.
3. **Compose a letter** Have pairs collaborate to compose a letter to Margie telling what it is like to go to school with other children. Instruct them to organize their letters into three paragraphs telling: what they like about going to school with other children; what they dislike about it; and if they think going to school alone or with others is better and why. Ask pairs to share their letters with other pairs. Based on the feedback, have pairs collaborate to revise their letters.
4. **Multi-level options** See MULTI-LEVEL OPTIONS on p. 310.

Across Content Areas: Science

Define Internet Terms

Use prior knowledge Write *Internet* on the board. Ask students to come up with as many words as they know related to the Internet. Have students give definitions when they can.

Answers
1. browser 2. URL 3. links 4. cursor

ASSESS

Have students list features of a science fiction story.

Using the Scientific Method

an excerpt from
a textbook
by Stephen Kramer

Objectives

Reading Recognize cause and effect relationships as you read an informational text.

Listening and Speaking Use information to raise unanswered questions.

Grammar Use *might* to show possibility.

Writing Write an informational text.

Content Science: Learn about sleep.

Chapter Materials

Activity Book: *pp. 169–176*
Audio: *Unit 5, Chapter 3; CD 2, Track 9*
Student Handbook
Student CD-ROM: *Unit 5, Chapter 3*
Teacher Resource Book: *Lesson Plan, Teacher Resources, Reading Summary, Activity Book Answer Key*
Teacher Resource CD-ROM
Assessment Program: *Quiz, pp. 79–80; Teacher and Student Resources, pp. 115–144*
Assessment CD-ROM
Transparencies
The Heinle Newbury House Dictionary/CD-ROM
Web site: http://visions.heinle.com

Objectives

Preview Read the objectives. *Ask: What objectives do you already know something about?* Have students give examples.

Use Prior Knowledge

Share Knowledge About Science Experiments

◾ Teacher Resource Book: *Web, p. 37*

Use prior knowledge *Ask: What are you studying in science right now? What other interesting things have you studied? What are some science terms you know?* Write terms students mention on the board. Organize words into a word web.

Use Prior Knowledge

Share Knowledge About Science Experiments

Science is the study of the natural world or the world around us. It explains why things are the way they are. "Using the Scientific Method" describes the steps for doing a science experiment.

A science experiment is a very careful plan or test. It helps scientists find out why something happens. It also can explain how something works.

What do you know about science experiments? Answer the questions below to gather your ideas:

1. Have you ever done a science experiment? What was it about?
2. What do you do in a science experiment? Ask questions? Make a plan? Observe or look carefully? Take notes?
3. With your class, discuss your experiences with science.

312   Unit 5 Explorations

MULTI-LEVEL OPTIONS *Build Vocabulary*

Newcomer Write the vocabulary words on the board. Point to each and use gestures or facial expressions to communicate its meaning. Then read the sentences and have students point to the correct vocabulary word, repeat it after you, and imitate the facial expression.

Beginning Write sentence *a.* on the board. Replace the underlined words with *will focus on.* Read the sentence emphasizing the vocabulary word. Use facial expressions to reinforce meaning. Have students read the sentence and imitate your facial expression. Introduce the other words in the same way.

Intermediate Have students use the vocabulary words to write sentences telling what they like to focus on and what makes them curious and frustrated.

Advanced Have students look up each vocabulary word in a thesaurus. Ask them to see if any synonyms could be used in the sentences.

Build Background

The Scientific Method

Scientists are people who ask questions and find out why things happen. To do this, scientists use the **scientific method.** The scientific method starts with an idea. This idea is called a **hypothesis.** The hypothesis can be about why and how something happens or it also can be about how people act.

Scientists then do an experiment to test the idea. The facts from the experiment are called the results. The results help the scientists learn if their hypothesis is true.

Many famous people have used the scientific method to discover new things. Do you know any famous scientists?

Content Connection
Scientists began to use the scientific method during the 1600s.

Build Vocabulary

Use a Dictionary to Locate Meanings and Pronounce Words

The selection includes words related to **behavior**—ways of acting.

1. Look up these words in a dictionary. With your teacher, pronounce the words and read the meanings.

Pronunciation	Meaning

a. curious /ˈkyʊriəs/ *adj.* interested in knowing about things: *I am curious; where did you buy that beautiful dress?*

b. focus

c. frustrated

2. Match the underlined words in the sentences with one of the words you looked up in the dictionary.
  a. He <u>will work for a long time</u> putting the pieces of a puzzle together.
  b. He <u>gets mad at the puzzle</u> and throws the pieces across the room.
  c. Your older brother or sister might <u>like to know</u>.

Write a sentence using each behavior word. Be sure you spell each syllable in the word correctly.

The Heinle Newbury House Dictionary   Activity Book p. 169   Student CD-ROM

Chapter 3 Using the Scientific Method   **313**

Content Connection
Social Studies

Build Background Have students work in groups. Ask each group to use books or Internet sources to research a scientist of the past. Have students report on when the scientist lived, where he or she was born, and identify a question the scientist answered about how something happens. (*Example:* Benjamin Franklin; 1700s; Massachusetts; How does electricity work?)

Learning Styles
Visual

Build Vocabulary Ask students to fold a piece of art paper into three parts. Have them write one of the vocabulary words in each third. Ask students to share what they know about computer emoticons, smiley-frowny faces, and other simple representations of feelings. Tell them to design an icon for each of the vocabulary words and draw it in the appropriate space on their pieces of art paper.

Build Background

The Scientific Method

1. **Reciprocal questioning** Have a student read the passage aloud to the class. Then have the student ask the class factual questions about the text.
2. **Content Connection** Modern science came into being in the 16th and 17th centuries when craft traditions merged with scientific theory and started the evolution of the scientific method.

Build Vocabulary

Use a Dictionary to Locate Meanings and Pronounce Words

Teacher Resource Book: *Personal Dictionary, p. 63*

1. **Understand abbreviations** Write on the board: *n, v, adj, adv, prep, pl.* Tell students that these abbreviations are used in dictionaries. Have them guess what they mean and give examples. (noun, verb, adjective, adverb, preposition, plural)
2. **Use new vocabulary** Ask questions to use new vocabulary. *Ask: Do you have any friends who are especially curious? When do you have to focus your attention? What subjects make you frustrated?*
3. **Reading selection vocabulary** You may want to introduce the glossed words in the reading selection before students begin reading. Key words: *gather, form, puzzle, measure, results, support, examine.* Instruct students to write the words with correct spelling and their definitions in their Personal Dictionaries. Have them pronounce each word and divide it into syllables.
4. **Multi-level options** See MULTI-LEVEL OPTIONS on p. 312.

Answers
2. **a.** focus **b.** frustrated **c.** curious

ASSESS

Have students explain what the scientific method is in their own words.

Text Structure

Informational Text

1. **Locate text features** Have students turn to the selection starting on p. 316 and locate the following features: bold type, italic type, lists with numbers.

2. **Connect to content classes** *Ask: In which classes do you read informational texts? Do you find them easier or harder to read than literature? Why do you think that is?*

Reading Strategy

Recognize Cause and Effect Relationships

1. **Identify cause and effect** Write on the board: 1. *I left food on a picnic table, so a bear came to our campsite. 2. I overslept because I didn't set my alarm. 3. She forgot her swimsuit; that's why she couldn't go swimming.* Have students identify the cause and effect in each sentence.

2. **Multi-level options** See MULTI-LEVEL OPTIONS below.

✓ ASSESS

Have students work in pairs to write a cause and effect sentence.

Text Structure

Informational Text

"Using the Scientific Method" is an **informational text.** It gives true information about a real-life topic. There are different kinds of informational texts. The author of this selection gives the process (directions) for doing an experiment. In an informational text, authors often use graphic features such as bold and italic type, bullets, and lists with numbers to organize the information. Look for the features of an informational text that are listed in the chart as you read.

Informational Text	
Facts	tell information that is true
Graphic Features	show the organization of a reading

Student CD-ROM

Reading Strategy

Recognize Cause and Effect Relationships

A **cause** is the reason why something happens. An **effect** is something that happens as a result of the cause. Authors sometimes present ideas using cause and effect. This helps them explain relationships.

Here are ways to find a cause and effect relationship. Ask "Did this happen *because* of that?" You might also ask "Did this *make* that happen?" If you can answer "yes" to these questions, you have found a cause and effect relationship.

Look at this sentence.

Ramona <u>forgot</u> to add sugar <u>so</u> the lemonade is not sweet.

Ramona forgot to add the sugar. This is the cause. The lemonade is not sweet. This is the effect. The lemonade is not sweet *because* Ramona forgot to add the sugar.

Look for cause and effect relationships as you read the selection. Remember to ask these questions to help you: "Did this happen *because* of that?" "Did this *make* that happen?"

Student CD-ROM

314 Unit 5 Explorations

MULTI-LEVEL OPTIONS *Reading Strategy*

Newcomer On the board, write *because* and *100%, A+,* or whatever you use to signify excellent work. Point to the grade on the paper. Hold up and read the word *because.* Mime studying a book. *Say: He got a* good grade because *he* studies. Repeat the process with other classroom examples, such as turning off a light switch.

Beginning Have students work in pairs. Write on the board and *say: There's a puddle of water on the floor.* Have one student draw the effect. Ask the other student to draw a cause, such as someone knocking over a glass. Tell the pair to present their work by having one show the effect, both saying *because,* and then the other showing the cause.

Intermediate Ask students to work in pairs to observe what is happening in their classroom. Have them list causes and effects. (*Example:* Effect: Papers are blowing off the desks. Cause: The window is open.)

Advanced Have students work in pairs to generate a list of cause and effect relationships they know about in nature. (*Example:* Birds fly south in the winter because they want to get away from cold weather.)

Using the Scientific Method

an excerpt from a textbook
by Stephen Kramer

315

Reading Selection Materials

Audio: *Unit 5, Chapter 3; CD 2, Track 9*
Teacher Resource Book: *Reading Summary,*
  pp. 107–108
Transparencies: #13, *Reading Summary*

Suggestions for Using Reading Summary

- Introduce new vocabulary or cognates.
- Cut the summary into strips, or jumble the sentences on an overhead transparency. Students put the sentences in order.
- Practice the reading strategy.
- Students read aloud or with a partner.
- Students paraphrase the summary.
- Students do a cloze activity.
- Students create a visual or graphic organizer, such as a timeline or storyboard, to illustrate the summary.
- Students paraphrase the summary.

Preview the Selection

1. **Interpret the image** Direct students to the photo. *Ask: What class are these students in? What do you think they are doing? Why are they wearing goggles? Why is safety important in a science laboratory?*
2. **Connect to theme** *Say: Remember that exploration can relate to exploring anything that is unknown. That is why we can think of science as a way of exploring.*

 Content Connection
Technology

Point out the computer in the picture on p. 315. Tell students that computers have become an important part of science experiments. *Ask: What are some of the ways you think computers can be useful to scientists?* (Conducting research on the Internet of what others have done; recording their own findings; figuring out formulas; writing up their results for others to read.)

Learning Styles
Interpersonal

Tell students that scientists often work in teams to do experiments. People on science teams cooperate with each other to be sure the experiment is carried out scientifically and safely. Ask students to look at the picture above. *Ask: What is each student doing to help with the experiment?*

Read the Selection

1. **Use art to preview text** Have students look at the illustrations on pp. 316–317. *Ask: How is the little boy feeling?* (angry, frustrated) *What is his sister wondering about on page 316?* (her brother's behavior) *What's the boy doing on page 317?* (putting a puzzle together) *This text is about using the scientific method to ask and answer questions.*

2. **Shared reading** Play the audio. Have students join in when they can.

3. **Identify topic** Have a volunteer read the first and last sentences of paragraph 1. *Ask: What is the topic of this paragraph?* (using the scientific method)

4. **Relate to personal experience** *Ask: Do you ever wonder why someone in your family behaves a certain way? Can you give an example? Do you have an idea or a hypothesis about why he or she behaves that way?*

Sample Answer to Guide Question
Missing a nap (cause) can make a younger brother act less patient (effect).

See Teacher Edition pp. 434–436 for a list of English-Spanish cognates in the reading selection.

Audio
CD 2, Tr. 9

Recognize Cause and Effect Relationships

What is one cause that can have an effect on how the younger brother acts?

You can probably think of some questions that the scientific method could help you answer. Perhaps you have a younger brother. You know that he is much harder to get along with when he misses his afternoon **nap.** But what is it about his behavior that makes him harder to get along with? How does he act differently? Let's use the steps of the scientific method to see how you could find the answer. 1

1. *Ask a question.* 2
   "How does my little brother act differently when he misses his afternoon nap?"

2. *Gather information about the question.* 3
   Watch your brother on days when he takes a nap and on days when he misses his nap. Ask your parents or brothers or sisters how he acts differently.

3. *Form a hypothesis.* 4
   "My little brother has less patience in the evenings on days he misses his nap than on days he takes a nap."

nap   a short sleep
gather   bring together

form   make up

316   **Unit 5** Explorations

MULTI-LEVEL OPTIONS *Read the Selection*

Newcomer Play the audio. *Ask: Is the selection about answering science questions?* (yes) *Is the first step to ask a question?* (yes) *Is the next step to ask someone the answer?* (no) *Do scientists guess the answer and test to see if they are right?* (yes)

Beginning Have students do a partner read aloud. *Ask: What is the selection about?* (doing science experiments) *What do scientists do first when they experiment?* (ask a question) *What is a hypothesis like?* (a guess) *What do scientists do to find out if their guess is right?* (test it)

Intermediate Ask students to do a reciprocal reading. *Ask: How do scientists begin an experiment?* (by deciding what question they are trying to answer) *In the example in the selection, how does the student test the hypothesis?* (by watching how the brother behaves)

Advanced Tell students to read silently. *Ask: Why is asking a question an important first step?* (because the experimenter needs to be clear about what he or she is trying to find out) *What is the relationship between the question and the hypothesis?* (The hypothesis is a guess about the answer to the question.)

5 **4. Test** *the hypothesis.*

Perhaps you've noticed that some evenings your little brother will work for a long time putting the pieces of a **puzzle** together. Other times he gets mad at the puzzle and throws the pieces across the room. You might decide to **measure** your brother's patience by checking how long he will work on putting together a puzzle.

> **Recognize Cause and Effect Relationships**
>
> What causes the little brother to throw the pieces across the room?

a. Pick five days when your brother 6 takes a nap. After dinner on those days give him a puzzle to put together. Count how many pieces he uses before **giving up.** This is the **control group.**

b. Pick five days when your 7 brother misses his nap. After dinner on those days give him a puzzle to put together. Count how many pieces he uses before giving up. This is the **experimental group.**

Control Group of 5 Days: Naps   **Experimental Group of 5 Days: No Naps**

---

test   try out

puzzle   a game in which stiff paper that has been cut into pieces is put back together

measure   find the total or size of

giving up   stopping doing something

control group   a group of people or objects used in an experiment to compare all other groups to

experimental group   a group of people or things that is being compared to the control group

Chapter 3   Using the Scientific Method   **317**

Read the Selection

1. **Do a jigsaw reading** Play the audio. Have groups read and prepare one part of the selection to teach to the class. Monitor that all students participate.
2. **Check comprehension** *Ask: How does the author suggest measuring the brother's patience?* (by checking how long he will work on putting together a puzzle) *Do you think this is a good way to measure his patience? Why or why not? Explain the control group and the experimental group.*
3. **Restate steps** Have groups review the four steps of the scientific method covered so far and restate them in their own words.
4. **Multi-level options** See MULTI-LEVEL OPTIONS on p. 316.

Sample Answer to Guide Question
Frustration might cause the little brother to throw the pieces across the room.

---

9 Punctuation

Periods for vertical lists

Have students find the first three steps in the scientific method listed on p. 316. *Ask: What punctuation mark is between the number of the step and the sentence telling about it?* (period) *Periods are used after the numbers in a list that goes down a page.* Have students look at p. 317 for more examples.

Apply Ask students to work in pairs to make a numbered list of steps for making an ice cream sundae or another simple process. They may either write or draw the steps. Remind them to put a period after each number.

Read the Selection

1. **Shared reading** Play the audio. Then have students take turns reading aloud with the audio.

2. **Speculate** Discuss with students other ways to measure how much patience the younger brother has. List each idea on the board. Talk about the pros and cons of each one.

Sample Answer to Guide Question
Using the same puzzle over and over might cause the brother to put it together more easily.

8　Of course, you would have to use puzzles that were all about the same **difficulty.** You would also have to be careful not to use one puzzle too many times, or your brother might begin to put it together more easily than the others.

> **Recognize Cause and Effect Relationships**
>
> If you used the same puzzle over and over, what would the effect on the experiment be?

9　However, if you did have enough puzzles, you could probably get a good idea of how much patience your brother had each evening. If your brother always put together more of the puzzle after taking a nap, he might also be more patient and easier to get along with. What if the **results** of your experiment don't **support** your hypothesis? Perhaps the number of puzzle pieces your brother puts together is not really a good measure of his patience. You might try to think of another way to measure how much patience he has.

---

difficulty how hard something is to do

results something that happens because of an action

support agree with

318 **Unit 5** Explorations

MULTI-LEVEL OPTIONS *Read the Selection*

Newcomer *Ask: Should your test answer your question?* (yes) *If your test does not work, can you try again?* (yes) *Should you share what you learn from your experiment?* (yes)

Beginning *Ask: What should your test answer?* (your question) *What can an experimenter do if the test does not answer the question?* (try again) *How can you share your experiment?* (tell someone)

Intermediate *Ask: What is the difference between control and experimental groups?* (The control group has the ordinary situation, like behavior after a nap. The experimental group is what you want to test, like the effect of missing a nap.)

Advanced *Ask: Would it work to have the little brother do puzzles sometimes and color sometimes for the test? Explain.* (No, because he might have more patience for one of these whether he had a nap or not.) *How might the results of this test be useful?* (The parents would make sure the child had a nap.)

10   If there is no evidence from any of your experiments to support your hypothesis, try a different one. A hypothesis you could test quite easily would be, "My brother cries more often in the evenings on days when he misses his nap."

Recognize Cause and Effect Relationships

What does the author say the effect is when the little brother misses his nap?

---

11   **a.** Pick five days when your brother takes a nap. Count the number of times he cries between 6:00 P.M. and 8:00 P.M. This is the control group.

b. Pick five days when your brother   12 misses his nap. Count the number of times he cries between 6:00 P.M. and 8:00 P.M. This is the experimental group.

Examine your results. Does your   13 brother really seem to cry more in the evenings on days when he misses his nap?

5. *Tell someone what you found.*   14

Your parents might be interested. Your older brother or sister might like to know. What you learned might make **babysitting** easier.

---

examine   look at carefully

babysitting   taking care of a child while the parents are away

---

❾ Punctuation

Colon for times

Tell students to find the times in paragraph 11. (6:00, 8:00) *Say: Look at the punctuation mark. It is a colon. The colon separates the hours from the minutes when we write times.* Write on the board: *12:15* and *9:30.* Point to the hours, then the minutes. Circle the colon.

Apply Work with students to write a schedule of what will happen in your classroom the rest of the day. (*Example: 12:00 lunch, 12:30 math, 1:15 physical education, and so on*)

Read the Selection

1. **Paired reading** Play the audio. Have students reread in pairs.

2. **Relate to personal experience** *Ask: What kinds of questions do you sometimes ask yourself? I often ask myself questions about my car, my computer, my CD player, and my dog.* Give a few example questions. Then have students give examples of things they wonder about.

3. **Make a hypothesis** Using examples from the discussion above, have students give hypotheses for the cause and effect of some of the questions. For example, *I think my car uses more gas in city driving because I stop and go so much.*

Sample Answer to Guide Question
The effect might be that the sister is more likely to help.

15 Everywhere you look there are questions you could use the scientific method to answer.

16 • Which kind of food does your dog like best?
  • Does your mother go to bed earlier on **weekday** nights or on **weekend** nights?
  • Do you eat more food on days when you go to school or on days when you stay home?
  • Does your father drive the car more on weekdays or on weekends?
  • Do dishes really get cleaner if you wash them in hot water instead of cold water?
  • Is your older sister more **likely** to help you if you say please?

> **Recognize Cause and Effect Relationships**
> What might be the effect of saying "please" to an older sister?

weekday Monday, Tuesday, Wednesday, Thursday, or Friday
weekend Saturday or Sunday

likely to be expected

320 Unit 5 Explorations

MULTI-LEVEL OPTIONS *Read the Selection*

Newcomer *Ask: Are there lots of science questions to answer?* (yes) *Do science experiments help you learn?* (yes) *Could you learn something no one else knows?* (yes) *Is it important to ask the right question?* (yes) *Is exploring science dull?* (no)

Beginning *Ask: What can you use the scientific method to find?* (answers) *To answer the question Which kind of food does your dog like best?, what would you have to change for the test?* (food) *What does the writer think science experiments are?* (exciting)

Intermediate *Ask: How can you find subjects for experiments?* (You can observe and ask questions about the world around you.) *How could you test the first question in the suggestion list?* (Give your dog several different kinds of food for several days and see which one he eats the most of.)

Advanced *Ask: What is another example of a question you could answer with the scientific method? (Example: Which food attracts ants?) How could you test it?* (Place bowls of different kinds of foods outside; count how many ants are in each bowl after one hour.)

17 There are thousands of questions you can ask and answer. You might learn some surprising things. You might learn something your parents or teachers didn't know. You might even learn something no one else ever knew. That's what makes science exciting. There are all kinds of new **discoveries** to be made. All you have to do is ask the right question—and know how to answer it.

> **Recognize Cause and Effect Relationships**
>
> What makes science exciting?

discoveries the finding of something new

About the Author

Stephen Kramer (born 1953)

Stephen Kramer has always loved science. He enjoys writing about it, too. Kramer also likes teaching science to fifth grade and high school students. He started a Web site for young people who like science. Kramer also likes to learn new things. He is learning to play the bagpipes (a musical instrument) for fun!

➤ Which of the following sentences do you think Stephen Kramer would most agree with? Why do you think so?
1. Science experiments are difficult and a lot of trouble to do.
2. Science experiments can be creative and fun.

Chapter 3 Using the Scientific Method **321**

 Spelling

Qu for the /kw/ sound

Ask: What sound do you hear at the beginning of question*?* (/kw/) *Look at paragraph 15 to see what letters make the sound.* (qu) *Find another example of* qu *making the /kw/ sound in paragraph 10.* (quite)

Apply Tell students that you are going to say some words that begin with the /kw/ sound. Ask them to write the words. *Say: quit, quack, quick.*

> **Evaluate Your Reading Strategy**

Recognize Cause and Effect Relationships
Say: You have practiced an important reading strategy. Now you can decide how well you have done. Does this statement describe how you read?

> As I read, I ask questions. I ask, "Did this happen *because* of that?" I also ask, "Did this *make* that happen?" I ask questions to understand cause and effect relationships and to understand how to do the steps in a process.

Read the Selection

1. **Relate to personal experience** Talk about scientific discoveries that students have found interesting or areas of science that students are curious about. *Ask: What kinds of science do you find interesting? Biology? Astronomy? Marine science?*
2. **Shared reading** Play the audio. Have students join in when they can.
3. **Multi-level options** See MULTI-LEVEL OPTIONS on p. 320.

Sample Answer to Guide Question
You might learn something surprising; you might learn something that no one else ever knew.

About the Author

Analyze facts Have students work in small groups to read the text aloud and come up with two questions to ask. They can also write an answer to the question. Then have groups exchange questions and compare answers to the guide question.

Answer
Sample: The author would most likely agree with sentence 2 because he thinks that science is fun and exciting.

Across Selections

Ask: What other selection about science and research did we read in this unit? ("Eye to Eye," p. 292.) *How is it different?* ("Eye to Eye" is written from the first-person point of view; it describes marine instead of behavioral research.)

Spelling, Punctuation, Capitalization

After the Reading Comprehension section, students will practice spelling, punctuation, and capitalization in the Activity Book.

Beyond the Reading

Reading Comprehension

Question-Answer Relationships

Sample Answers

1. A hypothesis is a guess about the answer to the question of a science experiment.
2. puzzles, a watch, paper and a pencil
3. When he doesn't get a nap, the boy is much harder to get along with, has less patience, and cries more.
4. The next step is to count how many pieces he uses before he gives up.
5. You could conclude that the brother is happier and better behaved when he has an afternoon nap.
6. This experiment could help a family understand why the boy is less patient without a nap and the importance of a nap.
7. Do teenagers eat more food for lunch at school or at home? What kind of food does my cat like best? Yes, because they are things I can measure.
8. Do teenagers eat more vegetables at school or at home?

Build Reading Fluency

Read Aloud to Engage Listeners

Model reading aloud with expression. Remind students to keep their eyes on the words as they read. This will help them with phrasing, intonation, and pronunciation.

Reading Comprehension

Question-Answer Relationships (QAR)

"Right There" Questions

1. **Recall Facts** What is a hypothesis?
2. **Recall Facts** What tools are used to find out about the younger brother's patience?

"Think and Search" Questions

3. **Compare and Contrast** Compare the brother's behavior when he naps with his behavior when he does not nap.
4. **Identify Steps in a Process** Look at paragraph 6. What step comes after the younger brother is given the puzzle to put together?

"Author and You" Question

5. **Draw Conclusions** The experiment you read about shows the brother crying more often without a nap. What conclusion can you make?

"On Your Own" Questions

6. **Generalize** How could an experiment like this help a family?
7. **Ask Questions** What questions would you like to ask and explore? Do you think you can use the scientific method to find the answers? Why or why not?
8. **Revise Questions** Discuss one of your questions above with a partner. Do you need to revise your question? If so, do it.

Activity Book
p. 170

Student
CD-ROM

Build Reading Fluency

Read Aloud to Engage Listeners

Reading aloud helps increase your fluency and expression. Learning to read with expression makes others want to listen to you.

1. Listen to the audio recording of "Using the Scientific Method."
2. Turn to page 316 and follow along.
3. Pay attention to phrasing and expression.
4. With a partner, read aloud paragraph 1 three times.
5. Read in front of the class with expression.

322 Unit 5 Explorations

MULTI-LEVEL OPTIONS *Elements of Literature*

Newcomer *Say: This piece was written to you. Listen for the word* you. Read aloud paragraph 5 or play the audio. Have students raise their hands every time the word *you* occurs.

Beginning *Say: Some selections are written to* you. *Raise your hand if you hear a sentence written to* you. Read the following sentences from Unit 5. *I was floating in clear, warm water.* (paragraph 1, p. 292) *They turned the pages.* (paragraph 3, p. 302) *Perhaps you have a younger brother.* (paragraph 1, p. 316)

Intermediate Have students look at books of science experiments to find other examples of direct address.

Advanced Ask students to rewrite the first three sentences of paragraph 1 in the third person. (Students can probably think of . . . could help them answer . . .) *Ask: How does this change the writing?*

Listen, Speak, Interact

Use Information to Raise Unanswered Questions

Stephen Kramer shows you how to use the scientific method to find the answers to two questions. He also gives some other questions you could answer using the scientific method.

1. Work with a small group. Reread the questions in paragraph 16 of the selection.
2. Choose one question from the list. Then talk about an experiment you could do to find out the answer.

3. Think of additional questions you could answer using the scientific method. Make a list of these questions with your group. Be sure to use a question mark at the end of each question. Which questions does your group find the most interesting? Which would you revise?
4. Present your best questions to the class. Make sure to use words from the reading selection in your questions and answers.

Elements of Literature

Recognize the Style of Direct Address

Style is how authors use language to express themselves. Style can include many elements, such as word choice and the use of long or short sentences.

In this selection, part of the style is **direct address.** This means that the author speaks directly to the reader using the pronoun *you.*

Perhaps you have a younger brother. (paragraph 1)

The author also uses direct address by writing words the reader might say. These words are in quotation marks.

"My little brother has less patience in the evenings on days he misses his nap than on days he takes a nap." (paragraph 4)

1. Look in paragraphs 2, 5, and 10. Find places in the selection where the author uses the pronoun *you.* Then find words the reader might say.
2. Why do you think the author writes the selection using this style? Does the style of direct address make the selection easier to understand? Why or why not?

Activity Book
p. 171

Student
CD-ROM

Chapter 3 Using the Scientific Method **323**

Content Connection
Math

Have students expand upon step 2 in Listen, Speak, Interact. Once they have decided upon a question and procedure, ask them to decide what mathematical procedures they might use in collecting and sharing their data. (*Examples:* measuring, graphing)

Learning Styles
Linguistic

Have students use direct address to tell how to do something, such as how to make their favorite sandwiches.

Listen, Speak, Interact

Use Information to Raise Unanswered Questions

▎ Teacher Resource Book: *Reading Log, p. 64*

1. **Categorize** Compile a list of the best questions from all the groups. Then ask students to group the questions into categories, such as questions about behavior, about pets, about school. Ask students which questions they think would make the best experiments. Have them explain why.
2. **Newcomers** Work with these students to brainstorm a list of questions together. Write the questions on the board. Have students copy them into their Reading Logs.

Elements of Literature

Recognize the Style of Direct Address

1. **Identify direct address** Have students look in other content area textbooks for examples of direct address. They can look in science, social studies, history, and health textbooks.
2. **Multi-level options** See MULTI-LEVEL OPTIONS on p. 322.

Answers

1. Paragraph 2: "How does my little brother act . . ." Paragraph 5: Perhaps you've noticed . . . You might decide to measure . . . Paragraph 10: If there is no evidence from any of your experiments . . . "My brother cries more often . . ."
2. *Possible answer:* Using direct address makes the text more personal and draws the reader into the text. Also, it makes readers think of their own situations and experiences.

 **ASSESS**

Have students identify direct address in paragraph 13.

Word Study

Use Greek Word Origins

Use a dictionary Have students use the dictionary to look up *method* and find related words listed after it. They may find *methodical* and *methodology*. Then ask them to look up other words with *bio–*, such as *biology* or *bionics*.

Answers
1. **a.** biography **b.** method

Grammar Focus

Use *Might* to Show Possibility

Review modal *might* Write on the board: *She might/may/could have tuna for lunch.* Tell your students these modals have very similar meanings. Point out that for the negative possibility, they can use *may not* or *might not*. However, *could not* means *not able* instead of *not possible*.

Answers
Examples: I might go the mall with my family. I might go to my friend's house.

ASSESS

Have students write sentences using *method* and *biography*.

Word Study

Use Greek Word Origins

Learning about a word's history and origin can help you understand its meaning. English has many words that come from Greek. Read this sentence from the selection:

> What if the results of your experiment don't support your <u>hypothesis</u>?

The word *hypothesis* comes from the Greek word *thesis*, which means "to set down." When you form a hypothesis you "set down," or present, an idea.

1. Look at the chart. First look at the meanings of the Greek words. Use these meanings to determine the meanings of the English words.

Greek Words	Meaning of Greek Words	English Word
meta hodos	with (meta) a way (hodos)	method
bios graph	life writing	biography

Choose from these meanings:
a. the story of a person's life
b. a process for doing something

2. Write the words and their meanings in your Personal Dictionary.

3. Check your answers in a dictionary.

Personal Dictionary   The Heinle Newbury House Dictionary   Activity Book *p. 172*   Student CD-ROM

Grammar Focus

Use *Might* to Show Possibility

Look at this sentence from the text:

> If your brother always put together more of the puzzle after taking a nap, he <u>might</u> also be more patient.

The modal verb *might* means *it is possible*. Use *might* with the simple form of a verb.

Subject	Modal Verb	Simple Verb
he	might	be

Think about next weekend. On a piece of paper, write two sentences about things that you might do.

I might go to the mall with my family.

Activity Book *pp. 173–174*   Student Handbook   Student CD-ROM

MULTI-LEVEL OPTIONS *From Reading to Writing*

Newcomer Have partners explain a process using a sequence chain. Tell them to draw a column of boxes connected with arrows. Instruct students to head each with the number of the step and the word *you*. (1. You, 2. You, and so on) Ask students to draw what to do in the boxes under the headings.

Beginning Have students work in pairs to write a process in a sequence chain. Ask them to number the steps and complete the sentence *You _____* with words and short phrases. (*Example: 1. You peel a banana 2. You put a stick in one end. 3. You dip it in chocolate.*) Tell them to include a picture to show each step.

Intermediate Have each pair share their first draft with another pair. Tell them to take turns reading their text aloud while the other pair mimes the steps. Ask students to notice whether there is any confusion about what to do. Then have pairs revise their texts.

Advanced Before students begin writing, ask them to decide whether they are writing for students their age, younger children, or adults. Ask them to determine what kind of background information and definition of terms might be helpful to their audience.

From Reading to Writing

Write an Informational Text

Work with a partner. Write three paragraphs that explain the process.

1. Brainstorm a list of things that you and your partner know how to do.
2. Choose one thing from your list. Write instructions on how to do it.
3. Use nouns correctly to show how many things are needed in each step.
4. Use the future tense with *will* to tell the reader how the process will help.

Activity Book
p. 175

Student Handbook

How to _____

Introduction
Tell about the process that you will explain.

Step-by-Step Instructions
Explain how readers can do the process.
1. First step.
2. Second step.
(Use as many steps as you need to.)

Conclusion
Summarize your writing.
Tell how the process will help your readers.

Across Content Areas

Learn About Sleep

When we sleep, we are having a time of rest. We do not know what is going on around us. It may seem like we are not doing anything as we sleep. Yet, this time of rest is a very important part of our lives.

Read each sentence below. Match each underlined word with the correct definition.

1. When we sleep, we sometimes have dreams that we remember after we wake up.
2. Our bodies repair themselves as we sleep. This is why it is important to sleep enough when we are sick.
3. We need to sleep enough to have the energy to do activities.

Definitions
a. heal, or become healthy
b. the power, or ability, to work and play
c. pictures and stories that form in the mind during sleep

In a small group, create a form that lists everyone's sleep habits over one week. Organize the form to include the days of the week, hours of sleep, and dreams. Revise your form as you correct spelling and grammar mistakes.

Activity Book
p. 176

Chapter 3 Using the Scientific Method **325**

From Reading to Writing

Write an Informational Text

1. **Provide visual aids** Suggest that students add simple diagrams or drawings to support and clarify steps in their informational texts. Remind them to write captions for each visual aid.
2. **Multi-level options** See MULTI-LEVEL OPTIONS on p. 324.

Across Content Areas: Science

Learn About Sleep

Relate to personal experience *Ask: How much sleep do you get every night during the week? On weekends? Do you sometimes remember your dreams?*

Answers
1. c 2. a 3. b

✓ ASSESS

Have students define *dream, repair,* and *energy* in their own words.

Reteach and Reassess

Text Structure Have students look at how-to books and identify topics, examples of facts, special type, headings, and numbered lists.

Reading Strategy Have students review "Eye to Eye"(p. 292) and identify examples of causes and effects. (Whales can swim faster than humans *because of* their 15-foot flippers.)

Elements of Literature Read to students a set of directions from an art project or other how-to book. Have them note examples of direct address.

Reassess Have students identify an effect in the classroom. (*Example:* The plant on the windowsill is turning brown.) Ask them to write a hypothesis about the cause. (It needs a cup of water each week.) Have them tell how they could test the hypothesis.

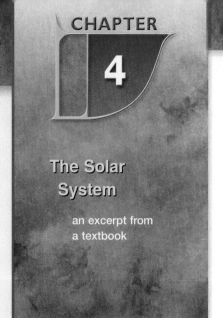

CHAPTER

4

The Solar System

an excerpt from a textbook

Into the Reading

Chapter Materials

Activity Book: *pp. 177–184*
Audio: *Unit 5, Chapter 4; CD 2, Track 10*
Student Handbook
Student CD-ROM: *Unit 5, Chapter 4*
Teacher Resource Book: *Lesson Plan, Teacher Resources, Reading Summary, Activity Book Answer Key*
Teacher Resource CD-ROM
Assessment Program: *Quiz, pp. 81–82; Teacher and Student Resources, pp. 115–144*
Assessment CD-ROM
Transparencies
The Heinle Newbury House Dictionary/CD-ROM
Web site: http://visions.heinle.com

Objectives

Preview Ask a student to read the objectives. Have students explain and give examples of terms they know in the objectives.

Use Prior Knowledge

Summarize What You Know on a Chart

Brainstorm Work with students to brainstorm things they would like to learn about the planets. If they need prompts, write these words on the board: *temperature, water, gravity, space exploration.*

Objectives

Reading Summarize information as you read an excerpt from a textbook.

Listening and Speaking Paraphrase to recall information.

Grammar Identify superlative adjectives.

Writing Outline an informational text.

Content Science: Compare planet orbits.

Use Prior Knowledge

Summarize What You Know on a Chart

The reading selection in this chapter gives information about three planets: Mercury, Venus, and Mars.

1. On a piece of paper, complete a KWL (**K**now, **W**ant to Know, **L**earned) Chart like the one here.

2. In the first column, list what you know about each of these three planets. In the second column, list what you want to know.

3. After you read the selection, list what you learned about each of these planets in your KWL Chart.

	What I Know	What I Want to Know	What I Learned
Mercury	It is close to the sun.		
Venus		Could humans live there?	
Mars			

326 Unit 5 Explorations

MULTI-LEVEL OPTIONS *Build Vocabulary*

Newcomer When showing students how to find and use dictionaries on the Internet, include translation dictionaries. Show them how they can enter a word from another language to find the English word.

Beginning Remind students that another resource to find meaning is by checking glossed words. Point out the glossed words on p. 330.

Intermediate Have students create a word map for *vast*. Tell them to look up the meaning in several sources, including the gloss for this selection, a dictionary, a thesaurus, and an online or CD-ROM dictionary or thesaurus, to get a full understanding of the word. Have them complete their maps by writing a sentence with *vast*.

Advanced Have students make a resource chart. On the left side of a paper, have them list different resources. Across the top, have them list types of information, such as definitions, synonyms, derivations, and pronunciation. Ask students to check off what each resource contains.

Build Background

Our Solar System

Our solar system is made up of the sun and all the objects that move around the sun. The sun is the star in the center of the solar system. Nine planets move around the sun. They are Mercury, Venus, Earth, Mars, Jupiter, Saturn, Uranus, Neptune, and Pluto.

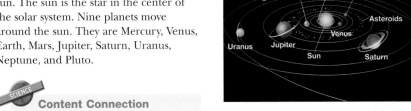

Content Connection
Smaller objects called comets and asteroids also move around the sun.

Build Vocabulary

Use Different Resources to Find Meaning

A **resource** is a tool that can help you research and find information.

1. A **table of contents** is a list of the sections or chapters of a book. It tells the page numbers where the section begins. Use the table of contents of this book to locate two favorite selections you read.

2. A **glossary** is a part of a book that gives the meanings of words. In this book, a glossary can be found at the bottom of each page of the reading selections. Find the word *gravity* in the glossary on page 330 of this book.

3. A **thesaurus** or **synonym finder** are books that you can use to find **synonyms** (words with similar meanings, such as *glad* and *happy*). Use a thesaurus or synonym finder to find a synonym for *vast*.

4. You can use the **Internet** to find a dictionary or a thesaurus. Type the keyword *dictionary* or *thesaurus* in a search engine to get started. Use a dictionary or the Internet to find the pronunciation of *mysterious*.

The Heinle Newbury House Dictionary   Activity Book *p. 177*   Student CD-ROM

Chapter 4   The Solar System   **327**

Cultural Connection

Build Vocabulary Have students create picture or word dictionaries to show meanings of ten words from another language. Instruct them to use resources, such as a print or electronic English-Spanish dictionary, to find definitions. Tell them to choose words for items that they use in school, such as books or computers. Have them teach a partner some of the words.

Learning Styles
Visual

Build Background Have students work in small groups to build simple models of the solar system. Tell them to use the picture at the top of p. 327, as well as books and Internet sites for ideas about what to show.

Build Background

Our Solar System

1. **Use illustrations to increase understanding** Bring in library books about the solar system. Have students look at illustrations and photos. Write key words from the new information and have students look up any new vocabulary.

2. **Content Connection** In 1611, Galileo used the recently invented telescope to discover dark spots on the sun. Chinese astronomers reported sunspots as early as 200 B.C.

Build Vocabulary

Use Different Resources to Find Meaning

Teacher Resource Book: *Personal Dictionary, p. 63*

1. **Identify additional resources** Ask: *Where do you go to get information for school assignments? What resources do you have at home? Do you ever go to a community or school library?*

2. **Reading selection vocabulary** You may want to introduce the glossed words in the reading selection before students begin reading. Key words: *gravity, orbit, energy, astronaut, distant, atmosphere, survive.* Instruct students to write the words with correct spelling and their definitions in their Personal Dictionaries. Have them pronounce each word and divide it into syllables.

3. **Multi-level options** See MULTI-LEVEL OPTIONS on p. 326.

Answers
1. *Examples:* "Roberto Clemente," p. 245 and "Nelson Mandela," p. 255; **3.** Vast-infinite, unlimited, boundless, endless; **4.** mysterious: /mɪˈstɪriəs/

 **ASSESS**

Say: Write three things you know about our solar system.

Text Structure

Informational Text

1. **Review features** *Ask: What other informational text have we read in this unit?* ("Using the Scientific Method") Have students turn to the selection on p. 316. *Ask: What were some of its features?* (facts, number lists, direct address) *That selection used direct address. Look at the new selection on p. 330. Does it use direct address?* (no)

2. **Multi-level options** See MULTI-LEVEL OPTIONS below.

Reading Strategy

Summarize Information

Summarize a paragraph Direct students to p. 321 and read aloud paragraph 17. Have small groups discuss the most important ideas in that paragraph and prepare a summary statement about it. For example: *Science is exciting because there are always questions to ask and discoveries to make.*

ASSESS

Ask: Why are headings useful in an informational text?

Text Structure

Informational Text

"The Solar System" is an **informational text.** Informational texts give information about a certain topic. When you read a textbook, you are reading an informational text. Look for the features of informational texts listed in the chart.

As you read "The Solar System," notice how these features help you understand new information.

Informational Text	
Informational Writing	uses details and facts to explain what something is or how something works
Headings	titles that tell you what the part of the text is about
Pictures and Charts	drawings, charts, and photos that help you understand what you read

Student
CD-ROM

Reading Strategy

Summarize Information

When you **summarize information,** you say or write down the most important ideas in a reading or part of a reading.

> *Dogs make great pets for many reasons. Most are very smart and loving and like to play. They also protect your house. Finally, walking a dog is good exercise.*
>
> *Summary: Dogs have several great qualities as pets.*

Follow these steps as you read this selection:

1. Look for the most important information in the first and last sentences of each paragraph.
2. If you cannot summarize by reading these sentences, ask yourself, "What is the paragraph mostly about?"
3. Write a summary of each paragraph. Then write a summary of the entire selection.

Student
CD-ROM

328 Unit 5 Explorations

MULTI-LEVEL OPTIONS *Text Structure*

Newcomer Examine a textbook with your students. Ask volunteers to point to examples of each of the features described on the chart at the top of p. 328.

Beginning Divide the class into groups of four. Give each student a slip of paper. Have them write one of the following on each of the slips: *fact, heading, picture, chart.* Have students use the slips to bookmark an example of each feature in one of their textbooks.

Intermediate Have students examine a section of a nonfiction book that they have not seen before. Ask them to preview the headings, pictures, and charts. Tell them to skim a page to find examples of the types of facts included. Ask students to predict the kind of information they think the section will contain.

Advanced Have students revisit a textbook chapter that they have already studied. *Ask: How did the author use the features listed on p. 328? How did the features help you understand the information? What other headings, pictures, charts, or facts would you have liked the author to include?*

The Solar System

an excerpt from a textbook

Starry Night, Vincent van Gogh, 1889.

329

Reading Selection Materials

Audio: *Unit 5, Chapter 4; CD 2, Track 10*
Teacher Resource Book: *Reading Summary,*
 pp. 109–110
Transparencies: #13, *Reading Summary*

Suggestions for Using Reading Summary

- Introduce new vocabulary or cognates.
- Cut the summary into strips, or jumble the sentences on an overhead transparency. Students put the sentences in order.
- Practice the reading strategy.
- Students read aloud or with a partner.
- Students paraphrase the summary.
- Students do a cloze activity.
- Students create a visual or graphic organizer, such as a timeline or storyboard, to illustrate the summary.
- Students paraphrase the summary.

Preview the Selection

1. **Interpret the image** Have students look at the art. *Ask: Do you think this is a realistic painting of the solar system? Why or why not? What do you like about it? The artist used many swirls and curves in the sky. What feeling does that give the night? What feeling do you get from this painting?*
2. **Learn about the artist** Explain that *Starry Night* was painted in 1889 by Vincent van Gogh, a Dutch post-impressionist painter. Have them locate the Netherlands on a map or globe. Van Gogh had a brief and tragic life (1853–1890), but he is one of the world's most widely recognized painters.
3. **Connect to theme** *Ask: What do you think people knew about the solar system in van Gogh's time? What kinds of exploration were taking place at the turn of the century?*

Content Connection
The Arts

Have students study the painting on p. 329. *Ask: What does this painting show? What do you think about the colors the artist used? What do you think the artist was trying to say about the solar system? How would you paint or draw the solar system?*

Learning Styles
Musical

Play excerpts of several pieces of classical music. After each, ask students to tell why they think the piece does or doesn't go well with the picture on p. 329. (*Example:* It goes well because it is quiet and mysterious like space.)

Read the Selection

1. **Shared reading** Play the audio. Have students join in when they can.
2. **Clarify terms** Ask questions to make sure students understand the key terms in the reading. *Ask: How do you know there's gravity on Earth?* (Things always fall down.) *Can you explain orbit in your own words?* (a planet's path around the sun) *Why is the sun so important to Earth?* (The sun generates energy in the form of light and heat.)

Sample Answer to Guide Question
The sun's energy gives warmth and light to Earth, and the gravitational pull keeps it in orbit around the sun.

See Teacher Edition pp. 434–436 for a list of English-Spanish cognates in the reading selection.

The Inner Planets

What is it like on other planets?

1 It's a good thing that Earth is part of the solar system. Without the pull of **gravity** between the sun and Earth, Earth would find itself traveling off into space. Without the sun's light and energy, Earth would be a very cold and dark world. However, Earth does **orbit** the sun and so it has a place in the solar system. But Earth is not the only planet that is affected by the sun's **energy** and gravity.

2 People have always wondered what it's like on other **bodies** in the solar system. The moon is the only place people have been able to visit in person to answer that question. On July 20, 1969, **astronaut** Neil Armstrong was the first human to set foot on the moon.

> **Summarize Information**
> In writing, summarize how Earth is affected by the sun's energy and gravity.

Audio
CD 2, Tr. 10

Earth orbiting the sun

---

gravity a natural force pulling objects to the ground
orbit a path in space followed by a planet, moon, or space vehicle

energy the power to do work
bodies objects
astronaut a person who flies into outer space

330 Unit 5 Explorations

MULTI-LEVEL OPTIONS *Read the Selection*

Newcomer Play the audio, pointing to parts of the illustrations named. *Ask: Is Earth part of the solar system?* (yes) *Have astronauts visited other planets?* (no) *Are other planets like ours?* (no) *Is this selection about all the planets?* (no)

Beginning Read the Reading Summary aloud. Then do a partner read aloud. *Ask: What is the topic of this selection?* (solar system) *Where have astronauts landed?* (on the moon) *Which planets will this selection tell about?* (Mercury, Venus, Earth, Mars)

Intermediate Have students do a paired reading. *Ask: How does the sun affect Earth?* (The sun warms it; the pull between the two keeps Earth in orbit in the solar system.) *What did astronauts accomplish by going to the moon?* (They explored and did experiments.)

Advanced Have students read silently. *Ask: Why do you think vehicles sent to explore other parts of the solar system did not have crews?* (The trips would have been too long, dangerous, and expensive.) *What is one thing you predict the author will tell about the inner planets?* (how they differ from each other)

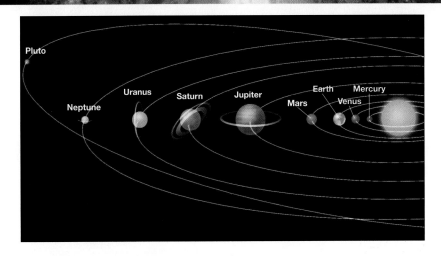

3   Six other **missions** visited the moon after that to explore, collect **samples,** and **conduct experiments.** Space **probes** sent from Earth without **crews** have been able to travel **vast** distances through the solar system. The probes have found that the planets in the solar system are very different from one another.

Summarize Information

Summarize orally the ways that people have learned about the planets in the solar system.

4   Find Mercury, Venus, Earth, and Mars on the map. They are the inner planets because they orbit closest to the sun. The outer planets—Jupiter, Saturn, Uranus, Neptune, and Pluto—orbit much farther away. In this lesson, you will learn how being in the solar system affects the inner planets.

missions   groups of people sent somewhere for a purpose
samples   single things that show what larger groups are like
conduct   do something

experiments   tests done to see if something works or happens
probes   space vehicles
crews   workers on a space vehicle
vast   wide in area, immense

Chapter 4 The Solar System   **331**

Read the Selection

1. **Paired reading** Have students read aloud in pairs. Have them list the facts they find on p. 331 and then compare their notes with a partner.
2. **Relate to personal experience** *Ask: Have you ever looked at the night sky through a telescope? What did you see? Do you know the name of any of the star constellations? Can you draw one on the board? Can you see any of the planets without a telescope?* (yes)
3. **Multi-level options** See MULTI-LEVEL OPTIONS on p. 330.

Sample Answer to Guide Question
There have been space missions to the moon to learn more about it, and they have sent space probes to other planets.

A   Capitalization

Planets

Ask: Look at paragraph 4. What do you notice about the names of the planets? (begin with capital letters) *Yes, they all begin with capitals because they are the names of places. The names of planets always begin with capital letters.*

   Apply Ask students to write three sentences about planets using the information on the diagram on p. 331.

Remind them to use capital letters for the names of planets. (*Examples:* Earth is bigger than Neptune. Venus is closer to the sun than Jupiter and Pluto.)

Read the Selection

1. **Preview the text** Have students look at the headings and illustrations. Have them tell you what they will be reading about. (the sun)

2. **Understand a diagram** Examine the diagram on p. 332 with students. *Say: Imagine that I have a ball on a string. Now I am swinging it around in a circle. I am the gravitational pull that keeps the ball in orbit. What will happen to the ball if I let it go? Will it continue in a circle? (No, because there is always a sideways force on it.)*

3. **Silent reading** Give students time to read silently. Then answer any questions they have.

4. **Draw a diagram to understand** Ask for volunteers to do a simple drawing or diagram showing the information in paragraph 6. (hydrogen atoms smashing into each other, forming helium, releasing energy)

Sample Answer to Guide Question
The most important information is that the sun is the center of the solar system, and all the planets orbit around it.

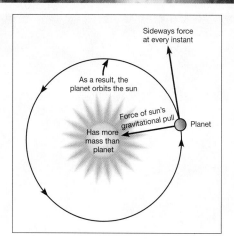

Sideways force at every instant

As a result, the planet orbits the sun

Force of sun's gravitational pull

Planet

Has more mass than planet

The Sun—The Shining Sphere

5   The sun is the largest, brightest, and hottest object in the solar system. It is also the center of the solar system. The sun has more **mass** than all the other objects in our solar system put together. As a result, **gravitational force** causes all the planets to orbit around the sun—even planets as **distant** as Neptune and Pluto.

> **Summarize Information**
> What is the most important information in this paragraph? Write your answer.

The powerful sun is mostly made of a gas called hydrogen. In turn, the hydrogen is made of tiny **particles** called atoms. At the sun's center, hydrogen atoms may reach temperatures as high as 15 million degrees Celsius (°C). The higher the temperature, the faster the atoms move. Some of the atoms move so fast that they **smash** into each other and form a gas called helium. And when the hydrogen atoms change into helium, they also **release** energy. The energy heats up the sun and makes it **shine.** The sun has enough hydrogen to stay hot and shining for about 4 billion years.   6

---

mass   generally speaking the amount of matter (material) in an object
gravitational force   what causes one object to move toward another object because of gravity
distant   far away

particles   very small pieces of something
smash   hit against something
release   let something go
shine   send out light

332   Unit 5   Explorations

MULTI-LEVEL OPTIONS *Read the Selection*

Newcomer *Ask: Is the sun the largest part of the solar system?* (yes) *Is the sun made of gas?* (yes) *Is Earth the closest planet to the sun?* (no) *Is Mercury larger than our moon?* (yes)

Beginning *Ask: What is the sun made of?* (hydrogen gas) *How long can the sun stay hot?* (4 billion years) *Which planet is closest to the sun?* (Mercury) *Which planet is about the same size as our moon?* (Mercury)

Intermediate *Ask: What is released when atoms of the sun's gas smash into each other?* (heat and light) *What do our moon, Earth, and Mercury have in common?* (rocks) *There are craters on Earth. How do you think they were formed?* (Meteorites crashed into Earth long ago.)

Advanced *Why would it be very hard to explore Mercury?* (It is very hot because it's so close to the sun.) *Is Mercury larger or smaller than Earth? How do you know?* (smaller; the text says that Mercury is about the size of the moon, and the moon is smaller than Earth.)

Mercury—The Hot and Cold Planet

7   The closest planet to the sun is Mercury. Because it is so close to the sun, it is difficult to study Mercury from Earth. The brightness of the sun makes it hard to see. **Spacecraft** flying past Mercury have sent back to Earth pictures and information about this planet.

Summarize Information

Write one sentence to summarize this paragraph.

8   In some ways, Mercury is similar to our moon. This small planet is only a little larger than our moon and, like the moon, it is covered by dust, rocks, and bowl-shaped holes called craters. Thousands of meteorites (mē'tē ɹ ĭtz) —chunks of rock from outer space— formed the craters by **crashing** into Mercury. You can see Mercury's rocky surface and some of its many craters in the picture shown below.

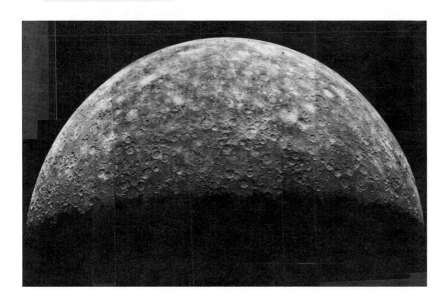

---

spacecraft   vehicles that fly in space   **crashing**   hitting onto something in a very hard way

Chapter 4   The Solar System   **333**

Read the Selection

▌ Teacher Resource Book: *Web, p. 37*

1. **Shared reading** Play the audio. Have volunteers join in for different parts of the selection.
2. **Use a graphic organizer** Draw a web on the board and write *Mercury* in the center. Have students come up and write terms and facts in the web. Then have them summarize what they know so far about the planet.
3. **Multi-level options** See MULTI-LEVEL OPTIONS on p. 332.

Sample Answer to Guide Question
Mercury is the closest planet to the sun, which makes it a hard planet to study.

 Spelling

Abbreviations for temperature

Ask students to reread paragraph 6 to find out how hot the sun is. (15 million degrees Celsius) *Say: The tiny circle and the capital* c *are abbreviations, a short way of saying* degrees Celsius. *The tiny circle stands for* degrees *and the* C *stands for* Celsius. Celsius *is one way of measuring temperature. The other way is Fahrenheit.* Write *degrees Fahrenheit* on the board. *Ask: How do you think we abbreviate this?* (°F)

Apply Write the following sentences on the board. Ask students to rewrite them with the abbreviations you have just discussed. *Water freezes at zero degrees Celsius.* (0°C) *Water freezes at 32 degrees Fahrenheit.* (32°F)

Read the Selection

Paired reading Play the audio. Then have students practice reading aloud in pairs. Have them practice summarizing paragraph 9.

Sample Answer to Guide Question
Mercury doesn't have enough atmosphere to regulate its temperature, so it gets very hot during the day but loses all its heat as soon as the sun stops shining on it.

9 When Mercury has **rotated** once around its **axis,** 59 Earth days have gone by. Long days combined with closeness to the sun and a very thin **atmosphere** explain how Mercury can be so hot and so cold. During the day, Mercury's thin atmosphere can't protect the planet from the sun's heating rays. The diagram below shows that daytime temperatures on Mercury can reach 407°C. At night, the atmosphere can't keep the heat in, so the temperature drops to about –183°C.

Summarize Information
Using your own words, orally summarize why Mercury is so hot during the day and so cold at night.

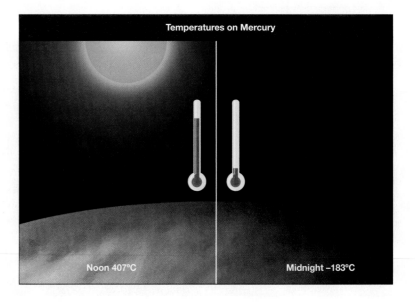

Temperatures on Mercury

Noon 407°C   Midnight –183°C

rotated   moved around something, especially in a circle

axis   a straight line around which an object turns

atmosphere   the air space above Earth or another planet

MULTI-LEVEL OPTIONS *Read the Selection*

Newcomer *Ask: Are days on Mercury hot?* (yes) *Are nights hot?* (no) *Is Venus almost the same size as Earth?* (yes)

Beginning *Ask: Describe days on Mercury.* (long and hot) *Describe nights.* (cold) *Which planet is about the same size as Venus?* (Earth)

Intermediate *Ask: Are days on Mercury shorter or longer than on Earth? Explain.* (Longer; it takes Mercury 59 times longer to rotate.) *What is something Venus and Earth have in common?* (winds, size) *How are they different?* (Venus has a thicker atmosphere.)

Advanced *Ask: Does Earth have a thinner or thicker atmosphere than Mercury? Explain.* (thicker, because our atmosphere protects us from heat and cold better) *Do you think humans could live on Venus? Explain.* (No, they would get crushed by the atmosphere just like the probes did.)

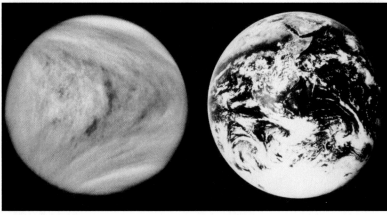

Venus

Earth

Read the Selection

Teacher Resource Book: *Web, p. 37*

1. **Reciprocal reading** Play the audio. Have volunteers read and then prepare questions on different parts of the text.
2. **Use a graphic organizer** Have students work in pairs to make an information web for Venus.
3. **Multi-level options** See MULTI-LEVEL OPTIONS on p. 334.

Sample Answer to Guide Question
Venus has a very thick and heavy atmosphere.

Venus—Cloudy Neighbor

10   Venus has a very thick atmosphere. The picture shows the thick, **swirling** clouds of **carbon dioxide** and acid that surround Venus. Powerful winds that move at speeds of over 300 kilometers per hour keep the clouds moving at all times. The atmosphere presses down on Venus like a very heavy blanket. In 1975, two large space probes from Earth landed on Venus. The probes lasted less than two hours before they were **flattened** by Venus's **crushing** atmosphere.

> **Summarize Information**
>
> In writing, summarize the most important information about Venus in this paragraph.

11   It takes Venus a little longer to rotate once around its axis than to **revolve** once around the sun. So, on Venus, a day is slightly longer than a year.

12   Compare the pictures of Venus and Earth. Venus is about the same size as Earth.

---

swirling   twisting and turning
carbon dioxide   a gas with no color, taste, or smell; people form carbon dioxide when they breathe out, but they cannot breathe in large amounts of carbon dioxide

flattened   made flat, crushed
crushing   able to crush or make flat
revolve   turn around something; move in a circle

Chapter 4 The Solar System   **335**

 Spelling

Irregular plurals

Ask: How do you usually make nouns plural? (add -*s* or -*es*) *Some words change their ending rather than adding letters. Find the word* axis *in paragraph 9. Write* axes *on the board. Say: Look at this word that means more than one* axis. *For this word, we change the* -is *to* -es *to make it mean more than one.*

Apply   *Say: In "Using the Scientific Method," there was a similar word. Ask* students to return to step 3 on p. 316 and find the word *hypothesis.* Write the word on the board and underline *is. Say: Tell me how to spell the word that means more than one* hypothesis. (hypotheses) Write the word on the board and underline *es.* Remind students to write with accurate spelling of inflections that change number or tense.

Read the Selection

Silent reading Play the audio. Then have students read the pages silently. Ask students to share their answers to the guide question.

Sample Answer to Guide Question
Venus's atmosphere is much thicker than Earth's, so it is very hot. Venus has no water, and its pressure is crushing.

Volcano on Venus

13   Like Earth, Venus has **mountains, valleys,** and **plains.** It even has a **volcano** bigger than any mountain on Earth. But Venus has no water. The heat on Venus is **unbearable**—about 450°C, enough to melt some kinds of metal! The thick atmosphere on Venus traps the sun's energy and holds it close to the surface, day and night. Venus is hotter than Mercury, even though Mercury is closer to the sun.

Life as we know it could not **survive** on Venus. Only rocks can **exist** in Venus's high temperatures and the crushing pressure of its atmosphere.

> **Summarize Information**
>
> Write a sentence summarizing how Venus is different from Earth.

---

mountains   very high hills
valleys   low areas of land between hills and mountains
plains   wide areas of flat land
volcano   a hill or mountain formed by hot, melted rock escaping from beneath the earth

unbearable   something that cannot be dealt with, accepted, or tolerated
survive   continue to live
exist   be

336   **Unit 5** Explorations

MULTI-LEVEL OPTIONS *Read the Selection*

Newcomer *Ask: Does Venus have mountains?* (yes) *Does it have rivers?* (no) *Is Mars smaller than Earth?* (yes) *Does Mars have seasons?* (yes)

Beginning *Ask: In what way is Venus like Earth?* (It has mountains, valleys, and plains.) *What is not found on Venus?* (water, humans) *Is Mars bigger or smaller than Earth?* (smaller) *What kind of nights does Mars have?* (very cold)

Intermediate *Ask: How is Venus similar to and different from Earth?* (same: mountains, valleys, plains; different: hotter, no water.) *How is Mars similar to and different from Earth?* (same: seasons, days, north and south poles; different: smaller, colder)

Advanced *Ask: Why wouldn't spacesuits protect visitors to Venus?* (The planet is so hot that it would melt them.) *Why does the author say* life as we know it could not survive? (Some other type of life that we don't know about could survive there.)

Mars—The Red Planet

14   Mars is a little bit like Mercury, a little bit like Venus, and a lot like Earth. As you can see in the picture, Mars looks **reddish.** Mars is about half the size of Earth.

Summarize Information

Which sentence in this paragraph contains the most important information? Write your answer.

15   As on Mercury, craters **dot** the surface of Mars. The nights are much colder than the days. As on Venus, the atmosphere of Mars is mostly carbon dioxide. But Mars's atmosphere is not thick enough to **trap** the sun's heat.

16   Like Earth, Mars has changing seasons, and days that are about 24 hours long. The average winter temperature on Mars is a **chilly** –125°C. Summer temperatures can sometimes get as high as 0°C. Mars also has north and south **poles.** The poles are covered with caps of frozen carbon dioxide, called dry ice. When the poles heat up, the ice caps melt and get smaller. When the poles cool down, the ice caps get larger.

Mars seen from space

reddish somewhat red	**chilly** a little cold
dot mark with small points	**poles** tops and bottoms of planets
trap catch something	

Chapter 4   The Solar System   **337**

Read the Selection

1. **Reflect on what you have learned** Have students turn back to their KWL charts and fill in what they have learned so far. Talk about what they still want to learn about the planets.
2. **Paired reading** Play the audio. Have students reread aloud with a partner.
3. **Multi-level options** See MULTI-LEVEL OPTIONS on p. 336.

Sample Answer to Guide Question
Mars is a little bit like Mercury, a little bit like Venus, and a lot like Earth.

 Punctuation

Apostrophe for possession

Remind students that in Unit 1 they learned that adding 's to a person's name shows that he or she owns something. Direct students to the last sentence in paragraph 13. *Ask: What word shows that the temperature and atmosphere belong to Venus?* (Venus's) *Does this word follow the rule about adding 's?* (yes) *What is odd about the word?* (It has two s's at the end.) *Yes, that does make the word look strange, but it is correct.*

Apply Call attention to the first sentence in paragraph 16. *Ask: How could we use a possessive to tell that the days on Mars are 24 hours long?* (Mars's days are 24 hours long.) Write the response on the board and have students tell you how to spell the first word. Remind students that it is important to write with accuracy when using possessives.

Read the Selection

1. **Summarize information** Have students summarize what we know and what we don't know about Mars. Then have them list the information on the board.
2. **Shared reading** Play the audio. Have students join in when they can.

Sample Answer to Guide Question
Mars might have had water millions of years ago, but now it is dry.

17   Some of the ice at the poles may also be frozen water. Mars might have had a lot of water millions of years ago. The many valleys and canyons on the surface of Mars could have been formed by **rushing** rivers. The flat areas could be the bottoms of lakes that dried up long ago. However, the surface is now dry and the air contains only **traces** of **water vapor.** Notice in the picture below that the surface of Mars is dry, reddish, and dusty. The redness comes from **rusted iron** in the rocks.

> **Summarize Information**
>
> Orally summarize the most important information in this paragraph.

Mars Polar Lander

---

rushing moving quickly
traces very small amounts
water vapor water that has changed from liquid to gas, and usually cannot be seen

rusted iron iron (a metal) that is covered with a reddish-brown material

338   Unit 5 Explorations

MULTI-LEVEL OPTIONS *Read the Selection*

Newcomer *Ask: Is it possible that Mars had water long ago?* (yes) *Is there water on Mars now?* (no) *Does Mars look red because of the sun?* (no) *Have scientists found signs of life on Mars?* (no)

Beginning *Ask: What do scientists think Mars may have had long ago?* (water) *What makes Mars look red?* (reddish rocks) *What have scientists studied from Mars?* (soil, air) *Do scientists think there could have been life on Mars?* (Some do.)

Intermediate *Ask: What clues has the land given that there may have been water on Mars?* (Some places look like rivers ran through them or lakes were there.) *Why is it likely that there is no life on Mars now?* (because there is no water, and living things need water)

Advanced *Ask: Why is it more likely that Mars had living things on it than other planets?* (Living things need water, and Mars may have had water.) *Why might astronauts be more likely to go to Mars than to other planets?* (because it may not be as dangerous to visit there as other planets; they may be more likely to find evidence of past life.)

View of Mars from space probe

18   Mars appears to be **lifeless** now. But does that mean there never was any life on Mars? In the summer of 1976, two space probes from Earth landed on the surface of Mars. The probes studied the air and the soil. They took pictures and sent the information back to Earth. Scientists found no signs of life after studying the information. Even so, some

scientists think Mars could **support** life. Perhaps someday astronauts will go to Mars to try to answer this **mysterious** question.

> **Summarize Information**
>
> Write one sentence that summarizes this paragraph.

---

lifeless without life
support maintain, keep something going

mysterious having no known cause

Read the Selection

1. **Shared reading** Play the audio. Have students join in when they can.
2. **Multi-level options** See MULTI-LEVEL OPTIONS on p. 338.

Sample Answer to Guide Question
Mars seems to be lifeless now, but scientists are not sure if there was once life on Mars.

Across Selections

Connect to unit theme *Say: In this selection, we explored the solar system. Look at the table of contents on p. 286. What else have we explored in this unit?* (whales, the future, human behavior) *What topic did you find the most interesting? Why?*

Spelling, Punctuation, Capitalization

After the Reading Comprehension section, students will practice spelling, punctuation, and capitalization in the Activity Book.

 Spelling

Ea for the long /e/ sound

Ask students to look at the second sentence in paragraph 18. *Say: Find the word that has a long /e/ sound.* (mean) *What vowels make that sound?* (ea) *Yes, ea is one way to spell long /e/.*

    Apply Say the following words. Have students write them: *team, neat, teach, beast, bead.*

Evaluate Your Reading Strategy

Summarize Information *Say: You have practiced an important reading strategy. Now you can decide how well you have done. Does this statement describe how you read?*

> I look for the most important information when I summarize. Summarizing information from a text helps me remember the most important parts of what I read.

Beyond the Reading

Reading Comprehension

Question-Answer Relationships

Sample Answers

1. Mercury, Venus, Earth, and Mars
2. hydrogen and helium
3. −125 degrees Celsius
4. They orbit farther away from the sun.
5. It's hard to study because its closeness to the sun makes it hard to see.
6. They both have craters, cold nights, and they have a thin atmosphere. Mars is not as hot or cold as Mercury, and Mars has north and south poles.
7. There is no water, the heat is unbearable, and the atmosphere is thick with crushing pressure.
8. It's like a very heavy blanket.
9. The pictures help me better understand the solar system by showing both the "big picture" of the solar system and what individual planets look like.
10. I think there was once water on Mars because there are valleys, canyons, and flat areas that could have been formed by water. There are traces of water vapor, and some ice at the poles may be frozen water.

Build Reading Fluency

Adjust Your Reading Rate to Scan

Explain that students need to adjust their reading to quickly scan the text to locate key words. Have them read the question then quickly scan to find the answer and identify key words.

Reading Comprehension

Question-Answer Relationships (QAR)

"Right There" Questions

1. **Recall Facts** List the inner planets.
2. **Recall Facts** Which gases create the light and heat from the sun?
3. **Recall Facts** What is the average winter temperature on Mars?

"Think and Search" Questions

4. **Explain** Why are Jupiter, Saturn, Uranus, Neptune, and Pluto called the outer planets?
5. **Identify Main Ideas** Why is it so difficult to study Mercury?
6. **Compare and Contrast** How is Mars the same or different from Mercury?
7. **Find Supporting Arguments** Why do scientists think that Venus cannot support life?

"Author and You" Question

8. **Describe** How does the author of "The Solar System" describe the atmosphere of Venus?

"On Your Own" Questions

9. **Evaluate** How does the illustrator's choice of pictures help you to understand the solar system?
10. **Evaluate Evidence** Based on "The Solar System," do you think that there was once water on Mars? Explain.

Activity Book
p. 178

Student
CD-ROM

Build Reading Fluency

Adjust Your Reading Rate to Scan

When you scan you adjust your reading rate to read fast. **Scanning** means glancing at the text for key words to help you answer questions. Work with a partner. Read aloud key words as you look for information. Write your answers on a piece of paper.

1. What astronaut first set foot on the moon?
2. Which planets are the "outer" planets?
3. What is the hottest object in the solar system?
4. What planet is closest to the sun?
5. Which planet has thick clouds of carbon dioxide?
6. Which planet looks reddish?

MULTI-LEVEL OPTIONS *Elements of Literature*

Newcomer Have students refer back to the selection and point to pictures that answer questions such as the following: *Ask: Which planet is the largest?* (Jupiter, p. 331) *What shape are craters?* (round, p. 333)

Beginning Reread aloud paragraph 4 with students' books closed. Work with students to generate three questions about the relative locations and sizes of the planets. Have students open their books to p. 331 and see if the diagram can help them answer their questions.

Intermediate Ask students to describe other graphic aids they might have added to the selection if they had written it.

Advanced After students have completed steps 1–4, ask them to review their list of questions. Tell them to identify one question that was not answered. Have each use a nonfiction resource to find the answer to the question and create a graphic aid showing the answer.

Listen, Speak, Interact

Paraphrase to Recall Information

Paraphrasing is another way to think about a reading selection and the information in it.

1. With a partner, reread the information in Build Background on page 327.
2. Close your books. On a note card, write the information that you learned in your own words.
3. Check your paraphrase against the original text. Is your paraphrase accurate?

Summarizing	Writing or saying the main ideas of a selection, or part of a selection. A summary is *shorter than* the original selection.
Paraphrasing	Retelling a selection or part of a selection in your own words, in writing or orally. A paraphrase can be *about the same length as* the original selection.

4. Share your paraphrase with the class. How are the paraphrases alike? How are they different?

Elements of Literature

Explore Graphic Aids

A **graphic aid** is a picture that tells you more about the information in a text. Many textbooks have graphic aids such as photographs, charts, and diagrams. Graphic aids help readers understand new and sometimes difficult information.

For example, paragraph 13 describes how Earth and Venus are similar and different. The photograph on the same page *shows* what Venus really looks like. This helps you understand the similarities and differences.

1. Reread paragraphs 3, 4, 7, and 8 without looking at the graphic aids. In your Reading Log, list any questions that you have about what you read.
2. When you have finished reading, look at the graphic aids for each of these paragraphs.
3. Examine how each of the graphic aids work to influence you.
4. Think about how the graphic aids helped you answer your questions. Which graphic aids helped you the most? Why?

Reading Log   Activity Book p. 179   Student CD-ROM

Chapter 4 The Solar System   **341**

Listen, Speak, Interact

Paraphrase to Recall Information

1. **Practice paraphrasing** Have students practice paraphrasing orally in small groups before they paraphrase information in writing.
2. **Newcomers** Point out to students that paraphrasing is a good study strategy when reading content material. Assign groups different paragraphs. Help them restate information in the paragraph and record their statements to share with the class.

Elements of Literature

Explore Graphic Aids

1. **Use graphic aids** Have students close their books and listen as you read paragraphs 3, 4, 7, and 8 aloud. Then have them look at the graphic aids and discuss how the aids helped them understand the material.
2. **Multi-level options** See MULTI-LEVEL OPTIONS on p. 340.

 **ASSESS**

Have groups of students discuss and write down the difference between paraphrasing and summarizing.

Home Connection

Point out that people use paraphrasing when they tell a friend or family member about something they have read in the newspaper. Read to students a paragraph from a newspaper article about a local issue or event. Ask them to practice paraphrasing the information with a partner. Then invite students to share their paraphrasing with someone at home.

Learning Styles
Visual

Have each student read a short encyclopedia article or other informational text about a topic that interests them. Ask them to choose a selection to read that does not include graphic aids. Instruct students to create a graphic aid to share what they learned about their topics. As an alternative, you may read an article to students.

Word Study

Recognize Words and Sounds with the Spelling *oo*

Define and clarify Have students repeat the examples after you, distinguishing the pronunciation between the two groups. List these words: *soon, soothe, loose, hoop, loom* and *hook, hoof, hood, soot.*

Grammar Focus

Identify Superlative Adjectives

1. **Discuss form** Point out the spelling changes with adjectives ending in *-e* (drop the *-e*), such as *closest,* and one-syllable adjectives ending in a vowel-consonant (double the final consonant), such as *hottest.*

2. **Use superlative adjectives** *Ask: Who is the funniest person in our class?* Continue asking about *nicest, tallest, youngest, oldest.* Write on the board the adjective with its superlative forms.

Answers

1. and 2. They are the inner planets because they orbit <u>closest</u> to the sun. The sun is the <u>largest</u>, <u>brightest</u>, and <u>hottest</u> object in the solar system.
3. close, large, bright, hot.

ASSESS

Say: Write two sentences about your family, using superlative adjectives.

Word Study

Recognize Words and Sounds with the Spelling *oo*

Some English words have two written vowels, but they are pronounced as one sound. The letters *oo* in the word *moon* are a diphthong. *Moon* contains two *o* vowels, yet you pronounce only one sound. It is only one syllable.

In English, *oo* is pronounced one of two ways. These two different sounds can be heard in the words *moon* and *good.* You must learn which way to pronounce *oo* for each word you read.

1. With a partner, pronounce each word in the chart. Use a dictionary to help you.
2. If you do not know the meanings of any of the words, use a dictionary and write the words' meanings in your Personal Dictionary.

Words Pronounced Like *Moon*		Words Pronounced Like *Good*	
cool	school	took	look
too	tool	book	cook
boot	root	foot	

3. Choose two *oo* words and write a sentence using each word.

Personal Dictionary   The Heinle Newbury House Dictionary   Activity Book p. 180   Student CD-ROM

Grammar Focus

Identify Superlative Adjectives

Superlative adjectives are adjectives that describe a noun compared with two or more other nouns. Superlative adjectives often end in *-est.* Look at this example:

Kai is the smart**est** person in the class.

The superlative adjective *smartest* describes Kai. It compares Kai with all the other people in the class.

1. Find two sentences that contain superlative adjectives in "The Solar System." Look in paragraphs 4 and 5.

2. Copy the sentences on a piece of paper. Underline the superlative adjectives.

3. Write the root word for each adjective. Note that adjectives ending in *-e* drop the *-e* before adding *-est.*

Activity Book pp. 181–182   Student Handbook   Student CD-ROM

MULTI-LEVEL OPTIONS *From Reading to Writing*

Newcomer Use a language experience approach to create a class outline in the form of two Main Idea Tables. Place the main ideas on the tabletops. Place supporting details on the legs. Make simple sketches to reinforce the meaning of the words and phrases on the tables.

Beginning Have pairs create outlines in the form of Main Idea Tables. After they have recorded their ideas in words and phrases, show them how to use Roman numerals to number the ideas on the tabletops and capital letters for details on the legs.

Intermediate Ask students to summarize the paragraphs orally. Have them use their outlines as notes. Each partner can tell about one of the paragraphs.

Advanced Review with students what they learned about summarizing on p. 328. Tell them to use their outlines to write summaries of the paragraphs. Remind them that summaries are another way to recall information.

From Reading to Writing

Outline an Informational Text

An **outline** shows the main ideas and supporting details in a text. Use Roman numerals (I, II, III, etc.) for main ideas. Use capital letters for subtopics, and use numbers for details.

1. With a partner, reread aloud paragraphs 7 and 8. Adjust your reading rate so that you can outline as you read. Read more slowly.
2. On a piece of paper, copy and complete this outline.
3. Use a computer to prepare and print your final outline.
4. Compare and contrast your outlines.

> **Mercury**
> I. Location
>   A. Closest planet to the sun
>   B. ____
>   1. Brightness of the sun—hard to see
>   2. Pictures from spacecraft
> II. Mercury compared to Earth's moon
>   A. ____
>   B. Surface
>   1. Dust
>   2. ____
>   3. ____

Activity Book p. 183   Student Handbook

Across Content Areas

Compare Planet Orbits

Read the list below. It shows about how long it takes for each planet to orbit around the sun in Earth years.

Mercury	88 days	Venus	224 days
Earth	1 year	Mars	2 years
Jupiter	12 years	Saturn	30 years
Uranus	84 years	Neptune	165 years
Pluto	247 years		

Note: There are about 365 days in 1 Earth year.

1. Which planet orbits around the sun in the shortest amount of time?
2. Which planet orbits around the sun in the longest amount of time?
3. Is Neptune closer to or farther from the sun than Venus? How do you know?

Work with a partner to write a news story about travel to other planets. Write a title and two paragraphs to organize your news story. Revise it as you correct spelling and grammar mistakes.

Activity Book p. 184

Reteach and Reassess

Text Structure Ask students to work in pairs. Assign each pair a science topic. Tell them to imagine that they are writing a textbook on the topic and identify one fact, one heading, and one graphic aid that they might include.

Reading Strategy Have students summarize information about one planet.

Elements of Literature Ask students to select three graphic aids from their science textbook. Have them identify a question that each graphic answers.

Reassess Have students reread a section of a textbook they have already studied. Have them paraphrase what they learned.

From Reading to Writing

Outline an Informational Text

1. **Outline format** Copy the outline onto the board. Call attention to the indentations and format. After students have done the activity in pairs, have volunteers complete the outline on the board.
2. **Connect to content areas** *Ask: In what other classes can you use outlines? Why do you think an outline can help you prepare for writing a paper? How do you think an outline can help you study?*
3. **Multi-level options** See MULTI-LEVEL OPTIONS on p. 342.

Answers
2. **B.** Difficult to study from Earth **A.** Little larger than moon **2.** Rocks **3.** Craters

Across Content Areas: Science

Compare Planet Orbits

Refer to graphic aids Have students look at the illustration on p. 327 to help them visualize the information.

Answers
1. Mercury (88 days) **2.** Pluto (247 years)
3. Neptune is farther from the sun because it takes much longer to orbit than Venus.

 **ASSESS**

Ask: What features do you use to create outlines? (Roman numerals, capital letters, and numbers)

Materials

Student Handbook
CNN Video: *Unit 5*
Teacher Resource Book: *Lesson Plan, p. 28;*
    Teacher Resources, pp. 35–64; Video Script,
    pp. 169–170; Video Worksheet, p. 177;
    School-Home Connection, pp. 147–153
Teacher Resource CD-ROM
Assessment Program: *Unit 5 Test, pp. 83–88;*
    Teacher and Student Resources,
    pp. 115–144
Assessment CD-ROM
Transparencies
The Heinle Newbury House Dictionary/CD-ROM
Heinle Reading Library: *The Invisible Man*
Web site: http://visions.heinle.com

Listening and Speaking Workshop

Give an Oral Report About Your Community

Review features of an oral presentation
Review planning an oral presentation. *Ask:*
What can you do to keep the audience's
attention? How can you use visuals?

Step 1: Choose a topic to present.
Brainstorm and list topics on the board. You
may give students the option of presenting to
an audience from another time period, such as
the 19th century or the 22nd century.

Listening and Speaking Workshop

Give an Oral Report About Your Community

> **Topic**
>
> Imagine that you are speaking to
> people who want to explore your
> community. Give an oral presentation
> in which you describe interesting
> places or things in your community.

Step 1: Choose a topic to present.

1. On a piece of paper, list three topics
   that you could present.
2. Choose the topic that you can
   research and that you know the
   most about.

**Step 2: Brainstorm three details that
support your topic.**

Use a chart like this one to organize
your ideas.

Topic: The Best Things to Do in My Community
Detail: go swimming at the pool
Detail: go boating on City Park Lake
Detail: watch a baseball game at the park

**Step 3: Think of an opening statement
that will get the audience interested.**

1. Ask a question, such as "Would you
   like to hear about the best things to
   do in my community?"

2. Give an opinion, such as "My
   community is a great place to have
   fun."
3. Compare your community to
   another place or thing. For example,
   "There are as many ways to have fun
   in my community as there are stars
   in the sky."

Step 4: Write your ideas on note cards.
Give examples and details.

**Step 5: Find or draw a picture that
shows something that you will describe.**

Step 6: Practice your presentation.

1. Practice your presentation in front
   of a partner. Use your note cards to
   help you remember what to say.
2. Ask your partner to complete the
   Active Listening Checklist. You will
   answer the Speaking Checklist.
3. Use the checklists to make your
   presentation better.

Step 7: Give your presentation.

1. Speak clearly and slowly. Make sure
   everyone can hear you.
2. Use your voice to show that you are
   excited about your topic.
3. If possible, record your presentation
   on audio or video. Review your
   presentation. How can you improve?

MULTI-LEVEL OPTIONS *Listening and Speaking Workshop*

Newcomer Have students
indicate their topic with a simple
map of the location. Instruct them
to draw several boxes on the
edges of their maps. Tell students
to sketch something in each box
to show examples of what a
person could see or do in this
community location. Have
students present their work.

Beginning Have students
make four note cards by
completing one of the following
sentences on each: *You can go to*
_____. *You can see* _____. *Then*
you can see _____. *You can see*
_____, *too.* Tell them to make
quick sketches on each card to
remind them of their ideas. Have
students read from the cards for
their presentations.

Intermediate Ask students to
include reasons that people would
enjoy visiting each of the sites
they describe.

Advanced Suggest that one
way to make their presentations
interesting is to include concrete
examples. Instruct students to tell
a brief anecdote or story about a
time they or someone they know
visited one of the sites described
in their presentation.

Active Listening Checklist

1. The opening statement was interesting: Yes / No

2. The details and supporting evidence helped me to understand the topic: Yes / No

3. The most interesting thing that I learned was _____ .

4. I understood the purpose of the presentation: Yes / No

Speaking Checklist

1. Did I prepare note cards on main points and details?

2. Did I speak clearly and loudly enough for people to hear me?

3. Did I hold up a picture to show what I was describing?

4. Did I use gestures?

Student Handbook

Viewing Workshop

View and Think

Discuss What People Are Exploring

People all over the world are exploring places such as the solar system to learn more about them. People are also exploring new ideas in computers, medicine, and science in order to make our lives better.

1. Go to a library. Find an article about a new idea or place that people are exploring today. You may use the Internet to search for an article. Use these keywords: *scientific discoveries, explorations, science news.*

2. Take notes and summarize as you read the article.
   a. What new idea or place is the article about?
   b. What did you learn about this idea or place from the article?
   c. Is it important to study this new idea or place? Why or why not?

3. Look for stories that tell about the new idea or place. Compare and contrast your article with the stories you find.

4. Make a chart with your class to show what you and your classmates found.

Further Viewing

Watch the *Visions* CNN Video for Unit 5. Do the Video Worksheet.

CNN Video

Apply and Expand **345**

Step 2: Brainstorm three details that support your topic.
Have students work in groups to create a wide variety of details.

Step 3: Think of an opening statement that will get the audience interested.
In groups have students help each other think of different interesting openings.

Step 4: Write your ideas on note cards.
Have students highlight the most important details with markers.

Step 5: Find or draw a picture that shows something you will describe.
Remind students to make the illustration big enough to be visible to the class.

Step 6: Practice your presentation.
Go over the Speaking Checklist and the Active Listening Checklist. Have students practice in small groups.

Step 7: Give your presentation.
Discuss other criteria for oral presentations, such as using a strong voice, maintaining eye contact, and holding interest.

ASSESS

Have students write one new thing they learned about their community.

Portfolio

Students may choose to record or videotape their presentations to place in their portfolios.

Viewing Workshop

View and Think

Research collaboratively Have students work in pairs to research using the Internet.

Cultural Connection

Ask students to recall or do research to find out about interesting places in another country. Have students draw or locate pictures of the places. Ask them to share with their classmates what makes these places special and interesting. Ask students to compare them to places they have seen or heard about in the United States.

Learning Styles
Intrapersonal

Ask students to explore their own thoughts about exploring. First, have them list or draw feelings that the idea of exploring gives them. (excited, scared, curious) Then ask them to list or draw places they would and would not like to explore. Have them record their thoughts in their Reading Logs.

Teacher Resource Book: *Reading Log, p. 64*

Writer's Workshop

Write a Research Report

Plan a research report Read and discuss the prompt. Have students begin their lists by thinking of different categories of animals, such as farm animals, city pets, birds, water mammals, and so on.

Step 1: Brainstorm what you would like to know about the animal.

Have students add other things they might like to know about animals.

Step 2: Research the animal and find answers to your questions.

Suggest to students that they put information about each question on a separate card and write down the source of information before they read.

Step 3: Record and organize information.

Have students work in pairs. Ask students to read their partner's information. Instruct them to identify information that is useful and information that should be added.

Step 4: Write a draft.

Students may find it helpful to put their information in outline form, and then check their outline against Step 4 to make sure they have included everything. Instruct them to use superlative adjectives to make their writing vivid and precise. If necessary, review Grammar Focus from Chapter 4.

Writer's Workshop

Write a Research Report

> **Prompt**
>
> In this unit, you learned about whales. Think of an animal that you would like to know more about. Write a research report about it.

Question: What does the animal eat?
Summary: Many snakes eat birds and mice.
Source: www.snakesaregreat.com

Step 1: Brainstorm what you would like to know about the animal.

1. What does the animal look like?
2. Where does the animal live?
3. What does the animal eat?
4. What interesting or amazing things does the animal do?

Step 2: Research the animal and find answers to your questions.

1. Find multiple sources about the animal. Use books from a library, or find information on the Internet. Use the animal's name as a keyword for your Internet search.
2. Use headings, tables of contents, and graphic features (maps, pictures, charts) to locate and organize information. Ask your teacher or librarian to help you interpret the information in the graphic features.
3. Revise your questions as you find information. Continue to research the answers.
4. Review your notes and your own knowledge to ask any questions you still need answers to.

Step 3: Record and organize information.

1. Evaluate your research. Decide if the information you find is useful.
2. Find information that answers your questions. Paraphrase it on a note card. *Be sure to use your own words.* Write your questions to help you organize your notes.
3. List the sources where you found the information. Use the citation format in your Student Handbook.
4. Use your own words to note additional information that is important or interesting.
5. Choose the information you will include in your report. The report outline in the next step will help you organize the information you paraphrased.

Step 4: Write a draft.

1. Write the introduction.
   a. Tell what your report is about.
   b. Explain why people should learn about the animal.
2. Write a **body** of three paragraphs. Each of these paragraphs explains a different idea.

MULTI-LEVEL OPTIONS *Writer's Workshop*

Newcomer Write on the board: *looks like? lives in? eats? habits?* Have students use pictures and other sources to find answers. Ask them to draw these answers on the appropriate sheets. Help students label the pictures and bind them into a booklet.

Beginning Have students copy the questions from step 1 onto separate sheets of paper. Ask them to use pictures, labels, and captions to answer the questions. Help them bind the pages into picture books to send to an elementary class.

Intermediate Divide the class into groups based on the classes of animals they wrote about: mammals, birds, reptiles, and so on. Ask each group to find out about that class and prepare an introduction. Have them choose a group member to read the introduction before individuals share their reports with the class.

Advanced Have students discuss a point of view for their audience. If they want to appeal to young readers, they might write from the animal's point of view. If they are writing about animals that people have as pets, they might want to use direct address. Third person might be best if they want the paper to sound scientific.

a. In each paragraph, state one idea about the animal.

b. Give details or examples that support each idea.

3. Write the conclusion. Explain why you think the animal is interesting.

4. Include a drawing of the animal.

5. List the sources you used, such as books or Web sites.

6. Give your report a title.

Title _____

☐ Tell what animal your report is about.
Explain why people should learn about the animal. _____

Idea 1: _____
Details and examples: _____

Idea 2: _____
Details and examples: _____

Idea 3: _____
Details and examples: _____

☐ Explain why you think the animal is interesting. _____

Sources: www.snakesaregreat.com
The Big Book of Snakes

Step 5: Revise and edit your draft.

1. Read your draft. Be sure you used details and examples in your body paragraphs. Did I correctly use the information that I found in my sources?

2. If you use a computer, use software, such as an online dictionary or thesaurus, to check your work. Also use the spell check and grammar check to revise and edit your draft.

3. Exchange drafts with a partner. Proofread each other's drafts. Then complete the Editor's Checklist for your partner's draft on a piece of paper.

4. With your partner, discuss how you could make your draft better.

5. Revise your draft to make it better. Also refer to the sources you used to help you clarify ideas and revise text.

 Editor's Checklist

1. The writer explained what the report is about. Yes / No

2. The writer explained why people should know about the animal. Yes / No

3. The writer used details and examples in each body paragraph. Yes / No

4. The writer listed sources. Yes / No

5. The writer used visuals. Yes / No

Step 6: Publish.

1. Rewrite your report in your best handwriting, or use a computer to type your report. Check for spelling and grammar errors.

2. Read your report to the class. Ask your science teacher to post it on the wall of your science class.

UNIT 5
Apply and Expand

Step 5: Revise and edit your draft.
Have students complete the Editor's Checklist after reading their partner's draft. Remind students to write in complete sentences. Suggest that they vary the types, such as using compound and complex sentences. Remind them to use appropriate punctuation for independent and dependent clauses.

Step 6: Publish.
After students have published and shared their reports, have them tell what was the most interesting thing they learned about the animal they researched.

 **ASSESS**

Have students list four steps they took in writing their research reports.

Portfolio

Students may choose to include their writings in their portfolios.

 Cultural Connection

Point out that students learned facts about animals by doing their reports. Suggest that another interesting thing to learn about animals is which ones are important to certain cultures. Remind students that in "Sadako and the Thousand Paper Cranes" they learned that cranes are considered lucky in some Asian countries. Have students ask people from different cultures about animals that have special meaning to them. Invite students to share what they learn.

Learning Styles
Natural

Suggest that another way to gather information for a report on an animal is through observation. Invite students who wish to do so to choose an animal in their environment, such as a pigeon, a worm, or a cat. Have them observe and record notes about behaviors as one source of information. Remind students to observe from a distance for their own safety and so that they will not alarm the animal.

Apply and Expand

Projects

Project 1: Explore Sources to Answer Science Questions

1. **Brainstorm questions for research** Help students think of questions to research. Ask students about what they are studying in science class or questions they may have about weather or health.

2. **Discuss different sources** Read the list of sources with students and discuss the advantages and disadvantages of each. For example, *say: Encyclopedias are usually just found in libraries. They have a lot of information, but sometimes it is more information than you can use.*

Project 2: Give a Presentation About an Explorer

Limit topic Talk with students about how to limit a topic. *Say: If the person is very famous or has explored many places, choose the most interesting one. Just focus on one or two things that the explorer did.*

Portfolio

Students may choose to include their projects in their portfolios.

Projects

These projects will help you learn more about explorations. Ask an adult for help if you need it.

Project 1: Explore Sources to Answer Science Questions

A source is a place where you can get information and answers to questions.

1. Work with a partner. Think of a science question. Write the question on a note card.
2. Go to a library. Ask the librarian where to find these sources:
   a. encyclopedias
   b. Internet access
   c. newspapers
   d. science books
   e. science magazines
3. List two sources that you could use to answer the question.

Question: Why do plants need sunlight to grow?

Sources: 1. An encyclopedia
              2. A person who grows plants

---

4. Report your question and answer to the class. Tell where you found the answer.
5. Think of a new question you formed as you researched. Use the information you found and your own knowledge. Where do you think you will find the answer?

Project 2: Give a Presentation About an Explorer

An explorer is a person who goes to a new place in order to learn about it.

1. Choose a famous explorer to research. Choose one from the list below or choose one on your own.
   a. Neil Armstrong
   b. Sacagawea
   c. Ferdinand Magellan
2. Research the explorer. Look for articles and stories about the explorer to compare and contrast how different sources tell information about him or her. You can use resources from a library. You can also use the Internet. (Use the explorer's name as a key word.)
3. Evaluate your research. Make sure the information you found is useful. Ask yourself the questions below. Write your answers on note cards to help you summarize and organize information. Write the answers in complete sentences.
   a. Where did the explorer go?
   b. When did the explorer go?
   c. What is this explorer famous for?
   d. Why is this explorer interesting?
4. Give a presentation on the explorer to the class. Use your note cards.
5. Use visuals such as photos, drawings, timelines, charts, and maps. Use these features to summarize and organize the information you found. Include captions that explain the visuals. Write the captions in complete sentences.
6. E-mail or write a letter to a friend or family member to further share your research.

MULTI-LEVEL OPTIONS *Projects*

Newcomer Work with students to find out about a particular explorer. Help students prepare skits with very simple dialogue to show things that the explorer did. Suggest that students make simple props and costumes to use in performing their skits for another class.

Beginning Have students work in small groups. Ask each to show on a map where their explorer traveled. Have them create a picture timeline to show what the explorer did. Tell students to write short captions for the pictures on their timelines.

Intermediate Ask students to role-play being the explorers that they have studied. As that person, have each student tell the class the story of one of his or her explorations. Encourage students to use the first-person point of view and speak expressively.

Advanced Ask each student to pair with another whose explorer had something in common with his/hers. For example, both may have been Spanish or both may have explored outer space. Have these pairs meet and create Venn diagrams comparing and contrasting their subjects.

Further Reading

The books below discuss exploration and discoveries. Read one or more of them. Write your thoughts and feelings about what you read in your Reading Log. After you read, answer these questions:

1. Which discovery did you find the most interesting?
2. Would you like to explore one of these places or ideas?
3. Can you connect the ideas and issues in these books to those found in the reading selections in this unit?

Dive!: My Adventures in the Deep Frontier
by Sylvia A. Earle, National Geographic Society, 1999. Sylvia Earle describes exploring oceans, learning about whales, and living in an underwater laboratory.

How to Think Like a Scientist: Answering Questions by the Scientific Method
by Stephen Kramer, HarperCollins Children's Books, 1987. This book teaches how the scientific method works by exploring everyday problems and questions.

Hallucination Orbit: Psychology in Science Fiction
edited by Isaac Asimov, Martin H. Greenberg, and Charles G. Waugh, Farrar, Straus and Giroux, 1983. Twelve science fiction stories explore how the human brain responds to strange situations. Authors include Roald Dahl, Isaac Asimov, and Jerome Bixby.

Exploring the Titanic
by Robert D. Ballard, Econo-Clad Books, 1999. The *Titanic* is a ship that sank in 1912. In 1986, it was discovered 12,690 feet (3,870 meters) below the ocean. This book describes the *Titanic,* the night it sank, and how the ship was explored more than 70 years later.

Can You Hear a Shout in Space?: Questions and Answers About Space Exploration
by Melvin Berger and Gilda Berger, Scholastic, Inc., 2001. This book describes what it is like to be in space. The book also talks about how the human body reacts to zero-gravity conditions.

1,000 Inventions & Discoveries
by Roger Francis Bridgman, DK Publishing, Inc., 2002. From millions of years ago to the present, there have been discoveries that have changed the world we live in. Each chapter of this book details an important period in the history of discoveries.

We Have Conquered Pain: The Discovery of Anesthesia
by Dennis Brindell Fradin, Simon & Schuster Children's, 1996. Four different doctors—Horace Wells, William Morton, Crawford Long, and Charles Jackson—claim to have discovered anesthesia in the 1840s. This book explores what each one did and how they fought for credit of the discovery.

Companion Web site   Reading Log   Heinle Reading Library The Invisible Man

---

Further Reading

1. **Read summaries** Have volunteers read the summaries. Ask students which books would interest them and why.
2. **Locate resources** Ask volunteers to check titles out from the library and bring them to class. Students can read the books during free time or for a special assignment.

Assessment Program: *Unit 5 Test, pp. 83–88*

Heinle Reading Library

The Invisible Man by H.G. Wells
In a specially adapted version
by Malvina G. Vogel

A quiet country village, a heavy snowstorm, a mysterious stranger . . . more than enough to rouse the townspeople to gossip and speculation. Who can he be, this suspicious-looking man who keeps his face hidden and his back to everyone? But when the stranger finally faces them, there are more questions than answers, and more terror of the most unspeakable kind, as outrage and murder put the once quiet countryside into the grip of an unstoppable madman. Ultimately, it is up to one man to solve the mystery and end the rampage, to reveal the identity of the faceless Invisible Man!

Visions Companion Site

http://visions.heinle.com
For additional student activities and teacher resources, see the Visions Companion Web site.

Unit Materials

Activity Book: *pp. 185–216*
Audio: *Unit 6; CD 2, Tracks 11–15*
Student Handbook
Student CD-ROM: *Unit 6*
CNN Video: *Unit 6*
Teacher Resource Book: *Lesson Plans, Teacher Resources, Reading Summaries, School-Home Connection, Video Script, Video Worksheet, Activity Book Answer Key*
Teacher Resource CD-ROM
Assessment Program: *Quizzes, Test, and End-of-Book Exam, pp. 89–108; Teacher and Student Resources, pp. 115–144*
Assessment CD-ROM
Transparencies
The Heinle Newbury House Dictionary/CD-ROM
More Grammar Practice workbook
Heinle Reading Library: *Moby Dick*
Web site: http://visions.heinle.com

Visions Staff Development Handbook

Refer to the Visions Staff Development Handbook for more teacher support.

Unit Theme: Connections

Clarify the theme word Have students look up *connection* in a dictionary. *Say: This unit is about* connections, *the relationships between people, things, or places.*

Unit Preview: Table of Contents

Use the table of contents Read the chapter titles and authors. *Ask: Which selections are probably based on facts?* ("The Boy King," "It Could Still Be a Robot," and "High-Tech Helping Hands")

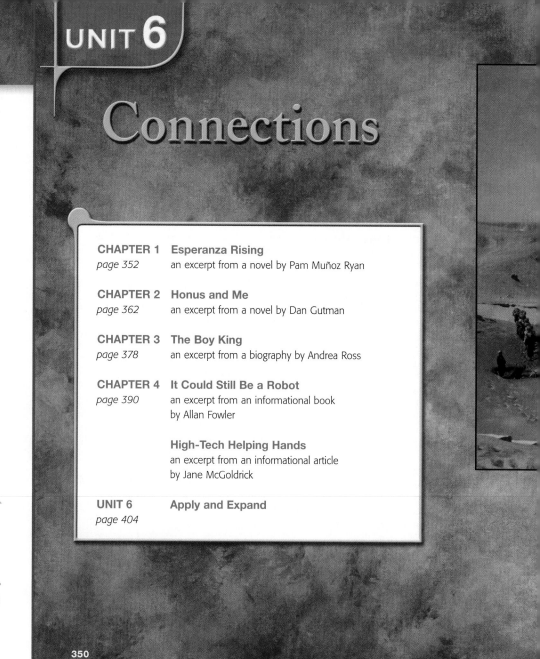

UNIT 6

Connections

350

UNIT OBJECTIVES

Reading
Make inferences as you read an excerpt from a novel • Identify the main idea and details as you read fiction • Identify cause and effect as you read a biography • Paraphrase to recall ideas as you read an informational text

Listening and Speaking
Distinguish between facts and opinions • Use persuasion • Ask and answer interview questions • Talk about advantages and disadvantages

Excavation of the Sphinx, Ernst Koener, 1883.

View the Picture

1. Describe what you see in the picture.
2. How does this picture show the theme of "connections"?

In this unit, you will read fiction, a biography, and informational texts. You will also practice writing these forms.

351

Grammar
Identify possessive adjectives
- Understand the past perfect tense • Understand modal auxiliaries
- Use adverbs of frequency

Writing
Write a fiction story • Write a paragraph
- Write a biography • Write a persuasive essay

Content
Social Studies: Learn about land forms
- Math: Use multiplication • Social Studies: Identify symbols • Science: Read an FAQ web page

View the Picture

1. **Art background** In 1883, the archaeologist Ernst Koerner excavated the Great Sphinx at Giza in Egypt. Considered to be one of the Seven Wonders of the World, the Sphinx is 70ft (20 m) high and 245ft (73m) long. Made of ashlar masonry between 2575 and 2465 B.C., it faces east, in front of Pyramid of Cheops, the tomb of an Egyptian pharaoh.

2. **Art interpretation** *Ask: Why do you think the ancient Egyptians built the Sphinx near the pharaoh's tomb?* (as a guard)

   a. **Make comparisons** *Say: Look at the shapes and lines of the pyramids behind the Sphinx. Compare these geometric structures to tombstones you might see in a modern cemetery. What do they tell you about the expectations and culture of ancient times?*

   b. **Speculate** *Ask: Why do you think the ancient Egyptians built the Sphinx? It is over 4000 years old. Why do you think it is so well preserved?*

   c. **Connect to theme** *Say: The theme of this unit is* connections. *In what ways are we connected to the ancient cultures?*

Answers
Sample answers: **1.** a huge stone sculpture and pyramids; people digging in the desert **2.** These structures are ancient, but they have survived for over 4000 years. Archaeologists excavate old places to help us understand and connect to ancient times and civilizations.

✓ **ASSESS**

Have students create a symbol to guard the school or their homes.

CHAPTER 1

Esperanza Rising

an excerpt from a novel
by Pam Muñoz Ryan

Into the Reading

Chapter Materials

Activity Book: *pp. 185–192*
Audio: *Unit 6, Chapter 1; CD 2, Track 11*
Student Handbook
Student CD-ROM: *Unit 6, Chapter 1*
Teacher Resource Book: *Lesson Plan, Teacher Resources, Reading Summary, Activity Book Answer Key*
Teacher Resource CD-ROM
Assessment Program: *Quiz, pp. 89–90; Teacher and Student Resources, pp. 115–144*
Assessment CD-ROM
Transparencies
The Heinle Newbury House Dictionary/CD-ROM
Web site: http://visions.heinle.com

Objectives

Preview Have a student read the objectives.
Ask: Which objective do you already know something about? A mountain is a land form. What other land forms can you name?

Use Prior Knowledge

Describe a Place That You Like to Visit

Use a graphic organizer Draw a Sunshine Organizer on the board and write a place you like to visit in the center. Have students ask you questions about your place. Fill in the answers. Then students can complete their own Sunshine Organizers in pairs.

Objectives

Reading Make inferences as you read an excerpt from a novel.

Listening and Speaking Distinguish between facts and opinions.

Grammar Identify possessive adjectives.

Writing Write a fiction story.

Content Social Studies: Learn about land forms.

Use Prior Knowledge

Describe a Place That You Like to Visit

What place do you like to visit? Is it indoors or outdoors? How would you describe it?

1. Copy this Sunshine Organizer. Use it to describe the place that you like to visit.
2. With a partner, ask and answer questions about the place. For example:

   What do you do there?

   Who do you see?

   When do you like to go there?

   How do you get there?

My Place — Who? What? When? Where? Why? How?

MULTI-LEVEL OPTIONS *Build Vocabulary*

Newcomer Act out the meanings of *gazing up* and *inched.* Have students imitate your actions and repeat the vocabulary word after you.

Beginning Act out *gazing up* and *inched.* Then say each vocabulary word, one by one, and ask students to act out the meaning as they say the words.

Intermediate Have students create a sentence for each vocabulary word. Tell them to leave a blank where the vocabulary word should be. Ask them to exchange papers with a partner and fill in the blanks in each other's sentences.

Advanced Have students use a thesaurus to identify a synonym for each word. (*Examples:* gazing – staring, tendril – wisp, inch – creep, patient – tolerant) *Ask: Do you think the word the writer chose is a better choice for the sentence than the synonyms you found? Why or why not?*

Build Background

Growing Grapes

The selection you will read takes place in a vineyard. A vineyard is an area of land where people grow grapes. Grapes grow on vines. Vines are plants that have long, thin stems. Grapes are grown around the world. They have been grown for thousands of years.

 Content Connection

The word *vineyard* comes from *vine* and *yard* (an area of land).

Build Vocabulary

Understand Words in Context

Read each sentence and use the **context** to help you understand the underlined word. The context is the information around the word. Check your answers with a partner. If you are not sure about an answer, look the word up in a dictionary.

1. The girl loved to walk with her father, <u>gazing</u> up at him as he spoke to her.
   a. looking at him for a long time
   b. looking away from him
2. He gently touched a green <u>tendril</u> that grew from the vine.
   a. piece of clothing
   b. a thin part of a plant

3. Little by little, she <u>inched</u> next to him.
   a. sat down
   b. moved very slowly
4. Her father told her to <u>be patient</u>, so she waited and lay silent.
   a. wait calmly for something
   b. sing a song

Write the words and their meanings in your Personal Dictionary.

Personal Dictionary   The Heinle Newbury House Dictionary   Activity Book *p. 185*   Student CD-ROM

 Content Connection
Science

Build Background Have small groups of students use books and Internet sites to research how grapevines grow. Ask each student in the group to illustrate one stage of the process. Have groups tape together their illustrations of the stages to form one continuous sequence strip.

Learning Styles
Visual

Build Vocabulary Ask each student to cut a sheet of paper into quarters. Have students draw a picture illustrating each vocabulary word in a different context than in the exercise above. Make a card for each vocabulary word. Have students hang their drawings on a wall under the appropriate cards. Provide time for students to see all the different contexts in which their classmates have shown the words.

Build Background

Growing Grapes

1. **Use prior knowledge** *Ask: What kinds of grapes can you buy in the store?* (green, red, white grapes) *What can you eat or drink that is made from grapes?* (juice, jelly, raisins from dried grapes)
2. **Content Connection** California is the number one producer of grapes in the United States, growing two-thirds of all grapes. New York state is the second biggest producer.

Build Vocabulary

Understand Words in Context

Teacher Resource Book: *Personal Dictionary, p. 63*

1. **Discuss reading strategy** Have students think about what they do when they come across unfamiliar words while they read. *Ask: Do you use the dictionary, do you guess the meaning, or do you skip the word and hope it's not important? Usually readers use many different strategies. Understanding words from context is a very useful strategy.*
2. **Reading selection vocabulary** You may want to introduce the glossed words in the reading selection before students begin reading. Key words: *valley, slopes, thumping, thud.* Instruct students to write the words with correct spelling and their definitions in their Personal Dictionaries. Have them pronounce each word and divide it into syllables.
3. **Multi-level options** See MULTI-LEVEL OPTIONS on p. 352.

Answers
1. a 2. b 3. b 4. a

 **ASSESS**

Have students work in pairs to write sentences with each of the four vocabulary words.

Text Structure

Fiction

Discuss types of fiction Ask students to think of other fiction they have read in this book. ("Gonzalo," p.122 and "The Fun They Had," p. 302) *Ask: Which one was science fiction?* ("The Fun They Had")

Reading Strategy

Make Inferences

1. **Analyze inferences** After reading the text and the chart, point out that sometimes you can make more than one inference about the information you read. *Say: Different inferences are based on experiences and opinions. Also, inferences about characters can change from the beginning of a story if new information is discovered. This is what makes reading fiction interesting—it is open to your interpretation.*
2. **Multi-level options** See MULTI-LEVEL OPTIONS below.

ASSESS

Have students write a sentence that states the difference between fiction and nonfiction.

Text Structure

Fiction

"Esperanza Rising" is from a novel, a story that fills a book. A novel is **fiction.** The author makes up the story. In this selection, you will find the features of fiction listed in the chart.

As you read the selection, look for the main character's traits and motivation. Also look for how the character changes.

Fiction	
Characters	the people in a story
Plot	the things that happen in a story
Character Traits	a character's qualities, such as friendly or honest
Character Motivation	the reason a character does something
Character Changes	changes in a character as the events take place

Student CD-ROM

Reading Strategy

Make Inferences

To understand characters in a story, you should **make inferences** about them. When you make an inference, you use the information in the text and your knowledge and experience to make a guess. Look at this example:

Tim yawned and closed his eyes.

Inference: Tim is tired.

1. Read the sentences in the chart. Do you agree with all these inferences?
2. As you read the selection, make inferences about the characters. Write your inferences in your Reading Log.

Text	Possible Inferences
Rita went to the window and looked outside. She gazed at her friends who were skateboarding. Sadly, she returned to her desk and opened her book.	**a.** Rita had to study. **b.** Rita doesn't like to study. **c.** Rita would like to be with her friends. **d.** Rita likes skateboarding.

Reading Log   Student CD-ROM

354 Unit 6 Connections

MULTI-LEVEL OPTIONS *Reading Strategy*

Newcomer Place items in several paper bags. In each bag, place pictures of tools or materials that a certain kind of worker in the school might use. For example, one bag might have a wooden spoon, a measuring cup, and a recipe. Have a volunteer open the bag and show the items. *Ask: Who does this bag belong to?* (cafeteria worker)

Beginning Place items in several paper bags. In each bag, place pictures of tools or materials that a certain kind of worker might use. For example, one bag might have a wooden spoon, a measuring cup, and a recipe. Have students work in pairs and make as many inferences as they can about the person who uses the items.

Intermediate *Say: Read the first paragraph on p. 356. What can you infer about the girl and her father?* (*Example:* They are good friends.) Have students defend their answers with a story detail and an idea from personal experience. (*Example:* They are spending time together. Good friends enjoy spending time together.)

Advanced *Say: Reread the paragraph on the chart. Write a paragraph to tell what Rita does next.* After students have completed their paragraphs, have them meet with partners and read each other's work. Tell students to make inferences about Rita based on the paragraph their partner has written.

ESPERANZA RISING

an excerpt from a novel
by Pam Muñoz Ryan

Reading Selection Materials

Audio: *Unit 6, Chapter 1; CD 2, Track 11*
Teacher Resource Book: *Reading Summary,*
    pp. 111–112
Transparencies: *#14, Reading Summary*

Suggestions for Using
Reading Summary

- Introduce new vocabulary or cognates.
- Cut the summary into strips, or jumble the sentences on an overhead transparency. Students put the sentences in order.
- Practice the reading strategy.
- Students read aloud or with a partner.
- Students paraphrase the summary.
- Students do a cloze activity.
- Students create a visual or graphic organizer, such as a timeline or storyboard, to illustrate the summary.
- Students paraphrase the summary.

Preview the Selection

1. **Interpret the image** Have students look at the photograph. *Ask: What feeling do you get from this art? What feeling do you get from the colors? Can you point to the house and the rows? What kind of climate do you think this is?*
2. **Connect to theme** *Say: The theme of this unit is connections. What kind of connection do you think this story may be about? Could it be a connection to Earth? Why do you think so?*

Community Connection

Work with the class to create a Venn diagram. Have them compare and contrast the scene above with the community in which their school is located. *Ask: What kind of work do you think people do here? How do you think they feel about the land? How is this similar to or different from what people do and think in our community?*

Teacher Resource Book: *Venn Diagram, p. 35*

Learning Styles
Linguistic

Ask students to look carefully at the picture on p. 355. *Say: Imagine that you are in this setting.* Have students create webs with a branch for each sense: sight, smell, sound, texture, and taste. Tell them to write descriptive words or phrases to portray what they would experience.

Read the Selection

1. **Listen for the main idea** Play the audio. Have students close their books and listen to the story. *Ask: What does the father want Esperanza to learn?* (to love the land)

2. **Shared reading** Read the text aloud. Have students join in when they can.

3. **Discuss images** Reread paragraph 2 aloud. *Say: The author writes that the valley breathes. This gives us the image that the valley is alive. What else in this paragraph adds to that image?* ("It gives us grapes . . . they welcome us . . . as if it had been waiting to shake his hand . . . you can feel it breathe . . . feel its heart beating.")

Sample Answer to Guide Question
He touches the tendril gently; it is precious to him, so he feels protective and careful of the plant.

See Teacher Edition pp. 434–436 for a list of English-Spanish cognates in the reading selection.

Audio
CD 2. Tr. 11

Aguascalientes, Mexico
1924

1 "Our land is alive, Esperanza," said Papa, taking her small hand as they walked through the gentle **slopes** of the vineyard. Leafy green vines draped the **arbors** and the grapes were ready to drop. Esperanza was six years old and loved to walk with her papa through the winding rows, gazing up at him and watching his eyes dance with love for the land.

2 "This whole **valley** breathes and lives," he said, sweeping his arm toward the distant mountains that guarded them. "It gives us the grapes and then they welcome us." He gently touched a wild tendril that reached into the row, as if it had been waiting to shake his hand. He picked up a handful of earth and studied it. "Did you know that when you lie down on the land, you can feel it breathe? That you can feel its heart beating?"

3 "Papi, I want to feel it," she said.

4 "Come." They walked to the end of the row, where the **incline** of the land formed a grassy **swell.**

5 Papa lay down on his stomach and looked up at her, patting the ground next to him.

6 Esperanza smoothed her dress and knelt down. Then, like a caterpillar, she slowly inched flat next to him, their faces looking at each other. The warm sun pressed on one of Esperanza's cheeks and the warm earth on the other.

7 She giggled.

8 "Shh," he said. "You can only feel the earth's heartbeat when you are still and quiet."

> **Make Inferences About Characters**
>
> How does the way Papa touches the tendril tell you about his feelings?

slopes   areas at an angle, like a hill
arbors   shelters of vines; frameworks covered with vines
valley   a low area of land between hills and mountains
incline   a hill
swell   a rounded hill

356   Unit 6   Connections

MULTI-LEVEL OPTIONS *Read the Selection*

Newcomer Play the audio. *Ask: Are the girl and her father walking on their grape farm?* (yes) *Does the father love his farm?* (yes) *Is the father teaching his daughter to farm grapes?* (no) *Is he teaching her to love the land?* (yes)

Beginning Read the Reading Summary aloud. *Ask: Where are the girl and her father?* (vineyard) *What does the father feel for his land?* (love) *What did the father want the girl to hear?* (the earth's heartbeat) *How did the girl feel in the end?* (happy)

Intermediate Have students do a paired reading. *Ask: What does the father want to pass on to his child?* (his love of the land) *How does he try to do this?* (by getting her to see that the land is alive) *Does the girl understand? How do you know?* (Yes, that is why she smiles at the end.)

Advanced Have students read silently. *Ask: At first, what does the girl think of her father's idea that the earth has a heartbeat? Explain.* (She thinks it is silly. She giggles.) *Do you think Esperanza may want to farm when she grows up? Why or why not?* (yes, because she is learning to love the land, too)

9   She swallowed her laughter and after a moment said, "I can't hear it, Papi."

10   "*Aguántate tantito y la fruta caerá en tu mano,*" he said. "Wait a little while and the fruit will fall into your hand. You must be patient, Esperanza."

11   She waited and lay silent, watching her Papa's eyes.

12   And then she felt it. Softly at first. A gentle **thumping.** Then stronger. A **resounding thud,** thud, thud against her body.

13   She could hear it, too. The beat rushing in her ears. *Shoomp, shoomp, shoomp.*

14   She stared at Papa, not wanting to say a word. Not wanting to lose the sound. Not wanting to forget the feel of the heart of the valley.

15   She pressed closer to the ground, until her body was breathing with the earth's. And with Papa's. The three hearts beating together.

16   She smiled at Papa, not needing to talk, her eyes saying everything.

17   And his smile answered hers. Telling her that he knew she had felt it.

> **Make Inferences About Characters**
>
> Was Esperanza patient? What tells you this?

---

thumping   a heavy sound
resounding   loud or booming

thud   the sound that a falling heavy object makes when it hits the ground

About the Author

Pam Muñoz Ryan (born 1951)

Pam Muñoz Ryan's grandparents moved from Mexico to the United States in the 1930s. Her grandmother told stories about her life. Pam Muñoz Ryan uses parts of her grandmother's stories in "Esperanza Rising."

➤ Why do you think Pam Muñoz Ryan uses her grandmother's stories in "Esperanza Rising"? What strategies do you think she uses to write?

Chapter 1   Esperanza Rising   **357**

---

th Spelling

Silent *u*

Have students find the word *guarded* in paragraph 2. Pronounce the word and write it on the board. *Ask: What letter is silent?* (u) Cross out the *u*. *Say: The letter* u *usually makes a sound, but sometimes it is silent. Here are some other words with silent* u. Write on the board: *guess, build, guest, guide, guitar.* Ask volunteers to cross out the silent *u.*

Evaluate Your Reading Strategy

Make Inferences *Say: You have practiced an important reading strategy. Now you can decide how well you have done. Does this statement describe how you read?*

> I make inferences when I read. Making inferences helps me understand the characters.

Read the Selection

1. **Paired reading** Have students read aloud with a partner.
2. **Dramatize the text** Ask volunteers to read the parts of Papa, Esperanza, and a narrator.
3. **Multi-level options** See MULTI-LEVEL OPTIONS on p. 356.

Sample Answer to Guide Question
In the end, she was patient; she "waited and lay silent" and felt the thumping.

About the Author

Relate to personal experience *Ask: Do you remember many stories that your grandparents or relatives have told you? Have you ever thought of writing them down? What would be an advantage to writing them down? Who might read these stories?*

Answers
Sample answers: She uses her grandmother's stories because they are an important part of her family and culture. The author uses words to help readers see, hear, smell, and feel things in the story as if they were really there.

Across Selection

Have students turn to the story "Gonzalo" on page 121. *Ask: How are these stories alike?* (They both relate to people's connection to Earth and younger people's connections to older relatives.)

Spelling, Punctuation, Capitalization

After the Reading Comprehension section, students will practice spelling, punctuation, and capitalization in the Activity Book.

Beyond the Reading

Reading Comprehension

Question-Answer Relationships

Sample Answers

1. grapes
2. She hears a thumping.
3. He says that when you are patient, things come to you; if she is patient, she will hear the sound.
4. She's laughing, so she doesn't hear anything. She stops laughing and listens quietly so she can hear the sound.
5. She feels happy to be with her father; she "loved to walk with her papa."
6. She becomes quiet and still and can hear the earth.
7. I think she feels hope because she can see the grapes that will grow and knows that the earth is full of life.
8. My aunt teaches all the cousins to drive because she is so calm and patient. Learning to be quiet and patient is something Esperanza's father teaches her.
9. I think it's both. The way she writes is very interesting, so she does entertain the reader, but she also tries to persuade the reader to be patient by showing that it is an important characteristic.

Build Reading Fluency

Read Silently and Aloud

Assessment Program: *Reading Fluency Chart, p. 116*

When students have completed the reading fluency activity, record their progress in the Reading Fluency Chart.

Reading Comprehension

Question-Answer Relationships (QAR)

"Right There" Questions

1. **Recall Facts** What does Esperanza's father grow on his land?
2. **Recall Facts** What does Esperanza hear when she lies down?

"Think and Search" Questions

3. **Explain** Why does Papa tell Esperanza to be patient?
4. **Resolve Problems** In paragraph 9, what problem does Esperanza have? How does she resolve it?

"Author and You" Questions

5. **Make Inferences About Characters** How does Esperanza feel at the beginning of the selection? How do you know this?

6. **Analyze Character Changes** How does Esperanza change at the end of the selection? How do you know this?

"On Your Own" Questions

7. **Analyze Character Traits** *Esperanza* means "hope" in Spanish. Do you think Esperanza has hope? Why?
8. **Compare Your Experiences** What family stories do you have? Make connections between one of your stories and "Esperanza Rising" by comparing the two.
9. **Draw Conclusions** What is the purpose of this story—to entertain you or to persuade you to do something? How do you know?

Activity Book   Student
p. 186   CD-ROM

Build Reading Fluency

Read Silently and Aloud

Reading silently for practice then reading aloud helps you read with expression and understanding.

1. Listen to the audio recording for "Esperanza Rising" on page 356.
2. Follow along with the reading.

3. Read silently paragraphs 1 and 2 two times.
4. With a partner read aloud both paragraphs.
5. Your partner will time your last reading.
6. Record your timing.

MULTI-LEVEL OPTIONS *Elements of Literature*

Newcomer Work together to list Esperanza's traits. Create a character-trait web. At the end of each branch, draw a symbol or simple drawing to show one of the character's traits. Have students point to aspects of the pictures or act out parts of the story related to that trait. Repeat the process for her papa's traits.

Beginning Have pairs of students create character-trait webs for the girl and her father. Have them write a trait at the end of each branch. (*Example:* loves the land) Have them write a phrase on the branch to show evidence from the story of that trait. (listens for heartbeat)

Intermediate Have students explain why they would or would not like to have Esperanza as a friend. Ask them to point out examples in the story of traits they like or dislike.

Advanced Have students identify a character from another selection that reminds them of Esperanza. Have them explain why they see the two characters as related. (*Example:* The son in "My Father Is a Simple Man" learned important things about life from his father as Esperanza did from hers.)

Listen, Speak, Interact

Distinguish Between Facts and Opinions

A **fact** is a statement that can be proved. An **opinion** is what someone thinks or believes.

1. Reread or listen to "Esperanza Rising."
2. Write down two facts found in the story. Also write down two of your opinions about the story.

For example:

Esperanza is six years old. (fact)

Esperanza is a good daughter. (opinion)

3. Read one of your facts or opinions to a partner. Your partner will tell you if it is a fact or an opinion.

Elements of Literature

Analyze Characters

Authors help you understand characters by describing how they behave.

"Our land is alive, Esperanza," said Papa, taking her small hand . . .

From Papa's actions, you can make an inference that he is a loving father. This is one of his traits.

Reread or listen to the story and **analyze the characters.** Copy and fill in the chart.

Activity Book p. 187   Student CD-ROM

	Esperanza	Papa
Traits What do they look like? How do they behave?		
Motivation Why do they do certain things?		*wants to teach Esperanza*
Conflict What problems do they have?		
Point of view What are their opinions? What do they like or not like?		
Relationships How do they feel about each other?	*admires her father*	
Changes How do they change?		

Chapter 1 Esperanza Rising **359**

Listen, Speak, Interact

Distinguish Between Facts and Opinions

1. **State facts and opinions** Before students do the activity, have them state facts and opinions about the classroom. Discuss how an opinion could be changed to a fact. For example, *This is a very small classroom* becomes *This classroom is the smallest in the school.*
2. **Newcomers** Work with these students in a small group to help them find facts and opinions in the reading.

Answers

Facts from the story: She was born in 1918. The story takes place in Aguascalientes. Her father grows grapes; he speaks Spanish. *Opinions from the story:* Esperanza is impatient. Her father is a good farmer. The vineyard is a beautiful place. Esperanza laughs a lot.

Elements of Literature

Analyze Characters

1. **Review descriptive adjectives** Before doing the activity, have students brainstorm adjectives to describe the characters.
2. **Multi-level options** See MULTI-LEVEL OPTIONS on p. 358.

Answers

Chart top to bottom: Esperanza–young, happy; motivated to be with her father; she's not quiet; she likes to be with her father; admires her father; she becomes quiet so she can hear the earth. Papa–thoughtful, kind; wants to teach Esperanza; sometimes it's hard to teach a child; loves his arbor and the earth; loves his daughter; becomes closer to his daughter.

ASSESS

Have students write two facts and two opinions about their school.

Home Connection

Ask each student to identify a family member or friend whom he/she admires. Ask students to fill out character charts for these people. Then have each student draw or write a paragraph summarizing the information on his/her chart. Suggest that students share the finished products with the people they have described.

Learning Styles
Natural

Remind students that Esperanza and her father enjoy observing nature together. Take students outdoors. Ask them to sit and observe an aspect of nature, such as clouds. Ask students to write facts about what they observe. (*Example:* white, moving east) Then have them write opinions. (*Example:* Clouds are beautiful.) As an alternative, students may look at pictures of aspects of nature.

Word Study

Distinguish Denotative and Connotative Meanings

Choose the right word Explain that it is important to choose words with the right connotation for an audience or purpose. Write on the board: *The child is skinny and bright.* Ask students to discuss the connotation of *skinny* and find a word with a more appropriate connotation. (slender, slim)

Answers
a. hang from with beauty (C), hang from (D)
b. a young, tender green stem (C), a green stem (D)

Grammar Focus

Identify Possessive Adjectives

Review homophones On the board, write: *its, it's.* Ask students to explain the difference and give sentences with each. Point out that there is no apostrophe in the possessive adjective. Repeat for *your/you're* and *their/they're/there.*

Answers
Paragraph 1: our land, her small hand, her papa, his eyes; Paragraph 2: his arm, his hand, its heart; Paragraph 5: his stomach; Paragraph 10: your hand; Paragraph 17: his smile.

ASSESS

Have students write two sentences using *its* and *our.*

Word Study

Distinguish Denotative and Connotative Meanings

All words have **denotative** meanings—the meaning that you find in the dictionary. Some words also have **connotative** meanings—attitudes or feelings connected to the word. For example:

"Esperanza . . . loved to walk with her papa, . . . gazing up at him . . ."

Gazing means *looking for a long time.* *Gazing* has the connotative meaning that you like or admire what you are looking at.

1. Copy the chart. Read the words and the meanings. Write *D* if the meaning is *denotative.* Write *C* if it is *connotative.*

Word	Meanings
a. drape	_____ hang from with beauty
	_____ hang from
b. tendril	_____ a young, tender green stem
	_____ a green stem

2. With a partner, choose one of the words and write a sentence using the connotative meaning.

The Heinle Newbury House Dictionary   Activity Book p. 188   Student CD-ROM

Grammar Focus

Identify Possessive Adjectives

A **possessive adjective** shows who or what owns something.

Jimmy brought <u>his</u> dog.

The possessive adjective *his* shows who owns the dog.

1. Find three examples of possessive adjectives in paragraphs 1, 2, 5, 10, and 17 of the story.

2. Write two sentences with possessive adjectives. Be sure to spell *its* correctly. Do not use the apostrophe (') as in *it's (it is).*

Possessive Adjectives	
I	**my**
you	**your**
he	**his**
she	**her**
it	**its**
we	**our**
they	**their**

Activity Book pp. 189–190   Student Handbook   Student CD-ROM

MULTI-LEVEL OPTIONS *From Reading to Writing*

Newcomer Ask each student to draw a character at the top of a piece of art paper. Tell students to use physical traits and actions to show the kind of person the character is at first. At the bottom, have students draw how their characters changed. In the middle, ask them to show events that caused the changes.

Beginning Have students draw a picture story. Ask them to begin by drawing a main character with words and phrases to describe him/her. Have students write captions to show how events changed the character. Ask them to use words and phrases to describe the character after the events.

Intermediate Point out that an important event, such as moving to a new country, can change a person. Give students the option of basing a story on how a child changed as a result of moving to the United States from another country.

Advanced Point out that fiction written about a particular time in history, historical fiction, often tells how an important event in the past changed a real or imaginary person. Suggest that students select a historical event to build into their stories.

From Reading to Writing

Write a Fiction Story

Write a story about how a character changes as events happen.

1. Make up a character. Use note cards to write down what they are like.
2. Decide on a character and a setting (the time and place) for your story.
3. Organize your story into three paragraphs. Remember to indent.
4. Use past tense verbs to show events that already happened.

Activity Book
p. 191

Student Handbook

Title _____

○ **Beginning**
The setting and the character's traits

○ **Middle**
Events

○ **End**
How the character changes

Across Content Areas

Learn About Land Forms

Earth is made up of different **land forms.** The words below are some types of land forms.

mountain _very high formation of land and rock_

plateau _a high area of flat land that has a drop on at least one side_

valley _a low area of land between high areas of land_

plain _a wide area of flat land_

The diagram here shows the shapes of different types of land forms. Copy the diagram and write the types of land in the

correct places. Match the land form word with the correct type of land.

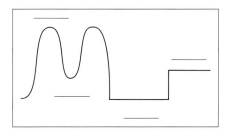

Activity Book
p. 192

Chapter 1 Esperanza Rising **361**

From Reading to Writing

Write a Fiction Story

1. **Create a round robin character** To help students think creatively, start a description of a character and have each student add a detail about this character. For example: _This character is a 15-year-old boy._ Then discuss how this character could change in a story.

2. **Write collaboratively** Students may work in pairs or small groups to write their stories. When they are finished, they should proofread their stories and display them in the room, with illustrations if possible.

3. **Multi-level options** See MULTI-LEVEL OPTIONS on p. 360.

Across Content Areas: Social Studies

Learn About Land Forms

Identify local land forms _Ask: What land forms are in our area? What other interesting land forms have you seen?_

Answers
From left to right: mountain, valley, plain, plateau

 **ASSESS**

Have students list features of a fiction story.

Reteach and Reassess

Text Structure Describe another event that might happen in the life of Esperanza, such as winning a contest for writing a short story about the farm. _Ask: How might this event change Esperanza?_ (_Example:_ She might decide to become a writer and set her stories on a farm.)

Reading Strategy Have students reread About the Author. Ask them what inferences they can make about Pam Muñoz Ryan based on what they read about her.

Elements of Literature Ask students to recall a character from a story they read in a previous unit of this book or a library book. Have them fill out a chart like the one on p. 359 to analyze the character.

Reassess Read a short biography of a person students have studied in Social Studies. Ask students what inferences they can make about the person.

CHAPTER 2

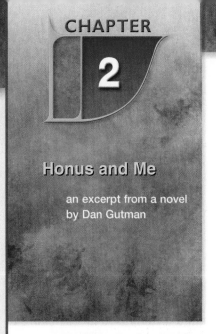

Honus and Me

an excerpt from a novel
by Dan Gutman

Into the Reading

Into the Reading

Objectives

Reading Identify the main idea and details as you read fiction.

Listening and Speaking Use persuasion.

Grammar Understand the past perfect tense.

Writing Write a paragraph.

Content Math: Use multiplication.

Chapter Materials

Activity Book: *pp. 193–200*
Audio: *Unit 6, Chapter 2; CD 2, Track 12*
Student Handbook
Student CD-ROM: *Unit 6, Chapter 2*
Teacher Resource Book: *Lesson Plan, Teacher Resources, Reading Summary, Activity Book Answer Key*
Teacher Resource CD-ROM
Assessment Program: *Quiz, pp. 91–92; Teacher and Student Resources, pp. 115–144*
Assessment CD-ROM
Transparencies
The Heinle Newbury House Dictionary/CD-ROM
Web site: http://visions.heinle.com

Objectives

Preview Have a student read the objectives. Ask volunteers to give examples of persuading someone.

Use Prior Knowledge

Discuss Objects That You Would Like to Collect

Compare preferences Take a class inventory of students' collections. *Ask: What is the most popular item to collect? What is the most unusual collection in the class? Do you have any friends or relatives with interesting collections? What do they collect?* If anyone has a card collection, have him/her describe it.

Use Prior Knowledge

Discuss Objects That You Would Like to Collect

Many people collect objects such as dolls or stamps as a hobby. They collect these objects because they like them. They usually keep these objects together as a group.

1. Work with three or four classmates.
2. Using one piece of paper and a pencil, write one kind of object that you collect or would like to collect.
3. Pass the paper and pencil to the next person. Each person will write what he or she collects or would like to collect.
4. After everyone has written an object, tell the group why you are interested in collecting your object.
5. Ask your group members questions about the objects that they are interested in.

362 Unit 6 Connections

MULTI-LEVEL OPTIONS *Build Vocabulary*

Newcomer Help students find pictures in magazines and books of people showing the emotions of the new vocabulary words. Point to each picture and say the word for the emotion it shows. Then have students act out or draw times when they feel each of the emotions.

Beginning Have students fold their papers into quarters. Ask them to copy one of the vocabulary words in each fourth. Have them draw pictures of people feeling each emotion. Tell students to show why the person is experiencing each emotion. Then help students use their understanding of each word to complete the sentences.

Intermediate Have students create a word wheel for each vocabulary word to develop their understanding further. Tell students to show a definition, synonym, related word, and their own sentence for each vocabulary word.

Advanced Point out that each sentence in Build Vocabulary tells about a feeling and the reason for it. Show students how to combine the short sentences in the exercise to form cause-effect sentences. For example, *Monica feels confused because she is not sure if she should stay or go.*

Build Background

Baseball Cards

Baseball cards are small cards with pictures of famous baseball players on them. The cards list facts about these baseball players. People began making baseball cards in the 1800s.

Most baseball cards do not cost a lot of money. Cards that are very old can be very valuable (cost a lot of money).

Content Connection
Honus Wagner was a baseball player in the early 1900s. One of his cards is probably the most valuable baseball card in the world.

LIONS

First Base

Arturo Ricardo

Build Vocabulary

Learn Words About Emotions

Emotions are feelings that people have. These words describe different emotions:

joyful very happy

confused not knowing what to do

guilty feeling that you have done something wrong or bad

confident feeling that you are very good at doing something

1. Copy the following sentences in your Personal Dictionary.
2. Complete each sentence with an emotion from the list.

a. Monica is not sure if she should stay or go. She is _____ .
b. Yuri feels bad. He was mean to his brother. He feels _____ .
c. Li is very happy because she won the game. She is _____ .
d. Antonio thinks that he will do very well on the test. He is _____ .

Personal Dictionary | The Heinle Newbury House Dictionary | Activity Book p. 193 | Student CD-ROM

Chapter 2 Honus and Me **363**

Content Connection
The Arts

Build Background *Say: Early baseball cards were* headshots, *such as the one on p. 365. Some of today's cards are* action shots *showing the player on the field. People who select the photos for cards must pick shots that are interesting and exciting.* Have small groups look through baseball books and magazines to find action shots of players. Ask each group to agree on a photo that they think would make a good baseball card and defend their choice.

Learning Styles
Musical

Build Vocabulary Point out that words are not the only way to tell about emotions. Music can also communicate feelings. Provide a collection of simple instruments, such as recorders, drums, tambourines, and harmonicas. Ask students to work in small groups to make musical sounds that they feel communicate each vocabulary word.

Build Background

Baseball Cards

1. **Use prior knowledge** Ask questions to find out what students know about collecting cards. Students may collect cards for other sports, such as football or basketball. *Ask: Where can you buy cards? How much do they usually cost? Why do you trade cards?*

2. **Content Connection** The first professional baseball team in the United States was the Cincinnati Red Stockings in 1869. In 1871, the National Association of Professional Baseball Players was organized, representing clubs in ten major cities.

Build Vocabulary

Learn Words About Emotions

Teacher Resource Book: *Personal Dictionary, p. 63*

1. **Brainstorm words about emotions** List adjectives students use in answering the following questions. *Ask: How are you feeling today? How do you feel when the last school bell rings? How do you feel during an oral presentation? How do you feel after taking a test?*

2. **Reading selection vocabulary** You may want to introduce the glossed words in the reading selection before students begin reading. Key words: *collector, discontinued, condition, worth, damage, fortune, deserved.* Instruct students to write the words with correct spelling and their definitions in their Personal Dictionaries. Have them pronounce each word and divide it into syllables.

3. **Multi-level options** See MULTI-LEVEL OPTIONS on p. 362.

Answers
a. confused b. guilty c. joyful d. confident

 **ASSESS**

Say: Write two sentences describing how you felt yesterday. You can say "I felt" or "I was."

Text Structure

Fiction

Identify conflict Have students turn to "Talking in a New Land" on p. 194. Give students a minute to review it. *Say: When there is a conflict, the characters need to solve a problem. What were the conflicts in this story and who were the conflicts between?* (Pai and Edite: she always had to translate for him. Pai and the lady: the lady wanted her dishes back.)

Reading Strategy

Identify the Main Idea and Details

1. **Identify details** Have students look at Build Background on p. 363. *Say: The main idea of this first paragraph is baseball cards. What are the details?* (small with pictures of players; list facts; started making them in 1800s; still made today)
2. **Multi-level options** See MULTI-LEVEL OPTIONS below.

ASSESS

Have students work in groups to describe a conflict. It can be a real conflict or something from a story or movie. They should tell who is involved and what the problem is.

Text Structure

Fiction

"Honus and Me" is **fiction.** It is an excerpt from a novel. Remember that a novel is a fictional story that fills a book. Look for the features of fiction listed in the chart as you read the selection.

Look for the conflict as you read or listen to "Honus and Me." Pay attention to the conflict and to point of view as you read. Who has the conflict? How would the story be different if told from the perspective of Joe's mother?

Student CD-ROM

Fiction	
Narrator	The narrator tells the story.
First-Person Point of View	When the narrator is a character in the story, the story is written in the first-person point of view. The narrator uses the pronouns *I, me, we,* and *us.*
Plot	The plot is made up of events in the story.
Conflict	The characters must solve a problem. The conflict can be between two characters or within one character.

Reading Strategy

Identify the Main Idea and Details

The **main idea** is the most important idea in a paragraph. It is often the first sentence. **Details** are facts or examples. They help you understand the main idea.

Maria likes to help people. She teaches children how to read. She also helps me with my homework. When I was sick, she cooked dinner for me.

Main Idea Maria likes to help people.

Details She teaches children how to read.
She helps me with my homework.
When I was sick, she cooked dinner for me.

Student CD-ROM

To Find the Main Idea	1. Read the whole paragraph.
	2. Ask, "What is this paragraph about?"
To Find Details	1. Think about the main idea.
	2. Find facts or examples that explain the main idea.

364 Unit 6 Connections

MULTI-LEVEL OPTIONS *Reading Strategy*

Newcomer Show students an action picture, such as one of a sporting event. Help them identify the main idea of the picture. (*Example:* The boy hit a home run.) Have them point out details in the illustration. (*Examples:* The crowd is cheering. His teammates look happy. The other team looks surprised.)

Beginning Have students look at an action picture. Ask them to use phrases to identify the main idea and several details.

Intermediate Read aloud a paragraph from a newspaper article about a local event or issue. Ask them to tell the main idea. Have them identify several supporting facts.

Advanced Have students read a short newspaper article about a local event or issue. Ask them to identify the main idea and support it with several details.

Honus and Me

WAGNER, PITTSBURG

an excerpt from a novel
by Dan Gutman

365

Reading Selection Materials

Audio: *Unit 6, Chapter 2; CD 2, Track 12*
Teacher Resource Book: *Reading Summary,*
    pp. 113–114
Transparencies: *#14, Reading Summary*

Suggestions for Using
Reading Summary

- Introduce new vocabulary or cognates.
- Cut the summary into strips, or jumble the sentences on an overhead transparency. Students put the sentences in order.
- Practice the reading strategy.
- Students read aloud or with a partner.
- Students paraphrase the summary.
- Students do a cloze activity.
- Students create a visual or graphic organizer, such as a timeline or storyboard, to illustrate the summary.
- Students paraphrase the summary.

Preview the Selection

1. **Interpret the image** Have students look at the photo. *Ask: What team does this person play with? When do you think this photo was taken? How is his uniform different from today's uniforms? Do you think Wagner is his first name or last name? What do you think his first name might be? Why?*
2. **Connect to theme** Remind students that the unit theme is *connections. Ask: How can you be connected to someone from long ago? What can you have in common with someone like this?* (similar interests, from same state or city, same likes and dislikes)

 Content Connection
Social Studies

Have small groups of students use nonfiction books and the Internet to find out about baseball in the 1900s when Honus Wagner was playing. Ask them to create a two-column chart to compare baseball then to modern baseball.

| Teacher Resource Book: *Two-Column Chart, p. 44*

Learning Styles
Visual

Ask: How much do you think you can tell about a person by looking at his or her face? Look at this picture of baseball player Honus Wagner. List describing words to tell what kind of person you think he is. Have students work in pairs to find biographies of Wagner on the Internet. Ask them to see whether the facts about the man support the traits they predicted by looking at his picture.

UNIT 6 • CHAPTER 2
Reading Selection

Read the Selection

1. **Discuss purpose of prologue** Read the prologue aloud. *Ask: What facts do we learn from the prologue?* (who the characters are, what Joe does for Miss Young, where he is at the beginning of the excerpt) *The prologue helps to set the scene for the story. The illustration also sets the scene. Where is Joe and what is he doing?* (He's in Miss Young's attic, cleaning it out.)

2. **Shared reading** Play the audio. Then have students join in when they can. Remind students to read with emotion because Joe is very excited about what he finds.

3. **Describe a character** Have students turn to the photo on p. 365 and describe Honus Wagner in their own words. Then have them describe Joe, using the illustration as a guide.

Sample Answer to Guide Question
These details help us understand what the man looks like: *young, brown hair parted in the middle, solemn expression, muddy gray shirt, navy blue collar.*

See Teacher Edition pp. 434–436 for a list of English-Spanish cognates in the reading selection.

Audio
CD 2, Tr. 12

Prologue

Joe Stoshack is the main character of "Honus and Me." Joe is in the seventh grade. He loves to collect baseball cards.

Joe lives with his mother. They do not have a lot of money. Joe sometimes works to get money. He gives some of the money to his mother. He uses the rest to buy baseball cards.

Miss Young is Joe's **elderly** neighbor. She has a job for Joe. She wants Joe to throw out everything in her **attic.**

Joe goes to Miss Young's house. He is cleaning out her attic. Suddenly, Joe sees a small piece of paper on the floor. He bends down and picks it up . . .

1   I turned over the card and looked at the other side. I **couldn't believe my eyes.**

2   It was a picture of a man's face. I **gasped. Instinctively,** I looked around to see if anybody was watching. Of course nobody was there.

3   The man in the picture was a young man, with short brown hair parted in the middle. He had a **solemn** expression on his face, with his head **swiveled** slightly so he

> **Identify the Main Idea and Details**
>
> The main idea of this paragraph is what the man in the picture looks like. What details help you understand the main idea?

---

elderly   old, aged

attic   a space under the roof of a house; people often put things that they do not use in an attic

couldn't believe my eyes   couldn't believe what I saw

gasped   breathed in quickly, usually because of surprise

instinctively   done from feeling, not from what you learned

solemn   serious

swiveled   turned

366   Unit 6   Connections

MULTI-LEVEL OPTIONS *Read the Selection*

Newcomer Play the audio. Then do a Quaker reading with students reading aloud their favorite parts of the text. *Ask: Is Joe a famous baseball player?* (no) *Is Joe a boy who likes baseball cards?* (yes) *Is Joe helping Miss Young?* (yes) *Does he find something important?* (yes)

Beginning Read the Reading Summary aloud. Have students do a paired reading. *Ask: Where is Joe?* (attic) *Who is he helping?* (Miss Young) *What does he find?* (baseball card)

Intermediate Have students read the selection silently. *Ask: How does Joe feel about his hobby? How do you know?* (It is important to him. He spends his extra money on it.) *How do you think Joe felt when he found the card? Explain.* (He was very excited because he knew it was valuable.)

Advanced Have students read silently. *Ask: What kind of boy do you think Joe is? Why?* (He is hard-working and helpful; he is earning money for his family and he is helping someone else.) *What do you predict Joe will do with the baseball card?* (Example: He will show it to Miss Young.)

was looking off to the left. His shirt collar was navy blue, and the shirt was muddy gray. It had four white buttons.

4   On the right side of his chest were the letters "PITTS" and on the left were the letters "BURG." There was no H.*

5   The **background** of the card was **burnt-orange.** There was a thin white border on all four sides. Across the bottom border, centered in the middle, were these magic words . . .

WAGNER, PITTSBURG

6   My breath came in short **bursts.** I suddenly felt warm. My heart was **racing.** My *brain* was racing. The **tingling sensation** was all over me, and stronger than I had ever experienced it.

7   No doubt about it. I had just **stumbled upon** a T-206 Honus Wagner card—*the most valuable baseball card in the world.*

> **Identify the Main Idea and Details**
>
> The main idea of this paragraph is that Joe is very excited. What details show that Joe is very excited?

* From 1890–1911, the city of Pittsburgh, Pennsylvania, was spelled "Pittsburg."

---

background   something behind something else

burnt-orange   an orange color that has a little red in it

bursts   things that happen suddenly and with force

racing   going very quickly

tingling sensation   a feeling that you get when you are excited, as if sharp things are touching your skin

stumbled upon   found by accident

Chapter 2 Honus and Me   **367**

Read the Selection

1. **Reciprocal reading** Write on the board: *Who, What, Where, When, How, Why.* Have volunteers read aloud and ask the class information questions.

2. **Speculate** *Say: Joe has just found something very valuable. What do you think he is imagining or thinking about? Do you think he is thinking about how he would spend the money? What's the first thing you would think about if you found something like this?*

3. **Locate derivations using dictionaries** Have students look at these glossed words and determine what words they are derived from: *bursts, racing, tingling, stumbled.* Have students check the derivations in a print, online, or CD-ROM dictionary.

4. **Multi-level options** See MULTI-LEVEL OPTIONS on p. 366.

Sample Answer to Guide Question
Details: *short bursts, felt warm, heart was racing, tingling sensation*

---

th Spelling

Voiced vs. unvoiced *th*

Write on the board: *think* and *them. Say: Repeat the words after me. Notice that your tongue touches your front teeth.* Then have students hold their fingers on their throats and repeat the words. *Say: Notice that you can feel your throat move when you say* them. *Can you feel it move when you say* think? (no) *Both words are spelled with* th, *but* th *makes a slightly different sound in each.*

Apply *Say: I am going to say some words with* th. *Repeat them after me. Raise your hand when you feel your throat move: there, thin, then, teeth, that, those.* (raise hands for *there, then, that, those*)

Read the Selection

1. **Choral reading** Divide the class into two groups, and have each group read alternate paragraphs with you. Do it twice so that each group reads all paragraphs.

2. **Summarize** Have the class summarize the story so far and write the summary on the board. For example, *Joe finds a rare old baseball card of Honus Wagner while cleaning out his neighbor's attic.*

3. **Relate to personal experience** *Ask: Have you ever found something really old in your house? What was it? Who did it belong to? How old was it? What is the oldest thing you have in your house?*

Sample Answer to Guide Question

Wagner didn't want to be on a baseball card because he was against smoking.

8   Every serious **collector** knows the **legend** behind the Wagner card. These early baseball cards were printed by tobacco companies and were included with their products. All the players agreed to be on the cards except for Honus Wagner, the **star shortstop** of the **Pittsburgh Pirates.**

9   Wagner was against cigarette smoking, and he didn't want his name or picture used to sell tobacco. He forced the American Tobacco Company to **withdraw** his card—but they had already started printing them. A small number of the cards reached the **public** before the card was **discontinued.**

> **Identify the Main Idea and Details**
>
> What is the main idea of this paragraph?

---

collector   a person who collects something, such as baseball cards

legend   a story about a person; the story may include real events and made-up events

star   very famous

shortstop   a position in baseball
Pittsburgh Pirates   a baseball team
withdraw   take back
public   the people in a country or an area
discontinued   stopped being made

368   **Unit 6**   Connections

MULTI-LEVEL OPTIONS *Read the Selection*

Newcomer *Ask: Was Honus Wagner against smoking?* (yes) *Did he let tobacco companies give out his card?* (no) *Were there lots of his cards?* (no) *Does Joe think he will get lots of money for the card?* (yes)

Beginning *Ask: Who gave out early baseball cards?* (tobacco companies) *Who stopped the tobacco company from giving out his card?* (Honus Wagner) *How many Honus Wagner cards are still around?* (about 40) *What can Joe do with the card?* (sell it)

Intermediate *Ask: How did Honus Wagner cards get so scarce?* (Only a small number of his were given out before Honus Wagner made the tobacco companies stop.) *How does Joe think the card will solve all his problems?* (He could sell it to get lots of money to help his family.)

Advanced *Ask: Why would tobacco companies give out baseball cards with their tobacco?* (to get more people to buy their brand) *What does Honus Wagner's action concerning his card show about him?* (He had strong beliefs, and he was willing to do something to show people how he felt.)

10   That's why the Honus Wagner card is so valuable. Only about forty of them are known to **exist** in the whole world, most of them in bad **condition.**

11   I just found No. 41, and it was *mint.* Nobody had *touched* it in over eighty years.

12   I knew the piece of **cardboard** in my hand was **worth** thousands of dollars, but I didn't know exactly how *many* thousands. I remembered that a few years ago some famous athlete had bought one at an **auction,** but I couldn't **recall** who he was or how much he paid for it. It was a **huge** amount of money, that was for sure.

13   All my problems, I suddenly realized, were solved. Or so I thought.

> **Identify the Main Idea and Details**
>
> What is the main idea of this paragraph?

exist   be

condition   how something is; for example, how something looks

mint   in new or excellent condition

cardboard   flat, stiff, thick paper

worth   how much money someone will pay for something

auction   a sale where items are sold to the person who offers to pay the most money

recall   remember

huge   very large

Chapter 2 Honus and Me   **369**

Read the Selection

1. **Paired reading** Play the audio. Then have students practice reading aloud in pairs. Ask volunteers to read parts of the story. Direct them to read with emotion to reflect how Joe was feeling.

2. **Multi-level options** See MULTI-LEVEL OPTIONS on p. 368.

Sample Answer to Guide Question
Joe knows that the card is worth a lot of money.

 Spelling

Abbreviation

Direct students to paragraph 11. *Ask: What does* No. *mean in the first sentence?* (number) *What is a clue that* n-o *means something different here?* (the period after it and capital *n*) *Yes, in this sentence,* n-o-period *is an abbreviation, a short way of writing* number.

    Apply Have students brainstorm other times when *No.* might be used to stand for number. List their responses on the board. (*Examples:* No. 15 bus, Player No. 26, question No. 2)

Read the Selection

1. **Predict character actions** Have students close their books. *Ask: What do you think Joe will do when he leaves Miss Young's? Do you think he will tell Miss Young what he found?*

2. **Silent reading** Play the audio. Then have students read silently.

Sample Answer to Guide Question
He was very careful not to bend it or damage it because this might decrease its value.

Identify the Main Idea and Details

What details show that Joe thinks the baseball card is very important?

14   I **slipped** the card in my backpack, being careful not to bend any of the corners or **damage** it in any way. A tiny **nick** in a card this rare might **decrease** its value by thousands of dollars.

15   Quickly, I gathered up the rest of the **junk** in the attic and **hauled** it out to the **curb.**

16   I had almost forgotten about Miss Young, but she called me over just as I was about to run home.

17   "Aren't you forgetting something, Joseph?"

18   She held out a five-dollar bill and shakily placed it in my **palm.** She grabbed my other hand and looked me in the eye.

19   "Thank you for helping out an old lady," she said seriously. "And because you did such a fine job, I want you to have *ten* dollars. I bet that's a lot of money to a boy your age."

---

slipped put in quickly and carefully	**junk** things that are no longer useful to someone
damage hurt, ruin	**hauled** carried
nick a small cut or mark	**curb** the edge of a sidewalk
decrease lessen	**palm** the inside part of the hand

370   Unit 6 Connections

MULTI-LEVEL OPTIONS *Read the Selection*

Newcomer *Ask: Does Joe take the card with him?* (yes) *Does he tell Miss Young about it?* (no) *Does he plan to keep the card?* (yes) *Does he think the card will help him?* (yes)

Beginning *Ask: Where does Joe put the card?* (in his backpack) *How much does Miss Young pay Joe for his work?* (ten dollars) *How does Joe feel?* (happy) *Who did Joe tell about the card?* (no one)

Intermediate *Ask: What are clues that Joe plans to sell the card?* (He puts it in his backpack without saying anything. He feels happy and fortunate.) *Are Miss Young and Joe talking about the same thing in paragraphs 22–23? Explain.* (No, she is talking about spending $10. He is talking about spending money from selling the card.)

Advanced *Ask: Why has Joe almost forgotten about getting paid?* (All of his thoughts are on the card and how much he will get for it.) *Reread paragraph 25. What does it tell you about Joe's beliefs about money?* (He believes it can solve all his problems and that it will give him power.)

20   Ten **bucks?** In my head I was thinking that I had a **fortune** in my backpack.

21   "Yeah, I could use ten dollars," I **sputtered.** "Thanks Miss Young."

22   "Buy something nice for yourself," she called out as I **dashed** away. "Money won't do *me* any good."

23   "I will," I called out as I left. "Believe me, I *will*."

24   Mom wouldn't be home from work for an hour or so. I grabbed my bike, hopped on, and started **pedaling** east on Chestnut Street past Sheppard Park and Founders Square.

25   As I **cruised** down the streets I was filled with an **overwhelming** feeling of joy. Happiness washed over my body. Nobody could touch me. Nobody could hurt me. Nobody could tell me what to do. It was a feeling I had never experienced before.

> **Identify the Main Idea and Details**
>
> What is the main idea of this paragraph?

Read the Selection

1. **Identify descriptive verbs** *Say: One way that an author makes a story very interesting or exciting to read is by using descriptive verbs. Look at paragraph 21. It says he "sputtered." What other word could the author have used? (said) Why is "sputtered" a more descriptive or interesting verb?* (It has the connotation of being nervous or surprised.) Have students read paragraphs 22–25 and identify other descriptive verbs. *(dashed, grabbed, hopped, cruised, washed)*

2. **Paired reading** Play the audio. Then have students reread aloud in pairs.

3. **Locate derivations using dictionaries** Have students look at these glossed words and determine what words they are derived from: *slipped, cruised, overwhelming.* Have students check the derivations in a print, online, or CD-ROM dictionary.

4. **Multi-level options** See MULTI-LEVEL OPTIONS on p. 370.

Sample Answer to Guide Question
Joe was filled with joy and happiness.

---

bucks   informal word for "dollars"
fortune   a very large amount of money
sputtered   spoke in an unclear way
dashed   left quickly

pedaling   moving the pedals of a bicycle with your feet
cruised   moving on a vehicle at a fast but comfortable speed
overwhelming   great; feeling an emotion very strongly

Chapter 2 Honus and Me   **371**

 A **Capitalization**

Names of public places

Say: Find Sheppard Park *and* Founders Square *in paragraph 24. These are the names of public places in Joe's town. What do you notice about the names of these places? Yes, both words in the names start with capital letters. We always start the names of public places with capital letters.*

Apply Have students work in small groups to draw simple maps of a location in their community where public places are found. Tell them to label these places and be sure to begin the names with capital letters.

Read the Selection

1. **Reciprocal reading** Play the audio. Then have volunteers read sections of the story and ask the class questions about it.

2. **Identify conflict** Remind students that a conflict can be between people or an internal conflict within a person. *Ask: Who is the conflict with?* (Joe has a conflict within himself.) *How would you summarize his conflict?* (Joe can't decide whether to give the card to Miss Young or to keep it because he found it.)

3. **Contrast pros and cons** Write on the board: *Pro – He should return the card. Con – He should keep the card.* Explain that *pro* means "in favor of" and *con* means "against something." Discuss and list the pros and cons for what Joe should do. Remind students that there is not always a right and wrong answer. Discuss when and if it is acceptable to withhold information.

Sample Answer to Guide Question
Joe felt badly when he realized it was not his card to take.

26   I didn't know if I should tell the whole world about my good **fortune,** or if maybe I shouldn't tell *anybody* in the world.

27   As I **whizzed** down the street, I felt like everyone was looking at me. I felt like everyone must somehow know what had happened to me. They knew what I had in my backpack. It was as if the news had instantly been picked up on **CNN** and **broadcast** around the **globe.**

> **Identify the Main Idea and Details**
>
> What is the main idea of this paragraph?

28   Those feelings lasted about a minute, when a different feeling came over me. A bad feeling. The baseball card wasn't mine to take, really. It was Miss Young's card. If anybody **deserved** to get rich from it, it was *her.* She had been nice enough to pay me *double* for cleaning out her attic, and I had **stolen** her fortune.

---

fortune luck	**globe** world
whizzed moved very quickly	**deserved** should; had a right to; was worthy of
CNN a news company	**double** two times as much
broadcast shown on television or played on the radio	**stolen** taken without permission or payment

372   Unit 6 Connections

MULTI-LEVEL OPTIONS *Read the Selection*

Newcomer *Ask: Is Joe very happy?* (yes) *Does he stay happy?* (no) *Does he start to feel bad about taking the card?* (yes) *Does he know the right thing to do?* (yes)

Beginning *Ask: How does Joe feel riding down the street?* (happy) *Then how does he start to feel?* (guilty) *How does he feel in the end?* (mixed up)

Intermediate *Ask: What makes Joe's feelings change?* (He starts to think about what he has done.) *How can you tell he is confused?* (He goes back and forth between thinking it is okay and not okay to keep the card.) *How does the story end?* (Joe still doesn't know what to do.)

Advanced *Ask: What hints can you find in the story about what Joe might do to solve his problem?* (In the story, Joe is a helpful and caring person. These are hints that he will tell the truth to his mother or Miss Young.) *Why do you think the author wrote this story?* (to tell a fun story that gets readers to think about a serious situation)

29 Almost as quickly, my brain came up with reasons I shouldn't feel badly. Miss Young herself said that money wouldn't do her any good, so why *shouldn't* I keep the card? After all, *she* told me to throw the stuff away. If I hadn't found the card, *she* wouldn't have found it. It would have ended up buried in a **landfill** someplace, worth nothing to anyone.

30 **Finder's keepers,** right?

31 And besides, I thought, Miss Young isn't going to live much longer.

32 I felt bad, again, thinking that last thought.

33 I was feeling very **mixed up.** Deep inside I knew the right thing would be to give Miss Young back her baseball card.

---

landfill   a place where garbage is buried and covered with dirt

finder's keepers   a saying; it means that the person who finds something gets to keep it

mixed up   confused, unsure of what to do

About the Author

Dan Gutman (born 1955)

Dan Gutman grew up in New Jersey. He became a writer when he was about 25 years old. He wrote for newspapers and movies. He even started a magazine for video games. Later, Gutman began writing about one of his favorite things—sports. Today, Gutman loves to write fiction for young people. He also visits schools to talk to students. He explains how reading and writing are fun.

➤ What advice do you think Dan Gutman would give Joe? Why do you think so?

Chapter 2   Honus and Me   **373**

 Spelling

Silent *h* after *w*

Ask: What consonant sound do you hear at the beginning of the word whizzed? *(/w/) Yes, that is the sound you hear. The word also has a silent consonant at the beginning. Look at paragraph 27 to find out what the silent letter is. (h) Find another word in that paragraph that starts with wh. (what)*

Apply   Have students find *wh* words in paragraph 28 *(when)* and 19 *(why)*.

Evaluate Your Reading Strategy

Identify the Main Idea and Details   *Say: You have practiced an important reading strategy. Now you can decide how well you have done. Does this statement describe how you read?*

> As I read a paragraph, I ask myself, "What is this paragraph about?" I also look for facts or examples that explain the main idea. Identifying the main idea and details helps me understand what I read.

Read the Selection

1. **Paired reading**   Have students read the selection aloud in pairs.
2. **Locate derivations using dictionaries**   Have students look at these glossed words and determine what words they are derived from: *whizzed, deserved, mixed.* Have students check the derivations in a print, online, or CD-ROM dictionary.
3. **Multi-level options**   See MULTI-LEVEL OPTIONS on p. 372.

Sample Answer to Guide Question
1. Miss Young said money wouldn't do her any good.
2. She was throwing the stuff away so she wouldn't have found it. 3. It would have ended up in a landfill.

About the Author

Analyze Details About the Author

Ask: What are three important details about the author? (Possible answers: He started writing at 25; he wrote for newspapers, movies, and a magazine; he writes about sports and fiction; he talks with students about reading and writing.) Some students may give *grew up in New Jersey* as an important detail. Talk about why this is not really an important detail.

Answer
Sample answer: I think Dan Gutman would tell Joe to give the card back to Miss Young because that is the only honest thing to do.

Across Selections

Say: In this story, Joe had an inner conflict. The main character in "Talking in the New Land" (p. 194) also had an inner conflict. Can you describe Edite's inner conflict? (Edite didn't want to translate for her father; she felt bad because she didn't want to help someone who she cared about.)

 **ASSESS**

Have students describe Joe's relationship with Miss Young.

Beyond the Reading

Reading Comprehension

Question-Answer Relationships

Sample Answers

1. Honus Wagner
2. Wagner, Pittsburg
3. It was on the floor in Miss Young's attic.
4. ten dollars
5. There were only a few cards printed and only 40 in existence.
6. Miss Young doesn't really need money for anything; she doesn't spend much and already has what she needs.
7. He was against cigarette smoking.
8. Joe is joyful and happy at first. When he realizes what he has done, he feels guilty.
9. It wasn't his to sell; she paid him double for his work; and he had stolen something that wasn't his to take.
10. I think Joe will resolve the conflict by doing what he knows is right. I think he will return the card to Miss Young.
11. I would return the card. Maybe I would ask for a reward.

Build Reading Fluency

Rapid Word Recognition

Rapid word recognition is an excellent activity for students who struggle with irregular spelling patterns. Time students for 1 minute as they read the words in the squares aloud.

Reading Comprehension

Question-Answer Relationships (QAR)

"Right There" Questions

1. **Recall Facts** Whose picture is on the baseball card that Joe finds?
2. **Recall Facts** What words are written at the bottom of that baseball card?
3. **Recall Facts** Where does Joe find the baseball card?
4. **Recall Facts** How much money does Miss Young give Joe?

"Think and Search" Questions

5. **Analyze Reasons** Why is the Honus Wagner card so valuable?
6. **Draw Conclusions** Why does Miss Young say, "Money won't do me any good"?
7. **Explain** Honus Wagner wanted the American Tobacco Company to stop making his baseball card. Why?

8. **Recognize Character Change** What is the first feeling that Joe has after he leaves Miss Young's house? How does his feeling change?

"Author and You" Questions

9. **Find Supporting Arguments** What are Joe's reasons for giving back the baseball card?
10. **Character Conflict** How do you think Joe will resolve his conflict? What will he do with the card?

"On Your Own" Question

11. **Support Your Opinion** What would you do with the baseball card? Why?

Activity Book
p. 194

Student
CD-ROM

Build Reading Fluency

Rapid Word Recognition

Rapidly recognizing words helps increase your reading rate. It is an important characteristic of effective readers.

1. With a partner, review the words in the box.
2. Read the words aloud for one minute. Your teacher will time you.
3. Count how many words you read in one minute.

believe	bursts	slightly	there	slightly
watching	there	bursts	slightly	there
there	breath	watching	believe	breath
slightly	slightly	there	watching	believe
breath	watching	believe	breath	bursts

MULTI-LEVEL OPTIONS *Elements of Literature*

Newcomer Show a few minutes of a video version of a story from your school library. Have students express the mood of this portion of the film through facial expression.

Beginning Remind students that timelines show important events that happened at certain times. *Say: We will make a mood line.* Draw a line on the board. Make simple sketches of main story events. Have volunteers draw faces under the events to show the mood the author created with each part.

Intermediate Have students create a mood line showing the main events of each part of the story and the moods the author created. Engage students in a discussion of what the author did to create each mood.

Advanced Have students recall how the author portrays Joe. (caring, helpful) *Ask: What if the author wanted to give the idea that Joe was dishonest and would probably keep the card? What might the author have done differently concerning the tone and mood of the story?*

Listen, Speak, Interact

Use Persuasion

People often use **persuasion** when they want other people to do or think something.

1. Copy and complete the paragraph.
2. Work with a partner. Suppose your partner is Joe. Persuade your partner to give back the baseball card. Use what you wrote in your paragraph.
3. As you speak, look at your partner. Use gestures to help make your point.

> Joe, you should _____
> _____. This is the right
> thing to do because _____
> _____.
> You should also do this because
> _____.
> If you do this, you will feel
> _____
> because _____.

Elements of Literature

Recognize Style, Tone, and Mood

Authors use **style, tone,** and **mood** to express themselves and help readers understand and enjoy their writing.

Read the following paragraphs aloud with a partner. Then answer the questions together.

1. Read paragraph 25. In this paragraph, the author uses short sentences. How does this style help show Joe's feeling?
2. Read paragraphs 8 and 9. What is the author's tone? Does he seem to approve or disapprove of Honus Wagner?
3. Read paragraphs 1 and 2. What mood does the author create at this point in the story? Fear? Suspense? Happiness?

Style	How the author uses language, for example: Long or short sentences Use of figurative language Informal or formal language
Tone	The author's attitude, for example: Positive attitude Negative attitude
Mood	The feeling the author wants you to get, for example: Suspense (wanting to know what happens next) Excitement Fear

Activity Book p. 195   Student CD-ROM

Chapter 2 **Honus and Me** **375**

Home Connection

Suggest that families often use sayings to remind children of the right thing to do. Have small groups meet to share their family sayings about honesty that might be useful in persuading Joe to do the right thing. (*Example:* Honesty is the best policy.)

Learning Styles
Kinesthetic

Point out that authors of books must use words to communicate their style, tone, and mood. Scriptwriters can also communicate these things through the facial expressions, gestures, and actions of actors. Have small groups use the Reader's Theater technique to act out the story. Have some students be the actors. Ask others to be the directors and tell the actors what to do to convey the mood and tone that they think Dan Gutman wanted to communicate.

Listen, Speak, Interact

Use Persuasion

1. **Review expressions of persuasion** *Say: You want to persuade me to not give any homework this week. What can you say to persuade me?* Write student responses on the board. Underline persuasive language such as *you should, if you, . . . you will, why don't you.*

2. **Analyze persuasive techniques** After students have listened to their partner's speech, have them analyze the persuasive techniques used. *Ask: What was the purpose of the speech?* (persuade) *What techniques did your partner use to persuade you?* Have them list the techniques. *Ask: What effect did the speech have on you? Did it persuade you to give back the baseball card? Why or why not?*

3. **Newcomers** Work with these students, helping them complete the paragraph. Then do the role-plays with them.

Elements of Literature

Recognize Style, Tone, and Mood

1. **Discuss point of view** Have students turn to the table of contents for Unit 5 (p. 286). For each selection, have students discuss whether it is first-person or third-person point of view. (first-person: "Eye to Eye"; third-person: "The Fun They Had," "Using the Scientific Method," "The Solar System")

2. **Multi-level options** See MULTI-LEVEL OPTIONS on p. 374.

Answers
1. Short sentences emphasize Joe's quick pace of thought and action and feeling of elation. 2. The tone is factual and strong; he approves of Wagner. 3. Words that convey a mood of suspense and surprise: *I couldn't believe my eyes; gasped; I looked around to see if anybody was watching.*

ASSESS

In small groups, have students reread paragraph 27. Have students identify the style, or how the author uses language. (repetition, figurative language)

Word Study

Use a Thesaurus or Synonym Finder

Teacher Resource Book: *Personal Dictionary, p. 63*

Find antonyms Have students find antonyms for these words from the reading: *elderly, nobody, solemn, excited, public, recall, huge, decrease, damage, guilty.*

Answers
1. a. joy **2. b.** important, worthwhile **3. c.** lessen

Grammar Focus

Understand the Past Perfect Tense

Teacher Resource Book: *Timelines, p. 39*

Use a timeline Draw a timeline on the board. From right to left, label it *today, yesterday afternoon, yesterday morning.* Above *yesterday morning,* write: *I had already taken a test. Say: I had already taken a test by yesterday afternoon.* Have students make up sentences about events that took place yesterday morning. Tell them to start their sentences with *By yesterday afternoon.*

Answers
1. had started **2.** had touched **3.** had been

ASSESS

Have students write two sentences about what they had already done by yesterday afternoon.

Word Study

Use a Thesaurus or Synonym Finder

A **thesaurus** and a **synonym finder** are books that list synonyms. **Synonyms** are words that have similar meanings. You can also use the Internet to locate synonyms. Do a search using the keyword *thesaurus* or *synonym.*

1. Read the following sentences. Look at the underlined words. Write one synonym for each underlined word. Use a thesaurus or synonym finder.
   a. <u>Happiness</u> washed over my body.
   b. I had found the most <u>valuable</u> baseball card in the world.
   c. A tiny nick might <u>decrease</u> its value by thousands of dollars.

2. In your Personal Dictionary, copy and complete a chart like the one here.

Word	Synonym
fast	quick
happiness	
valuable	
decrease	

Personal Dictionary   The Heinle Newbury House Dictionary   Activity Book *p. 196*   Student CD-ROM

Grammar Focus

Understand the Past Perfect Tense

When authors want to show that a past action took place before another action, they use the **past perfect tense.**

> I remembered that a few years ago some famous athlete <u>had bought</u> one.

The verb *had bought* is in the past perfect tense. This tense shows that the *buying* took place before the *remembering.*

To form the past perfect tense, use the auxiliary *had* plus the past participle. To form most past participles, add *d* or *ed* to the simple form of the verb. Some verbs have irregular past participles, such as *be/been.*

On a piece of paper, copy these sentences. Underline the past perfect tense verbs.

1. He forced the . . . Company to withdraw his card—but they had already started printing them.
2. Nobody had touched it in over eighty years.
3. She had been nice enough to pay me *double* for cleaning her attic.

Activity Book *pp. 197–198*   Student Handbook   Student CD-ROM

376   **Unit 6**   Connections

MULTI-LEVEL OPTIONS *From Reading to Writing*

Newcomer Have students locate or draw a picture of the item they would like to find. Ask them to mime finding it and showing their reaction.

Beginning Have students create a word web about the item they would like to find. Help them write the word for the item in the center. Show them how to write describing words for the item on one branch and words to tell their feelings about finding it on another.

Intermediate Point out that if the item they are describing is unfamiliar to many of their classmates, synonyms may be useful in describing it. Have students use comparisons using *like* or *as* that they learned in Unit 5, Chapter 1, to give their readers a clear picture of the item.

Advanced Challenge students to use the ideas in their paragraphs as the basis for fiction stories about finding the item. Suggest that they use Dan Gutman's work as a model.

From Reading to Writing

Write a Paragraph

In "Honus and Me," Joe finds something very special. Write a paragraph about an object that you would like to find.

1. Answer these questions:
   a. What is the object? Describe it for people who do not know what it is.
   b. Why would you like to find this object? How is it special?
   c. How would you feel if you found this object? Happy? Excited?
2. Use figurative language. Use a dictionary to find the denotative meaning of words. Then think about the connotative meaning.
3. Use the past perfect tense to show a past action that took place before another action.

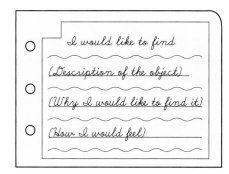

I would like to find

(Description of the object)

(Why I would like to find it)

(How I would feel)

Activity Book
p. 199

Student Handbook

Across Content Areas

Use Multiplication

In "Honus and Me," Miss Young pays Joe ten dollars instead of five dollars. Ten dollars is two times five dollars.

When you see the word "times" in math, it usually means that you have to **multiply.** The symbol × is used to mean "multiply."

$$2 \times 5 = 10$$

"$2 \times 5 = 10$" is an example of an **equation.** To read this equation aloud, you would say, "Two times five equals ten."

Answer these questions:

1. On another day, Miss Young paid Joe $15 instead of $5. Complete the equation: _____ $\times 5 = 15$.
2. How would you say the equation in **1**? Complete the sentence: Three _____ five _____ fifteen.

Activity Book
p. 200

Chapter 2 Honus and Me **377**

1. **Relate to personal experience** *Ask: Have you ever found something special, something that was not yours? What was it? Where did you find it? What did you do with it?* Brainstorm with students about things they would like to find. Direct them to think of objects other than money.
2. **Illustrate a paragraph** Have students illustrate their found objects and display their paragraphs in the classroom.
3. **Multi-level options** See MULTI-LEVEL OPTIONS on p. 376.

Across Content Areas: Math

Use Multiplication

Use prior knowledge *Ask: How do you write this multiplication: two times five equals ten?* Have a volunteer write the equation on the board. Have students dictate other equations to students at the board. Students may want to solve some of the problems.

Answers
1. 3 **2.** times, equals

 **ASSESS**

Have students write out this equation in words: $20 \times 2 = 40$.

Reteach and Reassess

Text Structure Have students create an advantage-disadvantage diagram showing the conflict Joe experienced in the selection and the pros and cons of not telling Miss Young about the baseball card he found.

Reading Strategy Ask students to use the chart on the bottom of p. 364 to determine the overall main idea of the story and the key supporting details.

Elements of Literature Have students review "Esperanza Rising" to discuss its

style, tone, and mood. Have students identify how the author created these.

Reassess Read aloud expressively a persuasive letter to the editor from your local newspaper. Ask students to identify the main idea and details used to persuade readers. Also, invite students to comment on the style, tone, and mood of the letter.

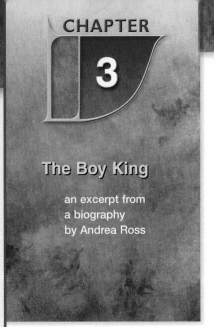

The Boy King

an excerpt from
a biography
by Andrea Ross

Objectives

Reading Identify cause and effect as you read a biography.

Listening and Speaking Ask and answer interview questions.

Grammar Understand modal auxiliaries.

Writing Write a biography.

Content Social Studies: Identify symbols.

Chapter Materials

Activity Book: *pp. 201–208*
Audio: *Unit 6, Chapter 3; CD 2, Track 13*
Student Handbook
Student CD-ROM: *Unit 6, Chapter 3*
Teacher Resource Book: *Lesson Plan, Teacher Resources, Reading Summary, Activity Book Answer Key*
Teacher Resource CD-ROM
Assessment Program: *Quiz, pp. 93–94; Teacher and Student Resources, pp. 115–144*
Assessment CD-ROM
Transparencies
The Heinle Newbury House Dictionary/CD-ROM
Web site: http://visions.heinle.com

Objectives

Preview Read the objectives. *Ask: What do you already know about biographies? What biographies have you read?*

Use Prior Knowledge

Leaders

Classify types of leaders *Say: Some people are born into leadership. For example, kings inherit their throne. Some leaders are elected. For some people, leading is their job. Others are natural leaders.* Ask students to give an example of each kind of leader.

Use Prior Knowledge

Leaders

A leader is a person who guides and connects with a group of people. There are different types of leaders. The president of a country guides the country's government and people. Your teacher guides your learning.

1. Think of leaders that you know about from your country, state, community, or school.
2. Write the titles and names of these leaders in a chart like the one shown. A title tells the kind of ruler the person is, for example, president, king, principal.

Leaders That I Know About	
Title	Name
Principal	Mrs. Rivera

3. Share the information from your chart with the class.
4. Compare leaders in your culture with leaders in other cultures. How are they the same? How are they different?

MULTI-LEVEL OPTIONS *Build Vocabulary*

Newcomer Say the vocabulary words slowly. Have students use a pencil or pen to gently tap out the syllables on their desks.

Beginning Write the vocabulary words on the board. Divide the words into syllables. Slowly say each word and point to each syllable. Then repeat the word and have students say the syllables with you. Ask students to note any familiar words formed by the syllables of the vocabulary words, such as *men* in *Tutankhamen*.

Intermediate Have students work in pairs. Tell each pair to pick five of the glossed words listed on pp. 382–385. Ask them to determine how many syllables are in each of the words they selected.

Advanced Have students look at the pronunciation key in a student dictionary. Show them how the key can help them decipher the pronunciation of words in the dictionary.

Build Background

Ancient Egypt

Egypt is a country on the continent of Africa. People who live in Egypt are called Egyptians. Thousands of years ago, kings and queens in Egypt were called pharaohs. The word *pharaoh* means "great house" in Egyptian. Very large buildings called temples and pyramids were built to remember pharaohs.

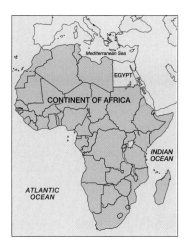

Content Connection

A **continent** is a very large area of land. It is surrounded by large bodies of water (oceans or seas).

Build Vocabulary

Look Up Syllables and Meanings of Words

Dividing a word into **syllables** is one way to learn to pronounce it. A syllable is a part of a word. For example, *teacher* has two syllables, *teach-er*. *Principal* has three syllables, *prin-ci-pal*. The dictionary breaks the words up into **syllables.** This helps you pronounce the words. For example:

Tut•ankh•a•men (an early king of Egypt)

1. Use a large dictionary to look up the words in the box.
2. Write the words, divided into syllables, in your Personal Dictionary.
3. Read the meaning in the dictionary. Then write it in your own words.

4. Work with your teacher to learn to pronounce the words. Listen for these words as you listen to the audio recording of the selection.
5. Listen to distinguish each sound in each word. Try to produce the sounds in the words that you hear.

archaeologist	antelope
hieroglyphics	papyrus

Personal Dictionary The Heinle Newbury House Dictionary Activity Book p. 201 Student CD-ROM

Chapter 3 The Boy King **379**

Content Connection
Technology

Build Vocabulary Tell students that some translation dictionaries on the Internet can help them with pronunciations. Use a search engine and the key words *translation, dictionary, pronunciation.* Demonstrate how to use one of the sites to help students see definitions and hear pronunciations.

Learning Styles
Visual

Build Background Tell students that they can learn a lot about how early Egyptians lived and what was important to them by looking at their art. Have students browse through art books or Web sites showing early Egyptian art. Ask them to make inferences about people and events shown in these works.

Build Background

Ancient Egypt

1. **Use a map** Have students locate Egypt on a globe or map. Have them identify other countries in the Middle East.
2. **Use resources** Bring in illustrated books or bookmark Internet sites about Egypt. Discuss climate, crops, animals, and pyramids.
3. **Content Connection** Earth's seven continents are Europe, Asia, Africa, North America, South America, Antarctica, and Australia. Continents make up about 29% of Earth's total area.

Build Vocabulary

Look Up Syllables and Meanings of Words

Teacher Resource Book: *Personal Dictionary, p. 63*

1. **Divide a word into syllables** Write on the board: *connections, president, example, king, government, biography, interview, excerpt.* Have students pronounce the words and draw lines to show the syllables.
2. **Reading selection vocabulary** You may want to introduce the glossed words in the reading selection before students begin reading. Key words: *historians, ancient, ruled, kingdom, tomb, injured, archaeologist.* Instruct students to write the words with correct spelling and their definitions in their Personal Dictionaries. Have them pronounce each word and divide it into syllables.
3. **Multi-level options** See MULTI-LEVEL OPTIONS on p. 378.

Answers

2. and 3. ar•chae•ol•o•gist (a person who studies human life through items of the past); an•te•lope (a fast, four-legged animal with horns); hi•er•o•glyph•ics (pictures representing words or sounds); pa•py•rus (water plant in Africa; paper made from it)

ASSESS

Ask: What continent is Egypt in? What do we call people who live in Egypt?

Text Structure

Biography

1. **Review features of a biography** *Ask: What features of a biography do you know?* (true story of someone's life, events, dates, third-person)

2. **Analyze sources** *Say: The Boy King was born in 1370 B.C. How many years ago was that?* (current year + 1370) *How do you think the author found out the information for the biography?* (historians, archaeologists) *Can we be sure that everything in this biography is a fact? Why not?*

3. **Multi-level options** See MULTI-LEVEL OPTIONS below.

Reading Strategy

Identify Cause and Effect

Practice the strategy Have students identify the cause and effect in these sentences: *When José doesn't get enough sleep* (cause), *he gets tired* (effect). *Martha was sick* (cause), *so she went to the doctor* (effect). *I was late* (effect) *because I forgot to set my alarm clock* (cause).

Answer

1. When José doesn't sleep enough (cause), he gets tired (effect).

ASSESS

Have students work in pairs to write two cause and effect sentences.

Text Structure

Biography

A **biography** is the story of a person's life. The author tells the events in chronological order (the order in which events happened). "The Boy King" is a biography about a young boy. This boy was a pharaoh in Egypt many years ago. In a biography, you will find the features shown in the chart.

As you read, look for these features. They will help you understand and recall information about the life of the boy king.

Biography	
Events in Chronological Order	things that happen in a person's life; they are presented in the order they happen
Dates	dates of birth, death, and important events
Details	information about the time and place in which the story happens

Student CD-ROM

Reading Strategy

Identify Cause and Effect

A **cause** is the reason why something happens. The **effect** is what happens because of the cause.

I am going to the library because I want a book.

Cause: I want a book.

Effect: I am going to the library.

Some words that often show cause and effect are *because*, *since*, *so*, and *when*.

1. Read this sentence. What is the cause? What is the effect?

    When José doesn't sleep enough, he gets tired.

2. Look for causes and effects as you read or listen to "The Boy King." Write the causes and effects in your

Reading Log. Use a chart like the one shown.

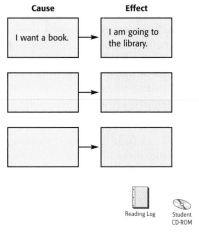

Reading Log   Student CD-ROM

MULTI-LEVEL OPTIONS *Text Structure*

Newcomer Draw a timeline chain on the board. Write dates and make simple drawings of a few important events from the life of someone familiar to students, such as another teacher or a famous person.

Beginning Divide your class into pairs and give each a picture book biography of a famous person. Have students draw a timeline to show a few key dates and events illustrated in the book.

Intermediate Have students review information in their social studies textbook or another nonfiction source about an important person in history. Help them identify the elements from the chart on p. 380.

Advanced Bookmark several short biographies of famous people from the past on the Internet. Divide the class into pairs and ask each to read one of the biographies. Have students identify the elements in the chart on the top of p. 380.

THE BOY KING

an excerpt from a biography
by Andrea Ross

381

Reading Selection Materials

Audio: *Unit 6, Chapter 3; CD 2, Track 13*
Teacher Resource Book: *Reading Summary,*
   pp. 115–116
Transparencies: #15, *Reading Summary*

Suggestions for Using
Reading Summary

- Introduce new vocabulary or cognates.
- Cut the summary into strips, or jumble the sentences on an overhead transparency. Students put the sentences in order.
- Practice the reading strategy.
- Students read aloud or with a partner.
- Students paraphrase the summary.
- Students do a cloze activity.
- Students create a visual or graphic organizer, such as a timeline or storyboard, to illustrate the summary.
- Students paraphrase the summary.

Preview the Selection

1. **Discover history of art piece** Have students look at the photo. *Say: This is a photo of an ancient Egyptian death mask of the Pharaoh Tutankhaten. It is from the tomb of the pharaoh and is about 21 inches high. It is made of gold inlaid with colored glass and semiprecious stones.*
2. **Connect** *Ask: Have you ever seen something like this in a museum? Have you seen masks from other cultures?*

Cultural Connection

Have students ask friends or family members to share information they know about historical rulers of other countries. Have them ask about the titles of the rulers, what kinds of powers they had, and how these leaders were chosen. Provide time for students to share what they find out through drawings or oral presentations.

Learning Styles
Interpersonal

Ask students to work with partners to discuss or act out how they would react if they were suddenly chosen to be the leader of their community. *Ask: How would you feel? What would you do first? Whom would you ask for help?*

Read the Selection

1. **Do a jigsaw reading** Assign paragraphs to small groups to prepare and "teach" to the class. Have them summarize the information and prepare questions to ask the class.

2. **Identify important details** Have pairs work together to make a list of the four or five most important details about Tutankhaten. Then discuss and list the details as a class. (*Possible details:* born in 1370 B.C., lived in El-Amarna, lived in a beautiful palace, was trained to be a pharaoh starting at about 4 years old)

3. **Analyze information** *Ask: How was Tutankhaten related to Queen Nefertiti and Akhenaten?* (Historians are not sure, but they think Akhenaten was probably his brother and the queen, his sister-in-law.) *Historians inferred that they were brothers. Why did they infer that? What happened when Akhenaten died?* (Tutankhaten became the new pharaoh.)

Sample Answer to Guide Question
The cause would be writing a wrong answer.

See Teacher Edition pp. 434–436 for a list of English-Spanish cognates in the reading selection.

---

1   How would you like to wake up one morning and be told that you are the ruler of your country? That is what happened over three thousand years ago to an Egyptian boy who was about nine years old.

2   Around 1370 B.C. a boy was born in a royal palace in Egypt. His name was Tutankhaten, which means "the living image of the sun god." He lived in a town in Egypt named El-Amarna during his early childhood, probably in the same palace as the pharaoh Akhenaten, and his wife, Queen Nefertiti. Most **historians** think Tutankhaten and Akhenaten were brothers, though no one knows for sure.

3   The walls of the palace were painted in rich, bright colors. The floors were decorated with colored clay tiles, and the furniture was covered with real gold. Beautiful gardens and pools around the palace helped keep the air cool.

4   In **ancient** Egypt the average **life span** was short by today's standards. Every boy in line for the throne had to be trained in case the time ever came for him to become a pharaoh.

Tutankhaten most likely started studying when he was about four years old. His education would have included learning hieroglyphics and mathematics. He would have written on papyrus, and if his answers were wrong, his **tutor** would have marked them in red ink.

> **Identify Cause and Effect**
>
> What would be the cause of getting marks in red ink?

Audio
CD 2, Tr. 13

B.C. Before Christ, the years before the birth of Christ in the Christian calendar
historians people who teach, study, and write about history

ancient very old
life span the number of years a person lives
tutor a teacher who helps students individually

MULTI-LEVEL OPTIONS *Read the Selection*

Newcomer Play the audio. *Ask: Did Tutankhaten live in Egypt?* (yes) *Did he live a very long time ago?* (yes) *Did he start studying to be king when he was nine years old?* (no) *Did he become king when he was nine years old?* (yes) *Did he play checkers?* (no)

Beginning Read aloud the selection. *Ask: Who is this selection about?* (Tutankhaten) *Where did he live?* (Egypt) *When was he born?* (1370 B.C.) *How old was he when he became king?* (nine) *What sports did he learn?* (wrestling, swimming, shooting a bow and arrow, driving a chariot)

Intermediate Have students do a reciprocal reading. *Ask: How did Tutankhaten get ready to become king?* (studied writing, math, horse riding, and shooting from the time he was four) *How do you think he reacted to becoming king so young?* (He may have been scared, but not too scared since he had prepared.)

Advanced Have students do a paired reading. *Ask: Why aren't people sure of some of the facts of Tutankhaten's life?* (because it was so long ago that people didn't keep the kinds of records we do) *Why were people's lives so much shorter in Tutankhaten's time?* (They did not have the medicines and hospitals we do today.)

5   Tutankhaten probably spent lots of time practicing sports. He would have learned to wrestle, swim, shoot a bow and arrow, and drive a two-horse chariot. When he stayed indoors, he might have played a game called *senet* that is not unlike today's checkers.

6   Eventually Tutankhaten's brother Akhenaten died. Tutankhaten was next in line for the throne, and he became the new king. He was about nine years old at the time. As part of becoming the new pharaoh,

Tutankhaten had to marry his seven-year-old niece, the daughter of Akhenaten. Since she was the royal **heiress,** their marriage gave Tutankhaten the **right** to the throne.

Identify Cause and Effect

What was the effect of Tutankhaten marrying?

---

heiress   a female legally in line to receive property   **right**   ownership

Chapter 3   The Boy King   **383**

Read the Selection

1. **Paired reading**   Play the audio. Then have students practice reading the selection in pairs.
2. **Compare activities**   *Ask: What activities did Tutankhaten do?* (wrestling, swimming, shooting a bow and arrow, and driving a chariot) *Which sports are no longer common?* (shooting a bow and arrow, driving a chariot)
3. **Multi-level options**   See MULTI-LEVEL OPTIONS on p. 382.

Sample Answer to Guide Question
Marrying the royal heiress gave Tutankhaten the right to the throne.

,   Punctuation

Hyphens in compound adjectives

Direct students to paragraph 5. *Ask: What kind of chariot or cart did Tutankhaten learn to drive?* (two-horse) Write the word on the board. Circle the hyphen. *Say: This describing word is made up of two words. It is a compound word. Some compound describing words have a short line called a hyphen joining the parts. We call these compound adjectives. Find another example in paragraph 6.* (seven-year-old)

Apply   Write on the board: *The wide eyed girl looked at the huge elephant. My dog is well behaved.* Ask students to place hyphens in the compound describing words. (wide-eyed, well-behaved)

Read the Selection

Teacher Resource Book: *Timelines, p. 39*

1. **Reciprocal reading** Play the audio. Then have volunteers read paragraphs and ask the class questions.
2. **Make a timeline** Have students work in small groups to make a timeline of Tutankhaten's life. Direct them to start with the year of his birth and record the events until his death. After groups have finished, have one group put their timeline on the board.

Sample Answer to Guide Question
He changed his name to include Amen, the god of the city his family was from.

---

7   Tutankhaten **ruled** successfully for the next few years with his wife. When he was about thirteen, the **temples** of Egypt displayed an **announcement** that praised all the things he had done to help the **kingdom.** These announcements were carved on flat pieces of stone. When he turned sixteen, Tutankhaten was considered a man and ruled the kingdom alone.

8   Tutankhaten was a great sportsman and seemed to like hunting particularly. Some of the objects from his **tomb** show him in a chariot aiming his bow at **ostriches.** He probably also hunted **gazelles** and **antelopes.**

9   Eventually, Tutankhaten decided to change his name to Tutankh*amen.* Amen was the god of Thebes, the city his family was from.

> **Identify Cause and Effect**
> How did the pharaoh's family background affect his decision to change his name?

---

ruled   governed, usually as a king or dictator
temples   buildings for religious worship
announcement   a formal letter or paper that makes public some information
kingdom   a country ruled by a king or queen

tomb   a burial room or grave with a monument over it
ostriches   large, flightless, African birds with long legs and necks
gazelles   animals like small deers
antelopes   any of various fast, hoofed, four-legged animals with horns

---

MULTI-LEVEL OPTIONS *Read the Selection*

Newcomer *Ask: Was Tutankhaten a good king?* (yes) *Did Tutankhaten change his name?* (yes) *Did he live to be an old man?* (no) *Was his tomb full of beautiful things?* (yes)

Beginning *Ask: How old was Tutankhaten when he could rule alone?* (16) *What kind of king was he?* (good) *How old was he when he died?* (about 17) *What do people remember about him?* (the riches in his tomb)

Intermediate *Ask: Why did Tutankhaten change his name?* (in honor of the place he was from) *Do you think Tutankhamen would have been famous if his tomb had not been found? Explain.* (no, because he did not live long enough to become famous as a ruler)

Advanced *Ask: How do you think Tutankhaten made decisions before he was 16?* (He must have had older relatives or family members that helped him.) *What was probably true about the king's tomb?* (It must have been big to hold so many treasures. It must have been well-protected or hidden to have the things in it last so long.)

10   When Tutankhamen was about seventeen, scholars think he somehow **suffered** a head **injury.** Perhaps he was **wounded** in **battle,** or maybe he was hurt while hunting. He might even have had enemies who were trying to kill him. We don't know for sure if this **wound** caused his death, but it is likely that he never recovered from it.

11   More than three thousand years later, an English **archaeologist** named Howard Carter found Tutankhamen's tomb. It **yielded** some of the most beautiful Egyptian treasures ever found and made the pharaoh's name famous all over the world. Though his rule was **short-lived**, Tutankhamen, "the boy king," will never be forgotten because of the riches he left behind.

Identify Cause and Effect

How did Howard Carter help the world remember Tutankhamen?

---

suffered   experienced pain, loss, or hardship
injury   a wound or damage
wounded   injured
battle   a fight between enemy soldiers
wound   a cut or other hurt cutting into the body

archaeologist   a person who studies human life and civilizations through items of the past such as buried houses, statues, pots, and so on
yielded   produced
short-lived   not lasting long

About the Author · Andrea Ross

Andrea Ross was born in New York. She started writing at the age of seven. Since then, she has written plays, stories for children, and a book for young adults. Ross says that writing "is like sunshine to my soul."

➤ What questions do you think Andrea Ross researched to write this selection?

Chapter 3   The Boy King   **385**

---

th Spelling

Open and closed syllables

Say: When there is a consonant at the end of a syllable, it is called a closed syllable. The vowel sound is usually short. Write and **say:** *had, flat, him.* Then **say:** *When a syllable ends in a vowel or a vowel + y, it is called an open syllable. The vowel sound is long.* Write and **say:** *day, also, be, family.*

Apply Have students underline words that end in open syllables. Write on the board: *country, sun, color, three, yesterday, king.* (underline *country, three, yesterday*)

Evaluate Your Reading Strategy

Identify Cause and Effect *Say: You have practiced an important reading strategy. Now you can decide how well you have done. Does this statement describe how you read?*

> When I do not understand the reason *why* something happened, I reread to identify the cause and effect. Identifying causes and effects helps me understand the events in a biography.

Read the Selection

1. **Discuss cultural traditions** *Ask: What traditions in ancient Egypt were different from ours?* (Rulers inherit a throne; the pharaoh studied with a tutor, not in a classroom; he became the new king when he was 9; he had to marry his 7-year-old niece; he was considered a man when he was 16.) *What traditions are similar?* (Children start learning at a young age; they learned math and writing; children enjoyed playing sports; he lived with relatives.)

2. **Paired reading** Play the audio. Have students reread aloud with a partner.

3. **Locate derivations using dictionaries** Have students look at these glossed words and determine what words they are derived from: *ruled, announcement, ostriches, gazelles, antelopes, archaeologist.* Have students check the derivations in a print, online, or CD-ROM dictionary.

4. **Multi-level options** See MULTI-LEVEL OPTIONS on p. 384.

Sample Answer to Guide Question
Howard Carter discovered Tutankhamen's tomb.

About the Author

Discuss author motivation *Say: Andrea Ross began writing when she was seven years old. Why do you think she started writing at an early age?* (She enjoys writing.) *What other detail supports your opinion?* (She says writing "is like sunshine to my soul.") *What is writing like for you?* Have students share their feelings about writing.

Answer
Sample answer: What were the important events in Tutankhamen's life? What were his interests? What happened while he was pharaoh?

Across Selections

Have students turn to the table of contents and locate the pages for the biography of Nelson Mandela. Give students time to review his biography. Compare and contrast the two leaders.

Beyond the Reading

Reading Comprehension

Question-Answer Relationships

Sample Answers

1. He was about 9.
2. "the living image of the sun god"
3. They lived in the same palace, and Tutankhaten became king when Akhenaten died.
4. His tomb yielded some of the most beautiful Egyptian treasures ever found.
5. I think he died of infection from his head wound because the ancient Egyptians didn't have antibiotics.
6. In Tutankhaten's time, the tradition was that leadership was passed down through men in a family, and a boy could become a king at any age. Kings were required to marry other royalty. In many countries today, leaders are elected; they can be men or women and must be at least 21 years old.
7. We both like sports.
8. The best thing about being king is that I can hunt any animal in my kingdom.
9. There would be many rules I would have to follow.
10. I could be a good leader because I encourage teamwork.

Build Reading Fluency

Repeated Reading

Assessment Program: *Reading Fluency Chart, p. 116*

As students read aloud, time the reading and count the number of incorrectly pronounced words. Record results in the Reading Fluency Chart.

Reading Comprehension

Question-Answer Relationships (QAR)

"Right There" Questions

1. **Recall Facts** How old was Tutankhamen when he became king?
2. **Recall Facts** What does Tutankhaten, the Boy King's original name, mean?

"Think and Search" Questions

3. **Make Inferences** Why do historians think Tutankhamen and Akhenaten were brothers?
4. **Analyze Cause and Effect** Why is Tutankhamen still famous today?

"Author and You" Questions

5. **Use Multiple Sources** How do you think Tutankhamen died? Draw a conclusion using information in this selection together with information from library books, encyclopedias, and the Internet.

6. **Compare Cultural Traditions** Compare and contrast the cultural tradition of leadership in Tutankhamen's time with today.
7. **Make Connections** Compare Tutankhamen's life with your own. What connections can you make with him?

"On Your Own" Questions

8. **Explain** If you were Tutankhamen, what do you think you would like best about being pharaoh? Explain your choice.
9. **Explain** What do you think you would like least about being pharaoh? Explain your choice.
10. **Speculate** Do you think that you would make a good leader? Why or why not?

Activity Book   Student
p. 202   CD-ROM

Build Reading Fluency

Repeated Reading

Repeated reading helps increase your reading rate and builds confidence. Each time you reread you improve your reading fluency.

1. Turn to page 382.
2. Your teacher or a partner will time you for six minutes.

3. With a partner, take turns reading paragraphs 1–2 aloud.
4. Stop after six minutes.

MULTI-LEVEL OPTIONS *Elements of Literature*

Newcomer Help students create an illustration of the main idea for each paragraph identified in Step 1. Then have students look at all the pictures together and think of a theme that connects them all.

Beginning Have students list key words and ideas from each of the paragraphs identified in Step 1. Have them use some of these ideas in creating a class statement of the theme.

Intermediate Have students review "Honus and Me." Ask them to identify its theme. Have them discuss possible themes for a next chapter for the story.

Advanced Have students read short stories from various cultures. Ask them to identify a theme for each. Have students who identified similar themes meet in groups to compare and contrast how the author approached the theme.

Listen, Speak, Interact

Ask and Answer Interview Questions

Suppose you are a news reporter. You have a chance to interview Tutankhamen to learn more about his life.

1. Write some questions you want to ask Tutankhamen. Some questions that are often asked in interviews are:
   a. When were you born?
   b. Where were you born?
   c. What do you do every day?
   d. What are some things that you like?
   e. How did you get your head injury?

2. Think about how Tutankhamen might answer. Use the reading to help you guess.
3. Ask your interview questions to a partner. Your partner will play the role of Tutankhamen and answer the questions.
4. Record your interview on video or audio. Review your recording. Is your interview believable? What would you do to improve it?

Elements of Literature

Discuss Themes Across Cultures

A reading presents a **theme.** A theme is an important topic that the author mentions several times in a reading selection.

1. With a partner, reread aloud paragraphs 4 to 9 of "The Boy King."
2. As you finish a paragraph, write down its main idea.
3. Use your main ideas to identify one theme in this part of the reading.

4. Discuss how the theme you identified is the same or different across other cultures.
5. Share with the class the theme that you found in "The Boy King."

Activity Book p. 203   Student CD-ROM

Listen, Speak, Interact

Ask and Answer Interview Questions

1. **Speculate about a character's personality** Discuss what sort of person students imagine Tutankhaten was. *Ask: Do you think Tutankhaten was a very smart young man? Do you think he was kind or selfish? Do you think he would answer questions politely? Do you think he was a very proud person?*

2. **Analyze speaker's credibility** After performing their interviews, have students analyze the credibility of their partner. *Ask: Did you believe your partner? How well did s/he play the role? Did you trust his/her words? Why or why not? What suggestions would you give your partner to be more credible or believable?* (example: be more confident, use stronger emotion, act more like the character, and so on)

3. **Newcomers** Work with these students to practice asking interview questions.

Elements of Literature

Discuss Themes Across Cultures

1. **Understand theme** Explain that reading selections can have more than one theme. Ask them to think of another theme for "Esperanza Rising." (Children learn values from their parents' actions.)

2. **Multi-level options** See MULTI-LEVEL OPTIONS on p. 386.

Answers

Sample answers: **2.** Paragraph 4: Boys are trained to be kings from age 4. Paragraph 5: He played lots of sports. Paragraph 6: His brother died, so he became king and was married. Paragraph 7: He was a successful ruler. Paragraph 8: He was a great sportsman and hunter. Paragraph 9: He changed his name to "Tutankhamen." **3.** Sons of kings were carefully educated and trained to be kings, and their lives were very structured. **4.** In our culture, everyone is educated, and leadership comes with ability to lead, not with birth.

 **ASSESS**

Have students write a brief description of the character Tutankhaten.

Content Connection
The Arts

Say: Songs have themes, too. Sometimes, it is easy to find the theme in a song because there is a line that is repeated over and over, a refrain, or chorus. Have students listen to a song, such as "This Land is Your Land." Have them identify and say in their own words the theme repeated in the chorus.

Learning Styles
Interpersonal

Tell students that when interviewers plan their questions, they also think about follow-up questions they might ask to get more information from the person. Have students think of follow-up questions they might ask related to two or three of the suggested questions. (*Example:* d. What are some things that you like? Why do you like them? Is there anything you don't like?)

Word Study

Recognize the Suffix -ian

Review suffixes On the board, write: *biologist, seismograph*. Underline the suffixes and help students remember other words they have studied with these suffixes.

Answers

2. musician (a person who writes, sings, or plays music); mathematician (a person who studies math); librarian (a person who directs or works in a library)

Grammar Focus

Understand Modal Auxiliaries

Model use of modal auxiliaries *Say: I know some things about my grandparents, but I don't have all of the facts. For example, my grandfather would have gone to school in Los Angeles because he was born there. He might have walked to school. What can you tell me about your older relatives?* Have students share information.

Answers

1. would 2. might

ASSESS

Have students copy and complete these sentences: *When I was young, I might _____. When my _____ was a child, _____ would _____.*

Word Study

Recognize the Suffix -ian

A **suffix** is a group of letters added to the end of a root word.

Most histor**ian**s think Tutankhaten and Akhenaten were brothers.

Historians has the suffix *-ian*. This suffix can mean "a person who works with or studies something." The root of *historians* is *history*. A historian is a person who studies history, or past events.

1. Read the words in the box. Read the root words below each word. Use a dictionary if you don't know a root word.

musician	mathematician	librarian
music	mathematics	library

2. What is the meaning of each word? Use the meaning of the suffix to help you. Check your ideas in a dictionary.

3. Ask your teacher to help you pronounce the words.

The Heinle Newbury House Dictionary Activity Book p. 204 Student CD-ROM

Grammar Focus

Understand Modal Auxiliaries

Read these sentences from the selection and notice the words in **bold** type:

He **would** have learned to wrestle, swim, . . . and drive a two-horse chariot. When he stayed indoors, he **might** have played a game called *senet* . . .

In grammar, words like *would* and *might* are called **modal auxiliaries.** Modal auxiliaries are often used in the **perfect** form to express past time.

Complete each sentence with *might* or *would*.

Perfect Modal Auxiliaries			
Subject	Modal Auxiliary	Have	Past Participle
They	might *or* would	have	learned many sports.

1. In my school, you _____ have studied U.S. history in eighth grade.
2. He _____ have given the book to Yeny.

Activity Book pp. 205–206 Student Handbook Student CD-ROM

MULTI-LEVEL OPTIONS *From Reading to Writing*

Newcomer Ask someone from the school's faculty or staff to visit your class. Help students find out basic information about him/her. Then have each student illustrate one fact about the person. Bind the pages together to form a booklet about the subject. Invite the person back to see the finished product.

Beginning Have students create their biographies in the form of fact sheets. Ask them to use dates, words, and phrases to show what they learned about their subjects.

Intermediate Suggest that students use headings to organize the information they learn about their subjects. For example, they may have sections titled *Early Life, Present Activities,* and *Future Goals.*

Advanced Remind students that they learned in Chapter 2 that a writer creates a mood and tone for each piece. Before students write, have them consider what attitudes they want to communicate about the subjects of their biographies and what feelings about the person they want to inspire in their readers.

From Reading to Writing

Write a Biography

Write a short biography of a friend.

1. Interview a friend to find out about his or her life. Ask these questions:
   a. When were you born?
   b. Where were you born?
   c. Where do you live now?
   d. Where do you go to school?
   e. What is your family like?
   f. What are your favorite things to do?

You may ask other questions.

2. Write your friend's answers on a piece of paper. Use your interview answers to write three paragraphs.
3. Form compound sentences with *and* or *but*.
4. Combine some of your sentences to form complex sentences with *because, if, when*.
5. Use transition words such as *then, next, finally*.

Activity Book
p. 207

Student
Handbook

Across Content Areas

Identify Symbols

Hieroglyphics are **symbols** that show meanings. A symbol is a picture, sign, or mark that stands for something else.

People in Egypt used hieroglyphics to write words long ago. In English writing, we use the letters of the alphabet to write words. However, we also use symbols to give information.

1. Copy the chart on a piece of paper.
2. Read the sentences in the first column. Use context clues to figure out what the symbols mean.
3. Choose the correct word from the box. Write the word in your chart.
4. What other symbols do you know?

	Symbol	Meaning
I paid $5 for lunch.	$	
The postcard had this message: I ♥ New York.	♥	
We moved the car when we saw this sign: ⊘	⊘	

> dollars
> love
> not allowed

Activity Book
p. 208

Reteach and Reassess

Text Structure Have students make a timeline of key events discussed in the biography they read.

Reading Strategy Have students draw or write a cause and effect statement about what most likely caused Howard Carter to search for Tutankhamen's tomb.

Elements of Literature Read a short story to students. Have them draw or write a sentence telling the theme.

Reassess Read a short biography of a well-known historical figure to students. *Ask: What caused this person to be well-known today?*

From Reading to Writing

Write a Biography

1. **Brainstorm** Before students interview, have them think of other questions to ask. Suggest questions such as: *When you were very young, what games did you play? Who was your favorite cartoon character?* Point out that questions with *why* can elicit answers with *because* and *since*, reflecting cause and effect.
2. **Compose an interview form** Ask pairs to collaborate to create a form for their interview. Instruct them to organize the form into questions and answers. Have pairs practice the interview using the form. Then instruct them to collaborate to revise the form based on their practice.
3. **Organize information** Have students think about how to organize their information into three paragraphs. For example, the first paragraph could be about where the person was born, where he or she lives, and where he or she goes to school. The second paragraph could be about the person's family, and the third paragraph could be about special interests.
4. **Multi-level options** See MULTI-LEVEL OPTIONS on p. 388.

Across Content Areas: Social Studies

Identify Symbols

Explain symbols Have volunteers come to the board to draw and explain other symbols they know, including symbols from other cultures.

Answer
Top to bottom: dollars, love, not allowed

ASSESS

Have students create a symbol to represent a sport or other school activity they enjoy.

CHAPTER

4

Into the Reading

It Could Still Be a Robot

an excerpt from an informational book by Allan Fowler

High-Tech Helping Hands

an excerpt from an informational article by Jane McGoldrick

Reading Materials

Activity Book: *pp. 209–216*
Audio: *Unit 6, Chapter 4; CD 2, Track 14*
Student Handbook
Student CD-ROM: *Unit 6, Chapter 4*
Teacher Resource Book: *Lesson Plan, Teacher Resources, Reading Summary, Activity Book Answer Key*
Teacher Resource CD-ROM
Assessment Program: *Quiz, pp. 95–96; Teacher and Student Resources, pp. 115–144*
Assessment CD-ROM
Transparencies
The Heinle Newbury House Dictionary/CD-ROM
Web site: http://visions.heinle.com

Objectives

Preview Read the objectives. *Ask: What do you already know about informational texts?*

Use Prior Knowledge

Talk About Machines

Identify machines at school Ask students to brainstorm a list of all the machines that people use at school. (*Examples:* computers, TV monitors, calculators, telephones, intercoms, school buses) Then have groups divide the list into categories.

Answers

Sample answers: **a.** computers **b.** airplanes, trains **c.** microwave oven, food processor **d.** cell phones, fax machines

Objectives

Reading Paraphrase to recall ideas as you read an informational text.

Listening and Speaking Talk about advantages and disadvantages.

Grammar Use adverbs of frequency.

Writing Write a persuasive essay.

Content Science: Read an FAQ web page.

Use Prior Knowledge

Talk About Machines

Machines are tools that help people do things. For example, a car is a machine that helps people travel. Most people use many machines in their lives.

1. With a partner, think of different types of machines that people use. What machines help people do these things?
   a. research information
   b. travel long distances
   c. cook
   d. communicate
2. Write your ideas in a web. Add other machines as supporting evidence that people use many machines.

3. Present your web to the class. Tell about how these machines help people.

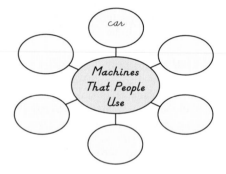

MULTI-LEVEL OPTIONS *Build Vocabulary*

Newcomer *Say: Chat means talk.* Use a friendly facial expression and act out chatting with a student volunteer. *Say: Gossip means talk.* Use a mean look and act out pointing to a student and whispering a secret to another student.

Beginning Have students work in pairs. Tell them to copy one of the following on each of four stick-on notes: *device, gadget, fume, smell.* Ask them to look through magazines or catalogs to find an example of a device and a gadget and something related to fumes and smells. (*Examples:* vacuum, automatic dog feeder, car exhaust, perfume)

Intermediate Have students create four-column charts. Tell them to head each column with one vocabulary word. Challenge them to list as many examples of each as they can in one minute.

Advanced Ask each student to write a paragraph about a fictitious device for getting rid of fumes. Tell them to try to use all four vocabulary words from numbers 1–2 in their paragraphs.

Build Background

Robots

You will read two selections about robots. Robots are special types of machines. They are controlled by computers. They are programmed to do certain jobs. This means that robots are made with instructions that tell them to do something. Most robots are made to help people do things. Some can be used to do dangerous jobs. Other robots can explore places that are far away. Robots can even help people who are disabled (not able to do certain tasks).

Content Connection

The first robots were made in the 1950s. They were used to help make things like cars.

Build Vocabulary

Distinguish Denotative and Connotative Meanings

In Chapter 1 of this unit, you learned about **denotative** and **connotative meanings.** Turn to page 360 and review that information.

Sometimes two words have similar denotative meanings, but their connotative meanings are different. Read these two sentences and then look at the chart:

They were **chatting** at the party.

They were **gossiping** at the party.

Word	Denotative Meaning	Connotative Meaning
chat	to talk	to talk informally
gossip	to talk	to tell private, untrue, or hurtful things

Read the meanings of these pairs of words. Which word has a connotative meaning? Which word has a denotative meaning?

1. **a.** device—an electrical or mechanical machine
   b. gadget—a small tool or machine that is often inexpensive and sometimes unnecessary
2. **a.** fume—a bad gas or smell
   b. smell—something that you sense with your nose or a feeling about something

Activity Book p. 209   Student CD-ROM

Community Connection

Build Vocabulary *Ask: In what stores in our community can people buy gadgets or mechanical devices? Where might people smell fumes in this area? What causes those fumes? What are describing words for some other smells in our community? What causes these smells?*

Learning Styles
Mathematical

Build Background Provide books and Web sites where students may learn basic facts about robots. Ask each student to draw a design for a robot to do a specific job. Tell students to think about how large their robots would have to be to do their jobs. Ask students to show the dimensions of the devices on their diagrams.

Build Background

Robots

1. **Use personal experience** Ask students to share examples of robots they have read about or seen in movies. *Ask: Do robots look like humans? Are robots always helpful?*
2. **Content Connection** The term *robot* is from the Czech word *robata* meaning "compulsory labor."

Build Vocabulary

Distinguish Denotative and Connotative Meanings

Teacher Resource Book: *Personal Dictionary, p. 63*

1. **Use connotative meanings** Have students use *gossip, gadget,* and *fume* in sentences.
2. **Clarify meaning and usage** Have students use print, online, or CD-ROM dictionaries and thesauruses to clarify the denotative and connotative meaning and usage of *tiny/puny* and *block/obstruct.*
3. **Reading selection vocabulary** You may want to introduce the glossed words in the reading selections before students begin reading. Key words: *factories, program, engineers, consumers, devices, feedback, limbs.* Instruct students to write the words with correct spelling and their definitions in their Personal Dictionaries. Have them pronounce each word and divide it into syllables.
4. **Multi-level options** See MULTI-LEVEL OPTIONS on p. 390.

Answers
1. **a.** denotative **b.** connotative
2. **a.** connotative **b.** denotative

ASSESS

Have students draw or describe a robot they would like to own or build.

Text Structure

Informational Text

Identify graphic features Direct students to p. 51. *Ask: What graphic feature helped you see the difference between facts and opinion?* (two-column chart) Do the same for p. 331 "The Solar System" (drawing) and the facing page (photographs).

Reading Strategy

Paraphrase to Recall Ideas

1. **Apply strategy to content class** *Ask: Do you paraphrase ideas in other classes? In which classes would it be especially useful? When you do your homework tonight, practice paraphrasing what you are studying. You can write it down or paraphrase it orally. See if it helps you study.*
2. **Multi-level options** See MULTI-LEVEL OPTIONS below.

ASSESS

Have students tell you three features of an informational text.

Text Structure

Informational Text

You will read two selections, "It Could Still Be a Robot" and "High-Tech Helping Hands." Both selections are **informational texts.** Informational texts explain a subject. These selections have the graphic features listed in the chart.

As you read, record sentences that give facts and examples. Notice how the graphic features help you understand what you read.

Informational Text	
Facts	things that are true
Examples	details that show how information is true
Graphic Features	photographs, drawings, and charts

Student CD-ROM

Reading Strategy

Paraphrase to Recall Ideas

To **paraphrase** is to say or write something you read in your own words. Paraphrasing important parts of a text as you read can help you remember the information.

As you read "It Could Still Be a Robot" and "High-Tech Helping Hands," paraphrase some of the paragraphs. To paraphrase, do the following:

1. Read the paragraph until you are sure you understand it.
2. Close your book.

3. On a piece of paper, write the information that you read in your own words.
4. Open your book again and compare your paraphrase to the paragraph. Did you include all of the information?
5. Revise your paraphrase.

Student CD-ROM

MULTI-LEVEL OPTIONS *Reading Strategy*

Newcomer Read and demonstrate directions to do a simple task, such as playing connect-the-dots. Have students "paraphrase" by acting out or telling the steps they saw you do.

Beginning Read aloud a brief description of a device, such as an electric alarm clock, from an ad or catalog. Point to the features as you read about them. Work with students to create a class paraphrase of the description, using words and short phrases.

Intermediate Have each student write a short paragraph describing a device or gadget in his/her home. Have students meet with partners to read their paragraphs to each other. After a student has read his/her paragraph, ask the partner to paraphrase the description.

Advanced *Say: Paraphrasing can let someone know you have heard what he/she said. Tell a partner how you feel about the idea of robots doing jobs that humans do now.* Have students paraphrase their partners' feelings. Suggest that they start with statements such as *Do you mean . . .?* or *Are you saying . . .?*

It Could Still Be a Robot

an excerpt from an informational book
by Allan Fowler

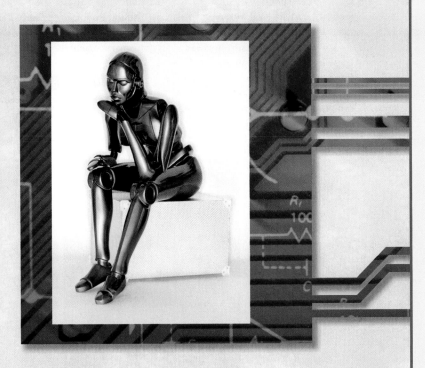

High-Tech Helping Hands

an excerpt from an informational article
by Jane McGoldrick

393

Reading Selection Materials
Audio: *Unit 6, Chapter 4; CD 2, Tracks 14–15*
Teacher Resource Book: *Reading Summary,
pp. 117–118*
Transparencies: #15, *Reading Summary*

Suggestions for Using Reading Summary

- Introduce new vocabulary or cognates.
- Cut the summary into strips, or jumble the sentences on an overhead transparency. Students put the sentences in order.
- Practice the reading strategy.
- Students read aloud or with a partner.
- Students paraphrase the summary.
- Students do a cloze activity.
- Students create a visual or graphic organizer, such as a timeline or storyboard, to illustrate the summary.
- Students paraphrase the summary.

Preview the Selections

1. **Interpret art** Have students look at the photo. *Ask: Do you think this is a real robot? Why or why not? Do you think that someday we will have robots like this? What would you think if you came to school one morning and your teacher was a super intelligent robot like this? How would you feel if you knew the robot could see everything, even when his head was turned?*
2. **Connect** Remind students that the theme of this unit is *connections*. Ask them to explain how they think robots might be "connected" to this theme.

Content Connection
Science

Say: You know that the reading selections in this chapter tell facts about robots. Look at the pictures on pp. 393–396. Based on what you already know about robots, which picture do you think is the most realistic? Which is the least? Ask students to write down their predictions and see if they have the same answers after reading the selections.

Learning Styles
Interpersonal

Have students make two-column charts with the headings *Yes* and *No*. Have students work in pairs to list tasks they think would be good ones for a robot to do and ones they think would not be good for a robot to do.

 Teacher Resource Book: *Two-Column Charts, p. 44*

Read the Selection

1. **Paired reading** Play the audio. Have students reread aloud with a partner.
2. **Relate to personal experience** Have a student read paragraph 3 aloud. *Ask: What movies or TV shows have you seen with robots? What did the robot look like? What was it able to do? In what ways was it like a human? Did it have emotions or a sense of humor?*

Sample Answer to Guide Question
Most robots today don't look like people, but in the future there might be androids.

See Teacher Edition pp. 434–436 for a list of English-Spanish cognates in the reading selection.

It Could Still Be a Robot
an excerpt from an informational book by Allan Fowler

1   It's shaped like a person. It walks like a person. It talks like a person and makes choices like a person. It seems to be alive. Is it a real person?

2   No, it's a robot, made in a factory—and covered with metal instead of skin.

3   You might have seen robots like these in movies or TV shows about the future or about life on other worlds.

4   Maybe someday, a long time from now, there will be androids—robots that look and act like real people.

5   Not yet, though. Most of the robots we have today don't look anything like people.

6   A robot could be an arm without a body . . . or just a box . . . and still be a robot. Robots aren't alive—since a robot is a machine. A robot is a "smart" machine.

Paraphrase to Recall Ideas

Paraphrase paragraphs 4, 5, and 6.

Audio
CD 2, Tr. 14

394   Unit 6   Connections

MULTI-LEVEL OPTIONS *Read the Selection*

Newcomer Play the audio. *Ask: Do robots look like people?* (no) *Do robots do some of the same jobs that people do?* (yes) *Can a robot do anything you want it to do?* (no) *Can robots do some jobs that people cannot do?* (yes)

Beginning Read the selection aloud. *Ask: Are robots more like people or machines?* (people) *What are some jobs a robot can do?* (paint, pick up things, move) *Where are robots used?* (factories)

Intermediate Have students read silently. *Ask: How is a robot different from a person?* (It's made in a factory and doesn't have skin.) *What vocabulary word from p. 391 best describes a robot?* (device) *Why might someone want a robot in his/her factory?* (They do some things faster or safer than people.)

Advanced Have students read silently. *Ask: Why do you think movies show robots in an unreal way?* (to make the movies scary or interesting) *What do you think* smart *in paragraph 6 means?* (able to do something well) *Give an example of something a robot could move or pick up that a human could not.* (*Example:* hot piece of steel)

7 Robots can do many of the things that people do, and some things people can't do.

8 But each robot is built to do only one thing or certain types of things.

9 Robots often do jobs that are unsafe for people to do.

10 **Factories** use robots to pour hot metal.

11 Your family's car was probably spray painted by a robot, because paint fumes are bad for people's health.

Paraphrase to Recall Ideas

Paraphrase paragraphs 9, 10, and 11.

12 Robot hands pick up things that are dangerous for people to touch.

13 Robots are used for tasks that would be boring or tiring for people.

14 Robots never get bored or tired.

15 They also do certain jobs better or faster than human beings can do them.

16 No person can handle very tiny objects as easily as these robot fingers can.

17 Some robots help people do things they cannot do for themselves.

18 Some robots move around. A robot might roll on wheels . . . or travel under water . . . or even fly like this robot plane that has no human pilot . . . and still be a robot.

---

factories buildings where things are made

Chapter 4 It Could Still Be a Robot *and* High-Tech Helping Hands **395**

Read the Selection

1. **Choral reading** Play the audio. Then divide the class into two groups and have each group read every other paragraph with you.
2. **Relate to personal experience** *Ask: Have you ever seen a real robot, either in real life or on TV? What was the robot doing? Here are some other examples of where you might see a robot: in a hospital surgery room, in a space exploration, in a factory, in an underwater ocean exploration.*
3. **Multi-level options** See MULTI-LEVEL OPTIONS on p. 394.

Sample Answer to Guide Question
Robots can safely do things that are dangerous for people to do, like pouring hot metal or spray painting a car.

 Spelling

Oi vowel sound

Call attention to the word *choices* in paragraph 1. Have students repeat the word after you. *Ask: What vowel sound do you hear in the middle of the word?* (/oi/) *Find another word in paragraph 4 that has the same sound.* (android) Tell students that the sound /oi/ can be spelled another way. Ask them to turn to p. 397 and find *enjoy* in paragraph 29. *Ask: How is the sound spelled in this word?* (oy)

Apply Write on the board: *toy, royal, soil, boy, avoid, coin.* Ask students to work in pairs to say each word and use it in a sentence.

Read the Selection

1. **Use a photo to preview** Have students look at the robot in the photo on p. 396 and speculate about what the robot can do.
2. **Reciprocal reading** Play the audio. Then have volunteers read sections aloud and ask the class questions.

Sample Answer to Guide Question
A robot arm might have fingers, a claw, or a tool, depending on the job.

19 But you won't often see a robot walking on two legs.

20 That's easy for you but hard for a robot.

21 Robots can go places where human beings can't go, such as the ocean bottom or the planet Mars.

22 At the end of a robot arm, there might be a hand with fingers . . . or a claw . . . or some kind of tool. It depends on what work the robot was built to do.

Paraphrase to Recall Ideas

Paraphrase paragraph 22.

23 Robots today are run by computers. If its computer **program** is changed, a robot might be able to change from one type of job to another.

24 This rolling robot has an electronic "eye," like a camcorder or a TV remote control.

25 The "eye" can tell if something is blocking the robot's path.

program a code of instructions for a computer

396 Unit 6 Connections

MULTI-LEVEL OPTIONS *Read the Selection*

Newcomer *Ask: Do robots usually have legs?* (no) *Do some robots have hands?* (yes) *Can robots work on other planets?* (yes) *Do robots have feelings?* (no)

Beginning *Ask: Where can a robot go that people cannot?* (the bottom of the ocean, other planets) *What makes a robot work?* (computer program) *What senses do robots seem like they have?* (sight, hearing, touch) *What don't they have that you have?* (feelings)

Intermediate *Ask: How does a robot move without bumping into things?* (An electric eye lets the robot know if there is something in its way.) *Reread paragraph 29. What is another example of something a robot cannot do?* (think, feel, love)

Advanced *Ask: How are a robot's senses different from yours?* (People are born with senses; scientists create instructions for robots so that they act as if they have senses.) *Why could you say a robot is only as good as the person that programs it?* (because if the instructions in the program aren't good, the robot will not work properly)

26   Then the robot can move around whatever is in its way.

27   Other robots are guided by sound or touch. So a robot could be said to see, hear, or feel . . . and still be a robot.

28   A robot might be keeping your school building from getting too warm or too cold. A robot might open doors for people . . . solve hard math problems . . . draw pictures . . . play a musical instrument . . . or spin tops . . . and still be a robot.

29   But it can't feel great or feel bad . . . enjoy a joke, a story, or a song . . . taste food . . . or love someone. Only human beings can do those things.

Paraphrase to Recall Ideas

Paraphrase paragraph 29.

About the Author   Allan Fowler

Allan Fowler was born in New York. He used to work for advertising agencies (companies that give information about products and services). He currently works as a freelance writer and lives in Chicago, Illinois. In addition to writing, Allan Fowler enjoys traveling.

► Why do you think Allan Fowler wrote this selection? To inform, to entertain, or to persuade?

Read the Selection

1. **Reciprocal reading** Play the audio. Then have volunteers read sections aloud and ask the class questions.

2. **Express personal opinions** *Ask: What's your opinion about using robots? For example, what would you think if you walked into a restaurant and robots were cooking the food, taking orders, and pouring drinks? Would you think that was a good or bad idea? Why?*

3. **Multi-level options** See MULTI-LEVEL OPTIONS on p. 396.

Sample Answer to Guide Question
There are many things only people can do.

About the Author

Analyze facts Have pairs of students write two questions about the author and then exchange questions with another pair to answer.

Answer
Sample answer: I think he wrote this selection mostly to inform.

ASSESS

Have students discuss what they would like a robot to do around their school.

---

th **Spelling**

Syllable boundary patterns

Write on the board: *bot/tom* and *ro/bot.* Underline the middle consonant(s). *Say: I have divided these two words into syllables. How did I know where to break them? I followed syllable rules. How many consonants are in the middle of* bottom*? (2) When there are two middle consonants, divide the word between them. How many consonants are in the middle of* robot*? (1) When there is one middle consonant, divide before it.*

Apply Write and pronounce the following: *fingers, today, compute, human, ocean.* Ask students to mark the syllables. (fin/gers, to/day, com/pute, hu/man, o/cean)

Read the Selection

1. **Use a photo to preview** Have students look at the photo on p. 399 and speculate about how a robot might help this person.
2. **Silent reading** Play the audio. Then have students reread silently.
3. **Group work** Have students work in small groups to write 4 or 5 questions about the selection. Then have groups exchange and answer the questions.

Sample Answer to Guide Question
Krista is one of several people who tests devices before they are sold.

See Teacher Edition pp. 434–436 for a list of English-Spanish cognates in the reading selection.

High-Tech Helping Hands
an excerpt from an informational article
by Jane McGoldrick

1 Krista is deaf and blind. To communicate, she often uses fingerspelling—forming shapes that stand for letters in the palm of the hand of her "listener." Krista helps **engineers** who work at the A.I. DuPont Institute in Wilmington, Delaware. They develop and test equipment to help people with **disabilities.** Krista is one of about a dozen young people with disabilities from the area who serve as **consumer** researchers before the **devices** are ready to be sold.

> **Paraphrase to Recall Ideas**
>
> Paraphrase the last sentence of paragraph 1.

2 "We ask the researchers to attend team meetings and give us ongoing **feedback,**" says director Richard Foulds. "They're a major part of our team."

3 Bern Gavlick, 16, has been testing a robot arm that attaches to his wheelchair. Because of his **cerebral palsy,** Bern cannot easily control the movements of his **limbs.** The arm can take a book off a shelf or open a door for him. Julia Nelson, 16, also has cerebral palsy. She tested a video game system designed for fun and fitness. "I love trying out the latest products," says Julia. "As a disabled teen, I'm looking to a future of trying to be independent," she adds. "It gives me hope that there are people working on products to help me achieve that goal."

Audio
CD 2. Tr. 15

---

engineers people who design machines or other products
disabilities illnesses or injuries that severely affect the brain or body
consumer someone who uses or buys things
devices equipment or machines designed for special purposes

feedback response
cerebral palsy a disease that affects the brain, muscles, and speech
limbs arms and legs

398 Unit 6 Connections

MULTI-LEVEL OPTIONS *Read the Selection*

Newcomer Play the audio. *Ask: Are Krista, Bern, and Julia robots?* (no) *Do they make machines?* (no) *Do they test new machines and robots?* (yes) *Do the machines help people who have disabilities (problems with their bodies)?* (yes)

Beginning Read the Reading Summary aloud. *Ask: Who helps by trying out new machines?* (Krista, Bern, Julia) *Who do the machines help?* (people with disabilities) *What is Bern trying out?* (robot arm) *What does the robot arm do?* (get books, open doors)

Intermediate Have students read silently. *Ask: How do the young people in the article help others?* (by testing machines for disabled people) *How do you think Bern feels about the robot he is testing?* (excited that it allows him to do things he can't do for himself)

Advanced Have students read silently. *Ask: How can robots and other devices make people with physical problems more independent?* (They can do things for themselves instead of depending on other people.) *How do you think Krista, Bern, and Julia feel about trying out equipment?* (happy to help others and themselves)

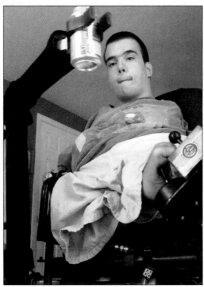

Robotic limbs help people with disabilities
achieve independence.

About the Author — **Jane McGoldrick**

Jane McGoldrick loves reading. When she was a little girl, she used to hide in a quiet place of her home and read all her favorite books. McGoldrick has written magazine articles for children and adults as well as books for children. In addition to writing, McGoldrick completed advanced university work in English and psychology. (Psychology is the study of how people act.)

➤ Why do you think Jane McGoldrick wrote this selection? Did she want to inform, to entertain, or to persuade?

Chapter 4 It Could Still Be a Robot *and* High-Tech Helping Hands **399**

Read the Selection

1. **Relate to personal experience** *Ask: Do you know someone with a disability who uses a device of some kind? Do you know a person with a disability who could use a robot if one were available? What would the robot do for that person? How would it improve the person's life?*
2. **Paired reading** Play the audio. Have students reread aloud with a partner.
3. **Multi-level options** See MULTI-LEVEL OPTIONS on p. 399.

About the Author

Analyze facts *Ask: What does the author love to do?* (read) *Where did she read when she was young?* (in a quiet place of her home) *Do you have a special place where you like to read?* Have students share their answers. Point out that libraries are good places to read because they are quiet and have many reading materials.

Answer
Sample answer: I think she wrote this selection to inform people.

Across Selections

Say: We read about robots in two other selections, "The Fun They Had" and "The Solar System." Direct students to reread p. 303 and p. 339. Ask: What did the authors call robots in their selections? (mechanical teacher, space probes)

Spelling, Punctuation, Capitalization

After the Reading Comprehension section, students will practice spelling, punctuation, and capitalization in the Activity Book.

 Punctuation

Dash

Direct students to the first sentence of paragraph 1, p. 398, and read it aloud.
Say: The short line in the sentence is a dash. What kind of information is after the dash? (It explains the word before the dash.) *We can use a dash to call attention to an explanation of a word or idea in a sentence.*

Apply Write on the board: *He bought a sander a tool for making wood smooth. Ask: Where should the dash go?* (between *sander* and *a*)

Evaluate Your Reading Strategy

Paraphrase to Recall Ideas *Say: You have practiced an important reading strategy. Now you can decide how well you have done. Does this statement describe how you read?*

As I read, I paraphrase by saying or writing what I read in my own words. Paraphrasing helps me recall ideas and better understand the text.

Beyond the Reading

Reading Comprehension

Question-Answer Relationships

Sample Answers

1. no
2. Paint fumes are bad for people's health.
3. the bottom of the ocean, the planet Mars
4. The "eye" can tell if something is blocking its path.
5. A robot can work with very tiny objects.
6. No, it's not. A robot is run by a computer, but a computer isn't always a robot.
7. Robots can know as many facts as people, but they probably can't make inferences as well or understand people's emotions.
8. Robots can help people write, communicate, move, and become more independent.
9. Robots are part of my life. They helped make the car my father uses to drive me to school. My grandmother could use a robot to help her shop for groceries since she has a hard time grabbing items off the shelf.
10. Androids might act as tour guides, bank tellers, or salespeople.
11. The robots in the first selection do not interact with people very much. They do mechanical things. The robots in the second selection help people do things they cannot physically do. Both kinds of robots help people live their lives.

Build Reading Fluency

Reading Chunks of Words

Explain that reading chunks of underlined words helps improve reading fluency. Ask students to listen as you model reading chunks before they practice aloud with a partner.

Reading Comprehension

Question-Answer Relationships (QAR)

"Right There" Questions

1. **Recall Facts** Do most robots look like people?
2. **Recall Facts** Why are robots used to spray paint cars?
3. **Recall Facts** Where can robots go that people cannot?

"Think and Search" Questions

4. **Explain** How can an electronic "eye" help a robot?
5. **Explain** What can a robot's hands and fingers do that a person's cannot?
6. **Draw Conclusions** Is a robot the same thing as a computer?

"Author and You" Questions

7. **Compare** Do you think robots are as smart as people? Why or why not?

8. **Identify Main Ideas** How can robots help people with disabilities?
9. **Make Connections** Use the information in the selections to make connections between robots and your life. Do you know someone who could use a robot to help them?

"On Your Own" Questions

10. **Predict** What kinds of things do you think androids might do?
11. **Find Similarities and Differences Across Texts** How are the robots described in the two selections similar? How are they different?

Activity Book p. 210   Student CD-ROM

Build Reading Fluency

Reading Chunks of Words

Reading chunks or phrases of words is an important characteristic of fluent readers. It helps you stop reading word by word.

1. With a partner, take turns reading aloud the underlined chunks of words.
2. Read aloud two times each.

> It's shaped   like a person.   It walks
> like a person.   It talks   like a person
> and makes choices   like a person.   It seems
> to be alive.   Is it   a real person?   No,
> it's a robot,   made in a factory
> —and covered with metal   instead of skin.

MULTI-LEVEL OPTIONS *Elements of Literature*

Newcomer Tell students that pictures in an article can support important ideas, too. Have them point to illustrations or elements of illustrations in the articles that support the important ideas in numbers 1–3.

Beginning Write the sentences for numbers 1–3 on the board. Underline the key words or draw simple sketches to reinforce their meaning. Then help students decide upon the correct answers as a class.

Intermediate Have students work in pairs. Ask each pair to find at least one more supporting fact for each important idea in the selections.

Advanced Have each student choose one of the three important ideas listed on p. 401. Ask them to use additional resources to find a supporting example *not* discussed in either reading selections.

Listen, Speak, Interact

Talk About Advantages and Disadvantages

An advantage is a good feature or benefit. A disadvantage is something that is negative and does not help.

1. Work with a group. Talk about the advantages and disadvantages of using robots. Use the following questions to help you brainstorm ideas.
   a. How can robots help us learn new things?
   b. What are some problems we can solve by using robots?
   c. What might happen if a robot broke down (stopped working)?
   d. Can using robots take jobs away from people?
2. Summarize your group's ideas and have one person present them to the class.

Elements of Literature

Analyze Text Evidence

Writers of informational texts often use examples to show how an important idea is true. Examples are **text evidence** because they support an important idea in the text.

Important Idea Robots do jobs that are unsafe for people.

Evidence That Supports an Important Idea Robots pour hot metal in factories.

Read the numbered sentences. Each one is an important idea. Choose the evidence—sentence **a** or sentence **b**—that best supports each important idea.

1. Robots are not real people.
   a. Some robots are covered with metal.
   b. Some robots are in movies.
2. Some robots move around.
   a. Some robots pick up tiny objects.
   b. Some robots roll on wheels.
3. Some robots go places where human beings cannot go.
   a. Some robots open doors for people.
   b. Some robots go to the planet Mars.

Activity Book p. 211   Student CD-ROM

Listen, Speak, Interact

Talk About Advantages and Disadvantages

1. **Formulate an opinion** After discussing advantages and disadvantages, have students come up with a statement expressing their opinion about robots. For example, *I think that the advantages of robots are greater than the disadvantages, but we need to be careful of how robots can have a bad effect on people's lives.*
2. **Newcomers** Work with these students to discuss the questions. Help them write their answers in the Reading Logs.

Answers
Examples: **2. a.** They can help explore space and the ocean. **b.** They can help us make jobs safer by doing jobs that are dangerous for humans. **c.** It would probably cause many problems and delays. A person would have to do what the robot did. **d.** Yes, they can.

Elements of Literature

Analyze Text Evidence

1. **Discuss the importance of evidence** *Ask: Why is it important to have evidence to support an idea? Is your position stronger if you support it with evidence?*
2. **Multi-level options** See MULTI-LEVEL OPTIONS on p. 400.

Answers
1. a 2. b 3. b

 **ASSESS**

In pairs, have students describe one advantage or disadvantage about using robots and support it with evidence.

 Content Connection
Social Studies

Have small groups work together. Assign each a device invented in the 1800s or 1900s, such as the automobile or electric light. Have group members answer the questions at the top of p. 401. Tell them to imagine they are students from the time their invention was first being used.

Learning Styles
Linguistic

Tell students that other types of supporting evidence include facts, statistics, and true-life stories (anecdotes). Have pairs work together. Ask each to select one of the important ideas at the bottom of p. 401. Tell them to use resources to find a fact, statistic, or anecdote that supports the idea.

Word Study

Learn Adverbs of Frequency

Review adverbs of frequency On the board, write: *never, rarely/seldom, sometimes, often, always.* Ask students questions about your class and have them answer using the adverbs. For example, *ask: Do I give you homework? Do I take attendance? Do I dismiss class early? Do we have tests? Do we work hard in class?*

Grammar Focus

Use Adverbs of Frequency

Use correct word order For additional practice, write scrambled sentences on the board for students to rewrite. Write:

1. *sleep/I/weekends/often/on/late*
2. *tired/Friday/I/afternoons/usually/on/am*

Answers

Examples: **1.** He sometimes visits his grandmother on weekends. **2.** Lon never lies. **3.** My room is always messy. **4.** I often watch that TV show.

ASSESS

Have students write sentences about themselves, using *never, sometimes, always.*

Word Study

Learn Adverbs of Frequency

Frequency is how often something happens. Some words to describe frequency are on the diagram.

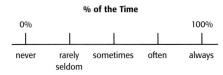

% of the Time

0% — never — rarely/seldom — sometimes — often — always — 100%

Copy the following sentences. Fill in each blank with an adverb of frequency that describes you.

1. I _____ eat carrots because they are good for me.
2. I'm _____ late for school because I _____ get up early.
3. I _____ help my little brother with his homework.

The Heinle Newbury House Dictionary

Activity Book p. 212

Student CD-ROM

Grammar Focus

Use Adverbs of Frequency

A **verb** is a word that tells the action of a sentence. **Adverbs of frequency** tell how often an action happens.

Robots <u>often do</u> jobs that are unsafe for people to do.

These charts show where to put adverbs of frequency in a sentence.

Rewrite these sentences and add an adverb of frequency.

1. He visits his grandmother on weekends.
2. Lon lies.
3. My room is messy.
4. I watch that TV show.

With the Verb *Be*			
Subject	Verb	Adverb	
She	is	never rarely sometimes often always	late.

With Other Verbs			
Subject	Adverb	Verb	
I	rarely	walk	to school.

Activity Book pp. 213–214

Student Handbook

Student CD-ROM

402   Unit 6   Connections

MULTI-LEVEL OPTIONS *From Reading to Writing*

Newcomer Have students work with two partners. Ask them to create three-panel persuasive brochures to share ideas about why people should use robots. Have each student draw one panel that shows an advantage of using robots. Provide time for groups to show their work to each other.

Beginning Help students create a language experience essay. After the essay is written, have students create collages or draw pictures showing the advantages of using robots. Display the essay. Hang the illustrations around it.

Intermediate Have students look at examples of persuasive pieces from newspapers or magazines. Discuss techniques the writers used to conclude their writing. Point out how they call readers to action. Remind students to conclude their persuasive essays with strong endings.

Advanced After first drafts are completed, have students work in pairs. Tell them to read their work aloud. Ask listeners to pretend to *dislike* the idea of using robots. Have the listener tell one thing in the essay he/she would argue with. Suggest that the writer add something to the essay to answer this argument.

From Reading to Writing

Write a Persuasive Essay

An essay is a piece of writing that is three to five paragraphs long. Essays can describe, tell a story, explain, or persuade.

Write a three-paragraph persuasive essay. Explain why people should use robots.

1. Paragraph 1: **Introduction**
   a. Tell what your essay is about.
   b. Write a sentence that tells why people should use robots. This is your **thesis statement.**

2. Paragraph 2: **Body**
   a. Write details that support your thesis statement. Use the advantages you talked about in Listen, Speak, Interact.
   b. Include examples.
3. Paragraph 3: **Conclusion**
   a. Restate your thesis.
4. Be convincing! You want readers to agree that people should use robots.

Activity Book   Student
p. 215   Handbook

Across Content Areas

SCIENCE

Read an FAQ Web Page

Internet sites often have **FAQ** pages. FAQ stands for Frequently Asked Questions. Usually an FAQ page is a list of questions. You click on the question to find its answer.

Read each numbered item below. Then find the question in the FAQs that you would click on to find the answer.

1. You want to know more about the word *robot*.
2. You are interested in the history of robots.
3. You want to know if robots are used in farming.

4. You are interested in how much people depend on robots.

FAQ's

Where does the word *robot* come from?

What do robots look like?

How are robots used?

When were the first robots built?

How many robots are there in the world?

How can I build a robot?

Activity Book
p. 216

Reteach and Reassess

Text Structure Show students a book or article about some type of modern technology, such as the Internet. Ask them to identify examples of each feature described on the top of p. 392.

Reading Strategy Have students paraphrase, through drawings or short paragraphs, what they learned in "High-Tech Helping Hands."

Elements of Literature Say: *An important idea from "High-Tech Helping Hands" was that disabled people help test*

devices being made for them. Ask students to find three supporting examples in the article.

Reassess Have students work in pairs. Ask each student to read aloud the essay he/she wrote. Then have the partner paraphrase one or two main ideas from the essay.

From Reading to Writing

Write a Persuasive Essay

1. **Compose an essay orally** Before students write, have them "tell" their essay to a partner. Explain that they will compose the essay orally. Have listeners ask questions to help writers make improvements.
2. **Peer edit** Have students edit each other's papers, checking that all of the items in the directions are included. Instruct them to check for correct capitalization and spelling.
3. **Multi-level options** See MULTI-LEVEL OPTIONS on p. 402.

Across Content Areas: Science

Read an FAQ Web Page

Relate to personal experience *Ask: Have you ever used an FAQ page on the Web? What information were you looking for? Sometimes when you buy a new device or machine, an FAQ page will be included. Have you ever gotten one?*

Answers
1. Where does the word *robot* come from? 2. When were the first robots built? 3. How are robots used? 4. How many robots are there in the world?

✓ ASSESS

Ask: What do you think robots will be used for 10 years from now?

Materials

Student Handbook
CNN Video: *Unit 6*
Teacher Resource Book: *Lesson Plan, p. 33;
Teacher Resources, pp. 35–64; Video Script,
pp. 171–172; Video Worksheet, p. 178;
School-Home Connection, pp. 154–160*
Teacher Resource CD-ROM
Assessment Program: *Unit 6 Test and End-of-
Book Exam, pp. 97–108; Teacher and
Student Resources, pp. 115–144*
Assessment CD-ROM
Transparencies
The Heinle Newbury House Dictionary/CD-ROM
Heinle Reading Library: *Moby Dick*
Web site: http://visions.heinle.com

Listening and Speaking Workshop

Give a Persuasive Speech

Step 1: Plan your speech.
Students can discuss reasons in small groups.
Suggest to students that they ask adults, such
as their parents, other teachers, or the principal,
for their opinions. They can also talk with any
friends who do wear uniforms to school.

Step 2: Write your speech.
Remind students that persuasion is stronger
when supported by facts or evidence. Have
students search the Internet for information on
this topic, using the key words *school uniforms*.

Listening and Speaking Workshop

Give a Persuasive Speech

Topic

Your school has decided to require
students to wear uniforms. Some
students think that this is a good idea.
Others do not. What is your opinion?
Present your opinion to the class. Use
the Internet to find facts, examples, or
quotations from experts to support
your position.

Step 1: Plan your speech.

1. Make a list of reasons for and
   against the topic.
2. Decide whether you are for or
   against the issue.

Arguments For	Arguments Against
Wearing school uniforms saves money.	Not wearing school uniforms teaches students to be individuals.

Step 2: Write your speech.

Introduction

1. Present the issue and your position.
2. Give a reason on the other side of
   the issue. Then explain why that
   reason is not a good one.
3. Explain that there are many good
   reasons to support your position.

Reasons and Supporting Evidence

1. Give three good reasons to support
   your position.
2. Use phrases like, "I am in favor of . . ."
   "I do not agree that . . ."
3. Support each of your reasons with
   examples or evidence.
4. Be careful not to exaggerate. You
   want to convince the listeners to
   believe you.

Conclusion

1. Tell what the issue means to you.
2. Urge your listeners to support you.

Step 3: Practice your speech.

1. Write a note card for each topic.
2. Use the Speaking Checklist.
3. Ask a partner to listen to you and
   give you feedback using the Active
   Listening Checklist.
4. Revise your speech based on your
   partner's feedback.

Step 4: Present your speech.

1. Speak clearly and loudly enough for
   everyone to hear you.
2. Use expression to show that you are
   convinced of your opinion.
3. If possible, record your speech on
   audio or video. You might also use
   presentation software. Present your
   speech to the class to support your
   position.

MULTI-LEVEL OPTIONS *Listening and Speaking Workshop*

Newcomer Tell those who like
the idea of uniforms to put plus
signs at the top of three pages.
Those who dislike the idea may
put minus signs at the tops of
three pages. Have students draw
their reasons for liking or disliking
the idea. Display the art under
"Pro" and "Con."

Beginning Meet with students
who are in favor of wearing
uniforms. Help them create an
illustrated list of reasons. Next,
meet with students who oppose
the idea and help them compile
an illustrated list of reasons for
their view. Provide time for both
groups to share their ideas with
the class.

Intermediate Ask students
if they have friends or family
members who go to schools that
require uniforms. Suggest that
they interview one of these
students and include his/her ideas
as supporting evidence.

Advanced Tell students that
an important part of planning
effective persuasive speeches is
to know what matters to their
audiences. Ask students to list
issues concerning uniforms that
would matter to students. (looks,
comfort, cost) Suggest that
students address some of these
issues in their speeches.

Speaking Checklist

Did you:

1. Have an interesting opening?

2. Support your reasons with facts and examples?

3. Tell listeners what the issue means to you?

4. Use vivid, specific words?

5. Look at the audience?

Active Listening Checklist

1. I liked _____ because _____ .

2. I want to know more about _____ .

3. I thought the opening was interesting. Yes / No

4. I understood the purpose of your speech. Yes / No

5. You used facts to support your opinion. Yes / No

Student Handbook

Viewing Workshop

View and Think

Compare Presentations of Technology

Science fiction movies often show worlds with new technology. Robots and computers are examples of technology.

1. Go to your library and borrow a video that shows a future world with technology. Watch the video and take notes about the technology that you see.

2. Watch television news for reports about how technology is helping people. Take notes.

3. What is the purpose of the video? To inform, entertain, or persuade? What is the purpose of the television news reports? What tells you this?

4. What did you like about the video and television news reports? What did you not like?

5. Compare how the video you watched and television news present information about technology. What ideas and points of view are presented? How do they influence you? How is the television news similar to the technology you saw in the video? How do the video and television news reports affect how you feel about technology?

Further Viewing

Watch the *Visions* CNN Video for Unit 6. Do the Video Worksheet.

CNN Video

Apply and Expand **405**

Step 3: Practice your speech.
Review with students the importance of a strong, clear speaking voice and good eye contact when presenting. Tell students to time their speeches and give them a suggested time of less than five minutes.

Step 4: Present your speech.
After students have listened to the speeches, have them analyze the persuasive techniques used. *Ask: What were some of the very persuasive reasons given? What techniques did the speakers use to persuade you?* Have them list techniques in small groups. *Ask: What effect did the speeches have on you? Did they cause you to change your opinion about school uniforms? Why or why not?*

 ASSESS

Have students write two sentences about how they have improved in their presentation skills.

Portfolio

Students may choose to record or videotape their speeches to place in their portfolios.

Viewing Workshop

View and Think

Teacher Resource Book: *Venn Diagram, p. 35*

1. **Locate resources** Assist students in locating videos to watch by contacting the school librarian. You may want to watch a little bit of a movie and a news report in class if students are unable to watch outside of class.

2. **Use a graphic organizer** Draw a Venn diagram on the board. Have volunteers fill in similarities and differences as the class discusses what they viewed.

Content Connection
Technology

Point out that not only were the presentations *about* technology, but technology was also used to communicate the information. Have students recall special effects that were seen and heard in both shows. Have them discuss how these special effects influenced the messages of the presentations.

Learning Styles
Kinesthetic

Ask: What kind of speaker is likely to be convincing? (confident, sincere) Engage students in discussing what kinds of facial expressions and body movements express confidence and honesty. (straight stance; strong, deliberate gestures; eye contact) Remind students to use these behaviors when they deliver their persuasive speeches.

Writer's Workshop

Write a Persuasive Letter to the Editor

Write a persuasive letter Read and discuss the prompt. If there is no school newspaper, suggest that students write the letter to the principal or local school committee.

Step 1: Brainstorm.
Point out to students that computers are expensive, so some reasons could suggest ways that the computers could save the school money. Schools are also concerned with student performance, so better school performance could be another reason.

Step 2: Arrange your ideas in logical order.
Have a volunteer write four of their reasons on the board. Model going through the list to determine the most logical order.

Step 3: Write a draft.
Students may write the letters collaboratively. If they do, after writing the draft, everyone in the group should make his/her own copy.

Writer's Workshop

Write a Persuasive Letter to the Editor

Prompt

Some schools provide a laptop computer (a small computer that you can carry) to every class. Do you think this is a good idea? Work with a partner to write a letter to the editor of your school or local newspaper. In your letter, state your position and try to persuade your readers that you are right.

Step 1: Brainstorm.
1. Make a list of all the reasons for or against this issue.
2. Decide what your position is on this issue.
3. Write your position in one or two lines.
4. Think of reasons to support your position. Write them in a chart like this.

Arguments For	Arguments Against
Every student would have access to the Internet.	It's very expensive to buy a computer for every student.

Step 2: Arrange your ideas in logical order.
1. What is your most important idea?
2. What is the least important idea?
3. Choose the ideas you want to include and number them in importance.

Step 3: Write a draft.
1. If possible write your draft on a computer.
2. Follow this model.

```
                              (Your Street)
                         (Your City, State)
                                    (Date)
(Newspaper Name)
(Newspaper Address)
To the Editor:
  [State the issue and why you
think it is important.]
    [State your opinion.]

  [Give at least three reasons
to support your opinion.]


  [Summarize your position and
ask the readers to support your
position. Ask them to take
action.]
  Sincerely,

[Your name]
```

MULTI-LEVEL OPTIONS *Writer's Workshop*

Newcomer Work with the class to create a language experience essay. Determine whether more students are for or against notebook computers. Have students choose a symbol, such as thumbs up or down, to show their position. Divide the page into parts. Have students draw reasons for their position in each part.

Beginning Have each student draw a notebook computer in a circle at the top of a piece of paper if they like the idea of students having computers. If they do not think this is a good idea, they can draw the same symbol with a slash through it. Help students list words and phrases to explain their positions.

Intermediate Before students begin to write, ask pairs to read a letter to the editor from a local newspaper. Have the pair discuss what was and was not convincing about the way the writer communicated. Ask students to keep in mind what they learned from their discussions as they draft their letters.

Advanced *Say: One of the most important parts of a persuasive essay is the introduction. The purpose of the introduction is not only to state a position, but also to get the audience to care about the issue so they will want to read your ideas. Brainstorm ways to start your essay and then choose the one that you think is most likely to get your readers interested.*

Step 4: Revise and edit.

1. Combine some of your sentences with conjunctions like *and, but, because, if,* or *when.*
2. Blend your paragraphs using transition words.
3. Read your letter carefully to find and correct typing or spelling errors. Use the spell check and grammar check on the computer to help you. Also use software, such as an online dictionary or thesaurus, to check spellings and definitions.
4. Check carefully for correct capitalization, punctuation, and use of apostrophes.
5. Use resources such as your Student Handbook.
6. Make sure your ideas are clear.
   a. Elaborate (explain) any difficult words or phrases.
   b. Delete (remove) any text that does not make sense or that is repeated.
   c. Add text to clarify.
   d. Rearrange sentences so that your ideas follow a logical order.
7. Make a second draft. Read it with your partner. Give each other feedback.

Step 5: Publish.

1. Prepare a final draft of your letter.
2. Create a class collection of the persuasive letters. Review them for their strengths and weaknesses.
3. Choose several letters to e-mail to the editor of your school or local newspaper. Set your goals as a writer based on your writing and the writing of your classmates.

The Heinle Newbury House Dictionary   Student Handbook

UNIT 6
Apply and Expand

Step 4: Revise and edit.
Have students dictate some sentences that could be combined with *because, if,* and *when.* Help make any corrections.

Step 5: Publish.
Display the letters for others to read and discuss. Ask students to select a few letters that would be the most persuasive to send to a local newspaper.

 ASSESS

Have students choose the letter they thought was the best and list three of its strongest features.

Portfolio

Students may choose to include their writing in their portfolios.

Content Connection
Math

Suggest that students research facts and figures related to notebook computers. Ask them to look up costs of these in ads. Tell students the average cost of school-related items, such as textbooks and field trips. Have them do some calculations, such as how many textbooks a school could buy for the cost of a computer. Ask students to include any relevant statistics in their letters.

Learning Styles
Visual

Tell students that another way to persuade people of their opinions is through political cartoons. Show a few examples from the editorial section of a local newspaper. Point out that these cartoons use exaggeration to get across their messages. Ask each student to create a political cartoon to reflect the message of his/her letter to the editor.

UNIT 6
Apply and Expand

Projects

Project 1: Tell a Story About Your Culture

1. **Select a person to interview** *Ask: Who in your family or community has a talent for telling an interesting and entertaining story?* Suggest to students that good storytellers would be good people to interview.
2. **Identify features of good storytelling** Model a brief family story of your own in a very matter-of-fact style. Then retell the story using intonation, pauses, and body language to give more drama to the story. Remind students to tell a story with a sense of drama.

Project 2: Make an Advertisement of a Robot

1. **Use realia as examples** Bring in some advertisements from newspapers or magazines to discuss features of effective ads. Point out that the visual element is very important and that the text of the advertisement is often very brief.
2. **Analyze advertisements** Display ads. Discuss which are the most effective and why.

Portfolio

Students may choose to include their projects in their portfolios.

Projects

These projects will help you learn more about making connections. You can make connections to the past by learning a story about your culture. You can make connections to the future by making a new robot.

Project 1: Tell a Story About Your Culture

Many families tell stories about something that happened in their culture. For this project, you will tell a story about your culture to a small group.

1. Think of an older family or community member you could interview.
2. Plan how you will interview this person. You may interview on the phone, in person, through the mail, or through e-mail.
3. Ask this person to share a story about something important that happened in the past. He or she may also share something funny that happened.
4. Ask the person some questions. You may want to ask:
   a. Who was with you?
   b. What happened?
   c. When did this event happen?
   d. Where did this event happen?
   e. Why was this event important?

You may think of more questions as you get information. Revise your questions as needed.

5. Take notes as the person tells the story. You may also want to record him or her speaking on audio or video. This will help you remember the story.
6. Work with a small group. Exchange stories. Tell the group the person's story. Then listen as your classmates share their stories.

Project 2: Make an Advertisement of a Robot

Work with a small group to design a new robot. Make an advertisement to tell about your robot. An advertisement is a notice or sign that tells about a product.

1. In a small group, brainstorm ideas.
2. Think about a task that many people need help with. Here are some examples: Students need help carrying books to school. People need help doing chores.
3. Think about how a robot could help people do this task. Review the ideas in Chapter 4 to help you.
4. Use poster board to make an advertisement for the robot.
   a. Give your robot a name. Draw the robot on a piece of poster board.
   b. Write a few exciting phrases to tell how the robot helps people.
   c. Use capitalization and punctuation to clarify and enhance your message.
   d. Be persuasive. You are making the advertisement so that people will want to buy the robot.
   e. Hang your poster in the class.

MULTI-LEVEL OPTIONS *Projects*

Newcomer Have students base their stories on family photos. Ask each to show a picture, identify the people, and tell the setting. The student can act out what was happening before, during, and after the photo was taken.

Beginning Tell students to ask their interview subjects to share items that are important to them, such as a doll from their childhood or a stone from a special place. Have students make models or pictures of the items. Ask them to show their artifacts, tell who owns the originals, and explain why they are important.

Intermediate Have students review "Esperanza Rising" (p. 357). Point out the Spanish sentence at the top of the page. *Say: Sometimes, writers include a word or a sentence in another language to make the story seem real.* Suggest that they include a few words from another language in their story.

Advanced Invite students to tell their stories in a cultural style that seems most comfortable to them. To find out about storytelling traditions, have students talk to family members or do some research.

Further Reading

The books listed below discuss the theme of connections. Choose one or more of them. Write your thoughts and feelings about what you read in your Reading Log. Take notes about your answers to these questions:

1. How is the theme of connections found in the books you read?
2. Make notes of something interesting you learned from what you read.

Esperanza Rising
by Pam Muñoz Ryan, Scholastic, Inc., 2002. Esperanza and her mother are forced to move from Mexico to Southern California. This is the true story of the author's grandmother, Esperanza Ortega.

Honus and Me
by Dan Gutman, Camelot, 1998. Joe finds a very valuable baseball card of Honus Wagner. Joe discovers that the baseball card allows him to travel through time. He travels back to 1909. He meets Honus Wagner and plays in the World Series.

Do You Remember the Color Blue?: And Other Questions Kids Ask About Blindness
by Sally Hobart Alexander, Puffin, 2002. The author of this book lost her sight at the age of 26. She describes how she adjusted to her loss of vision. She also describes what it is like to be blind.

History of Automobiles
by David Corbett, Barron's Educational Series, Inc., 1999. Automobiles play a huge role in today's world. This book follows the history of the automobile.

How to Build a Robot
by Clive Gifford, Franklin Watts, 2001. This book explains the process of making a robot that can walk and talk. It also explains the history of robots.

Phineas Gage
by John Fleischman, Houghton Mifflin, 2002. In 1848, Phineas Gage had a 13-pound iron rod shot through his head. He survived, but his personality changed. This change led scientists to study how brain damage affects people.

Tutankhamen's Gift
by Robert Sabuda, Scott Foresman, 1997. This book is a biography of the Egyptian pharaoh Tutankhamen. Tutankhamen became ruler at the age of ten.

Companion Web site

Reading Log

Heinle Reading Library Moby Dick

Further Reading

1. **Read summaries to select books** Read or have volunteers read the book summaries. Students may be intrigued with the interesting direction of the story "Honus and Me." Have students identify the book that they would like to read.
2. **Respond to literature** After reading a book, have students give an oral report or write a short book review.

Assessment Program: *Unit 6 Test, pp. 97–102;* End-of-Book Exam, *pp. 103–108*

Heinle Reading Library

Moby Dick by Herman Melville
In a specially adapted version by Shirley Bogart

"Call me Ishmael." So begins one of the greatest adventures ever written. Ishmael, a young school teacher who signs on board a whaling schooner, wants a change from his usual life. But life aboard the *Pequod* is more than a search for whales—it is a lifelong quest for revenge by the unbalanced Captain Ahab, who has vowed to destroy the great white whale who left him lame. But when these giants meet again, who will be the victor—or the victim?

Visions Companion Site

http://visions.heinle.com
For additional student activities and teacher resources, see the Visions Companion Web site.

Skills Index

■ Grammar, Usage, and Mechanics

■ Listening and Speaking

compare communication, 22,
129, 225, 348
deductive organization, 347
direct speech, 278
personification, 108, 115, 117
plot, 16, 56, 67, 108, 120, 202,
308, 354, 364
prologue, 292, 366
purpose of text
describe, 37
entertain, 23, 37, 101, 113,
139, 185, 397, 399
explain, 101, 113
express, 23, 139
influence/persuade, 23, 101,
139, 185, 265, 397, 399,
403, 404–405
teach/inform, 23, 37, 113, 185,
217, 325, 346, 392, 397,
399, 403
simile, 295

Literary Response
compare and contrast ideas,
themes, issues, 2, 4, 6, 8, 10,
11, 15, 22, 38, 44, 46–49,
50, 64, 88, 92, 108, 120,
128, 140, 149, 172, 202,
225, 249, 268, 269–275, 298,
308, 322, 340, 343, 345,
348, 378, 387, 400, 401
connect ideas, themes, issues, 15,
27, 43, 50, 54, 55, 77, 88,
118, 119, 128, 129, 132,
133, 149, 152, 153, 163,
189, 202, 207, 230, 239,
243, 249, 295, 298, 299,
300, 309, 326, 327, 345,
349, 353, 358, 379, 387,
389, 400, 409
interpret
through discussion, 2, 15, 89,
128, 129, 140, 145, 152,
173, 187, 219, 239, 249,
252, 263, 266, 277, 298,
309, 401
through enactment, 11, 23, 72,
89, 103, 144, 173, 178,
187, 226, 263
through journal writing, 11,
65, 73, 89, 94, 103, 115,
129, 134, 149, 159, 187,
227, 239, 277, 285, 290,
295, 309, 341, 349, 354,
380, 409
through literature review, 175,
222–223, 224–225
through media, 10, 145, 346
make connections, 3, 15, 27, 43,
50, 55, 77, 88, 118, 119,
128, 129, 133, 149, 152,
153, 163, 189, 202, 207,

239, 243, 251, 267, 289,
313, 326, 327, 349, 353,
358, 363, 379, 389, 400, 409
offer observations, 10, 22, 73, 88,
102, 103, 108, 114, 115,
128, 129, 140, 149
raise questions, 9, 37, 38, 64,
102, 141, 232, 295, 307,
314, 322, 323, 341, 346, 387
react, 172
speculate, 386
support responses
own experiences, 2, 38, 186,
190, 218, 248, 374
relevant aspects of text, 63,
172, 340, 343, 358, 374,
401

Literary Terms
abbreviations, 279
act, 11, 103
author, 23
body, 224, 403
characters, 4, 16, 56, 64, 68, 115,
178, 192, 203, 239, 244,
300, 354
main, 16, 38, 65, 118, 232, 239
minor, 16, 65, 239
characterization, 65, 67
changes, 67, 354, 358, 359, 361
conflict, 221, 226, 227, 359,
364, 374
motivation, 103, 186, 203, 354,
359
personification, 108, 115, 117
point of view, 11, 13, 44, 53,
120, 143, 203, 205, 221,
249, 251, 254, 268, 290,
297, 359, 364, 405
relationship, 64, 359
traits, 102, 202, 203, 248, 276,
308, 354, 359
conclusion, 67, 224, 403, 404
descriptive language, 28, 290,
297
dialogue, 65, 70, 178, 226, 263
direct address, 164, 278, 323
directions, 51, 154, 161
direct speech, 278
documentary, 223
elements of literature, 11
epilogue, 63
excerpt, 54, 118, 132, 162, 190,
252, 288, 312, 326, 352,
362, 378, 390
fiction, 56, 67, 120, 300, 354
figurative language, 290, 295,
297, 377
first-person point of view, 11, 13,
44, 53, 205, 221, 249, 254,
268, 290, 297, 364
free verse, 89

headings, 147, 148, 208, 219
historical fiction, 56
imagery, 28, 76, 78, 268, 277,
279, 295
introduction, 94, 224, 403, 404
lyrics, 154, 161
mood, 10, 128, 375
moral, 108
narrative fiction, 67, 120
narrator, 120, 178, 249, 364
novel, 56
personification, 108, 115, 117
perspective, 63, 262, 276
plot, 16, 56, 67, 108, 120, 202,
308, 354, 364
point of view, 11, 13, 44, 53, 120,
143, 203, 205, 221, 249,
251, 254, 268, 290, 297,
359, 364, 405
problem resolution, 67, 68, 120,
187, 192, 205, 358
prologue, 292, 366
quotations, 64, 65, 67, 70, 263,
278, 280, 323
refrain, 154
repetition, 78, 159, 161, 254, 263
reported speech, 278
rhyme, 28, 39, 89
rhythm, 28
scene, 187
science fiction, 300
setting, 16, 55, 56, 67, 68, 300,
309, 311, 361
simile, 295
stanza, 4, 28, 39, 78, 89, 91, 268,
277, 278, 279
style, 263, 323, 375
text evidence, 300, 340, 401
theme, 50, 129, 149, 189, 202,
387, 409
thesis statement, 221, 403
third-person point of view, 143,
249, 251
tone, 39, 64, 173, 265, 344, 375
topic, 68, 144, 208, 222, 280, 344
verse, 89, 154, 161

Purposes
adjust purpose, 65, 203, 204,
250, 263, 277, 281
appreciate writer's craft, 293
complete forms, 40, 159, 187,
239, 326
entertain, 23, 37, 101, 113, 139,
185, 397, 399
establish purpose, 9, 23, 37, 101,
113, 139, 140, 171, 185,
217, 259, 293, 307, 357,
397, 399
explain, 101, 113
inform, 23, 37, 113, 185, 217,
325, 346, 392, 397, 399, 403

Word Identification

adjectives, 296, 342, 360

context, 77, 88, 107, 191, 207, 253, 289, 353, 389

derivations, 12

dictionary, 27, 40, 41, 55, 70, 93, 104, 116, 119, 130, 142, 147, 160, 163, 177, 191, 220, 221, 225, 231, 240, 264, 267, 278, 283, 289, 310, 313, 324, 327, 342, 347, 353, 377, 379, 388, 407

glossary, 267, 327

language structure, 12, 24

letter-sound correspondences, 342, 379

meanings, 12, 24, 40, 43, 52, 70, 77, 78, 93, 104, 116, 119, 130, 142, 177, 220, 221, 231, 250, 253, 267, 278, 289, 296, 299, 310, 311, 313, 324, 325, 327, 353, 360, 379, 388, 389, 391

prefixes, 104, 204, 250

pronunciation, 3, 39, 220, 231, 289, 313, 327, 342, 379, 388

root words, 52, 90, 104, 204, 240, 264, 278, 342, 388

    Greek, 90, 220, 324

    Latin, 221, 310

suffixes, 40, 52, 240, 264, 278, 388

Writing

Connections

authors

    challenges, 171

    feelings/perspective, 7, 21, 38, 63, 262, 275, 276, 290, 292–293, 294, 308, 321, 373

    purpose, 9, 10, 23, 37, 101, 113, 139, 140, 171, 185, 217, 259, 293, 307, 345, 357, 397, 399

    strategies used, 173, 314, 357, 359

collaboration with other writers, 117, 118, 152, 176, 252, 298, 325, 362, 390, 406

correspondence

    e-mail, 348, 407, 408

    mail, 161, 225, 348, 408

Forms

advertisement, 279, 408

biography, 251, 282–283, 389

editorial, 406–407

fable, 117

fiction, 67, 311, 361

forms, 205, 297, 325

historical fiction, 67

informational text, 143, 221, 325, 343

instructions, 51, 325

interview, 144, 284, 408

job application form, 297

legend, 241

letter, 53, 161, 224–225, 348, 406–407

letter to the editor, 406–407

literature review, 175, 222–223, 224–225

lyrics, 161

narrative, 13, 25, 41, 53, 67, 70, 105, 131, 297

narrative fiction, 67, 131

news report/story, 105, 148, 284, 343

opinion, 175, 280

order form, 205

paragraph, 41, 105, 175, 282, 311, 325, 377, 389

personal narrative, 13, 41, 53, 70, 105, 297

persuasive

    essay, 403

    letter to the editor, 406–407

    poster, 408

    speech, 265, 404

poem, 28, 39, 91, 279

poster, 72, 148, 408

presentation, 280–281, 347, 348, 404

questions, 144, 284, 344, 348, 408

radio program, 226

report, 72, 143, 148, 222–223, 284, 343, 346–347

research paper, 346–347

review, 175, 222–223, 224–225

rules, 146

science fiction, 311

song, 161, 223

speech, 265, 348, 404

story, 25, 105, 311, 343

storyboard, 226

summary, 148, 189, 325, 345, 348

Inquiry and Research

cluster map, 146

concept map/web, 3, 54, 76, 91, 92, 146, 230, 252, 266, 279, 295, 390

evaluation, 146, 308, 348

learning log, 11, 65, 103, 115, 129, 134, 149, 159, 187, 227, 239, 277, 285, 290, 295, 309, 341, 349, 354, 380, 409

on-line searches, 221, 282, 345, 346

organize ideas, 3, 54, 76, 91, 92,

105, 117, 146, 148, 161, 164, 230, 241, 251, 252, 266, 280, 282, 295, 325, 328, 344, 345, 346, 348, 352, 361, 390, 406

outline, 134, 136–139, 282, 283, 343, 346–347

periodicals, 148, 348

presentations, 280–281, 323, 346–347, 348, 390, 404

prior knowledge, 2, 14, 26, 42, 54, 76, 92, 102, 106, 118, 132, 152, 162, 176, 190, 206, 230, 242, 252, 266, 279, 288, 298, 312, 326, 352, 362, 378, 390

questions, 7, 9, 41, 94, 284, 293, 307, 321, 322, 323, 341, 345, 346, 348, 377, 385, 389, 408

scientific questions, 322, 323, 341, 348

sources, citation of, 221, 346, 347

summarize ideas, 146, 148, 189, 203, 224, 325, 326, 328, 330, 332–333, 335–337, 339, 341, 345, 348

take notes, 39, 93, 141, 222, 280, 282, 341, 344, 345, 348, 404, 408

technology presentations, 68, 147, 265, 280, 343, 344, 404

timelines, 164, 244, 265, 282

Literary Devices

descriptive language, 28, 290, 297

figurative language, 290, 295, 297, 377

first person point of view, 11, 13, 44, 53, 205, 221, 249, 254, 268, 290, 297, 364

point of view, 13, 290, 359, 364

Purpose

appropriate form, 12, 52, 130, 204, 324, 325, 342

appropriate literary devices, 11, 13, 28, 44, 53, 205, 221, 249, 254, 268, 290, 295, 297, 359, 364, 377

audience and purpose, 70, 147

    appropriate style, 323, 375, 404

    appropriate voice, 344, 345, 404

ideas, 3, 54, 76, 91, 92, 117, 118, 146, 230, 252, 266, 282, 295, 324, 328, 344, 345, 346–347, 390, 406

precise wording, 405

purposes

    compare, 297, 343, 344, 345, 378

develop, 40, 239
discover, 323, 346
entertain, 23, 37, 101, 113,
139, 185, 397, 399
explain, 101, 113
express, 23, 39, 70, 139
influence/persuade, 23, 101,
139, 185, 265, 392, 397,
399, 403, 404–405,
406–407, 408
inform, 23, 37, 113, 185, 217,
325, 344, 345, 346, 397,
399, 403
problem solve, 67, 68, 120,
187, 205
record, 91, 251, 284, 294, 345
reflect on ideas, 2, 41, 54, 76,
91, 92, 146, 230, 252, 266,
282, 295, 328, 344, 345,
346–347, 390
transitions, 53, 67, 70, 164, 225,
241, 282, 389, 407

Writing Process
analyze writing, 22, 40, 71, 309
develop drafts, 13, 25, 41, 53, 67,
70, 91, 105, 117, 131, 143,
144, 146–147, 148, 161, 175,
189, 205, 221, 222, 224,
241, 251, 265, 279, 282–283,
297, 311, 323, 325, 343,
346–347, 361, 377, 389, 392,
403, 404, 406–407
edit drafts, 71, 117, 147, 148,
225, 283, 325, 347, 407
evaluate writing, 347
criteria, 347
others' writing, 71, 147, 225,
283, 344, 347, 407
own writing, 71, 147, 225, 283,
344, 347, 387, 407
prewriting strategies
brainstorming, 72, 91, 144,
222, 226, 252, 266, 295,
311, 325, 344, 346, 406,
408
graphic organizers, 40, 117,
146, 164, 295, 344, 406
logs, 11, 65, 89, 94, 103, 115,
129, 134, 149, 159, 187,
227, 239, 277, 285, 290,
295, 309, 341, 349, 354,
380, 409
notes, 39, 105, 222, 280, 282,
344, 345, 348, 361, 404,
408
paraphrase, 346
proofread, 71, 117, 147, 225,
283, 347, 407
publish, 71, 117, 147, 225, 283,
343, 347, 407

reference materials, use of, 24,
70, 72, 116, 119, 142, 146,
147, 148, 160, 191, 221,
224, 225, 282, 283, 313,
342, 346, 347, 377, 379, 407
resource materials, use of, 40,
41, 72, 146, 148, 251, 282,
345, 348, 404, 407
review collection of written
works, 71, 225, 407
revise drafts, 70, 71, 105, 117,
144, 147, 148, 161, 205,
224–225, 283, 297, 323, 325,
347, 392, 404, 407, 408
technology, use of, 68, 71, 144,
146, 147, 205, 265, 280,
282, 283, 297, 343, 346,
347, 387, 404, 407
text features
biography, 244, 281, 380
boldface, 205, 219
bullets, 205
essay, 403
fable, 108, 115, 117
fiction, 120, 300, 354, 361, 364
folktale, 16
font, 205, 225
informational text, 134, 143,
208, 219, 221, 314, 325,
328, 343, 392, 401
interview, 94
italics, 133, 205
legend, 232
literature review, 224
narrative, 4, 25, 41, 68, 70,
105, 108, 120, 192, 290
narrative fiction, 67, 120, 131
novel, 56
personal narrative, 4, 44, 53,
70, 105, 192, 290
persuasive essay, 403
persuasive letter to the editor,
406–407
persuasive speech, 404
poem, 4, 28, 39, 78, 268
research report, 346–347
science fiction, 300
sequence of events, 11, 322
song, 154, 159
speech, 254, 348, 404
story, 68, 361

▪ Viewing and Representing

Analysis
interpret and evaluate meaning,
1, 10, 13, 23, 69, 71, 75,
114, 145, 151, 187, 223,

229, 281, 287, 289, 340,
345, 346, 348, 351, 387, 405
media
compare and contrast, 10, 69,
145, 223, 281, 340, 345,
405
effect, 23, 158
electronic media, 69, 145, 223,
281, 345, 405
to entertain, 223, 405
to influence/persuade, 223,
341, 405
to inform, 223, 345, 405
print media, 345, 348
purpose, 223, 405
technology presentations, 68,
265, 280, 281, 404, 405
video, 69, 145, 223, 281, 344,
345, 387, 405
visual media, 1, 8–9, 13, 29–37,
43, 54, 68, 69, 75, 114,
141, 145, 151, 223, 229,
281, 287, 308, 311, 328,
340, 341, 344, 345, 346,
347, 348, 351, 387, 392,
405
point of view, 405
visuals, 1, 8–9, 13, 29–37, 43, 54,
68, 69, 75, 114, 141, 151,
229, 281, 287, 308, 311,
328, 340, 341, 344, 345,
346, 347, 348, 351, 392

Interpretation
choice of style, elements, media,
346
important events and ideas, 68,
69, 281, 290, 295, 328, 340,
345, 351, 405
media to compare ideas, 1, 10,
69, 145, 223, 281, 340, 345,
405
point of view, 405

Production
assess message, 23, 344
audio recording, 144, 344, 387,
404, 408
media, 344
mural, 105
technology, 68, 144, 147, 265,
280, 283, 387
video, 23, 280, 344, 387, 404, 408
visuals, 2, 11, 13, 41, 54, 68, 69,
71, 72, 91, 105, 117, 143,
147, 230, 265, 277, 280,
283, 297, 344, 345, 347,
348, 408

Credits

Credits **419**

Pp. 381–385, THE BOY KING. Reprinted by permission of SPIDER magazine, December 2000, Vol. 7, No. 12 © 2000 by Andrea Ross. Audio rights: From "The Boy King" from SPIDER magazine, December 2000, Vol.7, No. 12. Copyright © 2000 by Andrea Ross. Used by permission of the author.

Pp. 394–397, IT COULD STILL BE A ROBOT. From *It Could Still Be a Robot* by Allan Fowler. Copyright © 1997 by Children's Press®, a division of Grolier Publishing Co., Inc. Reprinted by permission.

Pp. 398–399, HIGH-TECH HELPING HANDS, by Jane McGoldrick. "High-Tech Helping Hands" from *National Geographic World,* March 1996. Copyright © 1996 by National Geographic Society. Reprinted by permission.

Illustrators

Mark Andresen: p. 356 (© Mark Andresen/Scott Hull Associates); **Don Baker:** pp. 316–320 (© Don Baker/Kolea Baker); **Kristin Barr:** p. 7 (© Kristin Barr/Irmeli Holmberg); **Clem Bedwell:** pp. 110–112 (© Clem Bedwell/Wilson-Zumbo Illustration Group); **Bob Dombrowski:** pp. 193–200 (© Bob Dombrowski/Artworks Illustration); **Andrea Eberbach:** pp. 80–86 (© Andrea Eberbach/Scott Hull Associates); **George Hamblin:** pp. 301–306 (© George Hamblin/Wilkinson Studios, LLC); **Ken Joudrey:** pp. 270–272 (© Ken Joudrey/Munro Campagna); **John Kastner:** pp. 30–37 (© John Kastner/The Beranbaum Group); **William Low:** pp. 121–126 (© William Low/Morgan Gaynin Inc.); **Ron Mahoney:** pp. 366–372 (© Ron Mahoney/Wilkinson Studios, LLC); **Mapping Specialists, Ltd.:** pp. 3, 41, 43, 55, 77, 93, 107, 119, 133, 163, 175, 191, 241, 243, 253, 292, 379; **Kay McCabe:** p. 247 (© Kay McCabe/The Beranbaum Group); **Precision Graphics:** pp. 131, 311, 327, 331, 332, 334; **Elizabeth Rosen:** p. 274 (© Elizabeth Rosen/Morgan Gaynin Inc.); **Elizabeth Sayles:** pp. 57–62 (© Elizabeth Sayles/Cornell & McCarthy, LLC); **Winson Trang:** pp. 180–184 (© Winson Trang/Square Moon); **Paula Wendland:** pp. 18–20 (© Paula Wendland/Wilkinson Studios, LLC); **Kris Wiltse:** pp. 234–237 (© Kris Wiltse/Morgan Gaynin Inc.); **Jean Wisenbaugh:** pp. 49, 53 (© Jean Wisenbaugh/Lindgren & Smith)

Author Photos

p. 7 (Ralph Fletcher); p. 9 (Carmen Lomas Garza); p. 21 (Andrew Matthews); p. 37 (Miriam Nerlove); p. 87 (Madeleine Dunphy); p. 113 (Lynette Dyer Vuong); p. 127 (Paul Fleischman); p. 139 (Mary Pope and Will Osborne, © Paul Coughlin); p. 171 (Zlata Filipovic, © Alexandra Boulat/SIPA Press); p. 185 (Suzanne Barchers); p. 201 (Edite Cunhã); p. 261 (Nelson Mandela, © Reuters NewMedia Inc./CORBIS); p. 273 (Luis Omar Salinas, © Arte Publico Press Photo Archives); p. 275 (Liz Ann Báez Aguilar); p. 293 (Sylvia Earle, © Macduff Everton/CORBIS); p. 307 (Isaac Asimov, © Douglas Kirkland/Corbis); p. 321 (Stephen Kramer, © Chris Kramer); p. 357 (Pam Muñoz Ryan); p. 373 (Dan Gutman); p. 385 (Andrea Ross); p. 399 (Jane McGoldrick)

Photos

Art Resource: (All © Art Resource) p. i-1 (*Children asking for 'posada' (La procesion),* Diego Rivera, oil on canvas, © Schalkwijk/Art Resource, NY); p. 329 (© The Museum of Modern Art/Licensed by SCALA/Art Resource, NY); p. 383 (© Scala/Art Resource, NY)

Bridgeman Art Library: p. 355 (*Vineyard, Provence,* by Eric Hains, oil on canvas © Bridgeman Art Library)

Cape Cod Times: p. 399 (© Vincent DeWitt/Cape Cod Times)

CORBIS: (All © Corbis) p. 5 (© Paul Barton/CORBIS); p. 29 (© Paul Barton/CORBIS); pp. 45 & 46 (© Richard T. Nowitz/CORBIS); p. 47 (© Vanni Archive/CORBIS); p. 48 (© Jonathan Blair/CORBIS); p. 63 (© David Samuel Robbins/CORBIS); pp. 74–75 (*Tiger in a Tropical Storm (Surprise!)* by Henri Rousseau © National Gallery Collection; By kind permission of the Trustees of the National Gallery, London/CORBIS); p. 79 (© Philadelphia Museum of Art/CORBIS); p. 95 (© Lucidio Studio Inc./CORBIS); p. 96 (© Alan Schein Photography/CORBIS); p. 98 (© John Henley/CORBIS); p. 99 (© Dean Conger/CORBIS); p. 100 (© John-Marshall Mantel/CORBIS); p. 109 (© Tim Davis/CORBIS); p. 136 (© Michael & Patricia Fogden/CORBIS); p. 137 (© Kevin Schafer/CORBIS); p. 138 (© Australian Picture Library/CORBIS); pp. 150–151 (© Flip Schulke/CORBIS); p. 155 (© James Marshall/CORBIS); p. 179 (© Christie's Images/CORBIS); p. 206 (© Tom & Dee Ann McCarthy/CORBIS); p. 213 (© Michael Keller/CORBIS); pp. 228–229 (© Philadelphia Museum of Art/CORBIS); p. 233 (© Dallas and John Heaton/CORBIS); p. 245 (© Bettmann/CORBIS); p. 246 (© Bettmann/CORBIS); p. 251 (© David Butow/CORBIS SABA); p. 255 (© David Turnley/CORBIS); p. 256 (© Jonathan Blair/CORBIS); p. 257 (© Charles O'Rear/CORBIS); p. 258 (© Peter Turnley/CORBIS); p. 260 (© David Turnley/CORBIS); p. 261 (© Reuters NewMedia Inc./CORBIS); p. 269 (© Paul Barton/CORBIS); pp. 286–287 (*Drawing of a Winged Shuttle Craft* © Bettmann/CORBIS); p. 288 (© Amos Nachoum/CORBIS); p. 289 (© Brandon D. Cole/CORBIS); p. 291 (© Amos Nachoum/CORBIS); p. 330 (© 1996 CORBIS; Original image courtesy of NASA/CORBIS); p. 333 (© CORBIS); p. 335 (© NASA/Roger Ressmeyer/CORBIS); p. 337 (© Stocktrek/CORBIS); p. 338 (© AFP/CORBIS); pp. 350–351 (© Christie's Images/CORBIS); p. 353 (© Bernardo Bucci/CORBIS); p. 365 (© Kit Kittle/CORBIS); p. 382 (© Sandro Vannini/CORBIS); p. 384 (© Roger Wood/CORBIS); p. 395 (© Reuters New Media Inc./CORBIS)

Getty Images: (All © Getty Images) p. 135 (© Joel Sartore/Getty Images); p. 209 (© SW Productions/Getty Images); p. 210 (© Jodi Cobb/National Geographic/Getty Images); p. 336 (© Jim Ballard/Getty Images); p. 381 (© Getty Images); p. 393 (© Zac Macaulay/Getty Images); p. 394 (Craig van der Lende/Getty Images)

Index Stock Imagery: (All © Index Stock Imagery) p. 14 (© 2002 Indexstock.com); p. 17 (© 2002 Indexstock.com); p. 396 (© 2002 Indexstock.com)

Magnum Photos: p. 170 (© Paul Lowe/Magnum Photos)

Photo Edit: (All © Photo Edit) p. 211 (© Jeff Greenberg/Photo Edit); p. 212 (© Michael Newman/Photo Edit); p. 214 (© Michelle D. Bridwell/Photo Edit); p. 216 (© Michael Newman/Photo Edit); p. 315 (© David Young-Wolff/Photo Edit)

NASA: p. 339 (© NASA/Spacepix.net)

SIPA Press: p. 165 (© Alexandra Boulat/SIPA Press); p. 166 (© Alexandra Boulat/SIPA Press); p. 167 (© Alexandra Boulat/SIPA Press); p. 168 (© Alexandra Boulat/SIPA Press); p. 171 (© Alexandra Boulat/SIPA Press)

Teacher Edition Index

Author and Reading Selection Index

Skills Index

■ Grammar, Usage, and Mechanics

■ Listening and Speaking

Teacher Edition Index

social studies, 3, 6, 15, 27, 41, 43, 55, 77, 93, 107, 119, 143, 153, 163, 175, 177, 191, 207, 231, 241, 243, 253, 265, 267, 279, 299, 313, 361, 363, 379, 389, 391; TE/45, 55, 103, 153, 203, 231, 253, 263, 299, 313, 365, 401

technology, TE/17, 93, 163, 219, 225, 277, 301, 315, 379, 405

Critical Listening

cultural connection, TE/159, 347

evaluate spoken message, 23, 144, 145, 222, 223, 280, 281, 344, 345, 404, 405, 407; TE/265

  content, 11, 69, 103, 115, 144, 222, 281, 345, 405

  credibility, 103, 115, 345, 387, 404

  delivery, 69, 103, 115, 144, 281, 322, 345, 387; TE/265

monitor understanding, 16, 18–21, 69, 231, 345, 405; TE/98, 112, 124, 138, 194, 271, 303, 317

multi-level options, TE/158

perception of message, 23, 273, 281

persuasive techniques, 173, 265, 375, 404–405

seek clarification, 69, 295

speaker, 190

  feelings/perspective, 7, 21, 38, 63, 262, 275, 276, 290, 292–293, 294, 308, 321, 373

  nonverbal message, 89, 129; TE/113

  opinion, 186, 187, 248, 280, 344, 348, 374, 404

  purpose, 223, 345, 404–405; TE/246

  verbal message, 129, 273, 281, 345, 405; TE/113

  verifiable fact, 404, 405

Culture

connect, 409; TE/23, 29, 57, 89, 147, 159, 209, 243, 345, 381

experiences, 2, 3, 26, 27, 41, 50, 54, 69, 107, 153, 186, 187, 190, 191, 358, 386, 408; TE/1, 32, 37, 51, 58, 61, 75, 93, 122, 125, 151, 154, 156, 161, 178, 195, 207, 211, 212, 214, 246, 247, 270, 274, 299, 300, 302, 316, 320, 321, 325, 331, 347, 357, 368, 377, 381, 394, 395, 399, 403

home connection, TE/193, 341, 375

ideas, 15, 88, 118, 132, 152, 177, 230, 239, 298, 299, 309, 345, 387

information, 2, 15, 43, 53, 55, 69, 72, 77, 93, 119, 133, 153, 163, 177, 191, 207, 231, 243, 253, 267, 299, 353, 363, 379, 386, 389

insights, 15, 26, 50, 69, 128, 152, 153, 187, 191, 207, 353

language use, 15, 90, 107, 118, 119, 129, 142, 152, 177, 190, 243, 267

oral traditions, 15, 22, 107, 177, 231, 238, 408

Presentations

body movement/gesturing, 23, 39, 68, 89, 265, 345, 375

community connection, TE/155, 187

conversation, 173

cross-cultural, 72

descriptions, 28, 39, 50, 78, 88, 128, 140,

158, 238, 248, 280–281, 295, 340, 352; TE/361, 366

dialogue, 65, 70, 178, 226, 263; TE/111, 199

discussion, 2, 42, 89, 106, 128, 129, 140, 145, 152, 162, 173, 176, 187, 219, 230, 239, 249, 266, 277, 298, 309, 312, 362, 401

dramatic reading, 23, 187; TE/201, 237, 357

evaluate

  others' presentations, 69, 103, 115, 145, 223, 281, 344, 345, 405; TE/265

  own presentations, 69, 145, 223, 265, 280, 281, 344, 345, 387, 405

expressive, 23, 39, 68, 89, 91, 186, 263, 265, 322, 345, 375

home connection, TE/121, 255

ideas, 309, 344, 390, 401

informative, 348, 378

interview, 103, 144, 284, 387, 408

legend, 239

literary response, 309, 341, 401

multi-level options, TE/10, 68, 72, 140, 144, 222, 226, 262, 280, 344, 348, 404, 408

narrative, 68; TE/131

news report, 148, 284

nonverbal, 89, 129; TE/181, 183

oral report, 72, 148, 222–223, 284, 344–345, 347; TE/227, 403, 409

paraphrase, 22, 203, 218, 294, 308, 341; TE/257, 273

persuasive, 173, 265, 375, 404–405

questions, 323, 348, 352, 387, 408

rehearse, 23, 39, 68, 115, 144, 148, 222, 280, 344, 404; TE/261

report, 72, 148, 222–223, 284, 344, 347

role-play, 11, 15, 23, 72, 89, 103, 144, 173, 178, 187, 226, 263; TE/348

software, 265, 404

song, 239

speech, 263, 265, 404

story, 68; TE/205

Purpose

build reading fluency, 294, 400

determine purpose, 23, 223, 259, 345; TE/84, 239

distinguish intonation patterns, 159, 161; TE/159, 272

distinguish sounds, 15, 159, 161, 342, 379

eliminate barriers, 23, 282, 408

organize, 68, 222, 280, 344, 404

persuade, 173, 375, 404–405

produce intonation patterns, 159, 161, 322; TE/159

produce sounds, 15, 159, 161, 322, 342, 379

recall details, 141, 187, 276; TE/246

summarize, 64, 114, 144, 172, 189, 195, 198, 203, 238, 276, 328, 331, 334, 338, 341, 401; TE/21, 60, 97, 111, 302, 319, 368

take notes, 39, 93, 222, 341, 348, 404, 408

understand major idea, 38, 69, 145, 158, 238, 345, 405; TE/100, 126, 302, 356

understand supporting evidence, 63, 187, 340, 344, 345, 374, 390, 401, 404; TE/100, 126, 302, 309

■ Reading

Comprehension

analyze

  characters, 4, 6, 16, 56, 64, 65, 102, 115, 178, 186, 203, 238, 308, 358, 359; TE/196, 199, 200, 202, 306, 382

  reasons, 374

  settings, 309; TE/60, 302, 309

  text evidence, 238, 300, 340, 401

  text types, 64

author

  feelings/perspective, 7, 21, 38, 63, 262, 275, 276, 290, 292–293, 294, 308, 321, 373

  purpose, 9, 23, 37, 101, 113, 139, 140, 171, 185, 217, 259, 293, 307, 357, 397, 399

  strategy, 173, 314, 357

build background, 3, 15, 27, 43, 55, 77, 93, 107, 119, 133, 153, 163, 177, 191, 207, 231, 243, 253, 267, 289, 299, 313, 327, 353, 363, 379, 391

captions, 134, 141, 147; TE/136

cause and effect, 22, 56, 58–63, 114, 172, 178, 180–185, 294, 314, 316–321, 380, 382–385, 386

chronology, 42, 43, 53, 67, 244, 246–247, 248, 251, 282, 283, 380; TE/261

compare and contrast, 4, 6, 8, 10, 15, 22, 38, 44, 46–49, 50, 64, 88, 92, 108, 120, 128, 140, 172, 218, 225, 268, 269–275, 308, 322, 340, 345, 348, 400; TE/201, 232, 234, 253, 372, 385

connect, 3, 15, 27, 38, 43, 50, 54, 55, 77, 88, 93, 107, 119, 128, 129, 133, 152, 153, 163, 177, 189, 191, 202, 207, 218, 231, 239, 243, 251, 253, 267, 289, 299, 313, 326, 327, 349, 353, 358, 363, 379, 386, 389, 390, 400, 409

  community connection, TE/79, 355

  home connection, TE/341

details, 4, 120, 187, 208, 221, 294, 308, 344, 364, 380, 403; TE/111, 382

dialogue, 65, 178, 263; TE/111, 199

draw conclusions, 10, 50, 88, 114, 120, 122–127, 128, 140, 172, 248, 262, 276, 284, 290, 292–293, 322, 358, 374, 400; TE/37

draw inferences, 22, 38, 88, 114, 128, 140, 154, 156–157, 158, 186, 202, 238, 253, 254, 256–260, 262, 290, 300, 302–307, 354, 356–357, 358, 386; TE/6, 191, 272

evaluate, 64, 224, 238, 294, 308, 340

experience for comprehension, use of, 2, 38, 162, 172, 190, 218, 358; TE/xii, 1, 32, 37, 51, 58, 61, 122, 125, 195, 274, 302

explain, 38, 88, 129, 140, 145, 158, 186, 202, 217, 259, 262, 276, 293, 294, 340, 358, 374, 386, 400

fact and opinion, 51, 94, 96–101, 309, 359, 392

generalize, 322

graphic organizers, 26, 328, 341, 346

  bar graph, 13

  charts, 12, 16, 26, 40, 42, 51, 56, 68, 70, 104, 107, 115, 119, 132, 143, 145,

Teacher Edition Index

■ Writing

◼ Viewing and Representing

◼ Assessment

◼ Learning Styles

Activity Book Contents

Activity Book Contents

Student CD-ROM Contents

Unit 1: Traditions and Cultures

Chapter 1: Family Photo *and* Birthday Barbecue

"Birthday Barbecue" by Carmen Lomas Garza
Build Vocabulary: Learn Words for Family Members
Capitalization: Titles and Names
Text Structure: Poem and Personal Narrative
Reading Strategy: Compare and Contrast
Elements of Literature: Recognize First-Person Point of View
Word Study: Identify Compound Words
Grammar Focus: Use Present Continuous Tense Verbs

Chapter 2: Coyote

Build Vocabulary: Learn Words for Animal Sounds
Spelling: Irregular Plurals
Text Structure: Folktale
Reading Strategy: Read Aloud to Show Understanding
Elements of Literature: Understand Author's Purpose
Word Study: Use a Thesaurus or Synonym Finder to Find Synonyms
Grammar Focus: Identify Subjects and Verbs in Sentences

Chapter 3: Thanksgiving

Build Vocabulary: Learn Words for Foods
Spelling: *To, Two,* or *Too*
Text Structure: Poem
Reading Strategy: Describe Mental Images
Elements of Literature: Identify Rhyme
Word Study: Analyze the Suffix *-ful*
Grammar Focus: Use Subject Pronouns

Chapter 4: Turkish Delight

Build Vocabulary: Identify Words That Show Time
Spelling: Abbreviations for Units of Measure
Text Structure: Personal Narrative
Reading Strategy: Compare Text Events with Your Own Experiences
Elements of Literature: Directions
Word Study: Recognize Root Words and the Suffix *-ish*
Grammar Focus: Use the Verb *To Be* with Complements

Chapter 5: Sadako and the Thousand Paper Cranes

Build Vocabulary: Identify Words about Setting
Punctuation: Apostrophes
Text Structure: Novel Based on a True Story
Reading Strategy: Identify Cause and Effect
Elements of Literature: Understand Characterization
Word Study: Recognize Adjectives Ending in *-ed*
Grammar Focus: Recognize Possessive Nouns

Unit 2: Environment

Chapter 1: Here Is the Southwestern Desert

Build Vocabulary: Use Context to Understand Words
Spelling: Word Endings
Text Structure: Poem
Reading Strategy: Describe Images
Elements of Literature: Recognize Free Verse
Word Study: Recognize Word Origins
Grammar Focus: Identify the Simple Present Tense

Chapter 2: Subway Architect

Build Vocabulary: Take Notes as You Read
Punctuation: Italics for Emphasis
Text Structure: Interview
Reading Strategy: Distinguish Facts from Opinions
Elements of Literature: Understand Character Motivation
Word Study: Learn about the Prefix *sub-*
Grammar Focus: Identify Questions

Chapter 3: Why the Rooster Crows at Sunrise

Build Vocabulary: Understand Words in Context
Punctuation: Quotations
Text Structure: Fable
Reading Strategy: Identify Main Idea and Details
Elements of Literature: Review Personification
Word Study: Learn about Words with Multiple Meanings
Grammar Focus: Identify Object Pronouns

Chapter 4: Gonzalo

Build Vocabulary: Use Word Squares to Remember Meanings
Capitalization: Titles, Countries, and Languages
Text Structure: Narrative Fiction
Reading Strategy: Draw Conclusions
Elements of Literature: Discuss the Theme
Word Study: Identify Compound Words
Grammar Focus: Recognize Comparative Adjectives

Chapter 5: Rain Forest Creatures

Build Vocabulary: Use Text Features
Punctuation: Exclamation Points
Text Structure: Informational Text
Reading Strategy: Outline Information to Understand Reading
Elements of Literature: Examine Visual Features
Word Study: Learn Word Origins
Grammar Focus: Identify the Subject and Verb of a Sentence

Unit 3: Conflict and Cooperation

Chapter 1: We Shall Overcome

Build Vocabulary: Learn Words about Freedom
Punctuation: Commas for Cities and States
Text Structure: Song Lyrics
Reading Strategy: Make Inferences
Elements of Literature: Recognize Repetition
Word Study: Recognize Homographs
Grammar Focus: Talk about the Future Using *Will* and *Shall*

Chapter 2: Zlata's Diary

Build Vocabulary: Find Antonyms in a Thesaurus
Spelling: *There, Their,* and *They're*
Text Structure: Diary
Reading Strategy: Recognize Sequence of Events
Elements of Literature: Identify Tone
Word Study: Form Contractions
Grammar Focus: Use Verbs with Infinitives

Chapter 3: The Peach Boy

Build Vocabulary: Define Words Related to Nature
Punctuation: Commas for Direct Address
Text Structure: Play
Reading Strategy: Analyze Cause and Effect
Elements of Literature: Recognize Problems and Resolutions
Word Study: Identify Homophones
Grammar Focus: Use Compound Sentences with *And*

Chapter 4: Talking in the New Land

Build Vocabulary: Use Synonyms to Find Meaning
Capitalization: Family Names
Text Structure: Personal Narrative
Reading Strategy: Summarize to Recall Ideas
Elements of Literature: Analyze Character
Word Study: Learn the Prefix *dis-*
Grammar Focus: Use *Could* and *Couldn't*

Student CD-ROM Contents

Chapter 5: Plain Talk About Handling Stress

Build Vocabulary: Learn Words Related to Stress in Context
Spelling: *ph* Spelling with /f/ Sounds
Text Structure: Informational Text
Reading Strategy: Identify Main Idea and Details
Elements of Literature: Use Headings to Find Information
Word Study: Locate Meanings, Pronunciations, and Derivations of Words
Grammar Focus: Recognize Complex Sentences with *If*

Unit 4: Heroes

Chapter 1: The Ballad of Mulan

Build Vocabulary: Evaluate Your Understanding of Words
Spelling: Silent *k* in *kn*
Text Structure: Legend
Reading Strategy: Make Predictions
Elements of Literature: Determine Main and Minor Characters
Word Study: Use the Suffix *-ly*
Grammar Focus: Use Prepositional Phrases

Chapter 2: Roberto Clemente

Build Vocabulary: Recognize Baseball Terms
Spelling: Abbreviations
Text Structure: Biography
Reading Strategy: Use Chronology to Recall and Locate Information
Elements of Literature: Recognize Third-Person Point of View
Word Study: Understand the Prefix *un-*
Grammar Focus: Identify Prepositional Phrases of Time

Chapter 3: Nelson Mandela *and* The Inaugural Address, May 10, 1994

"The Inaugural Address, May 10, 1994" by Nelson Mandela
Build Vocabulary: Infer Meanings of Homonyms
Punctuation: Ellipses
Text Structure: Biography and Speech
Reading Strategy: Draw Inferences
Elements of Literature: Analyze Style in a Speech
Word Study: Identify the Suffix *-ion*
Grammar Focus: Recognize Commands with *Let*

Chapter 4: My Father Is a Simple Man *and* Growing Up

Build Vocabulary: Use a Web to Remember Meaning
Spelling: *ui, ch,* and *tch*
Text Structure: Poem
Reading Strategy: Compare and Contrast
Elements of Literature: Recognize Imagery
Word Study: Identify the Suffix *-er*
Grammar Focus: Recognize Reported Speech

Unit 5: Explorations

Chapter 1: Eye to Eye

Build Vocabulary: Use Context to Identify Correct Homophones
Spelling: *oa* Spelling for the Long /o/ Sound
Text Structure: Personal Narrative
Reading Strategy: Draw Conclusions about the Author
Elements of Literature: Analyze Figurative Language
Word Study: Recognize Compound Adjectives
Grammar Focus: Recognize the Simple Past Tense

Chapter 2: The Fun They Had

Build Vocabulary: Explore Multiple Meaning Words
Capitalization: Months
Text Structure: Science Fiction
Reading Strategy: Make Inferences from Text Evidence
Elements of Literature: Analyze Setting

Word Study: Use Latin Root Words to Find Meaning
Grammar Focus: Use Dependent Clauses with *Because*

Chapter 3: Using the Scientific Method

Build Vocabulary: Use a Dictionary to Locate Meanings and Pronounce Words
Spelling: *qu* Spelling for the /kw/ Sound
Text Structure: Informational Text
Reading Strategy: Recognize Cause and Effect Relationships
Elements of Literature: Recognize the Style of Direct Address
Word Study: Use Greek Word Origins
Grammar Focus: Use *Might* to Show Possibility

Chapter 4: The Solar System

Build Vocabulary: Use Different Resources to Find Meaning
Punctuation: Possessives with Apostrophes
Text Structure: Informational Text
Reading Strategy: Summarize Information
Elements of Literature: Explore the Purpose of Graphic Aids
Word Study: Recognize Words and Sounds with the Spelling *oo*
Grammar Focus: Identify Superlative Adjectives

Unit 6: Connections

Chapter 1: Esperanza Rising

Build Vocabulary: Understand Words in Context
Spelling: Silent *u*
Text Structure: Fiction
Reading Strategy: Make Inferences about Characters
Elements of Literature: Analyze Character
Word Study: Distinguish Denotative and Connotative Meanings
Grammar Focus: Identify Possessive Adjectives

Chapter 2: Honus and Me

Build Vocabulary: Learn Words about Emotions
Capitalization: Public Places
Text Structure: Fiction
Reading Strategy: Identify the Main Idea and Details
Elements of Literature: Recognize Style, Tone, and Mood
Word Study: Use a Thesaurus or Synonym Finder
Grammar Focus: Understand the Past Perfect Tense

Chapter 3: The Boy King

Build Vocabulary: Look Up Pronunciations and Meanings of Words
Punctuation: Hyphens in Compound Adjectives
Text Structure: Biography
Reading Strategy: Identify Cause and Effect
Elements of Literature: Discuss Themes Across Cultures
Word Study: Recognize the Suffix *-ian*
Grammar Focus: Understand Perfect Modal Auxiliaries

Chapter 4: It Could Still Be a Robot *and* High-Tech Helping Hands

Build Vocabulary: Distinguish Denotative and Connotative Meanings
Punctuation: Dashes
Text Structure: Informational Text
Reading Strategy: Paraphrase to Recall Ideas
Elements of Literature: Analyze Text Evidence
Word Study: Learn Meanings of Adverbs of Frequency
Grammar Focus: Use Adverbs of Frequency

English-Spanish Cognates

Unit 1: Traditions and Cultures

Unit 1, Chapter 1
Family Photo, *page 5*

different	diferente
directions	direcciones
family	familia
generations	generaciones
group	grupo
photo	foto
poem	poema

Birthday Barbecue, *page 8*

baby	bebé
barbecue	barbacoa
decorate	decorar
much	mucho
narrative	narrativa
personal	personal

Unit 1, Chapter 2
Coyote, *page 17*

air	aire
bank	banco
bison	bisonte
colors	colores
coyote	coyote
disk	disco
divided	dividió
finally	finalmente
fruits	frutas
gallop	galopar
Indian	indio
lions	leones
my	mi
rocks	rocas
salmon	salmón
sound	sonido

Unit 1, Chapter 3
Thanksgiving, *page 31*

American	americano
baby	bebé
native	nativo
November	noviembre
piece	pieza
prepared	prepararon
special	especial

Unit 1, Chapter 4
Turkish Delight, *page 46*

adult	adulto
almonds	almendras
arrange	arreglar
celebrations	celebraciones
center	centro
classes	clases
community	comunidad
contribute	contribuir
cream	crema
during	durante
especially	especialmente
family	familia
famous	famoso
funeral	funeral
important	importante
lemon	limón
limited	limitado
medium	mediano
name	nombre

part	parte
person	persona
plate	plato
poetry	poesía
reason	razón
reflective	reflexivo
region	región
religious	religioso
respect	respetar
rituals	rituales
rural	rural
society	sociedad
solidarity	solidaridad
survive	sobrevivir
the rest	el resto
tolerance	tolerancia
traditions	tradiciones
Turkey	Turquía
volleyball	voleibol

Unit 1, Chapter 5
Sadako and the Thousand Paper Cranes, *page 59*

bomb	bomba
caused	causó
continues	continua
different	diferente
difficult	difícil
familiar	familiar
famous	famoso
figured	figurado
honor	honor
hospital	hospital
Japan	el Japón
leukemia	leucemia
mysteriously	misteriosamente
parasol	parasol
part	parte
person	persona
pieces	piezas
poem	poema
radiation	radiación
real	real
statue	estatua
story	historia
surprised	sorprendió
visitor	visitante

Unit 2: Environment

Unit 2, Chapter 1
Here Is the Southwestern Desert, *page 75*

cactus	cactus
coyote	coyote
desert	desierto
spines	espinas

Unit 2, Chapter 2
Subway Architect, *page 91*

architect	arquitecto
art	arte
clear	claro
decide	decidir
design	diseñar
employees	empleados
ideas	ideas
inspector	inspector
interested	interesado
millions	millones
murals	murales
New York	Nueva York

opinion	opinión
paint	pintar
part	parte
plan	planes
project	proyecto
sculptor	escultor
sign	señal
space	espacio
special	especial
station	estación
system	sistema
trains	trenes
visitor	visitante

Unit 2, Chapter 3
Why the Rooster Crows at Sunrise, *page 105*

animals	animales
appear	aparece
atmosphere	atmósfera
desperate	desesperado
different	diferente
discuss	discutir
finally	finalmente
horizon	horizonte
moment	momento
offered	ofreció
respect	respeto
silent	silencioso
situation	situación

Unit 2, Chapter 4
Gonzalo, *page 117*

algebra	álgebra
apartment	apartamento
baby	bebé
block	bloque
busses	buses
different	diferente
enemies	enemigos
English	inglés
equation	ecuación
exact	exacto
finally	finalmente
focused	enfocado
garden	jardín
gestures	gestos
Indian	indio
language	lenguaje
math	matemáticas
Mexicans	mexicanos
north	norte
packets	paquetes
planet	planeta
plaza	plaza
practically	prácticamente
practice	practicas
public	público
Salvadorans	salvadoreños
studied	estudió
totally	totalmente
vacant	vacante

Unit 2, Chapter 5
Rain Forest Creatures, *page 131*

animals	animales
camouflage	camuflaje
capture	capturar
colors	colores
creature	criatura
crocodiles	cocodrilos
different	diferente
flowers	flores
fruits	frutas

insects	insectos
millions	millones
natural	natural
nocturnal	nocturno
plants	plantas
predators	predatores
prey	presa
protection	protección
sense	sentido
special	especial
use	usar

Unit 3: Conflict and Cooperation

Unit 3, Chapter 1
We Shall Overcome, *page 155*

civil	civil
dignity	dignidad
justice	justicia

Unit 3, Chapter 2
Zlata's Diary, *page 165*

airport	aeropuerto
attack	atacar
bombs	bombas
bus	bus
capital	capital
center	centro
constantly	constantemente
destroyed	destruido
diary	diario
different	diferente
enemies	enemigos
explosion	explosión
family	familia
humanity	humanidad
idea	idea
inhuman	inhumano
Italy	Italia
march	marcha
members	miembros
natural	natural
part	parte
peace	paz
phone	teléfono
separate	separar
stations	estaciones
terrible	terrible
train	tren

Unit 3, Chapter 3
The Peach Boy, *page 179*

appreciate	apreciar
castle	castillo
continued	continuaron
creatures	criaturas
explained	explicó
favor	favor
floating	flotando
fortune	fortuna
front	frente
idea	idea
island	isla
Japan	Japón
monkey	mono
narrator	narrador
peck	picar
pheasant	faisán
possible	posible
studied	estudió
treasures	tesoros

English-Spanish Cognates

Unit 3, Chapter 4
Talking in the New Land,
page 193

air	aire
certainly	ciertamente
circle	círculo
company	compañía
dense	denso
disappear	desaparecer
discovered	descubrió
dividend	dividendo
escape	escapar
fragrant	fragrante
ignore	ignorar
important	importante
interrupted	interrumpió
lilac	lila
nervous	nervioso
porch	porche
Portugal	Portugal
Portuguese	portugués
premium	premio
stomach	estómago
telephone	teléfono
tone	tono
voice	voz

Unit 3, Chapter 5
Plain Talk About Handling Stress,
page 209

ability	abilidad
accept	aceptar
activity	actividad
affect	afectar a
basis	base
completed	completado
completely	completamente
confrontation	confrontación
consequence	consecuencia
control	control
cooperation	cooperación
correctly	correctamente
counselor	consejero
create	crear
crisis	crisis
disaster	desastre
doctor	doctor
exercise	ejercicio
family	familia
garden	jardín
ideas	ideas
impact	impacto
important	importante
impossible	imposible
individual	individual
irritable	irritable
limited	limitado
list	lista
member	miembro
mental	mental
method	método
minimize	minimizar
moment	momento
music	músico
natural	natural
nervous	nervioso
occur	occurir
opportunity	oportunidad
painted	pintado
particularly	en particular
peace	paz
physical	físico
pleasure	placer

prevent	prevenir
priority	prioridad
problem	problema
productivity	productividad
professional	profesional
psychiatrist	psiquiatra
psychologist	psicólogo
quality	calidad
reduce	reducir
relax	relajar
satisfaction	satisfacción
sense	sentido
serious	serio
situation	situación
special	especial
strategy	estrategia
suggestions	sugerencias
tennis	tenis
tense	tenso
tension	tensión
traffic	tráfico
tranquility	tranquilidad

Unit 4: Heroes

Unit 4, Chapter 1
The Ballad of Mulan, *page 233*

appeared	apareció
attacking	atacando
bank	banco
battles	batallas
bridle	brida
camel	camello
camped	acampó
comrades	camarada
emperor	emperador
enemy	enemigo
escort	escolta
excitement	exitación
family	familia
favorite	favorito
fierce	feroz
finally	finalmente
frail	frágil
generals	generales
glory	gloria
honor	honor
invaders	invasores
markets	mercados
miles	millas
mounted	montó
noble	noble
palace	palacio
peak	pico
possible	posible
poster	póster
prepare	preparar
respect	respeto
soldiers	soldados
surprise	sorpresa
titles	títulos
triumphant	triunfante
troops	tropas
victorious	victorioso
voice	voz

Unit 4, Chapter 2
Roberto Clemente, *page 245*

athletes	atletas
baseball	béisbol
coast	costa
continue	continuar

heritage	herencia
humanitarians	humanitarios
important	importante
league	liga
legacy	legado
medicine	medicinas
national	nacional
part	parte
pirates	piratas
receive	recibir
tragic	trágico
unfortunately	desafortunadamente
victims	víctimas

Unit 4, Chapter 3
Nelson Mandela, *page 255*

Africans	africanos
biography	biografía
chief	jefe
education	educación
family	familia
fortunately	fortunadamente
future	futuro
hero	héroe
important	importante
inclination	inclinación
leader	líder
millions	millones
nation	nación
patriot	patriota
politician	político
prediction	predicción
president	presidente
prince	príncipe
prison	prisión
prisoner	prisionero
servant	serviente
silent	silencioso
various	varios

The Inaugural Address,
May 10, 1994, *page 260*

Africa	África
dedicate	dedicar
heroes	héroes
heroines	heroínas
inaugural	inaugural
justice	justicia
peace	paz
reality	realidad
reconciliation	conciliación
reign	reinar
sacrificed	sacrificaron
salt	sal
united	unido

Unit 4, Chapter 4
My Father Is a Simple Man,
page 269

applause	aplauso
benefit	beneficioso
convince	convencer
education	educación
patience	paciencia
perpetual	perpetuo
poem	poema
pretense	pretexto
price	precio
provider	proveedor
reality	realidad
scholars	escolares
simple	simple

Growing Up, *page 274*

architect	arquitecto
delicious	delicioso
doctor	doctór
famous	famoso
poem	poema
students	estudiantes

Unit 5: Explorations

Unit 5, Chapter 1
Eye to Eye, *page 291*

actions	acciones
animals	animales
associated	asociado
bus	bus
clear	claro
coast	costa
determine	determinar
direction	dirección
floating	flotando
Hawaii	Hawai
humans	humanos
impossible	imposible
islands	islas
miles	millas
move	mover
northern	del norte
ocean	océano
or	o
orchestra	orquesta
photographer	fotógrafo
plants	plantas
scientist	científico
sounds	sonidos
studies	estudia
system	sistema
tropics	trópicos
vibrate	vibrar
vocalizing	vocalizando

Unit 5, Chapter 2
The Fun They Had, *page 301*

adjusted	ajustado
attic	ático
code	código
completely	completamente
diary	diario
different	diferente
dispute	disputar
fraction	fracción
geography	geografía
hour	hora
insert	insertar
inspector	inspector
lessons	lecciones
mark	marca
mechanical	mecánico
millions	millones
page	página
progress	progreso
proper	propio
real	real
regular	regular
stories	historias
stupid	estúpido
superior	superior
television	televisión

Unit 5, Chapter 3
Using the Scientific Method,
page 315

control	controlar
count	contar
different	diferente
difficulty	dificultad
evidence	evidencia
examine	examinar
experimental	experimental
group	grupo
hypothesis	hipótesis
idea	idea
information	información
interested	interesado
method	método
number	número
patience	paciencia
pieces	piezas
results	resultados
scientific	científico
surprising	sorprendente

Unit 5, Chapter 4
The Solar System, *page 329*

acid	ácido
air	aire
appears	aparece
areas	áreas
astronaut	astronauta
atmosphere	atmósfera
atom	átomo
billion	billón
canyon	cañón
carbon	carbono
center	centro
compare	comparar
crater	cráter
different	diferente
difficult	difícil
distance	distancia
distant	distante
energy	energía
exist	existir
experiment	experimento
explore	explorar
form	formar
formed	formado
formed	formaron
gas	gas
gravity	gravedad
helium	helio
hydrogen	hidrógeno
information	información
Jupiter	Júpiter
kilometers	kilómetros
lake	lago
lesson	lección
map	mapa
Mars	Marte
Mercury	Mercurio

metal	metal
mission	misión
mysterious	misterioso
Neptune	Neptuno
north	norte
objects	objetos
orbit	órbita
planets	planetas
Pluto	Plutón
pole	polo
protect	proteger
rays	rayos
rocks	rocas
Saturn	Saturno
scientists	científico
season	estación
similar	similar
solar	solar
space	espacio
study	estudiar
surface	superficie
survive	sobrevivir
system	sistema
temperature	temperatura
Uranus	Urano
valleys	valles
vapor	vapor
Venus	Venus
volcano	volcán

Unit 6: Connections

Unit 6, Chapter 1
Esperanza Rising, *page 355*

arbor	árbol
distant	distante
formed	formó
fruit	fruta
guard	guardar
moment	momento
patient	paciente
resounding	resonante
silent	silencioso
sound	sonido
stomach	estómago
valley	valle

Unit 6, Chapter 2
Honus and Me, *page 365*

athlete	atleta
attic	ático
baseball	béisbol
bike	bicicleta
buttons	botones
cards	cartas
centered	centrado
character	carácter
collar	collar
collector	coleccionista
company	compañía

condition	condición
cruised	cruzó
different	diferente
discontinued	discontinuado
dollars	dólares
double	doble
exactly	exactamente
exist	existir
expression	expresión
famous	famoso
forced	forzó
fortune	fortuna
globe	globo
hour	hora
included	incluido
instinctively	instintivo
legend	leyenda
letters	letras
magic	mágico
minute	minuto
name	nombre
number	número
palm	palma
paper	papél
pirates	piratas
problems	problemas
products	productos
public	público
reasons	razones
rest	resto
rich	rico
sensation	sensación
serious	serio
seriously	seriosamente
solemn	solemne
tobacco	tabaco

Unit 6, Chapter 3
The Boy King, *page 381*

ancient	antiguo
announcement	anuncio
antelope	antílope
archaeologist	arqueólogo
battle	batalla
caused	causó
colors	colores
decided	decidió
decorated	decorado
during	durante
education	educación
Egyptian	egipcio
enemies	enemigos
family	familia
famous	famoso
gardens	jardines
gazelle	gacela
heiress	heredera
hieroglyphics	jeroglíficos
historians	historiadores
image	imagen
included	incluido

marked	marcado
mathematics	matemáticas
name	nombre
objects	objetos
painted	pintado
palace	palacio
papyrus	papiro
particularly	en particular
practicing	practicando
probably	probablemente
riches	riqueza
royal	real
sports	deportes
studying	estudiando
suffered	sufrió
temple	templo
throne	trono
tomb	tumba
treasures	tesoros

Unit 6, Chapter 4
It Could Still Be a Robot,
page 393

certain	cierto
control	controlar
depends	depende
electronic	electrónico
future	futuro
human	humano
instrument	instrumento
machine	máquina
metal	metal
objects	objetos
ocean	océano
painted	pintado
person	persona
pilot	piloto
planet	planeta
program	programa
remote	remoto
robot	robot
story	historia
touch	tocar
types	tipos

High-Tech Helping Hands,
page 398

area	area
communicate	comunicar
engineers	ingenieros
equipment	equipo
forming	formando
goal	gól
independent	independiente
institute	instituto
letters	letras
movements	movimientos
products	productos
system	sistema